Time Out

South of France

timeout.com/southoffrance

D0452168

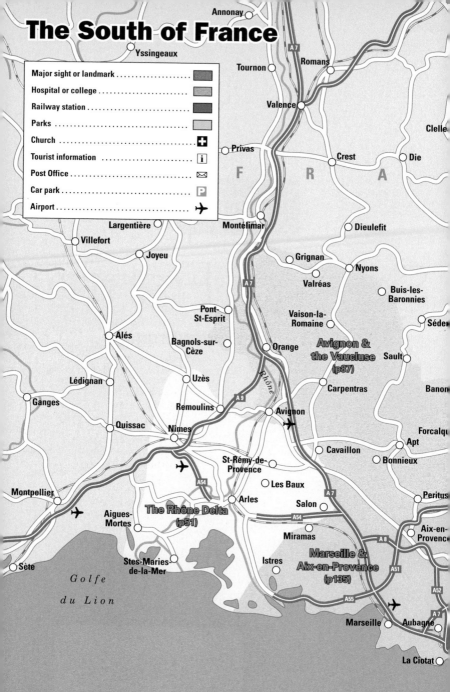

Time Out Guides Ltd
Universal House
251 Tottenham Court Road
London W1T 7AB
United Kingdom
Tel: +44 (0)20 7813 3000
Fax: +44 (0)20 7813 6001
Email: guides@timeout.com
www.timeout.com

Published by Time Out Guides Ltd, a wholly owned subsidiary of Time Out Group Ltd.
Time Out and the Time Out logo are trademarks of Time Out Group Ltd.

© **Time Out Group Ltd 2009**
Previous editions 2000, 2002, 2004, 2006.

10 9 8 7 6 5 4 3 2 1

This edition first published in Great Britain in 2009 by Ebury Publishing.
A Random House Group Company
20 Vauxhall Bridge Road, London SW1V 2SA

Random House Australia Pty Ltd 20 Alfred Street, Milsons Point, Sydney, New South Wales 2061, Australia

Random House New Zealand Ltd 18 Poland Road, Glenfield, Auckland 10, New Zealand

Random House South Africa (Pty) Ltd Isle of Houghton, Corner Boundary Road & Carse O'Gowrie, Houghton 2198, South Africa

Random House UK Limited Reg. No. 954009

For further distribution details, see www.timeout.com.

ISBN: 978-1-84670-034-7

A CIP catalogue record for this book is available from the British Library.

Printed and bound by Firmengruppe APPL, aprinta druck, Wemding, Germany.

The Random House Group Limited supports The Forest Stewardship Council (FSC), the leading international forest certification organisation. All our titles that are printed on Greenpeace approved FSC certified paper carry the FSC logo. Our paper procurement policy can be found at http://www.rbooks.co.uk/environment.

Time Out carbon-offsets its flights with Trees for Cities (www.treesforcities.org).

Contents

Introduction

With the 'discovery' of the Côte d'Azur in the 1920s, the South's mighty tourist industry was set in motion – and a powerful myth was born. Blame the artists and writers whose work made the Riviera a byword for bohemian sophistication and belle-époque elegance, forever imbued with the glittering promise of Raoul Dufy's colour-saturated canvases of bathers, palm-fringed promenades and sailing boats, or the glamour of Scott Fitzgerald's brittle, beautiful socialites and despair-tinged decadence.

Inland Provence is similarly hard to separate from its idealised image, shaped by everyone from Van Gogh to Peter Mayle. Its name alone is enough to conjure up a series of painterly vignettes: fields of lavender and tangled vineyards stretching under a cloudless sky; games of *pétanque* on plane tree-shaded squares; and tumbledown, mimosa-clad stone *mas*, enticing stressed urbanites with their promise of rural bliss.

Spend a week or two exploring and you may well encounter all of the above – but that's by no means the full story. The bleakly beautiful saltmarshes of the Camargue and the studenty social scene in Avignon are much a part of the South as its yacht-filled harbours and perched medieval villages, and equally worthy of a visit. Times have changed, and the chameleon South is busy reinventing itself for the 21st century, from rough diamond Marseille's rebirth as a cultural hub to Nice's daring, art-dotted piazza. Even the age-old Southern wine scene is changing, with a once-unthinkable swing from reds to rosés, and a small but influential band of organic and biodynamic wine producers.

While there's no point denying that much of the South is firmly on the tourist trail, it's always possible to find a path less trodden. If the beach doesn't appeal, try spending your summer hiking in the mountainous hinterlands of the Var or Southern Alps; in winter, take advantage of low-season rates and the balmy southern climate by spending a weekend in Nice, exploring its art galleries and restaurants at your own unhurried pace. A land that's rich in Roman remains and Modernist masterpieces, overcrowded beaches and unspoilt coves, exquisite restaurants and tacky tourist traps, the South is whatever you choose to make of it. *Elizabeth Winding, Editor*

Around the South

THE RHONE DELTA

The region that inspired Cézanne and Van Gogh is a landscape of contrasts, bounded by the arid limestone peaks of the **Alpilles** to the north and the wide open salt marches of the **Camargue** to the south. Amid this natural splendour, **Arles** and **Nîmes** are home to some of the best-preserved Roman remains in France, while the market town of **St-Rémy** is as chic as it is charming.
► *For more, see pp49-84.*

AVIGNON & THE VAUCLUSE

Centuries under Papal rule left **Avignon** with a rich cultural heritage, which it supplements with a flourishing arts festival. Lovers of opera, meanwhile, make for **Orange**, where the Roman theatre makes a magnificent backdrop for the annual Choregies event. The bucolic **Drôme Provençale** and **Luberon** have struck tourist gold with picture-perfect hill villages, vineyards and chateaux.
► *For more, see pp85-132.*

MARSEILLE & AIX

After an overdose of Riviera glamour and beautiful perched villages, **Marseille** brings a welcome change of pace. Chaotic and charismatic, the age-old port is a city on the up, thanks in part to its thriving contemporary arts agenda. It's also within easy reach of the fishing village of **Cassis** and the unspoilt seaside **Calanques**. Further inland, **Aix** is an unerringly elegant city with a spirited cultural scene.
► *For more, see pp133-174.*

THE VAR

Beaches abound along this stretch of coast, ranging from the beach clubs of **plage de Pampelonne**, where teeny bikinis and sizeable wallets are *de rigueur*, to the peaceful charms of the **Iles de Hyères**. **St-Tropez** epitomises Riviera glitz, but head into the Var's mountainous hinterland and you're immersed in a different world, with glorious scenery stretching as far as the eye can see.
► *For more, see pp175-228.*

THE RIVIERA & SOUTHERN ALPS

The South's mighty tourism industry was born on these shores, and the glamour of the belle époque lingers on in **Cannes**'s plush palace hotels, **Nice**'s palm-lined promenade and the private villas of **Cap Ferrat**. Artists also flocked here, leaving a rich legacy of artistic treasures in its museums, galleries and chapels. Inland, olive groves give way to mountains and gorges – and even a ski slope or two.
► *For more, see pp229-312.*

Best of the South

BEACH LIFE

White sand beaches and turquoise waters fringe the island of **Porquerolles** (*see p189*), a car-free paradise that feels a world away from the Riviera crowds. Best reached by boat from Cassis, the **Calanques** (*see p159*) are similarly unspoilt, with crystal clear inlets and not an ice-cream kiosk in sight. Those not averse to a pebble or two should head for the lovely **Mala plage** (*see p274*) in Cap d'Ail – it's secluded, but worth seeking out. If you don't mind sharing your stretch of sand, St-Tropez's famous **plage de Pampelonne** (*see p199*) is lined with toned, tanned bodies and bling-filled beach clubs.

MODERN ART MECCAS

Brilliant light, vibrant landscapes and moneyed patrons have long drawn artists to the South, and a rich artistic legacy remains. Nice's haul includes the **Musée Matisse** and **Musée National Message Biblique Marc Chagall** (for both, *see p260*). In St-Paul-de-Vence, the fortunate few staying at the **Colombe d'Or** (*see p303*) can admire works by the likes of Picasso, Matisse and Braque; fortunately, the **Fondation Maeght** (*see p301*) is open to everyone. Chapels also appealed to the modern masters: don't miss Matisse's **Chapelle du Rosaire** (*see p302*), Cocteau's **Chapelle Notre-Dame-de-Jérusalem** (*see p205*) and the **Chapelle de St-Pierre-des-Pêcheurs** (*see p272*), or Picasso's *La Guerre et la Paix* in the **Musée National Picasso** (*see p234*).

CELEBRITY-SPOTTING

Celebrities can't seem to keep away from St-Tropez. The epicentre of the scene remains the exclusive **Les Caves du Roi** (*see p196*), where pop stars, playboys and an assortment of other A-listers regularly hit the champagne. On Pampelonne beach, **Club 55** (*see p200*) is another perennially popular spot, allowing for discreet celeb-spotting from behind your shades. Alternatively, head for Cannes in festival time: the lobby's awash with A-listers at the **Martinez** (*see p239*), where suites are taken over by haute-couture labels for last-minute frock fittings. Stars fleeing the madding crowds, meanwhile, check in at the **Hôtel du Cap Eden-Roc** (*see p247*). After dark, head for **Bâoli** (*see p238*) to party with *le beau monde*.

WILDLIFE-WATCHING
In addition to its white horses and bulls, the **Camargue** (*see p80*) is home to an astonishing array of birdlife, from herons and plovers to terns and sandpipers. Even the most amateur of twitchers will be able to spot the flocks of pink flamingos. On the border with Italy, the rugged **Parc du Mercantour** (*see p307*) is a romantic wilderness, where the inhabitants run from badgers and bears to wolves and golden eagles. Alternatively, check out Monaco's clifftop **Musée Océanographique** (*see p283*), where an enormous whale skeleton resides alongside sharks, sea turtles and a live coral reef.

WINE REGIONS
You can't visit the South without touring a vineyard or two – and there's an abundance from which to choose. Pay homage to the mighty reds of **Châteauneuf-du-Pape** (*see p35*) or the increasingly famed **Bandol** (*see p182*) appellation, or sample the crisp whites of **Cassis** (*see p162*). Up-and-coming regions worth seeking out include **Gigondas** and **Rasteau** (*see p110*) or the compact **Baux-de-Provence** (*see p65*) region, where *vignerons* have embraced organic and biodynamic cultivation.

HIKES & WALKS
With their sheer drops and vertiginous views, the inland **Gorges du Verdon** (*see p226*) make for high-adrenaline hikes. Less of a scramble, though equally lovely, is the public footpath that winds around the **Cap Ferrat** peninsula (*see p276*), skirting luxury villas, secluded beaches and windswept cliffs. Alternatively, follow the iconic Grand Prix street circuit through the tightly-packed heart of **Monaco** (*see p280*) on foot – and marvel at how Formula 1's finest whip round its hairpin bends.

Time Out South of France

Editorial

Editor Elizabeth Winding
Copy Editors Ismay Atkins, Simon Cropper, Jan Fuscoe
Listings Editors Carlos Pineda, Julien Sauvalle
Proofreader Tamson Shelton
Indexer Jonathan Cox

Managing Director Peter Fiennes
Editorial Director Ruth Jarvis
Series Editor Will Fulford-Jones
Business Manager Dan Allen
Editorial Manager Holly Pick
Assistant Management Accountant Ija Krasnikova

Design

Art Director Scott Moore
Art Editor Pinelope Kourmouzoglou
Senior Designer Henry Elphick
Graphic Designers Kei Ishimaru, Nicola Wilson
Advertising Designer Jodi Sher

Picture Desk

Picture Editor Jael Marschner
Deputy Picture Editor Lynn Chambers
Picture Researcher Gemma Walters
Picture Desk Assistant Marzena Zoladz
Picture Librarian Christina Theisen

Advertising

Commercial Director Mark Phillips
International Advertising Manager Kasimir Berger
International Sales Executive Charlie Sokol
Advertising Sales (South of France) Carlos Pineda

Marketing

Marketing Manager Yvonne Poon
Sales & Marketing Director, North America & Latin America Lisa Levinson
Senior Publishing Brand Manager Luthfa Begum
Marketing Designer Anthony Huggins

Production

Group Production Director Mark Lamond
Production Manager Brendan McKeown
Production Controller Damian Bennett
Production Coordinator Julie Pallot

Time Out Group

Chairman Tony Elliott
Group General Manager/Director Nichola Coulthard
Time Out Communications Ltd MD David Pepper
Time Out International Ltd MD Cathy Runciman
Group IT Director Simon Chappell
Head of Marketing Catherine Demajo

Contributors

Introduction Elizabeth Winding. **History** Natasha Edwards, Elizabeth Winding (*No Pain, No Gain* Simon Cropper). **The South of France Today** Lizzy Davies. **Provençal Food & Wine** Richard James, Rosa Jackson. (*Market Forces, Profile: Rosé* Jamie Ivey). **The Artistic South** Natasha Edwards. **The Festive South** Julien Sauvalle (*Hitting a High Note* Stephen Mudge). **Nîmes & the Pont du Gard** Stephen Mudge. **St-Rémy & Les Alpilles** Jamie Ivey (*Death in the Afternoon* Simon Cropper, *Wine Tour: Les-Baux* Richard James). **Arles** Stephen Mudge (*Profile: Rencontres d'Arles* Natasha Edwards). **The Camargue** Stephen Mudge. **Avignon** Stephen Mudge. **Orange & Around** Stephen Mudge. **Carpentras & Mont Ventoux** Stephen Mudge (*Buried Treasures* Rosa Jackson). **The Drôme Provençale** Isabel Pitman, Elizabeth Winding. **The Luberon** Jamie Ivey. **Marseille** Natasha Edwards. **Cassis, the Calanques & La Ciotat** Tristan Rutherford & Kathryn Tomasetti (*Wine Tour: Cassis* Richard James). **Aix-en-Provence** Natasha Edwards. **Toulon & the Western Côte** Elizabeth Winding (*Wine Tour: Bandol* Richard James). **Hyères to Les Maures** Tristan Rutherford & Kathryn Tomasetti. **St-Tropez** Tristan Rutherford & Kathryn Tomasetti. **St-Raphaël & the Estérel** Sarah Fraser. **Brignoles & the Ste-Baume** Sarah Fraser. **Draguignan & the Central Var** Sarah Fraser. **The Gorges du Verdon** Sarah Fraser. **Cannes** Elizabeth Winding. **Antibes to Cagnes** Rosa Jackson. **Nice** Elizabeth Winding (*A Corking Night Out* Rosa Jackson). **The Corniches** Tristan Rutherford & Kathryn Tomasetti. **Monaco & Monte-Carlo** Natasha Edwards (*A Walk in the Fast Lane* Tristan Rutherford). **Roquebrune to Menton** Rosa Jackson. **Grasse & the Gorges du Loup** Sarah Fraser. **Vence & St-Paul** Rosa Jackson. **Into the Alps** Rosa Jackson (*Frozen Assets* Cyrus Shahrad). **Directory** Alexia Loundras.

Maps john@jsgraphics.co.uk.

Illustrations Ruth Winding.

Photography Charlie Pinder, except: page 16 Getty Images; page 23 Topfoto; page 37 Bridgeman Art Library; pages 41, 222, 278 Karl Blackwell; pages 42, 45 Elizabeth Carecchio; page 78 Grégoire Alexandre; page 302 © Succession H Matisse/Dacs 2008. The following images were provided by the featured establishments/artists: page 46, 78, 309, 310.

The Editor would like to thank Jan Fuscoe, Ruth Winding, Kari Clouston and all contributors to previous editions of *Time Out South of France*, whose work forms the basis for parts of this book.

About the Guide

GETTING STARTED

The five sections in this guide are arranged in a roughly west-to-east order; each one begins with an introduction and a map of the region. All the individual areas start with background history and sightseeing highlights, followed by details on where to eat, drink and stay (in bigger towns, these venues have been marked on our maps with coloured bullets like this: ❶), and tourist information. We also give travel directions; however, note that public transport options around inland rural areas are very limited.

THE ESSENTIALS

For practical information, including visas, disabled access, emergency numbers, useful websites and local transport, please see the Directory. It begins on page 314.

THE LISTINGS

All listings were checked and correct at press time. However, arrangements can alter at any time, and economic conditions can cause prices to change rapidly.

The very best venues, the must-sees and must-dos, have been marked with a red star (★). We've also marked sights that offer free admission with a FREE symbol, and budget restaurants with a € symbol.

THE LANGUAGE

A few basic French phrases go a long way. You'll find a primer on page 326.

PHONE NUMBERS

The area code for all venues in this guide (apart from Monaco) is 04. From outside France, dial your country's international access code (00 from the UK, 011 from the US) or a plus symbol, followed by the French country code (33) and then the number as listed in the guide, but omitting the initial '0'. So, to reach the Musée Matisse in Nice, dial +33.4.93.81.08.08.

Monaco has its own country code of 377, but no internal area codes. For Monaco, dial your country's access code or a plus symbol, followed by 377 and the number.

FEEDBACK

We welcome feedback on this guide, both on the venues we've included and on any other locations that you'd like to see featured in future editions. Please email us at guides@timeout.com.

Time Out Guides

Founded in August 1968, Time Out has grown from humble beginnings into the leading resource for anyone wanting to know what's happening in the world's greatest cities. Alongside our influential what's-on weeklies in London, New York and Chicago, we publish more than 20 magazines in cities as varied as Beijing and Beirut, and a range of travel books that includes more than 50 City Guides and the newer Shortlist series. The company remains proudly independent, still owned by Tony Elliott four decades after he launched Time Out London.

Written by local experts and illustrated with original photography, our books also retain their independence. No business has been featured because it has advertised, and all restaurants and bars are visited and reviewed anonymously.

ABOUT THE EDITOR

Elizabeth Winding is a staff editor at Time Out Guides. As well as editing *Time Out South of France*, she is the editor of *1,000 Things to Do in Britain*, and writes regularly for *Time Out London*.

A full list of the book's contributors can be found opposite. Note that we have also included details of our writers in selected chapters spread throughout the guide.

In Context

Menton.
See p290.

History

From Ice Age penguins to sun-seeking tourists.

TEXT: NATASHA EDWARDS

Since prehistoric man first settled here in around 27,000 BC, the South of France has had a tumultuous history. Thanks to its natural harbours, fertile plains and favourable climate, the region has been invaded by all the big-hitters, from Gauls and Greeks to Romans and Franks – leaving a rich legacy for archaeologists and camera-toting tourists.

More recent conflicts have also left their mark on the South, from the mighty forts that guarded Marseille's harbour from invaders (and dissuaded its rebellion-prone inhabitants from double-crossing Louis XIV) to the Allied bombs at the end of World War II, which razed Toulon's old town to the ground. Yet the South's history is also one of prosperity: soaring Roman arenas and aqueducts, grand chateaux and stately 19th-century mansions testify to its wealth. Tourism, too, has shaped this region, ever since wintering 19th-century British and Russian aristocrats first discovered the Riviera's charms.

PENGUINS IN PROVENCE?

Ancient cave paintings found in the Grotte Cosquer in the Calanques put the first date of human habitation in the South of France at around 27,000 BC. Judging from the images, palaeolithic man lived alongside penguins as well as the more familiar bison and horses – but then the paintings do date back beyond the last Ice Age. Later, Neolithic communities settled in the fertile lands near present-day Nice and Monaco, or sheltered in caves in the Verdon gorges. Then, in 1200 BC, the Gauls began to migrate from the Rhine Valley into France and Italy. The southernmost front of this advance developed into the Ligurian culture, which stretched from Spain into Italy. Skilled metalworkers and stone carvers, the Ligurians lived in *oppidums* (fortified villages) such as that at Entremont, near Aix.

Western civilisation first came to Provence with the Phocaean Greeks, who founded the colony of Massalia (Marseille) in about 600 BC. By the fifth century BC, Massalia was so powerful it was minting its own money and had begun to plant colonies along the coast at Nikaïa (Nice), Olbia (Hyères), Taureontum (Les Lecques) and Agde, as well as inland at Arles. The Greeks planted vines and olives, and the pan-Mediterranean trade in wine, olive oil and other goods soon filtered through to neighbouring Celtic areas.

THE RISE OF ROME

Marseille took the Roman side during the Carthaginian Wars, a smart move that stood it in good stead when Rome went annexing beyond the Alps towards the end of the second century BC. Called in by Marseille to help the city repulse a Celtic attack, the Romans stayed on, destroying the Oppidum of Entremont and founding the city of Aquae Sextiae (now Aix-en-Provence) in 122 BC. In recognition of its support, Marseille was allowed to remain an independent state within Roman territory.

The main reason, however, for expansion into the South of France was the need to secure the land route to Spain: the Via Domitia. Built in around 120 BC, it had staging posts at Apt, Beaucaire and Nîmes. By 118 BC Rome controlled the whole coast westwards to the Pyrenees, and large swathes of the hinterland. The Romans subdued by colonisation, with vast numbers of settlers attracted by the promise of free land. The Celtic town at Vaison-la-Romaine became a semi-autonomous federated city; Narbonne, further west, became the capital of Gallia Narbonensis – also known, more simply, as 'Provincia'. After 115 BC the Celtic tribe of the Cimbri and the Germanic Teutons mounted a series of raids on Provence, culminating in a humiliating defeat for the Romans at Orange in 105 BC.

Under the Pax Romana, Gallia Narbonensis became a model province, supplying grain, olive oil and ships to the ever-hungry empire. In return, it was treated more as an extension of the motherland than a colonial outpost, with impressive aqueducts, baths, temples and amphitheatres built at cities such as Aix, Arles, Nîmes, Orange and Glanum (St-Rémy). Further east the Romans constructed the port of Fréjus, Cemenelum (Nice) and a ring of fortified settlements in the eastern Var. Marseille was eclipsed after it supported Pompey against Caesar in the Civil Wars (*see p136*). Besieged in 49 BC, its possessions were transferred to Arles, Narbonne and Fréjus – though it remained a centre of scholarship.

DIVIDED WE STAND

The Christian community emerged in the early fifth century, with the foundation of the St-Honorat monastery on the Iles de Lérins and the Abbaye de St-Victor in Marseille. The latter was the centre of a monastic diaspora that gave the South a generous sprinkling of abbeys, ensuring that the land was worked even in times of crisis – although the monks could be as tyrannical in exploiting the peasantry as any feudal landlord.

After the fall of the Roman Empire in 476, the bishoprics maintained some semblance of order in spite of invasions by Visigoths and Ostrogoths, but when the Franks eventually gained control there followed a period of anarchy. Roman embellishments fell into ruin, and fields returned to swampland. The new rulers looked north rather than south, and the Mediterranean trade that had sustained cities like Arles and Marseille gradually dried up.

The three-way partition of the Carolingian Empire between the three sons of Louis I in the Treaty of Verdun in 843 made the Rhône a frontier, and provided the basis for the later division between Provence and Languedoc. In 931 the kingdom of Provence – one of many fragments of Charlemagne's former empire – was allied with Burgundy. Over the next couple of centuries, imperial rule gave way to out-and-out feudalism, as local lords used brute force and taxes to subdue the territory around their strongholds. The Saracens terrorised the coast and launched inland raids from their base in the Massif des Maures, until they were driven out by William I, Count of Arles, in 974, confirming the power of the kingdom of Arles, which became part of the Holy Roman Empire.

From the end of the 11th century, more efficient agriculture, the revival of trade and the rise of the guilds funded new religious foundations, such as the impressive Abbaye de St-Gilles in the Camargue, and the restoration of Arles's Cathédrale St-Trophime. A sober, pared-back style of Romanesque also evolved at the great Cistercian foundations of Silvacane, Senanque and Thoronet. Northern French Gothic, which had its beginnings at St-Denis in the 12th century, was slower to percolate down, but a few fine edifices were built – including Avignon's Palais des Papes and the Basilique St-Maximin-la-Ste-Baume.

Some time in the 11th century, a small local dynasty had felt confident enough to award itself the title of Counts of Provence. When the line died out in 1113, the title passed to the House of Barcelona, which became the nominal ruler of the area (neighbouring Languedoc, meanwhile, passed to the Counts of Toulouse). However, the larger cities soon asserted their independence, setting up governments known as Consulates. In the country, local bosses such as the Lords of Les Baux and Count of Forcalquier put up fierce resistance to those claiming higher authority. Barcelona's sway over Mediterranean France was helped along by language. Provençal, the eastern dialect of Occitan or *langue d'Oc,* was a close cousin of Catalan. Out of the apparent anarchy and the frequent shifts in the balance of power among warring *seigneuries*, a distinctive local culture emerged, which reached its fullest expression in the poetry and ballads of the troubadour poets.

Château de Tarascon.

'The last Count of Provence, Raymond-Bérenger V, was also one of the shrewdest, marrying all four daughters to kings or future kings.'

PRINCES AND POPES

Provence was spared the destruction visited on south-western France during the Albigensian Crusade against the Cathars. But the crusade altered the balance of power in the South: the Counts of Toulouse were crushed, and Languedoc passed to the French Crown in 1271 – bar the Comtat Venaissin (including Avignon, Carpentras, Cavaillon and Fontaine-de-Vaucluse), which Philippe III of France gave to the Papacy in 1274.

The Counts of Provence emerged as sole rulers of the land between the Rhône and the Alps. The last Count of Provence, Raymond-Bérenger V, was also one of the shrewdest and most cultured. He dealt with the increasingly muscular power of France in a masterful piece of dynastic planning, marrying all four daughters to kings or future kings: the eldest, Marguerite, to Louis IX of France, Eleanor to Henry III of England, Sanchia to Richard of Cornwall and, in 1246, Beatrice to Charles d'Anjou, brother of Louis IX, thus bringing Provence under Angevin rule.

The Anjou princes ruled for two and a half centuries. They made Aix their administrative capital, although, until they were chased out of Sicily in 1282, they preferred to reside in Palermo or Naples. Good King René (1434-80) likewise concentrated first on Italy, until he lost Naples to Aragon in 1442. Thereafter he split his time between Angers and Provence, establishing his court at Aix and building a lavish chateau at Tarascon. His reign was longer and more stable than most, and the poet-king encouraged a minor artistic revival from his court. The administrative reforms introduced by the last Count of Provence were continued with the establishment of the *états généraux*, a regional assembly that could raise taxes and take over the reins of government in times of crisis. The last of the local warlords, the Baux family, retreated to Orange, setting off the dynastic daisy chain that would lead to the latter becoming a corner of Protestant Holland in the 16th century.

In 1306 French-born pope Clement V made good use of papal bolthole the Comtat Venaissin, transferring his court first to Carpentras and then to Avignon, and ushering in the Papacy's 70-year 'Babylonian captivity'. When the Jews were expelled from France, first in 1306 by Philippe le Bel and again in 1394 under Charles VI, they found refuge in the papal enclave, where fine synagogues survive at Carpentras and Cavaillon. The Avignon Papacy spurred an economic, intellectual and cultural renaissance in the region, with new industries such as glass-making, paper manufacture and melon-growing, and the rise of an artistic school, now known as the Provençal Primitives. Enguerrand Quarton and Nicolas Froment, King René's court painter, were the leading figures of the school, which developed a Flemish-influenced style of crystalline painterly detail. To the east, in the territory of Nice (grabbed by the House of Savoy in 1388) and its mountainous hinterland, Niçois painter Louis Bréa and Piedmontese imports Giovanni Canavesio and Jean Baleison founded a distinctive school between the mid-15th and mid-16th centuries.

EARTHLY UNION AND HEAVENLY DISCORD

Charles du Maine, René's nephew, survived his uncle by only a year. Dying without an heir in 1481, he bequeathed Anjou, Maine and Provence (excluding Savoy, Monaco and the Comtat Venaissin) to portly King Louis XI of France. After trying strong-arm tactics for the first three years, France decided to allow Provence at least the illusion of independence, with the Act of Union (1486) granting the region substantial autonomy within the French state. A *parlement* was established at Aix in 1501, but there were still several pockets of resistance – notably Marseille, which stoutly defended its republican traditions. Francis I subdued the city with the fort on the Ile d'If and used the Marseille shipyards in the Italian wars, waged against his arch-enemy the Holy Roman Emperor Charles V; Charles V replied by besieging the city in 1523.

On the ground, religion became the dominant issue. Protestantism had achieved a firm foothold in Provence, especially among the rural poor. Even before Luther, the Waldensian or Vaudois sect – whose tweaking of Catholic doctrine was more than enough for them to be branded heretical – had put down roots in the Luberon, where feudal landlords encouraged them to repopulate the land after the Black Death. The movement was brutally put down in April 1545, when entire Vaudois villages were massacred. This was just the start of the Wars of Religion, which really kicked in when French Calvinism – or Huguenotism – spread through France in the 1550s. There were Protestant enclaves in Orange, Haute-Provence and the Luberon, but the main seedbed of the new faith lay in Nîmes, where three-quarters of the population were Huguenot. The 1560s saw atrocities on both sides, with most of the Huguenots of Orange massacred in 1563, and a Catholic massacre in Nîmes in 1567. In 1593 the first Bourbon monarch, the Protestant Henri de Navarre (Henry IV), converted to Catholicism and assumed power. To reconcile the warring factions he issued the Edict of Nantes (1598), which guaranteed civil and religious liberties to Protestants.

Under Louis XIII and his minister Cardinal Richelieu, the Catholic Counter-Reformation reached its apogee. Flamboyant baroque churches were built at l'Isle-sur-la-Sorgue, Martigues and in Italian-ruled Nice, while sculptor and architect Pierre Puget built his masterpiece, Vieille Charité, in Marseille. In 1638 Queen Anne of Austria, still childless after 22 years of marriage to Louis XIII, made a pilgrimage to Cotignac to pray for a son; she subsequently visited Apt in 1660 in gratitude for the birth of Louis XIV.

In 1685 Louis XIV, encouraged by his fervently Catholic mistress Madame de Maintenon, revoked the Edict of Nantes, leading to massacres of Protestants in Nîmes and Arles; Protestant churches were demolished and schools closed. The main effect, though, was to deprive Nîmes and Uzès of their industrious Huguenot manufacturers, who emigrated in their thousands. A few did convert, though, and stayed on to make silk and the sturdy blue linen 'de Nîmes' that English merchants called 'denim'.

THE SUN KING'S IRON RULE

By the 17th century, the history of the South was bound up with France. Of use to Paris as a source of fruit, olive oil, wine, textiles and taxes, and as a builder of ships for royal wars, the Midi was drained of funds and, at the same time, kept firmly in line by the increasingly centralised state and absolutist rule of the Sun King ('*l'état c'est moi*') Louis XIV. When restless Marseille dared to set up a rebel council in 1658, Louis XIV turned the town's cannons on itself and built a new fort to keep an eye on the unruly citizens. Toulon became the main base of the Mediterranean fleet, which was busy waging war against the Spanish.

Marseille took a further body blow in 1720, when a visiting Syrian ship caused one of the last big outbreaks of plague in the West, killing 50,000 people in the city alone. A plague wall was built, stretching as far as the Luberon, but the disease spread all the same. Nonetheless, the 18th century was also a time of growing prosperity. A wealthy bourgeoisie developed in the cities where industries thrived: textiles at Nîmes, salt at Aigues-Mortes and Hyères, furniture at Beaucaire, faïence in Marseille and Moustiers, perfumery and leather tanning in Grasse. In the 'parliamentary' city of Aix (capital of the *états généraux* administrative area of Provence), a caste of politicians with plenty of time on their hands built themselves sumptuous townhouses and lavish country *bastides*.

THE END OF THE ANCIEN REGIME

Resentment of Paris and its taxes continued to simmer, fuelled by bad harvests and rising unemployment. When the Revolution broke out in 1789, Provence was swift to join. Among its primary movers was the Comte de Mirabeau, elected as *député* of Aix when the Third Estate was finally convened later that year. The dockers of Marseille were particularly active, taking the forts of St-Jean and St-Nicolas in an echo of the storming of the Bastille.

'Defiance was nurtured in the shipyards of Toulon and Marseille, and most of the South threw its weight behind the 1848 Revolution.'

The republic's battle-hymn 'La Marseillaise' was in fact written by Alsatian Rouget de l'Isle, and was only associated with Marseille after having been adopted by its Jacobin national guard (*les Féderés*) on the march to Paris in 1792.

The Revolution was anti-clerical as well as anti-royal. Religious foundations and churches became state property and religious festivals were replaced by the cult of the Supreme Being. There were some lucky escapes: Toulon cathedral survived as an arms depot; St-Maximin-la-Ste-Baume was saved by an organ rendition of 'La Marseillaise' by Napoleon's brother Lucien. The papal enclave of the Comtat Venaissin was reincorporated into France in 1791, and in 1792 Revolutionary forces took Nice (subsequently handed back to Italy in 1814). Anarchy broke out across France, with counter-revolutionary uprisings brutally put down by Robespierre's Terror of 1793, notably in Marseille and Toulon. The British took advantage of the confusion to occupy Toulon in 1793; they were sent packing by artillery commanded by a rising military star, 24-year-old Napoleon Bonaparte. In 1799, after a military coup, he became First Consul, and declared himself Emperor in 1804.

One of the legacies of the Revolution was a further weakening of regional autonomy with the abolition of the *états généraux* and the carving up of France in 1790 into centrally administered *départements*. Though he had undergone his military training in Antibes and Toulon, Bonaparte had little affection for Provence – a feeling that was entirely mutual. Defeated in 1814, Napoleon was exiled to Elba. His return to France and flight north to Paris through the Alps are commemorated by the Route Napoléon, but his reinstatement was brief. After Waterloo, the monarchy was restored under Louis XVII.

The radical spirit endured, despite heavy losses sustained during the 1832 cholera epidemic. Defiance was nurtured in the shipyards of Toulon and Marseille, and most of the South threw its weight behind the 1848 Revolution, which saw the monarchy again overthrown and Louis-Napoleon Bonaparte, the nephew of Napoleon I, elected first President and in 1852, Emperor Napoleon III. The glittery Second Empire was a period of colonial and industrial expansion. The Suez Canal opened in 1869 and the spread of colonial France quadrupled Marseille's port traffic; stately boulevards, a new cathedral and the Palais Longchamp were built in celebration. Steamships poured out of the shipyards of La Ciotat and La Seyne-sur-Mer, and the coastal railway, an impressive feat of engineering with its tunnels and viaducts, reached Nice by 1865 and Monaco by 1868.

The last major territorial reshuffle took place in 1860, when Napoleon III received Nice and its mountainous hinterland from the House of Savoy in return for his diplomatic neutrality during the unification of Italy. Monaco was now a one-town state, having lost Roquebrune and Menton in 1848 when the inhabitants revolted against the Grimaldis's exorbitant taxes. Ironically, it was his principality's isolation and threatened bankruptcy that spurred Charles III to reinvent Monaco as the gambling capital of Europe, opening its first casino in 1863.

PROVENCE RESURGENT?

At the same time as the industrial revolution, tourism arrived in the South, initially in the form of winter stop-offs for aristos. In 1822 the promenade des Anglais, then a picturesque footpath, was laid out by the English colony in Nice. In 1834 Lord Brougham wintered in Cannes. Russians and English, including Queen Victoria, began flocking to the Riviera.

The 19th century also witnessed the rediscovery of Provence's ancient heritage. By the end of the century, Arles's Roman Arènes had been cleared, Viollet-le-Duc had restored the ramparts of Avignon and excavation had started at Vaison-la-Romaine. While the

IN CONTEXT

centralised administrative and education system meant Provence was more a part of France than ever, and the Provençal language had largely died out except in remote rural communities, there was an ever-present current of Catholic fundamentalism that created different reactionary minorities. Some, led by Frédéric Mistral, pursued the revival of the Provençal language and traditions; others supported Action Française, the proto-Fascist movement founded by Southerner Charles Maurras in Paris in 1899. Mistral, author of epic Provençal poem *Mirèio* (*Mireille*), was one of seven poets who founded the Félibrige movement in Avignon in 1854; he won the Nobel Prize for Literature in 1904.

The early 20th century became the era of the great waterfront hotels, as tourism surged: between 1890 and 1910, the number of foreigners visiting Nice each year grew almost six-fold to more than 150,000. The bourgeoisie, however, continued to winter in the country; only in the 1920s did French artists, designers and socialites begin to descend on Le Midi. American railroad magnate Frank Jay Gould opened up the summer season in Juan-les-Pins, and the artistic avant-garde and modernist architects began building radical new villas.

Though World War I was a distant, rain-soaked northern affair, it took its toll among provençal conscripts, and Fréjus found a curious role as an acclimatisation zone for colonial troops. In the 1930s France saw its first socialist government under Leon Blum's Front Populaire, enthusiastically supported in the South – and the arrival of paid holidays for all.

World War II marked the South. After Paris fell in June 1940 and nominal rule of France was transferred to Maréchal Pétain in Vichy, the South became part of the *zone libre* or free France (except Menton, which was occupied by the Italian army) – not that this prevented the creation of a number of internment camps for aliens, notably at Les Milles, near Aix. Marseille served as an important escape route. Then, from autumn 1942, the South was occupied by German troops. Hardest hit were the naval ports of Marseille and Toulon, ravaged by both Allied bombing and retreating Germans in 1944. Groups of *maquis*, the Resistance, hid out in the hills. The Alpes-Maritimes were occupied by Italian troops until the fall of Italy in September 1943, when they were replaced by Germans. The liberation of Provence by Allied forces based in North Africa came in August 1944, in an attack that centred on the Var. A 250,000-strong wave of Allied manpower landed on provençal shores between Toulon and Cannes, and gradually recaptured the major cities.

THE MODERN SOUTH

Post-war reconstruction was responsible for some of the architectural horrors that dog the South; lax or corrupt planning departments did the rest, suffocating the Côte d'Azur in concrete in an attempt to deal with mass tourism and the urban housing shortage. Environmental damage is another worry. Heavy industry played its part, with the the salt marsh of the Etang de Berre, west of Marseille, becoming a huge oil dump; wild fires – destroying a fifth of the Massif des Maures in 2003 – remain a concern each summer.

In the 1980s Mitterrand granted the regions limited autonomy, and the centralising impetus of the previous centuries began to be reversed. The regional assembly is largely about economic power, however, and with its large number of expat second-homers and immigrants, from outside and within France, has a less fierce sense of regional identity than the Pays Basque and Brittany. Nonetheless, Provençal lessons are now available in schools and dual-language street signs have appeared.

The economy of the South remains skewed, with big disparities between rich and poor, the highest property prices outside Paris, above-average unemployment and a population that soars in summer and plummets in winter. Marseille, France's second city, is a success story of the new South, however, shedding its somewhat shady image and set to become European Capital of Culture in 2013. While conventions and congresses bolster the economies of Nice and Cannes, much of the South remains dependent on tourism. The TGV has brought the South closer than ever to Paris, with trains arriving at Marseilles in under to four hours and Nice in less than six, while the influx of tourists (increasingly, second-homers) remains a source of revenue and a cause of muttering in local cafés.

No Pain, No Gain

The life and times of the South's most scandalous son.

In the scorebook of French grand villains, Donatien Alphonse François de Sade is by no means the most wicked: that honour belongs to the likes of 15th-century child-murderer Gilles de Rais, or serial killer Hénri Landru. But for sheer renown, the Frenchman whose name echoes in a word more widely used even than 'Napoleonic' or 'chauvinist' (and Chauvin, being fictional, doesn't really count) is top dog; and although many Anglophones know him only as a champion pervert, at home he's reckoned by good authorities to be one of the finest writers of all time. No mean feat for a man who spent 27 years behind bars.

Although de Sade was born in Paris, he inherited the family chateau in the Luberon, set on a rocky terrace overlooking the tranquil village of Lacoste (*see p121*). In 1771, partly to escape police investigation of his increasingly wild debaucheries in Paris, he moved there with his wife and their three children, and spent a fortune renovating its 42 rooms. He added a small theatre and invited fellow aristocrats to attend performances of works by Voltaire, Diderot, and Chamfort – directed by de Sade himself, and a great success.

But in June 1772, not for the first time, scandal struck. At an orgy in Marseille involving the marquis, his valet and four young girls, de Sade had handed out cantharidin, better known as the aphrodisiac Spanish fly. The girls fell ill, and two accused Sade of poisoning, which was serious, and sodomy, which was worse. The court of Marseille tried him in absentia and condemned him to death; Sade spent the next few years travelling by night or disguised as a priest, with the occasional secret return to Lacoste. On one occasion he was caught and imprisoned at Miolans, but his wife bribed the guards and he escaped.

In 1777, he made the mistake of showing his face in Paris, and spent the next 12 years in prison at Vincennes and in the Bastille, where he alleviated the tedium by writing graphic tales of orgies, rape, sodomy and torture, including *120 Days of Sodom* and *Justine*. Freed at the outbreak of the Revolution, he triggered new scandals and earned another death sentence that he only escaped by luck, with the timely death of Robespierre. More trouble followed the publication of *Justine*, and in 1801 he was thrown into prison once more; after reportedly attempting to seduce his male fellow-prisoners, he was transferred to Charenton lunatic asylum, where he died 13 years later at the age of 74.

The South of France Today

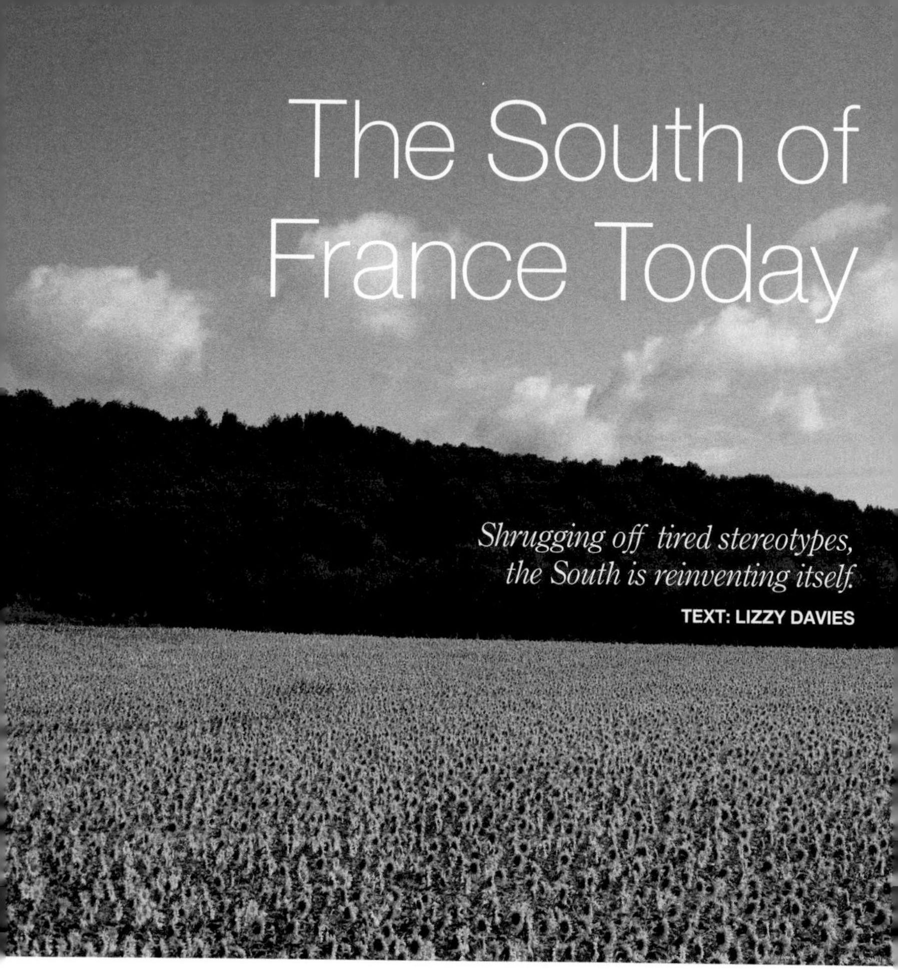

Shrugging off tired stereotypes,
the South is reinventing itself.

TEXT: LIZZY DAVIES

Azure skies and translucent, turquoise seas. Terracotta roofs and tumble-down farmhouses. Sleepy hillside villages, bustling, sun-kissed harbours and beautiful people with perma-tans lounging on their yachts. Cypress trees, olives and pines. Pastis and *pétanque*...

It's hard to talk about the South of France without resorting to cliché. In a part of the world where aesthetic perfection is always around the corner, this is hardly surprising – but it's also a great shame, because there's so much to the region that defies glib generalisation and lazy stereotype. Sure, there are sweltering, sandy beaches, and a chameleon light that changes colour with the clock, but there's also a lot more. Look a little closer, past the ten-a-euro picture-postcard images, and you'll find a reality that's more complex, more characterful – and infinitely more intriguing.

Based in France,
Lizzy Davies
writes for the
Guardian *and*
the Observer.

'There was no one at Antibes this summer except me, Zelda, the Valentinos, the Murphys, Mistinguett, Rex Ingram, Dos Passos, Alice Terry, the MacLeishes, Charlie Brackett, Maude Kahn, Esther Murphy, Marguerite Namara, E Phillips Oppenheim, Mannes the violinist, Floyd Dell, Max and Crystal Eastman, ex-Premier Orlando, Etienne de Beaumont – just a real place to rough it, an escape from all the world.'
– F Scott Fitzgerald, in a letter to John Peale Bishop, 1925

In his frustrated quest for peace and quiet, poor old Scott brilliantly summed up one of the first lessons of the South of France: it may be your idea of the perfect holiday, but it's also everyone else's. The region that sweeps like a jagged half-moon around the coastline, from the foothills of the Alps in the east to the Rhône Delta in the west, is the jewel in the crown of a country with the largest tourism industry in the world. Its tides ebb and flow with the visitors that surge on to its shores every day, week and month.

For the locals, this is a double-edged sword. Many towns and villages live off tourism money, their best bet for survival in the modern world. In the summer, both obvious seaside resorts and tiny provençal villages swarm with non-natives. It's hard to know which tourists the southerners regard with more distrust: the package-tour foreigners with sunburned noses and bum-bags, the millionaire foreigners with designer handbags and sprawling villas, or the Parisians with… well, their ineffable, unshakeable Parisian-ness.

The British have long been a fixture in the South; Fitzgerald's summertime hangout was even dubbed 'Angle-tibes' for its sheer concentration of English expats. The Americans, Germans and Italians have also been showing up for decades. From Angelina Jolie and Brad Pitt's $60-million Miraval chateau to David and Victoria Beckham's villa in the Var, celebrities of every nationality have made themselves feel at home. So, too, have President Nicolas Sarkozy and Carla Bruni, his supermodel-turned-singer wife. And now, for the first time since their pre-Revolution Riviera heyday, the Russians are coming. In St-Tropez, ground zero of the 'blingski' invasion, taxi drivers tell of five-minute journeys paid with €500 bills, and waiters speak of £6,000 bottles of wine left half-full on tables. This summer, Russian billionaire Mikhail Prokhorov was reported to have shelled out $750 million for the world's most expensive home, a villa set in 20 acres of grounds in Villefranche-sur-Mer.

MONEY, MONEY, MONEY

However, this kind of influx brings problems. Perhaps more in parts of the South than anywhere else in France, local people sometimes feel as if they're being pushed aside in the race to become a more lucrative magnet for tourists. Aside from the resentment that these divisions can create, especially in the poverty-stricken social-housing projects inland, there are more concrete drawbacks. Travelling down the Côte d'Azur in peak season, it's easy to see that although the tourist industry is keeping many places afloat, it's also killing off some of the spirit of the South that attracts visitors in the first place. In some hot spots, property prices have risen out of the reach of ordinary families, and many key workers can't afford to rent (let alone buy) in the towns where they work. In others, locals fear that their indigenous culture is being wiped out by holiday resorts and amusement parks.

In St-Tropez, an ongoing war of words crystallises all these issues. Led by Jean-Claude Molho, a 76-year-old photojournalist whose tranquil retirement has been marred by the constant thundering of millionaires' choppers over his otherwise idyllic home, the residents are urging the authorities to clamp down on so-called 'cowboy' helicopter pilots who pander to the whims of their wealthy clients and land wherever, whenever they choose. The activists, some of whom have lived in the environs for decades, accuse the local government of favouring a tiny minority of rich visitors at the expense of an entire population. For their part, the authorities say they cannot afford to put off such a lucrative section of society, as this particular town – perhaps more than any other in France – is reliant on it for its daily bread. It may be true, but it doesn't make it any more pleasant for long-suffering locals. It's a small-scale debate, but it's based on a fundamental question that affects the entire region: to whom does the South really belong?

IN CONTEXT

'Even the time-worn provençal heartlands are responding to the needs of a new century.'

GROWING PAINS

In a different context, the same question is also asked when the immigration debate raises its ugly head – which happens all too often. Lying just across the Mediterranean from North Africa, the South has historically attracted a sizeable proportion of France's low-income immigrant workers. Many live on sprawling suburban estates, their unemployment rate far higher than the national average. Most can no more enjoy the glamorous side to the Côte d'Azur than their billionaire neighbours can imagine what it must be like to live on the minimum wage of €8.71 per hour.

When Jean-Marie Le Pen shockingly swept to second place in the presidential elections of 2002, his far-right party's unrivalled bedrock of support proved to be the South. The biggest Front National vote of all came from Beaucaire, a picturesque town on the banks of the Rhône where the winding inner-city streets are referred to as 'the Kasbah' because of their large immigrant population. Thankfully, the threat of that year's 'earthquake' has now receded, largely because those who voted FN six years ago found a mainstream candidate who's tough enough on immigration to win their trust – in 2007, large parts of the South turned from Le Pen to Sarkozy. But two of the FN's most ringing endorsements came from the Vaucluse (16.8 per cent of the vote) and Beaucaire's Gard (15.4 per cent) *départements*, and the atmosphere in many places remains tense.

REINVENTING THE REGION

Amid this bad feeling, Marseille stands proud as the exception to the rule. Bold, brash and refreshingly down-to-earth, France's largest city was the only one of the country's metropolises not to riot in autumn 2005. With an 800,000-strong population that includes 200,000 Muslims, 80,000 North African Jews and 80,000 Armenians, it's an ethnically mixed melting pot where the inhabitants, in the words of one resident, 'just rub along'.

Until now, Marseille has been strangely reticent about pushing itself into the limelight, despite its urban model receiving almost universal praise. Unlike almost every other town in the South, it doesn't show any great desire to attract the most tourists or win the most Michelin stars. But in 2008, the city's authorities pulled off something of a coup: against stiff competition from Lyon, Bordeaux and Toulouse, the scrappy cosmopolitan underdog won the battle to become the European Capital of Culture in 2013. Over the next four years, €98 million will be poured into the city's coffers to give the Marseillais the arts scene they deserve. After years of staying under the radar, the birthplace of France's national anthem is putting itself back on the map.

It's not the only place in the South that's harnessing its natural charms to a new lease of life. Around 200 kilometres up the coast, the sleepy town of Nice is getting a shot of adrenalin thanks to Christian Estrosi, its newly elected motorcycle-racing mayor, who wants to turn the seaside resort into the first 'green' city of the Med through a raft of environmental policies such as lowering the cost of public transport. Even the time-worn provençal heartlands are responding to the needs of a new century. When not struggling to cope with leaks from the local Tricastin nuclear plant, the entire Drôme region is reinventing itself as France's first organic *département*, complete with 'bio' farms, vineyards, markets and essential oils, and finding a flourishing new market among clean-living, eco-friendly tourists. Just don't ask too many questions about radiation levels.

But these unlikely new developments are every bit as much a part of the South of France as the terracotta roofs and cypress trees of popular imagination. Town and country, native and foreign, past and present, grit and glamour – all meet here, in all their glorious contradictions. Just try and leave the clichés at home.

IN CONTEXT

Provençal Food & Wine

Days of wine and rosé – plus feasts of provençal fare.

TEXT: ROSA JACKSON & RICHARD JAMES

*Food writer **Rosa Jackson** writes about Provence and Paris for a global array of publications and teaches provençal cookery (www. petitsfarcis.com).*

__Richard James__ lives in the South of France and is the editor of www. winewriting.com. He also contributes to a number of wine and travel publications, including Decanter.

With gleaming fruit and vegetables piled high on its market stalls, and a reputation as a foodie mecca, Provence seems like a land of plenty. Yet the difficult landscape and often-extreme weather conditions have long forced locals to make ingenious use of modest ingredients. Before becoming the star of a Disney film, ratatouille was simply a way to use up vegetables that might be past their best: its name translates as 'an unappetising mix'. In the niçois speciality *tourte de blettes*, swiss chard fills in for fruit in a sweet tart. Meat is never taken for granted – most southerners would rather tuck into *daube* (cheap cuts of beef stewed in red wine with herbs and orange zest) than a fillet. Robust peasant fare lies at the heart of provençal cuisine, and continues to inspire even the most high-flying of chefs, in the kitchens of Provence's myriad Michelin-starred establishments.

Vines, meanwhile, have thrived across the region since time immemorial, cultivated here even before the Romans arrived in 122 BC. A bewildering array of appellations occupy its sun-baked plains and limestone hills, some household names such as Châteauneuf-du-Pape and Côtes de Provence, others barely known beyond the *département* borders – and crying out to be discovered.

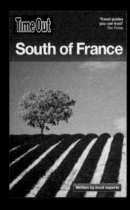

Provençal Food

Although the Vaucluse and the Var produce a high proportion of the fruit and vegetables sold across France, it's still worth seeking out the small farmers at local open-air markets (see p31 **Market Forces**): their selection of produce might be smaller and less perfect looking, but you'll be rewarded with a more intense flavour and the satisfaction of having met the person who produced your food. On a Saturday morning at the cours Saleya market in Nice, recipes whizz around like volleyballs on a patch of sandy beach, with the odd decisive spike as a *grand-mère* wins the last word in a heated culinary debate. Shoppers exchange tips for making *les petits farcis* (stuffed vegetables designed to use up leftover meat), while the organic tomato specialist hand-picks the ripest specimens in shades of yellow, pink, green, orange and occasionally red for his customers. More experienced cooks buy kilos of purple figs for jam-making (they know the season only lasts a few weeks), while novices get advice on how to deep-fry courgette flowers. No wonder so few people here own more than a couple of cookbooks.

VIVE LA DIFFERENCE: REGIONAL SPECIALITIES

Similar scenes take place in markets across Provence – with a few key differences. Just a few kilometres away in Cagnes-sur-Mer, fresh fish is more bountiful than in Nice. Menton, meanwhile, has its own subtropical microclimate, some of the world's best lemons and an Italian-influenced cooking style (unsurprising, given its proximity to the border). Glitzy Cannes quietly houses the finest collection of small fruit and vegetable producers on the Côte d'Azur in its Forville market, while on the Vieux Port in Marseille you can watch little wooden fishing boats deliver the live catch. St-Tropez, with its daily fish market, serves as a magnet not just for luxury yachts but also for serious foodies. Inland, fish gives way to beef, lamb and, in the Camargue, slow-cooked bull's meat.

In the Rhône Valley, the food often takes a back seat to some of the world's most sensual red and white wines. Elsewhere, crisp, chilled rosé makes a perfect match for summer fare, while bold provençal reds, particularly the celebrated Bandol, take over in winter. Provence is probably the only region in France where it's perfectly acceptable to put ice cubes in a glass of white or rosé, so don't be shy about following the locals' lead.

Hard winters, when the populace is whipped by the Mistral, call for rib-sticking dishes such as long-simmered *daube*. Leftover *daube* is used to stuff vegetables, while *pan bagnat* is salade niçoise stuffed into a bun, all the better for taking into the fields. Though the original versions of these dishes were always delicious, they were rarely refined – and that's where the current generation of chefs comes in. The stars of provençal cooking – **Alain Llorca** at the Moulin de Mougins (see p242); **Jacques Chibois** at the Bastide St-Antoine in Grasse (see p294); **Franck Cerutti** at the Louis XV in Monaco (see p284); vegetable maestro **Jean-Luc Rabanel** in Arles (see p75); **Christian Etienne** in Avignon (see p94); **Daniel Hébet**, at his outstanding bistro Le Jardin du Quai in l'Isle-sur-la-Sorgue (91 avenue Julien Guigue, 04.90.20.14.98, www.lejardinduquai.com) – bring finesse to peasant cooking, using technical prowess to let the ingredients speak for themselves.

It would be dishonest to pretend, however, that just being in Provence is a guarantee of good food. Marvellous ingredients are there for the taking, but not all chefs bother seeking them out. With so many potential victims coming through their doors in high season, they easily fall prey to cynicism – particularly near the seafront (with some notable exceptions). If you hope to get to the heart of provençal cooking, it pays to do some research – and perhaps rent a *gîte* or apartment with a kitchen, so you can try out the recipes for yourself.

MEAT AND POULTRY

Beef, a provençal favourite, might be grilled with herbs, simmered in a *daube* or sautéed with morels. In the Camargue look out for dark, tender bull's meat (*taureau*), simply grilled or stewed in a hearty *boeuf à la gardiane*. Sheep raised in Les Alpilles, the Crau plain and

'Thrift is at the heart of provençal cooking, and the less noble parts of the animals are also used.'

Haute Provence (most famously around Sisteron) produce tender lamb, which might be roasted with rosemary, summer savory or whole heads of garlic; *daube à l'avignonnaise* features lamb rather than beef. Game includes rabbit, hare and wild boar from the *garrigues* (brush hillsides) and woodland, which find their way into rich stews and saucissons. Rabbit is also stewed with white wine, herbs, tomatoes and sometimes tapenade. Few recipes exist for chicken in the provençal repertoire, though anise-spiked *poulet au pastis* is a classic; *canard aux olives* is a typically southern way to prepare duck.

Thrift is at the heart of provençal cooking and the less noble parts of the animals are also used, as in the *pieds et paquets* of Marseille (stuffed tripe and sheep's feet stewed in wine) or the type of *porchetta* found in Nice (whole pig, stuffed with its deboned meat, herbs, tripe and liver). Charcuteries along the coast sell delicious Italian-style sausages.

FISH

Coastal Provence has developed a splendid battery of fish and shellfish dishes, though given that there is barely enough fish to go around these days, you shouldn't assume that every fish restaurant sells the local catch. A limited amount of mostly very expensive fish is sold at the Marseille, St-Tropez, Cannes, Antibes and Cagnes-sur-Mer fish markets or delivered direct to seashore restaurants (some of which have their own fishing boats). The celebrated bouillabaisse is found all along the coast, although Marseille is its acknowledged home; a group of restaurateurs even signed a charter to defend the authentic recipe. Bouillabaisse is traditionally served in two courses: first the saffron-tinted soup, accompanied by toasted baguette, fiery rouille and a sprinkling of gruyère, then the fish. Purists insist on 12 varieties of fish and shellfish, but the three essentials are *rascasse* (scorpion fish), *grondin* (red gurnard) and *congre* (conger eel). Outside Marseille be sure to try *soupe de poissons*, made of tiny rockfish that are cooked with tomato, onion, saffron and chilli pepper and served with croutons, gruyère or parmesan and rouille.

Less well-known but equally delicious is *bourride*, a creamy, garlic-spiked fish soup made from one or more of John Dory, sea bass and monkfish, and bound with aïoli. If you're lucky, you may find *poutargue*, the pressed, salted grey mullet roe that is a speciality of Martigues. Mussels are raised in the bay of Toulon and are popular on the Var coast, eaten *à la marinière* (with white wine, onions and shallots), *à la provençale* (with white wine, tomatoes, onion and garlic) or gratinéed. Other fish preparations include sea bass grilled with fennel or baked in a salt crust, and red mullet with tapenade. *Brandade de morue*, salt cod soaked in milk and puréed with olive oil, is a speciality of Nîmes (salt cod came to Provence hundreds of years ago through trade with Scandinavia). Some of the best meals consist of just-out-of-the-sea fish, chosen at table, then charcoal-grilled. Expect to pay by weight (allow roughly 400g-500g per person).

FRUIT AND VEGETABLES

The quality and variety of the vegetables and fruit are generally superb, whether they come from fields and orchards along the Durance and Var rivers or from tiny coastal gardens. As a result, this part of France is a paradise for vegetarians – although specifically vegetarian menus are rare. As well as ratatouille, other favourites include *artichauts à la barigoule*, *tomates provençales* (slow-baked tomatoes topped with breadcrumbs and garlic), *soupe au pistou* (provençal minestrone) and courgette-blossom fritters. There are also all manner of stuffed vegetables and baked *tians* (gratins named after the dish in which they are cooked). And what could be simpler or more delicious than grilled red peppers, served cold and drizzled with olive oil?

Market Forces

An insider's guide to provençal markets.

Lourmarin market.

At the height of summer, a provençal market is a bustling beast. The August sun beats down, cars are parked at every conceivable angle, and the narrow aisles between the stalls are thronged. Amid the colourful parade of parasols, it's easy to assume that everything is authentic. Beware: plenty of traders have embraced the global economy and discovered cheaper goods elsewhere; provençal-patterned tablecloths from the Far East, lavender sachets from Bulgaria – even vegetables from the wholesale market.

The best advice is to turn up early, ask plenty of questions as to provenance and above all shadow the locals; they'll know the traders who grow their own veg, or harvest and sell their own lavender, and will shun the summer interlopers trying to make a quick buck out of the tourists. They might even lead you up a side street to where a neighbour is selling figs and apricots fresh from the garden.

RECOMMENDED MARKETS

Lourmarin's Friday morning market (*see p123*) has grown into one of the biggest in the Luberon. Visited out of season, it's a delight; in summer, visit early to avoid the crowds. Under the shady avenue of plane trees, you can buy everything from fresh fruit and vegetables to handcrafted olive-wood ornaments. Don't miss Martine the honey lady, whose pitch is by the post office. She sells over ten different types of honey, from lavender to forest, depending on the location of the hives. In early summer she harvests asparagus, selling huge bundles at bargain prices.

Another good bet is **Ansouis** (*see p123*) on Sunday morning. Even at the height of summer the market retains a local feel, with ten or so stalls grouped around the small square. Best of all is Barbara's butcher's van, its counter full of spread-eagled rabbits and unidentifiable cuts of meat (not for the squeamish). The real attraction is the unique blend of spices she uses on her *poulet* and *pintard roti* – the spit-roast chicken and guinea fowl are so good that market traders have flown in from South Africa to learn from her.

Finally, try **L'Isle-sur-la-Sorgue** (*see p127*) on a Sunday morning. Its antique and *brocante* stalls draw the tourists, but head for the town centre, away from the rushing waters of the Sorgue, and you can find some great stalls. In late autumn, Paul the mushroom man sets up opposite the church. He spends the early hours of the morning high on the hillside hunting for *lactaires*, *girolles* and *trompettes de la morte*, before hotfooting it into town to sell his mud-covered produce.

IN CONTEXT

Fish market, Marseille.

In spring, the region produces some of the best white, green and violet-tipped asparagus in France, followed by a summer abundance of aubergines, peppers, courgettes (look out for yellow and round varieties) and tomatoes. Artichokes are usually of the violet, almost chokeless, variety and can be eaten raw once they are trimmed. Humbler chickpeas, broad beans and fennel also feature in traditional recipes, as do *blettes* (swiss chard) – which make their way into tarts, stews, pasta, stuffings for fish and meat, and even desserts. *Epeautre* (spelt), grown on Mont Ventoux, has made a bit of a comeback, and excellent rice is still grown in the Camargue. Autumn brings squash, wild mushrooms and pumpkins, and winter is the time for truffles in the Drôme, Luberon and Var.

Delicious orange-fleshed *melon de Cavaillon* have been grown here since being introduced by the Avignon papacy in the 14th century. Other fruit cultivated in the region includes early strawberries from Carpentras, cherries, apricots, table grapes, peaches, plums, citrus fruits of all kinds in winter and a sumptuous glut of figs in late summer.

CHEESE

Dairying is limited, but you'll find plenty of farmhouse goat's and ewe's cheeses at markets. Look out for unctuous *banon*, made in the area around Forcalquier with goat's milk, wrapped in a chestnut leaf and aged to a pungent runniness; *picodon*, a small, young, tangy goat's cheese from north Provence; *pelardon*, similar to *picodon*, but aged and very firm; and *brousse de Rove*, a ricotta-like soft, mild, fresh cheese made from goat's or ewe's milk and used to fill ravioli or eaten drizzled with olive oil or honey. *Brocciu*, produced in Corsica with ewe's milk, is similar. Higher in the mountains, some farmers produce big round *tommes* (mild-flavoured or quite strong), made with cow's milk.

THE RESTAURANTS

At the grandest establishments, with their famous chefs, you'll eat sublime food and pay sublimely ridiculous prices. Locals tend to patronise these places only on special occasions or for lunch, when many renowned kitchens offer relatively affordable menus.

Otherwise they are more likely to seek out good value, accepting less silverware and perhaps a single waiter or waitress in exchange for cooking that's spot on.

The traditional emphasis on vegetables, olive oil and fish or small quantities of meat in the provençal diet already perfectly matches today's health concerns, but the southern restaurant scene has not stood still. If many restaurants delight in trad Provence, with print tablecloths and the comforting reassurance of age-old *daubes* and *tians*, other eateries are renewing southern cuisine with the creative use of seasonal, regional produce or by introducing cosmopolitan touches. Outside influences are not new: the Italian kitchen had a strong impact in Nice – for a long time part of the kingdom of Genoa – and Italianate gnocchi and ravioli (the latter often filled with *daube*) are common, alongside all sorts of other local snacks. Marseille cuisine goes well beyond bouillabaisse; the city boasts superb ethnic restaurants, reflecting the kaleidoscopic variety of people who've settled there. The city has large Italian, Spanish, North African, Greek and Armenian communities, and these cuisines have influenced many chefs.

When possible, think carefully before choosing your restaurant – €30 per person can buy you a feast in a bistro headed by a passionate chef, but these are not exactly thick on the ground in tourist hotspots. Be especially cautious in high season, when restaurants often hire unqualified staff. A worthwhile alternative is *tables d'hôtes*, offered in many B&Bs, where the hosts prepare a simple country-style meal; if they are doing this, chances are they want to share their love of the local food. Sometimes there is nothing more satisfying than a picnic on the beach with some local cheese and *fougasse* (flatbread cooked with olives or vegetables) and a bottle of chilled rosé.

Restaurants are generally relaxed in France. Although you shouldn't come to the table in a bathing costume unless you're right on the beach, ties are rarely required and T-shirts and shorts are usually fine. However, the French are often well dressed (think smart-casual), especially in the evening. Seaside showbiz destinations can be distinctly glitzy (gold jewellery and tans, real or fake, required), while haute cuisine establishments, even in a village, can be as dressy as Paris – if not more so. Finally, don't expect menus to be in English (though many are); for restaurant- and food-related vocabulary, *see p327*.

Provençal Wine

Despite the region's unimpeachable wine-making pedigree, local *vignerons* aren't resting on their laurels. Until recently, the provençal wine scene was generally more sedate – and certainly less vociferous – than its winegrowing neighbours in the more activist Languedoc and Catalan-hearted Roussillon. However, winemakers have reacted quickly to adapt to changing tastes at home and abroad – particularly the spiralling popularity of pink wine (*see p34* **Profile: Rosé**).

The relatively hot and dry southern climate favours a wealth of red grape varieties, from cabernet to cinsaut, sauvignon to syrah – and Provence is home to some big-hearted (and world-renowned) reds. White wine is rarer, with a few honourable exceptions. Cassis is probably the most famous white wine-producing area; look out, too, around La Londe-les-Maures. Other areas that might surprise you with their whites include certain villages in the southern Rhône Valley – among them king of reds Châteauneuf-du-Pape, where several estates are also highly regarded for their textured, creamy and nutty whites, which can age magnificently; ditto the Gigondas area. The grape varieties you'll come across include rolle (also called vermentino), sémillon, ugni blanc, marsanne, roussanne, grenache blanc, clairette and bourboulenc.

There's a long tradition of making fruity, dry rosés in the Mediterranean – and Provence is the quintessential land of rosé, in quantity if not always quality: rosés make up three-quarters of some appellations' production. Not just for summer, many have the fruitiness of a red, to match the hearty local cuisine, yet retain the crisp bite of a chilled white. The best, and the dearest (though it's a bit of a cheek charging the same price as for cask-aged

IN CONTEXT

Profile Rosé

The rosé revolution: how pink became the new white.

**THREE
TO TRY**
**Château Saint
Estève de Néri**
(Ansouis, 04.
90.09.90.16).
Pale and light
– a perfect
aperitif.

**Domaine
Saint André
de Figuière**
(La Londe-les-
Maures, 04.94.
00.44.70). A
perfumed and
delicate rosé.

**Château de
Roquefort**
(Roquefort La
Bédoule, 04.
42.73.20.84).
An ideal match
for grilled fish
and meat.

Horror of all horrors: 2008 saw a seismic shift in the wine world, an event that affronted the quivering noses and delicate palates of wine buffs everywhere. The French, sticklers in the classification of great vintages and ever resistant to change, woke up to the shameful news that as a nation they consumed more rosé than white wine. The most educated drinkers in the world had stopped sipping buttery Burgundies and turned to rosé. What was going on?

In the 1980s, pink wine was synonymous with hangovers and upset stomachs – and generally little more than a byproduct of red wine-making. To beef up the flavour of their reds, *vignerons* bled a little of the juice from the barrel at an early stage of fermentation. The resulting liquid had a pink tinge; winemakers would add sulphur to preserve its life then keep it in a barrel at the back of the cellar, selling it to anyone brave or ignorant enough to ask for rosé.

But towards the end of the '90s a revival began. Every year, thousands of litres of unsold

French wine were being thrown away or converted into fuel. Acres of vines were being ripped up in a desperate bid to combat overproduction, and sending a Christmas case of wine to the bank was no longer enough to stave off the threat of foreclosure. Vineyards were in crisis, but one group of winemakers were doing well: those who made good rosé.

The technique was simple. Take a red grape or combination of red grapes and control the amount of time the juice spent in contact with the skin. The longer the contact, the deeper the rosé's hue. Some winemakers stayed up all night testing the wine every hour to create the perfect tint; others quickly pressed the grapes for the faintest hint of colour.

Customers were rediscovering their taste for rosé. Stricter drink-driving rules meant people felt uncomfortable quaffing heavy reds and heady whites, and there was a perception – not always accurate – that pink wine was less alcoholic. By 2000, rosé was seriously hip. Kate Moss was snapped on the Côte d'Azur with a bottle peeking from her Chanel bag, and beach clubs held wild parties, fuelled by rosé bottles so big that scantily clad waitresses had to kneel to pour from them.

Winemakers responded by creating better and better wines, with some increasingly dry styles and rosés left to mature in oak to add flavour and complexity. These days, smart restaurants will even decant certain rosés to allow them to breathe – a practice that once would have seen any self-respecting wine waiter laughed out of his profession.

reds), are often from Bandol, Les Baux, Tavel and parts of Côtes de Provence. They are made from 'free-run' juice, drained or 'bled' off from crushed red grapes, after steeping in the skins for a few hours to pick up a hint of colour. The juice is then fermented fairly cool to preserve the fresh aromas and fruity overtones. Only the sturdier, more expensive rosé styles get better after over a year or so in bottle, so buy the youngest vintage possible.

Opportunities to visit vineyards abound throughout the region. The bigger vineyards are likely to have set seasonal opening hours and run regular tasting sessions and tours, while smaller establishments might be one-man operations, open by appointment only. In either case, it's best to call in advance. Harvest time (from late August to late September) is an exciting time to visit, although the owner or winemaker will probably be too busy to attend to vistors personally. Some estates charge a small fee for a full tasting and tour, but most provide both for nothing – although you're expected to buy something, even if it's just a bottle or two. A note of caution for those on the tasting trail: France has strict (and strictly enforced) drink-driving laws, with a maximum blood alcohol level of 0.5 g/l, compared to 0.8 g/l in the UK. If you don't like the idea of tasting-and-spitting, choose a compact route and cycle.

Suggested tours of four very different wine regions appear later in this book: the almost entirely organic Baux-de-Provence appellation (see p65); the relatively undiscovered wine villages of Gigondas and Rasteau (see p110); the justly famed red- and rosé-producing Bandol (see p182), overlooking the sea in the western Var; and white-wine producing Cassis (see p162). There are also some interesting wines to be had in the bijou Bellet appellation, tucked away in the hills behind Nice (see p260).

CHATEAUNEUF-DU-PAPE – THE KING OF REDS?

Châteauneuf-du-Pape needs little introduction; winemakers here have done a sterling job of creating an image of red wine nirvana revered around the globe. Good matches for the opulent, warming reds include game, lamb, cured sausage or gruyère, but it's pricey stuff: most start at €10-€15, with much higher prices for top estates. The central grape varieties are grenache, syrah and mourvèdre (plus more obscure ones such as counoise), which usually get very ripe in the hot summers and dry pebbley soils this area is known for. It'll be interesting to see whether these heady reds, with up to 14 per cent alcohol, will retain their popularity now that lighter wines are coming into vogue.

Although the appellation is surprisingly sprawling, a number of fantastic producers cluster around the village of Châteauneuf itself. Esteemed names include **Domaine Chante Cigale** (av Louis Pasteur, 04.90.83.70.57, www.chantecigale.com), **Domaine du Pégau** (av Imperiale, 04.90.83.72.70, www.pegau.com), **Château Fortia** (rte d'Avignon, 04.90.83.72.25, www.chateau-fortia.com), **Château Mont-Redon** (chemin du Maucoil, 04.90.83.72.75, www.chateaumontredon.fr) and **Domaine La Roquette** (Vignoles Brunier, 3 rte Châteauneuf, Bédarrides, 04.90.33.00.31, www.brunier.fr). Enthusiasts should also check out the **Maison des Vins** (8 rue Maréchal Foch, Châteauneuf-du-Pape, 04.90.83. 70.69), which stocks over 90 different domaines. It's much harder to get an invitation to exclusive names such as **Château de Beaucastel** (chemin de Beaucastel, Courthezon, 04.90.70.41.00, www.beaucastel.com), **Château la Nerthe** (rte de Sorgues, 04.90.83. 70.11, www.chateaulanerthe.fr), **Château Rayas** (rte Courthézon, 04.90.83.73.09, www. chateaurayas.fr) and **Domaine du Vieux Télégraphe** (Vignoles Brunier, 3 rte Châteauneuf, 04.90.33.00.31, www.vieuxtelegraphe.com) – but nothing ventured, nothing gained. For further information on the appellation, see www.chateauneuf.com.

FROM THE COTES DE PROVENCE TO THE MASSIF DES MAURES

Getting your head around the vast Côtes de Provence (www.vinsdeprovence.com) region is no mean feat: the appellation covers some 20,000 hectares (49,400 acres), stretching across the Var towards Marseille to the west and Grasse to the east. So many vineyards and villages mean very diverse terrain, producers and personalities. The end results range from cheap and cheerful (though very drinkable) supermarket plonk to some pretty serious

IN CONTEXT

bottles, all labelled with the same AOC badge. To make things easier, growers have been creating a handful of sub-appellations, such as Côtes de Provence Fréjus and Côtes de Provence Sainte-Victoire. If you're planning a wine-buying expedition, it pays to concentrate on a specific area and try to get acquainted with the best producers within it.

Shadowed by the Massif des Maures range, the scenic stretch from Hyères to St-Tropez has several quality-minded estates. To start, there's a pocket of vineyards north-west of Hyères around La Crau: try **Domaine de Mont-Redon** (2496 rte de Pierrefeu, 04.94.57.82.12, www.mont-redon.net), which also produces its own olive oil. La Londe-les-Maures is another good starting point, with over 20 producers – check out **Château Sainte-Marguerite** (Le Haut Pansard, 04.94.00.44.44, www.chateausaintemarguerite. com), which produces full-bodied, concentrated reds, lively rosés and an unusual white.

Between La Londe and Bormes-Les-Mimosas, on the winding route de Léoube, two names to note are **Domaine de la Sanglière** (No.3886, 04.94.00.48.58, www.domaine-sangliere.com) and **Château de Brégançon** (No.639, 04.94.64.80.73, www.chateau-de-bregancon.fr). Not far from St-Tropez, near Gassin, there's one of the grandest Cru Classés (an old unofficial classification): the **Château Minuty** (rte de Ramatuelle, 04.94.56.12.09).

AIX & WESTERN PROVENCE

The western chunk of Provence is Coteaux d'Aix country, spreading from the Durance to the sea and from the Rhône to Montagne Ste-Victoire. Just outside Aix, two names to look out for are the **Château des Gavelles** and **Château Beaulieu** (04.42.50.20.19, www.pgadomaines.com): at Gavelles, sample the classic, zingy rosé and solid, tangy red; at Beaulieu, the juicy but elegant rosé. East of Aix, Ste-Victoire has given its name to a recently carved out Côtes de Provence sub-region (www.vins-sainte-victoire.com), centred on Trets. Growers are furious about the TGV line extension to Nice that will cut right through their vineyards; will they win their case? On the way there, there's also the blink-and-miss-it Palette AOC, which serves up the odd reasonable red.

Moving on to the elevated terrain between Cuers and Le Luc, try **Domaine du Grand Cros** near Carnoules (D13, quai Grand Cros, 04.98.01.80.08, www.grandcros.fr) and, north of Brignoles, **Domaine des Aspras** (chemin Pont Frac, quartier Aspras, 04.94.59. 59.70, www.aspras.com) in Correns, which produces a delicate, classy Cuvée Tradition rosé. Brad and Angelina were 'spotted' in this village before they landed at nearby organic estate **Château Miraval** (off D554, 04.94.86.39.33, www.miraval.com), close to Le Val. Some of its vineyards lie in the Coteaux Varois AOC, which takes in 28 villages around Brignoles between the craggy Ste-Baume and Bessillons ranges.

Another impressive estate in the area is the beautifully set **Château Lafoux** in Tourves (RN7 between St-Maximin & Tourves, 04.94.78.77.86, www.chateaulafoux.com), with its subtly perfumed, deliciously fruity rosé. Look out, too, for the **Château Val-Joanis** (D973 exit 15, 04.90.79.20.77, www.val-joanis.com), in the über-fashionable Côtes du Luberon.

NIMES & NORTH-WESTERN PROVENCE

In the Rhône Delta, a gladiator's spear-throw from the ancient city of Nîmes, is the increasingly dynamic Costières de Nîmes AOC (www.costieres-nimes.com). The estates spread out to the south of the city, with growers tending to focus on red wine and rosé; two notable estates are the **Château de Campuget** (mas du Campuget, Manduel, 04.66.20.20.15, www.campuget.com) and the organically farmed **Domaine Pastouret** (rte de Jonquières, Bellegarde, 04.66.01.62.29, www.domaine-pastouret.com).

In the Alpilles, the village of Les Baux is at the centre of a small but thriving organic wine scene (*see p65* **Wine Tour**), with some notable estates. North of here, in the Vaucluse, Côtes du Ventoux is another mountain-shadowed, undiscovered and red-dominated inland region. Set to the north of the Luberon, its 100 domaines and 15 co-operatives are dotted across the eastern side of Carpentras. Try the **Château de l'Isolette** (rte de Bonnieux, Apt, 04.90.74.16.70), or see www.cotes-ventoux.com for five suggested wine trails and a comprehensive list of estates.

The Artistic South

Avant-garde art and the Côte d'Azur.

TEXT: NATASHA EDWARDS

Natasha Edwards writes on contemporary art, French design, food and travel for Elle Decoration, the Independent, Condé Nast Traveller, the Daily Telegraph, and Contemporary.

If, for some artists, the appeal of the South lay in its brilliant colours, its flora and vegetation, its burning light and strong shadows – the Montagne Sainte-Victoire for Cézanne, mimosa for Bonnard, the endless sea for Signac – for others it lay in the rise of the new leisure activities of yachting and bathing, and the antics of the Riviera set.

Artists were the pioneers to first colonise the South – helped by the advent of the railway, which made it newly accessible from Paris and beyond, and allowed a constant dialogue with the artistic currents going on in Paris, New York and Moscow. In the first half of the 20th century, Provence and the Côte d'Azur became the cosmopolitan playgrounds of the rich and the avant-garde. Artists, writers, composers, choreographers, photographers and film-makers mingled with wealthy patrons: Gertrude Stein, the Murphys and the Goulds in Juan-les-Pins, and the Comte and Comtesse de Noailles in Hyères.

After World War II, the world's art spotlight shifted from France to the USA. However, the South remained a creative hub, thanks to the numerous artists who continued to work there (including Nicolas de Staël, Marc Chagall, Victor Vasarely, Max Ernst and Dorothea Tanning). The 1950s and '60s brought a new artistic resurgence in the shape of the Ecole de Nice movement, whose concerns were far removed from the beaches and *plein air* painting of its predecessors.

Wanted. Jumpers, coats and people with their knickers in a twist.

From the people who feel moved to bring us their old books and CDs, to the people fed up to the back teeth with our politicians' track record on climate change, Oxfam supporters have one thing in common. They're passionate. If you've got a little fire in your belly, we'd love to hear from you. Visit us at **oxfam.org.uk**

Be Humankind ⊗ Oxfam

'Van Gogh's relationship with the South was more visceral than Cézanne's.'

THE SOUTHERN SCENE

It took **PAUL CEZANNE** (1839-1906), a native of **Aix-en-Provence**, to focus on the southern landscapes. Cézanne sought the 'permanent truth' behind the region, as opposed to the transient impressions of the Impressionists. In 1871, escaping the Franco-Prussian war, he painted the fishing village and the coast at **L'Estaque** near Marseille; he returned frequently in the 1870s and '80s. The 'red roofs on a blue sea' drew him here, but he was put off by the advance of progress: first gas, and then electric lights along the quays. From the 1880s, Cézanne turned increasingly to the area around Aix and the unspoiled savagery of **Montagne Ste-Victoire**. Influenced by the rationality of Poussin, his ordering of nature on canvas – 'Nature must be treated by the cylinder, the sphere, the cone…' – led towards a new conception of perspective.

In February 1888, **VINCENT VAN GOGH** (1853-90) arrived in Arles and went on to paint many of his most celebrated works in a period of feverish activity, staying first in a hotel and then renting a room at the house seen in *The Bedroom at Arles* and *The Yellow House*. His work explored the landscape and its monuments, such as **Les Alyscamps** and the boats at **Saintes-Maries-de-la-Mer**, but his relationship with the South was more visceral than Cézanne's: he wanted to understand not the underlying structure but the underlying emotion of the glaring provençal landscapes. Van Gogh was joined in 1888 by Gauguin, with whom he quarrelled incessantly. After a dispute, when Van Gogh cut off his ear, he checked into the asylum of St-Paul-de-Maussole on the edge of **St-Rémy**; in the year he spent here, he painted some 150 canvases, including *Irises* and *The Olive Grove*.

JOINING THE DOTS

Keen yachtsman **PAUL SIGNAC** (1863-1935) discovered **St-Tropez** as early as the 1890s, painting the port, the peninsula's rocky bays and the place des Lices. His port paintings seem infected by the wildness of the coast: he began to play with large blocks of colour, interested not just in the chronometric colour but in geometric structure as his paintings of the sea become broad, horizontal bands of shimmering dots. Signac was joined by fellow Neo-Impressionists Maximilien Luce and Theo van Rysselberghe; then, in 1904, he invited Albert Marquet, Henri Manguin, Henri-Edmond Cross and Henri Matisse, whose canvas *Luxe, Calme et Volupté* is influenced by Signac's divisionism and illustrates part of his continuing attempt to resolve the relationship between line and colour. The works of many of these painters can be seen in the **Musée de l'Annonciade** (*see p195*) in St-Tropez.

Although the Impressionists are largely associated with Paris, Normandy and the Ile de France, **AUGUSTE RENOIR** (1841-1919) first visited the South with Monet in the 1880s. In 1907, he bought the Domaine des Collettes in **Cagnes-sur-Mer**, where he built a house and studio (now the Musée Renoir; *see p250*). The southern light heightened Renoir's palette: he painted his late, garish *Les Grandes Baigneuses* in the garden, using housemaids as models, and some charming portraits of his youngest son Claude, such as *Coco Writing*. However, he complained that the sun was too dazzling. With his fingers nearly crippled by arthritis, he turned increasingly to sculpture in his final years.

In 1906, **GEORGES BRAQUE** (1882-1963) visited **L'Estaque** in what proved to be a crucial moment in the transition between his Fauvist and Cubist periods. Braque's Fauvist paintings of the port are a rhythm of pink waves. But by 1908, when he again spent summer in L'Estaque, Braque had seen the light in the form of Picasso's revolutionary (and as yet unexhibited) *Les Demoiselles d'Avignon*. His works of that summer show a new concern with structural planes, and a more sober palette dominated by greens and ochres. In this sense, Braque was influenced not just by Picasso but by Cézanne, the original Cubist.

IN CONTEXT

SOUTHERN LIGHTS

For **PIERRE BONNARD** (1867-1947), the '*affolant*' (maddening) southern light pushed art further towards chromatic patterns in which the solidity of outlines and perspective are broken down. In 1926, Bonnard bought a house at **Le Cannet** on the outskirts of Cannes; his large canvases of its garden and intimate domestic interiors are marked by a vibrant dematerialisation of form. Sometimes reworking canvases over many years, he painted the nature around him: the view from his window of village rooftops and brilliant yellow mimosa, the vegetation touched by light and shadow.

The inter-war period heralded a new age of sun worship and a new cult of the body. As the avant-garde mixed with the jet set, the Riviera became a meeting place for artists, writers and photographers such as Man Ray, Lee Miller, Pablo Picasso, Robert Capa and André Masson, who drew inspirations from the Mediterranean light, the uncommercialised provençal culture and the Riviera set's lack of restraint and unconventional behaviour.

Always flirting with different styles, **FRANCIS PICABIA** (1879-1953) was a forerunner of much contemporary art in his use of text, his questioning of the idea of authorship and his use of popular imagery. He moved to the South in 1925, spending more than 20 years in **Mougins**. He was both a satirist of Riviera society and a part of it, with his passion for cars (he owned 127) and the extravagant fancy-dress balls he organised in the casino at Cannes, such as the Bal des Cannibales. A move in his art from Dadaist machines to *Monstres* (caricatures of famous old masters using Ripolin household paint) and the more dreamy, mythological canvases of his overlapping 'transparencies' was also reflected in the design of the Château de Mai, the house he built for himself, which remained in a constant state of flux as he added more terraces, a swimming pool, turrets and an atelier.

MATISSE IN NICE

After an initial visit to St-Tropez alongside Signac, **HENRI MATISSE** (1869-1954) paid his first visit to **Nice** in 1917; from 1919 onwards, he spent half the year there. After the often dark tones of his early period, his work showed a noticeable lightening of palette, and the increasingly cosmopolitan city also proved a spur to his interest in oriental, Greek and African art. But despite his long friendships with Bonnard and Picasso, Matisse essentially remained isolated on the hill of Cimiez (now home to the Musée Matisse; *see p260*), developing an interest in blocks of colour and stark patterns. His **Chapelle du Rosaire** in Vence (*see p302*) is the ultimate expression of these dual impulses: simplified line drawings on white-tiled walls are juxtaposed with lucent yellows, greens and blues in stained-glass.

After initial visits to **Collioure** in south-west France and to L'Estaque in 1908 with Friesz and Braque, it was the festive aspects of the seaside that dominated the work of **RAOUL DUFY** (1877-1953). Save the brilliant blue skies and the addition of some palm trees, his fascination with beach holidays, regattas and casinos, and the sense of narrative in his bravura decorative style, is much the same whether they were painted in **Deauville** in Normandy or along the Promenade des Anglais in Nice.

PICASSO AND PALS

For **PABLO PICASSO** (1881-1973), bathers and the human body were a recurrent subject, as he ceaselessly explored different styles and media. His *Baigneuses Regardent un Avion*, painted in 1920 at **Juan-les-Pins**, and his curious, sand-covered tableaux-reliefs of the 1930s, made at much the same time as André Masson's automatic sand paintings in Antibes, show his affinity with the Surrealists. Other works celebrate the Mediterranean as a place of myths and archetypes, in which Pan, centaurs and the Minotaur – a sort of alter-ego – appear alongside local fishermen.

In 1946, Picasso moved south with Françoise Gilot, his new love. The pair spent four months in Antibes (now home to the **Musée Picasso**; *see p245*), where he painted the triptych *La Joie de Vivre*, before moving along the coast to **Vallauris**. Picasso discovered pottery here; he also painted the allegorical panels of *La Guerre et La Paix* for the chateau's deconsecrated chapel (*see p234*), while creating innovative 'assemblages' of found objects,

Atelier Cézanne. *See p39.*

such as the *Petite Fille Sautant à la Corde* (Little Girl Skipping), cast from a basket. Later, with new partner Jacqueline Roque, Picasso moved to Villa La Californie above Cannes and the Château de Vauvenargues on the edge of the Montagne Ste-Victoire, working on his last artist and his model paintings and his reworkings of Velasquez's *Las Meninas*.

Known for his abstract paintings, composed of thick blocks of colour painted with a palette knife, Russian-born artist **NICOLAS DE STAEL** (1914-55) bought a house at **Ménerbes** in the Luberon in the early 1950s after paying visits to the **Côte Bleue**, Antibes and **Bormes-les-Mimosas**. After moving to a house on the ramparts in Antibes in 1954, his works became more recognisably figurative, as he painted the chateau, fish and seagulls. *Le Grand Concert* (on display at the Musée Picasso; *see p245*) and *L'Orchestre*, his final works, were both painted after going to a concert of Schoenberg and Webern in Paris, days before his suicide in March 1955.

The dreamlike canvases of **MARC CHAGALL** (1887-1985) reveal his ability to combine colour, narrative and a personal iconography marked by Russian folklore, Greek mythology and the Bible. After moving to the USA to escape Nazi persecution during World War II, Chagall returned to France in 1947, settling in **Vence** in 1950. While here, he painted the huge late Old Testament canvases that form the centrepiece of Nice's **Musée National Marc Chagall** (*see p260*). He also made sculptures, stained glass and pottery at the Atelier Madoura in **Vallauris**, and his first mosaic for the Fondation Maeght.

LITTLE REVOLUTIONS

The 1950s and '60s saw a burst of artistic activity in **Nice**, centred around the group dubbed the Ecole de Nice by art critic Pierre Restany. Although it had links with Nouveau Réalisme (the French equivalent of pop art), Fluxus and Supports-Surfaces, the Ecole de Nice was more about a sense of energy and creation than a particular style. Along with Martial Raysse and Arman, one of its key figures was Nice-born **YVES KLEIN** (1928-62), who brought to the movement a sense of anarchy in an oeuvre that combined painting and art actions. Klein is best known for his monochromes, notably his trademark IKB (International Klein Blue) canvases and blue sponges, but he also found fame for his fire paintings and '*anthropométries*', which used the female body as a 'living paintbrush' in a form of literal figurative painting that was both painting and art performance in one.

The Festive South

*The South takes centre stage,
with a packed calendar of events.*

TEXT: JULIEN SAUVALLE

The South of France revels in a year-round programme of festivals and events. From the heady glamour of Cannes's Film Festival to the quirky charms of Avignon's fringe scene, there's plenty to keep visitors and locals entertained.

Celebrations such as Arles's Fête des Gardians pay tribute to the traditional southern way of life, along with the religious festivals and feast days still celebrated across the region. Bullfighting also features heavily in the cultural calendar, along with *course camarguaise* – a less bloodthirsty local variant on Spanish-style *corrida*.

Beyond tradition, the South is also a stage for artistic innovation. For cutting-edge photography, there's the Rencontres d'Arles; for ground-breaking theatre, the lively Festival d'Avignon. Music festivals, meanwhile, run from sophisticated jazz soirées to renowned opera events – along with a smattering of world music, rock and electronica events.

There are sporting thrills to be had at the Tennis Master Series in Monte-Carlo, or the exhilarating Grand Prix de Monaco. The yachting regatta brings a touch of old-school glamour to Antibes, as vintage yachts race along the coast.

INFORMATION

Tourist offices can supply information on local events, as well as the excellent (and free) *Terre de Festivals* booklet, which covers arts events in the Provence-Alpes-Côtes d'Azur region (information can also be found online at www.regionpaca.fr. Tickets can be bought at tourist offices, branches of Fnac (www.fnac.com) or through agencies like France Billet (08.92. 69.21.92, www.francebillet.com).

SPRING

FREE Transhumance
Throughout rural Provence, including St-Rémy-de-Provence, La Garde-Freinet, St-Etienne-de-Tinée & Riez. **Date** May-June.
Late spring sees the traditional movement of flocks from winter to summer pastures. Hundreds of sheep are driven through the villages to the sound of flutes and tambourines. Ask local tourist offices for details.

The Rhône Delta

Feria Pascale
Arènes, Arles (08.91.70.03.70/www.arenes-arles.com). **Tickets** €17-€92. **Date** Good Fri-Easter Mon.
Arles's famous Roman arena is the venue for three days of Spanish-style bullfighting.

FREE Fête des Gardians
Arènes & various venues, Arles (04.90.18.41.20/ www.tourisme.ville-arles.fr). **Date** 1 May.
Every year, the Camargue's *gardians* (who watch over the region's herds of horses and bulls) get together to elect a new captain of the Confrérie des Gardians brotherhood – and, every three years, a new 'Queen of Arles'. Festivities incorporate traditional bands and daring displays of horsemanship.

Feria de Pentecôte
Arènes, Nîmes (08.91.70.14.01/www.arenesde nimes.com). **Tickets** €22-€100. **Date** late May-early June.
Corridas during the main *feria* in Nîmes (held in the amphitheatre) are accompanied by an orchestra, and there are lively parties throughout the city.

FREE Pèlerinage de Mai
Stes-Maries-de-la-Mer (04.90.97.82.55/ www.saintesmaries.com). **Date** 24-25 May.
Romanies from across Europe gather to honour their patron saint, Black Sarah, who, legend has it, met Mary Magdalene, Mary Jacob and Mary Salome when they arrived by boat from Palestine (*see p82*). On Sarah's saint day (24 May), a procession bears her relics from the church to the sea to be blessed by a priest. The next day is devoted to Mary Salome and Mary Jacob, whose relics get the same treatment.

Avignon & the Vaucluse

FREE Ascension Day
Cavaillon (Office de Tourisme 04.90.71.32.01/ www.cavaillon-luberon.fr). **Date** late May.
Locals dress up in provençal costumes for this traditional *corso* (parade), which features decorated carnival floats and bands.

FREE Fête de la Vigne et du Vin
Avignon, Châteauneuf-du-Pape, Gigondas & other villages (04.90.84.01.67/www.fetedela vigneetduvin.com). **Date** May.
On the Friday and Saturday of Ascension weekend, the Vaucluse celebrates its three wine appellations – the Côtes du Rhône, Côtes du Luberon and Côtes du Ventoux – in a wine village set up in front of the Palais des Papes. On the Saturday, wine cellars and vintners from across the region offer tastings.

The Var

FREE Festival International des Arts de la Mode et de Photographie à Hyères
Villa Noailles, Hyères (04.98.08.01.98/www. villanoailles-hyeres.com). **Tickets** free (advance bookings only). **Date** end Apr.
Before a jury of industry professionals (the likes of Christian Lacroix, Tyler Brûlé and Kim Jones), ten young designers present their catwalk collections, and ten photographers show off their portfolios. There are also temporary fashion, photography and art exhibitions.

FREE La Bravade
St-Tropez (Office de Tourisme 04.94.54.82.29/ www.ot-saint-tropez.com). **Date** early-mid May.
To honour the arrival of the headless martyr Torpes (alias St Tropez) in AD 68, locals dress as sailors, musketeers and traditional provençaux for three days of processions.

The Riviera & Southern Alps

Le Printemps des Arts
Various venues, Monte-Carlo (00.377-93.25. 54.08/www.printempsdesarts.com). **Tickets** €17-€40; €6-€10 reductions; free under-12s. **Date** 1st 3wks Apr.
Monte-Carlo's arts festival features around 30 international acts, including the Ballet de Monte-Carlo.

Tennis Master Series Monte-Carlo
Monte-Carlo Country Club (00.377-97.98.70.00). **Tickets** €10-€135. **Date** 1wk mid Apr.
International men's hard-court tournament.

Cannes Film Festival
Cannes (04.92.99.84.22/www.festival-cannes.fr). **Tickets** vary. **Date** 2wks mid May.

IN CONTEXT

The legendary film extravaganza brings a fortnight of deal-brokering and frantic paparazzi activity to Cannes. It's almost impossible to get tickets to Official Selection films, but you can buy tickets for Directors' Fortnight and Critics' Week films.

Grand Prix de Monaco

Monaco (00.377.93.15.26.00/www.grand-prix-monaco.com). **Tickets** €70-€450. **Date** last Sun in May.

Monaco is said to be the most difficult and dangerous circuit of the Formula 1 world championship (*see p280* **A Walk in the Fast Lane**). Book ahead.

Fête de la Rose

Grasse (04.97.05.57.90/www.ville-grasse.fr). **Tickets** €7.50; free under-12s. **Date** mid May.

Grasse celebrates its famous flowers, with troubadours, fire-eaters and comedians performing in the streets, an artisan market and roses galore.

SUMMER

FREE Fête de la Musique

Across France (www.fetedelamusique.culture.fr). **Date** 21 June.

Concerts fill streets throughout the nation on the longest day of the year. Expect everything from rock, hip hop and jazz to pumping electro.

FREE Bastille Day (le Quatorze Juillet)

Across France. **Date** 14 July.

Fireworks and *bals des pompiers* (open-air parties at fire stations) commemorate 1789's storming of the Bastille, which sparked the French Revolution.

The Rhône Delta

Festival Uzès Danse

Various venues, Uzès (04.66.03.15.39/www.uzesdanse.fr). **Tickets** €6-€25. **Date** 1wk late June.

Formerly the Festival de la Nouvelle Danse, this week of contemporary dance events spotlights unknown European choreographers and dance acts.

FREE Fête de la Tarasque

Tarascon (Office de Tourisme 04.90.91.03.52/www.tarascon.org). **Date** 1wk end June.

St Martha's miraculous victory over an amphibious Rhône-dwelling beast is celebrated with music, bull-running, feasting and a grand parade.

Rencontres d'Arles

Various venues, Arles (04.90.96.76.06/www.rencontres-arles.com). **Tickets** *Exhibitions* free-€11. *Day pass* €21-€26. *Unlimited pass* €40. **Date** 1wk early July.

With a wealth of exhibitions, curated collections and a lively fringe festival (www.voies-off.com), this is a major event on the contemporary photography

scene (*see p78*). The festival proper lasts for just a week, but exhibitions continue until mid September.

Suds à Arles

Various venues, Arles (04.90.96.06.27/www.suds-arles.com). **Tickets** free-€30. **Date** 1wk mid July.

This world music festival attracts groups from across the globe. Check out the free concerts, plus dance and music classes and film screenings.

Nuits Musicales d'Uzès

Various venues, Uzès (04.66.62.20.00/www.nuitsmusicalesuzes.org). **Tickets** €8-€40. **Date** 2wks early July.

Classical, baroque, jazz and traditional music concerts are staged in historic halls.

La Feria Provençale

St-Rémy-de-Provence (Office de Tourisme 04.90.92.05.22). **Tickets** vary. **Date** 3 days mid Aug.

Three tense days of *abrivado* (herding bulls into the ring), *bandido* (taking them out again) and *encierro* (releasing them briefly) lead up to a single *corrida portugais* (Portuguese-style bullfight).

Avignon & the Vaucluse

Festival d'Avignon

Various venues, Avignon (information 04.90.27.66.50/reservations 04.90.14.14.14/www.festival-avignon.com). **Tickets** €3-€36. **Date** July.

More than 60 years on, Avignon remains a prestigious meeting point for some of the most avant-garde names in performing arts. The focal point for activities is the impressive Palais des Papes.

Avignon Off

Avignon (Maison d'Off Bureau d'Accueil, Conservatoire de Musique, pl du Palais, www.avignon-off.net). **Tickets** €9-€14. **Date** July.

Rather than cherry-picking from hundreds of applications, Avignon's fringe allows anyone to perform – so long as they can negotiate local-authority red tape and find a venue. The presence of fire-eaters, jugglers, sundry vaudevillians and a good many alt-musos can be assumed.

Festival de la Correspondance

Grignan (04.75.46.55.83/www.grignan-festival correspondance.com). **Tickets** €8-€25. **Date** 5 days early July.

Nearly 100 writers and actors, mostly French, celebrate the art of the letter through readings and other events, such as calligraphy and writing workshops.

FREE Festival de la Sorgue

L'Isle-sur-la-Sorgue (Office de Tourisme 04.90.38.04.78/www.oti-delasorgue.fr). **Tickets** free. **Date** July.

Singing competitions and a race between flower-decorated punts along the island's canals are hotly

IN CONTEXT

Hitting a High Note

From major festivals to select soirées, the summer opera scene is thriving.

Opera-loving Brits seem happy to put on full evening dress, brave rush-hour traffic and head for the rain-sodden countryside for an evening of music, clutching a picnic hamper of soggy sandwiches and a bottle of warm chardonnay. Observing such English stoicism, even cheer, during a summer thunderstorm at Grange Park, a French visitor was heard to mutter, 'We'd never pay to go through this'. She had a point: on the other side of the Channel, opera audiences are far more high-maintenance.

Happily, the South of France is blessed with a more clement climate, which is why the alfresco **Chorégies d'Orange** (*see p46*) can attract up to 10,000 opera fans, who park their *derrières* on the hard steps of the Roman amphitheatre for a line-up that rivals that of Italy's Verona festival.

The **Festival International d'Art Lyrique** (*see p46*) in stylish Aix-en-Provence is a little more sophisticated, with performances taking place within the confines of an air-conditioned opera house. What these two venerable events lack, though, is the exclusivity that Britain's three Gs (Garsington, Grange Park and Glyndebourne) exude – something a new wave of smaller scale (but impeccably chic) events aims to change.

When millionaire fashion designer Pierre Cardin bought the ruins of the Château de Lacoste – once the home of the Marquis de Sade – he decided to launch an opera festival of his own. His **Festival de Lacoste** (www.festivaldelacoste.com) takes place in a quarry near the chateau, where the circular stone performing area has more than a hint of Gothic decadence. Thanks to some spot-on programming and the determination of the event's glamorous artistic director, Eve Ruggieri, celebrities abound and it's become a hot ticket.

Ruggieri is also the director of the annual **Musiques au Coeur** (*see p47*) festival. Here, rising stars perform in the verdant grounds of the Villa Eilenroc – a grand 19th-century villa, designed by Charles Garnier (the architect behind the Paris and Monte-Carlo opera houses).

The picnics and prolonged dinner intervals beloved of the Glyndebourne set have yet to catch on with Francophone audiences, but in an attempt to encourage the trend, the cast of **Les Azuriales** (www.azurialopera.com) opera festival join the audience for dinner in the glorious gardens of the Villa Ephrussi-de-Rothschild on the Cap-Ferrat. Not surprisingly, this sun-drenched take on an English country-house opera festival was dreamt up by an English woman, Sarah Holford. Crowds are encouraged to dress smartly – with black tie and tuxedos a hot prospect for gents on sultry summer evenings – to create the modern equivalent of an 18th-century soirée. The festival may not have an orchestra, but its intimate, exclusive feel means tickets are highly sought-after.

IN CONTEXT

contested by locals from five neighbouring areas, while non-combatants are free to enjoy the floating markets and street theatre.

Vaison Danses
Théâtre Antique, Vaison-la-Romaine (04.90.28.84.49/www.vaison-danses.com). **Tickets** €10-€38. **Date** 3wks early July.
Ballet, latino, tango and flamenco performers take centre stage during this three-week festival.

Les Estivales de Carpentras
Théâtre de Plein Air, Carpentras (04.90.60.46.00/ www.ville-carpentras.fr). **Tickets** €15-€32. **Date** 2wks from mid July.
A multidisciplinary line-up of music, dance and plays, staged in an open-air theatre.

Chorégies d'Orange
Théâtre Antique, Orange (04.90.34.24.24/www. choregies.asso.fr). **Tickets** €4-€200. **Date** mid July-early Aug.
See p45 **Hitting a High Note**.

FREE Festival du Melon
Cavaillon (04.90.71.73.02/www.cavaillon-luberon.fr). **Date** 2 days early July.
Cavaillon plays host to street performances, a procession with floats and horses and a melon market.

Festival International de Quatuors à Cordes
Luberon (04.90.75.89.60/www.festival-quatuors-luberon.fr). **Tickets** €18-€23; €8 reductions; free under-12s. **Date** late July-early Sept.
Leading string quartets perform in the Abbaye de Silvacane and churches in Fontaine-de-Vaucluse, L'Isle-sur-la-Sorgue, Goult, Roussillon and around.

Marseille & Aix

FREE Fête de la St-Pierre
Martigues (Office de Tourisme 04.42.42.31.10/ www.martigues-tourisme.com). **Date** end June.
A statue of St Peter, patron saint of fishermen, is carried to the port, where fishermen and their boats are blessed. The feast day is also marked in La Ciotat, Cassis and Marseille.

Festival de Marseille
Marseille (information 04.91.99.00.20/box office 04.91.99.02.50/www.festivaldemarseille.com). **Tickets** €6-€27. **Date** 3wks July.
Marseille's annual festival hosts international contemporary dance, theatre and music performances.

Festival International d'Art Lyrique
Aix-en-Provence (04.42.17.34.34/www.festival-aix.com). **Tickets** €15-€185. **Date** July.
See p45 **Hitting a High Note**.

Festival International de Piano
La Roque d'Antheron (04.42.50.51.15/ www.festival-piano.com). **Tickets** €15-€51. **Date** mid July-mid Aug.
Eminent concert pianists perform in the park of the Château de Florans and seven other venues.

Musique à l'Empéri
Château de l'Empéri, Salon-de-Provence (04.90. 56.00.82/www.festival-salon.fr). **Tickets** €10-€26. **Date** early Aug.
Chamber music, from Mozart to Strauss, is played in the chateau's courtyard.

The Var

FREE Draguifolies
Draguignan (04.94.50.59.59/www.theatresen dracenie.com). **Date** 2wks early July.
Circus, dance, theatre, concerts, juggling and fire-eating all play a role in this ten-day street festival.

Jazz Festival de Ramatuelle
Ramatuelle (04.94.79.10.29/www.jazzfestival ramatuelle.com). **Tickets** €25-€35. **Date** mid Aug.
Jazz bands, trios and quartets give concerts in Ramatuelle's outdoor amphitheatre.

The Riviera & southern Alps

FREE Voiles d'Antibes
Port Vauban, Antibes (04.92.91.60.00/ www.voilesdantibes.com). **Date** 4 days early June.

Festival International d'Art Lyrique.

Classy sailing boats race round the Cap d'Antibes in this classic regatta. A 'village' next to the port hosts parties during the four-day event.

FREE Les Baroquiales

Roya & Bévéra valleys, Sospel (04.93.04.15.80). **Tickets** €8-€20. *Street performances* free. **Date** 4 days early July.

Sospel's rich baroque heritage is celebrated with concerts and evening outdoor theatre performances.

Biennale de Céramique Contemporaine

Musée de la Céramique, Vallauris (04.93.64. 71.83/http://biennale.vallauris.free.fr). **Tickets** €1. **Date** late June-mid Nov.

This biennial festival (the next will be in 2010) showcases contemporary European ceramics.

Jazz à Juan

Juan-les-Pins (04.97.23.11.10/www.antibes juanlespins.com). **Tickets** €20-€64. **Date** 2wks mid July.

Enjoy jazz on the beach at this hip festival. Its 1960s inception featured Miles Davis and Ella Fitzgerald; in 2008, Didier Lockwood and Al Jarreau took to the stage. The Jazz Off fringe festival has cheaper alternative gigs.

Nice Jazz Festival

Jardins de Cimiez, Nice (information 08.92.70. 74.07/box office 08.92.68.36.22/www.nicejazz festival.fr). **Tickets** €31-51; €9-€36 reductions; free under-3s. **Date** mid-late July.

Jazz concerts are staged in the stylish Roman arena at this poppier alternative to Jazz à Juan. In recent years, line-ups have included the likes of Rufus Wainwright, Diana Krall and Pink Martini.

FREE Festival International d'Art Pyrotechnique de Cannes

Palais des Festivals, Cannes (04.92.99.33.83/ www.festival-pyrotechnique-cannes.com). **Tickets** free. **Date** July-Aug.

International pyrotechnicians, all of them winners of the Vestals d'Argent prize for the best displays, compete for the ultimate Vestals d'Or award.

Musiques au Coeur

Villa Eilenroc, Cap d'Antibes (04.92.90.54.64/ www.antibes-juanlespins.com). **Tickets** €50-€75. **Date** early July.

See p45 **Hitting a High Note**.

Les Nuits du Sud

pl du Grand Jardin, Vence (04.93.58.40.17/www. nuitsdusud.com). **Tickets** €17; €12 reductions; €75 5-night pass; free under-12s. **Date** 4wks mid July-mid Aug.

Laid-back Vence speeds up a gear for this series of Latin American and world music outdoor concerts.

Festival de Musique

parvis St-Michel, Menton (04.92.41.76.95/www. musique-menton.com). **Tickets** €10-€48; €9-€39 reductions. **Date** end July-mid Aug.

Founded in 1950, this chamber and classical music festival features concerts by trios and orchestras, performed on the cobbles outside the Basilique St-Michel in Menton's old town.

Festival Pantiero

Palais des Festivals et des Congrès, Cannes (04.92.99.33.83/www.festivalpantiero.com). **Tickets** €25 1-night pass; €50 4-nights pass. **Date** 4 nights early Aug.

A new open-air music festival, with an eclectic selection of house, electro-pop, hip-hop, dub and reggae bands performing by Cannes's old harbour.

AUTUMN

FREE Journées du Patrimoine

Across France (www.culture.gouv.fr). **Date** 3rd wknd in Sept.

Historic buildings across France open up to the public for this annual architectural heritage weekend.

Avignon & the Vaucluse

FREE Fête de la Veraison

Châteauneuf-du-Pape (04.90.83.71.08/www. ccpro.fr). **Date** 1st wknd in Aug.

Harking back to medieval times, this wine festival has stalls run by local vintners and artisans, dressed in traditional costumes, selling everything from local olive oil to antique jewellery.

Marseille & Aix

Fête du Livre

Cité du Livre, Aix-en-Provence (04.42.91.98.88/ www.citedulivre-aix.com). **Tickets** free-€8. **Date** mid Oct.

The literary festival brings heavyweight guests (Nobel winners Pinter, Grass and Naipaul have all featured) and book-related talks, events and debates.

Fiesta des Suds

Docks des Suds, Marseille (information 04.91.99. 00.00/reservations 08.25.83.38.33/www.dock-des-suds.org). **Tickets** €10-€35. **Date** Oct.

The programme at this eclectic world music festival runs from reggae and salsa to rock and electro, reflecting Marseille's multi-ethnic population.

The Var

FREE Monaco Fête Nationale

Monaco (00.377-93.15.28.63/www.visitmonaco. com). **Date** 18-19 Nov.

The Monegasque National Festival is celebrated with fireworks, a funfair and parades.

IN CONTEXT

WINTER

Avignon & the Vaucluse

FREE Messe des Truffes

Chapel-le-Notre-Dame, Richerenches (04.90.28. 05.34/www.richerenches.fr). **Date** 15 Jan.
A special mass honours St Antoine, patron saint of *trufficulteurs*. The choicest truffles are later auctioned to raise funds for repairs to the church roof.

Les Hivernales

Various venues, Avignon & Vaucluse (04.90.82. 33.12/www.hivernales-avignon.com). **Tickets** €10-€16. **Date** Feb.
Selected dance companies – from ballet through to contemporary – perform in venues around Avignon.

Marseille & Aix

FREE La Chandeleur

Abbaye St-Victor, Marseille (04.96.11.22.60/ www.saintvictor.net). **Date** 2 Feb.
To mark Candlemas, a candlelit procession weaves behind the Black Virgin of the Abbaye St-Victor.

The Var

FREE Fêtes de la Lumière

St-Raphaël (Office de Tourisme 04.94.19.52.52/ www.saint-raphael.com). **Date** mid Dec-early Jan.
Throughout the Christmas period, St-Raphaël is aglow with lights. There's also a Christmas market, street theatre groups, kids' shows and musicians.

Le Corso Fleuri

Bormes-les-Mimosas (Office de Tourisme 04.94. 01.38.38). **Tickets** €5. **Date** 19 Feb.
A colourful parade of floats covered in flowers celebrates spring, with locals dressed in flamboyant costumes. Folk and brass bands fill the streets.

The Riviera & Southern Alps

FREE Exposition de Noël

Seillans (04.94.50.45.46/www.seillans.fr). **Date** mid-late Dec.
Christmas market, concerts and a live nativity scene take place in this beautiful medieval village.

Festival de Danse

Palais des Festivals & other venues, Cannes (04.92.99.33.83/www.festivaldedanse-cannes.com). **Tickets** €10-€42. **Date** Nov.
This contemporary dance festival is held every two years (the next is in 2009).

FREE Midnight Mass

Eglise St Pierre Es Liens, Fontvieille (Office de Tourisme 04.90.54.67.49/www.fontvieille-provence.com). **Date** 24 Dec.

In traditional provençal fashion, Fontvieille's midnight mass celebrates Christmas with an offerings ceremony for which locals dress up in Arlesian costume, accompanied by musicians.

FREE Rallye Automobile Monte-Carlo

Monaco (Office de Tourisme 00.377-92.16. 61.16/www.rallyemontecarlo.fr). **Date** 1wk mid Jan.
Up and running for three-quarters of a century, this annual event sees rally drivers careering up into the snow-capped mountains and back down into Monaco again.

Festival International du Cirque de Monte-Carlo

Espace Fontvieille, Monaco (00.377-92.05.23.45/ www.montecarlofestivals.com). **Tickets** €10-€160. **Date** 1wk late Jan.
Created back in the 1970s by the late Prince Rainier of Monaco, the festival has become one of the most prestigious international events in circus arts and acrobatics. Book tickets in advance.

Carnaval de Nice

Nice (08.92.70.74.07/www.nicecarnaval.com). **Tickets** €15-€25. **Date** 2wks mid Feb.
Some of the most fabulous carnival processions in the world saunter down the promenade des Anglais, their satiric intent inspired by Le Roi des Dupes – the Lord of Misrule. The 125th edition of the carnival is celebrated in 2009 with a 'Masquerade' theme.

Fête du Citron

Menton (Office de Tourisme 04.92.41.76.76/ www.fêteducitron.com). **Tickets** €12-€22. **Date** 2wks mid Feb.
This festival sees locals displaying extravagent sculptures of lemons and citrus-themed floats.

FREE Fête du Mimosa

Mandelieu-La Napoule (Office de Tourisme 04.92.97.99.27/www.ot-mandelieu.fr). **Date** 1wk mid Feb.
The week-long celebrations at this charming village start with the election of the Reine du Mimosa (Queen of Mimosa) and floral exhibitions, and culminate with a carnival and the exhilarating *bataille des bonbons* (battle of sweets).

FREE Napoléon à Golfe-Juan

Golfe-Juan (Office de Tourisme 04.93.63.73.12/ http://napoleon.golfe.juan.free.fr). **Date** 1st wknd in Mar.
A 400-strong Napoleonic army reconstructs the ambitious Corsican's landing on these shores from Elba in 1815 – complete with a battle fought by armed and mounted soldiers. Locals, kitted out in period dress, head to the beach on Sunday afternoon to sight Napoleon's ship.

The Rhône Delta

The **Pont du Gard**. *See p59*.

Introduction

A river runs through this enchanting – sometimes unearthly – landscape.

A centuries-old trading route, the mighty River Rhône lies at the heart of this region – and has irresistably shaped its history. The Romans sailed upriver and settled here, leaving a rich legacy: **Arles** and **Nîmes** evoke the empire's heyday with their magnificent amphitheatres and Roman remains. Near **St-Rémy**, the ancient city of Glanum is an atmospheric mosaic of Celtic, Greek and Roman remains – the result of centuries of successive occupation.

Yet the delta's cities, despite their myriad tourist attractions, remain living, workaday towns with year-round populations and busy cultural programmes. Although Arles capitalises on its Roman history and Van Gogh connection (the hot-headed Dutchman painted many of his best-known works here), it also looks to the future with its forward-thinking photography festival. Chic St-Rémy, meanwhile, combines its rich Renaissance heritage with a fashionable café society and chichi shopping scene.

Efforts to tame the river itself are age-old – and ongoing. The **Pont du Gard** aqueduct was an early feat of engineering, bringing water across the dry limestone plateau to nourish Nîmes. The river has also been dammed and channelled to irrigate the fertile flood plain and keep out the sea from the flat marshes of the Camargue. But water remains a perpetual battle: flash floods hit the area a few years ago, destroying bridges in the Gard in 2002 and flooding large areas of Arles, Beaucaire and the Camargue in 2003, when a dam was breached.

Down by the sea, the **Camargue** and **Grande Crau** are eerily beautiful flatlands with exceptional birdlife and gigantic skies. Further inland are the jagged **Alpilles**, with their dramatic mountain scenery and bizarre perspectives – notably at lofty **Les Baux-de-Provence**, part-medieval stronghold and part bauxite mining village. The surrounding hills, dotted with olive groves and vineyards, hide some top-class gastronomic destinations.

The Rhône Delta region is united by a passion for bull-fighting and the gentler *course camargaise*, but there are also more rustic festivities, such as the Transhumance moving of flocks in St-Rémy, the Fête de la Tarasque in **Tarascon**, and the vibrant annual Romany gathering at **Stes-Maries-de-la-Mer**.

The Best of The Rhône Delta

Standout sights, restaurants and hotels from across the region.

SIGHTSEEING
Make time to visit the amphitheatres in **Nîmes** (see p53) and **Arles** (see p72) – along with the latter's **Théâtre Antique** (see p73) and ancient burial ground, **Les Alyscamps** (see p72). If you've seen enough Roman remains, head for Nîmes's lovely **Jardin de la Fontaine** (see p55), where statues watch over the 18th-century formal gardens.

Despite high season crowds, the medieval walled city of **Aigues-Mortes** (see p83) and perched village of **Les Baux-de-Provence** (see p64) are both gloriously dramatic – though in very different ways.

SPORTS & ACTIVITIES
Riding the Camargue's white horses is a quintessential provençal experience, with a wealth of ranches to choose from (see p82).

WHERE TO STAY
Shut yourself away in Asian-inspired luxury at St-Rémy's sleek **Hôtel Les Ateliers de l'Image**, or enjoy the rural seclusion of out-of-town **La Maison du Paradou** (for both, see p64). If you prefer to be in the centre of the action, book into Arles's stylish **Grand Hôtel Nord Pinus** (see p77), a favourite with bullfighters. In Nîmes, **Jardins Secrets** (see p59) pairs elegant decor with a heavenly walled garden and hammam.

PLACES TO EAT
Michel Kayser has won two Michelin stars at **Alexandre** in Nîmes (see p56). To sample the handiwork of another starred chef at modest rates, try Jean-Luc Rabanel's **A Côté** (see p75) in Arles – a bistro offshoot of his more upscale establishment a few doors down.

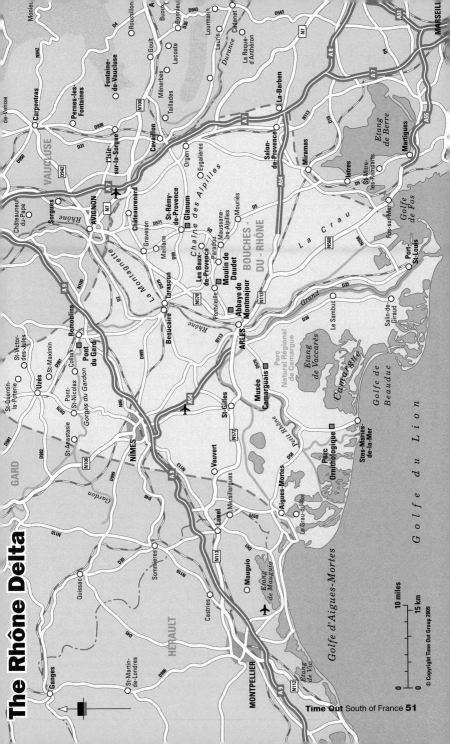

The Rhône Delta

Nîmes & Pont du Gard

Feeling bullish? Explore Nîmes' 2,000-year history.

Like Arles, Nîmes is famed for its imposing Roman arena – but while **Arles** is a sleepy provincial town, **Nîmes** has something of the truculence of a big city, and wears its macho bullfighting credentials on its sleeve. With its lively café society, airy modern art museum and colourful *ferias*, there's a definite buzz around town.

Just north of Nimes, the triple-decker Roman **Pont du Gard** aqueduct has stood firm through the centuries; nearby, the charming town of **Uzès** exudes Italianate elegance and is a mecca for art-lovers. Outdoor types might prefer exploring the plunging **Gorges du Gardon** – or taking to the water in canoes.

NIMES

This is not a genteel tourist destination, but a vibrant city with rough edges. Even the town's emblem of a crocodile and a palm tree – brought here by Roman legionnaires who had served in Egypt – is edgy, while 'les Crocos' (members of the local football team) are not to be messed with. If you are at ease with bullfighting, the Pentecostal *feria* in May shows the town at its most colourfully Spanish, with cafés plying paella and sangria spilling out on to the pavements. In keeping with the town's tough image, its hard-wearing cotton of white warp and blue weft – already referred to as 'denim' (*de Nîmes*) in London by 1695 – became a contemporary icon when Levi Strauss used it to make trousers for Californian gold-diggers.

It was a Celtic tribe that first discovered the great spring – Nemausus – that gave the city its name. Such a convenient stop on the Via Domitia between Italy and Spain was bound to attract imperial attention, and by 31 BC the Romans had moved in, building roads and ramparts, baths and fountains – not to mention the amphitheatre and Pont du Gard aqueduct, which supplied water to a metropolis that now numbered 25,000 people.

After the collapse of the Roman Empire, Nîmes declined in importance, wracked by war and religious squabbles. It has always been non-conformist, welcoming the 12th-century Cathar heretics and becoming a major centre of Protestantism in the 16th century, which saw the town heavily embroiled in the Wars of Religion. After the revocation of the Edict of Nantes in 1685, many Protestants emigrated or converted to Catholicism, but the town prospered through the 17th and 18th centuries from dye-making and textile production.

Sightseeing

The centre of Nîmes is compact enough to explore on foot, with most of the sights clustered inside *l'Ecusson* ('the shield'), a triangle formed by boulevards Gambetta, Victor Hugo and Amiral Courbet.

At the northern end of boulevard Victor Hugo, the **Maison Carrée** is a superbly preserved Roman temple, surrounded by a marble-paved open space on the site of the Roman forum. Its classical lines are daringly echoed by Norman Foster's glass and steel **Carré d'Art**, a modern art museum and library.

To the east lies the heart of Nîmes, the partially pedestrianised old town. Shops and cafés are tucked within Romanesque arches, walls are half-stripped of modern accretions to reveal the ancient stonework beneath, and

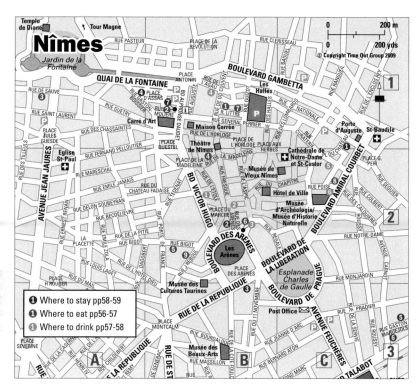

many 17th- and 18th-century mansions have been beautifully restored. Rue Nationale, tracing the line of the Via Domitia, leads between the covered Halles and the Porte Auguste, one of the city's original Roman gates.

On rue de l'Aspic, the Hôtel Fontfroide has a 17th-century double spiral staircase, while there are three early Christian sarcophagi embedded in the porch of the Hôtel Meynier de Salinelles. The place du Marché, where the corn market was once held, is adorned with a fountain by Martial Raysse, a modern take on the crocodile tied to a palm tree theme. On place des Herbes stands the much-altered **Cathédrale de Notre-Dame et St-Castor**. Next door, the elegant former bishop's palace contains the **Musée de Vieux Nîmes**, full of local curiosities and decorative arts. On boulevard Amiral Courbet, the **Musée d'Archéologie** and **Muséum d'Histoire Naturelle** are housed in an old Jesuit college; the adjoining chapel is used for temporary exhibitions. Near the Office du Tourisme to the west of Les Halles is the **Ilot Littré**. Once the dyers' and spinners' district, this part of the city has been carefully restored: cleaned-up 17th- and 18th-century façades conceal lovely courtyards.

At the southern tip of the shield stands the vast **Arènes**, an imposing Roman amphitheatre that's now used for bullfights and concerts. If you don't approve of the full-blown Spanish-style *feria*, try the gentler Course Camarguaise (*see p66* **Death in the Afternoon**). Nearby, the **Musée des Cultures Taurines** gives further insights into the art of bullfighting. The elegant **Musée des Beaux-Arts** lies a few streets south of the rue de la République.

West of the city centre from place Antonin, elegant 17th- and 18th-century patricians' houses line the canal along quai de la Fontaine, which leads to the **Jardin de la Fontaine**, an exquisite 18th-century formal garden.

Also to the north of the central triangle, in rue de la Lampèze, is the **Castellum**, remnants of a Roman water tower. Water arrived here from the Pont du Gard and was distributed across the city through thick lead pipes, from the ten holes still visible in the basin wall.

★ Les Arènes

bd des Arènes (04.66.21.82.56/www.arenes-nimes.com). Feria box office: 4 rue de la Violette (08.91.70.14.01). **Open** *June-Aug* 9am-7pm

Jardin de la Fontaine.

daily. *Apr, May, Sept* 9am-6.30pm daily.
Mar, Oct 9am-6pm daily. *Jan, Feb, Nov, Dec*
9.30am-5pm daily. Closed for *feria* & concerts.
Admission €7.70; €5.90 reductions; free under-
7s. **Credit** MC, V. **Map** p53 B2.

Dating from 90 to 120 AD, and encircled by two tiers
of 60 stone arcades, this is a Roman amphitheatre of
perfect classical proportions. The arcades surround
the corridors and *vomitoria* (exits), and the great oval
arena – named for the *arènes*, or sands, that were
spread to soak up the blood. The amphitheatre is an
amazing feat of engineering, constructed out of vast
blocks of stone from two local quarries. You can still
sit on the original stone benches and see the podium
for the president of the games and sockets for the
poles that held a huge awning to shelter the crowd.
For the best views, climb to the top tier of seats, traditionally reserved for slaves and women. The original games included gladiatorial fights, as well as
the spectacle of slaves and criminals being thrown
to animals; dogs were set on porcupines to get the
blood flowing and the crowd excited. *Photo p56.*
▶ *Another splendid Roman amphitheatre can be
found in Arles (see p72).*

★ Carré d'Art

*16 pl de la Maison Carrée (04.66.76.35.70/
library 04.66.76.35.50).* **Open** 10am-6pm Tue-
Sun. **Admission** €5; €3.70 reductions; free
under-10s. **No credit cards. Map** p53 B1.

The Foster-designed Carré d'Art is a masterful play
of transparency and space, housing both the Musée
d'Art Contemporain and the vast Bibliothèque Carré
d'Art, a library and media centre. The art gallery is
constructed around a light-filled atrium strung with
glass staircases, and provides an excellent overview
of French art since 1960, with works by Boltanski,
Klein, Raysse and Lavier. The top floor is occupied
by a lovely rooftop restaurant, Le Ciel de Nîmes.

FREE Cathédrale de Notre-Dame et St-Castor

pl aux Herbes (04.66.67.27.72). **Open** 8.30am-
noon daily. **Admission** free. **Map** p53 C2.

Nîmes's cathedral isn't what it was. Founded in
1096, it was – like much of the town – wrecked during the 16th-century Wars of Religion, and the bulk
of the current building is a 19th-century reconstruction of a 17th-century building. The remains of a
Romanesque frieze, sculpted with Old Testament
scenes, are visible on the façade, but the interior
owes more to the Romano-Byzantine style of 19th-
century architect Henri Antoine Révoil.

Jardin de la Fontaine & Tour Magne

quai de la Fontaine (04.66.58.38.00). **Open**
Gardens Apr-mid Sept 7.30am-10pm daily. Mid
Sept-Mar 7.30am-6.30pm daily. *Tour Magne* June-
Aug 9am-7pm daily. Sept 9.30am-1pm, 2-6pm
daily. Apr, May 9.30am-6.30pm daily. Mar, Oct

9.30am-1pm, 2-6pm daily. Jan, Feb, Nov, Dec
9.30am-1pm, 2-4.30pm daily. **Admission** *Gardens*
free. *Tour Magne* €2.70; €2.30 reductions; free
under-7s. **No credit cards. Map** p53 A1.

The bubbling spring at the heart of these lovely gardens was the reason the Romans named the city
Nemausus, after its Celtic tutelary god. In the 18th
century, formal gardens were laid out by Jacques
Philippe Mareschal. A complex system of reservoirs
distributed clean water, which had been sadly lacking in the city since the Pont du Gard aqueduct was
abandoned. Nowadays the still, green pools and
canals, overlooked by balustraded terraces and marble nymphs and cupids, provide a retreat from the
summer heat. Here, too, are the ruins of the so-called
Temple of Diana, part of a Roman sanctuary. High
on Mont Cavalier, on the edge of the garden, the
Tour Magne was part of Nîmes's pre-Roman ramparts. Its viewing platform (140 steps up) provides
a good view over the city and *garrigue*. *Photo p57.*

Maison Carrée

pl de la Maison Carrée (04.66.21.82.56). **Open**
June-Aug 10am-7pm daily. *Apr, May, Sept* 10am-
6.30pm daily. *Mar* 10am-6pm daily. *Oct* 10am-
12.30pm, 2-6pm daily. *Jan, Feb, Nov, Dec* 10am-
1pm, 2-4.30pm daily. **Admission** €4.50; €3.70
reductions; free under-7s. **No credit cards.**
Map p53 B1.

Not *carré* (square) at all, this rectangular Roman temple was built in the first century BC and dedicated to
Augustus's deified grandsons. With a great flight of
steps leading up to finely fluted Corinthian columns,
adorned with a sculpted frieze of acanthus leaves, it
has always inspired hyperbole. Arthur Young, an
18th-century British traveller, called it 'the most light,
elegant and pleasing building I have ever beheld' and
Thomas Jefferson, after failing to import it to
America, had it copied as the model for the Virginia
state capitol. A 20-minute audio-visual experience
takes you back to Roman times. *Photo p56.*

FREE Musée d'Archéologie et d'Histoire Naturelle

13bis bd Amiral Courbet (04.66.76.74.94). **Open**
10am-6pm Tue-Sun. **Admission** free. **Map** p53 C2.

The archaeology museum is a treasure trove of
Roman statues, coins, sarcophagi, entablatures and
mosaics, as well as gorgeous glass. Upstairs are more
everyday items, from oil lamps to cosmetic jars.
Sharing the premises, the natural history museum
includes Iron Age menhirs, a good anthropological
collection and stuffed bears, tigers and crocodiles.

Musée des Beaux-Arts

rue Cité Foulc (04.66.67.38.21). **Open** *July, Aug*
10am-6pm Tue, Wed, Fri-Sun; 10am-9pm Thur.
Sept-June 10am-6pm Tue, Wed, Fri-Sun; 10am-
9pm every 2nd Thur. **Admission** €5.10; €3.60
reductions; free under-10s. **No credit cards.**
Map p53 B3.

THE RHONE DELTA

Maison Carrée. *See p55*.

The imposing façade of this early 20th-century building leads into a beautiful exhibition space. Seven 18th-century paintings by Nîmes-born Charles-Joseph Natoire hang in the skylit central atrium, illustrating the story of Antony and Cleopatra, but the main draw is *The Marriage of Admetus*, a huge Roman mosaic. The eclectic collection also includes Jacopo Bassano's *Susanna and the Elders*, Rubens's *Portrait of a Monk* and *The Mystic Marriage of St Catherine* by Giambono.

Musée des Cultures Taurines

6 rue Alexandre Ducros (04.66.36.83.77). **Open** 10am-6pm Tue-Sun. **Admission** €4.90; €3.60 reductions; free under-10s. **No credit cards. Map** p53 B3.

Exploring the history and culture of bullfighting, the museum's collection ranges from extravagant toreador's costumes and posters of bullfights to eight plates designed by *feria* fan Picasso.

FREE Musée de Vieux Nîmes

pl aux Herbes (04.66.76.73.71). **Open** 10am-6pm Tue-Sun. **Admission** free. **Map** p53 C2.

This modest museum, housed in the 17th-century bishop's palace, was founded in 1920. The collection, much of it displayed as reconstructed interiors, comprises locally made furniture, pottery and fabrics, including some early denim, shawls and silks.

Where to eat

Alexandre

2 rue Xavier Tronc (04.66.70.08.99/www.michel kayser.com). **Open** *July, Aug* noon-1.45pm, 7-9.30pm Wed-Sun. *Sept-June* noon-1.45pm, 7-9.30pm Wed-Sat; noon-1.45pm Sun. **Main courses** €45-€55. **Menus** *Lunch* €44. *Dinner* €62-€107. **Credit** AmEx, DC, MC, V.

An unglamorous setting near the airport does nothing to diminish the impact of chef Michel Kayser's top-class cuisine. His take on local specialities is highly inventive, yet classical in technique: his version of local *brandade de Nîmes* is not to be missed.

Au Plaisirs des Halles

4 rue Littré (04.66.36.01.02/www.auxplaisirs deshalles.com). **Open** noon-2pm, 7-10pm Tue-Sat. **Main courses** €20-€30. **Menus** *Lunch* €21.50. *Dinner* €27-€60. **Credit** MC, V. **Map** p53 B1 ❶

Light and sophisticated cooking is served in a sleek, wood-panelled dining room at this busy bistro – or in the flower-filled courtyard. The menu ranges from pasta and seafood to classic meaty fare (roast pigeon with green beans, say, or calf's liver with onions).

€ La Bodeguita

3 bd Alphonse Daudet (04.66.58.28.27/www. royalhotel-nimes.com). **Open** noon-2.30pm, 5.30-11pm Mon-Sat. **Tapas** €3.50-€15. **Credit** MC, V. **Map** p53 B1 ❷

The city's Spanish leanings shine through here. Take a seat on the terrace and order up a feast of calamares, *albondigas* and patatas bravas. The restaurant hosts flamenco, jazz and poetry soirées.

★ € Le Bouchon et l'Assiette

5bis rue de Sauve (04.66.62.02.93). **Open** noon-1.45pm, 7-9.30pm Mon, Thur-Sun. **Main courses** €16-€20. **Menus** *Lunch (Mon-Fri)* €17. *Dinner* €27-€45. **Credit** AmEx, DC, MC, V. **Map** p53 A1 ❸

Lionel Geiger is one of the most adventurous chefs in town, using spices from his globe-trotting to enliven an inviting seasonal menu. Staff are friendly, and prices affordable.

★ Le Darling

40 rue de la Madeleine (04.66.67.04.99/www.le darling.com). **Open** 7-9.30pm Mon, Tue, Thur-Sun. **Mains** €29-€35. **Menus** €42-€45. **Credit** MC, V. **Map** p53 B2 ❹

THE RHONE DELTA

Vincent Croizard's eaterie is one of the hottest in Nîmes. Dishes are fashionably identified by their principal ingredient, with their intricacies revealed in the small print: wasabi, fig leaves and liquorice are unexpected flavours you might encounter.

L'Exaequo
11 rue Bigot (04.66.21.77.96/www.exaequo restaurant.com). **Open** noon-2pm, 7-10pm Mon-Fri; 7-10pm Sat. **Main courses** €14-€20. **Menus** *Lunch* €15-€19. *Dinner* €26-€53. **Credit** MC, V. **Map** p53 B2 ❺
Fashionably understated decor and a delightful shady courtyard make L'Exaequo a chic place to dine – but it has substance as well as style. Play it safe with a tasty haute cuisine hamburger, or opt for the more daring kangaroo carpaccio.

Le Lisita
2 bd des Arènes (04.66.67.29.15/www.le lisita.com). **Open** noon-2pm, 8-10pm Tue-Sat. **Main courses** €32-€38. **Menus** *Lunch* €35. *Dinner* €49-€76. **Credit** AmEx, DC, MC, V. **Map** p53 B2 ❻
This town centre restaurant goes from strength to strength, serving modern, market-sourced southern cooking in an airy, elegant dining room. Dishes such as the courgettes stuffed with local salt cod *brandade* are swiftly becoming modern classics.

★ Marché Sur la Table
10 rue Littré (04.66.67.22.50). **Open** noon-2pm, 7.30-10pm Wed-Sun. **Main courses** €17-€20. **Menus** *Lunch* €23. *Dinner* €33. **Credit** MC, V. **Map** p53 B1 ❼
The menu at this friendly bistro is based on the best local produce of the day, with dishes chalked up on a blackboard. Its high-quality regional cuisine has won this place a devoted following, so do reserve.

€ Nicolas
1 rue Poise (04.66.67.50.47). **Open** noon-1.45pm, 7-9.45pm Tue-Fri; 7.30-9.45pm Sat. **Main courses** €12-€18.50. **Menus** €13.50-€25. **Credit** DC, MC, V. **Map** p53 C2 ❽
This friendly, family-run establishment has exposed stone walls, sleek lighting and the requisite bull-fighting photos. Expect generous portions of home-style cooking at down-to-earth prices.

€ Les Olivades
18 rue Jean Reboul (04.66.21.71.78). **Open** noon-1.45pm, 7-10pm Tue-Sat. **Main courses** €12-€15. **Menus** *Lunch* €12. *Dinner* €22. **Credit** MC, V. **Map** p53 B2 ❾
An intriguing mix of wine shop and restaurant in a backstreet near Les Arènes. Browse the potent wines of the region before enjoying some traditional local cuisine, washed down with a glass or two.

Where to drink

Le Café Olive
22 bd Victor Hugo (04.66.67.89.10). **Open** 9am-1am Mon-Sat. **Main courses** €9.50-€14. **Credit** MC, V. **Map** p53 B2 ❶
Old stone and contemporary furniture meet in this pleasant café, which offers pan-Mediterranean cuisine, margaritas, and concerts and revues.

Courtois
8 pl du Marché (04.66.67.20.09). **Open** *July, Aug* 8am-midnight daily. *Sept-June* 8am-7.30pm daily. **Main courses** €9.80-€12.50. **Credit** AmEx, MC, V. **Map** p53 B2 ❷
This mirrored belle époque café is a Nîmes institution for tea, coffee, hot chocolate and cakes; simple meals are also offered. The terrace is a sunny spot to dawdle over your coffee and croissant.

THE RHÔNE DELTA

Jardin de la Fontaine. *See p55.*

La Grande Bourse

2 bd des Arènes (04.66.67.21.91/www.la-grande-bourse.com). **Open** noon-midnight daily. **Main courses** €10-€18. **Menus** *Lunch* €14.50. *Dinner* €19.50-€27.50. **Credit** MC, V. **Map** p53 B2 ❸

Brightly painted in Pompeian red and gold, this celebrated café-brasserie has a terrace looking across to the amphitheatre, and is an irresistible spot for a drink. Its brasserie-style food can be hit and miss.

Haddock Café

13 rue de l'Agau (04.66.67.86.57). **Open** 11am-3pm, 7pm-1am Mon-Fri; 7pm-1am Sun. **Main courses** €9-€15. **Menus** *Lunch* €11. *Dinner* €15-€20. **Credit** AmEx, MC, V. **Map** p53 B1 ❹

This alternative café hosts a busy schedule of live music and debates for a bright young local crowd. There's good moules-frites to be had too.

Lulu Club

10 impasse de la Curaterie (04.66.36.28.20/www.lulu-club.com). **Open** midnight-late Fri, Sat. **No credit cards**. **Map** p53 C2 ❺

A long-standing gay bar and disco, Lulu is a welcoming spot, with a good range of visiting DJs.

Le Mazurier

9 bd Amiral Courbet (04.66.67.27.48). **Open** 7am-midnight daily. **Main courses** €10-€15. **Menus** *Lunch* €11. *Dinner* €13.50-€20. **Credit** MC, V. **Map** p53 C2 ❻

Drop by this sweetly old-fashioned belle époque brasserie for a leisurely morning coffee over the newspaper on its terrace, or a pastis at the zinc bar.

Shopping

The best shopping is in the old town. For food, the covered market of **Les Halles** (rue des Halles, 7am-1pm daily) is unrivalled: pick up some excellent cheeses and dried meats. There's also a Monday flea market on boulevard Jean Jaurès. Streets near the amphitheatre abound in bullfighting memorabilia, ranging from pure tat to full outfits and vintage prints.

The following shops are open Monday to Saturday, unless specified otherwise. The tiny **F Nadal** (7 rue St-Castor, 04.66.67.35.42) sells olive oil from vats, handmade soaps, herbs, honey, coffee, spices and brandade. Long-established boulangerie-pâtisserie **Maison Villaret** (13 rue de la Madeleine, 04.66.67.41.79) is the place to buy Nîmes's other speciality: jaw-breaking almond *croquants*. For regional wines, visit the **Costières de Nîmes** (19 pl Aristide Briand, 04.66.36.96.20, closed Sat & Sun).

Founded in Nîmes, fashion group **Cacharel** still has a boutique in town (1898 av Mar Juin, 04.66.02.01.38). The **Marie Sara** boutique (40bis rue de la Madeleine, 04.66.21.18.40, closed Mon & Sun), owned by a famous former bullfighter, is another chic clothes shop.

Arts & entertainment

For local entertainment listings, pick up the freebie *Nîmescope* and regional *César*, or check out www.sortiranimes.com.

Le Sémaphore

25 rue Porte de France (04.66.67.83.11/www.semaphore.free.fr). **Tickets** €5.90; €5 reductions; €4 under-12s. **Credit** MC, V.

Le Sémaf offers an imaginative programme of international art house flicks.

Théâtre de Nîmes

1 pl de la Calade (04.66.36.65.00/box office 04.66.36.65.10/www.theatredenimes.com). **Open** *Box office* 11am-1pm, 2-6pm Tue-Sat. **Tickets** €11-€45. **Credit** AmEx, DC, MC, V.

This pretty vintage theatre brings a thrilling range of theatre, music and dance to the town.

Where to stay

Most hotels put up their prices during *ferias*, so check ahead to avoid expensive surprises.

€ Hôtel Central

2 pl du Château (04.66.67.27.75/www.hotel-central.org). **Rates** €40-€50 double. **Rooms** 15. **Credit** MC, V. **Map** p53 C1 ❶

Just opposite the Acanthe du Temple, this clean, inexpensive hotel makes a useful base in the centre of town. The top-floor bedroom has a great view of the Tour Magne too.

€ Hôtel de l'Amphithéâtre

4 rue des Arènes (04.66.67.28.51). **Rates** €41-€70 double. Closed Jan. **Rooms** 15. **Credit** AmEx, MC, V. **Map** p53 B2 ❷

Surprisingly smart for the price, this nicely restored 18th-century building has a lovely staircase, antique furniture and large, white-tiled bathrooms.

Hôtel Le Cheval Blanc

1 pl des Arènes (04.66.76.05.22). **Rates** €105-€200 double. **Rooms** 32. **Credit** AmEx, MC, V. **Map** p53 B2 ❸

This friendly, modern hotel is directly opposite the amphitheatre. Make sure you nab a room at the front, then bask in the magnificent view; it's particularly majestic at night, in all its floodlit glory. Rooms and suites are simply furnished but comfortable, with whitewashed walls and wooden floors.

Hôtel Imperator

15 rue Gaston Boissier (04.66.21.90.30/www.hotel-imperator.com). **Rates** €190-€255

Marie Sara.

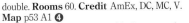

Map p53 A1 ❹
Unremarkable from the outside, Imperator has a
lovely inner courtyard and garden. Its restaurant is
the most attractive in town, although the cooking is
a little over-elaborate for some tastes.

★ Jardins Secrets
*3 rue Gaston Maruejols (04.66.84.82.64/
www.jardinssecrets.net).* **Rates** €195-€220
double. **Rooms** 12. **Credit** AmEx, DC, MC, V.
Map p53 C3 ❺
The secret garden in question belongs to this chic
newcomer, whose sybaritic pleasures include luxurious, modern bedrooms and a swimming pool and
spa, which soothe away the aches and pains of visiting toreadors and tourists.

La Maison de Sophie
*31 av Carnot (04.66.70.96.10/www.hotel-
lamaisondesophie.com).* **Rates** €150-€290 double.
Rooms 8. **Credit** MC, V. **Map** p53 C3 ❻
The eponymous Sophie welcomes people into her
stately *hôtel particulier* with inimitable style. Rooms
are elegantly appointed, while the delightful garden,
with its own little swimming pool, is another draw.

Le Royal Hôtel
*3 bd Alphonse Daudet (04.66.58.28.27/www.royal
hotel-nimes.com).* **Rates** €60-€110 double. **Rooms**
23. **Credit** AmEx, DC, MC, V. **Map** p53 B1 ❼
This fashionable little hotel is studiously casual,
with artfully distressed walls and friendly propri-
etors. Rooms vary considerably in size, with a minimalist look that tends towards the spartan.
▶ *Visit the lively ground-floor restaurant, La
Bodeguita, for good Spanish tapas (see p56).*

Resources

Hospital
Hôpital Carémeau *pl Prof Robert Debré
(04.66.68.68.68).*

Police
8 rue Rangueil (04.66.36.75.06).

Post office
19 bd Gambetta (04.66.36.32.60).

Tourist information
Office de Tourisme *6 rue Auguste
(04.66.58 38.00/www.ot-nimes.fr).* **Open**
July, Aug 8.30am-8pm Mon-Fri; 9am-7pm Sat;
10am-6pm Sun. *Apr, May, June, Sept* 8.30am-
7pm Mon-Fri; 9am-7pm Sat; 10am-6pm Sun.
Oct-Mar 8.30am-6.30pm Mon-Fri; 9am-6.30pm
Sat; 10am-5pm Sun.

North of Nîmes
PONT DU GARD
No picture can convey the awesome scale of
the triple-decker Pont du Gard, which rises
to a lofty 49 metres (161 feet), and is the largest
aqueduct the Romans ever built. The gigantic
blocks of limestone, some weighing as much
as six tons, were hauled into place by pulleys,
wheels and huge numbers of slaves. During
the devastating floods of 1988 and 2002, it stood
firm while lesser bridges collapsed – perhaps
due to its slight bow, which allows it to
withstand great water pressure. The aqueduct

originally carried drinking water from the springs in Uzès across the Gardon river to Nîmes, along a 50-kilometre (30-mile) route, much of it passing through underground channels dug out of solid rock. Fragments of water channels and lost aqueduct arches still litter the area, marked with a signposted trail.

The **Public Information Centre** (08.20.90.33.30, www.pontdugard.fr, €7) provides a film (the English version is screened at 3pm daily), an exhibition and hands-on activities for children. Simply crossing the bridge is a magical experience, though – and there's a little beach on the riverbank, with swimming when water levels are high enough.

UZES & THE GARDON

There could hardly be more of a contrast between bullfighting Nîmes, with its heat and dust, and charming Italianate Uzès. Often dubbed 'the Tuscany of France', the town was designated a *ville d'art* in 1962. Its pale limestone buildings have been beautifully restored – and despite a multitude of antique shops and arty boutiques, the town still has soul, making it a favourite location for historical films such as *Cyrano de Bergerac*. Its thriving market is heaven for foodies, while the locally grown violet garlic is among the best in France. The pungent root has its own festival on 24 June, while the third Sunday in January is set aside to celebrate another underground treasure: the local truffles.

A powerful medieval bishopric and later a major centre of Protestantism, Uzès prospered from its linen, serge and silk industries in the 17th and 18th centuries. It was also an important ducal seat, and lays claim to having been the first duchy in France. Within the ring of boulevards along the former ramparts, the arcaded **place aux Herbes** sums up Uzès, coming alive for the market (Wed morning

& all day Sat), which is a great source of olives, baskets, provençal fabric and pottery. Behind the square, a web of small streets and squares lead to the **Duché d'Uzès**, where the duke lives on, Republicanism notwithstanding. A guided tour includes a visit to the dungeons, complete with a holographic ghost.

Beyond the ramparts, the 17th-century **Cathédrale St-Théodorit** (open 9am-6pm Mon-Sat) contains a superb 18th-century organ. The earlier **Tour Fenestrelle**, a round, arcaded bell tower reminiscent of Pisa, is the only part of the Romanesque cathedral to survive the Wars of Religion. Next door, the late 17th-century bishop's palace houses the **Musée Georges Borias**, with its local pottery and paintings: it also pays tribute to novelist André Gide, born here in 1869.

On impasse Port Royal, the **Jardin Medieval** contains a remarkable collection of carefully labelled local plants and medicinal and culinary herbs. The excavated **Fontaine d'Eure**, a spring that originally carried water to Nîmes via the Pont du Gard, is a short walk from Uzès town centre (take chemin André Gide out of town to the Vallée de l'Alzon).

Between Uzès and Nîmes, the Gorges du Gardon are the most spectacular of a series of deep river gorges; they are visible from **Pont St-Nicolas** on the D979, where a fine, seven-arched medieval bridge spans the chasm. To walk along them, take a detour through Poulx, taking the D135 then the D127, to pick up the GR6 footpath through the depths; at the north-east end, the village of Collias has wonderful views. You can also explore the gorges on the water by hiring canoes (04.66.70.08.61, www.canoe-france.com, closed Nov-Mar, €20-€44).

Duché d'Uzès

pl de Duché, Uzès (04.66.22.18.96/www.duche-uzes.fr). **Open** *July-Aug* 10am-1pm, 2-6.30pm daily. *Sept-June* 10am-noon, 2-6pm daily. **Admission** €14; €4-€10 reductions; free under-7s. **No credit cards**.

Jardin Medieval

impasse Port Royal, off rue Port Royal, Uzès (04.66.22.38.21). **Open** *Apr-June, Sept* 2-6pm Mon-Fri; 10.30am-12.30pm, 2-6pm Sat, Sun. *July, Aug* 10.30am-12.30pm, 2-6pm daily. *Oct* 2-5pm daily. Closed Nov-Mar. **Admission** €4; €2 reductions; free under-16s. **No credit cards**.

Musée Georges Borias

Palais de l'Evêché, pl de l'Evêché, Uzès (04.66. 22.40.23). **Open** *Feb, Nov, Dec* 2-5pm Tue-Sun. *Mar-June* 3-6pm Tue-Sun. *July, Aug* 10am-noon, 3-6pm Tue-Sun. *Sept, Oct* 3-6pm Tue-Sun. Closed Jan. **Admission** €2; €1 reductions; free under-5s. **No credit cards**.

Where to stay & eat

Close to the Pont du Gard, the **Vieux Castillon** (10 rue Turion Sabatier, Castillon-du-Gard, 04.66.37.61.61, www.vieuxcastillon.com, double €200-€472) is an upmarket option, with glorious rural views and a lovely pool. In nearby Collias, the **Hostellerie le Castellas** (Grande Rue, 04.66.22.88.88, www.lecastellas.fr, closed Jan & Feb, double €145-€270, menus €32 lunch, €57-€104 dinner) has a palm-filled garden, a restaurant and a pool.

In Uzès itself, family-run **La Taverne** (9 rue Xavier Sigalon, 04.66.22.13.10, www.lataverne-uzes.com, menus €24-€32) offers a refined, modern take on regional cuisine, and operates a simple but tasteful hotel across the street (No.4, double €57-€62). Built around a delightful 15th-century manor house, the **Hôtel du Général d'Entraigues** (pl de l'Evêché, 04.66.22.32.68, www.leshotelsparticuliers.com, double €60-€170) has a charming terrace and swimming pool. The **Hostellerie Provençale** (1-3 rue de la Grande Bourgade, 04.66.22.11.06, www.hostellerie provencale.com, double €85-€135) offers nine quietly stylish, comfortable bedrooms, and a warm welcome. For simpler accommodation **Le Patio de Violette** (chemin Trinquelaïgues, 04.66.01.09.83, double €60-€75) has a pool, no-frills rooms and a simple restaurant.

For stylish dining in Uzès, try the fashionable **Les Trois Salons** (18 rue du Dr Blanchard, 04.66.03.10.81, menus €22 lunch, €39-€57 dinner), set in a beautiful *hôtel particulier*. Its Swedish chef, Tobias Eriksson, serves sophisticated, modern cuisine.

Les 80 Jours (2 pl Albert 1er, 04.66.22.09.89, closed Sun, Wed Sept-June, menus €19 lunch, €30-€39 dinner) is named in honour of the travels of Jules Verne, though the cooking stays comfortingly local: a perfectly cooked rack of lamb, for instance, or *supions* (squid) on a bed of peppers. For a quick meal, the **Bistrot de Grezac** (pl Belle Croix 04.66.03.42.09, mains €12-€15.50, menu €18.50-€26.50) offers brasserie-style fare.

Five kilometres outside Uzès, the village of St-Siffert is home to **L'Authentic** (pl de l'Ancienne Ecole, 04.66.22.60.09, closed Mon-Wed, menus €20 lunch, €28-€38 dinner). Set in the old schoolhouse, its menu is based on fresh, seasonal southern produce; book ahead.

In Arpaillargues, four kilometres from Uzès, the 18th-century **Château d'Arpaillargues** (Hôtel Marie d'Agoult, 04.66.22.14.48, www.chateaudarpaillargues.com, closed Nov-Mar, double €70-€208, mains €19-€25, menus €28 lunch, €50 dinner) has traditional but tasteful rooms, plus summer barbecues by the pool. In nearby Serviers-Labaume, Numo and Odino Domenichini run the acclaimed **L'Olivier**

(04.66.22.56.01, www.l-olivier.fr, double €70, menu €22 lunch, €43-€65 dinner). Its enticing Italian-influenced menu might include pappardelle with rabbit and herbs, or sea bream with peperonata and basil; upstairs are five attractive rooms.

Those keen to develop their own culinary skills should head for the **Clos du Léthé** (Hameau de St-Médiers, 04.66.74.58.37, www.closdulethe.com, double €170-€270), an impeccably stylish *chambre d'hôte* that also offers cooking classes.

Resources

Tourist information

Uzès Office de Tourisme *Chapelle des Capucins, pl Albert 1er, 30700 Uzès (04.66.22.68.88/www.uzes-tourisme.com).* **Open** *June, Sept* 9am-6pm Mon-Fri; 10am-1pm, 2-5pm Sat, Sun. *July, Aug* 9am-7pm Mon-Fri; 10am-1pm, 2-5pm Sat, Sun. *Oct-May* 9am-12.30pm, 2-6pm Mon-Fri; 10am-1pm Sat.

GETTING THERE & AROUND

By air

The **Aéroport de Nîmes-Arles-Camargue** (04.66.70.49 49, www.nimes-aeroport.fr) is 10km south-east of Nîmes. A shuttle bus heads to the town centre and train station (€4.30).

By bus

STD Gard (04.66.29.27.29) runs several buses (daily except Sun) between Nîmes and Avignon and Nîmes and Uzès (some Uzès buses stop at Remoulins for the Pont du Gard and a few continue to St-Quentin-la-Poterie). There are also three buses daily to Avignon via Remoulins for the Pont du Gard (none Sun) and three between Uzès and Avignon. **Cars de Camargue** (04.90.96.36.25) runs a service between Nîmes and Arles (four daily Mon-Sat, two Sun). **TCN** (04.66.38.15.40) runs the useful little La Citadine bus, which runs in a big loop from the station, passing a good many of the principal sights.

By car

For Nîmes, coming south from Lyon/Orange or north-east from Montpellier, take the A9 autoroute, exit 50. West from Arles, take the A54 autoroute, exit 1. For Uzès, take the D979 from Nîmes. Pont du Gard is 14km south-east of Uzès on the D981, 20km (12 miles) north-east of Nîmes on the N86 (take the Remoulins exit from the A9); from Avignon take the N100 then the D19.

By train

Nîmes is on the Paris–Avignon–Montpellier line, with a TGV link direct to Paris (around 3hrs). The *gare routière* is behind the train station.

St-Rémy & Les Alpilles

Chic towns and fortified villages perch amid the craggy Alpilles hills.

While Luberon residents still shiver in the long winter shadows, **Les Alpilles** dons its summer wardrobe over a month earlier. Plane trees throw a dappled canopy over the streets, vines sprout and the baking hot plains are adorned with olive trees and lush bougainvillea. English royals started visiting in the 1960s, and today there's a host of fashionable boltholes in the lea of the Alpilles.

Stylish, self-assured **St-Rémy-de-Provence** sits in a dramatic setting at the northern foot of the hills. Birthplace of Nostradamus and home to the asylum that sheltered Van Gogh, it's a favoured escape for Paris's creative elite – the St-Germain-des-Prés of the south.

ST-REMY-DE-PROVENCE

On first impressions, you might wonder what all the fuss is about. The circular boulevards of Victor Hugo, Mareau, Mirabeau and Gambetta are permanently clogged with traffic, its fumes spilling over the roadside cafés. But this chaotic exterior hides a warren of cobbled streets, where fountains trickle in quiet corners, squares are dotted with shady benches and bijou boutiques rub shoulders with traditional shops (the town still has a horse butcher).

One of the major festivals celebrated in the town is May Day, which brings flowers, music, donkey-drawn carts and a children's fair. The Fête de Transhumance on Whit Monday, meanwhile, recreates the exodus of flocks into the Alpilles for the summer. Expect to see up to 4,000 sheep paraded through town, accompanied by donkeys and goats. In summer, Tuesday evenings (7-11.30pm, mid July-mid Sept) bring the Marché des Createurs in place de la Mairie, where craftsmen display their work. Contact the tourist board for further information (*see p64*).

For an olfactory treat, head to the **Musée des Arômes et des Parfums**, which is dedicated to the fragrant herbs and plants of Provence. Here you'll find antique perfume stills, gorgeously ornate bottles and all kinds of heady potions made from essential oils.

The august **Collégiale St-Martin** church was rebuilt in 1820 after the original structure caved in, and has a 5,000-pipe modern organ, used for summer recitals (5pm Sat July-Sept). Follow the street to the right of the church into the old town, where squares with burbling fountains and Renaissance *hôtels particuliers* give a sense of St-Rémy's illustrious past.

On place Favier, the 15th-century Hôtel de Sade, built on the site of Roman baths, was the family mansion of the Marquis de Sade (*see p23* **No Pain, No Gain**); today it's the **Musée Archéologique**. Closed for renovation until 2009, its collection of fragments found at Glanum (*see p63*) includes stunning temple decorations and a stone lintel with hollows carved to hold the severed heads of enemies. Across the square, the **Musée des Alpilles Pierre-de-Brun** occupies a handsome 16th-century mansion, once home to the Mistral de Mondragon family. Lack of personnel has kept the museum closed in recent years, though the art exhibition on its ground floor is open.

The 18th-century Hôtel Estrine is now the **Centre d'Art Présence Van Gogh**, with themed exhibitions and reproductions of Van Gogh's work. It also houses changing displays of contemporary art and a permanent exhibition on the father of Cubism, Albert Gleize, who lived in St-Rémy for the last 15 years of his life.

From May 1889 Van Gogh spent a year under the care of nuns in the psychiatric asylum adjoining the pretty **Monastère St-Paul-de-Mausole**. Just south of the town, it has a Romanesque chapel and a cloister, with an exhibition of *art brut* created by patients. Van Gogh's own stay was remarkably fertile; *Olive Groves* and *Starry Night* were among the 150 paintings he produced here.

Beyond the monastery are the fascinating archaeological sites of **Les Antiques** and **Glanum** (rte des Baux, 04.90.92.23.79). Les Antiques consists of an impressively preserved mausoleum, embossed with lively reliefs, and a triumphal arch that once marked the entrance to the ancient city of Glanum. A Celto-Ligurian site of pilgrimage in the fifth and sixth centuries BC, Glanum's heyday came with the Roman occupation in 49 BC. Its ruins – an intriguing jumble of Celtic, Greek and Roman remains – were long hidden under river silt, and excavations only began in the 1920s. Today, models and plans help make sense of the immense site and once-thriving town, with its public baths, basilica and forums.

Centre d'Art Présence Van Gogh

Hôtel Estrine, 8 rue Estrine (04.90.92.34.72/ www.ateliermuseal.net). **Open** *May-Sept* 10am-12.30pm, 2-7pm Tue, Thur-Sun; 10am-7pm Wed. *Mar, Apr, Nov, Dec* 10am-12.30pm, 2-6pm. Closed Jan-Mar, 3wks Nov. **Admission** €3.20; €2.30 reductions; free under-12s. **No credit cards**.

Monastère St-Paul-de-Mausole

Centre d'Art Valetudo, Maison de Santé St-Paul (04.90.92.77.00/www.cloitresaintpaul-valetudo. com). **Open** *Apr-Sept* 9.30am-7pm daily. *Nov-Mar* 10.30am-7pm daily. Closed Jan. **Admission** €4; €3 reductions; free under-12s. **No credit cards**.

Musée des Alpilles Pierre-de-Brun

Hôtel Mistral de Mondragon, 1 pl Favier (04.90.92.68.24/www.ateliermuseal.net). **Open** (ground floor only) *Jan, Feb, Nov, Dec* 2-5pm Tue-Sat. *Mar-June, Sept, Oct* 10am-noon, 2-6pm Tue-Sat. *July, Aug* 10am-12.30pm, 2-7pm Tue-Sat & 1st Sun of mth. **Admission** €3; €2 reductions; free under-10s. **No credit cards**.

★ Musée Archéologique

Hôtel de Sade, rue du Parage (04.90.92.64.04). **Open** Closed until late 2009. Call for details.

FREE Musée des Arômes et des Parfums

34 bd Mirabeau (04.32.60.05.18/www.florame. fr). **Open** *Apr-Sept* 10am-12.30pm, 2-7pm daily. *Oct-Mar* 10am-12.30pm, 2-7pm Mon-Sat. **Admission** free.

Where to eat

The straightforward decor of **Alain Assaud** (13 bd Marceau, 04.90.92.37.11, closed Wed, lunch Thur & Sat, Nov-late Dec, Jan-mid Mar, menus €28-€44) belies the chef's sophisticated seasonal cuisine and exquisite desserts. Good-value **La Gousse d'Ail** (6 bd Marceau, 04.90. 92.16.87, www.la-goussedail.com, closed Thur, Jan-Mar, menus €12-€34) has music nights on Wednesdays in summer; specialities include leg of lamb with garlic cream and local *taureau*.

Occupying a stately 18th-century townhouse, François Perraud's **La Maison Jaune** (15 rue Carnot, 04.90.92.56.14, closed Jan-Feb, Mon, lunch Tue, menus €36-€66) offers a modern take on provençal cooking. **Xa** (24 bd Mirabeau, 04.90.92.41.23, closed lunch, dinner Wed, Nov-mid Mar, menu €27) has a short but inviting menu, ranging from seafood to curry.

The appealing **Bistrot Decouverte** (19 bd Victor Hugo, 04.90.92.34.49, www.bistrot decouverte.com, mains €18-€25) has a splendid wine list and simple menu, based on top-notch ingredients; don't miss the chocolate fondant. For a light lunch in a brasserie atmosphere, try **Café des Variétés** (32 bd Victor Hugo, 04.90.92.42.61, menus €19.50-€39).

Monastère St-Paul-de-Mausole.

Shopping

With its well-heeled visitors in mind, St-Rémy has plenty of sophisticated shops. Inventive *chocolatier* **Joël Durand** (3 bd Victor Hugo, 04.90.92.38.25, www.chocolat-durand.com) is perfect for presents, including gleaming bars of lavender- or cardamom-infused chocolate. A few doors up at **Le Petit Duc** (No.7, 04.90.92.08.31), Dutch-born pastry chef Hermann Van Beek and his French wife Anne Daguin have resurrected a delicious array of ancient biscuit recipes. Among them are pine nut *pignolats*, found in the *Traité des Fardements et des Confitures* – written in 1552 by none other than Nostradamus.

The outer boulevards have been colonised by international brands such as **Vilebrequin** (17 bd Victor Hugo, 04.32.60.06.10) whose brightly-patterned swimming shorts are ubiquitous around town in August. For more unique pieces try **Le Grand Magasin** (24 rue de la Commune, 04.90.92.18.79), where you can buy everything from handmade jewellery to contemporary clothing. **NM Deco** (9 rue Hoche, 04.90.92.57.91), meanwhile, is great for cashmere, silk and linen. Market day in St-Rémy is Wednesday.

Where to stay

The **Domaine de Valmouriane** (petite rte des Baux, 04.90.92.44.62, www.valmouriane. com, double €145-€340, menus €33-€80) is an idyllic stone *mas*. Set in a pine forest, halfway between St-Rémy and Les Baux, it has a library, bar, restaurant and pool, and is surrounded by herb-scented gardens. In town, the **Hôtel Les Ateliers de l'Image** (36 bd Victor Hugo, 04.90.92.51.50, www.hotelphoto.com, closed Jan, double €165-€600) is a sleek boutique hotel, partly housed in the town's old cinema and music hall. There's a pool in the landscaped gardens, and the restaurant serves sushi as well as more traditional fare (menus €28-€43).

Even more central is the **Hôtel Gounod Ville Verte** (pl de la République, 04.90.92.06.14, www.hotel-gounod.com, double €110-€220), with its friendly staff, chic tearoom and quirky mix of modern and antique decor. Another option is the newly opened **La Maison du Village** (10 rue du 8 Mai, 04.32.60.68.20, www.lamaisonduvillage.com, €150-€190 suite), a gorgeous townhouse with five opulent suites. Family-run **Le Castelet des Alpilles** (6 pl Mireille, 04.90.92.07.21, www.castelet-alpilles. com, closed Nov-Mar, double €71-€98) is rustic but comfy, with rooms overlooking the garden.

Just outside town, the intimate **Mas des Carassins** (1 chemin Gaulois, 04.90.92.15.48, www.masdescarassins.com, closed Jan, Feb,

double €99-€208, menu €28.50) is a beautiful stone farmhouse with a pool and large gardens. For those with a little more cash to splash, the **Château des Alpilles** (rte D31, 04.90.92.03.33, www.châteaudesalpilles.com, closed Jan-Mar, double €175-€270, menu €20-€42) is a grand 19th-century manor house, now kitted out as a quietly luxurious hotel.

Resources

Internet
Café des Variétés *32 bd Victor Hugo (04.90.92.42.61).* **Open** *June-Sept* 7am-midnight daily; *Oct-May* 7am-2am daily.

Tourist information
Office de Tourisme *pl Jean Jaurès, St-Rémy-de-Provence (04.90.92.05.22/www.saintremy-de-provence.com).* **Open** *Easter-Oct* 9am-12.30pm, 2-6.30pm Mon-Sat; 10am-noon Sun. *Nov-Easter* 9am-12.30pm, 2-6pm Mon-Sat.

LES ALPILLES & AROUND

The bone-white limestone outcrop of the Alpilles is one of the more recent geological formations to be thrust up from the earth's crust, and it shows: there are no smooth, time-worn edges here, just dramatically barren rock stretching south from St-Rémy. On a spur dominating the range, its surreal rock forms accentuated by centuries of quarrying, is the bizarre eyrie of **Les Baux** (in Provençal, *baou* means 'rocky spur'): not, as it appears from below, a natural phenomenon, but a fortified village with its own ruined château.

The medieval Lords of Baux were a fiercely independent lot, swearing allegiance to no one and always ready to resort to bloodshed. Their court, however, was renowned for its chivalry: only ladies of the highest birth and learning were admitted, and quibbles over questions of gallantry were often referred here. In 1372 the sadistic Raymond de Turenne became guardian of Alix, the last princess of Les Baux. Dubbed 'the scourge of Provence', he terrorised the countryside for miles around, making his prisoners leap to their death from the castle walls. On Alix's death, a subdued Baux passed to Provence, then France, only to raise its head again as a Protestant stronghold in the 17th century – after which Cardinal Richelieu ordered that its walls and castle be razed.

In 1822, the aluminium ore bauxite (named after the place) was discovered in the deserted village, changing its fortunes; its wild and windswept landscapes subsequently made it a fashionable destination among travellers. Below the ruined castle, the winding streets and noble mansions have been restored and

Wine Tour Les Baux

Richard James recommends the pick of the local vineyards.

Centred around the medieval village of Les Baux-de-Provence, this unique wine region has quietly garnered quite a following. It comprises a dozen estates, set in eight villages – a perfect compact tour for those in pursuit of lush, rustic red wines and full-on rosés. Look out, too, for the annual Les Baux two-day wine festival, held in May.

Grape-wise, syrah and cabernet sauvignon are harmoniously blended with warm-blooded Mediterranean varieties such as grenache and mourvèdre. What makes Les Baux so special, though, is that 85 per cent of the vineyards are organically farmed or run on biodynamic principles (also incorporating planetary and atmospheric elements).

Among the rising band of biodynamists are Jean-Louis and Anne-Marie Charmolüe of the **Château Romanin** (rte de Cavaillon, St-Rémy, 04.90.92.45.87, www.romanin. com). Located near the airfield, it produces seductive, smoky reds. Back towards St-Rémy, **Domaine Hauvette** (Voie Aurelia, quartier de la Haute Galine, St-Rémy, 04.90.92.03.90) is also run on biodynamic principles, with characterful reds based mainly on grenache and, unusually, cinsault. Heading east again, off the D99 before the turning for Eygalières, is the family-run **Domaine de Terres Blanches** (rte de Cavaillon, chemin 107628, St-Rémy, 04.90.95.91.66), whose 'Aurelia' red is a classic syrah-cabernet sauvignon blend.

Moving on to Les Baux, head south from St-Rémy on the D5 until you see the **Mas de la Dame** (04.90.54.32.24, www.masdeladame.com) on the right. Here, sisters Anne Poniatowski and Caroline Missoffe make award-winning whites, reds and rosés. Along the D27, and offering wonderful views of Les Baux, is **Mas Sainte-Berthe** (04.90.54.39.01, www.mas-sainte-berthe.com), where Christian Nief produces a rich white made from grenache blanc and roussanne, and traditional reds that age well.

Over in Mouriès is **Domaine de Lauzières** (04.90.47.62.88, www.lauzieres. com), where Jean-Daniel Schlaepfer's three reds include Sine Nomine, a sumptuous table wine that breaks the rules by using the petit verdot grape. **Jean-André Charial** (04.90.54.56.54, www. oustaudebaumaniere.com), meanwhile, makes a fruity, powerful red that goes under the enigmatic name of L'Affectif.

Finally, in St-Etienne-du-Grès you'll find **Château Dalmeran** (04.90.49.04.04), producing a chunky, tasty red that grows more complex with age, and **Domaine de Trévallon** (04.90.49.06.00, www.domaine detrevallon.com) – the Dürrbach family left the AOC, as its delicious biodynamically reared reds are built from much more cabernet sauvignon than is allowed.

are visited by two million people a year. In summer it can be overpowering, as visitors sweat their way to the summit and jostle in the narrow, cobbled streets, lined with trinket-touting shops. Most daytrippers make their way back by 6pm, however, so evenings tend to be less frenetic.

The **Musée Yves Brayer** houses many of the 20th-century artist's vigorous oil paintings of the region, and also hosts two temporary exhibitions a year. Meanwhile, the **Fondation Louis Jou** (Grande Rue, 04.90.54.34.17, open by appointment), in the 16th-century Hôtel Jean de Brion, displays the presses, wood blocks and manuscripts of the Spanish-born etcher and typographer. The **Musée des Santons** (pl Louis Jou, 04.90.54.34.39) has a collection of traditional local nativity figures, made from clay, wax, glass and even bread.

The village's star attraction, though, is the **Château des Baux**. It's an impressive sight, with breathtaking views and sheer drops to the plateau below. Allow a good hour to walk along the battlements and explore the remnants of the once-mighty stronghold, with its crumbling towers, dovecote, Gothic chapel and leper's hospital; a free audio-guide is available.

From the edge of the escarpment there are views across the savage, unearthly rocks of the Val d'Enfer (literally, 'hell valley'), said to have inspired Dante's *Inferno* and the backdrop for Cocteau's *Le Testament d'Orphée*. Walkers can follow the GR6 footpath through the valley (access from D27) and along the crest of Les Alpilles. The vast **Cathédrale d'Images**, a disused bauxite quarry, makes a dramatic setting for audio-visual shows with thousands of images projected on to the floor, ceiling and

THE RHONE DELTA

THE RHONE DELTA

Death In the Afternoon

Bullfighting is still going strong in these parts – but not without controversy.

Probably the easiest way to start a row in the South of France is to wonder aloud whether bulls should be taunted for sport. Yes, says the man with the thick arms, who insists that it's a vital expression of provençal culture; no, says the woman in the dolphin T-shirt, such sports are cruel, barbaric, medieval; and with persuasion and compromise apparently impossible, the dispute runs and runs. If you try asking the bull what he thinks, he just snorts.

French bull-baiting, or *tauromachie*, comes in two main flavours. The healthier option is the *course camarguaise*, which, like the more familiar and far messier *corrida*, pits two legs against four inside an arena. The *raseteur*, all in white, has to hook a series of ribbons, pompoms and twists of braid from the charging animal's horns and head, and because the Camargue bull is lighter and more agile than the Spanish breed used in *corridas*, this is far from easy. If the *raseteur* jumps out of the arena, the bull is quite capable of clearing the wall to follow him, and injuries are common: one *raseteur* was badly gored at Aigues-Vives in June 2008 and almost died.

But at least the *course* doesn't kill the bull. Indeed, the bull (*biòu* or *cocardier*) is as much a star as the *raseteur*, and the *abrivado* (ceremonial procession of bulls through the streets to the arena) draws big crowds. This young sport – first played in the 19th

century and only given formal rules in 1966 – is not a universal southern hit, however. Marseille's council banned a proposed *course* in late 2008 (the city hasn't seen *tauromachie* for 40 years), and animal rights campaigners want a total ban.

That goes double for *corridas*, and in summer 2007 the Société pour la Protection des Animaux, France's RSPCA, produced some hard-hitting TV ads to show what a nasty business a *corrida* is. Still accessible on the SPA's website (www.spa.asso.fr), they show bulls with blood pouring from their mouths and bubbling from their punctured flanks. A snippet of undercover video shows the illegal but widespread practice of *afeitado*, the sawing off of five to ten centimetres of the bull's horns before it enters the arena; this alters the bull's perception of distance, and is in itself excruciatingly painful.

Frustratingly for the SPA, the ads were too gory to get past the broadcasting watchdog – even though anyone, of any age, is allowed to attend the real thing. The blocking triggered a bitter national row, with French and foreign celebrities including Twiggy, Brigitte Bardot and Jean-Claude Van Damme petitioning President Sarkozy to overturn it; as one side howled about censorship, the other roared about the protection of French heritage. Sarkozy, so far, has done nothing, no doubt because bullfighting is a big earner, with an estimated annual revenue of €100 million; indeed, he himself has been seen at bullfights.

Tauromachie certainly delivers local colour – but do you want to help fund it? Read up and decide for yourself. The *corrida* is the preserve of the Fédération des Sociétés Taurines de France (www.torofstf.com); for the *course camarguaise*, see www.ffcc.info. The most prestigious course is the Cocarde d'Or, held in Arles (*see p73*); the season (900 events) runs from February to November throughout the Rhône Delta and the Camargue. The *corrida* is held even more widely.

walls; the theme changes annually. The quarries are cool (16°C/61°F), so bring a jumper.

The lower slopes of Les Alpilles are covered with vineyards, producing renowned Les Baux reds and rosés (*see p65* **Wine Tour**) and Coteaux d'Aix whites. In the heart of Les Alpilles, the tiny village of **Eygaliéres** is really too pretty for its own good, filled with overpriced interiors shops and restaurants. However, the delightful 12th-century Chapelle St-Sixte, set on a spartan, luminous hillside speckled with olive and almond trees, lifts the spirits. Pagan rites were once performed on the hill, and one ritual endures: on the day of a couple's engagement, the future husband drinks spring water from his fiancée's hands. If they don't marry within a year, legend has it that he'll die.

The **Moulin Jean-Marie Cornille** (rue Charloun Rieu, 04.90.54.32.37, www.moulin-cornille.com), a traditional olive mill in the picturesque town of **Mausanne-les-Alpilles**, offers guided tours of its premises on Tuesday and Thursday mornings, with the opportunity to buy its fruity green olive oil. To the south-west, **Fontvieille** boasts a literary landmark, the **Moulin de Daudet** (allée des Pins, 04.90.54.60.78, closed Jan, €2.50). Alphonse Daudet's *Letters from my Windmill* (1860) captures the essence of life in the south, though he was accused of caricaturing the locals; to find some modern-day characters, visit Friday morning's market. Daudet never actually lived in his windmill, preferring a friend's nearby chateau, but the view from the pine-scented hilltop is delightful. Just outside town are the remains of a Roman aqueduct that carried water from Les Alpilles to Arles.

Further along the road towards Arles is the **Abbaye de Montmajour**, founded by the Benedictines on a great rock surrounded by marshland. The 12th-century church, crypt and cloisters have been painstakingly pieced together over the past century, while the interior, used for exhibitions, is plain and serene. It's at its most human in the tiny tenth-century chapel of St Peter (closed for restoration for the foreseeable future), with hermits' cells and an altar gouged out of a cave. Ask for the keys to the **Chapelle St-Croix**, but be prepared to hand over a form of ID in return; it's best to call a few days in advance.

French Air Force flying school jets and hard-sell Nostradamus heritage make an unlikely pairing at the sprawling commercial crossroads of **Salon-de-Provence** on the eastern edge of the Crau. In the **Maison de Nostradamus**, where the astrologer and doctor wrote his *Centuries* and lived from 1547 until his death in 1566, a 40-minute audio tour talks you through various kitsch waxwork tableaux.

More atmospheric is Nostradamus's tomb – a simple tablet set into the wall in the Gothic **Collégiale de St-Laurent** beyond the city wall. The Romano-Gothic church of St-Michel in the old town is also worth a look, as are two surviving gateways: Tour de Bourg Neuf, guarded by a black Virgin, and Porte de l'Horloge, topped by a wrought-iron belfry. Looming over Salon is the **Château de l'Emperi**, built between the tenth and 13th centuries for the bishops of Arles, and today home to a 26-room military museum and assorted Napoleonic memorabilia.

Modern town life centres around the Hôtel de Ville, the cafés of place Croustillat and the shops of cours Gimon, while the morning market is held on Wednesday.

Abbaye de Montmajour

rte de Fontvieille, Fontvieille (04.90.54.64.17). **Open** *Apr-Sept* 10am-7pm daily. *Oct-Mar* 10am-6pm daily. **Admission** €6.50; €4.50 reductions. **Credit** MC, V.

▶ *North-west of Beaucaire, the Abbaye St-Roman (see p69) is also well worth a detour.*

Cathédrale d'Images

rte de Maillane, Les Baux-de-Provence (04.90.54.38.65/www.cathedrale-images.com). **Open** *Mar-Sept* 10am-7pm daily. *Oct-Jan, mid Feb-Mar* 10am-6pm daily. Closed Jan-mid Feb. **Admission** €7.50; €3.50 reductions; free under-8s. **Credit** DC, MC, V.

★ Château des Baux

rue du Trencat, Les Baux-de-Provence (04.90.54.55.56/www.château-baux-provence. com). **Open** *Mar-May* 9am-6.30pm daily. *June, Sept, Oct* 9am-7pm daily. *July, Aug* 9.30am-8.20pm daily. **Admission** €7.60; €3.85-€5.70 reductions; free under-7s. **Credit** MC, V.

Château de l'Emperi

Montée du Puech, Salon-de-Provence (04.90. 56.22.36). **Open** 10am-noon, 2-6pm Mon, Wed-Sun. **Admission** €3; €2.30 reductions; free under-7s. **No credit cards.**

Maison de Nostradamus

rue Nostradamus, Salon-de-Provence (04.90.56. 64.31/www.salon-de-provence.org). **Open** 9am-noon, 2-6pm Mon-Fri; 2-6pm Sat, Sun. **Admission** €3.05; €2.30 reductions; free under-7s. **No credit cards.**

Musée Yves Brayer

Hôtel des Porcelet, pl François de Herain, Les Baux-de-Provence (04.90.54.36.99/www.yves brayer.com). **Open** *Apr-Sept* 10am-12.30pm, 2-6.30pm daily. *Oct-Mar* 10am-12.30pm, 2-5.30pm daily. Closed Tue Oct-Mar. **Admission** €4; free under-18s. **Credit** AmEx, MC, V.

THE RHONE DELTA

Where to stay & eat

In Les Baux, the tranquil, 300-year-old **Mas d'Aigret** (D27A, 04.90.54.20.00, www.mas daigret.com, closed Jan, double €100-€195, menu €34) is perched below the fortress, with its restaurant built into the rock. The **Reine Jeanne** (Grande Rue, 04.90.54.32.06, www.la reinejeanne.com, closed Jan, double €50-€70, menus €16-€31) is an inexpensive alternative with glorious views across the valley; the restaurant serves reliable regional dishes.

Tucked away amid the fig trees just off the main road leading up to Les Baux, **L'Oustau de Beaumanière** (val d'Enfer, 04.90.54.33.07, www.oustaudebaumaniere.com, closed Jan, Wed Nov-Apr, double €200-€430) oozes understated glamour. Set in a 16th-century farmhouse, it has airy, elegant rooms and a Michelin-starred restaurant (menus €120-€175). The **Cabro d'Or** (Mas Carita, rte d'Arles, 04.90.54.33.21, www.lacabrodor.com, closed Nov-mid Dec, double €160-€415) is another plush option, with beautiful decor and exquisite food, served on a romantic garden terrace (closed lunch Mon, Sun, mains €44-€47).

In Le Paradou (between Arles and St-Rémy), **La Maison du Paradou** (2 rte de St-Roch, 04.90.54.65.46, www.maisonduparadou.com, double €285) is a gorgeous, wisteria-draped *mas*, with five rooms and a small heated pool. Just outside the village, the **Hameau des Baux** (chemin de Bourgeac, 04.90.54.10.30, www.hameaudesbaux.com, double €195-€280) occupies a cluster of stone buildings, basking in an olive grove. Its beamed rooms are kitted out in calm hues and dotted with antiques; outside there are tennis courts and a pool. On the edge of the village, **Le Bistrot du Paradou** (57 av de la Vallée des Baux, 04.90.54.32.70, closed Sun, lunch Mon, 2wks Oct, May, menus €43-€49) offers a daily changing menu: Friday brings *aïoli*, a feast of salt cod, snails and vegetables served in rich garlic mayonnaise. Another good stop for regional cuisine is **La Place** (65 av de la Vallée des Baux, 04.90.54.23.31, closed Tue winter, menus €21-€32).

If you're travelling with children, or don't want anything fussy and formal, **La Peiriero** (34 av des Baux, 04.90.54.76.10, closed mid Nov-Mar, double €89-€210, menu €28) is a friendly hotel with a lovely pool, built into a former quarry. There are plenty of activities available, including badminton and boules.

In the centre of Mausanne-les-Alpilles, **L'Oustaloun** (pl de l'Eglise, 04.90.54.32.19, www.loustaloun.com, closed 3wks Feb, 3wks Nov, double €55-€85) has eight rooms in a 16th-century abbey, and a restaurant serving regional cuisine (menu €20-€30).

Château de Tarascon.

To make the most of Eygalières, stay at the **Hôtel Mas du Pastre** (quartier St-Sixte, 04.90.95.92.61, www.masdupastre.com, closed mid Nov-mid Dec, double €125-€180), a charming *mas* with a heated pool, jacuzzi and hammam; in the garden, two gypsy caravans have been converted into rooms. For dinner, book a table at smart **Chez Bru** (rue de la République, 04.90.90.60.34, www.chezbru.com, closed Mon, lunch Tue, mid Nov-mid Dec, double €130-€200, menus €95-€120), where hot young Belgian chef Wout Bru draws a well-heeled clientele. Two chic bedrooms and five suites allow gastronomes to stagger upstairs after a heavy meal.

In Fontvieille, the **Auberge La Régalido** (1 rue Frédéric Mistral, 04.90.54.60.22, www.la regalido.com, double €100-€270, closed Nov-Mar) offers accommodation and old-fashioned haute cuisine (restaurant closed Mon, Tue, lunch Sat, menus €15-€40) in an ancient olive mill. Among the many casual bistros, **Le Patio** (117 rte du Nord, 04.90.54.73.10, www.lepatio-alpilles.com, closed Wed, 2wks Feb, 2wks Nov, dinner Tue in winter, lunch Tue in summer, menus €18-€34) is notable for its all-inclusive menus and home-cooking; it has a pleasant courtyard and small garden for alfresco dining.

Salon's **Hôtel Vendôme** (34 rue Maréchal Joffre, 04.90.56.01.96, www.hotelvendome.com, double €44-€56) is housed in a 19th-century building and has a pretty garden. Five kilometres outside town is the **Abbaye de Ste-Croix** (rte du Val de Cuech, D16, 04.90.56.24.55, www.hotels-provence.com, closed Nov-Mar, double €182-€509), where the monks' cells have been converted into quiet, luxurious rooms; most have private gardens or roof terraces. The restaurant draws local bigwigs (closed lunch Mon June-Aug, lunch Mon, Tue-Fri Apr, May, Sept, Oct, menus €78-€120).

The **Hostellerie Domaine de La Reynaude** in Aurons (04.90.59.30.24, www. domainedelareynaude.com, double €63-€126, menu €33-€38) is a converted 16th-century coaching inn. Bedrooms are comfortable and modern, but the main draw is the large pool, plus tennis and volleyball courts. You can also hire bikes to explore the idyllic countryside.

Resources

Tourist information

Les Baux Office du Tourisme *Maison du Roi, Les Baux-de-Provence (04.90.54.34.39/www. lesbauxdeprovence.com).* **Open** 9am-6pm Mon-Fri; 10am-5.30pm Sat, Sun.

Salon Office de Tourisme *56 cours Gimon, Salon-de-Provence (04.90.56.27.60/www.visits alondeprovence.com).* **Open** *July, Aug* 9.30am-6.30pm Mon-Sat; 9.30am-12.30pm Sun. *Sept-June* 9.30am-12.30pm, 2-6pm Mon-Sat.

BEAUCAIRE & AROUND

Set on the flat planes either side of the Rhône, far from the magical scenery of Les Alpilles and surrounded by industrial hinterlands, Beaucaire and Tarascon are, in fact, surprisingly enjoyable towns. Provided the Mistral isn't blowing, that is: the wind farm to the south is testimony to the speed of the chilling wind, which whips down the Rhône Valley from the Alps to spread its icy fingers across Provence.

Midway along the Roman road that linked Italy with Spain, **Beaucaire** (known to the Romans as Ugernum) was the site of one of the great medieval fairs of Europe. Thousands of merchants would sail their vessels up the river to sell silks, spices, pots, skins, wines and textiles here. Later, the town became known for its finely made furniture and mirrors.

Today, shabby streets conceal its former prosperity, but intricate architectural details can still be found in its sculpted windows and doorways. Dominating the town, the **Château de Beaucaire** (04.66.59.26.72, €10, €7 reductions) is now a picturesque ruin. It's off-limits to the public, except during the daily afternoon falconry displays. The surrounding garden contains the **Musée Auguste-Jacquet**, where odds and ends from Roman Beaucaire are beautifully displayed.

On the opposite bank of the Rhône, **Tarascon** is synonymous – to the French at least – with its fictional resident Tartarin, Alphonse Daudet's bumbling antihero. The town is dominated by its white-walled 15th-century chateau, the favourite castle of Good (as in good-living) King René. To satisfy the king's love of material comforts, the **Château de Tarascon** (bd du Roi René, 04.90.91.01.93) was richly decorated with spiral staircases, painted ceilings and tapestries: today, only the ornately carved courtyard and graceful interior hint at its lavish past. The old town huddles around the castle, with covered medieval arcades and the 15th-century Cloître des Cordeliers on the rue des Halles. There's also a market on Tuesdays and Fridays. The **Musée Souleiado** recounts the history of the local textile industry; Tarascon was a major producer of *les indiennes*, the printed cottons that have become an emblem of Provence.

Four kilometres north-west of Beaucaire, the **Abbaye St-Roman** is an extraordinary fifth-century abbey with chapels, cells, altars and 150 tombs hewn out of sheer rock. **Mas des Tourelles** (4294 rte de St-Jilles, 04.66.59.19.72, www.tourelles.com), four kilometres south-west on the D38, is a working re-creation of an ancient Roman winery; the addition of authentic ingredients such as fenugreek, honey and seawater means its wines are an acquired taste. South towards Arles, **Le Vieux Mas** (rte de Fourques, 04.66.59.60.13, www.vieux-mas.com) is a faithful reconstruction of an early 1900s provençal farmhouse, with farm animals, tools and regional products.

North of Tarascon, La Montagnette hill is famous for its herbs, made into a medicinal-tasting liqueur by monks at the 19th-century Abbaye St-Michel-de-Frigolet – *férigoulo* being the Provençal word for thyme. East of here, between St-Rémy and Avignon, is the fertile Petite Crau plain, important for market gardening. Stop off at sleepy **Graveson**,

THE RHONE DELTA

INSIDE TRACK
A BEASTLY TALE

According to local lore, Tarascon was once terrorised by the **Tarasque**, a scaly, river-dwelling beast with a taste for human flesh. In the ninth century, though, along came St Martha, who tamed the monster, sprinkled it with holy water and led it into town – where the townspeople promptly hacked it to bits. On the last weekend of June, an effigy of the dread beast is paraded through the streets amid fireworks and bullfights (*see p44*).

which has a Romanesque church and the **Musée Auguste Chabaud**, dedicated to the powerful landscape paintings and disturbing portraits of the eponymous artist (1882-1955).

Pleasant **Maillane** is the birthplace of Frédéric Mistral, the founder of the Félibrige movement (*see p22*), whose house and garden (now the **Museon Mistral**) have been preserved as he left them.

★ Abbaye St-Roman

D999 (04.66.59.19.72/www.abbaye-saint-roman. com). **Open** *Apr-June, Sept* 10am-6pm daily. *July, Aug* 10am-6.30pm daily. *Oct-Mar* 2-5pm Sat, Sun & school hols. **Admission** €5.50; free under-12s. **No credit cards.**

★ Musée Auguste Chabaud

cours National, Graveson (04.90.90.53.02/ www.museechabaud.com). **Open** *June-Sept* 10am-noon, 1.30-6.30pm daily. *Oct-May* 1.30-6.30pm daily. **Admission** €5; €3 reductions; free under-12s. **No credit cards.**

★ Musée Auguste-Jacquet

In the chateau gardens, Beaucaire (04.66.59. 90.07). **Open** *Apr-Oct* 10am-12.30pm, 2.15-6pm Mon, Wed-Sun. *Nov-Mar* 10am-noon, 2-5.15pm Mon, Wed-Sun. **Admission** €4.60; €1.30 reductions; free students. **No credit cards.**

Musée Souleiado

39 rue Proudhon, Tarascon (04.90.91.50.16/ www.souleiado.com). **Open** 10am-5pm Tue-Sat. **Admission** €6.50; €3.05 reductions; free under-12s. **No credit cards.**

Museon Mistral

11 av Lamartine, Maillane (04.90.95.84.19). **Open** *Apr-Sept* 9.30am-noon, 2-6.30pm daily. *Oct-Mar* 10am-noon, 2-4.30pm Tue-Sun. **Admission** €4; €3 reductions; free under-12s. **No credit cards.**

Where to stay & eat

The **Hôtel des Doctrinaires** (6 quai du Général de Gaulle, 04.66.59.23.70, www.hotel doctrinaires.com, closed mid Dec-mid Jan, double €55-€85, menus €20-€45) in Beaucaire is set in a 17th-century doctrinal college. The guestrooms don't quite live up to the impressive vaulted reception, but the restaurant's traditional cuisine is popular with locals. A cheaper option is the attractive but basic **Hôtel Napoléon** (4 pl Frédéric Mistral, 04.66.59.05.17, doubles €36-€71). It has six bedrooms and a small restaurant with an outdoor terrace; most guests opt for the good-value half board at €36. The town's most fashionable bistro is the small, hidden-away

L'Ail Heure (46 rue du Château, 04.66.59. 67.75, www.lailheure.fr, menus €17-€37). Book ahead to sample chef Luc Andreu's modish cooking: foie gras with artichoke, perhaps, followed by magret in truffle sauce.

In Tarascon, the **Hôtel Echevins** (26 bd Itam, 04.90.9101.70, www.hotel-echevins.com, double €62-€73) is housed in a beautiful 18th-century building, while **Rue du Château** (24 rue du Château, 04.90.91.09.99, www.chambres-hotes.com, double €82-€90) is a charming B&B.

Resources

Tourist information

Beaucaire Office de Tourisme *24 cours Gambetta, Beaucaire (04.66.59.26.57/www.ot-beaucaire.fr).* **Open** *Apr-Sept* 8.45am-12.15pm, 2-6pm Mon-Fri; 9.30am-12.30pm, 3-6pm Sat. *Oct-Mar* 8.45am-12.15pm, 2-6pm Mon-Fri.

Châteaurenard Office de Tourisme *11 cours Carnot, Châteaurenard (04.90.24.25.50).* **Open** *July, Aug* 9am-noon, 2-5.45pm Mon-Sat; 10am-noon Sun. *Sept-May* 9am-noon, 2-5.45pm Mon-Sat.

Tarascon Office de Tourisme *59 rue des Halles, Tarascon (04.90.91.03.52/www.tarascon. org).* **Open** *July, Aug* 9am-1pm, 2-6pm Mon-Sat; 9.30am-12.30pm Sun. *Sept, June* 9.30am-12.30pm, 2-6pm Mon-Sat; 2-6pm Sun. *Oct-May* 9am-12.30pm, 2-5.30pm Mon-Sat.

GETTING THERE & AROUND

By bus

Cartreize (08.00.19.94.13, www.lepilote.com) is an umbrella organisation for buses within the Bouches du Rhône, including services between Avignon and Les Baux via Châteaurenard and St-Rémy, St-Rémy and Tarascon (Mon-Sat), Arles and St-Rémy, Arles and Marseilles via Salon-de-Provence, Avignon and Maillane via Châteaurenard and Graveson.

By car

For St-Rémy, take A7 exit 25, then the D99 between Tarascon and Cavaillon. Or, south of Avignon, take the N570 and the D571, via Châteaurenard. Les Baux is 8km south of St-Rémy by the D5 and the D27. Tarascon and Beaucaire are reached by the N570 and the D970 from Avignon or the D999 from Nîmes. Salon is at the junction of the A7 (exit 27) and the A54 (exit 14/15) or by the N113 from Arles.

By train

Frequent TGVs serve Avignon and Nîmes, while local trains run between Tarascon, Arles and Avignon. Salon-de-Provence has several trains a day from Avignon; for Marseille or Arles, you'll need to change trains at Miramas.

Arles

Roman Arles looks to the future…

The town of **Arles** has long been labelled a bastion of tradition. Its ladies don traditional costumes – complete with lace fichus, shawls and bonnets – at the drop of a hat, bullfighting *ferias* are big news, and there are a wealth of museums and Roman remains to potter round.

Yet despite its conservative image, Arles is making waves on the arts scene. Its annual photography festival is an increasingly cutting-edge affair – and plans to create a new multi-million-euro contemporary art and photography complex are afoot. Superstar architect Frank Gehry, who designed the Guggenheim museum in Bilbao, is in charge of transforming the ex-railway yard into a vast artistic city, due to open by 2012.

ARLES

A Greek trading port as early as the sixth century BC, Arles's moment of glory came in 49 BC, when it backed Julius Caesar's bid to break Marseille's stranglehold on both sea trade and the Via Domitia land route from Rome to Spain. Caesar was victorious – and while Marseille was stripped of its riches (*see p136*), Arles's heyday had arrived. Trading in imports from the Orient, the city flourished.

Dark Ages battles took a relatively minor toll on the town and, by the Middle Ages, Arles had regained its clout. At its height, the kingdom of Arles included Burgundy and part of Provence – and in 1178, Holy Roman Emperor Frederick Barbarossa pitched up and was crowned King of Arles in the newly finished cathedral.

Gradually, as the sea retreated, Marseille took over as the most important port; then, in the 19th century, railway traffic killed off its river traffic. Despite its key role in Frédéric Mistral's Félibrige movement (*see p23*), Arles has never really regained its lost glory.

Today, Arles wears its history with ease. Its ancient monuments are not museum pieces, but part of the urban fabric: the great Roman arena is encircled by the old town like a snail in its shell, while newer buildings snuggle up to the walls of the Cathédrale St-Trophime. Roman vestiges crop up embedded in buildings around the medieval town – a brooding, atmospheric knot of narrow streets, built to provide protection from the chilly blasts of the Mistral.

Arles is irrevocably linked with Van Gogh, who arrived here in February 1888 in search of southern light and colour, only to find the city covered in thick snow. Undaunted, he rented the 'yellow house' and began working furiously. In just 15 months (punctuated by the odd stay in the town asylum, a dispute with Gauguin and the lopping off of his own ear), he produced some 300 canvases. In April 1889, he checked himself into the asylum at nearby St-Rémy.

At the time, the good citizens of Arles, like everybody else, rejected the unbalanced Dutchman. Now somewhat embarrassed by not owning a single Van Gogh painting, the city makes do with a mock-up of one of his most famous subjects, the **Café de la Nuit** (*see p77*), and the **Espace Van Gogh** bookshop and arts centre. The **Fondation Van Gogh**, however, pays the right sort of homage to the much-misunderstood genius, with a superb collection of works by contemporary masters.

Sightseeing

The best view of Arles is from the top tier of the Roman **Arènes**, looking across terracotta roofs and ochre walls to the River Rhône. Adjacent to the Arènes are the crumbling remains of the **Théâtre Antique**, described by Henry James as 'the most touching ruins I had ever beheld'. They now provide an atmospheric backdrop for an outdoor theatre season in June and July.

Down the hill on place de la République stands the great Romanesque **Cathédrale**

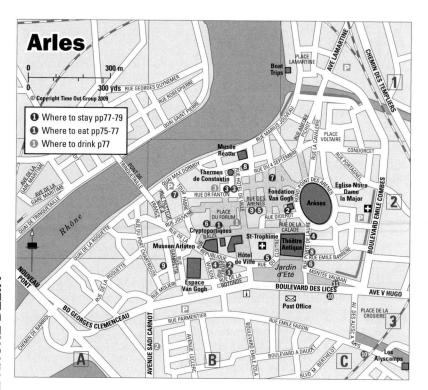

THE RHONE DELTA

St-Trophime, its doorway embellished with magnificent 12th-century sculptures. Here, too, is the imposing Hôtel de Ville, with its 17th-century classical façade and celebrated vaulting. Accessible from the vestibule is the Plan de la Cour, a small medieval square that is home to the 13th-century Palais des Podestats. Extending beneath the Hôtel de Ville are the **Cryptoportiques**, underground chambers of obscure purpose, dug out by the Romans.

A block away is Frédéric Mistral's pet project, the **Museon Arlaten**, devoted to local folklore, crafts and costumes. It's housed in a 16th-century mansion, with a courtyard built round the columns of the original Roman forum.

Arles's markets take place on nearby boulevard des Lices on Saturdays, moving to boulevard Emile Combes on Wednesdays. Both offer fruit, vegetables and fish, and a vast array of spices, herbs, charcuterie and bric-a-brac. More bric-a-brac can be found on the boulevard des Lices on the first Wednesday of the month.

Place du Forum, next to the original forum site, remains the centre of Arlesian life, buzzing with cafés and restaurants. A statue of Frédéric Mistral looks over it all, leaning on his stick and

looking, as he himself complained, as if he's waiting for a train. From here, stroll to the banks of the Rhône, where you can walk along the quays, visit the **Thermes de Constantin** baths or admire the work of modern masters in the **Musée Réattu**, set in a lovely old priory.

Near the museum is a small antiques enclave; check out Antiquités Maurin (4 rue de Grille, 04.90.96.51.57), crammed with furniture, paintings and objets d'art, or Livres Anciens Gilles Barbero (3 rue St-Julien, 04.90.93.72.04) for antiquarian books, photos and postcards.

At the southern end of rue de l'Hôtel de Ville and the Jardin d'Eté, the shady, café-lined boulevard des Lices is great for observing *le tout Arles*, especially on Saturday mornings, when the market offers vibrant Southern colours and smells. Local cheese, olives, ham and sausages – donkey is the local speciality – are all good buys.

Further south, the crumbling necropolis of **Les Alyscamps** lies on the ancient Aurelian Way from Rome. It's a wonderfully melancholy place to stroll, though the best of the tombs and sculptures now reside in the **Musée de l'Arles Antique**, west of the old centre.

Les Alyscamps

av des Alyscamps (04.90.49.38.20/www.tourisme. ville-arles.fr). **Open** *Mar, Apr, Oct* 9am-noon, 2-6pm daily. *May-Sept* 9am-6.30pm daily. *Nov-Feb* 10am-noon, 2-5pm daily. **Admission** €3.50; €2.60 reductions; free under-12s. **No credit cards. Map** p73 C3.

From its beginnings as a pre-Christian necropolis until well into the Middle Ages, Les Alyscamps was one of the most fashionable spots in Europe to spend eternity. Corpses from up-country were parcelled up and floated down the Rhône with the burial fee in their mouths, to be fished out from Trinquetaille bridge by the gravediggers. By the Renaissance, though, many of the magnificent stone sarcophagi had been looted; in the 19th century the railway cut through one end of the cemetery. But the remaining avenue of tombs is still as atmospheric as when Van Gogh painted it. Here, too, is the tiny, ruined church of St-Honorat, with the marks where St Trophimus is said to have kneeled to bless the spot.

Les Arènes

rond-point des Arènes (04.90.49.59.05/box office 04.90.96.03.70/www.arenes-arles.com). **Open** varies. **Admission** €5.50; €4 reductions; free under-12s. **No credit cards. Map** p73 C2.

One of the oldest amphitheatres in the Roman world, Les Arènes was built in the first century AD. Like Nîmes, it once had three storeys, but the top floor was plundered for stone in the Middle Ages. The rabble that constructed a slum within its walls a few centuries later was only cleared out in 1825, when restoration began. For a taste of Roman-style bloodlust, come for a bullfight, when the arena echoes with spectators' cries. It's also used for the less bloodthirsty local variant on bullfighting, *course camarguaise* (*see p66* **Death in the Afternoon**). The season gets under way with the April *feria* and the *gardian* festival on 1 May; it culminates in early July with the award of the coveted Cocarde d'Or. Tickets are usually available on the gate, but book ahead for the *feria* and Cocarde d'Or.

FREE Cathédrale St-Trophime

pl de la République (04.90.49.38.20). **Open** *Church* 8.30am-6.30pm daily. *Cloister* Nov-Feb 10am-5pm daily. Mar, Apr, Oct 9am-6pm daily. May-Sept 9am-6.30pm daily. **Admission** *Church* free. *Cloister* €3.50; €2.60 reductions; free under-12s. **No credit cards. Map** p73 B2.

A church has stood here since the fifth century, though the current Romanesque cathedral was built in the 12th century to house the relics of St Trophimus, a third-century bishop of Arles. Its nave is hung with Aubusson tapestries and 17th-century Dutch paintings, and dotted with Roman sarcophagi – but it's the portal that takes your breath away. A vivid carving shows Christ in glory, with life-size apostles depicted in the columns below. A frieze shows the Last Judgement, with souls being dragged

off to hell in chains or given to the saints in heaven. The cloister features a surprisingly harmonious blend of Romanesque and 14th-century Gothic sculptures, while carved columns and capitals portray a profusion of biblical stories. *Photos p74.*

Cryptoportiques

rue Balze (04.90.49.38.20). **Open** *Mar, Apr* 9am-12.30pm, 2-6pm daily. *May-Sept* 9am-noon, 2-6.30pm daily. *Oct* 9am-noon, 2-6pm daily. *Nov-Feb* 10am-noon, 2-5pm daily. **Admission** €5.50; €4 reductions; free under-12s. **No credit cards. Map** p73 B2.

These chilly, slightly sinister horseshoe-shaped Roman underground galleries were constructed to support the hillside foundations of the forum, and may also have been used as a religious sanctuary or to store grain. During World War II, they sheltered members of the Resistance.

FREE Espace Van Gogh

pl du Dr Félix Rey (04.90.49.36.37). **Open** 6am-9pm daily. **Admission** free. **Map** p73 B3.

Comprising a library, bookshop and exhibition space, this cultural centre is set around a garden courtyard in the hospital where Van Gogh was treated after he cut off his ear.

▶ *Next door, the Jardin des Arts (38 rue de la République, 04.90.96.10.36) is a charming tearoom and restaurant, with a leafy interior courtyard.*

★ Fondation Van Gogh

Palais de Luppé, 24bis rond-point des Arènes (04.90.49.94.04/www.fondationvangogh-arles. org). **Open** *Apr-June* 10am-6pm daily. *July-Sept* 10am-7pm daily. *Oct-Mar* 11am-5pm Tue-Sun. **Admission** €7; €5 reductions; free under-12s. **Credit** MC, V. **Map** p73 C2.

Work by contemporary artists in tribute to Van Gogh include a Hockney chair, a Rauschenberg sunflower in acrylic yellow and blue on steel, plus works by Bacon, Rosenquist, Lichtenstein and Viallat, and photographs by Doisneau and Cartier-Bresson.

INSIDE TRACK
PILGRIM'S PROGRESS

If you've got the time (and energy), consider walking part of the **Chemin d'Arles**, one of four medieval French pilgrimage routes to Santiago-de-Compostela. Less busy than the Le Puy route, the path leads through Montpellier, Toulouse and Oloron before reaching the Spanish border at Col du Somport in the high Pyrenees, and on to Puente-la-Reina. Here, it merges with the other pilgrim routes and leads the faithful (and footsore) on to Santiago.

Cathédrale St-Trophime. *See p73.*

Musée de l'Arles Antique

presqu'Ile du Cirque Romain (04.90.18.88.88/
www.arles-antique.cg13.fr). **Open** *Apr-Oct*
9am-7pm daily. *Nov-Mar* 10am-5pm daily.
Admission €5.50; €4 reductions; free under-
12s, all 1st Sun of mth. **Credit** MC, V.
On the fringes of the Roman circus, this modern blue
triangle designed by Henri Ciriani houses the many
antiquities unearthed in Arles. The collection ranges
from statues, pottery, jewellery, glass and mosaics
to maps, models and town plans. Look out for the
carved sarcophagi from Les Alyscamps, many dating from the fourth century AD or earlier.

★ Musée Réattu

10 rue du Grand Prieuré (04.90.49.37.58). **Open**
Mar-June, mid Sept-Oct 10am-12.30pm, 2-6.30pm
daily. *July-mid Sept* 10am-7pm daily. *Nov-Feb*
1-5pm daily. **Admission** €7; €5 reductions;
free under-12s. **No credit cards. Map** p73 B2.
The museum showcases works by its founder, artist
Jacques Réattu, along with a collection of more modern work by Léger, Dufy, Gauguin and others. Most
notable are the 57 Picasso drawings, donated by the
artist in 1972 to thank Arles for amusing him with
its bullfights. Also by Picasso is a delicious render-
ing of Lee Miller as an Arlésienne, painted in 1937.

€ Museon Arlaten

29 rue de la République (04.90.93.58.11/www.
museonarlaten.fr). **Open** *Apr, May, Sept* 9.30am-
noon, 2-5.30pm Tue-Sun. *June-Aug* 9.30am-
12.30pm, 2-6pm daily. *Oct-Mar* 9.30am-noon,
2-4.30pm Tue-Sun. **Admission** €1; free all 1st
Sun of mth. **No credit cards. Map** p73 B2.
Frédéric Mistral used the money from his 1904
Nobel Prize for Literature to set up this museum,
devoted to local traditions and costumes. Attendants
wear Arlésienne costume and captions are in French
and Provençal only. The best exhibits are a bizarre
haul of traditional talismans, which include a fig
branch burned to encourage maternal milk and a
ring made from a horseshoe nail, intended to ward
off haemorrhoids.
▶ *You can pick up your own Arlésienne costume*
or gardian cowboy shirt at La Nouvelle Arlésienne
(12 rue Président Wilson, 04.90.93.28.05).

Théâtre Antique

rue du Cloître & rue de la Calade (04.90.49.38.20).
Open *Mar, Apr, Oct* 9am-noon, 2-6pm daily.
May-Sept 9am-6.30pm daily. *Nov-Feb* 10am-noon,
2-5pm daily. **Admission** €3; €2.20 reductions;
free under-12s. **No credit cards. Map** p73 C2.
Dating from the first century BC, this Roman theatre once seated over 10,000 spectators. Today, its
tumbledown columns and fragments of carved
stones are a romantic backdrop for summer theatre
and music performances. Vestiges of the original
tiered stone benches remain, along with two great
Corinthian columns, once used as a gallows.

Thermes de Constantin

*pl Constantin (04.90.49.38.20/www.tourisme.
ville-arles.fr).* **Open** *Mar, Apr* 9am-12.30pm,
2-6pm daily. *May-Sept* 9am-noon, 2-6.30pm daily.
Oct 9am-noon, 2-6pm daily. *Nov-Feb* 10am-noon,
2-5pm daily. **Admission** €5.50; €4 reductions;
free under-12s. **No credit cards. Map** p73 B2.
At the fourth-century AD Roman baths, you can still
see the vaulted caldarium, warm bath, and the
bricks of the underfloor heating system.

Where to eat

★ € A Côté

*21 rue des Carmes (04.90.47.61.13/www.bistro-
acote.com).* **Open** 9am-10pm daily. **Main
courses** €8-€18. **Credit** MC, V. **Map** p73 B3 ❶
This plucky new bistro is an economic way to discover the genius of chef Jean-Luc Rabanel, with simple food served all day at reasonable prices. It's ideal
for a glass of wine and some upmarket tapas.

L'Atelier de Jean-Luc Rabanel

*7 rue des Carmes (04.90.91.07.69/www.rabanel.
com).* **Open** noon-2pm, 7.30-10pm Wed-Sun.
Menus *Lunch* €45. *Dinner* €75. **Credit** MC, V.
Map p73 B3 ❷
One of the great culinary success stories of the region,
Rabanel began cooking at the famed Chassagnette
(*see p81*), but has taken his reputation and market-
fresh produce to downtown Arles. The seven-dish
tapas-style lunch is a feast you won't forget.

Au Brin de Thym

*22 rue du Dr Fanton (04.90.49.95.96/www.au
brindethym.com).* **Open** noon-1.30pm, 7-9.30pm
Mon, Thur-Sun; 7-9.30pm Wed. **Main courses**
€15-€24. **Menus** €18-€30. **Credit** MC, V. **Map**
p73 B2 ❸
This intimate restaurant – all white beams, white
tablecloths and bunches of lavender – serves tasty
provençal cuisine, a flavoursome selection of local
goat's cheese, and delicious home-made puddings.

Bistrot La Mule Blanche

*9 rue du Président Wilson (04.90.93.98.54/www.
restaurant-mule-blanche.com).* **Open** noon-2pm,
7.30-10pm Mon-Sat. **Main courses** €8-€20.
Menus *Lunch* €17. **Credit** MC, V. **Map** p73 B3 ❹
Be prepared to wait for a seat on the palm-shaded
terrace of this popular address in the centre of town.
The lengthy menu provides a good selection of simple grilled fish and meat, big salads and pasta.

La Charcuterie Bouchon Lyonnais

*51 rue des Arènes (04.90.96.56.96/www.la
charcuterie.camargue.fr).* **Open** noon-1.30pm,
7.30-9.30pm Tue-Sat. **Main courses** €8-€22.
Credit MC, V. **Map** p73 B2 ❺
This Lyonnais bistro initially comes as something
of a surprise in a provençal stronghold, but has

broadened its culinary appeal and is now a popular
local haunt, with good produce and precise cooking.

★ Le Cilantro

*29/31 rue Porte de Laure (04.90.18.25.05/www.
restaurantcilantro.com).* **Open** *July, Aug* noon-
2pm, 7.30-10pm Tue-Fri; 7.30-10pm Mon, Sat.
Sept-June noon-2pm, 7.30-10pm Tue-Fri; 7.30-
10pm Sat. **Menus** *Lunch* €24-€29. *Dinner* €65-
€85. **Credit** MC, V. **Map** p73 C3 ❻
Michelin-starred chef Jérome Laurent drags Arles's
culinary scene into the 21st century with his inventive, sophisticated, modern cookery. The style can
be a little precious, but the perfect antidote to one
too many typically provençal menus.

L'Entrevue

*pl Nina Berbenova (04.90.93.37.28/www.
restaurant-lentrevue.com).* **Open** *May-Sept*
9.30am-3pm, 7-11pm daily. *Oct-Apr* 9.30am-3pm,
7-11pm Mon-Sat; 7-11pm Sun. **Main courses**
€14-€22. **Menu** €27. **Credit** V. **Map** p73 B2 ❼
Part of the Actes Sud complex, this couscous restaurant has a terrace overlooking the river and a lively
atmosphere, drawing a young intellectual crowd.

€ L'Escaladou

23 rue Porte de Laure (04.90.96.70.43). **Open**
noon-2pm, 6.30-11pm Mon, Tue, Thur-Sun. **Main
courses** €8.50-€16. **Menus** €18-€24. **No credit
cards. Map** p73 C2 ❽
This old-fashioned (and affordable) restaurant
serves simple provençal dishes (including a delicious
aïoli), accompanied by local wines. It's popular with
locals and tourists alike – and deservedly so.

★ € La Gueule du Loup

39 rue des Arènes (04.90.96.96.69). **Open** *Mar-
Sept* 7.45-9.45pm Mon; noon-1.30pm, 7.45-9.45pm
Tue-Sat. *Oct-Feb* noon-1.30pm, 7.45-9.45pm Tue-
Sat. **Menus** *Lunch* €12-€17. *Dinner* €22-€29.
Main courses €14-€24. **Credit** DC, V, MC.
Map p73 B2 ❾
Access to this beamed, intimate little bistrot is via
the deliciously fragrant kitchen, passing members
of the Allard family en route. The food is sophisti-
cated and tasty (braised bull in red wine, say, or
monkfish with saffron), but you need to book ahead.

Le Jardin de Manon

14 av des Alyscamps (04.90.93.38.68). **Open**
Mid Mar-mid Sept noon-2pm, 7-10pm Mon, Thur-
Sun; noon-2pm Tue. *Mid Sept-mid Mar* noon-
2pm, 7-10pm Mon, Thur-Sat; noon-2pm Tue.
Main courses €17-€26. **Menus** €22-€46.
Credit AmEx, MC, V. **Map** p73 C3 ❿
Restaurants are in relatively short supply down by
the Alyscamps and, as its name suggests, Manon
has a delightful garden for alfresco dining. The interior, like the menu, features local colour combined
with contemporary touches.

THE RHONE DELTA

€ Le Malarte

2 bd des Lices (04.90.96.03.99). **Open** *May-Oct*
noon-3pm, 7-10pm daily. *Nov-Apr* noon-3pm,
6-8pm daily. **Main courses** €11-€17. **Menus**
€15-€20. **Credit** V. **Map** p73 C3 ⑪
Boulevard des Lices is packed with slightly tacky
brasseries and cafés, but you can have an enjoyable
meal at the Malarte. It's a family-run establishment,
serving copious portions of local cuisine.

Where to drink

Café de la Nuit

11 pl du Forum (04.90.96.44.56). **Open** *Summer*
9am-2am daily. *Winter* 9am-11.30pm daily. **Main
courses** €13-€22. **Credit** MC, V, AmEx. **Map**
p73 B2 ①
This central café has a great people-watching terrace, a lofty interior painted in vibrant Van Gogh
colours and a bar decorated to look somewhat like
his painting of the same name. Simple dishes are
best, washed down with a carafe of inexpensive wine.
▶ *If this place is full, the Bistrot Arlésien at No.5
(04.90.96.07.22) is a firm favourite with locals.*

Cargo de Nuit

*7 av Sadi Carnot (04.90.49.55.99/www.cargode
nuit.com).* **Open** *Oct-June* varies. **Admission**
€5-€18. **Credit** MC, V. **Map** p73 B2 ②
Head here for world music, rock, techno and jazz.
The restaurant has been replaced by a lounge bar,
where you can take a break from the concert.

Chez Ariane

2 rue du Dr Fanton (04.90.52.00.65). **Open** 7.30-
11pm Wed-Sun. **Main courses** €13-€16. **Credit**
MC, V. **Map** p73 B2 ③
This welcoming wine bar offers an excellent choice
of organic wines, along with well-prepared *plats du
jour* and fine charcuterie selections.

Arts & entertainment

For entertainment listings, pick up free
fortnightly listings mag *César.*

★ Actes Sud

*23 Place Nina Berberova (Cinéma 08.92.68.47.
07/Hammam 04.90.96.10.32).* **Open** *Bookshop*
9am-7pm Mon-Fri. *Cinema* varies. *Hammam* Men
5.30-10pm Mon, Wed, Thur, Sat. Women 9am-5pm
Mon, Sat, Sun; 9am-10pm Tue-Fri. **Admission**
Cinema €5.50. *Hammam* from €13.
This sprawling riverside arts complex houses its
own publishing house, arts cinema and hammam,
next door to L'Entrevue restaurant (*see p75*).

Théâtre d'Arles

*bd Georges Clemenceau (04.90.52.51.51/www.
theatre-arles.com).* **Open** *Box office* 11am-1pm,
3-6.30pm Tue-Sat. **Tickets** €2-€21. **Credit** MC, V.

Hôtel l'Arlatan. *See p79.*

The theatre offers music and lectures as well as
plays – though the interior is now a rather anonymous raked amphitheatre.

Théâtre de la Calade

*Le Grenier à Sel, 49 quai de la Roquette
(04.90.93.05.23/www.theatredelacalade.org).*
Open *Box office* 10am-12.30pm, 2-6pm Mon-Fri.
Tickets €6.50-€17. **No credit cards.**
Based in an old salt warehouse, this adventurous
theatre group hosts visiting companies, jazz performances and workshops, as well as its own shows.

Where to stay

★ Grand Hôtel Nord Pinus

*pl du Forum (04.90.93.44.44/www.nord-
pinus.com).* **Rates** €160-€295 double. **Rooms**
25. **Credit** AmEx, DC, MC, V. **Map** p73 B2 ①
This bullfighters' favourite, opened in the 19th century, is dramatically decorated with heavy carved
furniture, Peter Beard's giant black and white photos, *feria* posters and mounted bulls' heads. It also
has an elegant bar and brasserie. It's set on the place
du Forum, so you're in the thick of the action.

★ € Hôtel de l'Amphithéâtre

*5/7 rue Diderot (04.90.96.10.30/www.hotel
amphitheatre.fr).* **Rates** €55-€95 double. **Rooms**
28. **Credit** AmEx, DC, MC, V. **Map** p73 C2 ②
Set in a restored 17th-century building, this pleasant little hotel is decorated with warm old tiles, yellow walls and original wrought-iron banisters.
Rooms can be on the small side.

Profile Rencontres d'Arles

Arles through a lens.

Come summer, Arles resounds to the sound of clicking shutters, as the **Rencontres d'Arles** (www.rencontres-arles.com) comes to town. Kicking off in June and winding down in mid September, it's one of the longest-running photography festivals in the world – and, thanks to its energetic director, François Hébel, a force to be reckoned with on the arts scene.

Hébel's gift for persuading big names to come on board as guest curators has given the Rencontres a new lease of life, and won it valuable column inches. Martin Parr did the honours in 2004, and in 2008 Hébel persuaded Arles-born Christian Lacroix to take the reins. The town's prodigal son made a triumphant return to his hometown, whose vivid colours and bullfighting tradition have so shaped his flamboyant designs.

Lacroix's pick included such luminaries as Richard Avedon, Paolo Reversi, Peter Lindbergh and Françoise Huguier, along with rising talents such as Tim Walker and Achinto Bhadra. But the Rencontres is also about making new discoveries, with the best of the year's graduates from Arles's photography school, the SFR Jeunes Talents show and the Discovery Award. Then there's the 'off' fringe scene, with its *salon des réfusés* and a busy agenda of exhibitions and events, which colonise hotels, restaurants and galleries around town, and spill into the streets.

As its name suggests, though, there's more to the Rencontres ('meetings') than its exhibitions – especially during the opening week, which brings workshops, lectures, debates and night-time events in the Théâtre Antique. There's also the one-night 'La Nuit de l'Année', which pays tribute to photojournalism. Visitors stroll through town until 3am, admiring the press agencies' past year's work, displayed in school playgrounds, monasteries and houses around Arles.

In 2008, the festival took on a new dimension with its expansion into a complex of former SNCF railway repair sheds on the edge of town, renamed **Le Parc des Ateliers**. The industrial, edgy space is a far cry from the existing exhibition sites in the old town: Romanesque cloisters, Gothic churches, elegant townhouses and the former Bishop's Palace. Instead, visitors found themselves wandering round huge, semi-derelict brick hangars – some still with railway tracks running across the concrete floors, or trade union emblems daubed on the walls.

Even more dramatic changes are afoot, with plans to create the €100 million **Foundation Luma** at the Parc des Ateliers. Resembling a series of precariously stacked boxes, the vast artistic 'city', designed by Frank 'Bilbao Guggenheim' Gehry, will contain exhibition space, archives, studios, a restaurant and gardens – and underscore Arles's determination to become a year-round centre for photographic creativity. Final plans for the building are set to be announced at the Rencontres d'Arles in 2009, and it's due for completion by the start of 2012.

JOIN THE AFTER-PARTY
For the '**Afters**', organised in association with the **Cargo de Nuit** (*see p77*), the Parc des Ateliers resonates to electro beats, hip hop and vintage soul, as festival-goers party until dawn.

Hôtel l'Arlatan

26 rue du Sauvage (04.90.93.56.66/www.hotel-arlatan.fr). Closed Jan. **Rates** €85-€155 double. **Rooms** 47. **Credit** AmEx, MC, V. **Map** p73 B2 ❸
Built over part of the Roman basilica, this provençal mansion has a wealth of period details and antiques. There's an elegant salon with a vast fireplace, an enclosed garden courtyard and a pool. *Photo p77.*

Hôtel le Calendal

5 rue Porte de Laure (04.90.96.11.89/www.lecalendal.com). Closed Jan. **Rates** €99-€119 double. **Rooms** 38. **Credit** AmEx, DC, MC, V. **Map** p73 C2 ❹
This romantic hotel occupies several cleverly linked old buildings around a large, shady garden. Sunny rooms look over either the Théâtre Antique or the garden, while the *salon de thé* serves good light meals.

€ Hôtel le Cloître

16 rue du Cloître (04.90.96.29.50/www.hotel cloitre.com). Closed Nov-mid Mar. **Rates** €50-€70 double. **Rooms** 30. **Credit** AmEx, MC, V. **Map** p73 B2/3 ❺
Set in a narrow street near the Roman theatre, this place is good value for money. The Romanesque vaulted dining room is splendid, while rooms feature exposed stone walls and simple, rustic decor.

Hôtel du Forum

10 pl du Forum (04.90.93.48.95/www.hoteldu forum.com). Closed Nov-mid Mar. **Rates** €80-€150 double. **Rooms** 38. **Credit** AmEx, DC, MC, V. **Map** p73 B2/3 ❻
An old-fashioned hotel right in the centre of things, the Forum has a private garden and swimming pool – a huge plus point during the torrid summers. The bar is where Picasso set up camp during the *feria*.

€ Hôtel la Muette

15 rue des Suisses (04.90.96.15.39). **Rates** €45-€58 double. **Rooms** 18. **Credit** V. **Map** p73 B2 ❼
La Muette may be a budget hotel, but it's hardly lacking in charm, with thick stone walls and decent rooms, simply furnished in a very basic provençal style. The building dates back to the 12th century.

€ Hôtel du Musée

11 rue du Grand Prieuré (04.90.93.88.88/www.hoteldumusee.com.fr). Closed Jan. **Rates** €48-€68 double. **Rooms** 28. **Credit** AmEx, DC, MC, V. **Map** p73 B2 ❽
This small hotel occupies a 16th-century mansion, with breakfast served in the leafy inner courtyard. Rooms have an old-fashioned but comforting feel, and are decorated with antiques.

L'Hôtel Particulier

4 rue de la Monnaie (04.90.52.51.40). **Rates** €189-€239 double. **Rooms** 15. **Credit** AmEx, DC, MC, V. **Map** p73 B3 ❾

For a pampering stay in serene and elegant surrounds, book into the Hôtel Particulier. It's a majestic 19th-century mansion-turned-exclusive hotel, with a Roman-style swimming pool in the central courtyard, a sauna and massages.

Jules César

9 bd des Lices (04.90.52.52.52/www.hotel-jules cesar.fr). **Rates** €160-€250 double. **Rooms** 58. **Credit** AmEx, DC, MC, V. **Map** p73 C3 ❿
Now a swish hotel, the César was once a Carmelite convent. The mother superior might be shocked today by the luxury of her former bedroom, the sun-loungers and swimming pool and the pricey gourmet restaurant.

RESOURCES

Hospital
Hôpital Général Joseph Imbert *quartier Haut de Fourchon (04.90.49.29.29).*

Police station
1 bd des Lices (04.90.18.45.00).

Post office
5 bd des Lices (04.90.18.41.15).

Tourist information
Office de Tourisme *esplanade Charles de Gaulle, bd des Lices, Arles (04.90.18.41.20/ www.arlestourisme.com).* **Open** *Apr-Sept* 9am-6.45pm daily. *Oct-Mar* 9am-4.45pm Mon-Sat; 10am-12.45pm Sun.

GETTING THERE & AROUND

By air
Arles is about 20km (12 miles) from Nîmes-Arles-Camargue airport. A taxi takes roughly half an hour and should cost about €30.

By bus
Cars de Camargue (04.90.96.36.25) runs buses between Nîmes and Arles three times daily on weekdays, and twice a day on Sat (none Sun), and four buses Mon-Fri between Arles and Stes-Maries-de-la-Mer. **SNCF** (08.92.35.35.35) runs three or four buses daily (Mon-Sat) to Avignon. **Cartreize** (08.00.19.94.13, www.lepilote.com) runs a service between Arles and St-Rémy.

By car
The A54 goes through Arles, with exit 5 bringing you nearest to the centre. Otherwise take the N570 from Avignon.

By train
Arles station is on the main coastal rail route, and connects with Avignon for the TGV service to Paris.

THE RHONE DELTA

The Camargue

White horses, wetlands and wildlife – welcome to cowboy country.

Eerily beautiful, the **Camargue** is a vast, flat plain that lies between the Grand and Petit Rhône rivers. Its marshland, dunes, pasture and salt-water *étangs* (lagoons) are best appreciated from horseback – but beware the merciless mosquitoes. Stretching across some 140,000 hectares (345,950 acres) of land, this is one of Europe's most important wetlands, and a designated National Park.

Aside from Arles, the Camargue's only major towns are **Stes-Maries-de-la-Mer**, a place of pilgrimage for the Roma people, and medieval **Aigues-Mortes**, surrounded by salt marshes.

AROUND THE AREA

It wasn't until the Middle Ages that the marshes were settled by Cistercians and Templars; though the landscape looked bleak, there was money to be made in salt harvesting. As the powers of the religious orders declined in the 16th century, the Camargue passed into the hands of cattle- and horse-raising *gardians*, descendants of whom, dressed in black hats and high leather boots, still herd small black fighting bulls on horseback.

Riding remains one of the best ways to explore the region, and survey its extraordinary flora and fauna. Here, you can spot purple herons and pink flamingos, black bulls and grey ponies, wild boar and beavers, bulrushes and samphire, pastures and paddy fields. Be sure to bring binoculars to take a closer look.

The reserve centres on the Etang de Vaccarès, a body of brackish water covering 6,500 hectares (16,000 acres). Boat trips explore the network of canals, all charging around €10; try **Tiki III** (Le Grau-d'Orgon, 04.90.97.81.68, www.tiki3.fr, closed mid Nov-mid Mar), **Aventure en Camargue** (Aigues-Mortes, 06.03.91.44.63), or **Les Péniches Isles de Stel** (Aigues-Mortes, 04.66.53.60.70, www.islesdestel.camargue.fr).

The **Musée de la Camargue**, housed in a converted sheep shed between Arles and Stes-Maries-de-la-Mer, explores Camargue life on a 19th-century *mas* (farm) and the role of the *gardians*, as well as providing information on its nature trails. By the Etang de Ginès, the **Maison du Parc Naturel & Regional de la Camargue** (Pont de Gau, rte d'Arles, Stes-Maries-de-la-Mer, 04.90.97.86.32, www.parc-camargue.fr, closed Fri Oct-Mar) is an excellent introduction to the wetlands habitat, with an interactive permanent exhibition and temporary shows exploring specific ecological issues.

For those who need help identifying the local birdlife, the **Parc Ornithologique de Pont de Gau** is a 60-hectare (148-acre) reserve, with seven kilometres of birdwatching trails along the Ginès lagoon and aviaries for injured birds.

The 20-kilometre (12.5-mile) walk from Stes-Maries-de-la-Mer to the salt-processing town of **Salin-de-Giraud** runs along a dyke that was built in 1857 to protect the wetlands from the sea, offering panoramic views across the reserve. The dyke is off-limits to cars, though mountain bikes are tolerated. If you don't want to part with your vehicle, various points on the D37 and C134 roads allow glimpses of herring gulls and black-headed gulls, herons, avocets and egrets as well as the slender-billed gull and the red-crested pochard, which breed nowhere else in France. Most impressive of all, though, are the 20,000 flamingos that roost on the Vaccarès lagoon. East of the lagoon is the vast **Réserve Nationale Camargue** at La Capelière, where you can survey the wildlife from observation platforms.

The hamlet of **Le Sambuc** is home to the **Musée du Riz** (rte de Salin-de-Giraud, 04.90.97.29.44, €4.50), which explores the vital role rice plays in local agriculture: an important cash crop, it also absorbs salt from the soil, enabling other cereals to grow. For solitude, strike out along the sea wall walk to the beach at the Pointe de Beauduc, or the huge empty beach of Piémanson at the mouth of the Grand Rhône. If the walk to Beauduc seems a hike too far, and your car has decent suspension, its beach can be reached from Salin-de-Giraud by what the tourist office coyly calls '*voies pittoresques*'. It's a bumpy ride over an unmade track, crossing an otherworldly lunar landscape of salt marshes. The beach, meanwhile, is as uncommercialised a seaside experience as you're likely to find in the Mediterranean.

Across the salt lagoons, west of Arles, **St-Gilles-du-Gard** was an important medieval port forced to turn to agriculture when the sea receded. The village is dominated by its abbey church, founded by Cistercian monks as a rest stop on the pilgrimage route to Compostela. Huguenot forces wreaked havoc on the 12th-century Romanesque building during the Wars of Religion, leaving only the façade and the rib vaulting of the crypt intact; the rebuilt 17th-century version is half the size of the original, but the elaborate carving on the portals rivals that of St-Trophime in Arles (*see p73*). Opposite, the Maison Romane is a superb 12th-century house, and birthplace of Pope Clement IV. It now houses the **Musée de St-Gilles** (04.66.87.40.42, closed Sun & Jan), with a fine collection of medieval sculpture and a room dedicated to the ornithological wonders of the Camargue. St-Gilles's market is on Thursdays and Saturdays.

Musée de la Camargue

Mas du Pont de Rousty, D570 (04.90.97.10.82/ www.parc-camargue.fr). **Open** *Apr-Sept* 9am-6pm daily. *Oct-Mar* 10am-5pm Mon, Wed-Sun. **Admission** €5; €2.50 reductions; free under-10s. **Credit** AmEx, MC, V.

Parc Ornithologique de Pont de Gau

rte d'Arles, 4km from Stes-Maries-de-la-Mer (04.90.97.82.62/www.parcornithologique.com).

Open *Apr-Sept* 9am-sunset daily. *Oct-Mar* 10am-sunset daily. **Admission** €7; €4 reductions; free under-4s. **Credit** MC, V.

Réserve Nationale Camargue

rte de Salin de Badon, La Capelière (04.90.97.00. 97/www.reserve-camargue.org). **Open** *Apr-Sept* 9am-1pm, 2-6pm daily. *Oct-Mar* 9am-1pm, 2-5pm Tue-Sun. **Admission** €3; €1.50 reductions. **Credit** AmEx, MC, V.

Where to stay & eat

East of the Etang de Vaccarès, **Le Mas de Peint** (Le Sambuc, 04.90.97.26.96, www.masde peint.com, closed mid Nov-mid Dec, mid Jan-mid Mar, double €205-€395, restaurant closed Wed lunch July-Aug; lunch Tue, Thur Sept-June, menu €57) is the height of Camargue chic, with its stone floors, linen sheets, beams and log fires. The owner is happy to show you his bulls and let you ride his horses (€40/2hrs). **La Chassagnette** (rte de Sambuc, 04.90.97.26.96, menus €22-€37 lunch, €44-€60 dinner) may have lost its acclaimed chef to Arles (*see p75* L'Atelier de Jean-Luc Rabanel), but remains a fine restaurant under Armand Arnal, who makes excellent use of the organic garden produce.

Nearer the Etang, the **Mas de St-Bertrand** (Salin de Giraud, 04.42.48.80.69, www.mas-saint-bertrand.com, closed mid Nov-Jan, double €40-€65, mains €10-€13, menus €19-€30) offers basic rooms and Camargue delicacies, including *tellines*. Almost next door is the legendary **Chez JuJu** (Salin de Giraud, 04.42.86.83.86) due to reopen in April 2009. Edith and Manu Camacho cook up some of the best grilled fish in the world – though it'll cost you €5.60 per 100 grams. Neither place accepts credit cards.

Parc Naturel & Regional de la Camargue.

THE RHONE DELTA

In St-Gilles, **Le Cours** (10 av François Griffeuille, 04.66.87.31.93, www.hotel-le-cours. com, closed mid Dec-mid Mar, double €53-€75) is a friendly, simple place to stay: its restaurant serves honest country food (menus €11.50-€34) and is a local favourite. Nearby is the luxury *chambre d'hôte* **Domaine de la Fosse** (rte de Sylvéréal, 04.66.87.05.05, www.domainede lafosse.camargue.fr, double €115-€145), set in a beautiful 17th-century building with five tastefully restored bedrooms.

Resources

Tourist information
St-Gilles Office de Tourisme *1 pl Frédéric Mistral, St-Gilles-du-Gard (04.66.87.33.75/ www.ot-saint-gilles.fr).* **Open** 9am-noon, 1.30-5.30pm Mon-Fri; 9am-noon, 2-5pm Sat.

STES-MARIES-DE-LA-MER

Strategically positioned at the centre of the Camargue, where the Petit Rhône meets the sea, Stes-Maries is best known for its Mary Magdalene connection. Soon after the death of Christ, the legend goes, Mary Magdalene, Mary Salome, Mary Jacobe, Maximin and assorted companions were cast out from Palestine in a boat with no oars or sail. Miraculously washing up on the shores of Stes-Marie, they were met by Black Sarah the gypsy (who, others say, travelled from the Holy Land with Mary, and was her Egyptian maid). The local populace converted en masse, and Sarah was adopted by the Roma as their patron saint. Maximin became the bishop of Aix, while Mary retreated to a solitary cave in the Ste-Baume (*see p210*).

The town is dominated by its magnificent 12th-century fortified church – and there is a real sense of worship in its crypt, where hundreds of candles burn around an effigy of Black Sarah. The best time to visit, though, is in May, when Roma from all over Europe and the Middle East make a pilgrimage here. The exuberant three-day gathering involves dancing and traditional music, culminating in a procession to the sea bearing statues of Mary Salome, Mary Jacobe and Black Sarah aloft.

With its long, sandy beach, cheap cafés and souvenir shops, Stes-Maries is now primarily a tacky seaside resort – though there is a proper market on Monday and Friday mornings. The low-rise hacienda-style second homes and seaside tat won't encourage you to linger, but head off down the road that follows the *plage est* (€3/car). The further you go the fewer tourists you'll see, and the impressive salt marshes and vast, deserted beaches are a glimpse of the real Camargue.

Back in town, the **Musée Baroncelli** (rue Victor Hugo, 04.90.97.87.60, closed mid Nov-Apr)

Wild Horses

Come to the Camargue and enjoy being taken for a ride.

The roads round these parts are lined with a seemingly endless succession of ranch-style stables and hotels, all offering a quick trot on the magnificent white Camargue horses. The quality varies enormously – and a brief circuit of well-trodden paths, perched atop docile, nose-to-tail nags, misses the point. Galloping across the wetlands like a real *gardian* is what's required for the genuine spaghetti western fantasy. Whole day hacks can be arranged, including picnic lunches or overnight stays in *cabanes*: traditional thatched lodges, set against the Mistral.

There's nothing like choice to confuse the eager punter, so head to the tourist office in Stes-Maries (*see p83*) and explain exactly what you're looking for. One of the best riding schools is **Les Chevaux du Vent** (rte d'Arles, 04.90.54.70.99, www.les chevauxduvent.fr) – a serious institution that caters for professionals and amateurs alike. Around Stes-Maries, the **Brenda-Centre de Tourisme Equestre** (Mas St-Georges, Astouin, 04.90.97.52.08, www.brendatourismeequestre.com) and **Cabanes de Cacharel** (Hôtel Mas des Aliscornes, rte d'Arles, 04.90.97.83.41, www.camargueacheval.com) are both reputable stables. If you're staying in the area, your hotel may well have a preferred stable or its own horses.

Expect to pay €20-€30 for two hours, or €80-€110 for a day (including lunch). If you want to become a real cowboy, there's even a course run by the **Manade Salierène** (Mas de Capellane, 04.66.87. 45.57, www.manadesalierene.com). *Manadiers* are the bull breeders who, assisted by the *gardians*, supply the handsome beasts for both table and fights; happily, Camargue-style bullfights involve collecting rosettes from the bull rather than a public execution (*see p66* **Death In the Afternoon**).

is named after the Marquis Folco de Baroncelli, a 19th-century aristocrat who became a Camargue cowboy. The museum celebrates his life and local traditions but lacks regular opening times and cutting-edge presentation. More interesting is the **Château d'Avignon**, a grand 18th-century chateau between Stes-Maries and Arles. In the late 19th century, wine merchant Louis Noilly-Prat transformed it into an up-to-the-minute home, which had electric light 30 years before it became widely available.

Château d'Avignon

rte d'Arles (04.90.97.58.60). **Open** *Apr-Oct* 9.45am-5.45pm Tue-Sun. *Nov-Mar* 9.45am-4.45pm Fri, last Sun of mth. **Admission** €3; €1.50 reductions; free under-18s. **No credit cards**.

Where to stay & eat

Just outside Stes-Maries-de-la-Mer begins a long stretch of ranch-style hotels, ranging from rustic affairs to luxurious retreats. Pride of place goes to the **Mas de la Fouque** (rte du Bac du Sauvage, 04.90.97.81.02, www.masdela fouque.com, double €190-€390), whose stylish rooms have wooden balconies overlooking a lagoon; some have two-seater baths for added romance. Another good choice is **Le Pont des Bannes** (rte d'Arles, 04.90.97.81.09, www.pont desbannes.com, double €130-€169), a chic converted hunting lodge with a romantic lakeside annexe and whitewashed *cabanes*. On the same road, the **Auberge Cavalière** (04.90.97.88.88, www.aubergecavaliere.com, double €140-€252, menus €32-€42) also has thatched *cabanes* and an excellent restaurant. At the edge of town, the **Hotel des Rièges** (rte de Cacharel, 04.90.97.85.07, www.hoteldes rieges.com, double €65-€75) is a Camargue-style ranch with more modest prices.

North-west of Stes-Maries, **Hostellerie du Pont de Gau** (rte d'Arles, 04.90.97.81.53, www.pontdegau.camargue.fr, closed Jan-mid Feb, Wed mid Nov-Easter; menus €22-€54) offers serious traditional cooking and good service. **Lou Mas Dou Juge** (rte du Bac du Sauvage, Pin Fourcal, 04.66.73.51.45, www.le masdujuge.com, double €77-€92) is a seven-room *chambre d'hôte* on a working farm on the Petit Rhône. Dedicated cowboys can also book self-catering *gardian* cabins (details from Stes-Maries-de-la-Mer tourist office, *see right*).

For a seaside-resort atmosphere but no culinary sophistication, head for **Chez Boisset** (1 av de la République, 04.90.97.84.77, www. chez-boisset.camargue.fr, mains €10-€20). The **Brûleur de Loups** (67 av Gilbert Leroy, 04.90.97.83.31, closed Tue dinner, Wed & mid Nov-Dec, menus €17-€40) has sea views and serves regional specialities.

Resources

Tourist information

Office de Tourisme *5 av Van Gogh, Stes-Maries-de-la-Mer (04.90.97.82.55/www.saintes maries.com)*. **Open** *Apr-June, Sept* 9am-7pm daily. *July, Aug* 9am-8pm daily. *Mar, Oct* 9am-6pm daily. *Nov-Feb* 9am-5pm daily.

AIGUES-MORTES

Visible for miles around, the fortress-like medieval town of **Aigues-Mortes** ('dead waters', from the Latin) stands on the western edge of the Camargue. As the one historic must-see in the region, it is besieged by coach-loads of day trippers in summer.

Once set by the sea, it now stands several kilometres inland, surrounded by salt marshes and Listel gris vineyards. This would be nobody's first choice for urban development, but Louis IX wanted to set out on a crusade from his own port rather than using the then-provençal Marseille. Realising take-up for his new town would be low, he offered generous tax and trade incentives. During the Hundred Years War the Burgundians seized the town, only to have it snatched back by the Armagnacs, who, after slaughtering their enemies, stored the salted corpses in the Tour de Bourguignons. Receding sea and silting-up of the canals led to the town's decline in the 15th century.

The best way to get an overview of the town and surrounding area is to walk around the monumental ramparts, punctuated by massive towers. The most spectacular is the thick-walled 13th-century **Tour de Constance**. Although it contains a small chapel, it is principally remembered as a prison, initially for political opponents of the Templars, then, notoriously, for the Protestant women of the Cévennes in 1685.

The **Eglise Notre-Dame-de-Sablons** is the oldest monument in town, but has suffered from too many refits over the centuries, culminating in the modern stained glass of Claude Viallat. The magnificent baroque Chapelle des Pénitents Blancs and Chapelle des Pénitents Gris are worth seeing – though visits have to be arranged through the tourist office. Place St-Louis, the main square, is a lively hub, with exhibitions in the town hall in summer and a market on Wednesday and Sunday mornings. While you're here, don't miss the delicious *fougasse* bread at **Olmeda** (32 rue Emile Jamais, 04.66.53.73.42, closed Wed Nov-Mar), a speciality of the town.

Salt is sold everywhere, from standard table salt to rough, grey organic crystals, adored by foodies. To learn rather more than you need to know about its production, you can be taken by bus from the tourist office to the **Salins du Midi** (04.66.51.17.10, www.salins.com, closed

THE RHONE DELTA

Nov-Feb). You can also visit the **Caves de Listel** (Domaine de Jarras, 04.66.51.17.00, www.listel.fr, closed Sat, Sun) to swig some of the famed flinty rosé – one of the most reliable pink wines in France.

North-east of Aigues-Mortes, the **Château de Teillan** was the former priory of the Abbaye de Psalmody, which sold the land for Aigues-Mortes to Louis IX. It's a fascinating building: in summer, the gardens and 18th-century orangery are well worth a visit.

Urban development of the contemporary kind has expanded the ports of Le Grau-du-Roi and Port Camargue into unappealing resorts; the quay of seafood restaurants at Le Grau-du-Roi has a certain cheap and cheerful charm, though.

Château de Teillan
Aimargues (04.66.88.02.38). **Open** *Mid July-Aug* 3pm-7pm Tue-Sun. **Admission** €4; €2.50 reductions; free under-12s. **Credit** MC, V.

Tour de Constance & Ramparts
Logis du Gouverneur, pl Anatole France (04.66. 53.61.55). **Open** *May-Aug* 10am-7pm daily. *Sept-Apr* 10am-5.30pm daily. **Admission** €6.50; €4.50 reductions; free under-18s. **Credit** MC, V.

Where to stay & eat

The restaurants on the main square are ideal for an aperitif, but for dinner locals head to **Coco** (19 rue Jean Jaurès, 04.66.53.91.83, closed

mid Nov-Dec, menu €14), an inexpensive grill and pizzeria. For a more sophisticated meal, try **Le Café de Bouzigues** (7 rue Pasteur, 04.66.53.93.95, www.cafedebouzigues.com, menu €27-€30), where modern regional cuisine (including local bull) is served in the colourful courtyard. **L'Oustau Camarguais** (2/4 rue Alsace Lorraine, 04.66.53.79.69, www.oustau. info, menus €19-€38) offers local specialities and a lively atmosphere. Nearby, the evenings-only **La Salicorne** (9 rue Alsace Lorraine, 04.66.53.62.67, www.la-salicorne.com, menus €38-€56) serves an imaginative bistro menu.

Within the city walls, the best place to stay is the **Villa Mazarin** (35 bd Gambetta, 04.66.73. 90.48, www.villa-mazarin.camargue.fr, closed mid Jan-mid Feb, double €114-€255) with its indoor pool and relaxing garden. The **Hôtel Les Templiers** (23 rue de la République, 04.66.53. 66.56, www.hotellestempliers.fr, double €105-€250) has been elegantly restored, while a more old-fashioned atmosphere reigns at the **Hôtel St-Louis** (10 rue Amiral Courbet, 04.66.53.72.68, www.lesaintlouis.fr, closed late Nov-mid Mar, double €79-€102). The charming **L'Hermitage de St-Antoine** (9 bd Intérieur Nord, 06.03.04. 34.05, www.hermitagesa.com, double €64) is a well- appointed, peaceful *chambre d'hôte*.

Resources

Tourist information
Office de Tourisme *pl St-Louis, Aigues-Mortes (04.66.53.73.00/www.ot-aiguesmortes.fr).* **Open** *June-Sept* 9am-6pm daily. *Oct-May* 9am-noon, 1-6pm Mon-Fri; 10am-noon, 2-6pm Sat, Sun.

GETTING THERE
By car
Leave the A54 at exit 4 and take the D570 to Stes-Maries-de-la-Mer. For Aigues-Mortes take the D570 from Arles or Stes-Maries and then the D58.

By train/bus
The nearest SNCF station is Arles, from which several buses a day run to Stes-Maries. You can take a train or bus to Aigues-Mortes with **STDG** (04.66.29.27.29) from the TGV station in Nîmes.

Aigue-Mortes. *See p83.*

Château de
Grignan.
See p116.

Introduction

Urban culture and rural bliss in the heart of inland Provence.

Until 1793, Avignon remained part of a prosperous enclave with independent status from France, the Comtat Venaissin – which also took in Cavaillon, Carpentras, Fontaine de Vaucluse and L'Isle-sur-la-Sorgue. Here, the popes held sway – making **Avignon** a centre of scholarship and artistic excellence. Relics of its 14th century glory days include cardinals' palaces, the majestic Palais des Papes, and an abundance of museums and artistic treasures. The Comtat also became a refuge for persecuted Jews, resulting in a Jewish heritage that is unique in France, with beautiful synagogues at **Carpentras** and **Cavaillon**.

Beyond its urban centres, the land-locked Vaucluse takes in the hilly terrain spreading north and east of the Rhône. It may not be named after a river (as is the case with most French *départements*), but it does derive its name from a water source: the *val clausa* or closed valley, where water bubbles out of a deep pool at **Fontaine-de-Vaucluse**. Today, the **Luberon** is at the forefront of provençal rural chic. Idyllic scenery, attractive villages

that have stayed largely within their historic limits, imposing chateaux, remote abbeys and plenty of old stone *mas* ripe for conversion are combined with the social gloss of villages like **Gordes** or **Lourmarin** – all within easy reach of a cultural fix in Avignon or Aix. The lower-key but equally lovely **Drôme Provençale** is fast following in its wake; its truffle harvest is another draw for *bon viveurs* and restauranteurs.

On the eastern edge of the Luberon, in the sparsely populated Alpes de Haute-Provence *département*, **Forcalquier** has more provincial feel, with traces of a once-powerful past as an independent Comté. North of Avignon, **Orange** and **Vaison-la-Romaine** offer impressive Roman remains, and there are some globally famed wine-producing villages.

The Luberon massif, the ragged **Dentelles de Montmirail**, the **Baronnies** and the bleak **Mont Ventoux** all offer plentiful opportunities for walking, riding, cycling and rock-climbing. This region has a healthy, outdoorsy feel, yet it never seems too wild – you're seldom too far from a vineyard or sophisticated restaurant.

The Best of Avignon & the Vaucluse

Standout sights, restaurants and hotels from across the region.

SIGHTSEEING

Admire Avignon's Papal legacy at the **Palais des Papes** (*see p93*) and **Musée du Petit Palais** (*see p92*) – then fast forward to the 20th century with the **Collection Lambert** (*see p91*), a stunning showcase of post-1960s art. Artistic masterpieces also abound at the tiny **Musée Albert André** (*see p105*) in the village of Bagnols. In Orange, don't miss the wonderfully-preserved **Théâtre Antique** (*see p103*).

Alternatively, visit a vineyard or two in **Châteauneuf-du-Pape** (*see p104*) or **Gigondas** (*see p112*), browse the antiques at **L'Isle-sur-la-Sorgue** (*see p126*), or wander through the astonishing, ochre-hued **Colorado de Rustrel** (*see p130*).

WHERE TO STAY

Avignon's **Hôtel de la Mirande** (*see p99*) tops the luxury stakes, along with the hilltop hideaway of the **Hostellerie de**

Crillon-le-Brave in Mont Ventoux (*see p111*). More modern, but equally enticing, is the **Domaine des Andéols** (*see p129*), hidden away in the Luberon. This is also a region of charming *chambres d'hôtes*, such as the **Lumani** (*see p98*) in Avignon.

PLACES TO EAT

For exquisite fine dining, reserve a table at Avignon's **Christian Etienne** (*see p94*) or **La Mirande** (*see p95*). Further off the beaten track, try the **Pré du Moulin** (*see p103*), Lourmarin's **Auberge La Fenière** (*see p124*), or the simpler likes of the **Auberge du Beaucet** (*see p128*).

NIGHTLIFE

Jam-packed during the festival, Avignon's lively clubs and music venues include the **Red Zone** and **Delirium**. There's a thriving gay scene too, centering on **Le Cid Café** (for all, *see p96*).

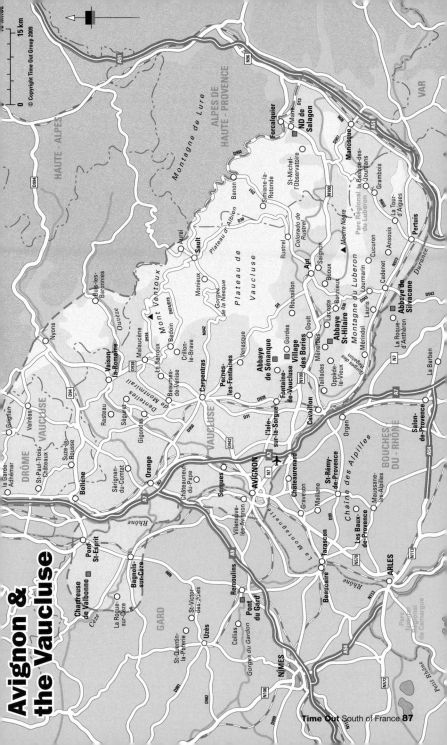

Avignon & the Vaucluse

Avignon

Artistic Avignon draws a cultured crowd.

Avignon is a town of many faces. Home to the papacy for over a century, it is crowned by the awe-inspiring medieval Palais des Papes, and still holds a wealth of artistic treasures. Modern times have brought a lively student life, thriving gay community and troubled suburban sprawl – though the city centre's ancient walls protect tourists from its grittier side. The annual performing arts festival is a vibrant artistic free-for-all, with a lively fringe scene (Avignon Off) to rival that of Edinburgh.

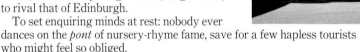

To set enquiring minds at rest: nobody ever dances on the *pont* of nursery-rhyme fame, save for a few hapless tourists who might feel so obliged.

ABOUT THE CITY

Approaching the city along the banks of the Rhône, the Rocher des Doms – with its gleaming virgin on top of the Cathédrale Notre-Dame-des-Doms – makes an imposing sight. Four kilometres of beautifully preserved ramparts add to the effect: sadly, ubiquitous 19th-century architect and 'improver' Viollet-le-Duc didn't stop at adding frilly crenellated tops to the sturdy walls, but also filled in the moat. Just outside the walls stands the city's other top tourist attraction: the celebrated *pont*. Only four arches of the original 22 remain, together with a tiny Romanesque chapel, but the 12th-century Pont St-Bénezet still exerts its fascination.

In 2001, a sleek new TGV station suddenly put Avignon within easy reach of Paris. For stressed urbanites, the dream of leaving the capital and opening an upmarket B&B or a chic designer gallery became a glorious possibility. An influx of skips and scaffolding followed, along with a surge of new bars, hotels, shops and restaurants – and a rise in house prices.

The festival over, Avignon used to revert to being a sleepy provincial town. Now the artistic adventure continues year round, thanks

---

About the author
Stephen Mudge *is the French correspondent for* Opera News, *and also writes about food and travel for* Time Out *and the BBC.*

to a busy programme of student-led theatre, music and exhibitions. Anyone who remembers the 1970s will feel immediately at home in the city, with its whiff of bohemia and joss sticks, and penchant for alternative therapies.

History

Avignon started life as a Neolithic settlement on the Rocher des Doms. Under the Romans, it flourished as a river port, but it wasn't until the 12th century, when Avignon's clergy became a power to be reckoned with, that the town started to think big, building towers, the Romanesque cathedral and St-Bénezet bridge.

In 1306, French pope Clément V brought his court from turbulent Rome to the safety of the independent, Vatican-owned Comtat Venaissin. After his death in 1314, six further popes saw no reason to relocate to Rome. Their 68-year 'Babylonian captivity', as furious Italians branded it, utterly transformed the quiet provincial backwater. The population soared, and artists, scholars, architects, weavers and jewellers flocked to find patronage. The virtue industry fostered vice in equal measure: 'A sewer,' sniffed Petrarch, 'the filthiest of cities.'

Gregory XI, elected in 1370, was badgered by the persuasive St Catherine of Siena into returning to the Holy See. He took her advice, went back, and promptly died in 1378. The Italians elected a Roman pope, but the French were loath to lose their hold on the reins of power and swiftly elected Clement VII in

Avignon. The rival popes excommunicated each other, sparking the Great Schism – which finally ended 40 years later, when all sides agreed on the election of Martin V in 1417.

Even after the popes returned to Italy, Avignon remained papal territory. Without French censorship, and far enough from Rome to escape Vatican checks, the town flourished as an artistic, religious and publishing centre. This continued when the town was returned to France in 1791: it was to Avignon that the Félibrige (the 19th-century organisation for the promotion of Occitan culture) turned to get its provençal-revival works into print.

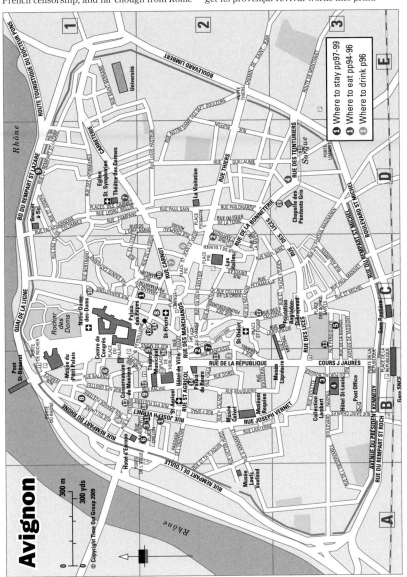

AVIGNON & THE VAUCLUSE

SIGHTSEEING

The terraced gardens of the **Rocher des Doms**, perched above the Rhône, are a good place to begin a visit. A miniature vineyard, sloping down the northern flank, signals Avignon's role as capital of Côtes du Rhône: an example of every grape variety is represented, with the full gamut harvested during the Ban des Vendanges festival in September. The view ranges across the city – 'its closely knitted roofs of weathered tile like a pie crust fresh from the oven', as Lawrence Durrell wrote – and over the Rhône to Villeneuve-lès-Avignon.

Jutting into the river below are the four surviving arches of the **Pont St-Bénezet**, reached by walking along the only section of the city walls open to the public. Between the Dom and the bridge, the **Musée du Petit Palais**, a former cardinal's palace, has a superb collection of early Italian and provençal paintings, and religious sculptures.

The massive bulk of the **Palais des Papes**, more like an ogre's castle than a pontiff's palace, shares its square with **Cathédrale Notre-Dame-des-Doms** and the swagged and furbelowed former Hôtel des Monnaies (mint), now the Conservatoire de Musique. Before entering the Palais, get a sense of its solidity by walking along rue de la Peyrollerie to see its towers. A tacky fleet of mini tourist trains (www.petittrainavignon.com) tour Avignon's sights between March and October, leaving from place du Palais (€7).

Further south, place de l'Horloge is the centre of town life, with its cafés, grand 19th-century Hôtel de Ville and **Théâtre Municipal**. The square gets its name from the Gothic clock tower, Tour du Jacquemart, although the painted wooden figurines of Jacquemart and his wife have taken retirement from ringing the hour. Children will love the square's gilded

carousel, though, with its prancing horses. South of here, busy rue de la République is the town's main shopping thoroughfare. To the west lies the smart part of town, its streets packed with fashionable restaurants and beautifully restored mansions. On rue St-Agricol, the 15th-century carved doorway of the **Eglise St-Agricol** (open 4-5pm Sat) has been restored, as has the church's 16th-century painting of the Assumption by Avignon artist Simon de Châlons. An alley off rue St-Agricol leads to the 15th-century **Palais du Roure**, where the aristocratic poet Folco Baroncelli was born, and where Frédéric Mistral edited *Aïoli*, his journal in Provençal.

Rue Joseph Vernet is a shopaholic's dream, with designer stores set in a parade of 17th- and 18th-century *hôtels particuliers*. At No.65, the **Musée Calvet** displays sculpture and paintings in the colonnaded galleries of an elegant 18th-century palace; one wing is also home to the **Muséum Requien d'Histoire Naturelle**. Further south, on rue Victor Hugo, the **Musée Louis-Vouland** is a lavishly decorated showcase for 18th-century French furniture and faïence. Nearby, an 18th-century mansion houses the cutting-edge contemporary art of the **Collection Lambert**.

On rue Portail Boquier, check out the dramatic juxtaposition of historic and modern architecture at the **Hôtel Cloître St-Louis**, a former monastery. On one side of the cloister, the Espace St-Louis is used for art exhibitions and becomes a box office during the festival.

East of rue de la République, on a spacious square, the lovely **Eglise St-Didier** was built in the simple, single-aisled provençal Gothic style. Around the corner in rue Laboureur, admire the artworks at the **Fondation Angladon-Dubrujeaud**; nearby, the **Musée Lapidaire** displays ancient sculpture in an old Jesuit chapel. Across rue des Lices, not far from the tourist office, lies shady place des Corps-Saints. Stretched in front of the 14th-century Chapelle de St-Michel et Tous-les-Saints, it becomes a sea of café chairs in summer.

Heading east, rue du Roi René has several fine 17th- and 18th-century mansions; at No.22 a plaque records that in 1327, this was where Italian poet Petrarch first set eyes on Laura, the woman he was to idolise for the rest of his life. At its far end, the riverside rue des Teinturiers is one of Avignon's most atmospheric streets, dotted with the waterwheels of the 19th-century dye works that gave the street its name. These days, the street is home to a boho mix of cafés, second-hand bookshops and art galleries. At No.8 the **Chapelle des Pénitents Gris**, crouched at the end of a tiny bridge, was founded in the 13th century. Legend has it that the chapel witnessed its own mini-version

---

**INSIDE TRACK
UNDYING LOVE**

Avignon's **Hôtel d'Europe** (see p98) has long been a favourite with visiting lovers, among them the eloping Brownings and philosopher John Stuart Mill and his wife Harriet Taylor. When Harriet died there of lung complications in 1858, Mill was so distraught that he bought a house overlooking the **Cimetière St-Véran** (av Stuart Mill, 04.90.80.79.95), where she was buried, furnishing it with the contents of their last hotel room. When he died in 1873, he was buried beside her in the shady cemetery.

Collection Lambert.

of the parting of the Red Sea during the floods of 1433, when the waters are said to have curled back on either side of the aisle, allowing the consecrated host to be carried out safe and dry. North-east of here, bikes can be hired from **Aymard** (80 rue Guillaume Puy, 04.90.86.32.49, closed Mon, 2wks in Aug).

The partly pedestrianised streets north of place St-Didier are the heart of the medieval town. Once shabby, with empty statue niches and pigeon-daubed churches, it's smartened up considerably in recent years. **Place Pie** is home to Avignon's covered food market (7am-1pm Tue-Sun), while to the north, in place St-Pierre, the Gothic **Eglise St-Pierre** (open 2-5pm Thur, 2-6.30pm Fri, Sat) has finely carved walnut doors and a handsome belfry.

The winding streets behind the Palais des Papes lead to rue Banasterie and the **Chapelle des Pénitents Noirs** (open 2-5pm Sat), which has a sumptuous baroque interior painted to the last inch with gold leaf and cherubs. On nearby rue des Escaliers Ste-Anne, the **Utopia** arts cinema is one of Avignon's liveliest cultural centres. Opposite, the Porte de la Ligne gateway emerges beside the Rhône, close to the jetty where a free ferry nips across to the grassy Ile de la Barthelasse every 15 minutes in summer. The island is home to the **Piscine de la Barthelasse** (04.90.82.54.25, closed Sept-Apr), an Olympic-sized open-air pool that's perfect for when the city gets too hot to bear.

Back inside the walls on the lively place des Carmes, the **Eglise St-Symphorien**, originally a Carmelite convent, has a 15th-century Gothic façade and some fine wooden statues inside. Its 14th-century cloisters now rub shoulders with one of Avignon's oldest theatre companies, the **Théâtre des Carmes**. This is the university district, packed with bars, cafés and second-hand bookstores.

ᴿᴿᴱᴱ Cathédrale Notre-Dame-des-Doms

pl du Palais (04.90.86.81.01/www.cathedrale-avignon.fr). **Open** 8am-6pm daily. **Admission** free. **Map** p89 C1.

Apart from the Romanesque porch and a rather fine marble throne, most vestiges of the church's 12th-century origins have been obliterated by subsequent alterations: a baroque gallery, a rebuilt tower and a golden statue of the Virgin perched on its pinnacle.

★ Collection Lambert

Hôtel de Caumont, 5 rue Violette (04.90.16.56. 20/www.collectionlambert.com). **Open** *July, Aug* 11am-7pm daily. *Sept-June* 11am-6pm Tue-Sun. **Admission** €9.50; €2-€8 reductions; free under-6s. **Credit** MC, V. **Map** p89 B3.

Housed in a stately 18th-century *hôtel particulier*, this formidable collection, on extended loan from Parisian art dealer Yvon Lambert, spans the 1960s to the present. Three annual temporary exhibitions and site-specific commissions keep things fresh, while the main collection is particularly strong on conceptual and minimalist art, taking in painting, sculpture, installation, video and photography by international artistic heavyweights such as Nan

Goldin, Jean-Michel Basquiat, Julian Schnabel and Cy Twombly. There's also a good bookshop, and a lovely courtyard café.

FREE Eglise St-Didier
pl St-Didier (04.90.86.20.17). **Open** 8am-6.30pm daily. **Admission** free. **Map** p89 C2.
This pretty example of provençal Gothic has delicate 14th-century Italian frescoes in the north chapel. In the Chapelle St-Bénezet are relics of the bridge-building saint himself, or his skull at least.

★ Fondation Angladon-Dubrujeaud
5 rue Laboureur (04.90.82.29.03/www.angladon. com). **Open** 1-6pm Tue-Sun (closed Mon & Tue in winter) **Admission** €6; €1.50-€4 reductions; free under-7s. **No credit cards**. **Map** p89 C3.
The marvellous collection displayed in this 18th-century mansion was amassed by 19th-century Paris couturier Jacques Doucet – an avid collector. It was eventually inherited by his great-nephew and his wife, Jean and Paulette Angladon-Dubrujeaud, who bequeathed it to the museum. On the ground floor, a remarkable line-up of paintings includes works by Degas, Picasso, Cézanne and Modigliani – as well as the only Van Gogh in Provence. Upstairs, a series of rooms display paintings, antiques and objets d'art to lavish effect.

Musée Calvet
65 rue Joseph Vernet (04.90.86.33.84/www. fondation-calvet.org). **Open** 10am-1pm, 2-6pm Mon, Wed-Sun. **Admission** €6; €3 reductions; free under-12s. **No credit cards**. **Map** p89 B2.
This beautiful fine art museum displays its collection in elegant, colonnaded rooms built around a central courtyard. The ground floor has Gobelins tapestries and medieval sculpture, while its 18th- and 19th-century French paintings include works by the Avignon-based Vernet family and David's *La mort de Bara*. A good modern section showcases works by Bonnard, Vuillard, Sisley, Manet and Dufy; look out, too, for Camille Claudel's sculpture of her brother Paul, who had her incarcerated in a nearby mental asylum when her relationship with Rodin became too scandalous.

★ Musée du Petit Palais
pl du Palais (04.90.86.44.58/www.petit-palais.org). **Open** June-Sept 10am-6pm Mon, Wed-Sun. Oct-May 10am-1pm, 2-6pm Mon, Wed-Sun. **Admission** €6; €3 reductions; free under-12s. **No credit cards**. **Map** p89 B1.
Several lesser habitations were razed to the ground to make way for the Petit Palais, built in 1317 for Cardinal Berenger Fredoli. Subsequent inhabitants each made their mark on the palace: in the late 15th century, its Renaissance façade and tower were added by Cardinal Giuliano della Rovere, the future Pope Julius II. It now houses magnificent medieval

paintings, frescoes and sculptures, many rescued from churches destroyed in the Revolution. Don't miss the sarcophagus of Cardinal Jean de Lagrange, with its anatomically realistic depiction of a decaying corpse, and his brutally mutilated tomb effigy.

★ Musée Lapidaire
27 rue de la République (04.90.85.75.38/www. musee-lapidaire.org). **Open** June-Sept 10am-6pm Mon, Wed-Sun. Oct-May 10am-1pm, 2-6pm Mon, Wed-Sun. **Admission** €2; €1 reductions; free under-12s. **No credit cards**. **Map** p89 B3.
Avignon's archaeological collection is superbly displayed in this 17th-century Jesuit chapel as part of the Fondation Calvet. As well as Greek, Gallo-Roman and Etruscan sculpture, mosaics and glass, it is rich in Egyptian sculpture, *stelae* (inscribed slabs) and *shabtis* (small statues of servants, buried with the dead to serve them in the afterlife). The Gallo-Roman selection has a depiction of the Tarasque of Noves, the local man-eating monster.

Musée Louis Vouland
17 rue Victor Hugo (04.90.86.03.79/www. vouland.com). **Open** July-Sept noon-6pm Tue-Sun. Oct-June 2-6pm Tue-Sun. Closed Feb. **Admission** €6; free under-12s. **No credit cards**. **Map** p89 A2.
A 19th-century *hôtel particulier* with trompe l'oeil ceilings houses the largely 18th-century decorative arts collection of former resident Louis Vouland. A preserved-meat salesman, Vouland spent 50 years acquiring furniture and porcelain, including faïence from Les Moustiers, Montpellier and Marseille, and

Palais des Papes. *See p93.*

Ming porcelain. Among the 19th-century paintings are works by Avignon artists Claude Firmin, Clément Brun and Pierre Grivolas.

FREE Muséum Requien d'Histoire Naturelle
67 rue Joseph Vernet (04.90.82.43.51/www. museum-avignon.org). **Open** 9am-noon, 2-6pm Tue-Sat. **Admission** free. **Map** p89 B2.
Founded in 1840, this old-fashioned natural history museum is packed with rocks, minerals, stuffed animals and fossils. Buried in the archives is John Stuart Mill's collection of dried flowers and herbs, while temporary exhibitions have focused on everything from crystals to local insect life.

★ Palais des Papes
pl du Palais (04.90.27.50.73/www.palais-des-papes.com). **Open** *Mar-June, mid Sept-Nov* 9am-7pm daily. *July-mid Sept* 9am-8pm daily (9pm during festival). **Admission** *Mid Mar-Oct* €10.50; €8.50 reductions; free under-8s. *Nov-early Mar* €8.50; €7 reductions; free under-8s. **Credit** MC, V. **Map** p89 C1.
More like a fortress than a palace, the labyrinthine Palais des Papes is an unmistakeable power statement. The interior is strangely empty after the devastation wreaked during the Revolution, when it was used as a prison and barracks; soldiers chipped off bits of fresco to sell, but exquisite fragments remain. The Palais comprises two interlocking parts: the forbidding Palais Vieux, built in the 1330s for Pope Benedict XII, and the more showy Palais Neuf,

tacked on a decade later by Clement VI. Wander at will (an audioguide is included in the entry fee) or join a guided tour. Across the main courtyard from the ticket office is the Salle de Jésus, the antechamber of the papal council room, where frescoes from the cathedral are displayed. Next door, the Chapelle St-Jean has delightful frescoes (c1346) by Matteo Giovanetti, Clement VI's court painter. Upstairs, the ceiling of the Grand Tinel banqueting hall was once coloured blue and studded with gold stars to resemble the sky, while the kitchens, with their huge pyramid-shaped chimney, could cater for 3,000 guests. There are more Giovanetti frescoes, lavish with lapis lazuli and gold, in the Chapelle St-Martial.

Beyond the Salle de Parement (robing room), Benedict XII's tiled study was only discovered in 1963. The papal bedchamber is followed by the Chambre du Cerf, Clement VI's study, where some charming frescoes exude the spirit of courtly love. Next is the vast Chapelle Clémentine, which was barely large enough to hold the college of cardinals when it gathered in conclave to elect a new pope. Through the Chamberlain's Room, whose raised stone slabs mark the spot where papal treasure was discovered, stairs lead up to the battlements, with dramatic views over the city. Back on the ground floor, the Grande Audience hall has a bevy of biblical prophets frescoed by Giovanetti.

Palais du Roure
3 rue Collège du Roure (04.90.80.80.88). **Open** *Guided tour* 3pm Tue or by appointment. *Library* (open for research) 9am-noon, 2-5.30pm Mon-Fri. **Admission** €4.60; €2.30 reductions. **No credit cards.** **Map** p89 B2.
The birthplace of Marquis Folco de Baroncelli-Javon, who devoted his life to writing poetry, breeding bulls and preserving Camarguais traditions, has a charming courtyard with fragments of frescoes and a splendid carved doorway. It is now a literary archive and library, museum of local culture, and headquarters of the Festival Provençal, an autumn festival of theatre and music in the Provençal language (for details contact the tourist office, *see p99*).
▶ *For more on course camarguaise, see p66.*

★ Pont St-Bénezet
rue Ferruce (04.90.27.51.16/www.palais-des-papes.com). **Open** *Mar-June, mid-Sept-Nov* 9am-7pm daily. *July-mid Sept* 9am-8pm daily (9pm

---

INSIDE TRACK
CUT-PRICE CULTURE

The free Avignon-Villeneuve **PASSion** pass gives 20 to 50 per cent reductions on most museums and sights in Avignon and Villeneuve-lès-Avignon. Ask at the tourist office (*see p99*) for details.

AVIGNON & THE VAUCLUSE

during festival). *Nov-Feb* 9.30am-5.45pm daily. **Admission** *Mid Mar-Oct* €4.50; €3-€3.50 reductions. *Nov-mid Mar* €3.50; €2-€3 reductions. *Combined ticket* (Palais & bridge) €11-€13; €8.50-€10 reductions. **Credit** MC, V. **Map** p89 B1.

Construction of the original pont d'Avignon was begun in 1185 by a shepherd boy from the Ardèche, who later became St Bénezet. Divinely inspired to build a bridge, he lifted the first massive stone, convincing the sceptical populace that it was possible. When completed, the bridge had 22 arches and was nearly a kilometre long. It played a key role in the town's development, although in 1660, after a huge flood, the Avignonnais finally gave up the unequal maintenance struggle. Today, only four arches and a tiny fisherman's chapel remain; a small museum in the reception area explains the history. Despite the song, it seems unlikely that anyone ever danced on the narrow, busy structure. It's more likely that locals danced *sous le pont* (under the bridge): the Ile de la Barthelasse, which the bridge used to cross, was a favourite R&R spot during the Middle Ages.

Where to eat

★ Les 5 Sens

18 rue Joseph Vernet (04.90.85.26.51/www. restaurantles5sens.com). **Open** 11.30am-2.30pm, 7.30-11pm Tue-Sat. Closed 1st 2wks Aug, Feb, school hols. **Menus** *Lunch* €20. *Dinner* €42. **Credit** AmEx, MC, V. **Map** p89 B2 ❶
The sleek, Indian-influenced interior may be a touch too modern for some tastes, but the courtyard is delightful – and there's no doubting the quality of chef Thierry Baucher's beautifully presented contemporary cuisine.

€ Au Tout Petit

4 rue d'Amphoux (04.90.82.38.86/www.au toutpetit.fr). **Open** noon-2pm, 7-10.30pm Mon, Tue, Thur-Sat; noon-2pm Wed. **Menus** *Lunch* €11. *Dinner* €15-€24. **Credit** MC, V. **Map** p89 C2 ❷
The chef at this teeny restaurant offers inventive, modestly priced 'cuisine ré-créative', introducing modern accents to classic dishes. The team are also firm believers in the beneficial properties of a good home-made soup, which can be bought to take away.

€ Le Café de la Comédie

15 pl Crillon (04.90.85.74.85). **Open** 7am-1am (7am-3am during festival) Mon-Sat. Closed Aug & 1wk Feb. **Main courses** €8-€9. **Credit** DC, MC, V. **Map** p89 B2 ❸
In a calm, spacious square that's liberally dotted with restaurants, Café de la Comédie attracts a fascinating mixed clientele – including celeb chef Keith Floyd, who once claimed it as his local caff. Sit back under a plane tree and gaze upon the Renaissance façade of Avignon's first theatre.

€ Caves Breysse

41 rue des Teinturiers (04.32.74.25.86). **Open** *Restaurant* noon-2.30pm Tue-Fri. *Bar* 6am-11pm daily. Closed Aug. **Main courses** €10-€15. **Credit** MC, V. **Map** p89 D2 ❹
A relaxed wine bar on the fashionable rue des Teinturiers, Caves Breysse invites you to explore the wines of the region by the glass. An excellent pit stop for a lunchtime *plat du jour*, it's equally well suited to early-evening aperitifs.

★ Christian Etienne

10 rue de Mons (04.90.86.16.50/www.christian-etienne.fr). **Open** noon-2pm, 7-9.30pm Tue-Sat. **Main courses** €32-€45. **Menus** *Lunch* €35. *Dinner* €65-€120. **Credit** AmEx, DC, MC, V. **Map** p89 C2 ❺
In the shadow of the Palais des Papes, this is one of Avignon's most ambitious restaurants. Etienne's cuisine is sophisticated and seasonal – so summer might bring a menu devoted to the humble tomato, featuring such delights as braised lamb with baby fennel and dried tomatoes, and tomato mousse with aubergine caviar. If you're on a budget, book in for the modestly priced lunchtime menu.

€ L'Echapée Belle

11 rue de la Balance (04.90.82.52.61). **Open** *Sept-June* noon-10pm Mon-Sat. *July, Aug* noon-10pm daily. **Mains** €11.50-€15. **Credit** MC, V. **Map** p89 B1 ❻
Spices and exotic seasonings liven up the *plats du jours* at this new tearoom-cum-restaurant. It's also a great place to enjoy a delicious piece of cake and reviving cup of tea.

€ L'Entrée des Artistes

1 pl des Carmes (04.90.82.46.90). **Open** noon-2pm, 7.30-10.30pm Mon-Fri. **Menus** €21-€26. **Credit** V. **Map** p89 D1 ❼
On the pretty place des Carmes, this appealing bistro offers simple but well-prepared dishes based on good, fresh ingredients. The occasional modern flourish keeps diners on their toes.

L'Epicerie

10 pl St-Pierre (04.90.82.74.22). **Open** noon-2.30pm, 7.30-10.30pm Mon-Sat (open Sun during festival). Closed mid Oct-Mar. **Main courses** €17-€25. **Credit** MC, V. **Map** p89 C2 ❽
This laid-back bistro has an idyllic setting: a pretty, cobbled square, right next to the magnificent Eglise St-Pierre. Crowds of locals and tourists head here to admire the view and fill up on the nicely executed Mediterranean menu and *pichets* of local wine.

★ La Fourchette

17 rue Racine (04.90.85.20.93). **Open** 12.15-1.45pm, 7.15-9.45pm Mon-Fri. **Menus** *Lunch* €26. *Dinner* €32. **Credit** MC, V. **Map** p89 B2 ❾

La Fourchette's reasonable prices and excellent cuisine have won it a diehard local following – so it's always best to book ahead. The menu combines classic dishes (including a very good *daube*, served with macaroni) with lighter, more modern combinations.

Le Grand Café

La Manutention, 4 rue des Escaliers Ste-Anne (04.90.86.86.77/www.legrandcafe-avignon.com). **Open** noon-midnight Tue-Sat. **Menus** *Lunch* €20. *Dinner* €28. **Credit** AmEx, DC, MC, V. **Map** p89 C1 ❿

Set in a warehouse-like converted army supplies depot next to the Utopia cinema, this place attracts a lively, bohemian crowd. Glimmering candles and huge mirrors make it an atmospheric spot for dinner, while the menu is unpretentious but inviting.

Hiély Lucullus

5 rue de la République (04.90.86.17.07/www. hiely-lucullus.com). **Open** noon-2pm, 7-10pm Mon-Fri; 7-10pm Sat. Closed 1wk Jan. **Menus** *Lunch* €25-€35. *Dinner* €45-€95. **Credit** MC, V. **Map** p89 B2 ⓫

The stately, wood-panelled dining room at Hiély Lucullus is where the buttoned-up bourgeoisie of the town head for a traditional feast. Quality food is assured – just don't go there expecting a boisterous crowd or cutting-edge cuisine.

L'Isle Sonnante

7 rue Racine (04.90.82.56.01). **Open** noon-2pm, 7-10pm Tue-Sat (daily during festival). Closed lunch Aug. **Menus** €25-€38. **Credit** AmEx, MC, V. **Map** p89 B2 ⓬

Close to the town hall, this cosy, rustic restaurant serves provençal specialities with a contemporary twist, alongside traditional dishes such as flavoursome stuffed courgette flowers.

Michel Peyaud

20 rue St-Etienne (04.90.85.27.56). **Open** noon-2pm, 7.30-10.30pm Tue-Sat. **Mains** €15-€30. **Menus** €28. **Credit** MC, V. **Map** p89 B1 ⓭

Michel Peyaud cooked up quite a reputation for himself down on the place Crillon, and is now going solo in this long, rather featureless room – opened in September 2008. Prices are reasonable, and it's definitely worth a punt.

La Mirande

4 pl de la Mirande (04.90.85.93.93/www.la-mirande.fr). **Open** 12.30-2pm, 7.30-10pm Mon, Thur-Sun. Closed Jan. **Main courses** €38-€45. **Menus** *Lunch* €35. *Dinner* €80-€105. **Credit** AmEx, DC, MC, V. **Map** p89 C21 ⓮

Under hotshot young chef Julien Allano, La Mirande is a quietly luxurious place to dine, whether you eat in the rose garden or 15th-century dining room; save room for artful desserts from pastry chef Gaëtan Orlando. Tuesday and Wednesday nights bring an informal *table d'hôte* (€92), where a feast is whipped up before your eyes in the 19th-century kitchens.

Numéro 75

75 rue Guillaume Puy (04.90.27.16.00/www. numero75.com). **Open** noon-2.15pm, 8-10pm Mon-Sat. **Menus** *Lunch* €26-€30. *Dinner* €32.50. **Credit** MC, V. **Map** p89 D3 ⓯

Set inside a beautifully converted former *hôtel particulier* that once belonged to the Pernod family, Numéro 75 also has a lush walled garden. Young lovers and families crunch over the gravel to sample its Mediterranean menu; it might not be the best haute cuisine in town, but it's a romantic spot.

L'Opéra Café

24 pl de l'Horloge (04.90.86.17.43). **Open** 9am-1am daily. **Main courses** €12-€28.50. **Menus** *Lunch* €13.50. *Dinner* €25-€35. **Credit** DC, MC, V. **Map** p89 B2 ⓰

The smartest of the cafés that crowd around place de l'Horloge, this essay in modern city chic is lacking in local atmosphere. Still, it's a good place for a languid, late-afternoon drink.

★ Piedoie

26 rue des Trois Faucons (04.90.86.51.53). **Open** *July* 12.30-3pm, 7.15-10.30pm daily. *Aug-June* 12.30-3pm, 7.15-10.30pm Mon, Thur-Sun. **Menus** €17-€49. **Credit** MC, V. **Map** p89 C2 ⓱

Numéro 75.

Rue Joseph Vernet.

Thierry Piedoie's cluttered, intimate restaurant has an enticing menu of regional favourites, cooked with a light modern hand. Produce is fresh and carefully sourced, and this is the place to enjoy a spectacular white truffle salad in season.

▶ *Hankering to get your hands on some truffles to create your own masterpieces? See p114.*

Simple Simon Tea Lunch
26 rue de la Petite Fusterie (04.90.86.62.70).
Open noon-7pm Mon-Sat. Closed Aug.
Main courses €11-€17. **Credit** MC, V.
Map p89 B2
This slice of Britain, complete with beams, English china and swirly carpets, should bring solace to any *rosbifs* missing home; the tea and cakes are generally superior to the savoury offerings.

Woolloomooloo
16bis rue des Teinturiers (04.90.85.28.44/ www.woolloo.com). **Open** 11.45am-2pm, 7.30pm-midnight daily. **Menus** *Lunch* €15-€18. *Dinner* €23-€42. **Credit** MC, V. **Map** p89 D3
The honorary HQ of Avignon's arty crowd buzzes with brooding students and neophyte playwrights, who fuel their creativity with 'world food' (tandoori chicken, North African lamb) and veggie platters.

Where to drink

Le Bokao's
9bis quai St-Lazare (04.90.82.47.95/www.bokaos. fr). **Open** 10pm-5am Wed-Sat. **Admission** free. **Credit** AmEx, DC, MC, V. **Map** p89 D1

This converted barn, beside the Rhône and just beyond the ramparts, has been elevated from mere bar to full-blooded nightclub. The playlist comprises pumping disco, house and techno.

Le Cid Café
11 pl de l'Horloge (04.90.82.30.38/www.lecid cafe.com). **Open** 6.30am-1am daily. **Credit** MC, V. **Map** p89 B2
Avignon's most popular gay bar is also its most central, standing proud on the place de l'Horloge. The laid-back crowd is mixed by day, gay by night, when DJs play to different themes: disco on Monday, Latino music on Wednesday, house at weekends.

★ Delirium
1 rue Mignard (04.90.85.44.56/www.le delirium.net). **Open** 9pm-2am Thur-Sat (daily during festival). **Admission** *Membership* €2. **No credit cards. Map** p89 B3
This relaxed, late-opening members' club pitches itself as a modern-day cultural salon, with exhibitions, music and performance art. Anything goes, from tuba-toting musicians to tango dancers.

L'Esclave
12 rue du Limas (04.90.85.14.91/www.esclave bar.com). **Open** *Sept-July* 11pm-dawn Mon-Sat. *Aug* 11pm-dawn daily. **Admission** free. **Credit** MC, V. **Map** p89 B1
This central gay disco has a surprisingly cosmopolitan feel despite its intimate proportions: nights include bears' dance parties.

Pub Z
58 rue de la Bonneterie (04.90.85.42.84). **Open** noon-1.30am Mon-Sat. Closed 2wks Aug. **Admission** free. **No credit cards. Map** p89 C2
A life-size zebra welcomes you into this striped bar, which is popular with a regular crowd of rockers and students. There's a happy hour (7.30-8.30pm), art shows and a DJ at weekends.

The Red Lion
21-23 rue St-Jean-le-Vieux (04.90.86.40.25). **Open** 6pm-1am Mon-Sat. **Admission** free. **Credit** AmEx, MC, V. **Map** p89 C2
This boisterous British pub is popular with students thanks to its extended happy hour (5-8pm). Guinness is on tap, but put aside any thoughts of real ale – though grub includes fish and chips. There's rock and blues on Tuesdays, Wednesdays and Sundays.

The Red Zone
25 rue Carnot (04.90.27.02.44/www.redzone djbar.com). **Open** 9pm-3am daily. **Admission** free. **Credit** AmEx, DC, MC, V. **Map** p89 C2
Very red and very popular, this bar-club close to the university is where the youth of Avignon come after a night's drinking on place Pie. Every night of

the week you can dance to anything from funk and electro to house and 'ethnic fusion salsa'.

Shopping

The indoor **Les Halles** market in place Pie is open from 7am to 1pm Tuesday to Sunday. It's a disappointing building, but a great place to stock up on fabulous olives, goat's cheese and seafood from the outstanding fishmonger. The **place des Carmes** hosts a flower market on Saturday mornings, and a flea market on Sunday mornings. All shops are open from Monday to Saturday unless stated.

Rue de la République is the main shopping drag, with high street names such as Zara, H&M, Monoprix and Fnac. Peeling off down the pedestrian rue des Marchands is a maze of clothes shops and boutiques. **Mouret** (No.20, 04.90.85.39.38, www.chapelier.com) is Avignon's oldest shop – an enchanting hatter frozen in the 1860s. Further east down rue Bonneterie, **Liquid** (No.37, 04.90.85.19.89) is amply stocked with the region's Côtes du Rhône. **Hermès** has a grand corner premises on place de l'Horloge (No.2, 04.90.82.61.94).

On rue St-Agricol, provençal food paradise **La Tropézienne** (No.22, 04.90.86.24.72, www.latropezienne.net) sells *calissons*, nougat and *papalines* (pink, spiky-coated chocolates infused with local oregano liqueur). Opposite, ice-cream shop **Deldon** (No.35, 04.90.85.59.41) is a good summer heat-buster.

Rue Joseph Vernet is great for sophisticated togs, with **Cacharel** (No.8, 04.90.86.19.19), **Comptoir des Cotonniers** (No.27, 04.90.14.63.84) and **Ventilo** (No.28, 04.90.85.27.40). **Pierre Tissier** (No.85, 04.90.82.12.58) is a shoe-lover's paradise, while **Les Olivades** (No.56, 04.90.86.13.42) sells top-quality provençal fabrics by the metre. Sinfully good chocolate-maker **Puyricard** has an outpost at No.33 (04.90.85.96.33). At No.3, **Le Vigneron Rebelle** (04.90.85.46.67, www.le-vigneron-rebelle.com) favours interesting wines from smaller producers.

Running parallel, the rue Petite Fusterie is an interiors hotbed, with antiques and garden furniture at **Hervé Baume** (No.19, 04.90.86.37.66). Second-hand English books can be found at **Shakespeare** (155 rue Carreterie, 04.90.27.38.50, closed Mon, Sun), which doubles up as a tearoom.

Arts & entertainment

AJMI

La Manutention, 4 rue des Escaliers Ste-Anne (04.90.86.08.61/www.jazzalajmi.com). **Tickets** €5-€15. Available through agencies or 30mins before show. **No credit cards**.

AJMI has been promoting jazz and improvised music in Avignon since 1978. Now using the same venue as the Utopia (*see p97*), it is still keenly developing dynamic and creative jazz, even going so far as to create its own record label, AJMISeries.

[FREE] La Galerie MMB

20 rue de la Balance (04.90.85.17.21). **Open** *Oct-June* 2-6pm Mon; 10am-noon, 2.30-6.30pm Tue-Sat. *July-Sept* 9am-7pm daily. **Admission** free.

Marie-Marguerite Buhler's contemporary art space displays Thomas Ghislaine's work, along with temporary exhibitions; recent examples include the sombre architectural photography of Hervé Perdriel and the abstract work of Guillaume Lavigne.

Théâtre des Carmes

6 pl des Carmes (04.90.82.20.47/www.theatre descarmes.com). **Tickets** €10-€15. **Credit** MC, V.

Avignon's oldest theatre company, Carmes is firmly committed to radical theatre. It was also one of the founders of the 'Off' fringe festival.

Théâtre du Chien qui Fume

75 rue des Teinturiers (04.90.85.25.87/ www.chienquifume.com). **Open** *Box office* 1hr before show. Closed Aug. **Tickets** €10-€25. **No credit cards**.

Director Gérard Vantaggioli keeps this theatre buoyant throughout the year with new productions, exhibitions and *chansons françaises*. A free show on the last Friday of the month welcomes new theatre, song, dance and circus acts.

Théâtre Municipal

20 pl de l'Horloge (04.90.82.81.40/www.opera theatredavignon.fr). **Open** *Box office* 11am-6pm Mon-Sat; 11am-12.30pm Sun. **Tickets** €5-€60. **Credit** MC, V.

The main permanent opera house-cum-theatre in Avignon, the Théâtre Municipal stages official festival productions in July and a good season of opera and ballet, but also top variety acts and comedy.

★ Utopia

La Manutention, 4 rue des Escaliers Ste-Anne (04.90.82.65.36/www.cinemas-utopia.org/ avignon). **Open** *Box office* 11am-11pm daily. **Tickets** €6; €4 noon screening. **No credit cards**.

Avignon's main *version originale* (original language) cinema is a cultural hub, with a packed programme and a good bar-bistro. It has a smaller offshoot at 5 rue Figuière (04.90.82.65.36).

Where to stay

Expect rates to shoot up for the duration of the Avignon festival (for dates, *see p44*).

★ La Banasterie

11 rue de la Banasterie (04.32.76.30.78/www.
labanasterie.com). **Rooms** 5. **Credit** MC, V. **Map** p89 C2 ❶
Set in a charming 16th-century house, this upmarket B&B is set in one of the old town's most atmospheric streets. Its rooms are named after great chocolates of the world, and decorated in rich, welcoming hues – with complimentary chocs on arrival.

€ Hôtel de Blauvac

11 rue de la Bancasse (04.90.86.34.11/
www.hotel-blauvac.com). **Rates** €65-€97 double.
Rooms 16. **Credit** AmEx, DC, MC, V. **Map** p89 B2 ❷
Overlooking a winding street leading to the place de l'Horloge, the Blauvac's 17th-century premises are full of character. Its high-ceilinged rooms are simply furnished, but decent value for money.

€ Hotel Boquier

6 rue du Portail Boquier (04.90.82.34.43/
www.hotel-boquier.com). **Rates** €48-€66 double.
Rooms 12. **Credit** MC, V. **Map** p89 B3 ❸
Not far from the tourist office, this 18th-century building has been sympathetically transformed into a budget hotel. Its airy bedrooms are sparsely furnished, but the agreeable public spaces and hospitable owners make this a competitive choice.

Hôtel Cloître St-Louis

20 rue Portail Boquier (04.90.27.55.55/
www.cloitre-saint-louis.com). **Rates** €145-€240
double. **Rooms** 80. **Credit** AmEx, DC, MC, V.
Map p89 B3 ❹
The 16th-century cloister, chapel wing and fountain courtyard of a former monastery make an imposing setting for this smart hotel – along with a contemporary steel and glass extension by Jean Nouvel. Rooms are less impressive than the exterior, but there's a nice walled garden and small rooftop pool.

€ Hôtel Colbert

7 rue Agricol Perdiguier (04.90.86.20.20/www.
avignon-hotel-colbert.com). Closed Nov-Feb.
Rates €55-€108 double. **Rooms** 15. **Credit**
AmEx, MC, V. **Map** p89 C3 ❺
One of a cluster of budget hotels on a tiny street in the middle of town, Le Colbert has clean, cheerfully decorated rooms, with air-conditioning. In summer, you can breakfast in the charming little courtyard.

Hôtel d'Europe

14 pl Crillon (04.90.14.76.76/www.hotel-d-
europe.fr). **Rates** €169-€475 double. **Rooms** 41.
Credit AmEx, DC, MC, V. **Map** p89 B2 ❻
Picasso, Charles Dickens, Tennessee Williams and Jackie Onassis are some of the past guests at this 16th-century mansion, which opened as a hotel in 1799. Rooms are traditional but not too fussy, while suites have their own private terraces. The hotel has

its own smart bar and restaurant, while cookery lessons can be arranged with chef Bruno d'Angelis.

Hôtel de Garlande

20 rue Galante (04.90.80.08.85/www.hotel
degarlande.com). Closed mid Jan-mid Feb. **Rates**
€75-€115 double. **Rooms** 10. **Credit** AmEx, DC,
MC, V. **Map** p89 C2 ❼
The welcome is warm and the decoration tasteful at this cosy but elegant little hotel. Its central location means you're in the thick of the action too.

★ Le Limas

51 rue du Limas (04.90.14.67.19/www.le-limas-
avignon.com). **Rates** €100-€150 double. **Rooms**
4. **No credit cards. Map** p89 B1 ❽
Starck bathroom fittings and Le Corbusier furniture contrast with the period features in this lovely 18th-century mansion, now a *chambre d'hôte*. Breakfast is served on the roof terrace in summer, with superb views over Avignon and the Palais des Papes.

★ Lumani

37 Rempart St-Lazare (04.90.82.94.11/
www.avignon-lumani.com). Closed mid Nov-mid
Dec, Jan, Feb. **Rates** €90-€130 double. **Rooms** 5.
Credit MC, V. **Map** p89 D1 ❾
The owners of this chic guesthouse are artists; Jean is a musician, while Elizabeth paints. Downstairs, three beautiful living rooms open on to a central courtyard, while the five rooms and suites are simple, stylish and immaculately kept.

Le Mas de Capelou

1336 chemin des Poiriers, Ile de la Barthelasse
(04.90.85.81.77/www.masdecapelou.com). **Rates**
€80-€135 double. **Rooms** 3. **No credit cards.**
The Ile de la Barthelasse is a welcome green lung for Avignon in the sultry months, and this *chambre d'hôte* is an authentic 17th-century country home. There are two spacious, light-filled rooms and one suite with its own terrace – plus a fabulous pool.
▶ *On a budget? The Ile is also home to the lovely*
Camping du Pont d'Avignon (04.90.80.63.50,
www.camping-avignon.com) and its outdoor pool.

€ Hôtel Le Médiéval

15 rue Petite Saunerie (04.90.86.11.06/www.
hotelmedieval.com). Closed Jan. **Rates** €58-€90
double. **Rooms** 35. **Credit** MC,V. **Map** p89
C2 ❿
A fine 17th-century mansion has been converted into this charming small hotel, with an attractive flower-filled courtyard and impressive sweeping staircase. Some of the simply furnished rooms are studios, which include a useful kitchenette for longer stays.

★ € Hôtel Mignon

12 rue Joseph Vernet (04.90.82.17.30/www.hotel-
mignon.com). **Rates** €59-€72 double. **Rooms** 16.
Credit AmEx, MC, V. **Map** p89 B2 ⓫

Le Limas.

A sweet little hotel on a fashionable street, the Mignon offers small but good-value rooms and lovely welcoming staff. The breakfast room is so small that, to cater for the overspill, some lucky volunteers get breakfast in bed.

Hôtel de la Mirande
4 pl de la Mirande (04.90.14.20.20/www.la-mirande.fr). **Rates** €310-€540 double. **Rooms** 20. **Credit** AmEx, DC, MC, V. **Map** p89 C2 ⑫
Aubusson tapestries, antique furniture, Pierre Frey fabrics and Venetian chandeliers transport you back in time at this 18th-century cardinals' palace, although 21st-century luxuries abound. The restaurant, La Mirande, is highly regarded (*see p95*).

€ Hôtel du Parc
18 rue Agricol Perdiguier (04.90.82.71.55/http://perso.modulonet.fr/hoduparc). **Rates** €36-€47 double. **Rooms** 14. **Credit** MC, V. **Map** p89 C3 ⑬
A few doors up from the Colbert, the Parc's balconies cascade with greenery and offer views of flower-filled place Agricol Perdiguier. The rustic, stone-walled interior is comfortable and clean, but there are no 'distracting' TVs in the rooms.

Villa Agapé
13 rue St-Agricol (04.90.85.21.92/www.villa-agape.com). **Rates** €100-€180 double. **Rooms** 3. **No credit cards. Map** p89 B2 ⑭
This neatly decorated townhouse has the enormous advantage of a small private swimming pool and terrace, which is almost unheard of within the city

walls. Its owner, Madame de La Pommeraye, extends a charming welcome to her house guests.

RESOURCES

Hospital
Hôpital Général Henri Duffaut *305 rue Raoul Follereau (04.32.75.33.33).*

Police station
Commissariat Central *bd St-Roch (04.90.16.81.00).*

Post office
La Poste *cours Président Kennedy (04.90.27. 78.00).* **Open** 8am-7pm Mon-Fri; 8am-noon Sat.

Tourist information
Avignon Office de Tourisme *41 cours Jean Jaurès, Avignon (04.32.74.32.74/www.ot-avignon.fr).* **Open** *Apr-June, Aug-Oct* 9am-6pm Mon-Sat; 10am-5pm Sun. *July* 9am-7pm Mon-Sat; 10am-5pm Sun. *Nov-Mar* 9am-6pm Mon-Fri; 9am-5pm Sat; 10am-noon Sun.

VILLENEUVE-LES-AVIGNON

Villeneuve-lès-Avignon may be just a short bus trip across the Rhône, but the atmosphere couldn't be more different. In torrid weather the town provides a haven of peace after the bustle of Avignon, dotted with 13th-century homes for visiting cardinals, and a handful of sights.

This small settlement came into its own in 1307, when King Philippe le Bel decided it was a prime location for keeping an eye on papal goings-on across the river. A heavily fortified 'new town' (hence Villeneuve) sprang up, plus a watchtower, the **Tour Philippe le Bel**, that grew higher as Avignon became more powerful. Energetic souls can climb to the top of this defensive tower, which stood at the end of the pont St-Bénézet.

Fine views also abound from the massive ramparts of the 14th-century **Fort St-André**, inside which are the remains of the **Abbaye St-André**. Bewitching terraced gardens lead to a tiny Romanesque chapel, a ruined 13th-century church and a touching graveyard with sarcophagi laid out like beds. Below the fort, the **Chartreuse du Val de Bénédiction** was once the largest Carthusian monastery in France. The charterhouse has been painstakingly restored, removing all signs of the depredations suffered during the Revolution when, to add insult to injury, the tomb of Pope Innocent VI, who founded the monastery in 1352, was turned into a white marble rabbit hutch. There are monks' cells resembling little terraced cottages, as well as a laundry, kitchen, prisons and a herb garden. A small chapel off the cloître du Cimetière (an enchanting open-air theatre venue during the festival) has exquisite frescoes by Matteo Giovanetti. 'Chocolat' guided tours on winter Sundays culminate in a fireside tea of hot chocolate and cake. The Chartreuse acts as a state-funded centre for playwrights, whose recorded voices can be heard echoing through the buildings, reading the fruits of their labours.

The **Musée Pierre de Luxembourg** is a former cardinal's residence that is filled with four floors of art, including a delicately carved ivory Virgin and Child and 16th- and 17th-century religious paintings by Mignard and de Champaigne. The highlight is Enguerrand Quarton's extraordinary *Coronation of the Virgin* (1453-54). The entire medieval world view is represented in the painting's detailed landscape and depiction of human activity.

Just south of the museum, the 14th-century **Collégiale Notre-Dame** has works by Mignard and Levieux, a lavish 18th-century altarpiece and a copy of Enguerrand Quarton's *Pietà* (the original is in the Louvre). Market day in Villeneuve is Thursday; there's also a flea market on Saturdays.

★ Chartreuse du Val de Bénédiction

58 rue de la République (04.90.15.24.24/ www.chartreuse.org). **Open** *Apr-Sept* 9.30am-6pm daily. *Oct-Mar* 9.30am-5pm Mon-Fri; 10am-5pm Sat, Sun. **Admission** €6.50; €4.50 reductions; free under-18s. **Credit** AmEx, DC, MC, V.

FREE Collégiale Notre-Dame

pl du Chapitre (04.90.25.61.33). **Open** *Apr-Sept* 10am-12.30pm, 2-6.30pm daily. *Oct-Mar* 10am-noon, 2-5pm daily. **Admission** free.

AVIGNON & THE VAUCLUSE

Abbaye St-André.

Fort St-André & Abbaye St-André
*montée du Fort (fort 04.90.25.45.35/abbey
04.90.25.55.95).* **Open** *Fort* mid May-Sept
10am-1pm, 2-6pm daily. Oct-mid May 10am-1pm,
2-5pm daily. *Gardens* Apr-Sept 10am-12.30pm,
2-6pm Tue-Sun. Oct-Mar 10am-12.30pm, 2-5pm
Tue-Sun. *Abbey* by appointment. **Admission**
Fort €5; €3.50 reductions; free under-18s. *Abbey
& gardens* €5; free under-13s. **No credit cards**.

Musée Pierre de Luxembourg
3 rue de la République (04.90.27.49.66). **Open**
Apr-Sept 10am-12.30pm, 3-7pm daily. *Oct-Mar*
10am-noon, 2-5.30pm Tue-Sun. Closed Feb.
Admission €3; €2 reductions; free under-18s.
No credit cards.

Tour Philippe le Bel
rue Montée de la Tour (04.32.70.08.57).
Open *Apr-mid June* 10am-12.30pm, 2.30-
6.30pm Tue-Sat. *Mid June-Sept* 10am-12.30pm,
1.30-7pm daily. *Oct-Mar* 10am-noon, 2-5pm
Tue-Sun. Closed Feb & Mon mid Sept-mid June.
Admission €2; €1.50 reductions; free under-18s.
No credit cards.

Where to stay & eat

Villeneuve's hotels absorb the overflow from
the Avignon festival, but are also worth
considering in their own right. The luxury
option is **Le Prieuré** (7 pl du Chapitre,
04.90.15.90.15, www.leprieure.fr, closed Jan,
€205-€295 double), an exquisitely restored
14th-century archbishop's palace with a library,
garden, pool and gourmet restaurant (menus
€45-€92, closed Mon Sept-June). Almost as
elegant is **La Magnaneraie** (37 rue Camp
de Bataille, 04.90.25.11.11, www.hostellerie-
la-magnaneraie.com, closed Jan, €115-€245
double, menus €26 lunch, €33-€80 dinner), with
smart modern rooms in a 15th-century building,
complete with a leafy garden, pool and an
excellent restaurant. A more intimate choice
is the 17th-century **Hôtel de l'Atelier** (5 rue
de la Foire, 04.90.25.01.84, www.hoteldelatelier.
com, closed Jan, €56-€109 double), an airy,
modern-rustic guesthouse with a delightful
breakfast terrace.

Villeneuve also has a few upmarket *chambres
d'hôtes*, notably the elegant **La Vigne** (28
rue de la Monnaie, 04.90.89.50.31, €77-€93
double) and **Les Jardins de la Livrée** (4bis
rue Camp de Bataille, 04.90.26.05.05, www.la-
livree.oxatis.com, €60-€90 double), which has
a swimming pool and four simple rooms.

Under the arcades in the town centre,
Aubertin (1 rue de l'Hôpital, 04.90.25.94.84,
closed Mon, Sun & last 2wks Aug, menus €35-
€49) is one of Villeneuve's leading restaurants,
offering creative regional cuisine by celebrated

chef Jean-Claude Aubertin. Another popular
choice is the more traditional **La Banaste** (28
rue de la République, 04.90.25.64.20, closed
lunch & Thur except July-Aug, menus €28-€46).

Resources

Tourist information
Villeneuve Office du Tourisme *1 pl
Charles David, Villeneuve-lès-Avignon (04.90.
25.61.33/www.villeneuvelesavignon.fr/tourisme).*
Open *Sept-June* 9am-12.30pm, 2-6pm Mon-Sat.
July 10am-7pm Mon-Fri; 10am-1pm, 2.30-7pm Sat,
Sun. *Aug* 9am-12.30pm, 2-6pm daily.

GETTING THERE & AROUND
By air
Caumont-Avignon (www.avignon.aeroport.fr)
airport is 8km outside the city. Flights go to
London City airport via Paris Orly; there are
about 20 buses a day to the centre from nearby
Lycée Agricole.

By bus
The main **bus station** is on av Montclar
(04.90.82.07.35), next to the Centre Ville train
station; buses run from Avignon to Aix, Arles,
Carpentras, Cavaillon, l'Isle-sur-la-Sorgue, Nîmes
and Orange, or further afield to Marseille, Nice
and Cannes. Town buses and services to the TGV
station are run by **TCRA** (04.32.74.18.32, www.
tcra.fr). To get from Avignon to Villeneuve, take
the No.11 or the summer Bâteau Bus from allée
de l'Oulle.

By car
Coming south, take the A7 autoroute; from the
Perpignan/Montpellier direction take the A9,
exiting at Avignon nord or sud. When leaving the
town be sure to go towards the correct motorway.

By taxi
If you're in Avignon, contact **Taxis Radio
Avignonnais** (place Pie, 04.90.82.20.20). Long
waits are common during the festival.

By train
Avignon is at the junction of the Paris–Marseille
and Paris–Montpellier lines. The **Gare Centre
Ville** has frequent links to Arles, Nîmes, Orange,
Toulon and Carcassonne. The **Gare TGV**
(08.92.35.35.35, www.tgv.com) is 4km south
of Avignon. A bus service (*navette*) leaves from
the station at the arrival of each train, taking
passengers to the Gare Centre Ville, and leaves
from the centre for the Gare TGV every 15mins.
From July to September, a **Eurostar** (www.
eurostar.com) service travels direct from London
to Avignon in 6hrs 30mins. At other times of the
year you must change in Lille or Paris.

Orange & Around

Wine, Romans and song: a feast for the senses.

A small town with a big Roman past and quite a reputation in the opera world, monumental **Orange** nestles among some of the finest vineyards in France.

To the west, the mighty River Rhône is spanned by the seemingly endless arches of the ancient **Pont-St-Esprit** and the bustling market town of **Bagnols-sur-Cèze**; there's more wine to the south in the famous **Châteauneuf-du-Pape**, surrounded by sweeping views and carefully-tended vineyards that stretch enticingly into the distance. This is a region of France where the grape is king, and the opportunities to sample the local wines are many and varied.

ORANGE

For opera fans, Orange is synonymous with the annual Chorégies d'Orange festival, when the great Roman amphitheatre comes alive with the greatest voices in the world. The monumental theatre may initially seem out of proportion with the modestly sized town, but the Roman city of Arausio, founded in 35 BC, was four times as large as Orange is today.

Declining sharply in the Dark Ages, the town's fortunes picked up in the 12th century, as an enclave governed by troubadour-prince Raimbaut d'Orange. In 1530, it passed to a branch of the German House of Nassau, and gave its name to Nassau's Dutch principality 14 years later. Thereafter, Orange became a Protestant buzzword, finding its way into Ulster's Orange Order and the Orange Free State, and the town attracted Protestant refugees from across Provence during the Wars of Religion.

The Nassaus clung on to their little piece of France, and in 1622 Maurice de Nassau built an impressive chateau and fortifications. Sadly, he used stones from the Roman monuments that hadn't already been destroyed by barbarians, and only the Arc de Triomphe and the Théâtre Antique survived the pillage. In 1673, Louis XIV ordered the destruction of the chateau; in 1713, the Treaty of Utrecht finally gave the principality to France.

Geographically and emotionally, the magnificent **Théâtre Antique** dominates the town. What sets it apart from other Roman theatres is the unrivalled state of preservation of its stage wall, a sandstone screen 36 metres (118 feet) high that Louis XIV referred to as 'the finest wall in my kingdom'. In its heyday, the amphitheatre hosted everything from political meetings to sporting events, but in the fourth century it was abandoned. It wasn't until the 19th century that restoration began, and the spectacular **Chorégies d'Orange** (*see p45* **Hitting a High Note**) was born. Seats sell out months ahead, so forward planning is key.

The new glass and steel awning above the stage is not the architectural sacrilege that some had feared, and provides relatively discreet protection to the wall at no cost to the theatre's astonishing acoustics. In June, **Orange se Met au Jazz** (call the tourist office; *see p104*) offers a salient contrast to the Chorégies, with amateur musicians shaking up the Roman stones.

In a 17th-century building opposite the theatre's main entrance, the **Musée Municipal** houses a collection of Roman artefacts, including a unique series of cadastres. These marble tablets map the streets, administrative divisions and geography of the Orange region over the course of three successive Roman surveys. On the top floor is an unexpected curiosity: a selection of post-Impressionist paintings by Welsh artist Frank Brangwyn.

The traditional printed cotton cloth known as *indiennes* is celebrated in a series of paintings by 18th-century artist GM Rossetti, while modern-day *indiennes* can be tracked down next door at **La Provençale** (5 pl Sylvain, 04.90.51.58.86). There's a Thursday morning market, and top butcher **Au Charolais** (4 rue Grande Fusterie, 04.90.34.13.09) has a tempting selection of tarts and charcuterie for picnics; buy cakes at the **Pâtisserie Blaise** (3 rue de la République, 04.90.34.06.23), founded in 1878.

On top of the hill of St-Eutrope is a pleasant park, home to the ruins of Maurice de Nassau's chateau and the open-air **Piscine des Cèdres** (04.90.51.38.68, open July & Aug 10am-7pm daily) pool – a delight during the dry, dusty summers. At other times of the year, cool off in the covered **Plein Ciel** (chemin Queyradel, 04.90.51.38.11, open Sept-end June daily).

The old town, in front of the Roman theatre, is a tight knot of twisting streets. Although it provides little architectural competition for the towering classical monuments, the once-scruffy area is being sympathetically restored and has smartened up considerably in recent years. With its fine Romanesque porch, the cathedral of **Notre-Dame-de-Nazareth** is worth a look, and there are plenty of attractive, shady squares.

On the northern edge of town, the **Arc de Triomphe** is Orange's other great Roman monument. The triumphal arch spans the former Via Agrippa, which linked Lyon to Arles. Built in 20 BC, it's the third largest arch of its kind in the world; the north side is a riot of carving. Just out of town is the **Palais du Vin** (A7, exit 22, 04.90.11.50.00), where you can buy wine from over 150 independent producers.

★ Théâtre Antique/ Musée Municipal

rue Madeleine Roch (04.90.51.17.60/www. theatreantique.com). **Open** *Mar, Oct* 9.30am-5.30pm daily. *Apr, May, Sept* 9am-6pm daily. *June-Aug* 9am-7pm daily. *Nov-Feb* 9.30am-4.30pm daily. **Admission** €7.70; €5.90 reductions; free under-7s. **Credit** MC, V.

Where to stay & eat

The most comfortable hotel in the town centre is the **Hôtel Arène Kulm** (pl de Langes, 04.90.11.40.40, www.hotel-arene.fr, double €74-€140); its 35 air-conditioned rooms are set on a paved square. Pretty in pink on the edge of the arena, the **Hôtel St-Jean** (1 cours Pourtoules,

---

INSIDE TRACK
THE HOT TICKET

Orange may officially be the hottest town in France, but if you manage to score a ticket for the **Chorégies d'Orange**, remember that the biting chill of the Mistral can creep in towards midnight: take some extra layers or a rug.

04.90.51.15.16, www.hotelsaint-jean.com, double €55-€110) is an attractive budget choice, as is the funky **Herbier d'Orange** (8 pl aux Herbes, 04.90.34.09.23, www.lherbierdorange.com, double €37-€50). There's also the **Saint Florent** (4 rue du Mazeau, 04.90.34.18.53, www.hotel saintflorent.com, double €40-€77) – though its modern art is an acquired taste. If a pool and sophisticated home comforts appeal, there are two charming *chambres d'hôtes*: **Justin de Provence** (chemin Marcadier, 04.90.69.57.94, www.justin-de-provence.com, double €110-€195) and **Villa Aurenjo** (121 rue François Chambovet, 04.90.11.10.00, www.villa-aurenjo.com, double €60-€180).

Orange finally got an interesting modern bistro with the opening of **Alons'O Bistro** (58 cours Aristide Briand, 04.90.29.69.27, closed Thur & Sat lunch, menus €17-€25), run by acclaimed chef Pascal Alonso of the superb **Pré du Moulin** (04.90.70.14.55, www.predumoulin. com, closed Feb, Mon & Tue lunch, mains €35-€45, menus €39-€79) in nearby Sérignan-du-Comtat. Alternatively, **Parvis** (55 cours Portoules, 04.90.34.82.00, menus €17-€42) serves imaginative food made with local produce in its cool, beamed dining room.

In the centre of town, **Le Forum** (3 rue du Mazeau, 04.90.34.01.09, menus €18-€36) has a classical menu and a solid reputation. Out of season, the **Brasserie le Palace** (7 rue de la République, 04.90.34.13.51, menus €20) is the

L'Arc de Triomphe.

locals' favourite diner, with an €8 *plat du jour*, but during the Chorégies, the **Festival Café** (5 pl de la République, 04.90.34.65.58, mains €10) provides one of the best pre-opera menus. For a cup of tea or a light meal, try the charming **Côté Jardin** (23 rue Victor Hugo, 04.90.30.28.36, mains €11); hillside **La Cantina** (60 montée Julia Barthet, 04.90.30.92.84, mains €10, menu €16) is a great place for pizza.

The nearby village of Uchaux is home to the exclusive **Château de Massillan** (chemin Hauteville, 04.90.40.64.51, www.chateau-de-massillan.com, closed Nov-Mar, double €185-€450), which has a fine restaurant and pool. For simpler tastes, there's *chambres d'hôte* **Les Convenents** (04.90.40.65.64, www.les convenents.com, double €95-€105) and two excellent restaurants: the upmarket **Côté Sud** (rte d'Orange, 04.90.40.66.08, www.restaurant cotesud.com, closed Wed May-Sept, Mon & Tue evening Oct-Apr & mid Dec-mid Jan, menus €24-€47) and the less elaborate **Le Temps de Vivre** (Les Farjons, 04.90.40.66.00, menu €30), with an inviting terrace and locally based fare.

Resources

Tourist information

Office de Tourisme *5 cours Aristide Briand, Orange (04.90.70.88/www.otorange.fr)*. **Open** *Apr-June* 9am-6.30pm Mon-Sat; 10am-1pm, 2-6.30pm Sun. *July-Aug* 9am-7.30pm Mon-Sat; 10am-1pm, 2-7pm Sun. *Oct, Nov-Mar* 10am-1pm, 2-5pm Mon-Sat.

CHATEAUNEUF-DU-PAPE

The road from Orange to Châteauneuf-du-Pape, the town that gives its name to the potent papal wine, is one of the most spectacular in the region. Once you get to Châteauneuf itself, you'll find offers to taste and buy are insistent; the place is dominated by wine shops, and the tourist office has a comprehensive list of vineyards offering visits that involve more than simply sipping and spending. For our recommendations, *see p32*. Another good strategy is to pick a chateau whose wine you've enjoyed in a local restaurant, and seek it out.

The original vineyards were planted at the behest of the Avignon popes, who summered here in the 14th-century castle built by wine-lover John XXII. The stringent rules regarding yield and grape varieties that were laid down in 1923 proved to be a far-sighted blueprint for France's *appellation d'origine contrôlée* regulations, sealing the reputation of the local red wine – a meticulous blend of at least eight varieties, dominated by grenache.

The alluvial soil is sprinkled with heat-absorbing pebbles, which retain the warmth of the sun; this, along with the widely spaced vines and cloud-dispersing Mistral, contributes to the high alcoholic content and complex nose of the wine, more at home with a winter stew than a summer salad. More recently, white Châteauneuf-du-Pape (with a minimum of five grapes) has made a name for itself, though tight regulations have no truck with fashionable rosé.

Châteauneuf-du-Pape.

Though low on sights, Châteauneuf-du-Pape is agreeably smart and tastefully restored, with a bustling centre and a market on Friday morning. Not surprisingly, there are several wine events, notably the Fête des Vignerons on 25 April, when the new wine is tasted, and the pseudo-medieval Fête de la Véraison on the first weekend in August, which marks the moment when the grapes begin to colour.

Little remains of the Château des Papes itself, but the views across the vineyards and up to the Mont Ventoux are superb. One winemaker, Père Anselme, had the bright idea of opening a museum to celebrate the area's winemaking tradition, the **Musée du Vin**. The baskets, pruners and suchlike are interesting enough, but the shop and tasting room do limit your choice of winemaker.

FREE Musée du Vin

Le Clos (04.90.83.70.07/www.brotte.com). **Open** *July-Sept* 9am-1pm, 2-7pm daily. *Oct-June* 9am-noon, 2-6pm daily. **Admission** free.

Where to stay & eat

Unpretentious **La Garbure** (3 rue Joseph Ducos, 04.90.83.75.08, www.la-garbure.com, closed Mon & Sun Nov-Apr, 1wk Jan, double €59-€82, menus €16 lunch, €23-€45 dinner) provides simple accommodation on the main street; a little further along is **Le Pistou** (15 rue Joseph Ducos 04.90.83.71.75, mains €9-€14, menus €16-€45), serving enormous salads in summer as well as its namesake pesto soup.

In the centre of town, **La Mère Germaine** (3 rue du Commandant Lemaître, 04.90.83.54.37, www.lameregermaine.com, double €50-€78, menus €16-€105) offers an extravagant seven-course pontifical meal for €105, with a different wine accompanying every course; more modest (and far cheaper) menus are also offered.

For one of the loveliest views in town, the unsophisticated **Verger des Papes** (4 rue du Château, 04.90.83.50.40, www.vergerdespapes. com, menus €20 lunch, €29 dinner) has a splendid terrace up by the chateau; you can also buy wines from its cellar.

For something more elaborate, the classy **Château des Fines Roches** (rte de Sorgues, 04.90.83.70.23, www.chateaufinesroches.com, double €119-€309, menus €25-€35 lunch, €38-€85 dinner), a 19th-century pile set in a vineyard, has a good – though rather pricey – restaurant. In the heart of the vineyards, **La Sommellerie** (rte de Roquemaure, 04.90.83.50.00, www.la-sommellerie.fr, closed Jan, double €74-€113, menus €30 lunch, €45-€62 dinner) combines an inspired regional restaurant and extremely comfortable rooms; outside, there's a good-sized pool.

Resources

Tourist information

Office de Tourisme *pl Portail, Châteauneuf-du-Pape (04.90.83.71.08/www.ccpro.fr).* **Open** *July, Aug* 9.30am-7pm Mon-Sat; 10am-1pm, 2-6pm Sun. *Sept-June* 9.30am-12.30pm, 2-6pm Mon-Sat.

PONT-ST-ESPRIT & BAGNOLS-SUR-CEZE

The 19 arches of the 'Bridge of the Holy Spirit', spanning the Rhône as it enters Provence, are spectacular even 700 years after they were built. The town of **Pont-St-Esprit** itself was badly bombed in World War II and then, in 1951, found itself at the centre of a scandal when its bread was mysteriously poisoned. But the Spiripontains, as the inhabitants are sweetly called, have put this dark episode behind them, and the rather gloomy town comes alive for its Saturday morning market.

The religious paintings and artefacts of the **Musée d'Art Sacré du Gard** are displayed in the *maison des chevaliers*, a well-preserved merchant's house inhabited by the Piolenc family for six centuries; it's worth a look even if you're not agog to see the collection. The works of 20th-century painter Benn, whose mysterious spirituality is particularly at home here, are currently displayed in the **Musée Paul Raymond**, formerly the grand town hall.

Nearby **Bagnols-sur-Cèze** has one of the best markets in the area (every Wednesday), its stalls laden with olive oil, wine, garlic, cheese and charcuterie. While shopping, check out rue Crémieux, which runs up to the arcaded place Mallet. The street is lined with fine 16th- to 18th-century townhouses; admire the riotous gargoyles at No.15 and browse the organic food shop housed in its courtyard.

On the second floor of the town hall, a 17th-century mansion on place Mallet, is the town's big cultural draw: the **Musée Albert André**. In 1923, a fire destroyed the museum's patchy and parochial collection of daubs, and painter Albert André, then its curator, launched an appeal (with the help of his friend Renoir) to the artists of France to fill the empty walls. They responded in force, and the museum is a snapshot of early 20th-century figurative art, with works by Renoir, Signac, Bonnard, Matisse and Gauguin. Samples of the town's rich archaeological finds, Celtic-Ligurian and Gallo-Roman, are housed in the **Musée d'Archéologie Léon Alègre**.

Perched above the River Cèze, ten kilometres west of Bagnols, **La Roque-sur-Cèze** is a gorgeous village with a fine Romanesque church, approached by an ancient single-track bridge. Downstream, the Cèze cuts through limestone to form the spectacular **Cascade de Sautadet** – though bathers should beware, as this stretch of the river is treacherous. North of La Roque, in the middle of a romantic oak forest, is the 13th-century **Chartreuse de Valbonne** monastery, which produces its own Côtes du Rhône wine. You can visit the richly decorated baroque church and the cloisters, or stay in its basic monastic accommodation.

Chartreuse de Valbonne

St-Paulet-de-Caisson (04.66.90.41.24/vineyard 04.66.90.41.00/www.chartreusedevalbonne.com). **Open** *May-Aug* 10am-1pm, 1.30-7pm daily. *Sept-Apr* 10am-noon, 1.30-5.30pm daily. **Admission** €5; €2.50 reductions; free under-10s. **Credit** AmEx, DC, MC, V.

★ FREE Musée Albert André

pl Mallet, Bagnols (04.66.50.50.56). **Open** 10am-noon, 2-6pm Tue-Sun. Closed Feb. **Admission** free.

FREE Musée d'Archéologie Léon Alègre

24 av Paul Langevin, Bagnols (04.66.89.74.00). **Open** 10am-noon, 2-6pm Tue, Thur, Fri. Closed Feb. **Admission** free.

FREE Musée d'Art Sacré du Gard

2 rue St-Jacques, Pont-St-Esprit (04.66.39.17.61). **Open** *July* 10am-7pm Tue-Sun. *Aug-June* 10am-noon, 2-6pm Tue-Sun. Closed Feb. **Admission** free.

FREE Musée Paul Raymond

pl de l'Hôtel de Ville, Pont-St-Esprit (04.66.39.09.98). **Open** *June-Sept* 10am-noon, 3pm-7pm Tue-Sun. *Oct-May* 10am-noon, 2pm-6pm Wed, Thur, Sun. Closed Feb. **Admission** free.

Where to stay & eat

In Pont-St-Esprit, the **Auberge Provençale** (av du Général-de-Gaulle, 04.66.39.08.79, double €35, hotel & restaurant closed Sun, menus €10-€23) has very simple accommodation and a popular restaurant. Good value provençal fare is served at **Lou Recati** (6 rue Jean-Jacques, 04.66.90.73.01, closed Mon & Sun, menus €20-€30). Just outside town is the charming *chambre d'hôte* **Le Mas Canet** (chemin de Gavanon, St-Paulet de Caisson, 04.66.39.25.96, www.mascanet.com, double €65).

A few kilometres west of Bagnols is the luxurious **Château de Montcaud** (rte d'Alès Combe, Sabran, 04.66.89.60.60, www.chateau-de-montcaud.com, closed Nov-mid Apr, double €180-€370, restaurant closed lunch, mains €25-

€32, menus €78-€88, bistro closed Sat & Sun, mains €11-€17). Its restaurant, Les Jardins de Montcaud, offers sophisticated country cooking in a stone *mas*; the charming bistro has a simpler menu. The **Château du Val de Cèze** (69 rte d'Avignon, 04.66.89.61.26, www.sud-provence.com, double €99) has a brace of comfortable bungalows in its grounds.

The best bet in the centre of Bagnols is the **Hotel-Bar des Sports** (3 pl Jean Jaurès, 04.66.89.61.68, www.hotel-des-sports.fr, double €49), which has tidy rooms above a popular bar; place Mallet has several casual restaurants with tables dotted around the square.

At La Roque-sur-Cèze, **Le Mas du Bélier** (rte de St-Laurent, 04.66.82.21.39, www.mas dubelier.com, closed Mon & Tue Oct-Mar, menus €13-€28) is a popular waterside inn with simple cuisine.

Resources

Tourist information

Bagnols-sur-Cèze Office de Tourisme
Espace St-Gilles, av Léon Blum, Bagnols-sur-Cèze (04.66.89.54.61/www.ot-bagnolssurceze.com). **Open** *June-Sept* 9am-7pm Mon-Fri; 10am-1pm Sat. *Oct-May* 9am-6pm Mon-Fri; 10am-1pm Sat.
Pont-St-Esprit Office de Tourisme
Résidence Welcome, 1 av Kennedy, Pont-St-Esprit (04.66.39.44.45/www.ot-pont-saint-esprit.fr). **Open** *June-Sept* 9am-7pm Mon-Sat; 9.30am-12.30pm Sun. *Sept-May* 9am-6pm Mon-Fri; 9am-12.30pm Sat.

GETTING THERE & AROUND

By bus

Rapides du Sud-Est (04.90.34.15.59) runs 12 buses between Avignon and Orange daily except Sun. **Cars Auran** (04.66.39.10.40, www.carauran.fr) runs daily buses between Avignon, Pont-St-Esprit and Bagnols-sur-Cèze. **Sotra Ginaux** (04.75.39.40.22) runs daily buses from Mon to Fri (less frequent in the school holidays) between Orange and Pont-St-Esprit, from Avignon to Aubernas via Pont-St-Esprit, and from Aubernas to Bagnols.

By car

Orange (A7, exit 21) is 30km (19 miles) north of Avignon. For Pont-St-Esprit and Bagnols-sur-Cèze take exit 19 off the A7, and then the N86. For Châteauneuf-du-Pape, take the D68 from Orange or N7 and D17 from Avignon.

By train

Orange station (av Frédéric Mistral, 04.90.11.88.00) is on the main Paris–Avignon–Marseille line. A few TGVs stop here, making Paris–Orange a useful possibility.

AVIGNON & THE VAUCLUSE

Carpentras
& Mont Ventoux

Fertile plains meet soaring hills in the verdant Vaucluse.

The truffle heartland of Provence, **Carpentras** is set on a fertile plain, sheltered from the worst of the Mistral's rage. It's another story on the windswept heights of the gigantic **Mont Ventoux**, which looms over the landscape and presents a gruelling challenge to intrepid cyclists. To the east lie its foothills, the dramatic, jagged-edged **Dentelles de Montmirail**.

Stretching to the north are some of the most prestigious vineyards in France, and the charming town of **Vaison-la-Romaine**; set on the banks of the River Ouvèze, it's best known for its impressive Roman remains.

CARPENTRAS

During the Middle Ages, Carpentras came to prominence as the capital of the Comtat Venaissin, a countrified Vatican City embedded in France. It remained under papal control for centuries, only becoming part of France after the Revolution. These days it's a busy town, with traffic roaring along its ring road past the 14th-century city gate, the **Porte d'Orange** – a far cry from the two-wheeled chariots from which the town takes its name.

The atmospheric **Musée Sobirats**, an 18th-century townhouse bequeathed to Carpentras by pre-Revolutionary nobleman Armans de Châteauvieux, has become a decorative arts depot filled with a jumble of Marseille pottery, Aubusson tapestries and Louis XV furniture, all donated by local residents. Up the road, the lofty 17th-century **Chapelle du Collège** (rue du Collège, 04.90.60.22.36) puts local modern art on the high altar. Meanwhile, the concierge of the **Musée Comtadin-Duplessis** guards the region's customs and history with the world's largest key, unlocking primitive local paintings and decoy bird-calls made by Carpentras son Théodore Raymond. Five kilometres away in St-Didier, his great-grandson continues to dupe owls and cuckoos at his **Eco-Musée** (pl Neuve, 04.90.66.13.13, www.appeaux-raymond.com).

Topped by an early 20th-century bell tower, the mainly 15th-century **Cathédrale St-Siffrein** (pl St-Siffrein, closed Mon, Sun) is a hotchpotch of styles and epochs. Its Gothic-style southern door is known as the Porte des Juifs: when Philippe le Bel expelled the Jews from France, many fled to the papal-controlled Comtat Venaissin, only to be bullied into Catholic baptism. It's said they passed through this door on their way to conversion; note the odd carving of rats gnawing on a globe above the door. Poky chapels line the dark, baroque interior towards the resplendent Treasury, its entrance adorned with the 'Saint Mors' relic – a horse bit made of two nails taken from the Cross, a symbol featured in the town's crest since the 13th century. Behind the cathedral is a Roman triumphal arch, which lacks the grandeur of its big brother in Orange but has an interesting carving of chained prisoners on its eastern side.

Next door, the **Palais de Justice** occupies the former bishop's palace, notable for its 17th-century Romanelli frescoes (the tourist office can arrange visits, *see p109*). An open-air theatre is erected here in the last fortnight of July for Les Estivales, a popular music and theatre festival. From here, you can explore the smart boutiques of the passage Boyer, built in the 19th century and inspired by Paris's covered thoroughfares.

Opposite the Hôtel de Ville is the oldest **Synagogue** to have survived in France. It dates from the 14th century, though it was largely rebuilt in the 18th. The main room is decorated in discreet 18th-century baroque style, but the most interesting part of the building is the lower floor, which has two ovens for baking unleavened bread, a *piscina* for women's purification rites and a prayer room dedicated to Jerusalem (men must wear a *copal*). Today, the Jewish community is considerably depleted, although its culture remains strong. Don't miss the Festival de Musiques Juives in early August, held in the Synagogue and the inner courtyard of the Hôtel-Dieu.

South of the centre, the **Hôtel-Dieu** is a splendid 18th-century hospital. Its hand-painted dispensary, open in summer, is a mesmerising collection of earthenware jars, glass bottles and drawers promising absinthe, opium poppies and dragon's blood. Its baroque chapel contains the tomb of Bishop d'Inguimbert, the hospital's founder and benefactor of many of the town's museums. With the medical services now trolleyed out of town, it's promised that the building will be transformed into a cultural centre, which will house the town's museum collections as well as a theatre.

Foodies should visit on the first Sunday of February for the **Fête de la Truffe** (http://melano.free.fr), when the crop of local 'black diamonds' is revealed by the *rabassiers* (truffle gatherers). A less costly local delicacy is the town's famous *berlingot*, a tetrahedral humbug. Founded in 1946, the **Confiserie du Mont Ventoux** is the last traditional *berlingot* workshop, which gives sugary demonstrations in its kitchen, by appointment (1184 av Dwight Eisenhower, 04.90.63.05.25, www.berlingot.net). To stock up on a wider range of regional delights, visit the well-stocked Tendance Saveurs (7 rue des Halles, 04.90.40.00.73, www.tendancesaveurs.com).

Musée Comtadin-Duplessis

234 bd Albin Durand (04.90.63.04.92). **Open** *Apr-Sept* 10am-noon, 2-6pm Mon, Wed-Sun. *Oct-Mar* by appointment. **Admission** €2 (with Musée Sobirats); free under-12s. **Credit** AmEx, MC, V.

Musée Sobirats

112 rue du Collège (04.90.63.04.92). **Open** *Apr-Sept* 10am-noon, 2-6pm Mon, Wed-Sun. *Oct-Mar* by appointment. **Admission** €2 (with Musée Comtadin-Duplessis); free under-12s. **No credit cards**.

FREE Synagogue

pl de l'Hôtel de Ville (04.90.63.39.97). **Open** 10am-noon, 3-5pm Mon-Thur; 10am-noon, 3-4pm Fri. Closed Jewish holidays. **Admission** free.

Cathédrale St-Siffrein. *See p107*.

Where to stay & eat

Hotels flank the town's western edge, notably the comfortably traditional **Le Comtadin** (65 bd Albin Durand, 04.90.67.75.00, www.le-comtadin.com, double €76-€99); in the centre, try **Le Fiacre** (153 rue Vigne, 04.90.63.03.15, www.hotel-du-fiacre.com, double €57-€90), a characterful *hôtel particulier* with spacious rooms and frescoes.

The hip bistro **Chez Serge** (90 rue Cottier, 04.90.63.21.24, www.chez-serge.com, closed Mon, Sun, menus €14-€26.50) serves the best food in Carpentras. Armenian Serge is one of the most knowledgeable wine men in the area, and his new chef Frédéric Maniet looks set for white and black truffle glory. **La Ciboulette** (30 pl de l'Horloge, 04.90.60.75.00, menus €17-€21) has a spacious courtyard below an ancient belfry, and serves regional specialities.

The fortified hilltop village of Venasque, 12 kilometres south-east of Carpentras, has postcard views of Mont Ventoux and its surrounding vineyards. **La Maison aux Volets Bleus** is a cosy and slightly funky *chambre d'hôte* (pl des Boviers, 04.90.66.03.04, www.maison-volets-bleus.com, closed mid Nov-mid Mar, double €75-€92), while **L'Auberge la Fontaine** (pl de la Fontaine, 04.90.66.02.96, www.auberge-lafontaine.com, closed Wed, menus €20-€38) hosts occasional concerts with dinner and has five minimalist suites (€125).

In Mazan, 15 kilometres from Carpentras, one of the Marquis de Sade's chateaux has become a luxury hotel: the best rooms at the **Château de Mazan** (pl Napoléon, 04.90.69.62.61, www.chateaudemazan.fr, closed Jan, Feb, double €98-€275, menus €42-€48) have their own private gardens. Its restaurant, **L'Ingénue**, has a magical terrace on which to savour Franck Pujol's fine modern cuisine.

Four kilometres south of Carpentras, the village of Monteux has a couple of interesting *chambres d'hôte* **Le Mas des Songes** (1631 impasse du Pérussier, 04.90.65.49.20, www.masdessonges.com, double €160-€200) has high-tech rooms straight out of a colour supplement; the simpler, 17th-century **Mas de l'Estiou** (2362 rte de Bédarrides, 04.90.66.91.83, www.lestiou.com, double €60-€80) serves moreish, homely food for just €23. For more exalted fare, try the **Saule Pleureur** (145 chemin de Beauregard, 04.90.62.01.35, menus €29-€89, closed all Mon, Sat lunch), whose new chef Laurent Azoulay makes his own bread and sources his products with care. After a fine meal here, you could treat yourself to a night at the **Domaine de Bournereau** (579 chemin de la Sorguette, 04.90.62.01.35, www.bournereau.com, double €90-€170), whose rooms are an elegant mix of antique and contemporary.

Resources

Tourist information

Office de Tourisme *97 pl du 25 Août 1944, Carpentras (04.90.63.00.78/www.carpentras-ventoux.com).* **Open** *July, Aug* 9am-1pm, 2-7pm Mon-Sat; 9.30am-1pm Sun. *Sept-June* 9.30-12.30pm, 2-6pm Mon-Sat.

PERNES-LES-FONTAINES

Pernes is known as the 'perle du Comtat', and the town's emblem of a pearl and sun can be seen on one of the town's 40 18th-century fountains, the Fontaine du Cormoran, crowned by a spread-winged cormorant. A stroll around this sleepy town is a rewarding, bucolic affair (the town only comes to life on market days); as a former capital of the Comtat Venaissin, Pernes has a certain miniature grandeur in its town planning, with fortified ramparts and no fewer than 14 important houses.

Cross the river Nesque through the **Porte Notre-Dame**, sole remnant of the 16th-century city walls and home to the chapel of Notre-Dame-des-Grâces. Here, too, is the 11th-century **Eglise Notre-Dame-de-Nazareth**; to visit, contact the tourist office, *see p110*. The tourist office can also arrange visits to the medieval **Tour Ferrande**, whose upper floors boast some well-preserved 13th-century frescoes depicting Charles d'Anjou's crusades. The tower overlooks the fontaine Guillaumin – dubbed the 'fontaine du gigot', thanks to its resemblance to a leg of lamb.

On rue du Donjon, the **Tour de l'Horloge** is all that remains of the chateau of the Counts of Toulouse, who ruled Pernes from 1125 to 1320. The town is also home to the **Maison Fléchier** (pl Fléchier, 04.90.61.31.04, closed Sept, Oct), which displays traditional costumes and locally made *santons* (Christmas crib figures), which you'll see for sale throughout the region. A lively *marché provençal* is held on Saturday, and there's a *marché paysan* on Wednesday nights in July and August.

Where to stay & eat

The **Domaine de la Nesquière** (rte d'Althen, 04.90.62.00.16, www.lanesquiere.com, double €75-€99) is a farm that offers horse riding, comfortable, frilly bedrooms, and a lavender-scented garden. One of the region's best restaurants clings to a rock face in the nearby village of Le Beaucet: **Auberge du Beaucet** (04.90.66.10.82, www.aubergedubeaucet.fr, closed Sun dinner, all Mon, menus €18-€42) has spectacular views from its rooftop terrace, and serves a sophisticated take on local produce, with a sensational array of goat's cheeses.

Four kilometres out of town, **Mas Le Bonoty** (chemin de la Bonoty, 04.90.61.61.09, www.bonoty.com, double €62-€95, menus €22-€55) offers simple rooms but more elaborate food. The goose-led **Dame l'Oie** (56 rue Troubadour Durand, 04.90.61.62.43, closed Mon, lunch Tue, 2wks Feb, menus €16-€29) remains a reliable spot for traditional cuisine, despite a change of ownership, and is a firm favourite with locals.

Resources

Tourist information

Office de Tourisme *pl Gabriel Moutte, Pernes-les-Fontaines (04.90.61.31.04/www.ville-pernes-les-fontaines.fr)*. **Open** *Apr-June, Sept, Oct* 9am-noon, 2-6pm Mon-Fri; 9am-noon, 2-5pm Sat (closed Sat in Oct). *July, Aug* 9am-noon, 2-6.30pm Mon-Fri. *Nov-Mar* 9am-noon, 2-5pm Mon-Fri; 9am-noon Sat.

MONT VENTOUX

The highest point in the Midi (1,909 metres/6,263 feet), **Mont Ventoux** is known as the Géant de Provence ('giant of Provence'). On a clear day you can see all the way to Corsica; Petrarch is considered the father of alpinism for climbing the mountain in 1336 just to admire the view. The lure of the limestone-crowned summit has proved irresistible to walkers and cyclists, and its 20 kilometres (12.5 miles) of pure ascent are the most gruelling stage of the Tour de France. British Olympic cyclist Tom Simpson collapsed and died near the top in the 1967 race, and the

---

Wine Tour Gigondas to Rasteau & beyond

Richard James recommends the pick of the local vineyards.

Lovers of red wine should explore the area around a few of the pretty hilltop wine villages to the east and north-east of Orange, where lush vineyards snuggle up against the jagged Dentelles de Montmirail. You could easily spend a couple of leisurely days touring around Vacqueyras, Gigondas, Séguret, Rasteau and Cairanne, even though the complete stretch is not greater than 20 kilometres (12 miles).

This is serious Côtes du Rhône-Villages country (www.vins-rhone.com), with some villages allowed to put their name on the label after those words, and others with their own separate village AOC. You'll find a fair few growers making spicy, chunky reds from grenache, syrah and mourvèdre to rival Châteauneuf-du-Pape. A little further south is Beaumes-de-Venise, famous for its delicious, sweet fortified Muscats, as well as similarly hearty reds.

Start in Gigondas country (www.gigondas-vin.com), which is easily reached via the charming village of Vacqueyras from the south. Take the D7, then D8 towards La Bégude and, before crossing the river, you'll find Saurel-Chauvet, which encompasses two domaines: **La Bouscatière** and **Le Péage** (quartier la Beaumette, Gigondas, 04.90.70.96.80, www.saurel-chauvet.com). Expect spicy, full-on reds made mostly from old-vine grenache, and using more mourvèdre than most growers in this area.

Head back south on the D8 and take a left turn; they all lead into Gigondas eventually. It's not hard to find Gabriel Meffre's *caveau*, the **Domaine de Longue Toque** (04.90.12.30.21, www.gabriel meffre.com), once you've worked out the one-way streets. Meffre's is quite a big operation, but that doesn't stop it making great examples of the local wines.

Head north from Gigondas, passing through Sablet and on to postcard-pretty Séguret. After admiring its magnificent views, take the winding road out of the village into the hills towards Vaison-la-Romaine, where you'll eventually come to signposted **Domaine de Mourchon** (La Grande Montagne, 04.90.46.70.30, www.domainedemourchon.com), a leading estate set up by friendly Scots couple Walter and Ronnie McKinlay. They produce two impressive reds under the Côtes du Rhône-Villages Séguret AOC, Tradition and Grande Réserve.

Return to Séguret, then go north to the roundabout on the D977, and keep heading for Roaix (you have to cross the river), then follow signs south-west for Rasteau. The **Cave de Rasteau** is located on the main road (rte des Princes d'Orange, Rasteau, 04.90.10.90.10, www.rasteau.com); the front of the old cellar has been converted into a sleek stone and glass space. The range is good, and you must try the signature AOC Rasteau – a heady, port-like red that's great with mature cheeses or chocolate. The estate also organises wine trails and other events.

memorial to him has become a shrine. 'The Ventoux is a god of Evil, to which sacrifices must be made,' wrote the French philosopher Roland Barthes. 'It never forgives weakness and extracts an unfair tribute of suffering.'

Its name suggests wind (*vent*), and the military mast on the summit has been built to resist the fierce onslaught of the Mistral. Just below the summit on the northern face is a small ski resort, **Mont Serein** (chalet d'accueil 04.90.63.42.02). On its lower reaches, though, the mountain is far less hostile. A UNESCO-protected biosphere, it's home to *épeautre* (wild barley), poppies and, of course, Côtes du Ventoux vineyards.

The main D974 summit route forks off from the Vaison–Carpentras road at Malaucène, where the tourist office (*see below*) organises night climbs in summer. Just beyond Malaucène is the Source du Groseau spring, reputedly used by an ancient Celtic cult. The octagonal **Notre-Dame-de-Groseau**, formed by two chapels grafted together, is all that remains of an 11th-century monastery.

The big, bad climb up the mountain is on its western flank from the village of **Bédoin**, home to a fine, Jesuit-style church. **Bédoin Location** (chemin de la Feraille, 04.90.65.94.53, www.bedoin-location.com) hires out bikes and, for €46, takes visitors up in a bus so they can freewheel down. It also marks the start of a four-hour hike (for details ask the tourist office, *see right*); you can stock up on provisions at the market on a Monday. For a scenic warm-up, cut in on the quieter D19, which runs past the remains of a 17th-century aqueduct to the Belvedere du Paty above the hill village of **Crillon-le-Brave**. The gentlest, bluest ascent is east along the D164 from Sault, one of the main centres for lavender production.

Where to stay & eat

The 16th-century **Hostellerie de Crillon-le-Brave** (pl de l'Eglise, 04.90.65.61.61, www.crillonlebrave.com, closed Oct-Mar, double €230-€470, menus €44-€75) is one of the nicest hilltop retreats in Provence, with rooms that combine slick sophistication with provençal warmth. Within walking distance of here, the **Restaurant du Vieux Four** (04.90.12.81.39, closed Mon, lunch Tue-Sat, mid Nov-Mar, menu €27) is an old bakery offering cosy suppers, great views and truffles in season.

On the way to Bédoin, the homely **Moulin d'Antelon** (rte de Bédoin, 04.90.62.44.89, www.moulin-dantelon.com, double €66-€68) makes an ideal base for cyclists; at nearby St-Pierre-de-Vassols, **Les Conils** (04.90.12.79.49, double €60-€70), is a 17th-century *bastide* with simple rooms and a secluded pool. In Bédoin itself, the

good-value **Hôtel L'Escapade** (pl Portail l'Olivier, 04.90.65.60.21, www.lescapade.eu, closed Nov-Feb, double €52-€58) has ten rooms and a smart, welcoming restaurant (menus €14-€25). In the nearby village of Ste-Colombe, **La Garance** (04.90.12.81.00, www.lagarance.fr, double €50-€72) is a friendly old farm with a small pool. Nearby, **Le Guintrand** (04.90.12.82.61, www.leguintrand.com, double €55, menus €14-€22) is a friendly hotel and café, handy for some pre- or post-ascent R&R. Alternatively, push your starting line up Mont Ventoux with a cunning five-kilometre drive to **Le Mas des Vignes** (04.90.65.63.91, closed Mon, Oct-Mar, menus €35-€50), where you can enjoy fine regional food and spectacular views over the Dentelles de Montmirail.

For open-air accommodation, pitch up at the **Camping Municipal** (04.90.64.07.18, closed Oct-Apr, €3.30/person, tent pitch €2.85) above Sault; for more creature comforts, try the **Hostellerie du Val de Sault** (04.90.64.01.41, www.valdesault.com, double €124-€169, menus €39-€92), where you can hire a bike after enjoying Yves Gattechaut's gastronomic food.

Resources

Tourist information
Office de Tourisme *Espace Marie-Louis Gravier, pl du Marché, Bédoin (04.90.65.63.95/*

Mont Ventoux.

www.bedoin.org). **Open** *Mid June-Aug* 9am-12.30pm, 2-6pm Mon-Sat; 9.30am-12.30pm Sun. *Sept-mid June* 9am-12.30pm, 2-6pm Mon-Fri; 9.30am-12.30pm Sat.

LES DENTELLES DE MONTMIRAIL

The foothills of Ventoux are known as the Dentelles de Montmirail. *Dentelles* means lace in French, but the word's make-up includes tooth (*dent*), and the jagged landscape looks more like a dentist's nightmare than a doily. The limestone fangs poke up into the blue provençal sky like the set of a dinosaur movie; this range of photogenic hills is among the most painted, walked and climbed in the South of France. Along the hem of this lacy petticoat is a string of picturesque medieval villages, producing some of the finest wine in France.

Malaucène, on the road that separates the Dentelles from Mont Ventoux, is the jumping-off point for both. It's dominated by the 14th-century fortified church of St-Michel-et-St-Pierre, and has a market on Wednesdays. Set higher up, **Le Crestet** has the most filmic views, spanning the full amphitheatre of Ventoux, the wine valleys and the Baronnies hills. It's a charming spot, with steep alleys threading around an arcaded square, old stone houses and an 11th-century church; the 12th-century castle is closed to the public. Southwards in **Le Barroux**, another ruined 12th-century castle (04.90.62.35.21, closed Nov-Mar) sternly surveys the Vaucluse plain. Saffron once flourished here, before disappearing in the 19th century; it's now being grown again at **L'Aube Safran** (*see p113*).

Cross the Col de la Chaine from Malaucène for the unmissable vine-striped descent towards terraced **Beaumes-de-Venise**, famous for its sweet dessert wine. You can taste the wine at the young *cave* Domaine de la Pigeade (Le Cours, 04.90.62.90.00, www.lapigeade.fr). On the western flank is the tiny village of **Gigondas**, with the Col du Cayron pass towering above it. The village gives its name to the famous grenache-based red wine (*see p110* **Wine Tour**); indeed, this region is dotted with the celebrated medieval wine-producing villages of the Côtes du Rhône. Supermarket offerings will never be the same again once you've sampled a bottle of Sablet, Séguret, Rasteau or Cairanne; Cairanne also has a sense-titillating wine museum, the **Cave de Cairanne** (rte de Bollène, 04.90.30.82.05, www.cairanne.com).

Where to stay & eat

In Malaucène, **Hôtel de Domaine des Tilleuls** (rte de Mont-Ventoux, 04.90.65.22.31, www.hotel-domainedestilleuls.com, double €79-€95) is a useful base for Mont Ventoux and the Dentelles, and has a pool and garden. If you're cycling up Mont Ventoux, try **Les Ecuries du Ventoux** (quartier des Grottes, 04.90.65.29.20, closed Dec-Feb, dorm €14/person), a stable converted into a clean, efficient *gîte d'étape*. For more comfy lodgings, Le Crestet's **Mas d'Hélène** (quartier Chante-Coucou, 04.90.36.39.91, www.lemasd helene.com, closed Jan-Mar, double €55-€112) has soft provençal colours and a stunning pool.

L'Aube Safran (chemin du Patifiage, 04.90.62.66.91, www.aube-safran.com, closed mid Nov-mid Mar, double €100-€145) is an airy, polished *chambre d'hôte* with a pool and a

Quartier de la Villasse. *See p114.*

strong commitment to Barroux saffron and cuisine (menu €39, closed Jan). Also in Le Barroux is the hotel-restaurant **Les Géraniums** (pl de la Croix, 04.90.62.41.08, double €60-€65, menus €28-€38), with rather basic rooms but delicious cuisine and local foie gras. Nestled in vineyards, **Le Clos Saint Saourde** (rte de St-Véran, 04.90.37.35.20, www.leclossaintsaourde.com, double €120-€170) is an elegant contemporary conversion, set around a stone courtyard – the epitome of provençal chic. In Beaumes-de-Venise, village restaurant **Dolium** (pl Balma-Vénitia, 04.90.12.80.00, www.dolium-restaurant.com, menus €18-€55) runs occasional cookery courses and makes exciting use of local produce, such as the famous Caromb black figs.

Wine is the focus in Gigondas, where **Du Verre à l'Assiette** (pl du Village, 04.90.12.36.64, closed Dec-Mar), a curio-bedecked basement cellar and restaurant, serves charcuterie and salads (€8-€12). **L'Oustalet** (pl Gabrielle Andéol, 04.90.65.85.01, www.restaurant-oustalet.fr, menus €21-€75) is the place for a more adventurous meal as Cyril Glémot proves he's one of the most exciting and ambitious chefs in the area. On the last Friday of each month, he creates a feast based on one local product, from melons to mushrooms.

The **Restaurant-Hôtel Les Florets** (rte des Dentelles, 04.90.65.85.01, www.hotel-les-florets.com, closed Jan-mid Mar, double €68-€182), a short drive up into the vineyards, has a floral terrace where the family's own wine accompanies outstanding local dishes (menus €22-€28 lunch, €42-€50 dinner). At the foot of the village, sporty types use the basic **Gîte d'Etape des Dentelles** (04.90.65.80.85, closed mid Jan-Mar, dorm €15/person), where courses and information on climbing, mountain biking and hiking are on offer. A couple of kilometres east of Vacqueyras, the **Hôtel Montmirail** (04.90.65.84.01, www.hotelmontmirail.com, closed mid Oct-mid Mar, double €80-€115) is a rather imposing 19th-century pile, with colourful provençal fabrics in the bedrooms.

Stay among the vines in the simple **Domaine de Cabasse** (between Séguret and Sablet, 04.90.46.91.12, www.domaine-de-cabasse.fr, closed mid Nov-mid Mar, double €96-€132), which produces its own wine. The Côtes du Rhône villages also have a number of fine restaurants serving the local wine with top-notch food: in Sablet, **Les Abeilles** (4 rte de Vaison, 04.90.12.38.96, www.abeilles-sablet.com, menus €18-€55) has the perfect mix of modernity and classicism in its menu, while Séguret's **La Table du Comtat** (04.90.46.91.49, closed Sun, dinner Tue, 3 wks Feb, double €80-€110, menus €20-€48) uses thyme, olives and apricots from the region, and has simple rooms and spectacular views over the Dentelles.

INSIDE TRACK
FOOD, GLORIOUS FOOD

In autumn, local winemakers, chefs, artisan producers and hungry foodies flock to **Les Journées Gourmandes** (www.journees-gourmandes.com) in Vaison. The four-day celebration of all things edible brings food stalls, cookery demonstrations, competitions and olive-mill tours – plus the grand finale of the **Festivals des Soupes**. The latter is preceeded by three weeks of frenzied soup-making in Vaison and 14 surrounding villages, with villagers cooking up over 200 *bouillons*, *potages* and *veloutés*, vying for a place in the final; free tastings are held in every village.

Resources

Tourist information
Gigondas Office de Tourisme *pl du Portail, Gigondas (04.90.65.85.46/www.gigondas-dm.fr)*. **Open** *Apr-Oct* 10am-12.30pm, 2.30-6pm daily. *Nov-Mar* 10am-noon, 2-5pm Mon-Sat.
Malaucène Syndicat d'Initiative *pl de la Mairie, Malaucène (04.90.65.22.59)*. **Open** *June-Sept* 9am-noon, 2-5pm Mon-Sat. *Oct-May* 9am-noon, 2-5pm Mon-Fri.

VAISON-LA-ROMAINE

Nestling under Ventoux, Vaison offers culture, vivid Roman ruins and a great base for wine tasting and walking. Only a small area of the ancient Roman town has been excavated, and many treasures remain buried; there are two archaeological sites on the right bank of the Ouvèze (the **quartiers du Puymin** and **de la Villasse**), and a magnificent Roman bridge – which, unlike modern constructions, resisted a devastating flood in 1992. On the left bank of the river is the old town or *ville haute*, perched on a cliff with steep, cobbled medieval streets, pretty fountains and the ruined 12th-century chateau of the Comtes de Toulouse. Market day is Tuesday (and Thursday and Saturday in summer).

The admirably organised **Musée Théo Desplans** in the quartier de Puymin features statues, mosaics and domestic items; especially striking is a marble family group dating from 121 AD, showing a stark-naked Emperor Hadrian standing beside his elaborately dressed wife Sabina. Other highlights are a third-century AD silver bust, and floor mosaics from the Peacock villa. Behind the museum is the Roman amphitheatre, still the venue for Vaison's main cultural events. The most important summer festival is the prestigious **Vaison Danses** (www.vaison-danses.com), two weeks of modern dance, featuring world-class exponents like the late Maurice Béjart's Lausanne ballet or young American choreographer Alonzo King. Music fans can look forward to **Blues & Jazz in Vaison** in August (www.blues-jazz-vaison.com).

Past the tourist office is the **quartier de la Villasse**. The colonnaded main street, with its huge paving stones and vast scale, powerfully evokes Vaison's past prosperity. On either side of it stand the remains of shops, baths and villas, including the property where the silver bust was found. Whoever owned it was certainly wealthy; the 5,000-square-metre (53,820-square-foot) *domus* had its own baths and an extensive hanging garden.

Cathédrale Notre-Dame-de-Nazareth, a ten-minute walk away on avenue Jules Ferry, is a fine example of provençal Romanesque, with fine carving and pure lines. It was built on the ruins of a Roman basilica, and here and there antique components can be seen recycled in the 11th-century structure. The peaceful, intricately carved cloisters are filled with sculptures, including a curious horned Byzantine Christ. North of the cathedral, the Romanesque Chapelle de St-Quentin (closed to the public) has a unique triangular apse, based on an earlier Roman temple. The area around the chapel was a Roman necropolis, and archaeological digs have unearthed a wealth of objects.

Musée Théo Desplans, Quartiers de Puymin & de la Villasse

Open *Nov-Feb* 10am-noon, 2-5pm daily. *Mar, Oct* 10am-12.30pm, 2-5.30pm daily. *Apr, May* 9.30am-6pm daily. *June-Sept* 9.30am-6.30pm daily. **Admission** €8; €3.50 reductions. **No credit cards**.

Where to stay & eat

The 16th-century **Hostellerie le Beffroi** (rue de l'Evêché, 04.90.36.04.71, www.le-beffroi.com, closed mid Dec-mid Mar, double €75-€115) has superb views in the old town and a restaurant (closed Tue, Wed lunch Nov-mid Mar, menus

---

Buried Treasures

Why truffle trading can be a grubby business.

As the narrow streets of Carpentras ring with the cheerful shouts of market sellers on a Friday, a more discreet scene is taking place at the Café de l'Univers on place Aristide Briand. A small group of men in heavy coats and broad-brimmed hats huddles around a table, dangling small bags from an antique set of scales. Prices are quietly muttered; cash changes hands.

From November to March, the same ritual takes place in towns across Provence, which now produces 80 per cent of truffles sold in France. Although the French have prized the jet-black tuber melanosporum, also known as the *truffe du Périgord*, for hundreds of years, the stakes are now higher than ever. In the last 100 years, France's annual truffle production has plummeted from around 1,000 tons to an estimated 30 to 60 tons, much of which is sold on the black market. The decline started after World War I, with the planting of vines in previously forested areas and the neglect of truffle-producing trees; agricultural chemicals are also blamed for today's poor crop. Black truffles now sell for €700-€800 a kilo to brokers who deal directly with the truffle harvesters.

Although truffle markets are open to the public, it can be a risky business for the average shopper. The markets are watched by the French fraud squad, as well as experts appointed by the growers, but unscrupulous sellers still try to pass off the less potent *truffe brumale* or the notoriously flavourless *truffe chinoise* as tuber melanosporum. Some even dye the paler summer truffles with iron oxide or the juice of preserved truffles to achieve the coveted charcoal colour.

In response to such scams, the town of **St-Paul-Trois-Châteaux** has introduced a truffle market whose aim is to make the *truffe du Tricastin*, one of the finest melanosporum truffles, accessible to the general public. After inspection by three experts, the truffles are brushed, sorted and weighed on certified scales, then sold in bags bearing the name of the truffle growers' association. When it comes to an earthy black tuber, things don't get any more transparent than this.

Truffles abound in provençal restaurants during the winter, reaching their aromatic peak in January. The availability of truffles in the area means few chefs will cheat outright, but bear in mind that the word *truffe* might refer to a less-coveted variety – perhaps the tuber uncinatum or *truffe de Bourgogne*, rather than the precious

€28-€45). Higher up **La Fête en Provence** (pl du Vieux-Marché, 04.90.36.36.43, www.hotella fete-provence.com, closed Wed, Nov-Mar, double €72-€100), with its girly decor, dreamy courtyard and tasty food. On the town's central square, the **Hôtel Burrhus** (1 pl de Montfort, 04.90.36. 00.11, www.burrhus.com, closed mid Dec-mid Jan, double €46-€82) has sleek modernist rooms.

Good *chambres d'hôtes* include **Jade en Provence** (Le Clos des Oliviers, av André Coudray, 04.90.28.81.60, www.jade-en-provence. com, double €75-€85) and characterful **L'Evêché** in the old town (rue de l'Évêché, 04.90.36.13.46, http://eveche.free.fr, double €78-€85), which also has a few suites.

Robert Bardot is Vaison's top chef, and one of the few celebrated cooks in France who rarely leaves his kitchens, under the Roman bridge at **Le Moulin à Huile** (quai Maréchal Foch, 04.90.36.20.67, www.moulin-huile.com, closed Mon, dinner Sun, menus €40-€75). **Auberge la Bertavelle** (12 pl Sus-Auze, 04.90.36.02.16, closed Mon, lunch Fri, Jan, menus €16-€50) serves local specialities, with a truffle menu in season. Another truffle restaurant is **Le Brin d'Olivier** (4 rue du Ventoux, 04.90.28.74.79, menus €18-€39), which has a welcoming hearth and a charming terrace with an olive tree. **Le Bateleur** (1 pl Théodore Aubanel, 04.90.36.28.04, menus €20-€38) serves classy provençal dishes like a superb vegetable tian, accompanied by excellent local wines.

Seven kilometres north-east is the lovely hilltop village of Faucon; sit and enjoy delicious tarts and bread from the **Boulangerie des Tilleuls** under its titular lime trees (pl des Tilleuls, 04.90.36.12.91, closed Tue, lunch Sun, mains €4-€8). **Le Laurier** (pl de la Mairie, 04.90.46.55.54, closed Mon, Tue, Nov-mid Mar, menus €19-€30) serves simple regional cuisine with a tasty line in wild rabbit and organic wine from the *vignerons* behind La Roche-Buissière.

At Entrechaux, seven kilometres out of town, **La Bastide des Gramuses** (04.90.46.01.08, www.lesgramuses.com, double €30-€100) is a 17th-century *chambre d'hôte* with a pool and pretty bedrooms. In the same village, the **St Hubert** (04.90.46.00.05, menus €16-€50) has been in the same family for 80 years, and serves fine game in season.

Resources

Tourist information
Office de Tourisme *pl Chanoine Sautel, Vaison-la-Romaine (04.90.36.02.11/www.vaison-la-romaine.com).* **Open** *Apr-June* 9am-noon, 2-5.45pm Mon-Sat; 9am-noon Sun. *July, Aug* 9am-12.30pm, 2-6.45pm daily. *Sept-mid Oct* 9am-noon, 2-5.45pm Mon-Sat; 9am-noon Sun. *Mid Oct-Mar* 9am-noon, 2-5.45pm Mon-Sat.

GETTING THERE & AROUND
By bus
Arnaud (04.90.63.01.82) runs three buses a day from Marseille to Carpentras, via Pernes-les-Fontaines; three daily from Orange to Carpentras; and an hourly service from Avignon. **Cars Comtadins** (04.90.67.20.25) runs four buses a day between Carpentras and Vaison-la-Romaine (also serving Malaucène); and two a day between Carpentras and Bédoin. **Cars Lieutaud** (04.90.36.05.22) runs buses from Orange to Vaison via Sablet, north of Gigondas.

By car
Take the A7 (exit 21) and the D950 to Carpentras. The D938 goes south to Pernes, north to Mont Ventoux and Vaison; the D7 heads to Beaumes-de-Venise and Gigondas.

By train
The TGV runs to Avignon, with some services stopping at Orange; you'll then need to take a bus.

---

melanosporum. Some 'truffle' dishes contain no more than truffle oil perfumed with a chemical compound – which should be reflected in the price.

To sniff out the real thing (in the forests, a task that's entrusted to dogs rather than pigs these days, as the latter's taste for the luxury tubers led to too many wrestling matches with their owners), time your visit to coincide with the truffle festivals in **Richerenches** (*see p48*) or **Ménerbes** (end December; *see p120*). Alternatively, attend a truffle market: there are good ones at **Richerenches** (av de la Rabasse, 10am-1pm Sat), **Carpentras** (pl Aristide Briand, 10am-1pm Fri), **St-Paul-Trois-Châteaux** (fontaine de l'Esplan, 10am-1pm Sun) and **Valréas** (rond-point du Monument aux Morts, 10am-1pm Wed).

Alternatively, dine at a truffle-serving restaurant. In Richerenches, friendly bistro **L'Escapade** (av de la Rabasse, 04.90.28. 01.46, www.escapade-resto.blogspot.com) serves updated provençal cuisine with a focus on truffles in winter. For an haute cuisine feast, try **Christian Etienne** (*see p94*), who is considered Avignon's truffle pope. In Carpentras itself, **Chez Serge** (*see p109*) serves truffle dishes year round, with special truffle nights on Thursdays.

The Drôme Provençale

Olive trees and sunflowers thrive in the garden of Provence.

Magnificent scenery abounds in the verdant **Drôme Provençale**, with its rolling fields of lavender, olive groves and almond trees. Though its natural beauty and historic assets (Roman bridges, pretty Romanesque churches and grand chateaux) draw the crowds, it retains an unspoilt feel – and there's always a quiet corner to escape to, in the wooded valleys or winding hillside trails.

There's plenty to please food-lovers, too, from the fruity olive oil pressed around **Nyons** to **Montélimar** nougat, and the precious truffles unearthed around the **Tricastin** plain.

THE TRICASTIN & GRIGNAN

Named after the Gaul tribe of the Tricastani, the **Tricastin** is a Rhône-side plain, best known for its black truffles and renowned AOC Coteaux du Tricastin wines. Of late, a less desirable association has emerged, after a uranium leak at the Tricastin nuclear power station in July 2008, leading to talk of the AOC changing its name.

The region's ancient capital, **St-Paul-Trois-Châteaux**, has zero chateaux, but is home to the textbook 12th-century Romanesque Ancienne Cathédrale on place de l'Hôpital. Next door, the **Maison de la Truffe et du Tricastin** has a permanent truffle exhibition and tastings on the second Sunday in February. The town is also home to a tightly regulated truffle market (*see p114* **Buried Treasures**).

Upriver, **Montélimar** is France's nougat capital. The knobbly slabs of almonds and honey have been big business here since the 17th century, and quality and prices remain high. The tourist office (*see p118*) can provide a list of weekday guided visits to the factories, most of which are in the industrial outskirts to the south of town. North of the town centre, the **Palais des Bonbons et du Nougat** is dedicated to all things sweet and sugary, also incorporating a playground and petting zoo.

East of here is the graceful *village perché* of **Grignan**, fragrant with old-fashioned roses (in full bloom in May and June). Its castle, the

Château de Grignan, is a sumptuous Renaissance-style stronghold, immortalised in the Marquise de Sévigné's famous letters. The lady herself is entombed in the 16th-century **Collégiale St-Sauveur**, while her memory is resurrected for the Festival de la Corréspondence in July (call the tourist office for details, *see p118*).

The 19th-century, columned *lavoir* du Mail dominates the marketplace, busy with stalls each Tuesday. For a shady stroll, head to the **Grotte de Rochecourbière**, a kilometre south of the public swimming pool. The Grotte cocoons a round stone table where the Marquise is said to have penned many of her letters.

South of Grignan, past the lollipop-stick-thin medieval tower at **Chamaret** (04.75.46.55.85, closed Sept-June), is the medieval hill village of **Suze-la-Rousse**. Its name is derived from the Celtic *uz* (meaning high place) and, allegedly, the auburn mane of one of the ladies of Château de Suze. The fortified **Château de Suze-la-Rousse** began life as a 12th-century hunting lodge for the Princes of Orange, before acquiring an Italianate grand courtyard that resonates to the sound of chamber music in July. The chateau houses the Université du Vin, which has its own vineyard with 70 different grape varieties. In September, the local harvest begins with wine tastings and dancing at the **Ban des Vendanges**; the Caves Coopératives (2 av des Alpes, 04.75.97.23.10) is a good year-round filling station for Coteaux du Tricastin.

Château de Grignan

Grignan (04.75.91.83.55). **Open** *July, Aug* 9.30-11.30am, 2-6pm daily. *Sept, Oct, Apr-June* 9.30-11.30am, 2-5.30pm daily. *Nov-Mar* 9.30-11.30am, 2-5.30pm Mon, Wed-Sun. **Admission** *Chateau* €5.50; €3.20 reductions; free under-11s. *Gardens* free. **Credit** V.

Château de Suze-la-Rousse

Suze-la-Rousse (04.75.04.81.44). **Open** *Apr-June, Sept-Oct* 9.30-11.30am, 2-5.30pm daily. *July, Aug* 9.30-11.30am, 2-6pm daily. *Nov-Mar* 9.30-11.30am, 2-6pm Mon, Wed-Sun. **Admission** €3.50; free under-11s. **Credit** AmEx, MC, V.

Maison de la Truffe et du Tricastin

rue de la République, St-Paul-Trois-Châteaux (04.75.96.61.29/www.maisondelatruffe.com). **Open** *Summer* 3-7pm Mon; 9am-noon, 3-7pm Tue-Sat; 10am-noon, 2-6pm Sun. *Winter* 9am-noon, 2-6pm Tue-Sat; 10am-noon, 2-6pm Sun. **Admission** €3.50; €2 reductions; free under-7s. **No credit cards**.

Palais des Bonbons et du Nougat

100 rte de Valence (04.75.50.62.66/www.palaisbonbons.com). **Open** *July, Aug* 10am-7pm daily. *Sept-June* 2-7pm Mon; 10am-12.30pm, 2-7pm Thur-Sat; 10am-12.30pm, 1.30-7pm Sun. Closed 3wks Jan. **Admission** €8; €5 reductions; free under-5s. **No credit cards**.

Where to stay & eat

In season, truffles permeate the menus of local restaurants. In St-Paul-Trois-Châteaux, try **L'Esplan** (15 pl de l'Esplan, 04.75.96.64.64, www.esplan-provence.com, closed lunch, late Dec-mid Jan, doubles €67-€114, menus €25-€52), which also uses local produce and herbs to great effect. On the outskirts of town, **Villa Augusta** (14 rue du Serre Blanc, 04.75.97.29.29, www.villaaugusta.fr, double €145-€400, menus €28-€75, restaurant closed Mon, dinner Sun) is an expensively restored 19th-century manor house, with plush rooms and a kitchen headed up by the renowned David Mollicone.

Meanwhile, **La Vieille France-Jardin des Saveurs** (chemin des Goudessards, 04.75.96.70.47, closed Nov-Apr, lunch, all day Mon, Tue Sept-June, mains €27-€32, menus €25-€110) serves a wonderfully regional menu: courgette flowers stuffed with brousse (ewe's milk cheese), say, followed by local lamb.

In Grignan, the **Café de Sévigné** (pl Sévigné, 04.75.46.51.82) is good for a scenic beer, while friendly **Hôtel Sévigné** (15 pl Castellane, 04.75.46.50.97, www.hotel-sevigne-grignan.com, double €66-€120), at the foot of the chateau, has Wi-Fi access and a restaurant (closed dinner Sun, all Mon, menus €12-€28).

Le Clair de la Plume (pl du Mail, 04.75.91.81.30, www.clairplume.com, double €98-€170) is a tasteful rural-chic hotel, with ten charming rooms, a trellised garden and a tearoom. Set in an old watermill, **La Maison du Moulin** (quartier petit Cordy, 04.75.46.56.94, www.maisondumoulin.com, double €75-€130, menu €30) is an exquisite B&B with decor worthy of a sleek interiors magazine, and a pool.

Hôtel la Bastide de Grignan (rte de Montélimar, 120 chemin de Bessas, 04.75.90.67.09, www.labastidedegrignan.com, menus €28-€48, double €65-€110) has smart, simply decorated rooms, some with views over the garden; on the same road, **La Table des Délices** (04.75.46.57.22, www.latabledes delices.com, menus €24 lunch, €34-€48 dinner, closed Mon, dinner Sun) serves polished provençal cuisine and a truffle menu in winter.

For dinner in Grignan, try **Coté Patio** (rue du Grand Faubourg, 04.75.46.59.20, closed 2wks Nov, mains €12-€19, menu €25), which serves truffle ravioli in its fountain courtyard, or **Le Poème de Grignan** (rue St-Louis, 04.75.91.10.90, www.lepoemedegrignan.com, closed Wed, menus €25 lunch, €28-€46 dinner).

Towards Suze-la-Rousse, **Campsite Les Truffières** (lieu-dit Nachony, 1100 chemin de Bellevue d'Air, 04.75.46.93.62, www.les truffieres.com, closed Oct-mid Apr, €13.50-€16.60/plot) has an outdoor pool. The peaceful **Les Aiguières** guesthouse (rue de la Fontaine d'Argent, 04.75.98.40.80, www.les-aiguieres.com, double €72-€82) offers spacious, elegant rooms; its garden, dotted with fig trees, has a pool and terrace.

AVIGNON & THE VAUCLUSE

Château de Grignan.

Further south is the plush **Château de Rochegude** (Rochegude, 04.75.97.21.10, www.chateauderochegude.com, double €170-€355, closed early Nov), a grandiose castle with a restaurant (closed Nov, dinner Sun-lunch Tue Dec-Apr, menus €16-€85), pool and tennis court; deer roam the park.

Resources

Tourist information
Grignan Office de Tourisme *pl du Jeu de Ballon, Grignan (04.75.46.56.75/www.guideweb.com/grignan)*. **Open** *Mar-June, Sept-Nov* 9.30am-12.30pm, 2-5.30pm Mon-Sat. *July, Aug* 9.30am-12.30pm, 2.30-7pm daily.
Montélimar Office de Tourisme *montée St-Martin, allées Provençales, Montélimar (04.75.01.00.20/www.montelimar-tourisme.com)*. **Open** 9am-12.30pm, 1.30-6.30pm Mon-Sat.
Suze-la-Rousse Office de Tourisme *av des Côtes-du-Rhône, Suze-la-Rousse (04.75.04.81.41/www.ot-suze-la-rousse.fr)*. **Open** *Sept-June* 9am-noon, 2.30-6pm Tue-Fri; 9am-noon Sat. *July, Aug* 9am-noon, 2.30-6.30pm Mon-Fri; 9am-noon, 2.30-4.30pm Sat.

NYONS

Author Jean Giono called Nyons 'paradise on earth': with its very own regenerative wind (the Pontias), perennial sunshine and a halo of olive groves, this antechamber to heaven is fast filling with taramasalata-pink retirement villas. Dubbed 'Petit Nice', Nyons shelters in a bowl of mountains at the opening of the Eygues Valley, pulling in visitors with its medieval place des Arcades, vaulted rue des Grands Forts and remains of a feudal chateau. The 13th-century **Tour Randonné** – a prison, rebuilt as a chapel in the 19th century – towers over the town and its busy Thursday morning market.

The most northerly olive-growing area in Europe, Nyons produces the mild and fruity black *tanche*, the first variety in France to be awarded an *appellation d'origine contrôlée*. The olive harvest festival is in early February, while July's **Les Olivades** brings tastings and night markets. Olive-pressing history tours are given at the **Musée de l'Olivier** (allée des Tilleuls, 04.75.26.12.12, admission €2) and the family-run **Les Vieux Moulins** (4 promenade de la Digue, 04.75.26.11.00/http://vieuxmoulins.free.fr, closed Nov, Jan-Mar, admission €4) on the banks of the Eygues. Olives are pressed next door at the **Moulin Autrand-Dozol** (04.75.26.02.52, shop closed Sun) and olive-related products, local wines and tours are available at the **Vignolis Coopérative du Nyonsais** (pl Olivier de Serres, 04.75.26.95.00). **La Scourtinerie** (36 rue de la Maladrerie, 04.75.26.33.52, www.scourtinerie.

Nyons.

com, closed Sat, Sun) is France's last workshop to make colourful, natural-fibre mats (originally used for olive-pressing) by hand.

Next to Les Vieux Moulins is the 'Roman' donkey bridge, an elegant single-arch crossing that was actually built in the 13th and 14th centuries. In summer, it's enveloped by the heady scent of lavender from the **Distillerie Bleu Provence** (58 promenade de la Digue, 04.75.26.10.42, www.distillerie-bleu-provence.com), where you can make your own eau de toilette.

For scenic walks, the Sentier des Oliviers takes you up through the olive groves, while the more challenging forest path along the Garde-Grosse mountain to the south affords soaring views. If you're driving in from Grignan, hug the foot of the mountain through the pretty village of Rousset-les-Vignes and take the lime-tree avenue towards **Venterol**, a radiant, picture-postcard village tumbling down the hillside, with a fine 17th-century bell tower.

Where to eat, drink & stay

If your palate needs some aromatherapy, lime-blossom and fig spike the beer at the friendly provençal microbrewery **Brasserie Artisanale du Sud** (69 av Frédéric Mistral, 04.75.26.95.75, www.la-grihete.com, closed Sun).

Stop for lunch at the **Café de la Bourse** (04.75.26.29.75, menus €17.50-€33.50) on the central place des Arcades, or head to nearby rue Victor Hugo, where **Le Petit Caveau** (No.9, 04.75.26.20.21, closed dinner Sun, all Mon, menus €25-€55) serves modern provençal cuisine in a vaulted dining room.

With its cypress-shaded walled garden, pool and shabby-chic decor, **Une Autre Maison** (pl de la République, 04.75.26.43.09, www.uneautremaison.com, closed Nov-Jan, double €60-€185) is a charming place to stay. There are only ten rooms; if you don't manage to nab one, you can still dine in the little restaurant (mains €18, menu €38), if you book ahead. Surrounded by olive trees and set just to the north of Nyons, **Hôtel La Picholine** (promenade de la Perrière, 04.75.26.06.21, www.picholine26.com, double €59-€80) offers comfortable rooms and a pool.

In Venterol, **La Ferme des Auches** (04.75.27.92.85, www.fermedesauches.com, closed Jan, Feb, double €46-€50) is a no-frills farmhouse *chambre d'hôte*, set among the vines; it also lets out a *gîte*.

Resources

Tourist information
Office de Tourisme *pl de la Libération, Nyons (04.75.26.10.35/www.paysdenyons.com).* **Open** *Apr-June* 9.30am-noon, 2.30-6pm Mon-Sat; 10am-1pm Sun. *July, Aug* 9am-12.30pm, 2.30-7pm Mon-Sat; 10am-1pm, 3-5pm Sun. *Jan-Mar, Oct-Dec* 9.30am-noon, 2.30-5.45pm Mon-Sat.

BUIS-LES-BARONNIES

Set in a heady landscape of apricot orchards and aromatic plants, the precipitous limestone Baronnies mountains south-east of Nyons are popular for rock-climbing, hiking and riding. Sheltered beside the River Ouvèze under the jagged Rocher St-Julien, sleepy **Buis-les-Baronnies** was the medieval capital of the Barons of Mévouillon. With the Renaissance façade of the Couvent des Ursulines (now used for art exhibitions) as its backdrop, the village enjoys a tranquillity interrupted only by the thud of *pétanque* and, during the July arts festival, drifting jazz and classical tunes. Since the 19th century, Buis has produced almost all of France's world-class lime-blossom, hand-harvested for the *tilleul* fair each July.

Aromatic and medicinal herbs are sold at the Wednesday market in place des Arcades, at *herborist* **Bernard Laget** (pl des Herbes, 04.75.28.16.42) or at the **Maison des Plantes Aromatiques et Médicinales**. Built into the medieval ramparts, the latter presents a small, fragrant display on lime-blossom and lavender, a herb garden, and an amusing 'smell organ'.

An hour's walk through terraced olive groves takes you to the hillside village of **La Roche-sur-le-Buis**, where the Chapelle des Pénitents is now a micro-museum of traditional farm instruments, its tiny graveyard cultivated into an enchanting 'symbolic plant garden'.

Maison des Plantes Aromatiques et Médicinales
14 bd Eysseric (04.75.28.04.59/www.maison desplantes.com). **Open** *July, Aug* 9am-12.30pm, 3-7pm Mon-Sat; 10am-noon, 3-6pm Sun. *Sept-June* 9.15am-noon, 2-6pm Mon-Sat; 10am-12.30pm, 2.30-6pm Sun. **Admission** €3.50; €1.50 reductions; free under-12s. **No credit cards**.

Where to stay & eat

In the centre of Buis-les-Baronnies, **La Fourchette** (pl des Arcades, 04.75.28.03.31, closed lunch Mon July & Aug, lunch Mon & dinner Sun Sept & Dec-June, menus €15-€38) serves refined regional cuisine under the arcades. The neighbouring **Hôtel les Arcades-Le Lion d'Or** (04.75.28.11.31, www.hotelarcades.fr, closed Dec-Feb, double €53-€65) boasts a charming garden, a pool and gentle wake-up calls from the fountain in the square. For ecclesiastical pomp, **L'Ancienne Cure** (2 rue du Paroir, 04.75.28.22.08, www.ancienne-cure.com, closed mid Nov-Mar, double €70-€113), holiday home of the bishop of Valence in the 15th century, is now a delightful *chambre d'hôte*, lavishly decorated with oriental antiques.

Resources

Tourist information
Office de Tourisme *14 bd Eysséric, Buis-les-Baronnies (04.75.28.04.59/www.buisles baronnies.com).* **Open** *July, Aug* 9am-12.30pm, 3-7pm Mon-Sat; 10am-noon, 3-7pm Sun. *Sept-June* 9am-noon, 2-6pm daily.

GETTING THERE & AROUND

By bus/train
The nearest train stations are Avignon, Orange and Montélimar. **Cars Lieutaud** (04.90.86.36.75) runs two buses daily except Sunday between Nyons and Avignon via Vaison-la-Romaine, and between Avignon and Buis-les-Baronnies. **Cars Dunevon** (04.75.28.41.54) runs two buses a day, except weekends, between Nyons and Buis. **Cars Teste** (04.75.00.27.90) runs five buses a day between Montélimar and Nyons via Grignan, and buses between Grignan and Nyons via Valréas. **Autocars Petit Nice** (04.75.26.35.58) runs five buses each day except Sunday, from Nyons to Vaison, with three return journeys. There are fewer buses in school holidays.

By car
Take exit 18 off the A7 autoroute, then the D133 and D541 for Grignan, or take exit 19 and the D994 for Suze-la-Rousse. Nyons is 20km (12 miles) from Grignan by the D941 and D538, and 30km (19 miles) from Buis by the D5, D46 and D538.

The Luberon

It's easy to fall for the Luberon's charms – but you won't be the first.

Hill villages, fortresses and chateaux dot the ever-lovely **Luberon**, declared a Parc Régional in 1977. Its heart is the limestone massif of the Montagne du Luberon, cut in two by the Aiguebrun Valley, which divides the Petit Luberon mountains to the west from the lofty Grand Luberon peaks to the east.

At three o'clock every Sunday afternoon, village streets from **Gordes** to **Lourmarin** suddenly empty, as the departure of the last TGV from Avignon to Paris draws nigh. The flying train enables countless Parisians to live a double life, swapping their soulless offices for weekends in idyllic rural *mas*. Add in the red-kneed, rosé-quaffing Brits – attracted by Peter Mayle's *A Year in Provence* – and high summer can be seriously overpowering.

For the rest of the year, thankfully, the Luberon remains largely unspoiled by the incomers, and you'll still find local farmers sipping a pastis down age-old stone backstreets. All the same, four-fold property price hikes as newbies renovate decrepit *bastides* have done nothing to ease the lot of locals.

NORTH LUBERON: FROM TAILLADES TO SAIGNON

Once important for stone quarrying, the rugged northern flank of the Montagne du Luberon is punctuated by picturesque hill villages and sweeping fields of vines. In winter, the canyons and crevices echo with the sound of guns as hunters pursue the ever-elusive wild boar, partridges and hares, known collectively as *gibier* (game). Come summer, the crack of the cartridge is replaced by the ringing of shop tills, a phenomenon that has led the locals to dub tourists the *gibier d'été* – summer's 'game'.

At the western edge of the ridge, tranquil **Taillades** is the village that best recalls the area's stone-quarrying past. Houses seem to sit on blocks of cut rock, and the remains of two chateaux – one fortified, one dating from the Renaissance – face each other across a ravine. A path climbs to a chapel perched over one former quarry, now an atmospheric outdoor theatre.

Hugging the N100, the main attraction in inconspicuous **Coustellet** is its summer farmers' market (Sun morning, Apr-Nov). You might also want to visit the **Musée de la Lavande**, where a film explains how the tiny purple flowers are distilled, and a smelling machine demonstrates the difference between true lavender and the hybrid *lavindin*. It's run by a family that still cultivates lavender high up on Mont Ventoux.

Oppède-le-Vieux, reached through narrow country lanes to the south, perfectly symbolises the rebirth of the Luberon. The old village was abandoned during the 19th century, but has been resettled since the 1960s by artists, potters and writers; it is still romantically overgrown. At the top are the restored Romanesque **Collégiale Notre-Dame-d'Alidon**, with its gargoyle-adorned bell tower, and the ruined **castle** of notorious baron Jean de Meynier. He was behind the brutal 1545 massacre of the Vaudois (or Waldensian) heretics, a proto-Protestant sect who populated many of the Luberon villages. Below the village, the *sentier vigneron* footpath follows quiet lanes amid vineyards, with discreet panels identifying different grape varieties.

On the crest of a hill just to the east, **Ménerbes** remains a clock-stopped stone village with fine doorways that point to a prosperous past. Artists Pablo Picasso, Nicolas de Staël and Dora Maar all spent some time

About the author
Jamie Ivey has written a trilogy of books about his life in the South of France, where he sells rosé, and is also the publisher of a lifestyle magazine dedicated to the Luberon and Les Alpilles region.

living here. At the top of the village, the turreted chateau (not open to the public) was once a Vaudois stronghold. On the plain below, you can visit the state-of-the-art cellars of the Domaine de la Citadelle, where Yves Rousset-Rouard, producer of the *Emmanuelle* films, has established himself as one of the area's most respected winemakers. A visit to the vineyard also takes in the corkscrews of the **Musée du Tire-Bouchon** (Domaine de la Citadelle, Le Chataignier, chemin de Cavaillon, 04.90. 72.41.58, www.museedutirebouchon.com, €5, €3.50 reductions). The **Maison de la Truffe et Vin** (pl de l'Horloge, 04.90.72.52.10) also has an excellent display in its cellars about the wines of the area.

Between Ménerbes and Lacoste on the scenic D109, a bumpy track leads to the isolated **Abbaye St-Hilaire**, the remains of a 13th-century Carmelite priory whose cloister, chapel and garden have been lovingly restored over many years by the Bride family.

With its fortified medieval gateways and cobbled streets, the tiny, semi-deserted village of **Lacoste** should not be missed. The ruined castle at the top was the home of the scandalous Marquis de Sade (*see p23* **No Pain, No Gain**) on and off for 30 years, until his imprisonment in 1786. Having been acquired by global fashion magnate Pierre Cardin, it now hosts a summer opera festival (*see p45*). From here, the road zigzags up the ramparts of Bonnieux.

Inhabited since Neolithic times, **Bonnieux** became a Templar *commanderie* and later a papal outpost, although it was reunited with France back in 1793. Its sights include a 12th-century hilltop church, reached via cobbled steps from rue de la République; a newer parish church in the lower village, which contains four 15th-century panel paintings; the tiny **Musée de la Boulangerie**; and the remains of the towers that once surrounded the village. North of Bonnieux, enroute to the Roman Pont Julien, the **Château de Mille** (D3, rte de Bonnieux, 04.90.74.11.94, www.chateau-de-mille.fr) is the oldest wine chateau in the Luberon, and a former summer residence of the Avignon papacy. You can't visit the chateau itself, but you can appreciate the exterior while buying a few bottles of wine.

In the lesser-known eastern half of the Luberon above Apt, the unspoiled village of **Saignon** stretches along a craggy escarpment between a square-towered Romanesque church and cemetery, and a rocky belvedere. Its remote location and mountain site made the nearby hamlet of **Buoux** an important refuge during the Wars of Religion: high on the hillside (take a stout pair of walking shoes) are the ruins of the **Fort de Buoux** (04.90.74.25.75, closed in bad weather, €3; €2 reductions), demolished

by Louis XIV to deter Huguenots from taking refuge here. A little further on, at the end of the secluded Aiguebrun Valley, rock climbers pepper the overhanging crags, and assorted footpaths lead to Sivergues and the stunning Mourre Nègre.

FREE Abbaye St-Hilaire

Ménerbes (04.90.75.88.83). **Open** *Summer* 9am-7pm daily. *Winter* 10am-6pm daily. **Admission** free; donations welcome.

FREE Collégiale Notre-Dame-d'Alidon

Oppède-le-Vieux. **Open** *July, Aug* 10am-7pm daily. *Apr-June, Sept-Nov* 10am-7pm Sat, Sun, or by appointment with the mairie (04.90.76.90.06). Closed Nov-Mar. **Admission** free.

Musée de la Boulangerie

12 rue de la République, Bonnieux (04.90.75. 88.34). **Open** *Apr-Oct* 10am-12.30pm, 2.30-6pm Wed-Sun. *Oct-Mar* Open for groups by appointment only. **Admission** €3.50; €1.50 reductions; free under-12s. **No credit cards**.

Musée de la Lavande

rte de Gordes, Coustellet (04.90.76.91.23/ www.museedelalavande.com). **Open** *Feb,Mar, Oct-Dec* 9am-12.30pm, 2-6pm daily. *Apr, May, Sept* 9am-1pm, 2-6.30pm daily. *July, Aug* 9am-7pm daily. Closed Jan. **Admission** €6; free under-15s. **Credit** *Shop* AmEx, DC, MC, V.

Collégiale Notre-Dame-d'Alidon.

Where to stay & eat

At Robion, on the road between Taillades and Coustellet, **Lou Luberon** (av Aristide Briand, 04.90.76.65.04, mains €9.80-€14, menus €12.90-€19.50, closed Tue, dinner Wed Apr-Sept, daily Oct-Mar) looks like a simple roadside bar but serves delicious salads and regional dishes. In Coustellet itself, Olivier Gouin took over the old family butcher **Maison Gouin** (pl du Marché Paysan, 04.90.76.90.18, closed dinner Wed, Sun, mid Nov-early Dec, menus €14-€36) and turned it into an haute cuisine restaurant, combined with a butcher's and upmarket deli. There's an informal, inexpensive menu at lunch, but it's a more dressed-up affair in the evening.

Lacoste's **Café de Sade** (pl de La Poste, 04.90.75.82.29, menu €15 lunch, closed mid Sept-mid Oct) offers sweeping views from its terrace, while the interior features the bar and grand piano from the old Maxime's bar in Monaco. The food is an unusual French/Thai/Moroccan fusion, with crab cakes, spring rolls and local Merguez sausages all jostling for space on the blackboard.

Over in Bonnieux, the semi-troglodyte **Le Fournil** (5 pl Carnot, 04.90.75.83.62, closed Mon, Tue, mid Nov-mid Dec, mid Jan-mid Feb, menus €21.80-€41) is the definition of low-key provençal style, with great service and an inventive menu that uses plenty of local produce. **Brasserie Les Terrasses** (cours Elzear Pin, 04.90.75.99.77, mains €8-€16, closed Wed Oct-June), an excellent pizzeria, offers views across the valley to Mont Ventoux.

On the *garrigue*-covered plateau above the village, **Le Bastide de Capelongue** (04.90.75.

89.78, www.capelongue.com, menus €70-€190, double €160-€320) has 17 airy, white and cream bedrooms, and the services of Michelin-starred chef Edouard Loubet. Off the D194, **Les Trois Sources** (chemin de la Chaone, 04.90.75.95.58, www.lestroissources.com, double €60-€140) is a lovely *chambre d'hôte* in an ancient building surrounded by mulberry trees. **Café de la Gare** (rte de la Gare, 04.90.75.82.00, mains €9-€17, menus €13-€22) is a popular, friendly restaurant in an old railway station, with terrific views and an outside terrace.

The remote **Auberge des Seguins** (Buoux, 04.90.74.16.37, double €50-€85), under the crags at the end of a valley, is a popular choice with walkers and rock climbers, and has a small *buvette* where you can stop for a drink. In Saignon, the **Auberge du Presbytère** (pl de la Fontaine, 04.90.74.11.50, www.auberge-presbytere.com, closed Jan-Feb, double €58-€145, restaurant closed Wed, menus €28-€38) overlooks the village square, with tables set out by the fountain in summer.

Chambre de Séjour Avec Vue (04.90.04.85.01, www.chambreavecvue.com, double €80) is an old house that has been transformed with a remarkable eye for colour and design by Kamila Regent; she invites artists in residence to work and exhibit in the house, while letting out three bedrooms and an apartment.

Resources

Tourist information
Bonnieux Office de Tourisme *7 pl Carnot, Bonnieux (04.90.75.91.90).* **Open** 2-6pm Mon; 9.30am-12.30pm, 2-6pm Tue-Sat.

Cucuron.

LOURMARIN & THE SOUTH LUBERON CHATEAUX

The southern edge of the range is known for its trio of Renaissance chateaux in Lourmarin, Ansouis and La Tour d'Aigue. One of the largest and liveliest Luberon villages, **Lourmarin**, with its cluster of grey-shuttered stone houses, belfry and medieval church, is becoming ever more chic with furniture and antiques shops opening every year. Tourism here remains civilised, though, with action centred on the main street, where Café Gaby and Café de l'Ormeau enjoy a friendly rivalry. The market is on a Friday morning.

Lourmarin was settled by Vaudois peasants and suffered in the merciless massacre of April 1545, when much of the village was temporarily abandoned. Rebuilt, it thrived in the 17th and 18th centuries as a centre of silk production. The Protestant temple now stands at the edge of the village. From here, rue du Temple leads to the 15th- to 16th-century **Château de Lourmarin**, which presents a fortified medieval aspect from one side and the large windows of the Renaissance from the other. The chateau narrowly escaped destruction in the Revolution; it was restored in the early 1900s and since 1925 has hosted artists- and writers-in-residence and chamber music concerts (summer only). Don't miss the cantilever staircase and extraordinary Renaissance fireplace, which combines classical Corinthian capitals with Native American figures from the newly discovered Americas. Albert Camus lived on the outskirts of the village and is buried in its cemetery.

West of Lourmarin, **Mérindol** is worth a visit not so much for its second homes of today as for the moving evocation of what used to be. Climb the waymarked route des Vaudois to a ruined village that is witness to the massacre of 1545, when Jean de Meynier, president of the Parlement d'Aix, sent in his troops to implement the Decree of Mérindol, which condemned the Vaudois as heretics. Within six days, 22 villages had been pillaged and burned, and an estimated 2,500 were dead. Mérindol was razed to the ground and its ruined citadel (now the Mémorial des Vaudois) remains a potent symbol; beyond, hilltop views stretch as far as the Alpilles, Montagne Ste-Victoire and Ste-Baume massif.

West of Mérindol, the **Gorges de Regalon**, provide a welcome breath of cool air. They are as pleasant for a stroll amid wild rosemary and shrubs as for making a start on the more ambitious walk to Oppède across the range. Although dry in summer, the gorge is apt to flood after heavy rain.

More workaday than chic Lourmarin, **Cadenet** has some charming stepped streets and ancient houses, as well as the small **Musée de la Vannerie**, devoted to basketmaking, once one of the town's principal activities; the market takes place on Monday mornings. There's a statue of the drummer boy of Arcole in the main square: born in the village, he saved French troops in the war against Austria in 1796. Of the chateau that once towered above the village, only the foundations remain.

East of Lourmarin on the D27, lovely, partly walled **Cucuron** is a tangle of narrow streets. On place de l'Horloge, a fortified bell-tower gateway leads to a ruined keep. The surprisingly large Eglise Notre-Dame-de-Beaulieu contains a fine baroque altarpiece and Gothic side chapels. Below, sunk into a rock, the **Moulin Huile Dauphin** olive press (La Clos la Treille, montée Galinier, 04.90.08.96.32, mill open Nov-Dec, shop open all year) makes deliciously fruity olive oil. On the square where the market is held on Tuesday mornings, the plane tree-shaded Bassin de l'Etang is a large stone water tank. Built in the 15th century to supply local flour mills, it's one of the most beautiful water features in Provence. From here, footpaths lead up the Mourre Nègre, the Luberon's highest point. Further east, the Luberon is quieter and less populated, with tiny, authentic villages like **Cabrières d'Aigues** and **La Motte d'Aigues** slumbering in the sunshine.

Ansouis is dominated by its Renaissance chateau, whose ramparts wind up around the mound. A visit takes in its baronial halls and massive kitchens, but the highlight is the terraced gardens. The Romanesque church is built into the edge of the castle's ramparts, and concerts are often held in the grounds in summer. In the town, the morning market on Sunday is the only real attraction.

Towards Pertuis – dull and traffic-clogged, but useful if you need a supermarket or a train – the **Château Val Joanis** (D973, rte de Cavaillon, Pertuis, 04.90.79.88.40, www.val-joanis.com, closed Sun Nov-Mar) combines wine-growing with beautiful terraced gardens. Further east at **La Tour d'Aigues**, amid rolling vineyards, are the remains of what was once the finest of all the Renaissance chateaux. Sadly, it was destroyed by fire way back in 1792; across ample defensive ditches, only the pedimented entrance and part of the wings survive, although in its magnificent heyday the chateau had a park, orangerie and exotic menagerie. Two museums, the **Musée des Faïences** and **Musée de l'Histoire du Pays d'Aigues**, are housed in the cellars.

In an area of vineyards, oak and pine forests lies **La Bastide de Jourdans**, founded in the 13th century and once a bustling centre of silk production, and the fortified medieval village of **Grambois**, where part of Marcel Pagnol's *La Gloire de Mon Père* was filmed.

AVIGNON & THE VAUCLUSE

Château d'Ansouis

rue Cartel, Ansouis (04.90.09.82.70/www. chateau-ansouis.com). **Open** (tours only) *Apr-Oct* 2-6pm Mon, Wed-Sun. **Admission** €6; €3-€4.50 reductions; free under-6s. **No credit cards**.

Château de Lourmarin

Lourmarin (04.90.68.15.23/www.chateau-de-lourmarin.com). **Open** *Jan* 2.30-4pm Sat, Sun. *Feb-Apr, Nov, Dec* 10.30-11.30am, 2.30-4pm daily. *May, June, Sept* 10-11.30am, 2.30-5.30pm daily. *July, Aug* 10-11.30am, 3-6pm daily. *Oct* 10.30-11.30am, 2.30-4.45pm daily. **Admission** €5.50; €2.50 reductions; free under-10s. **No credit cards**.

Musée de la Vannerie

La Glaneuse, av Philippe de Girard, Cadenet (04.90.68.24.44). **Open** *Apr-Oct* 10am-noon, 2.30-6.30pm Mon, Thur-Sat; 2.30-6.30pm Wed, Sun. Closed Nov-Mar. **Admission** €3.50; €1.50 reductions; free under-16s. **No credit cards**.

Musée des Faïences/Musée de l'Histoire du Pays d'Aigues

Château de la Tour d'Aigues (04.90.07.50.33/ www.chateau-latourdaigues.com). **Open** *Apr-June* 10am-1pm, 2.30-6pm Wed-Sat; 2.30-6pm Mon, Tue, Sun. *July-mid Aug* 10am-1pm, 2.30-6pm daily. *Mid Aug-Oct* 10am-noon, 2-6pm Wed-Sat; 2-6pm Mon, Tue, Sun. *Nov-Mar* 10am-noon, 2-5pm Wed-Sat; 2-5pm Mon, Tue, Sun. **Admission** €4.50; €2 reductions; free under-8s. **No credit cards**.

Where to stay & eat

Lourmarin has become the gourmet capital of the Luberon, thanks in part to Reine Sammut at **Auberge La Fenière** (D945, rte de Cadenet, 04.90.68.11.79, www.reinesammut.com, closed mid Nov-mid Dec, mid-end Jan, double €150-€315, restaurant closed Mon & lunch Tue, menus €46-€120). Working against the backdrop of a stylish modern *mas*, she's particularly good at starters, often using produce from her vegetable garden. There are cookery courses every Tuesday, and attractive rooms upstairs.

Le **Moulin de Lourmarin** (rue du Temple, 04.90.68.06.69, www.moulindelourmarin.com, closed mid Jan-mid Feb, double €165-€310) is a controversially converted but very comfortable watermill. A simple lunchtime menu (€25) is available in the courtyard; in the evening, under the auspices of chef Philippe Brun, the cooking is more serious (menus €32-€64).

When not in the mood for haute cuisine, locals enjoy laid-back **L'Antiquaire** (9 rue du Grand Pré, 04.90.68.17.29, closed Mon & Tue lunch in summer, Mon all day, Tue lunch, dinner Sun in winter, 3wks Nov-Dec, 3wks Jan-Feb, menus €20-€42) or the pan-Mediterranean flavours at **Maison Ollier Michel-Ange** (pl de la Fontaine, 04.90.68.02.03, closed Wed Easter-Oct, Tue & Wed Oct-Easter, all mid Nov-mid Dec, menus €21-€58), which has recently been refurbished. The former manager of the Auberge de Seguins in Buoux (*see p122*) has now taken over **L'Oustalet** (2 av Philippe Girard, 04.90.68.07.33, closed Mon), so superb, authentic cooking is assured. Prices are keen (menus €26-€28.50), and booking advised.

Well-hidden in the heart of the village, **Les Chambres de la Cordière** (impasse de la Cordière, rue Albert Camus, 04.90.68.03.32, www.cordiere.com, double €45-€70) has four characterful rooms (tiled floors, roll-top baths) in an ancient house, with a courtyard and a vaulted kitchen.

Amid vineyards two kilometres to the east of Lourmarin, **Le Mas de Guilles** (rte de Vaugines, 04.90.68.30.55, www.guilles.com, closed Nov-Mar, double €85-€200) is a cleverly converted *mas* with a swimming pool and tennis courts. At the Combe de Lourmarin, a short walk from the village, the friendly **Hostellerie du Paradou** (rte d'Apt, 04.90.68. 04.05, www.hotelparadou.fr, closed mid Nov-Jan, double €85-€135, menus €13-€35 lunch) is a stone *mas* with spacious lawns and nine simple rooms; the elegant restaurant now serves Thai food.

In Cadenet, **La Tuilière** (chemin de la Tuilière, 04.90.68.24.45, www.latuiliere.com, double €69-€85) offers five rooms in a big old house, with a ramshackle terraced garden, a small pool and a billiards table. The **Camping Val de Durance** (Les Routes, Cadenet, 04.90. 68.37.75, www.homair-vacances.com, closed Oct-Mar, pitch €24/two people) has well-spaced pitches, screened by trees. It overlooks a public lake with a little sandy beach, where swimming is permitted from May to September. The best restaurant is **L'Ardoise** (2 pl Tambour d'Arcole, 04.90.68.35.35, menu €18, closed Tue), which imports some much-needed chic from neighbouring Lourmarin and offers a modern take on provençal cooking.

In scenic Cucuron, good-value **L'Horloge** (55 rue Lèonce Brieugne, 04.90.77.12.74, closed dinner Tue-Wed, 2wks Feb, mains €18-€38, menus €18-€38), housed in vaulted cellars, is a cool retreat for some quietly creative provençal cooking. **La Petite Maison** (pl de l'Etang, 04.90.77.18.60, www.la-petitemaisondecucuron. com, closed mid Dec-mid Jan, menus €35-€55) is a favourite eatery among local fashionistas, with chef Eric Sapet serving imaginative versions of local staples. For pizzas, visit **La Remise** (bd du Nord, 04.90.07.53.44, closed Mon, mains €15-€30), which has a child-friendly garden at the rear. In Ansouis, **La Closerie** (bd des Platanes, 04.90.09.90.54, closed Wed, Thur, dinner Sun & all Jan, menu

€35) has a well-deserved reputation for serving excellent food at very competitive prices.

There are fewer options on the Luberon's eastern slopes, but the **Restaurant de la Fontaine** (pl de la Fontaine, 04.90.07.72.16, closed dinner Sun, all Mon, 10 Dec-10 Jan, menus €25-€35) in St-Martin-de-la-Brasque is justifiably popular. Grambois's welcoming **Auberge des Tilleuls** (moulin de Pas, 04.90.77.93.11, www.tilleuls.com, double €59-€109) provides five simple rooms and a good restaurant (menus €19-€39.50).

Resources

Tourist information

Ansouis Office de Tourisme *pl du Château, Ansouis (04.90.09.86.98/www.ansouis.fr).* **Open** *Apr-Sept* 10am-noon, 2-6pm daily. *Oct-Mar* 10am-noon, 2-5pm Wed-Sat. Closed Jan.
Cucuron Office de Tourisme *rue Lèonce Brieugne, Cucuron (04.90.77.28.37).* **Open** 9am-12.30pm, 2.30-6pm Mon-Fri.
Lourmarin Office de Tourisme *17 av Philippe de Girard, Lourmarin (04.90.68.10.77/ www.lourmarin.com).* **Open** 10am-12.30pm, 3-6pm Mon-Sat.
Mérindol Office de Tourisme *rue des Ecoles, Mérindol (04.90.72.88.50/www.cavaillon-luberon.fr).* **Open** *Sept-Apr* 9am-12.30pm, 1.30-5.30pm Tue-Sat. *Oct-Mar* 9am-12.30pm, 1.30-5.30pm Tue, Wed, Fri, Sat.

CAVAILLON

Cavaillon is most famous for being the melon capital of France: the juicy globes are celebrated in a festival in July (*see p46*), and crop up in everything from jam to chocolates. The town injects a dose of 'real life' into the Luberon – think housing estates, lounging youths and an absurd number of roundabouts – but

compensates with a thriving year-round arts scene, thanks to its **Scène Nationale** theatre (205 rue du Languedoc, 04.90.78.64.64, www.theatredecavaillon.com) and the **Grenier à Sons** (157 av du Général de Gaulle, 04.90.06.44.20) music venue.

In recent years, Cavaillon has been more commonly associated with militant farmers than with sightseeing, but past the anonymous periphery is an old town with relics from what was once an important medieval diocese. The market is wholesale only, except on Mondays when there is a lively food and general goods market. There are also a number of expensive delis and specialist food shops, including **Gérard Auzet** (61 cours Bournissac, 04.90.78.06.54), the baker who recently collaborated with Peter Mayle on his book *Confessions of a French Baker*.

The earliest visible reminder of Cavaillon's past is the spindly first-century AD **Arc Romain** (pl du Clos), bearing traces of sculpted flowers and winged victories. Behind it, a footpath zigzags the cliff to the medieval **Chapelle St-Jacques**, offering panoramic views and a lovely spot of green in the middle of town. At the foot of the Arc, peer into the time-capsule **Fin de Siècle** café. The raggedy old town is presided over by the Romanesque **Cathédrale Notre-Dame et St-Véran**, with its damaged cloister, octagonal tower and sundial. A relief on one altar refers to local melon cultivation, introduced by the Avignon popes. Outside, tree-shaded place Philippe de Cabassole has some fine 18th-century houses. The baroque façade of the Grand Couvent reflects Church power during the Comtat Venaissin; in the **Musée de l'Hôtel Dieu**, archaeological finds from a Neolithic settlement on St-Jacques hill are displayed in the former hospital and chapel.

Like nearby **Carpentras** (*see p107*), Cavaillon had a sizeable Jewish community, and its beautiful, light-filled **Synagogue** (built 1772-4) is one of the finest in France. The baby pink and blue upper level has bronze chandeliers, a rococo tabernacle and delicate ironwork, while the lower level doubled as a bakery. It was a bit of a last gasp: in 1791, the Comtat Venaissin was integrated into France and French Jews were given their liberty, marking the end of Cavaillon's ghetto. The town's Jewish population today is mainly of North African origin. The synagogue now contains the **Musée Juif Comtadin**, housing tabernacle doors from the earlier synagogue, and possessions of the community.

Musée de l'Hôtel Dieu
Grand-Rue (04.90.76.00.34). **Open** *May-Sept* 9.30am-12.30pm, 2.30-6.30pm Mon, Wed-Sun.

Admission (incl Synagogue/Musée Juif Comtadin) €3; €1.50 reductions; free under-12s. **No credit cards**.

Synagogue/Musée Juif Comtadin

rue Hébraïque (04.90.76.00.34). **Open** *Apr-Sept* 9am-12.30pm, 2.30-6.30pm Mon, Wed-Sun. *Oct-Mar* 9am-noon, 2-5pm Mon, Wed-Fri.

Admission (incl Musée de l'Hôtel Dieu) €3; €1.50 reductions; free under-12s. **No credit cards**.

Where to stay & eat

Cavaillon's hotels leave quite a lot to be desired, though old-fashioned **Hôtel du Parc** (183 pl François Tourel, 04.90.71.57.78, double €56-€68)

Antique and Chic

Find your very own piece of bygone Provence – at a price.

On a Sunday morning, at the height of the season, L'Isle-sur-la-Sorgue is busier than just about anywhere else in France. And with good reason: this mini-Venice is an antiques mecca. Dealers began settling here in the early 1960s, when the first *foires à la brocante* were held; these days, an estimated 300 sellers cluster along avenue de la Libération, avenue des Quatre Otages and around the station, many setting up stall in picturesque canalside locations. Each Sunday, the antiques shops and arcades (open 10am-7pm Mon, Sat, Sun) are joined by legions of junkier *brocanteurs*, who line avenue des Quatre Otages, while at Easter and on 15 August, antiques fairs flow over into nearby fields. Merchandise ranges from high-quality antiques and garden statuary to pedal cars and quirky collectibles, including many provençal items, such as gilt mirrors, armoires, printed fabrics, and local faïence pottery. There are also

architectural salvage specialists, offering old zinc bars, bistro fittings and the like.

The different arcades have different characters: two-storey **Quai de la Gare** (4 av Julien Guigue) is the most upmarket, with its fine 18th-century furniture, paintings and porcelain; **Village des Antiquaires de la Gare** (2bis av de l'Egalité), in a former carpet factory, is more ramshackle and boho; **Hôtel Dongier** (9 esplanade Robert Vasse) is set up as a series of smart interiors; **Isle-aux-Brocantes** (7 av des Quatre Otages) abounds in vintage garden furniture and 20th-century items.

Even if there are few true bargains (some shops seem to ship entire crates of furniture direct to stores in the USA, and it's common to hear sums being discussed in dollars), prices are lower than in Paris, where a fair number of the goods end up. Needless to say, the usual bargaining rules apply. Should you succumb, transport firms can ship your purchases around the world.

AVIGNON & THE VAUCLUSE

near the tourist office offers traditional style and a patio. There's no restaurant, but next door the belle époque café **Le Fin de Siècle** (46 pl du Clos, 04.90.71.12.27, closed Tue, Wed, menus €13-€28.50) has kept its mosaic frontage and large mirrors; upstairs is a restaurant which has a loose half-board arrangement with the Hôtel du Parc (call the hotel for details).

Other tempting tables include upmarket, old-fashioned **Prévôt** (353 av de Verdun, 04.90.71.32.43, closed Sun, 1wk Aug, 1wk Sept, menus €25-€35), famed for its inventive summer melon menu. For good-value provençal cuisine, try **Côté Jardin** (49 rue Lamartine, 04.90.71.33.58, closed all Sun, dinner Mon, dinner Tue in winter, all Feb, menus €23-€30), which has tables around a courtyard fountain, or **La Fontaine** (47 pl Castil Blaze, 04.90.71.78.01, closed lunch Sat, Sun, mains €12-€28, menus €14.50-€29.50).

Resources

Tourist information

Office de Tourisme *pl François Tourel, Cavaillon (04.90.71.32.01/www.cavaillon-luberon. com).* **Open** *July, Aug* 9am-noon, 2-6.30pm Mon-Sat; 9am-12.30pm Sun. *Sept-June* 9am-noon, 2-6pm Mon-Fri; 9am-noon Sat.

L'ISLE-SUR-LA-SORGUE & FONTAINE-DE-VAUCLUSE

L'Isle-sur-la-Sorgue is known as the 'Venise Comtadin' for its double (in places triple) ring of canals; charmingly, many households cross their thresholds over little stone bridges. Waterwheels recall a time when water powered the silk industry and, later on, the paper mills, and today the canals alleviate the worst of the summer heat. The other great attraction is France's largest concentration of antiques dealers outside Paris, strung out along the canals (*see left* Antique and Chic).

In the old town, head for the **Collégiale Notre-Dame-des-Anges** (pl de la Liberté, no phone, closed Mon, Sun), whose heavenly baroque interior is full of cherubim. Outside, place de la Liberté contains the pretty belle époque **Café de France**, some galleried houses and the town's tourist office, set in the old public granary. The former Musée Donadeï de Campredon, an elegant 18th-century *hôtel particulier*, is now the **Maison René Char**. As well as recreating the study of the Surrealist poet, who was born here in 1907, the museum hosts temporary exhibitions of modern art. There's a market on Thursdays and Sundays.

Seven kilometres upstream (along the D25), **Fontaine-de-Vaucluse** clusters around the source of the Sorgue river. After periods of heavy rain, water mysteriously gushes out of a sheer cliff-face into a jade-green pool, giving the ancient name Vallis Clausa ('closed valley') or Vaucluse to the whole *département*. Numerous divers, including the late Jacques Cousteau, have tried without success to find the source; their exploits, and the geological wonders of the area, are described in the underground museum **Le Monde Souterrain de Norbert Casteret**. Above the village is a ruined castle, built by monks to protect pilgrims visiting the tomb of dragon-slayer St Véran, while the pretty Romanesque church has a painting of St Véran and an 11th-century open altar table. Outside, a column commemorates Petrarch. Abandoned factories hint at Fontaine's more industrial past, notably paper-making for the Comtat Venaissin. Across the river, the **Musée Pétrarque** stands on the site where Italian Renaissance scholar Petrarch wrote his famous *Canzoniere*. Further up, past the mill, the **Musée d'Histoire 1939-1945 'L'Appel de la Liberté'** explores daily life during the occupation.

Le Beaucet is a pretty hillside village eight kilometres north of Fontaine-de-Vaucluse, which offers great views of the Vaucluse mountains, a fortified chateau, several restaurants and some interesting artisans' workshops, including Le Jardin de Robert, where two artists use the natural landscape to create living art works.

Between April and December, the Sorgue can be navigated by canoe between Fontaine-de-Vaucluse and Partage-des-Eaux. Canoes can be hired at **Canoë Evasion** (on D24 at Pont de Galas, 04.90.38.26.22, canoe hire €11-€17).

Maison René Char

20 rue du Dr Tallet, L'Isle-sur-la-Sorgue (04.90.38.17.41). **Open** 10am-1pm, 3-7pm Tue-Sun. **Admission** €6.50; €5.50 reductions; free under-14s. **Credit** MC, V.

Le Monde Souterrain de Norbert Casteret

chemin de la Fontaine, Fontaine-de-Vaucluse (04.90.20.34.13). **Open** *Apr-Sept* 10am-12.30pm, 2-6pm Tue-Sun. **Admission** €5.50; €4.50 reductions. **No credit cards**.

Musée d'Histoire 1939-1945 'L'Appel de la Liberté'

chemin du Gouffre, Fontaine-de-Vaucluse (04.90.20.24.00). **Open** *Mar-Sept* 10am-6pm Mon, Wed-Sun. *Oct-Dec* 10am-noon, 2-6pm Mon, Wed-Sun. Closed Jan, Feb. **Admission** €3.50; €1.50 reductions. *With Musée Pétrarque* €4.60; €2.80 reductions; free under-12s. **No credit cards**.

Musée Pétrarque

quai du Château Vieux, Fontaine-de-Vaucluse (04.90.20.37.20). **Open** *Apr-May, Oct* 10am-noon, 2-6pm Mon, Wed-Sun. *June-Sept* 10am-12.30pm,

1.30-6pm. Closed Nov-Mar. **Admission** €3.50;
€1.50 reductions. *With Musée d'Histoire* €4.60;
€2.80 reductions; free under-12s. **No credit cards.**

Where to stay & eat

Hungry antiques browsers are served by a
plethora of restaurants along the canals of
L'Isle-sur-la-Sorgue. One of the best is modish
bistro **Le Carré des Herbes** (13 av des
Quatres Otages, 04.90.38.23.97, closed Mon-
Thur Oct-Mar, menu €32). The stylish **Café du
Village**, within the Village des Antiquaires de
la Gare (closed Tue-Fri, dinner Mon, Sat, Sun,
menus €19-€22), serves imaginative, market-
inspired cooking (if you manage to arrive
within its limited opening times). The best new
restaurant is Michelin-starred **Le Vivier** (800
cours Fernande Peyre, 04.90.38.52.80, www.le
vivier-restaurant.com, closed lunch Thur-Sat,
all Mon, menus €43-€70), opened by Patrick
Fischnaller on one of the canals just outside
town, and serving modern French cuisine.

To maximise your antiques hunting time, stay
at the **Hôtel Les Nevons** (chemin des Nevons,
04.90.20.72.00, double €67-€89), a reasonably
priced central option with spacious rooms. Just
outside town, with affordable rooms, is the Best
Western outpost **Le Domaine de la Petite
Isle** (rte d'Apt, 04.90.38.40.00, double €51-€98).
For calm and characterful comfort, try the **Mas
de Cure Bourse** (carrefour de Velorgues,
04.90.38.16.58, double €75-€115, restaurant
closed lunch Mon in winter, all Jan, menus €27-
€51), an 18th-century coaching inn with rooms
à la provençale, a large garden and pool, set in
orchards three kilometres from town.

Fontaine-de-Vaucluse is strong on snacks and
ice-cream, as well as river trout. The **Hostellerie
Le Château** (quartier du Château Vieux,
04.90.20.31.54, closed lunch in winter, mains
€15-€30) is an attractive veranda restaurant in
a waterside setting. The 24 neo-provençal rooms
at the **Hôtel du Poète** (04.90.20.34.05, www.
hoteldupoete.com, closed late Dec-mid Feb,
double €70-€310) are set around imaginatively
landscaped gardens (and a pool) beside the river.

In Le Beaucet, **L'Auberge du Beaucet**
(04.99.66.10.82, www.aubergedubeaucet.fr,
closed Mon, Sun, Dec, Jan, mains €25, menu
€24 lunch) offers an excellent selection of local
Luberon and Ventoux wines, along with rustic
provençal cuisine.

Resources

Tourist information

**Fontaine-de-Vaucluse Office de
Tourisme** *chemin de la Fontaine, Fontaine-de-
Vaucluse (04.90.20.32.22).* **Open** 10am-1pm,
2-6pm daily.

L'Isle-sur-la-Sorgue Office de Tourisme
*pl de l'Eglise, L'Isle-sur-la-Sorgue (04.90.38.
04.78/www.oti-delasorgue.fr).* **Open** 9am-
12.30pm, 2.30-6pm Mon-Sat; 9am-12.30pm Sun.

APT

At first glance, there doesn't seem to be much
going on in Apt, with its industrial outskirts,
plane trees and sleepy squares along the
Calavon river. But on Saturday mornings the
town comes alive, thanks to the largest market
for miles around. It's busy all year, unlike some
of the more touristy offerings – and if the
weather's right, you'll find truffle vendors on
market mornings in December (*see p114*
Buried Treasures).

Place de la Bouquerie is the main access
point for the old town, via the narrow rue des
Marchands. The **Ancienne Cathédrale Ste-
Anne** throws an arch across the street. Now
demoted to the status of parish church, it's a
curious mix of Gothic and baroque, with crypts
dating from the fourth and 11th centuries. In
1660, Anne of Austria made a pilgrimage here
in thanks for the birth of Louis XIV, and gave
money to complete the Chapelle Royale. A
Roman sarcophagus, meanwhile, harks back to
the town's role as a staging post on Via Domitia.

The nearby **Maison du Parc** details the
flora, fauna and geology of the Parc Régional
du Luberon, and contains the **Musée de la
Géologie**. Next door, the **Musée de
l'Aventure Industrielle** traces the three
industries that brought prosperity to Apt in the
18th and 19th centuries: candied fruits; cream-
glazed and marbled earthenware; and ochre-
extraction. Today, although plenty of pottery
can be picked up at the market, only the **Atelier
Yvonne Rigo** (98 rue de la République, 04.90.
04.74.66, closed Sun) still makes the town's
traditional marbleware. **Aptunion** (N100,
quartier Salignan, 04.90.76.31.43) is the town's
biggest manufacturer of candied fruits. It runs
factory visits at 2.30pm from Monday to Friday,
with a shop that's open every day but Sunday.

FREE Ancienne Cathédrale
Ste-Anne

*rue de la Cathédrale (04.90.04.85.44/www.apt-
cathedrale.com).* **Open** *July-Sept* 8.30am-noon,
3-7pm Tue-Fri; 10am-noon Sat, Sun. *Oct-June*
8.30am-noon, 2-4pm Tue-Fri; 10am-noon Sat, Sun.
Treasury July-Sept (guided tours only) 11am,
5pm Mon-Sat; 11am Sun. **Admission** free.

FREE Maison du Parc

60 pl Jean Jaurès (04.90.04.42.00). **Open** *Apr-
Sept* 8.30am-noon, 1.30-6pm Mon-Fri, 8.30am-
noon Sat. *Oct-Mar* 8.30am-noon, 1.30-6pm
Mon-Fri. **Admission** free.

Musée de l'Aventure Industrielle
14 pl du Pastal (04.90.74.95.30). **Open** *June-Sept* 10am-noon, 3-6pm Wed-Sat; 2-5.30pm Sun. *Oct-May* 10am-noon, 2-5.30pm Wed-Sat. **Admission** €4; €2 reductions; free under-16s. **No credit cards**.

Where to stay & eat

At **L'Auberge du Luberon** (8 pl du Faubourg du Ballet, 04.90.74.12.50, double €58-€98, closed Nov; restaurant closed all Mon, lunch Tue, dinner Sun, Dec-Apr, menus €25-57), chef Serge Peuzin offers a special *menu aux fruits confits*, featuring Apt's speciality in every course; there are also 14 bedrooms. The **Bistrot de France** (67 pl de la Bouquerie, 04.90.74.22.01, mains €9.50-€16, closed Mon, Sun) stars in *A Year in Provence* but, despite the celebrity endorsement, still manages to offer reliably good regional fare. **La Fromagerie** (23 rue de Préfecture, 04.90.04.01.78, closed Mon-Wed, Sun, menu €17 lunch) is a must for cheese-lovers; it offers a huge range of *fromages* to take away, plus lunch plates with cheese, salads, bread and wine.

With the arrival of the **Domaine des Andéols** (Les Andéols, St-Saturnin-les-Apt, 04.90.75.50.63, www.domainedesandeols.com, double €250-€780) just north of Apt, the Luberon has gained a stunning boutique hotel. Olivier Massart created ten 'maisons' from the buildings of the family farm, where traditional tile and oak finishes merge with contemporary furniture, art and modern comforts such as plasma TVs. The grounds are a *tour de force*, while a fibre-optically lit staircase leads to the restaurant; its menus (from €68) use market produce and change nightly. There's also a low-key spa with a sauna, hammam and indoor pool, and an infinity pool overlooking the olive groves.

Resources

Tourist information
Office de Tourisme *20 av Philippe de Girard, Apt (04.90.74.03.18/www.ot-apt.fr).* **Open** *Mid June-mid Sept* 9.30am-7pm Mon-Sat; 9am-12.30pm Sun. *Mid Sept-mid June* 9am-noon, 2-6pm Mon-Sat.

GORDES & THE PLATEAU DE VAUCLUSE

A principal stamping ground for the *gauche caviar*, France's champagne socialists (or the *gauche tapénade*, as they are known further south), **Gordes** is almost too pretty for its own good. Its spectacular hillside setting is dominated by the turrets of its chateau, drystone walls and steep, stepped alleys. From a vantage point just outside the village, the view is magnificent, sweeping across the valley to the shadowy northern slopes of the Luberon, which seem almost to glow in the early evening light.

The rows of tasteful shops sell the usual provençal crafts and produce, and there's a market on Tuesday mornings. The **Château de Gordes** has a semi-permanent exhibition by the 20th century Belgian painter Pol Mara (don't believe the old posters you still see mentioning Vasarely), but otherwise the village is best enjoyed from the outside looking in. Note that parking for the village is a ten-minute walk from the centre.

To the west of Gordes, the **Village des Bories** is a group of restored, beehive-shaped drystone huts, inhabited between the 16th and 19th centuries. You'll find *borie* houses, stables and sheepfolds dotted all over the hillside, as well as a photo exhibition that shows similar drystone structures in other countries.

AVIGNON & THE VAUCLUSE

Gordes

North of Gordes, at the bottom of a wooded valley, is the **Abbaye Notre-Dame-de-Sénanque**. Founded in 1148, this is one of the great triumvirate (along with Silvacane and Thoronet) of provençal Cistercian monasteries. Set in lavender fields, the beautifully preserved Romanesque ensemble is still home to a monastic community.

Surrounded by strangely eroded outcrops of ochre-red rocks, **Roussillon** is among the most picturesque of all the Luberon villages – though it can get suffocated by tourists. The houses are painted in an orange wash, which makes the entire village glow. There are few sights as such, though the belfry-sundial of the **Eglise St-Michel** and the 18th-century façades on place de la Mairie are worth noting; the town's market is held on Thursday morning. To the left of the village cemetery, above a car park, the **Sentier des Ocres** (closed Nov-Mar, admission €2, free under-10s) footpath offers wonderful views amid peculiar rock formations, the result of ochre quarrying. On the D104 towards Apt, the former ochre works have reopened as the **Conservatoire des Ocres et Pigments Appliqués** (Usine Mathieu, D104, 04.90.05.66.69, www.okhra.com). Guided tours (July, Aug every 30min, 10am-noon, 2-6pm daily. Sept-June 11am, 3pm daily, €6) show how the rock was made into pigment.

Reached by small lanes south of the D22 towards Rustrel from Apt, undulating green countryside suddenly gives way to the vibrantly coloured **Colorado de Rustrel**, a valley littered with rocks long exploited for ochre pigment. Its dramatic colours vary from pale cream via yellows and orange to deep, russet red. Near the car park, a path descends to a picnic site and *buvette*, and relics of disused ochre works. Wear decent shoes and stick to the *sentiers* (colour-coded, waymarked paths), which lead you round some of the most spectacular turrets, chimneys and banks.

Abbaye Notre-Dame-de-Sénanque
3km N of Gordes on D177 (04.90.72.05.72/ www.senanque.fr). **Open** *Guided tours* 10.10am, 2.30pm, 3.30pm, 4.35pm Mon-Sat; 2.30pm, 3.30pm, 4.35pm Sun. Closed 2wks Jan, mornings Oct-Apr. **Admission** €7; €3-€5 reductions; free under-6s. **No credit cards.**

Château de Gordes
Gordes (04.90.72.02.75). **Open** 10am-noon, 2-6pm daily. **Admission** €4; €3 reductions; free under-10s. **No credit cards.**

Village des Bories
Les Savournins, Gordes (04.90.72.03.48). **Open** 9am-sunset daily. **Admission** €6; €4 reductions; free under-12s. **No credit cards.**

Where to stay & eat

In Gordes, **La Bastide de Gordes** (rte de Combe, 04.90.72.12.12, www.bastide-de-gordes.com, closed Jan, double €195-€875) is an upmarket hotel built into the ramparts, with great views and both an indoor and outdoor pool. The **Domaine de l'Enclos** (rte de Sénanque, 04.90.72.71.00, closed mid Nov-mid Mar, double €140-€180) is beautifully decorated and has a decent restaurant (menu €45); all ground-floor rooms have private gardens. Adjoining the chateau, **Café-Restaurant la Renaissance** (pl du Château, 04.90.72.02.02, mains €20-€32) has tables out on the square and was recently used as one of the locations for the Ridley Scott film adaptation of Peter Mayle's *A Good Year*.

David (pl de la Poste, 04.90.05.60.13, closed Jan, menus €33-€52) is the most reliable of the bistros and snack bars dotted about Roussillon, while the **Mas de Garrigon** (rte de St-Saturnin-d'Apt, 04.90.05.63.22, double €157-€197) is a traditional provençal farmhouse that provides nine very comfy rooms and a friendly welcome.

In Goult, just north of the N100 Avignon to Apt road, the **Café de la Poste** (pl de la Libération, 04.90.72.23.23, lunch only, closed Sun, Jan, menu €18) is another provençal restaurant to gain fame in Mayle's *A Year in Provence* – and also featured in Jean Becker's film *L'Eté Meurtrier*. Join locals and chic second-homers for gossip and home cooking. At the foot of the village is upmarket *chambre d'hôte* **La Grande Bégude** (06.62.31.85.01, www.la-grande-begude.com, double €150-€190), a tastefully converted old farmhouse with a swimming pool.

Resources

Tourist information
Gordes Office de Tourisme *Le Château, Gordes (04.90.72.02.75/www.gordes-village.com).* **Open** *July, Aug* 9am-7.30pm daily. *Sept-June* 9am-noon, 2-6pm Mon-Sat.

Roussillon Office de Tourisme *pl de la Poste, Roussillon (04.90.05.60.25/www.roussillon-provence.com).* **Open** *July, Aug* 10am-noon, 2-6pm Mon-Sat. *Sept-June* 1.30-5.30pm Mon-Fri.

MANOSQUE

This traditional Luberon town, with its sun-baked streets, is the birthplace of skincare company L'Occitane, whose fragrant body creams, candles and shower gels conjure up the smells of Provence in bathrooms from Norway to Japan. The company, now the town's main employer, has an outpost at 21 rue Grande and an outlet shop in the St-Maurice industrial zone, where factory tours are also offered.

Outside Manosque, housing and industrial parks now sprawl over the hillside and the traffic can be terrible. Within the city walls, though, narrow streets, squares and covered passageways give an interesting perspective on what the Luberon must have been like before it became so hip. Manosque is positively moribund on a Sunday out of season and liveliest on a Saturday, when a market takes over the centre.

Porte Saunerie leads into rue Grande, Manosque's main shopping street. At No.14, a plaque marks the house where novelist Jean Giono (1895-1970), son of a local shoemaker, was born. Note also the 18th-century balcony at No.23. There are two historic churches, **St-Sauveur**, which features in Giono's swashbuckler *Le Hussard sur le Toit*, and **Notre-Dame-de-Romigier** on place de l'Hôtel de Ville, which has a fine Renaissance doorway and a black Virgin inside.

The town's Giono link is exploited to the full with literary competitions, bookshops and walks on the theme of 'Jean Giono, poet of the olive tree'. The **Centre Jean Giono** (3 bd Elèmir Bourges, 04.92.70.54.54, closed mornings, all day Mon, Sun, €4), in an 18th-century *hôtel particulier*, has exhibitions and a permanent display about the writer's life and work. His own house, **Lou Paraïs** (montée des Vraies Richesses, 04.92.87.73.03), north of the old town, is open for guided visits on Friday afternoons (ring ahead).

Where to stay & eat

The **Pré Saint Michel** (rte de Dauphin Manosque, 04.92.72.14.27, www.presaint michel.com, double €60-€100) is a beautifully decorated hotel with a very good restaurant (menus €24-€40). **Hostellerie de la Fuste** (rte d'Oraison, 04.92.72.05.95, www.lafuste.com, doubles €110-180, restaurant closed dinner Sun, Mon Oct-June, 1wk Jan, 2wks Nov, menus €55-€87) is just outside Manosque, but worth the trip. Chef Daniel Jourdan has been there for over 40 years, cooking wonderful dishes such as the local Sisteron lamb or trout from the River Durance; it's popular, so book ahead. For the latest in upmarket chic, visit the newly opened **Couvent des Minimes** (chemin de Jeux Mai, Mane, 04.09.74.77.77, www.couventdesminimes. com, double €150-€425, menus €60-€90), a spa and hotel set in the grounds of a 17th-century convent, ten kilometres outside Manosque.

Resources

Tourist information
Office du Tourisme *pl du Dr Joubert, Manosque (04.92.72.16.00/www.ville-manosque. fr).* **Open** *July, Aug* 9am-7pm Mon-Sat; 10am-noon Sun. *Sept-June* 9am-12.15pm, 1.30-6pm Mon-Fri; 9am-12.15pm Sat.

PAYS DE FORCALQUIER

In the early Middle Ages, the Counts of Forcalquier rivalled those of Provence. The two were united in 1195, when Gersande, Comtesse de Forcalquier, married Alphonse, Comte de Provence; their son Raymond Bérenger V craftily succeeded in marrying all four of his daughters to future kings. Today, **Forcalquier** is light years from its illustrious past, but still a lively local centre. The main reason to visit is the big market on Monday mornings – so popular with traders that itinerant vendors seeking a space have to camp overnight to guarantee themselves a spot.

The sober Romano-Gothic Cathédrale Notre-Dame-du-Bourguet is almost as wide as it is long, with a triple nave and an impressive organ loft. The former Couvent des Visitandines now contains the Cinématographe cinema, the mairie and the **Musée Municipal**, where archaeological finds include a fine Roman head from nearby Lurs. Narrow streets next to the cathedral lead into the old town, where there are attractive houses on rue Béranger and a fancy Gothic fountain on place St-Michel. Climb past the *carrillon* up the wooded mound, where the citadel was replaced in 1875 with the octagonal Chapel Notre-Dame-de-Provence, with its neo-Gothic musician angels. Forcalquier's other

Forcalquier

AVIGNON & THE VAUCLUSE

main sight is its cemetery, north-east of the centre, with striking landscaped walls of yew.

At **Mane**, once a market halt on the Via Domitia, houses climb up in concentric curtain walls around the feudal castle (closed to the public). On the edge of the village, the **Prieuré Notre-Dame-de-Salagon** combines fascinating botanical gardens with an ethnographical museum. The 12th-century chapel has traces of medieval frescoes, as well as modern stained glass by abstract painter Aurélie Nemours, while priory buildings house exhibits on beekeeping and sage growing. There's also a reconstructed forge, but the highlight is the medieval garden, which reveals that turnips, parsnips and pulses were staples – quite different to what we now think of as provençal cuisine. Other gardens are planted with herbs, aromatic plants and flowers used in popular remedies. Just outside Mane, the **Château de Sauvan** is a carefully restored 18th-century building with extensive gardens.

The colony of white domes blistering out of the hillside above the village of **St-Michel-l'Observatoire** belong to the **Observatoire de Haute-Provence** (04.92.70.64.00, www.obs-hp.fr, tours Apr-July, Sept-Nov 2-4pm Wed, Aug 1.30-4.30pm Thur, €4, €2.50 reductions), a national astronomical research laboratory. The site was chosen thanks to its pure air and clear skies; its position on a promontory means the views are pretty amazing, too, even if you're not looking up. Meanwhile, the **Centre d'Astronomie** (plateau du Moulin Vent, 04.92.76.69.69, www.centre-astro.fr) runs observation evenings in July and August .

Château de Sauvan

Mane. (04.92.75.05.64). **Open** Tours *July-Aug* 3.30pm Mon-Sat. *Sept-mid Nov* 3.30pm Thur, Sat, Sun. *Feb-Mar* 3.30pm Thur, Sat, Sun. Closed mid Nov-Jan. **Admission** €6. **No credit cards**.

Musée Municipal

pl du Bourguet, Forcalquier (04.92.75.00.14). **Open** *Apr-Sept* 3-6pm Wed-Sat. Closed Oct-Mar. **Admission** €2; free under-18s. **No credit cards**.

★ Prieuré Notre-Dame-de-Salagon

Mane (04.92.75.70.50). **Open** *May-Sept* 10am-12.30pm, 2-7pm daily. *Oct-Dec, Feb-May* 2-6pm daily. Closed Jan. **Admission** €5; €2.60 reductions; free under-12s. **No credit cards**.

Where to stay & eat

In Forcalquier, you'll find several café-brasseries on place du Bourguet and around place St-Michel. **Grand Hôtel** (10 bd Latourette, 04.92.75.00.35, double €44-€48) offers basic but clean rooms in a good downtown location. **Hôtel la**

Bastide St Georges (rte de Banon, 04.92.75.72.80, www.bastidesaintgeorges.com, double €110-€170) is a relaxing option, with 17 well-decorated rooms and a good pool. Just outside town is the **Auberge Charembeau** (N100, rte de Niozelles, 04.92.70.91.70, www.charembeau.com, double €54-€108), set in an 18th-century farm, with seven hectares of land to explore and a pretty pool area and garden.

Resources

Tourist information

Office de Tourisme *13 pl du Bourguet, Forcalquier (04.92.75.10.02/www.forcalquier.com).* **Open** *June-Sept* 9am-noon, 2-7pm Mon-Sat; 10am-1pm Sun. *Oct-May* 9am-noon, 2-6pm Mon-Sat.

GETTING THERE & AROUND

By bus

Cars Sumian (04.91.49.44.25) runs a morning bus between Aix and Apt, via Cadenet, Lourmarin and Bonnieux. **Cars Arnaud** (04.90.38.15.58, www.voyages-arnaud.fr) runs buses between L'Isle-sur-la-Sorgue and Fontaine-de-Vaucluse or Avignon, none on Sun. Note that, at the time of writing, this service was in danger of being stopped – call to check. **Barlatier** (04.32.76.00.40) runs six buses a day between Avignon and Apt; four a day between Cavaillon and Avignon; four between Cavaillon and Apt; and four between Cavaillon and Forcalquier (all Mon-Sat only). **Express de la Durance** (04.90.71.03.00) runs two buses a day between Cavaillon and Gordes. There are no bus services to Roussillon.

By car

From the A7, take exit 25 for Cavaillon. The D2 runs from Cavaillon to Taillades and joins the N100, the Avignon–Apt–Forcalquier road, which rings the Montagne de Luberon. L'Isle-sur-la-Sorgue is on the N100 or by the D938 from Cavaillon. To the south, the D973 runs from Cavaillon to Cadenet and Pertuis, via Mérindol and Lauris. The only road across the range is the D943 from Cadenet via Lourmarin, which then forks to Apt (D943) and Bonnieux (D36). Manosque can be reached by the D973 and N96 or the A51 from Aix. For Cadenet from Aix, take the N7 and D543/D943 via Rognes.

By train

There's a TGV service to Avignon, with shuttle buses to L'Isle-sur-la-Sorgue and Cavaillon, or to Aix-en-Provence with three shuttles a day to Manosque. Local trains run from Avignon Centre Ville to Cavaillon and L'Isle-sur-la-Sorgue. Pertuis and Manosque are on the branch line from Marseille to Gap via Aix: Manosque-Gréoux-les-Bains station is 1.5km south of the centre.

Marseille & Aix

The **Vieux Port**.
See p137.

Introduction

A tale of two cities – and a glorious stretch of coastline.

As France's oldest city, **Marseille** has plenty to offer tourists – but it can also do very well without them, thank you very much. Marseille belongs to the Marseillais, and like any self-respecting *citadins*, they go on holiday in summer. But it's a great city to visit at any time of year – and is currently in the thick of a vast urban renewal programme.

With its beautifully preserved *hôtels particuliers*, elegant fountains and secluded squares, **Aix-en-Provence** exudes chic self-assurance. Paul Cézanne was born here, and has left a fascinating trail of former homes, studios, favourite cafés and painterly haunts. Follow in his footsteps from the artful jumble of his atelier in Aix-en-Provence to the wilder Montagne-Ste-Victoire and the abandoned quarries at Bibémus.

Although they may seem poles apart, rough-and-ready Marseille and polished Aix have far more in common than first impressions might suggest. For a start, both have a staunchly independent spirit (which, in both cases, helped to fuel the progress of the French Revolution). Both cities also have historic universities and thriving year-round cultural scenes. Aix hosts the prestigious Festival International d'Art Lyrique, while Marseille boasts an adventurous contemporary arts scene – and is set to become European Capital of Culture in 2013.

Despite Marseille's gritty edge, it has some postcard-perfect stretches of coastline on its doorstep, whose pristine beaches, stunning cliffs and tranquil fishing ports seem a world away from the urban rush. To the east, the city segues into the craggy outcrops and crystal-clear sea of the **Calanques**. Less well-known to outsiders are the **Côte Bleue**, the pretty stretch of coast west of Marseille, and the old fishing town of **Martigues**. Even in the heart of the city, though, boats bob in the Vieux Port, and every other street corner offers up a glittering vista of the Med – Marseille, it seems, has the best of both worlds.

The Best of Marseille & Aix

Standout sights, restaurants and hotels from across the region.

THINGS TO DO

Survey Marseille from the **Basilique Notre-Dame-de-la-Garde** (*see p141*), then stroll around Pierre Puget's **Centre de la Vielle Charité** (*see p143*). Art-lovers should check out the surrealist gems at the **Musée Cantini** (*see p144*), then brush up on Cézanne's *oeuvre* over in Aix. The **Musée Granet** (*see p167*) has a handful of his works, but for an insight into the man behind the masterpieces, visit the **Atélier Cézanne** (*see p168*) or **Carrières de Bibémus** (*see p172*).

Round your trip off with an evening at the **Ballet Preljocaj – Pavillon Noir** (*see p172*), Aix's daring new dance centre. Cultural overload? Surrender to the sun-drenched charms of the **Côte Bleue** (*see p157*) and the **Calanques** (*see p159*).

PLACES TO EAT

In Marseille, feast on bouillabaisse at **Le Miramar** or sample inventive seafood at **L'Epuisette** (for both, *see p150*). Aix's

varied dining scene, meanwhile, runs from the traditional **Bistro Latin** (*see p169*) to elegant Japanese eaterie **Yamato (Koji & Yuriko)** (*see p170*). To experience Southern café culture, quaff a café at the **Brasserie des Deux Garçons** (*see p169*), which has barely changed in centuries.

WHERE TO STAY

Spend a night in an architectural icon at Marseille's **Hôtel Le Corbusier** (*see p155*) or hang out at Aix's unexpectedly hip **Hôtel Cézanne** (*see p173*).

NIGHTLIFE

Get with the 'cours Ju' action at **Espace Julien** (*see p152*), plug into club culture at **Le Trolleybus** (*see p153*) or nab a terrace table at **Le Bar de la Marine** (*see p151*) and enjoy the view. In Aix, get friendly with the locals at the lively **Bar Brigand** (*see p170*) or **Le Sextius Mirabeau**, or work through the cocktail menu at **La Rotonde** (for both, *see p171*).

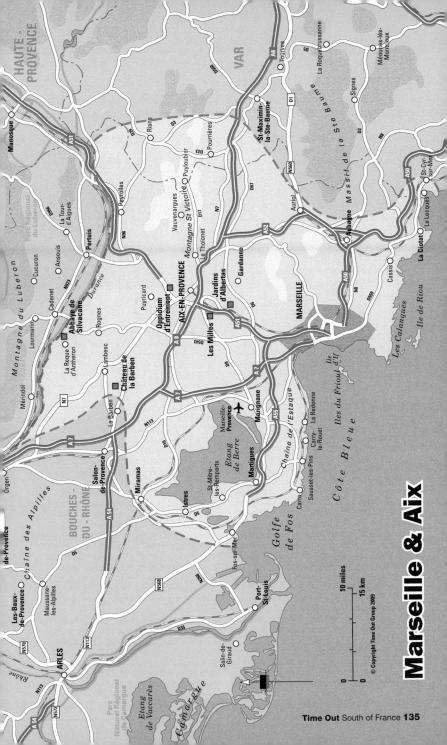

Marseille & Aix

Marseille

Brash and brimming with life, this age-old port has a vibrant charm.

In France's oldest city, medieval churches, Roman remains, 19th-century palaces and tiny cottages on hilly streets jostle with huge housing estates, louche cafés and avant-garde architecture. There may be glorious sea views at every turn, but **Marseille** is proudly, defiantly urban: not a seaside resort out to fleece tourists, but a year-round working city with a lively cultural scene, where you might just happen to join the locals for a swim on the beach.

For weekend getaways, head for the fishing ports, rocky inlets and sand and shingle beaches of the nearby **Côte Bleue**.

ABOUT THE CITY

If the *French Connection* movies and, more recently, Robert Guédiguian's *La Ville est Tranquille* haven't exactly painted a pretty bouillabaisse-suffused picture of the city, other images capture its upbeat energy: the omnipresent blue and white of football team Olympique de Marseille (OM); Luc Besson's *Taxi* films, packed with local humour and colour; and the nationwide success of France's most popular soap opera, *Plus Belle la Vie* (*see p140* **Life is Beautiful?**). Of late, Marseille has been undergoing an ambitious programme of urban renewal, which has brought a sleek new tramway; what's more, it has been chosen as the European City of Culture for 2013.

This is a city of fascinating contradictions. The sun almost always shines, but the ferocious winds of the Mistral chill the bones in winter. The architecture can be stunning but, despite much restoration in hand, many buildings are crumbling and Marseille has its share of modern eyesores. Yuppies dine in the Vieux Port's smart restaurants, while boy racers charge around in souped-up cars late at night. Some of the neighbourhoods behind the Vieux Port remain relatively poor, while the Corniche coastal road to the south is peppered with grand stucco villas. A dangerous reputation lingers, but the crime rate is no higher than in other major French cities and continues to drop.

Bouillabaisse, *méchoui* (roasted lamb), pizza and *nems* (spring rolls) illustrate the ethnic mix, but France's second-largest city offers so much more. Loud-mouthed and welcoming to those who appreciate their city, its citizens first and foremost consider themselves Marseillais.

History

Life in Marseille has revolved around the Vieux Port ever since a band of Phocaean Greeks sailed into the harbour in 600 BC. On that very day a local chieftain's daughter, Gyptis, was to choose a husband and the Greeks' dashing commander Protis clearly fitted the bill. The bride came with a dowry of land and a hill near the mouth of the Rhône, where the Greeks founded a trading post named Massalia.

By 500 BC, Massalia's trading routes extended throughout Mediterranean Europe and from Brittany to the Baltic. In 49 BC, though, Caesar besieged the city, leaving Massalia's Greeks with little more than their famous university and much-vaunted independence, which they were to lose and regain several times over the centuries.

In 1666, Louis XIV pulled down the city walls and expanded the port to the Rive Neuve, building a new arsenal, along with the Fort St-Nicolas. Marseille became France's leading port – and it was here, in 1720, that the plague came to Europe, via a ship that had come from Syria; 45,000 of Marseille's citizens were wiped out.

Marseille enthusiastically supported the Revolution, marching on Paris singing the anthem now known as *Le Marseillais*, only to turn monarchist under the First Empire and republican under the Second. By the time of

Vieux Port.

Napoléon III, Algeria had become a French *département*, leading to an enormous increase in shipping; a new port, La Joliette, was built in 1853. In 1869, when the Suez Canal opened, Marseille became the greatest boom town in Europe. As immigrants poured in from Spain, Greece and Italy, it acquired the astonishingly cosmopolitan population it maintains to this day.

More immigrants arrived following the independence of Tunisia in 1956 and Algeria in 1962, when the city received a mass exodus of French colonials, North African Jews and North Africans who had been involved in colonial administration. At the same time, the loss of the colonies hit its shipping trade. From 1954 to 1964 the population grew by 50 per cent, creating a severe housing shortage. New neighbourhoods sprang up to cope with the influx; areas of high unemployment throughout the 1970s and '80s, they became infamous for drug dealing and crime.

Yet while Jean-Marie Le Pen and his 'France for the French' extreme-right politics have gained ground elsewhere in the region, Marseille is one place where the melting pot seems to work – and the city was largely free of the suburban riots widespread in much of France in 2005. The city elected a socialist council from 1953 to 1995, but Jean-Claude Gaudin, the conservative mayor of Marseille since 1995, easily won the 2001 municipal elections and was narrowly re-elected in 2008.

SIGHTSEEING

Marseille takes in 57 kilometres (36 miles) of seafront, from L'Estaque in the north to the Calanques in the south (*see p159*). The city is laid out in 16 *arrondissements*, moving clockwise from the Vieux Port, then anticlockwise in an outer semi-circle.

Around the Vieux Port

The Vieux Port remains the emotional centre of Marseille life, as it has been for the past 26 centuries. It's a favourite place for a stroll, scene of the 14 July fireworks and somewhere for jubilant OM fans to celebrate after a victory. Fashionable bars and avant-garde theatres rub shoulders with ship's chandlers, while luxury yachts bob alongside the tiny fishing boats that deliver the day's catch to the market at quai des

> **INSIDE TRACK**
> **THE SUSPICIOUS SUN KING**
>
> Tellingly, the mighty cannons at the **Fort St-Jean** and **Fort St-Nicolas** used to face towards, rather than away from, the city: the rebellious Marseillais are still proud of this display of Louis XIV's doubts about their allegiance.

Marseille

0 — 200 m
0 — 200 yds

© Copyright Time Out Group 2009

Docks de la Joliette

Ferry to Château d'If & Iles de Frioul

Cathédrale de la Major

Ancienne-Major

St-Laurent

Musée de Docks Roma

Fort St-Jean

Memorial des Camps de la Mort

QUAI DE LA TOURETTE

AVENUE VAUDOYER

AVENUE DE LA TOURETTE

RUE SCHUMAN

RUE DE L'EVECHE

RUE ST FRANCOISE

MONTEE DES ACCOU

RUE ST LAURENT

RUE CAISSERIE

AVENUE ST JEAN

RUE DE LA LOGE

QUAI DU PORT

PI
VI

Jardin du Pharo

Anse de la Reserve

Fort St-Nicolas

Vieux

Ferry Boat

Club Nautique

BOULEVARD CHARLES LIVON

Basin de Carénage

Théâtre de la Cri

RUE DES CATALANS

RUE E DUCHESNE

RUE NEUVE SAINTE CATHE

CORNICHE

LE PHARO

ST MAURICE

PLACE ST VICTOR

Abbaye de St-Victor

RUE D'ENDOUME

RUE ROBERT

RUE SAINTE

RUE DE LA CROIX

AVENUE DE LA CORSE

BD DE LA CORDERIE

RUE DES LICES

Jardin Pu

Docks de la Joliette

La Friche

Gare St-Charles

RUE SAUVEUR TOBELEM

PLACE J. ETIENNE

RUE ABBE DAS

La Canebière

Vieux Port

RUE J ARCHER

AVENUE VAUVENARGUES

MONTEE DE L'ORATO

RUE D'ENDOUME

BD ANDRE

Corniche

Avenue du Prado

LAMBERT

BOULEVARD TELLENE

ST VICTOR

Stade Vélodrome

RUE DAVID

Stade

RUE SCUDERY

Basilique Notre-Dame-de-la-Garde

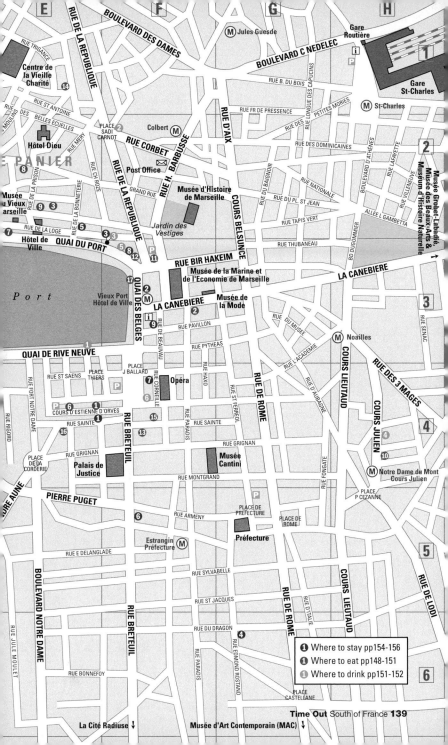

RUE TRIGANCE
RUE DE LA REPUBLIQUE
BOULEVARD DES DAMES
Jules Guesde
Gare Routière
BOULEVARD C NEDELEC
Gare St-Charles

Centre de la Vieille Charité
14
RUE ST ANTOINE
RUE MODULINS DES BELLES ECUELLES
RUE DE LA REPUBLIQUE
RUE B. DU BOIS
RUE LONGUE DES CAPUCINS
RUE FR DE PRESSENCE
St-Charles
RUE DES PETITES MORIES
RUE DES DOMINICAINES

Hôtel Dieu
PLACE SADI CARNOT
2
Colbert
RUE CORBET
RUE MERY
RUE DE LA REPUBLIQUE
RUE H. BARBUSSE
RUE D'AIX
RUE DU PL. ST JEAN
RUE NATIONALE
BOULEVARD D'ATHÈNES
RUE LAFAYETTE
RUE VILLENEUVE
Musée Grobet-Labadié Musée des Beaux-Arts & Muséum d'Histoire Naturelle

PANIER
Musée du Vieux Marseille
8
RUE CH PROZE
Post Office
GRAND RUE
RUE DE LA BONNETERIE
Musée d'Histoire de Marseille
Jardin des Vestiges
COURS BELSUNCE
RUE DU BAIGNOIR
RUE TAPIS VERT
ALLÉE L GAMBETTA
RUE DES DOMINICAINES
2

RUE DE LA PRISON
9
3
RUE DE LA LOGE
3
3
RUE THUBANEAU
BD DUGOMMIER

7
Hôtel de Ville
QUAI DU PORT
5
8
12
11
RUE BIR HAKEIM
Musée de la Marine et de l'Economie de Marseille
LA CANEBIERE

Port
17
QUAI DES BELGES
Vieux Port Hôtel de Ville
2
LA CANEBIERE
2
Musée de la Mode
RUE DU MUSÉE
RUE SENAC
3

QUAI DE RIVE NEUVE
1
i
9
RUE DE BEAUVAU
RUE PAVILLON
RUE PYTHEAS
RUE DE L'ACADÉMIE
RUE D'AUBAGNE
COURS LIEUTAUD
Noailles
RUE DES 3 MAGES

RUE ST SAENS
PLACE THIERS
PLACE J BALLARD
7
Opéra
6
RUE CORNEILLE
RUE HAXO
RUE ST FERREOL
RUE DE ROME

RUE FORT NOTRE DAME
P
6
1
COURS D'ESTIENNE D'ORVES
15
RUE SAINTE
RUE PARADIS
RUE SAINTE

RUE RIGORD
16
RUE SAINTE
13
RUE GRIGNAN
COURS JULIEN
10
4

PLACE DE LA CORDERIE
RUE GRIGNAN
Palais de Justice
RUE BRETEUIL
Musée Cantini
RUE FONGATE
Notre Dame du Mont Cours Julien

RUE AUNE
PIERRE PUGET
RUE MONTGRAND
PLACE P CEZANNE

BOULEVARD NOTRE DAME
6
RUE ARMENY
PLACE DE PREFECTURE
PLACE DE ROME
COURS LIEUTAUD
RUE DE LODI

RUE JULE MOULET
Estrangin Préfecture
Préfecture
5

RUE E DELANGLADE
RUE SYLVABELLE
RUE ST JACQUES
RUE DE ROME
RUE D'ITALIE

RUE BRETEUIL
RUE DU DRAGON
4

RUE BONNEFOY
RUE PARADIS
RUE EDMOND ROSTAND
PLACE CASTELLANE
6

❶ Where to stay pp154-156
❶ Where to eat pp148-151
❶ Where to drink pp151-152

La Cité Radiuse ↓
Musée d'Art Contemporain (MAC) ↓

Time Out South of France **139**

Belges (officially renamed quai de la Fraternité). You don't need to ask if the fish is fresh: the octopuses are still slithering and sea bream try valiantly to hop out of the tub. This eastern quay, bordered by cafés, stately hotels and the baroque church of St-Ferréol, is the departure point for ferries to Château d'If, the Iles de Frioul (*see p148*) and the Calanques (*see p159*).

From this vantage point, the two forts guarding the entrance to the port come into view: **Fort St-Jean** on the north bank and **Fort St-Nicolas** (which still belongs to the army and is closed to the public) on the south. The former, now a popular suntrap, was built in the 12th century and the latter under Louis XIV.

The quieter quai du Port, to the north, offers pleasant strolling. The Nazis – aided by the Vichy regime – were responsible for brutally reshaping this corner of the city. Then the historic St-Jean district, it was dynamited in February 1943, razing 1,500 old apartment buildings to the ground. The 25,000 inhabitants were cleared out of their homes in under 48 hours, events commemorated by an annual ceremony, when wreaths are laid in nearby place du 23 Janvier 1943, and in the **Mémorial des Camps de la Mort** around the corner. The medieval church of St-Laurent and its adjoining baroque chapel, just behind the fort, are all that remain of the old district.

The 1950s apartment blocks that line the quai, designed by architect Fernand Pouillon, look proud and elegant in their way. They are offset by the fine 17th-century Hôtel de Ville, with its twin pediments and baroque armorials, now surrounded by a grand new public space.

Remains of much earlier shipping activity can be seen in the nearby **Musée des Docks Romains**, while the **Maison Diamantée**, with its surprising diamond pointed façade, is a remainder of the prosperous merchants' houses that stood here in the 16th century. Behind this, steps lead up to the ancient, and gradually gentrifying, Le Panier district (*see p142*).

A small free ferry runs across the harbour between the Hôtel de Ville and place des Huiles

MARSEILLE & AIX

Life is Beautiful?

Not if you're a character from hit soap Plus Belle la Vie, *filmed in Marseille.*

By rights, it should be called 'Life just gets worse and worse', but *Plus Belle la Vie*, a tangled tale of murder, corruption and café life in Marseille, is the longest running, most popular French soap ever, with an audience that has increased from around a million when it first aired in 2004 to almost five million a night in 2008.

The reason for its popularity? A clever balance between suspense and humour, realism and utter absurdity, and appealing characters that are served by well-written dialogue, multiple storylines – rare in French TV drama – and a guaranteed cliffhanger at the end of every episode. Serial killers, hired assassins, poison pen letters, passionate affairs, divorce, blackmail, poisonings, long-lost children, missing twins, reformed prostitutes, mad surgeons, spies and KGB agents – you name it, *PBLV* has seen it. To keep it real there are also school exams, teenage love affairs, abortion, a gay couple, a racist policeman, AIDs and the perils of internet poker. The series is marked by lightening-fast changes of plot and sometimes even swifter changes of character – so Charlotte morphed from lovelorn clothes designer to adulterous wife and vengeful murderer; Vincent from wimpy, womanising architect to avaricious schemer.

If all this sounds slightly familiar, it's because any resemblance to *Eastenders* is entirely intentional. Production company Telfrance was inspired by the long-running London soap when it created the series. It's set in a fictional district, Le Mistral, that's clearly modelled on Marseille's Le Panier, with its ochre coloured houses and steep stairways. And just as *Eastenders* has its Queen Vic, Le Mistral's café is the focus for exchanging gossip and keeping the storylines coming at breakneck speed.

The series is filmed in Marseille on a vast complex of permanent interior and exterior sets constructed in studios in the Belle de Mai (*see p145*), as well as on location around the city, such as Parc Borély and the plage du Prado. If you catch an episode, you'll recognise Notre-Dame-de-Garde and the Vieux Port in the title credits too.

While mafia intrigues and corruption often play a starring role, the series also highlights the city's stunning scenery and the Marseillais gift for repartee. It's also brought fans flooding in to discover the 'real' Mistral – and to buy the T-shirt from the *PBLV* shop on place des 13 Cantons in Le Panier. To catch the latest scandalous storyline, tune in to an episode: it's shown on France 3 at 8.20pm, Monday to Friday.

on the opposite side, but it's just as quick to walk. On the other bank, the quai de Rive Neuve houses some of the city's hippest bars and clubs, including the **Bar de la Marine** and **Trolleybus**. Further along, towards the Corniche, is the **Palais du Pharo**, built on a site donated by the city to Napoléon III. He wanted an imperial residence while he embellished his leading Mediterranean port – although in the end, he never stayed there. Today, the palace contains a congress centre and auditorium. On the terrace is a striking bronze monument to those lost at sea, while the surrounding Parc du Pharo has a children's playground and panoramic views over the Vieux Port, the docks and along the Côte Bleue.

Behind quai de Rive Neuve, touristy eateries compete to sell discount bouillabaisse on the streets around place Thiars, although the broad cours d'Estienne d'Orves is worth a visit for its bars and the fine old Arsenal buildings. From here, climb up the stairs to rue Sainte, full of trendy restaurants and clothes shops. At its western end is the ancient **Abbaye de St-Victor**, a fascinating double-decker church that was once one of the most powerful abbeys in the South. Follow avenue de la Corse to reach Catalans beach, or take the steep but rewarding climb to the stripey neo-Byzantine basilica of **Notre-Dame-de-la-Garde**, the city's most famous – and audaciously stand-out – landmark.

★ FREE Abbaye de St-Victor

3 rue de l'Abbaye, 7th (04.96.11.22.60). M° Vieux-Port/54, 55, 61, 81 bus. **Open** 9am-7pm daily. **Admission** free. *Crypt* €2; free under-12s. **No credit cards**. **Map** p138 C4.
Looking more like a castle than a place of worship, this medieval church was built on the remains of an ancient necropolis. The earlier church, founded in the fifth century by St Jean Cassian, was the city's first basilica and the heart of a powerful abbey complex. Destroyed by Saracens in the 11th century, it was rebuilt in the 13th in a simple, massive Gothic style and fortified in the 14th century. On either side of the main altar, alcoves contain ornate reliquaries, witness to the medieval passion for collecting bones and other saintly memorabilia. Chunks of the earlier church remain in the convoluted crypt, part of it dug directly out of the rock, where finely carved sarcophagi include the tomb of St Victor, ground to death between two millstones by the Romans.

★ FREE Basilique Notre-Dame-de-la-Garde

montée de la Bonne Mère, 6th (04.91.13.40.80). Bus 60 from Vieux Port or Petit Train de la Bonne Mère. **Open** 7am-7pm daily. **Admission** free. **Map** p138 D6.
Topped by a massive gilded statue of the Virgin Mary and Child, this 19th-century basilica is the emblem of Marseille, and the most visited tourist site in Provence. Known locally as 'La Bonne Mère' ('the good mother'), it is deeply loved by Marseillais. The Byzantine-style interior is filled with remarkable ex-votos, including thanks for those saved from shipwreck and one for Olympique de Marseille. The mosaic floors were made in Venice, while alternating red and white marble pillars add to the richness of the surprisingly intimate chapel. Outside, the esplanade offers wonderful vistas in all directions.

Fort St-Jean

quai du Port, 2nd (04.96.13.80.90/www.musee-europemediterranee.org). M° Vieux-Port. **Open** (during exhibitions) 10am-noon, 2-7pm Mon, Wed-Sun. **Admission** €2; €1.50 reductions; free under-18s. **No credit cards**. **Map** p138 C2.
There's been a fortress here for centuries, although the oldest remaining part is the square tower built in the 15th century by Good King René. The fortress is currently used for temporary exhibitions, which prefigure the Musée National des Civilisations de l'Europe et de la Méditerranée. Due to open in 2012, with a modern extension designed by Rudy Ricciotti, the new museum will be based around the folk art and ethnographic collection of the former Musée National des Arts et Traditions Populaires in Paris.

Jardins des Vestiges/ Musée d'Histoire de Marseille

Centre Bourse, 1 sq Belsunce, 1st (04.91.90.42.22). M° Vieux-Port. **Open** noon-7pm Mon-Sat. **Admission** €2.50; €1 reductions; free under-10s. **No credit cards**. **Map** p138 F2.
While the foundations for the Centre Bourse shopping centre were being dug in the 1970s, remains of Marseille's original Greek walls and a corner of the Roman port were unearthed, preserved here in a sheltered garden. The splendid collection at the adjoining Musée d'Histoire ranges from vintage promotional posters to historical models of the city.

FREE Mémorial des Camps de la Mort

esplanade de la Tourette, 2nd (04.91.90.73.15). M° Vieux-Port or Joliette/83 bus. **Open** *June-Sept* 11am-6pm Tue-Sun. *Oct-May* 10am-5pm Tue-Sun. **Admission** free. **Map** p138 C2.
In January 1943, following orders from Hitler, Karl Oberg, head of the Gestapo in France, declared: 'Marseille is the cancer of Europe. And Europe can't be alive as long as Marseille isn't purified… That is why the German authorities want to cleanse the old districts and destroy them with mines and fire.' These chilling words resonate in a series of haunting and fascinating pictures that capture subsequent events, on display in a former bunker.

Musée des Docks Romains

pl Vivaux, 2nd (04.91.91.24.62). M° Vieux-Port/83 bus. **Open** *June-Sept* 11am-6pm Tue-Sun.

Oct-May 10am-5pm Tue-Sun. **Admission** €2;
€1 reductions; free under-10s. **No credit cards.**
Map p138 D2.
During post-war reconstruction in 1947, the remains
of a first-century AD Roman shipping warehouse
were discovered. This museum preserves the site
intact and documents maritime trade through terracotta jars, amphorae and coins.

Musée du Vieux Marseille (Maison Diamantée)

2 rue de la Prison, 2nd (04.91.55.28.68).
Mº Vieux-Port/49B, 83 bus. **Open** *June-Sept*
11am-6pm Tue-Sun. *Oct-May* 10am-5pm Tue-
Sun. **Admission** €3; €1.50 reductions; free
under-10s. **No credit cards**. **Map** p138 E2.
Reopened following painstaking renovation, the
Maison Diamantée, so named thanks to its diamond-
faceted Renaissance façade, was built in the late 16th
century, probably for a wealthy merchant.
Exhibitions focus on daily life in Marseille since the
18th century, with furniture, photographs and
provençal costumes.

Le Panier, La Joliette & Les Carmes

Le Panier, rising between quai du Port and rue
de la République, has been the traditional first
stop for successive waves of immigrants.
Today, it's at the top of the tourist itinerary.
It's hard to resist the charm of its narrow, hilly
streets, steep stairways and pastel-coloured
houses – think Italy-meets-Tunisia. Certain
Marseillais (the ones who don't live here)
still think of Le Panier as a dodgy area to be
avoided at night, but nowadays there is little
evidence to support such fears. Once a district
of prostitution and petty criminals, its
population is changing as artists, teachers,
students and arty professionals move in.
    Whether you take one of the stairways up
from the Vieux Port or any of the roads leading
to rue Caisserie, the striking **Hôtel Dieu** above
catches your eye. The hospital was founded in
the 12th century, although the present building,
with its galleried façade, was designed in 1753;
it's currently being converted into a plush hotel.
At the foot of the steep montée des Accoules,
the **Eglise Notre-Dame-des-Accoules** has
a remarkable spire and bell tower.
    After it has peaked, the montée des Accoules
runs down to gently animated place de Lenche.
On the site of the original Greek *agora* (place
of assembly), it is edged by a few bars,
restaurants and shops. Further north is the
stunning **Centre de la Vieille Charité**, built
as a poorhouse but now home to two museums
and a pleasant café. West of the Vieille Charité,
with an unimpeded line to God and the sea, is
the vast 19th-century **Cathédrale de la
Major** and its predecessor **l'Ancienne Major**.

Le Panier.

Behind Le Panier, the up-and-coming
La Joliette area, centred around the 1860s
Docks de la Joliette, is the focus of the
Euroméditerranée redevelopment project.
The bold plans, overseen by architects Yves
Lion and François Kern, embrace public
housing, a museum and aquarium, restaurants,
a theatre, offices and two hotels.
    Long a grimy, traffic-laden thoroughfare,
laid out in the 1860s to connect the old port
to the city's thriving new docks, busy rue de
la République is also changing. In line with
the area's transformation, it has been cleaned
up and floodlit to draw attention to its fine
Haussmann-style apartments, with their
fanciful doorways and wrought-iron balconies.
    Heading left down rue Jean Trinquet, some
unobtrusive, smelly steps just past rue Cathala
lead up to place des Grandes Carmes and a
hidden gem, **Eglise Notre-Dame-du-Mont-
Carmel** – currently undergoing restoration
to preserve its 300-plus statues, baroque interior
and many paintings. This spot offers a respite
and urban views across to Le Panier and the
imposing residential block on place Sadi Carnot,
once infamous as Nazi headquarters. Just
behind the church is the 17th-century **Halles
Puget**. Built as a fish and meat market, it was
first converted into a church, then a police
station. It has now been restored to its original,
temple-like open structure.

FREE **Cathédrale de la Major**

pl de la Major, 2nd (04.91.90.53.57). M°
Joliette. **Open** 10am-noon, 2-5.30pm Tue-Sun.
Admission free. **Map** p138 D1.
The largest cathedral built in France since the
Middle Ages, the neo-Byzantine Nouvelle Major was
started in 1852 and completed in 1893, with orien-
tal-style cupolas and a lustrous mosaic. The remains
of the 11th-century Ancienne Major, parts of which
date back to Roman times, lie in a state of disrepair.

★ **Centre de la Vieille Charité**

2 rue de la Charité, 2nd (04.91.14.58.80).
M° Joliette or Vieux-Port. **Open** *June-Sept*
11am-6pm Tue-Sun. *Oct-May* 10am-5pm
Tue-Sun. **Admission** *Each museum* €2; €1
reductions; free under-10s, all Sun morning.
Exhibitions €3; free under-10s, all Sun morning.
No credit cards. **Map** p138 E1.
Constructed from 1671 to 1749 as a poorhouse to
round up 'poor natives and errants', this ensemble
was designed by Marseille-born architect and sculptor Pierre Puget, and completed by his son François.
Open loggias surround its courtyard, dominated by
a magnificent domed chapel. The building was
reopened as a cultural complex in 1986, housing temporary exhibitions in the former chapel, along with
the Musée d'Archéologie Méditerranéenne and the
Musée des Arts Africains, Océaniens and
Amerindiens (MAAOA). The former has a superb
collection of archaeological finds, and the most
important Egyptian collection in France outside
Paris. MAAOA displays tribal art and artefacts
from Africa, the Pacific and the Americas.

FREE **Docks de la Joliette**

10 pl de la Joliette, 2nd (04.91.14.45.00/www.
euromediterranee.fr). M° Joliette. **Open** 9am-6pm
Mon-Sat. **Admission** free. **Map** p138 C1.
The handsome warehouses of this 19th-century port
run along the waterfront for almost a mile, and were
modelled on St Katharine Docks in London. They
were state of the art in 1866, but as traffic declined
and cargo shifted to containers, the buildings fell
into disuse and there were plans to demolish them.
Now brilliantly renovated by architect Eric Castaldi,
they form the centrepiece of the Euroméditerranée
redevelopment. The warehouses are occupied by a
diverse mix of companies, bars and restaurants: in
atrium 10.2, an information centre displays designs
and models of the entire scheme.

La Canebière, cours Julien
& the Préfecture

Running inland from the Vieux Port, La
Canebière (from *canèbe*: hemp in Provençal,
after a rope factory once located here) marked
the expansion of the city under Louis XIV and
long served as the dividing line between the
'poor' north and the 'rich' south of Marseille.

In its 19th-century heyday it was lined with
grand hotels and smart department stores;
now rather shabby in parts, it's dominated by
chain stores. Nonetheless, its faded wedding-
cake façades and lively multicultural
atmosphere still make for an interesting walk.
At No.168, stop off at the celebrated **Plauchut**
(04.91.48.06.67, closed Mon, Aug), a pâtisserie
and tearoom where the swirls and flourishes
of its art nouveau interior rival those of the
elaborate cakes and ice-creams.

At the Vieux Port end, by the Office du
Tourisme, rue Beauvau leads to the colonnaded
façade of the **Opéra de Marseille** (*see p154*).
Behind here is Marseille's smartest shopping
area, around rue Francis Davso, rue Paradis
and rue St-Férreol. Amid the jewellers and
designer labels of rue Grignan, a beautiful,
golden stone *hôtel particulier* contains the
Musée Cantini, a superb collection of early
20th-century art.

Just across La Canebière from the tourist
office, the Bourse et Chambre de Commerce,
decorated with ship carvings alluding to the
importance of the port, now contains the
**Musée de la Marine et de l'Economie
de Marseille**. Nearby, a building houses the
dynamic **Musée de la Mode** and a fashion-
industry trade centre. Beyond Métro Noailles,
the upper reaches of La Canebière have had a
facelift since the arrival of the tramway, with
pleasant pavement cafés along the tree-shaded
allées de Meilhan and a flower market on
Tuesday and Thursday mornings. At the top
end of La Canebière, you can't miss the twin
spires of the imposing **Eglise des Réformés**.

Around broad cours Belsunce stretches the
predominantly North African neighbourhood of
Belsunce, known for its handsome 18th-century
residences and considered the most likely place
to be mugged in the city. This may be unfair,
but best be wary of loitering lads in quiet
backstreets. It's also home to the tremendous
modern municipal library designed by Adrien
Fainsilber, constructed around the old entrance
of the Alcazar music hall. Rue d'Aix, lined with
North African pâtisseries and jewellers, leads
to the busy traffic junction of place Jules
Guesde – home to the imperial **Porte d'Aix**,
a triumphal arch built in 1825-33. The streets
east of the cours offer a vibrant snapshot of
modern-day Marseille: corner-shop mosques,
boutiques selling cheap fabrics and gadgets,
and sweetmeats of every kind. It's minutes
from the Vieux Port, but so different in mood
you might have spent 24 hours on a ferry.

On the other side of the Canebière, the
cours St-Louis is set to hold the future Grande
Mosquée de Marseille, while rue d'Aubagne
is packed with North African grocers selling
spices, sacks of couscous and loofahs.

Climb up the steps from here to the bohemian – if that means tastefully graffitied – cours Julien, home to a flower market on Wednesday and Saturday mornings, and an organic food market on Friday mornings. An eclectic array of boutiques, bookshops, French and ethnic restaurants, cafés with sun-soaked terraces, theatres and music venues make for a slightly uncomfortable contrast with less well-off locals, who also like to chill out here. Much of the city's youth music scene is centred around this area, bringing with it a vibrant streetlife.

Behind here, place Carli is home to second-hand booksellers and the elaborate, 19th-century **Palais des Arts** (04.91.42.51.50, www.regards-de-provence.com). The fanciful former public library and art school was designed by Henri-Jacques Esperandieu, architect of Notre-Dame-de-la-Garde and the Palais de Longchamp. These days, its ornate salons are used for exhibitions.

It's very different in mood to the pompous banks and 19th-century apartment blocks, strung with wrought-iron balconies, that line rue de Rome and rue de Paradis in the area around the Palais de Justice (law courts) and the regal Préfecture building. In front of it, cascading fountains, wide pavements much loved by skateboarders and an attractive square border the top of the busy shopping street of pedestrianised rue St-Ferréol.

Across the street is the American consulate, where Varian Fry sheltered several Surrealist artists in what was then France Libre, helping them to flee France during World War II. Behind the Préfecture, rue Edmond Rostand is the focus of the **Quartier des Antiquaires**, home to numerous small art galleries and antiques dealers. South of here, place Castellane marks the beginning of the broad avenue du Prado. At its centre, the Cantini fountain features marble statues symbolising the Durance, Rhône and Gardon rivers and the Mediterranean, with Marseille (naturally) on top of the column.

It's also worth visiting **Parc du XXVI Centenaire** on square Zino Francescatti. This agreeable 25-acre park is a recent – and as yet unfinished – addition in honour of Marseille's 26 centuries of history. Stemming from the site of the former Gare du Prado, it combines paved walkways, lawns and a stream between the old platforms – and is mercifully dog-free.

FREE Eglise des Réformés
1 rue Barbaroux, 1st (04 91 48 57 45). M° Réformés-Canebière. **Open** *4-6pm daily.* **Admission** free.
This handsome neo-Gothic church got its nickname from an order of reformed Augustine monks whose chapel stood on this site; its actual name is St-

Vincent-de-Paul. Founded in 1852, it wasn't consecrated until 1888 due to lack of funds. The two spires, one housing four bells, are 69m (226ft) high.

★ Musée Cantini
19 rue Grignan, 6th (04.91.54.77.75). M° Estrangin-Préfecture. **Open** *June-Sept* 11am-6pm Tue-Sun. *Oct-May* 10am-5pm Tue-Sun. **Admission** €3; €1.50 reductions; free under-10s. **No credit cards.** **Map** p138 F4.
In an elegant 17th-century mansion, Musée Cantini houses one of France's foremost collections of Fauve and Surrealist art, along with some fine post-war works. Highlights include a Signac of the port, Dufy from his early Cézannesque neo-Cubist phase and paintings by Camoin, Kupka, Kandinsky, Léger and Ernst. Upstairs the collection focuses on Surrealist and abstract artists, including Arp, Brauner and Picabia, along with works by Dubuffet and Bacon.
▶ *Léger fans should also check out Biot's Musée National Fernand Léger, near Antibes; see p248.*

Musée de la Marine et de l'Economie de Marseille
9 La Canebière, 1st (04.91.39.33.33). M° Vieux-Port. **Open** 10am-6pm daily. **Admission** €3; €1.50 reductions; free under-12s. **Credit** MC, V. **Map** p138 F3.
This grandiose former stock exchange, housing the city's Chamber of Commerce, was inaugurated by Napoléon III in 1860. The museum charts the maritime history of Marseille, with paintings, models, old maps and engravings, as well as celebrating ports of the world from Liverpool to Montevideo.

★ Musée de la Mode de Marseille
11 La Canebière, 1st (04.96.17.06.00/ www.espacemodemediterranee.com). M° Vieux-Port. **Open** *June-Sept* 11am-6pm Tue-Sun. *Oct-May* 10am-5pm Tue-Sun. **Admission** €3; €1.50 reductions; free under-10s. **No credit cards.** **Map** p138 F3.
Adjoining the Espace Mode Méditerranée, the fashion museum has more than 6,000 accessories and outfits, from the 1940s to the present. Selected pieces are displayed in changing exhibitions.

St-Charles, Longchamp & the Belle de Mai

One look around the Gare St-Charles when you get out of the train is enough to get an idea of the transformation this district is undergoing. Alongside the fine 19th-century train station, with its majestic entrance and imposing glazed train shed, is a gleaming new glass shopping mall with slippery marble floors, cafés, shops and the bus station ticket office. At the far end, landscaped with fountains and palm trees, a newly cobbled square leads to part of the University of Provence Marseille.

Beyond is the old industrial neighbourhood of Belle de Mai, which grew up in the 19th century with the arrival of the railway. Here, a former tobacco factory has become the thriving cultural centre **La Friche la Belle de Mai**. The surrounding area is hardly appealing on foot, although a former maternity hospital is set to be converted into a university arts faculty, and the south-east corner of Belle de Mai is to become the focus of a new Media Park as part of the Euroméditerranée project.

Further east of the station, boulevard Longchamp is crowned by the grandiose Palais Longchamp, which holds the **Musée des Beaux-Arts** and **Muséum d'Histoire Naturelle**. Behind the palace are attractive landscaped gardens, which stay open later than the museums. Just down the hill, the **Musée Grobet-Labadié** testifies to the moneyed lifestyle of a pair of 19th-century art collectors.

Much further out in the 13th *arrondissement*, heading past the bright blue landmark of the Hôtel du Département (seat of the Bouches-du-Rhône Conseil Général), designed by British architect Will Alsop, is the Château-Gombert district. Home to a *technopôle* (science and business park), as well as the delightful **Musée du Terroir Marseillais**, this is a charming little suburban village of winding roads where property is now highly sought-after. Hop on a bus and spend an afternoon wandering around and you'll soon see why.

★ La Friche la Belle de Mai

41 rue Jobin, 3rd (04.95.04.95.04/www.la friche.org). M° St-Charles/49A, 49B bus. **Open** 3-6pm Mon-Sat. **Admission** free.
A disused tobacco factory in the increasingly trendy Belle de Mai quarter, La Friche started life as an artists' squat. These days its vast concrete halls are home to numerous artistic, musical, theatrical, dance and media outfits, open to the public for performances, workshops and exhibitions. Names to look out for include Aide aux Musiques Innovatrices, Théâtre Massalia, Triangle France, Radio Grenouille and Georges Appaix's La Liseuse dance company.

Musée des Beaux-Arts & Muséum d'Histoire Naturelle

Palais Longchamp, bd de Longchamp, 4th. (04.91.14.59.50/www.museum-marseille.org). M° Longchamp-Cinq-Avenues. **Open** *Musée des Beaux-Arts* closed for renovation. *Muséum d'Historie Naturelle* 10am-5pm Tue-Sun. **Admission** *Muséum d'Histoire Naturelle* €4; €2 reductions; free under-10s. **No credit cards.**
No monument better expresses the ebullience of 19th-century Marseille than the Palais Longchamp. This ostentatious complex, inaugurated in 1869, was built to celebrate the completion of an 84km (52-mile) aqueduct bringing the waters of the Durance to the

drought-prone port. A massive horseshoe-shaped classical colonnade, with a triumphal arch at its centre and museums in either wing, crowns the hill. On the ground floor are works by sculptor and architect Pierre Puget, while the upper floors contain French, Italian and Flemish paintings from the 16th to 19th centuries. The natural history museum has zoological and prehistoric artefacts.

Musée du Terroir Marseillais

5 pl des Héros, 13th (04.91.68.14.38). M° La Rose then 5 bus. **Open** 9am-noon, 2-6.30pm Tue-Fri; 2.30-6.30pm Sat, Sun. **Admission** €4; €1.60 reductions; free under-6s. **No credit cards.**
Founded in 1928, the museum offers a charming insight into provençal culture. Its displays include hand-painted 18th-century dressers, faïence pottery, dolls and ancient kitchen gadgets such as a fig-drier.

Musée Grobet-Labadié

140 bd de Longchamp, 1st (04.91.62.21.82). M° Longchamp-Cinq-Avenues. **Open** *June-Sept* 11am-6pm Tue-Sun. *Oct-May* 10am-5pm Tue-Sun. **Admission** €2; €1 reductions; free under-10s. **No credit cards.**
This 1873 mansion houses the private art collection of a wealthy 19th-century couple. Scrupulously renovated, it offers an intriguing glimpse into cultivated tastes of the time, its collection ranging from 15th- and 16th-century Italian and Flemish paintings to Fragonard and Millet, medieval tapestries and 17th- and 18th-century provençal furniture and faïence.

La Corniche, Prado & the south-west

The Corniche Président JF Kennedy – known simply as **La Corniche** – carves along the coast from just beyond the Vieux Port to where the 8th begins near the Centre de Voile. Vantage points, craggy coves and little beaches along the way offer stunning views of the rocky coastline, offshore islands and spooky Château d'If. The sheltered, sandy **plage des Catalans**, encircled by cafés and restaurants, is the closest beach to the town centre. A little further along is the striking war memorial to the Poilus d'Orient – North Africans who served France in World War I. Beside it, steps descend to the picturesque **Vallon des Auffes** inlet, a bijou harbour lined with tiny cottages, narrow alleyways and a couple of upmarket eateries.

Sticking out on the exposed westerly tip is the equally sought-after **Malmousque** district. It has several rocky bays and a quay, which offer refreshing although unsupervised bathing points (the most popular are in front of the Foreign Legion base, down from rue de la Douane, anse de Maldormé and anse Fausse Monnaie) amid luxurious 19th-century villas.

Following the road south, the ominously named **plage du Prophète** is an attractive

MARSEILLE & AIX

Profile La Cité Radieuse

Life inside an architectural icon.

Children splash in the rooftop paddling pool, while a few feet away two Japanese tourists take photos of a concrete funnel, silhouetted like a sculpture against the sky. It's a curious dichotomy – but **La Cité Radieuse** (*see right*) is no ordinary apartment block.

Commissioned in 1945, it was the first of Le Corbusier's forays into mass housing. A 'vertical garden city', it was designed to create a model for social living – so as well as flats, the building encompassed shops, a crèche, a nursery school, a gym and a rooftop amphitheatre and paddling pool.

The ingeniously interlocking design means that while every apartment opens off a convivial central corridor or 'street', each then has another level, above or below, that spans the width of the building, giving every resident a sea and a mountain view. Inside, it's the attention to detail that impresses. The fitted kitchens, designed by Charlotte Perriand, were way ahead of their time, incorporating everything from extractor fans to saucepan racks. Downstairs, a pivoting bookcase has shoe storage hidden behind it, while a blackboard serves as a sliding door between two kids' rooms.

Locals once dubbed the Cité *la maison de fada* ('the madman's house') – but over 50 years on, attitudes have changed, with duplexes selling for prices that few Marseillais can afford. 'It has become very middle class,' says one of its residents, Jocelyne Gamus – a design aficionado who cherishes her flat's original features and has furnished it with Mouille lights and Perriand bookshelves. 'Fortunately, though, the school has an intake from the whole district, so a social mix still takes place among the children.'

'It has become a bit of a sect, with architects, people working in culture, English and Parisians,' confirms Dominique Gerberin, owner of the Hôtel Le Corbusier. 'But then it always was; before, there were lots of teachers. It has gone from being the fief of the communist gauche to the fief of the bobo (shorthand for bourgeois bohemian) gauche.'

An architectural bookshop, design gallery, architectural practice and accountancy firm have replaced the grocery shops

on the indoor 'rue commerçante' – although the bakery remains, and residents are battling for the return of the mini-supermarket, which was closed in 2008.

The hotel was part of the concept from the outset – and its carefully restored studios and budget-priced *cabines* offer visitors a unique opportunity to experience the Le Corbusier lifestyle. The hotel's guests, says Gerberin, fall into two camps. 'There are architecture students, architects and those in love with design, and there are those who arrive by chance. Either they run away immediately or they let themselves be guided; I take them around almost literally by the hand, so that they gradually understand the place. I take them up to the rooftop and say, "Look, this is the most wonderful view in the world..."'

TAKE A TOUR
Guided visits are organised by the **Office de Tourisme** (*see p157*); alternatively, ask at **Hôtel Le Corbusier** (*see p155*).

MARSEILLE & AIX

sandy beach. All of these sunspots can be reached by strolling down through the smart residential areas of Bompard and (hilly) Roucas Blanc, occasionally a challenging up-and-down walk. The No.73 bus offers a fun rollercoaster ride from Castellane via Périer down to Vallon de l'Oriol on the seafront. In addition, the less reliable 83 runs (or rather crawls) along the Corniche between the Vieux Port and Prado.

Along the top of the hill, past the rond-point du Prado on boulevard Michelet, stands the **Stade Vélodrome**, proud home to the city's beloved Olympique de Marseille. Further along, you can stop for a meal or spend the night at Le Corbusier's landmark **Cité Radieuse**. Heading south-west between Ste-Anne and Mazargues on avenue d'Haïfa – just before César's gigantic bronze sculpture of a thumb – the **Musée d'Art Contemporain** contains an adventurous collection of contemporary art.

The avenue du Prado ends at the **plage du Prado** in front of a bold marble copy of Michelangelo's *David*. Along this broad stretch of beach and seaside park (the Parc Balnéaire du Prado), you'll see David-like windsurfers being tossed about on the waves as they brave Marseille's fearsome Mistral. The long sequence of sand and shingle beaches, with its lawns, children's play areas and watersports facilities, was created using landfill from the construction of the metro. For those more interested in the *après-plage*, the Escale Borély is a complex of brasseries, bars and beach clubs. Across the road is the 42-acre **Parc Borély**, with its horseracing track, botanical gardens, lake and the 18th-century Château Borély – a haven for families, joggers and *pétanque* players.

Continuing on through Bonneveine and Vieille Chapelle, this stretch of beaches is Marseille at its most sporty and Californian – though the picturesque ports of **Pointe Rouge** and **Madrague de Montredon** remain typically Marseillais. La Madrague also has an unofficial gay 'beach', an isolated patch of rocks accessed from boulevard Mont-Rose.

Les Goudes is a 20-minute walk beyond here: a seemingly remote village, surrounded by barren outcrops, yet still within the city limits. With its small stone houses blending into the orange rock, it attracts fishing enthusiasts, divers and hikers, and is a great place to feast on fresh fish or wood-fired pizza. Even further out is the timeless village of **Callelongue**, which is dominated by the forbidding Massif de Marseilleveyre and too many cars at weekends.

★ La Cité Radieuse

*280 bd Michelet, 8th (hotel 04.91.16.78.00). M°
Rond-Point du Prado then 21, 22 bus.* **Open** For guided tours, ask at the hotel reception or at the Office du Tourisme. **Map** p138 G6.

La maison de fada ('the madman's house') is the locals' once-scornful but now affectionate name for Le Corbusier's 1952 reinforced-concrete apartment block, where the architect tried out his prototype for mass housing. Perched on stilts, the complex contains 340 flats (*see left* **La Cité Radieuse**), plus a hotel (*see p155*) and restaurant (*see p151*).

Musée d'Art Contemporain (MAC)

*69 av d'Haïfa, 8th (04.91.25.01.07). Bus 23,
45.* **Open** *Oct-May* 10am-5pm Tue-Sun. *Oct-May* 10am-5pm Tue-Sun. **Admission** €3; €1.50 reductions; free under-10s. **No credit cards.**
Map p138 F6.
Marseille's contemporary art museum, dedicated to post-1950s art, is located in a hangar-like space. Displays change regularly, mixing temporary exhibitions with selections from the permanent collection, which include Fluxus, *arte povera* and *nouveau réalisme*; recent acquisitions include works by Carsten Hollar, Jimmie Durham and Nan Goldin. The garden is dotted with sculptures by the likes of César (born in Le Panier), Absalon and Dietman.

Musée de la Faïence

*157 av de Montredon, 8th (04.91.72.43.47). M°
Castellane or Prado then 19 bus.* **Open** *June-Sept* 11am-6pm Tue-Sun. *Oct-May* 10am-5pm Tue-Sun. **Admission** €2; €1 reductions; free under-10s. **No credit cards. Map** p138 A6.
Surrounded by a magnificent park, Château Pastré was constructed in 1862 by a rich trading family. Today, it houses the Musée de la Faïence, celebrating the pottery industry that thrived in Marseille in the late 17th and 18th centuries.

FREE Stade Vélodrome (Olympique de Marseille)

*3 bd Michelet, 8th. Club office: 25 rue Negresco,
8th (04.91.76.56.09/www.om.net). M° Rond-*

INSIDE TRACK
CEZANNE IN THE SUBURBS

North-west of Marseille, the unassuming suburb of **L'Estaque** played an unlikely role in the history of modern art. A little fishing port when Paul Cézanne first visited in 1870, on the brink of becoming an industrial working-class suburb, its luminous light and colours astounded him. Over the years he returned to paint the landscape again and again, followed by the likes of Derain, Braque, Renoir and Dufy. Today, it's not easy to pick out the locations they immortalised: to help you spot them, follow the two-hour **Circuit des Peintres** route. Details are available from Marseille's tourist office (*see p156*).

Point du Prado. **Open** *Shop & museum*
10am-1pm, 2-6pm Mon-Sat. **Admission** free.
Map p138 F6.
This isn't a football stadium, it's a place of worship.
L'Olympique de Marseille commands the sort of fer-
vour that separatist movements might elsewhere. OM
has had a rollercoaster ride since winning the UEFA
Champions League in 1993, but came a respectable
third in the French premier division in the 2007-08
season. The second largest stadium in France, Stade
Vélodrome can hold 60,000 seated spectators: the best
seats (€70) are in the Jean-Bouin stand, but the Ganay
(max €60) also offers a relatively quiet viewpoint.
Tickets can be bought from the stadium on match
day, in advance from L'OM Café (3 quai des Belges,
Vieux Port) or by ringing 32 29 Allo OM.

Ile d'If & Iles de Frioul

The Ile d'If, a tiny islet of sun-bleached white
stone 20 minutes from the Vieux Port, is today
inhabited by salamanders and seagulls. Its two
most famous residents, though, are Edmond
Dantès and Abbé Faria, the main characters of
Alexandre Dumas's *The Count of Monte Cristo*.

To keep Marseille under control, François I
had a fortress built here in 1524 – so formidable
that it never saw combat and was eventually
converted into a prison. Thousands of
Protestants met grisly ends here after the Edict
of Nantes was revoked in 1685, but it was
Dumas who put If on the map by making it
the prison from which Dantès escaped: wily
administrators soon caught on and kept tourists
happy by hacking out the hole through which
Edmond slid to freedom in the story. The
chateau is quickly visited, so bring a picnic
and enjoy the clean seawater.

It's easy to combine a visit to the Château
d'If with the Iles de Frioul, a collection of small
islands. Aside from a few holiday flats by the
marina, they consist largely of windswept rock,
wonderfully isolated beaches and fragrant
clumps of thyme and rosemary. Ile Ratonneau
is also home to the impressive **Hôpital
Caroline**, constructed in the 1820s as a
quarantine hospital to protect Marseille from
epidemics. Today, it is a curious historic site
with terrific views, well worth the slog up the
hill. In June and July, it hosts the Nuits Caroline
– a series of night-time events ranging from
live jazz to open-air theatre (04.96.11.04.61).

Château d'If

Ile d'If, 1st (04.91.59.02.30). **Open** *May-Sept*
9.30am-6.30pm daily. *Oct-Apr* 9am-5pm Tue-Sun.
Admission €8; €3.10 reductions; free under-18s.

Ferries

GACM (04.91.55.50.09, www.answeb.net/
gacm) runs regular crossings (Tue-Sun, less

frequent Oct-May), many of which stop at If
and Iles de Frioul. A return ticket for one island
costs €10, with €5 reductions; both islands costs
€15, with €6.50 reductions. Under-3s go free,
and credit cards aren't accepted.

WHERE TO EAT

Les Arcenaulx

*25 cours d'Estienne d'Orves, 1st (04.91.59.80.
30/www.les-arcenaulx.com). M° Vieux-Port.*
Open noon-2pm, 8-11pm Mon-Sat. Closed 1wk
Aug. **Menus** €36-€55. **Credit** AmEx, DC, MC,
V. **Map** p138 E4 ❶
In a strikingly converted former arsenal building,
this restaurant is set in an antiquarian bookshop,
publishers and kitchen shop-cum-épicerie. A chic
dinner rendezvous for Marseille's chattering classes,
it serves modern southern cooking (pan-fried pork
with rosemary, chorizo and caponata, say).

Baie des Singes

Cap Croisette, Les Goudes, 8th (04.91.73.68.87).
Open Mon-Sat (phone for details). Closed Sept-
mid Apr. **Main courses** €15-€50. **Credit** V.
Even though getting here involves arriving by boat
or scrabbling over a rocky promontory, you won't
be the first: ex-president Chirac and a host of TV personalities have already done it. And you can see why
– with the bare white rock and blue seas, you could
be on a Greek island. The speciality is fresh, grilled
fish, presented in a basket for you to choose from.

La Boutique du Glacier

*1 pl Général de Gaulle, 1st (04.91.33.76.93).
M° Vieux-Port.* **Open** 7.45am-7.15pm Mon-Sat;
7.45am-1pm, 3.30-7.15pm Sun. **Main courses**
€2.40-€4.50. **Menus** €7.40-€9.40. **Credit** MC, V.
Map p138 F3 ❷
Despite its snappy wood-and-marble makeover, this
tearoom thankfully continues to attract nice old
dears, who come here to feast on decadent cakes and
ice-creams.

Le Café des Epices

*4 rue du Lacydon, 2nd (04.91.91.22.69).
M° Vieux-Port.* **Open** noon-3pm, 8-11pm Tue-Fri;
8-11pm Sat. **Menus** €15-€30. **Credit** MC, V.
Map p138 E2 ❸
Expect deft spicing and inventive takes on traditional favourites by haute-cuisine trained young
chef Arnaud de Grammont – though prices have shot
up since it opened. Reserve, as there are just a handful of tables in the slick interior and on the terrace.

Le Charles Livon

*89 bd Charles Livon, 7th (04.91.52.22.41/
www.charleslivon.fr). Bus 83.* **Open** 8-11pm Mon,
Sat; noon-2pm, 8-11pm Tue-Fri. Closed 2wks in
July. **Menus** *Lunch* €19. *Dinner* €39-€64.
Credit AmEx, MC, V. **Map** p138 B3 ❹

L'Epuisette. *See p150.*

This sleek minimalist bistro stands opposite the Parc du Pharo. The elegant, modern cooking makes excellent use of regional produce; quail prepared three ways, perhaps, or john dory with fennel. The €19 lunch *formule* is a steal.

Chez Fonfon
140 Anse du Vallon des Auffes, 7th (04.91. 54.89.08/www.chez-fonfon.com). Bus 83. **Open** 7-9.45pm Mon (June-Aug only); noon-1.45pm, 7-9.45pm Tue-Sat. **Main courses** €24-€28. **Menus** €42-€55. **Credit** AmEx, MC, V.
A Marseille institution, Chez Fonfon's quietly stylish dining room overlooks the picturesque harbour of the Vallon des Auffes. If you don't feel like bouillabaisse, try the fresh catch of the day, chargrilled or flambéed with pastis.

Chez Michel
6 rue des Catalans, 7th (04.91.52.30.63/www. restaurant-michel.com). **Open** noon-2pm, 7.30-9.30pm daily. Closed mid Feb-2 Mar. **Main courses** €30-€60. **Credit** AmEx, MC, V. **Map** p138 A3 ❺
This Marseille institution, looking across the Anse des Catalans, is a failsafe choice for bouillabaisse or bourride. Fresh fish are expertly de-boned by sea-weathered waiters, and served with garlicky rouille.

★ La Côte de Boeuf
35 cours d'Estienne d'Orves, 1st (04.91.54. 89.08). M° Vieux-Port. **Open** noon-2pm, 7.30-11.15pm Mon-Sat. **Main courses** €23-€60. **Credit** AmEx, MC, V. **Map** p138 E4 ❻

After all the fish, this two-storey bistro in a converted warehouse behind the port is heaven for carnivores. Go for the namesake house speciality: a vast côte de boeuf for two, served sliced and deliciously rare in the middle. The other draw is the legendary wine list – one of the most extensive in France.

Le Crystal
148 quai du Port, 2nd (04.91.91.57.96). M° Vieux-Port/83 bus. **Open** *May-Sept* 9am-2am daily. *Oct-Apr* 9am-6pm Mon, Sun; 9am-2am Tue-Sat. **Main courses** €7-€25. **Credit** MC, V. **Map** p138 E2 ❼
With its red leatherette banquettes and Formica tables, this groovy café has bags of 1950s-diner appeal. In sunny weather, though, the foliaged terrace is hard to resist.

INSIDE TRACK
REAL-DEAL BOUILLABAISSE

For the quintessential Marseille dish of bouillabaisse – which, insist the Marseillais, can only be authentically made here – seek out a well-reputed establishment such as **Chez Fonfon** (*see left*) or **Le Miramar** (*see p150*), be prepared to pay at least €40 per person, and ideally order 48 hours in advance. As bouillabaisse is always a two-course meal (the soup, followed by the fish), don't order a starter.

MARSEILLE & AIX

€ Cup of Tea

1 rue Caisserie, 2nd (04.91.90.84.02). M° Vieux-Port. **Open** 8.30am-7pm Mon-Fri; 9.30am-7pm Sat. **Menus** €3-€6. **Credit** AmEx, MC, V. **Map** p138 E2 **8**

One part tearoom, one part bookshop, this fabulous little place in Le Panier is one of the best pit stops in town. All manner of teas and coffees are available, plus various pastries (€3), quiche and salad (€5) or the huge, garden-fresh *salade composée* (€6.50).

★ L'Epuisette

156 rue de Vallon des Auffes, 7th (04.91.52.17. 82/www.l-epuisette.com). Bus 83. **Open** 12.15-2pm, 7.45-10pm Tue-Sat. Closed 4 Aug-2 Sept. **Menus** €45-€90. **Credit** AmEx, DC, MC, V.

Young wonder-chef Guillaume Sourrieu continues to impress at this seafood restaurant, dramatically set on a craggy stone finger surrounded by the Med. Try lobster tagine with spring vegetables, or goat's cheese-stuffed lamb medallions. Among the desserts, chocolate brownie with pistachios, rose ice-cream and wild strawberries is heavenly. *Photo p149.*

La Fabrique

3 pl Jules Verne, 2nd (04.91.91.40.48). M° Vieux-Port. **Open** noon-2pm, 8pm-midnight daily. **Menus** *Lunch* €15-€30. *Dinner* €26-€30. **Main courses** €11-€19. **Credit** MC, V. **Map** p138 E2 **9**

This hip restaurant has a louche, loungey feel. Low seating, even lower lighting, chilled-out tunes: you get the picture. But that's not to say food takes a back seat – great mains could be anything from a simple risotto to *papillote de rouget aux agrumes*.

€ Le Jardin d'à Côté

65 cours Julien, 6th (04.91.94.15.51). M° Notre-Dame-du-Mont or Noailles. **Open** noon-2.30pm Mon-Sat. **Menus** €10-€30. **No credit cards**. **Map** p138 H4 **10**

The nicest restaurant on 'cours Ju', this trad bistro offers a warm welcome, tasty, well-priced food, and a terrace that's perfect for people-watching. A typical dish would be rich, hearty *daube* with a creamy polenta to soak up the juices. Quaffable house wine is served in handy, lunchtime-sized carafes.

€ La Kahena

2 rue de la République, 1st (04.91.90.61.93). M° Vieux-Port. **Open** noon-2.30pm, 7-10.30pm daily. **Menus** €12-€16. **Credit** MC, V. **Map** p138 F3 **11**

This is one of the best North African restaurants in the city centre, as evidenced by its popularity (book at the weekend), and you'll struggle to eat three courses. To start, try the *chorba* (spicy chickpea broth), calamares or a substantial salad. The merguez are good, as is the fish couscous.

Le Miramar

12 quai du Port, 2nd (04.91.91.10.40/www. bouillabaisse.com). M° Vieux-Port. **Open** noon-

2pm, 7-10pm Tue-Sat. Closed 2wks Jan, 3wks Aug. **Menus** €55-€70. **Credit** AmEx, DC, MC, V. **Map** p138 F3 **12**

A legendary address for bouillabaisse, this Vieux Port restaurant has Christophe Buffa in the kitchen, and has recently been expanded to add a few extra tables. Sample the fishy delicacy in the '50s-vintage portside dining room or out on the busy terrace, or enrol on one of the bouillabaisse cooking courses.

€ La Part des Anges

33 rue Sainte, 1st (04.91.33.55.70/www.lapart desanges.com). M° Vieux-Port. **Open** 9am-2am Mon-Sat; 9am-1pm, 6pm-2am Sun. **Menus** €15-€30. **Credit** MC, V. **Map** p138 F4 **13**

This smart wine bar and restaurant hunts down wines from across France, including undiscovered off-the-wall growers, and sells many by the glass. There's simply prepared, casually presented food to sustain the crowds, including hearty cheese and charcuterie boards.

Le Péron

56 Corniche JF Kennedy, 7th (04.91.52.15.22). Bus 83. **Open** noon-2.15pm, 8-10.15pm daily. **Menus** €22-€72. **Credit** AmEx, MC, V.

Despite several changes of chef, this remains one of Marseille's most fashionable addresses, so you'll need to book ahead. The dark-wood decor is sleek and modern, the sea view one of the very best in town, and the cooking inventive and accomplished.

Pizzaria Etienne

43 rue Lorette, 2nd (no phone). M° Vieux-Port. **Open** 7.30-11pm Mon-Sat. **Menus** €28. **No credit cards.** **Map** p138 E1 **14**

Owner Stéphane Cassaro is a legendary Panier personality. Pizza is considered a starter here and main courses are enormous. Pasta can be disappointingly mushy, so go for meat, or fried squid with garlic.

€ PP Maulio

24 rue Sainte, 1st (04.91.33.46.13). M° Vieux-Port. **Open** noon-2pm, 8-11pm Mon-Fri; 8pm-midnight Sat. **Menus** €15-€30. **Credit** MC, V. **Map** p138 F4 **15**

Corsican specialities (including incredible wood-fired pizzas – try the 'figatelli') are the name of the game at this cosy, popular bistro just behind the Vieux Port. The delicious wines also hail from the *île de beauté*. Service comes with a smile.

La Table à Denise

63 rue Sainte, 1st (04.91.54.19.74). M° Vieux-Port. **Open** 11.30am-2.30pm Mon-Fri; 7.30-10.30pm Sat. Closed mid July-mid-Aug. **Menus** €20-€30. **Credit** MC, V. **Map** p138 E4 **16**

With its brick walls, wooden tables and fado music playing in the background, this tiny, convivial local haunt is full of twangy Marseille accents. This is the place to come to experience some true southern

MARSEILLE & AIX

La Caravelle.

hospitality and home cooking, with dishes such as lamb simmered with aubergine purée, veal with artichokes or duck magret with figs and honey.

Une Table au Sud
2 quai du Port, 2nd (04.91.90.63.53/www.une tableausud.com). M° Vieux-Port. **Open** noon-2pm, 7.30-10.30pm Tue-Thur; noon-2pm, 7.30pm-midnight Fri, Sat. **Menus** €43-€58. **Credit** AmEx, MC, V. **Map** p138 F3 ⑰
After working for Alain Ducasse, chef Lionel Lévy opened this relaxed gourmet restaurant (incongruously located above a Häagen-Dazs café) and has quickly won a fine reputation – and a Michelin star – for his modern French cooking. Specialities include foie gras brûlée, and amazing squid dishes.

Le Ventre de l'Architecte
Le Cité Radieuse, 280 bd Michelet, 8th (04.91.16. 78.23). Bus 21. **Menus** *Lunch* €24. *Dinner* €50. **Open** noon-2pm, 8-10pm Tue-Sat. **Credit** MC, V.
Set in Le Cité Radieuse, the 'belly of the architect' has a suitably stylish black and white interior, while the terrace affords superb views. Chef Jérémy Bigoux delivers ambitious, creative cuisine, with unexpected flavours; pigeon with ginger polenta, say, or steamed red scorpion fish with citrussy artichoke salad.

★ € La Virgule
27 rue de la Loge, 2nd (04.91.90.91.11). M° Vieux-Port. **Open** noon-10pm Tue-Sat. **Main courses** €15-€30. **Menus** €19-€27. **Credit** AmEx, MC, V. **Map** p138 D2 ⑱

The bistro offshoot of La Table au Sud is much prized by casual foodies and Parisiennes down for the weekend, thanks to its fresh, lively bistro cooking; gazpacho served with fabulous cucumber sorbet, perhaps, or a fricassée of tiny octopus. The pavement terrace offers a perfect view up to Notre-Dame-de-la-Garde across the port.

WHERE TO DRINK

★ Le Bar de la Marine
15 quai de Rive Neuve, 7th (04.91.54.95.42). M° Vieux-Port. **Open** 7am-2am daily. **Credit** AmEx, V. **Map** p138 E3 ❶
This perennially trendy quayside bar, with its vintage zinc bar and cosy mezzanine, has a slightly raffish air and attracts a diverse crowd. In summer, tables on the terrace are keenly contested at lunchtime and during the *apéro* hour.

Café Parisien
1 pl Sadi Carnot, 2nd (04.91.90.05.77). M° Colbert or Vieux-Port. **Open** 8am-7pm Mon-Sat. **Credit** V. **Map** p138 F2 ❷
Drinks are quite pricey at this handsome 1901 belle époque café, but the atmosphere is stylish. It's an all-day affair, starting with breakfast and lively early-morning banter; tapas are served in the evening.

La Caravelle
34 quai du Port, 2nd (08.26.10.09.47). M° Vieux-Port. **Open** 7am-2am daily. **Credit** AmEx, MC, V. **Map** p138 E3 ❸

MARSEILLE & AIX

Marseille

Hidden up a flight of stars inside the Hôtel Bellevue (*see p154*), La Caravelle serves breakfast and lunch but is above all a boho cocktail bar. A handful of coveted tables on the narrow balcony offer an idyllic view of the Vieux Port.

Les Danaïdes
6 sq Stalingrad, 1st (04.91.62.28.51). M° Réformés-Canebière. **Open** 7am-9pm Mon-Sat. **Credit** MC, V.
In a tranquil square enclosed by hectic roads, this gay-friendly café has a large terrace out front. Busy at lunch, it offers stress-free drinking in the evening.

★ O'Cours Jus
67 cours Julien, 6th (04.91.48.48.58). M° Notre-Dame-du-Mont-Cours-Julien. **Open** 6.30am-7pm Mon-Sat. Closed Aug. **No credit cards**. **Map** p138 H4 ❹
This is one of the more bohemian cafés along cours Julien, and its small terrace attracts a big crowd for coffee, beer and snacks.

La Samaritaine
2 quai du Port, 2nd (04.91.56.06.48). M° Vieux-Port. **Open** *Summer* 6am-1pm, 7pm-midnight daily. *Winter* 6am-1pm, 7-9pm daily. **No credit cards**. **Map** p138 F3 ❺
Occupying a prime corner of the Vieux Port, this is a long-standing rendezvous for regarding the passing fauna over tea, an ice-cream or an aperitif.

L'Unic Bar
11 cours Jean Ballard, 1st (04.91.33.45.84). M° Vieux-Port. **Open** 10am-5pm Mon-Sat. **Credit** AmEx, V. **Map** p138 F4 ❻
Despite its seedy exterior and air of old portside bar, the Unic turns out to be a welcoming haunt for an eclectic range of late-night drinkers.

NIGHTLIFE & MUSIC VENUES

Most venues don't have box offices; tickets are available from Fnac and ticket agencies.

L'Affranchi
212 bd St-Marcel, 11th (04.91.35.09.19/ www.l-affranchi.com). Bus 15, 40. **Open** (concert nights) 9pm-3am. **Admission** €8. **No credit cards**.
Near the motorway towards Aubagne, L'Affranchi is a showcase for Marseille rap and reggae.

★ Espace Julien
39 cours Julien, 6th (04.91.24.34.10/infoline 04.91.24.34.19/www.espace-julien.com). M° Notre-Dame-du-Mont-Cours-Julien. **Admission** free-€21. **Open** varies. **Credit** varies.
This long-standing, very active venue on the boho 'cours Ju' has a packed musical programme, which

L'Intermédiaire.

ranges from international pop and blues to local electro; smaller bands and DJs play in the Café Julien.

New Cancan
3 rue Sénac-de-Meilhan, 1st (04.91.48.59.76/ www.newcancan.com). M° Réformés-Canebière. **Open** 6pm-6am daily. **Admission** free-€11. **Credit** AmEx, MC, V.
Marseille's largest gay club is little changed since the '70s and attracts a mixed, uninhibited crowd. Stage shows liven things up, as does the backroom.

FREE L'Intermédiaire
63 pl Jean Jaurès (04.91.47.01.25). M° Notre-Dame-du-Mont-Cours-Julien. **Open** 6.30pm-2am Mon, Tue; 5.30pm-2am Wed-Sat; 6.30pm-2am 1st Sun of mth. **Admission** free. **No credit cards**.
This hip jazz, blues and rock venue is crowded but friendly. Gigs are held at 10.30pm, Wednesday to Saturday, with jam sessions on Tuesdays and jazz on the first Sunday of the month.

Le Sports Beach Café
Escale Borély, 148 av Pierre Mendès France, 8th (04.91.76.12.35/www.sportsbeachcafe.fr). Bus 19. **Open** noon-3pm, 7pm-midnight Mon-Fri; noon-3.30pm, 7pm-midnight Sat, Sun. Closed Mon, Sun in winter. **Admission** free-€10 (incl 1 drink). **Credit** MC, V.
Among the beachside brasseries of the Escale Borély, this restaurant, lounge bar and club attracts Marseille's gilded youth for lunch round the pool by day and themed soirées (salsa, Latin, disco) by night.

152 Time Out South of France

Le Trolleybus

24 quai Rive Neuve, 7th (04.91.54.30.45/www.le trolley.com). Mº Vieux-Port. **Open** 11pm-dawn Wed-Sat. **Admission** free Wed-Fri; €10 Sat. **Credit** MC, V.

This sprawling harbourside club continues to pack in the punters, with different rooms offering techno, salsa, funk… and *pétanque*. An equally heterogeneous crowd goes from well-heeled young bankers to rappers in tracksuits.

Le Warm'Up

8 bd Mireille Jourdan Barry, 8th (04.96.14.06.30/ www.warmup-marseille.fr). Bus 15, 40. **Open** 8pm-2am Tue-Sat. **Admission** free Tue, Fri; €8-€12 Wed, Thur, Sat. **Credit** MC, V.

Marseille's answer to the super-club, Warm'Up has everything from a state-of-the-art sound system and heaving dancefloor to an oriental chill-out room and terrace bar, with a swimming pool and views of the distant hills. DJs spin diverse sets, from straight-ahead house through electro bleeps to spirited salsa.

SHOPPING

Marseille's main shopping district lies between La Canebière and the Préfecture. **Pâtisserie d'Aix** (No.2 rue d'Aix, 04.91.90.12.50) is famed for its Tunisian pastries, its shelves stacked high with pyramids of honey-drenched delights. Towards the Vieux Port, the **Centre Bourse** (17 cours Belsunce, 04.91.14.00.50) is the main shopping centre, with a Fnac store on the second floor. On the port itself is **La Maison du Pastis** (No.108, 04.91.90.86.77, www.la maisondupastis.com), crammed with a dizzying array of pastis, anisette and absinthe. Just back from the port, you can stock up on cubes of traditional Marseille soap at **La Compagnie de Provence** (1 rue Caisserie, 04.91.56.20.94). The classic is non-perfumed olive-oil green, but it also sells vanilla, jasmine and honey varieties.

Crossing back across La Canebière, rue St-Ferréol is lined with clothes shops and big chains, including the **Galeries Lafayette** department store (No.40, 04.96.11.35.00). Nearby rue de la Tour is a pedestrianised street behind the Vieux Port that has become a hub for local designers, led by flamboyant hat stylist **Manon Martin** (No.10, 04.91.55.60.95). Several designer boutiques have also sprung up on rue Francis Davso and rue Grignan. The latter is home to the likes of Cartier and Louis Vuitton, along with chic concept store **Marianne Cat** (No.53, 04.91.55.05.25), where hip clothes and accessories are mixed with 1930s and '40s furniture and modern design *objets*.

Rue Paradis offers Kenzo, MaxMara, Gérard Darel and Tara Jarmon. **Rive Neuve** (30 cours d'Estienne d'Orves, 04.96.11.01.01) is indicative of the designer boutiques now colonising

Marseille, with a cutting-edge selection of labels, including Alberta Ferretti, Camarlinghi, Paul Smith and Coast. On rue Sainte you'll find great shoes at **Créatis** (No.53, 04.91.54.21.73) and rising labels **Bérénice** (No.10, 04.91.33.97.80) and **Zadig et Voltaire** (No.4, 04.91.33.64.88). At No.136, the **Four des Navettes** (04.91.33. 32.12, www.fourdesnavettes.com) bakery was founded in 1781 and is famed for its boat-shaped *navette* biscuits.

Good homeware shops congregate around the Opéra, but for a quirkier selection of boutiques, head to rue Thubaneau or cours Julien. While you're there, pop into **Madame Zaza de Marseille** (73 cours Julien, 04.91.59.28.48) to browse the label's well-cut womenswear and collection of costume jewellery.

Nearby **G Bataille** (25 pl Notre-Dame-du-Mont, 04.91.47.06.23) is a magnificent *traiteur* (deli) and the perfect place to shop for wines and olive oil, or a picnic of delicious cheeses, salads, cold meats and pastries. Just off cours Lieutaud, which runs parallel to cours Julien, the **Librairie Internationale Maurel** (95 rue de Lodi, 04.91.42.63.44) is a specialist in English- and Italian-language books, with some Russian, German and Spanish material.

Marseille has some 30 markets, the most famous of which are the daily fresh fish market (*see p142*); the cours Julien (*see p143*); and the avenue du Prado (every morning, flowers Friday). Despite being a long way from the centre, the flea market (av du Cap-Pinède, 15th, bus 35 & 70) is worth a visit, with antiques and bric-a-brac sold Friday to Sunday.

ARTS & ENTERTAINMENT

Marseille has over 30 theatres and café-theatres and around 100 theatre companies, as well as its opera and ballet. For details of events, pick up weekly freebie *Marseille Hebdo*, Provence-wide *César* or the Marseille edition of *Métro*. In summer, the **Festival de Marseille** (*see p46*) programmes first-rate contemporary dance and music. Look out, too, for free concerts in Le Panier during **Soirs d'été** (04.91.91.09.28, www.fetedupanier.com), or jazz in the Palais de Longchamp gardens.

Dock des Suds

12 rue Urbain V, 2nd (04.91.99.00.00//www. dock-des-suds.org). Mº National. **Open** call for details. **Admission** varies. **No credit cards**.

The 5,000sq m (54,000sq ft) dock that hosts the Fiesta des Suds (*see p47*) is now programming music with a world and salsa bias all year round.

Dôme-Zénith

48 av St-Just, 4th (04.91.12.21.21/www.le-dome.com). Mº St-Just-Hôtel du Département/41,

53, 81 bus/Fluobus at night. **Open** call for details. **Admission** varies. **No credit cards**.
This vast modern venue is the place to catch international rock acts and stars of French *variété*, along with dance shows, musicals and big names from the stand-up comedy circuit.

FREE FRAC Provence-Alpes-Côtes d'Azur

1 pl Francis Chirat, 2nd (04.91.91.27.55). Mº Joliette. **Open** 10am-12.30pm, 2-6pm Mon-Sat. **Admission** free.
The Fonds Régional d'Art Contemporain has a wide-ranging collection of contemporary art, from global names to young artists. Works and special commissions are exhibited here at its gallery, and in schools, museums and cultural centres across the region.

Le Moulin

47 bd Perrin, 13th (04.91.06.33.94/www.le moulin.org). Mº St-Juste. **Open** *Box office* 7.30pm on day of performance. **Admission** €10-€22. **No credit cards**.
This converted cinema has become one of Marseille's main venues for visiting French and international rock, reggae and world music bands.

Opéra de Marseille

2 rue Molière, 1st (04.91.55.11.10). Mº Vieux-Port. **Open** *Box office* 10am-5.30pm Tue-Sat. **Tickets** €8-€60. **No credit cards**.
The original opera was one of the city's great 18th-century buildings. Partially burnt down in 1919, it was rebuilt in art deco style, preserving the original façade. Today, it holds performances of opera and the Ballet National de Marseille, directed by Marie-Claude Pietragalla.

Théâtre National de la Criée

30 quai Rive Neuve, 7th (04.91.54.70.54/www. theatre-lacriee.com). Mº Vieux-Port. **Open** *Box office* 10am-7pm (in person noon-6pm) Tue-Sat; limited evening opening. **Tickets** €10-€20. **Credit** MC, V.
This celebrated theatre was created from the city's former fish market in 1981. Director Jean-Louis Benoit, in partnership with producer and artistic consultant Frédéric Bélier-Garcia, is bringing an international slant to the operation.

Théâtre du Gymnase

4 rue du Théâtre Français, 1st (04.91.24.35.24/ box office 08.20.00.04.22/www.lestheatres.net). Mº Noailles. **Open** *Box office* 11am-6pm (in person noon-6pm) Tue-Sat. **Tickets** €20-€30. **Credit** MC, V.
This candy-box of a theatre, dating from 1834, was restored in 1986. Directed by Dominique Bluzet, it's one of the best-attended, most innovative theatres in France, staging its own take on everything from classics to contemporary drama.

WHERE TO STAY

€ Auberge de Jeunesse de Marseille Bonneveine

Impasse du Dr Bonfils, 8th (04.91.17.63.30/ www.fuaj.net). Mº Rond-Point du Prado then 44 bus. **Closed** mid Dec-Feb. **Rates** €11.45-€13.35/ person. **Rooms** 40. **Credit** DC, MC, V.
Just a stone's throw from the sea and very near the Calanques, this comfortable youth hostel is a good bet if you're looking for a back-to-nature holiday.

€ Etap Hôtel Vieux Port

46 rue Sainte, 1st (08.92.68.05.82/www.etap hotel.com). Mº Vieux-Port. **Rates** €65 double. **Rooms** 147. **Credit** AmEx, MC, V. **Map** p138 E4 ❶
The façade of this former arsenal building is gorgeous, even if the rooms of this budget chain hotel feel a bit like prison cells. Still, you can't beat the location or the price.

★ Hôtel Alizé

35 quai des Belges, 1st (04.91.33.66.97/www. alize-hotel.com). Mº Vieux-Port. **Rates** €73-€91 double. **Rooms** 39. **Credit** AmEx, DC, MC, V. **Map** p138 F3 ❷
It's worth paying a little extra for a room overlooking the Vieux Port, rather than the tiny courtyard. All are decorated in Impressionist-inspired autumnal colours, with sparkling modern bathrooms.

Hôtel Belle-Vue

34 quai du Port, 2nd (04.96.17.05.40/www.hotel-bellevue-marseille.fr). Mº Vieux-Port. **Rates** €92-€122 double. **Rooms** 18. **Credit** AmEx, MC, V. **Map** p138 E3 ❸
This historic hotel above La Caravelle bar (*see p151*) has 18 tastefully renovated rooms with immaculate bathrooms; try to get one facing the port. Pictures by local artists adorn the stairs.

Hôtel Edmond Rostand

31 rue du Dragon, 6th (04.91.37.74.95/www.hotel edmondrostand.com). Mº Castellane or Estrangin-Préfecture. **Rates** €80-€99 double. **Rooms** 15. **Credit** AmEx, DC, MC, V. **Map** p138 F3 ❹
This clean, friendly place in the antiques district behind the Préfecture is decent value and has adequate (though not spacious) air-conditioned rooms.

Hôtel Hermès

2 rue Bonneterie, 2nd (04.96.11.63.63/www.hotel marseille.com). Mº Vieux-Port. **Rates** €68-€85 double. **Rooms** 28. **Credit** AmEx, DC, MC, V. **Map** p138 E2 ❺
Though its rooms are small, this simple hotel is just steps from the Vieux Port, and offers good value for money. Three rooms on the top floor have small terraces with superb views of the harbour and Notre-Dame-de-la-Garde, and there's a rooftop sundeck too.

Hôtel Hermès.

Rooms are small but clean at this friendly little hotel, though it would help if the owners had taken some of the old furniture out when they put the new furniture in. All have air-conditioning and double glazing – useful, as small children seem to play football in front of the opéra until late at night.

★ Hôtel Résidence du Vieux Port
18 quai du Port, 2nd (04.91.91.91.22/www.hotel marseille.com). M° Vieux-Port. **Rates** €126 double. **Rooms** 50. **Credit** AmEx, DC, MC, V. **Map** p138 F3 ❽
One of the most sought-after places to stay in town, this 1950s building features balconies (except on the second floor) and unbeatable views across the Vieux Port to Notre-Dame-de-la-Garde. Some rooms are decorated in provençal style, while others have been refurbished to keep up the '50s feel.

Hôtel le Rhul
269 Corniche JF Kennedy, 7th (04.91.52.01.77/ www.bouillabaissemarseille.com). Bus 83. **Rates** €90 double. **Rooms** 16. **Credit** AmEx, MC, V.
Occupying a prime position on the Corniche, all the rooms at the Rhul have jaw-dropping sea views; some have spacious terraces. The restaurant is renowned for its bouillabaisse.

★ Hôtel Richelieu
52 Corniche JF Kennedy, 7th (04.91.31.01.92/ www.lerichelieu-marseille.com). Bus 83. **Rates** €55-€110 double. **Rooms** 21. **Credit** V.
Clinging perilously on to the seashore by the plage des Catalans, this charming hotel has bright paintings in the lobby and colourful murals of seagulls and sailing boats in the bedrooms. Rooms at the rear have incredible sea views, and some have mini-balconies – though a few share a loo on the landing.

★ Mercure Grand Hôtel Beauvau Vieux Port
4 rue Beauvau, 1st (04.91.54.91.00/www. mercure.com). M° Vieux-Port. **Rates** €165-€236 double. **Rooms** 72. **Credit** AmEx, DC, MC, V. **Map** p138 F3 ❾
This historic hotel, where Chopin and George Sand once stayed, overlooks the Vieux Port and has been luxuriously renovated. Rooms feature Napoléon III furniture and traditional provençal textiles; the duplexes are particularly good for families.

New Hôtel Bompard
2 rue des Flots-Bleus, 7th (04.91.99.22.22/ www.new-hotel.com). Bus 61. **Rates** €125-€140 double. **Rooms** 46. **Credit** AmEx, MC, V.
Tucked away in a quiet residential area near the Corniche, the Bompard has air-conditioned rooms in the old wing and extension, family apartments with kitchens, and four sumptuous provençal-style *mas* (€170-€200). There's a nice swimming pool and gardens, along with a guests-only restaurant.

Hôtel Le Corbusier
280 bd Michelet, 8th (04.91.16.78.00/www.hotelle corbusier.com). M° Rond-Point du Prado/21, 22 bus. **Rates** €59-€120 double. **Rooms** 21. **Credit** AmEx, DC, MC, V.
Modern architecture aficionados won't want to miss the chance to stay in this iconic building (*see p146* **La Cité Radieuse**). The Le Corbusier spirit is lovingly preserved, although the cheapest rooms, with a shared loo, resemble the monks' cells on which they were modelled. Pricier rooms are large and there are two studios with terraces, sea views and original Le Corbusier kitchens (not for use).

Hôtel du Palais
26 rue Breteuil, 6th (04.91.37.78.86/www.hotel dupalaismarseille.com). M° Estrangin-Préfecture. **Rates** €95-€125 double. **Rooms** 22. **Credit** AmEx, MC, V. **Map** p138 F5 ❻
Located near the Palais de Justice – handy for strolling around the Vieux Port, but far enough removed to be peaceful at night – the Palais is a smart, efficiently run place to lay your head.

€ Hôtel Relax
4 rue Corneille, 1st (04.91.33.15.87/http://relax hotel.free.fr). M° Vieux-Port. **Rates** €55-€60 double. **Rooms** 22. **Credit** MC, V. **Map** p138 F4 ❼

MARSEILLE & AIX

Le Petit Nice – Passédat

Anse de Maldormé, Corniche JF Kennedy, 7th (04.91.59.25.92/www.petitnice-passedat.com). Bus 83. **Rates** €250-€610 double. **Rooms** 13. **Credit** AmEx, DC, MC, V.

Perched on its own little promontory off the Corniche road, this luxurious villa has opulent air-conditioned rooms, a swimming pool and what some consider to be Marseille's top restaurant, renowned for chef Gérard Passedat's splendid seafood.

Pullman Palm Beach

200 Corniche JF Kennedy, 7th (04.91.16.19.00/ www.accorhotels.com). Bus 83. **Rates** €265-€315 double. **Rooms** 140. **Credit** AmEx, DC, MC, V.

This sleek 140-room chain hotel has stunning views of the bay and islands. Open spaces, huge windows and giant plants are combined with cutting-edge designs by Starck, Zanotta, Emu and Gervasoni; the final result is surprisingly warm and inviting. The saltwater pool is fed by a natural spring.

Radisson Vieux Port

38-40 quai de Rive Neuve, 7th (04.89.61.90.05/ www.marseille.radissonsas.com). M° Vieux-Port. Bus 83. **Rates** €235-€314 double. **Rooms** 189. **Credit** AmEx, DC, MC, V. **Map** p138 D3 ❿

The pick of the new bunch of business hotels is also a good holiday option, with a prime position on the Vieux Port. Spacious guestrooms have provençal or African-inspired decor, and are spread over two buildings with a rooftop swimming pool between the two. A generous breakfast buffet, colourful bar, gym and restaurant complete the facilities.

GETTING THERE

From the airport

Aéroport Marseille-Provence (04.42.14.14.14) is 25km (15.5 miles) north-west of Marseille near Marignane. It has two terminals, one for the main international airlines (www.marseille.aeroport.fr), the second (www.mp2.aeroport.fr) for low-cost carriers. 'La Navette' coaches (04.42.14.31.27) run

---

**INSIDE TRACK
FREEWHEELING**

Up and running since 2007, Marseille's municipal bike hire scheme, **Le Vélo** (www.levelo-mpm.fr), has been a great success. Use your credit card to purchase a €1 *abonnement courte durée* (seven-day subscription), then pick up a bike from one of the stations dotted around town. At the end of your journey, you can return the bike to any pick-up point. The first half hour of every journey is free; after that, it's €1 an hour.

---

every 20mins 6.15am-10.50pm to Gare St-Charles, and from the station to the airport 5.30am-9.50pm; the trip takes about 25mins and costs €8.50. A taxi to the Vieux Port costs around €40.

By boat

SNCM (61 bd des Dames, 2nd, 04.91.39.40.00, www.sncm.fr, M° Joliette) is the primary passenger line from the Gare Maritime de la Joliette for Sardinia, Corsica, Algeria and Tunisia.

By bus

The *gare routière* adjoins the train station (08.91.02.40.25, M° St-Charles). **Cartreize** (08.00.19.94.13, www.lepilote.com) is the umbrella organisation for all coach services in the Bouches-du-Rhône. **Eurolines** (04.91.50.57.55, www.eurolines.fr) operates coaches between Marseille and Avignon, Nice via Aix-en-Provence and daily coaches to Venice, Milan and Rome, Barcelona and Valencia. Note that the bus for Aix-en-Provence (buses every 5mins at peak times, buy ticket on the bus) currently leaves from the Porte d'Aix (pl Jules Guesde).

GETTING AROUND

By bus, tram & Métro

RTM (04.91.91.92.10, www.rtm.fr) runs a comprehensive network of bus routes, two Métro lines (5am-9pm Mon-Thur; 5am-12.30am Fri-Sun & OM match nights) and two tramlines. The same tickets are used on all three and can be bought in Métro stations (singles only) and at tabacs and newsagents displaying the RTM sign. A single ticket costs €1.70 and entitles the user to one hour's travel. The Carte Libertés (€6 or €12) offers five or ten journeys, each also lasting up to an hour. For unlimited travel, a one-day ticket is €4.50, a weekly pass (with photocard) €10.30. At night, a network of Fluobuses runs between the Canebière (Bourse) and outer districts.

By car

Marseille is served by three motorways. The A7-A51 heads north to the airport, Aix and Lyon; the A55 runs west to Martigues; and the A50 runs east to Toulon. The Prado-Carénage toll tunnel links the A55 to the A50.

By taxi

There are cab ranks on most main squares; alternatively, call **Marseille Taxi** (04.91.02.20.20), **Taxi Plus** (04.91.03.60.03) or **Taxi Radio Tupp** (04.91.05.80.80).

By train

The main station is the **Gare St-Charles** (08.10.87.94.79, www.sncf.com), with frequent high-speed TGV trains from Paris (coming from the UK it is also possible to change in Lille), the main coast route east to Nice and Italy, and west via Miramas and Arles. Branch lines run to Miramas via Martigues and the Côte Bleue, and to Aix and Gap.

RESOURCES

Hospitals

Hôpitaux Public de Marseille *(15 OR 04.91.49.91.91/www.ap-hm.fr).* The SAMU number (15) is also the central emergency number for all Marseille hospitals. **Hôpital de la Conception** *147 bd Baille, 5th (04.91.38.30.00). M° Baille.* **Hôpital Militaire Lavéran** *34 bd Lavéran, 13th (04.91.61.70.00/www.hia-laveran.fr). M° Malpassé then bus 38.*

Internet

Info-Café *1 quai Rive Neuve, 1st (04.91.33.74.98/www.info-cafe.com). M° Vieux-Port.* **Open** 9am-10pm Mon-Sat; 2.30-7.30pm Sun.

Police

Commissariat de Noailles, 66-68 La Canebière, 1st (04.88.77.58.00). M° Noailles.

Post office

Hôtel des Postes, rue Henri Barbusse, 1st (04.91.15.47.00). M° Colbert or Vieux-Port.

Tourist information

Office du Tourisme *4 La Canebière, 1st (04.91.13.89.00/www.marseille-tourisme.com). M° Vieux-Port.* **Open** 9am-7pm Mon-Sat; 10am-5pm Sun.

Around Marseille

MARTIGUES & THE COTE BLEUE

Beyond L'Estaque towards Carro is the **Côte Bleue**, much loved by Marseillais at weekends thanks to its sheer cliffs, small fishing ports and rocky beaches. This area is as easy to reach by train as by car – while the D5 meanders between inlets and over the red hills of the Chaine de l'Estaque, the railway chugs over a series of scenic viaducts along the coast (the *découverte* day ticket allows as many stops as you like). Tiny coves like Niolon and La Madrague-de-Gignac afford stunning views across the bay to Marseille. The main resorts are **Sausset-les-Pins**, which is very popular with families, and **Carry-le-Rouet**. **Carro** is a picturesque fishing port and a favourite with windsurfers. It's also worth stopping at **La Redonne**'s peaceful little harbour.

Inland, **Martigues** is a pretty though traffic-cluttered town of pastel houses, built alongside canals. It stands on the edge of the heavily industrialised (and polluted) Etang de Berre lagoon. The railway station is some way out towards Lavera, which means a long walk along main roads, or waiting for an infrequent bus. An alternative is to take the coach from Marseille or Aix to the bus station in the centre.

The town is the result of a merging of three villages in 1581: Jonquières, Ferrières and L'Ile Brescon, now linked by a series of bridges, Venice-style. In Jonquières, admire the wildly colourful baroque **Chapelle de l'Annonciade** (1664-71), then follow the road down to place Gérard Tenque and stroll around the plethora of shops and cafés. On L'Ile Brescon, the **Eglise de la Madeleine** is another fine baroque edifice with an ornately carved façade.

In Ferrières, the modern Théâtre des Salins contrasts starkly with the colour-washed fishermen's cottages. The **Musée Ziem** is a pleasant surprise, with works by Félix Ziem, Manguin, Loubon and Dufy.

🆓 Musée Ziem

bd du 14 Juillet (04.42.41.39.60). **Open** *July-Aug 10am-noon, 2.30-6.30pm Mon, Wed-Sun. Sept-June 2.30-6.30pm Wed-Sun.* **Admission** free.

Where to eat & stay

Locals in Sausset-les-Pins delight in the imaginative cooking at **Les Girelles** (rue Frédéric Mistral, 04.42.45.26.16, closed Mon, lunch Tue in July & Aug, Wed, dinner Sun Sept-June, Jan, menus €28-€38), which stages jazz concerts on summer evenings.

In Carro, friendly, family-oriented **Le Chalut** (port de Carro, 04.42.80.70.61, closed dinner Mon, all Tue, menus €17-€28) specialises in fish and shellfish. The **Auberge de la Calanque** (port de la Redonne, 04.42.45.95.01, mains €9-€12.50) serves appetising pizzas. In Martigues, try the baby calamares or delicate fish kebabs at **Le Miroir** (4 rue Marcel Galdy, 04.42.80.50.45, closed Mon, lunch Sat, dinner Sun & all Sun July-Aug, 1wk Nov, 2wks Dec, 2wks Easter, menus €14.50-€30). The **Hôtel Cigalon** (37 bd du 14 Juillet, 04.42.80.49.16, double €42-€75) is a simple, cheerfully furnished hotel.

Resources

Tourist information

Martigues Maison du Tourisme *Rond-point de l'Hôtel de Ville, Martigues (04.42.42. 31.10/www.ville-martigues.fr).* **Open** 9am-7pm Mon-Sat; 10am-1pm, 3-6pm Sun.

Cassis & the Calanques

The scenery is postcard-perfect… and the wine's not bad, either.

The setting for **Cassis**, one of France's prettiest fishing villages, is heavenly. Towering white cliffs, picturesque vineyards and white sandy beaches conspire to produce picture-postcard views, best enjoyed with a glass of the local white wine.

Out of season, this is a tranquil little place, where the main excitement comes from Sunday morning *pétanque* matches by the harbour. In summer, though, it's a different story, when Cassis becomes a chic mini-version of St-Tropez, and sun-worshippers and souvenir sellers abound.

Along the coast, the **Calanques** are a series of inlets in the precipitous limestone cliffs, dotted with tiny beaches and coves.

CASSIS

Early 20th-century artists, including Dufy, Matisse and Vlaminck, flocked to Cassis for the sea air and intense light, though sadly none of their works have made it into the small **Musée Municipal**, with its displays on local history and art. The town has two delightful public beaches: the main plage de la Grande Mer and the quieter plage du Bestouan, in a sheltered bay to the west of the port. The market is on Wednesday and Friday mornings.

The picturesque descent into Cassis takes you through a dozen top wineries, most producing the famed AOC Cassis white wine (*see p162* **Wine Tour**). The route des Crêtes (D141) climbs across Cap Canaille, the highest coastal cliff in Europe, to La Ciotat, with often nail-biting views. On foot, the Cap's summit can be reached in about an hour and a half, starting from the avenue du Revestel; less energetic hikers can tour the vineyards with the tourist office's free *vin et terroir* walking map.

The waters around Cassis offer some of the best diving in France. Scuba 'baptisms', lessons and undersea tours are conducted by both the **Centre Cassidian de Plongée** (3 rue Michel Arnaud, 04.42.01.89.16) and **Narval Cassis** (aboard the *Don Luis* in the port, or at 11 av de la Viguerie, 04.42.01.87.59).

FREE **Musée Municipal**

rue Xavier d'Authier (04.42.01.88.66). **Open** *Apr-Sept* 10.30am-12.30pm, 3.30-6.30pm Wed-Sat. *Oct-Mar* 10.30am-12.30pm, 2.30-5.30pm Wed-Sat. **Admission** free.

Where to stay & eat

Cassis is blessed with several enchanting hotels, but it's vital to book ahead in summer. Winston Churchill learned to paint while staying at **Les Roches Blanches** (rte des Calanques, 04.42.01.09.30, www.roches-blanches-cassis.com, closed Nov-mid Jan, double €135-€210); both the hotel and its classic French restaurant (dinner only except July & Aug, menus €39-€65) boast breathtaking views over Cap Canaille and the port. Back from the bustling promenade, **Le Provençal** (7 av Victor Hugo, 04.42.01.72.13, www.cassis-le-provencal.com, closed mid Oct-Dec, double €42-€85) is an cheap, popular option.

Le Cassitel (pl Clémenceau, 04.42.01.83.44, www.hotel-cassis.com, double €58-€90) offers provençal-themed rooms, some with harbour views. Two chic *chambres d'hôtes* are **Maison9** (9 rue du Dr Yves Bourde, 04.42.01.26.39, www.maison9.net, double €110-€195), in the middle of a vineyard with a private pool, and **Château de Cassis** (traverse de Château, 04.42.01.63.20, www.chateaudecassis.com, double €220-€690), in a castle midway up the Cap Canaille. A 15-minute walk out of town, **Camping les Cigales** (av de la Marn, 04.42.01. 07.34, www.campingcassis.com, closed mid Mar-mid Nov, €5.70/person & €4.80/pitch) is superb.

On the port, seafood purist **Nino** (2 quai Jean Jacques Barthélémy, 04.42.01.74.32, www.nino-cassis.com, closed Mon, menu €34) has harbour-fresh fish and crustaceans, and three delightful suites (€180-€300). At the end of the harbour, **Le Bistro** (av Am Ganteaume, 04.42.01.07.59, menu €27-€58) combines fine seafood with budget-friendly crispy pizzas and jugs of wine.

A hip, modern Italian addition is **Romano** (15 quai Barthélémy, 04.42.01.08.16, closed Mon, menus €25-€65). Gastronomes should seek out **La Villa Madie** (av du Revestel, anse de Corton, 04.96.18.00.00, www.lavillamadie.com, closed Mon, Tue lunch Apr-Sept, Mon, Tue, Sun lunch Oct-Mar, mains €48-€55), Jean-Marc Banzo's temple of fine provençal dining.

Resources

Tourist information
Office du Tourisme *quai des Moulins, Cassis (08.92.25.98.92/www.ot-cassis.com)*. **Open** *June-Sept* 9am-7pm daily; *Oct-May* 9.30am-12.30pm, 2.30-6pm Mon-Fri; 10am-12.30pm, 2.30-6.30pm Sat; 10am-12.30pm Sun.

THE CALANQUES

These spectacular gashes in the limestone cliffs between Marseille and Cassis were formed in the Ice Age when sea levels rose and flooded the deep valleys, leaving secluded bays and towering rock formations. The Calanques now form a rugged 5,000-hectare (12,355-acre) national reserve, where bushes, flowers, ferns and occasional trees cling to dry rocks, lined with trails that meander up cliffs, across mountain passes and even underwater. Eagles and falcons share the skies with seagulls, puffins and stormy petrels.

The Calanques closest to Marseille are flatter and wider than those towards Cassis. The best-known (and most visited in summer) are **Sormiou** and **Morgiou**, which are dotted with *cabanons*. Built from recycled driftwood and scrap, these run-down, century-old holiday huts are so cherished by Marseilleis families that they are passed from generation to generation, and are now listed buildings. There is no electricity on either Calanque, and only one telephone booth on Sormiou for emergencies. The setting is perfect for lazy swims, cliff diving or rock climbing. If you're planning to drive there, note that access is severely restricted in summer; the twisting, single-track fire-road is closed between 7am and 8pm from Easter to mid-September, though cars are allowed in for those with lunch reservations. For boat access from Cassis, *see p160*.

From the Cassis side, only the first Calanque, **Port-Miou**, is fully accessible by car. Boats sail to the other inlets, or you can walk along the *grande randonnée* (GR) hiking trail. The best climbing is up the 'finger of God' rock spur in **En-Vau**, which has a Thailand-esque bright-white sand beach. For hardened professionals, the cliffs of **Devenson** offer a serious challenge.

Cassis.

MARSEILLE & AIX

Where to stay & eat

La Presqu'Ile (quartier Port-Miou, 04.42.01.
03.77, www.restaurant-la-presquile.com, closed
Mon, menus €30-€48) serves up incredibly good
seafood overlooking the Med. **Le Nautic** (04.
91.40.06.37, closed Mon, dinner Sun, Nov-Jan,
mains €12.50-€40) is a lively bar-restaurant
on the port at Morgiou. **La Fontasse** hostel
(04.42.01.02.72, www.fuaj.org, closed mid Dec-
mid Mar, dorm €10.40 for YHA members) is
the only place to stay in the Calanques, a good
hour's walk from Cassis; bring food and water.

Getting to the Calanques

By boat
From Marseille, boats run by **Icard Maritime/
Marseille Côte Mer** (1 quai Marcel Pagnol,
04.91.33.03.29, http://visiter.calanques.free.fr)
leave from quai des Belges on the Vieux Port
daily in July and August, and on Wednesday,
Saturday and Sunday the rest of the year.

From Cassis, regular boats (Feb-Oct) from
the eastern end of the port serve one of three
Calanques circuits: prices are fixed at €13 for
three Calanques, €15 for five or €19 to motor
around all eight. You can be dropped off at
En-Vau or Morgiou in summer until 11am,
before hiking back. Tickets are available on
board, or from the yellow hut on quai St-Pierre
(04.42.01.90.83, www.calanques-cassis.com).

By bus
Marseille bus No.19 (04.91.91.92.10, www.rtm.fr)
from Prado or Castellane runs to La Madrague de
Montredon to reach the Calanques by footpath

GR98. Buses 21 and 21s go to the Université
de Luminy. Buses 22 and 23 from Prado to
Beauvallon or Les Beaumettes lead to Sormiou
and Morgiou.

By car
For details of the restricted access track, *see p159.*

LA CIOTAT &
ST-CYR-SUR-MER

A genteel summer residence since the mid 19th
century, **La Ciotat** has much of the charm of
neighbouring resorts, yet little of the expense.
Its six-kilometre sandy beach curves around
the Baie de la Ciotat to **St-Cyr-sur-Mer** and
its seaside suburb of **Les Lecques**.

The colourful fishing boats and maritime-
themed **Musée Ciotaden** point to a proud
seafaring past, but history hasn't always been
kind: in 1989, the Krupp dockyard closed and
10,000 people in a town of 30,000 lost their jobs.
The factories at the edge of the pretty port are
now a huge yacht club and bar complex. The
town has markets on Tuesday morning on
place du Marché, Sunday morning at the port,
and a farmers' market on Friday afternoon.

Among La Ciotat's most illustrious residents
were Auguste and Louis Lumière, who made
the world's first film: a clip of the Toulon to
Marseille train pulling into La Ciotat station.
Those present at the screening in 1895
apparently dived out of the way, fearing that
they'd be squashed by the oncoming engine.
The **Espace Lumière Michel Simon** on
rue Maréchal Foch relives the past with
photographs, posters and a film archive.

Sormiou.

The **Ile Verte**, surely the South of France's least visited island, is a 430-metre- (1,400-foot-) long paradise with walking trails and world-class snorkelling. Two Calanques – quieter and as geologically stunning as any in Cassis – lie just west of town. The first, **Mugel**, is nestled in the Parc du Mugel botanical gardens, while the breathtaking **Calanque de Figuerolles**, immortalised by Braque, features two of La Ciotat's most enchanting places to stay.

St-Cyr-sur-Mer's vibrant café life centres around the gilded replica of the *Statue of Liberty* on place Portalis, donated by sculptor Bartholdi. Its seaward extension, **Les Lecques**, is a clutter of shops and eateries, with a family-friendly promenade. Les Lecques claims to have been the Greek trading post of Tauroentum, and the **Musée de Tauroentum** displays the artefacts to prove it. Past the museum, a nine-kilometre footpath (marked in yellow) clings to the coast through old pines and oaks to La Madrague (2hrs to Port d'Alon) and Bandol (3hrs 30mins). Also in the vicinity is **Aqualand**, a self-explanatory fun park.

Aqualand

St-Cyr-sur-Mer (04.94.32.08.32/www.aqua land.fr). **Open** *Mid June-Aug* 10am-7pm daily. **Admission** €24; €17.50 reductions; free children under 1m. **Credit** AmEx, MC, V.

FREE Espace Lumière Michel Simon

20 rue Maréchal Foch, La Ciotat (04.42.08.69. 60). **Open** *July-Sept* 10am-7pm Tue, Sat; 3-6pm Wed. Fri. *Oct-June* 3-6pm Tue, Wed, Fri, Sat. **Admission** free.

Musée Ciotaden

1 quai Ganteaume, La Ciotat (04.42.71.40.99/ www.museeciotaden.org). **Open** *July-Aug* 4-7pm Wed-Mon. *Sept-June* 3-6pm Wed-Mon. **Admission** €3.20; €1.60 reductions; free under-12s. **No credit cards**.

Musée de Tauroentum

131 rte de La Madrague, St-Cyr-sur-Mer (04.94. 26.30.46). **Open** *June-Sept* 3-7pm Mon, Wed-Sun. *Oct-May* 2-5pm Sat, Sun. **Admission** €3; €1 reductions; free under-7s. **No credit cards**.

FREE Parc de Mugel

La Ciotat (guided visits 06.75.56.99.62). **Open** *Apr-Sept* 8am-8pm daily. *Oct-Mar* 9am-6pm daily. **Admission** free.

Where to stay, eat & drink

The **Yacht Club La Ciotat** (quai Port Vieux, 04.42.08.14.14, www.yclc.com, menus €29-€64) has taken over the old Krupp dockyard in La Ciotat and is now a giant entertainment complex,

---

**INSIDE TRACK
PADDLE POWER**

Kayaking around the Calanques is an unforgettable experience. To hire your own trusty kayak, call in at **Calankayak** in the port at Cassis (06.16.90.25.71, www.calankayak.com), where fees start at €60 per day.

much of it open-air, with panoramic port views, restaurants serving fusion food and concerts at weekends. On the harbour but serving hearty cuisine from the interior is **Table Le Jeanne** (29 quai François Mitterand, 04.42.08.18.17, closed Mon, Sun dinner, mains €15-€38). **Le Sirocco** (8 quai Ganteaume, 04.42.62.11.74, closed Mon, menus €14-€29) features simply prepared, harbour-fresh seafood and local lamb.

Of the handful of hotels in town, **Les Lavandes** (38 bd de la République, 04.42.08.42.81, www.hotel-les-lavandes.com, double €54-€60) is a simple option behind the port. More imaginative are the two *chambres d'hôtes* at Calanque de Figuerolles: the rustic **Les Falaises** (06.17.17.32.46, www.lesfalaises. org, double €75-€90), with its open fire and shared sun terrace, and the sweet bungalows of **Figuerolles** (04.42.08.41.71, www.figuerolles. com, double €37-€135, menus €36-€43) with its acclaimed restaurant, by the beach below.

On the beach road to Les Lecques, **Hôtel Le Marina** (18 av Franklin Roosevelt, 04.42.98.12.40, double €65-€85) occupies the seafront villa where the cinematic Lumière brothers once lived. In the seaside suburb itself, **Hôtel Petit Nice** (11 allée du Dr Seillon, 04.94.32.00.64, www.hotelpetitnice.com, closed Nov-mid Mar, double €111.50-€124) has a shady pool near the beach. **Riviera del Fiori** (04.94.32.18.20, closed Mon & Feb, menus €19.50-€28), on the new port of Les Lecques, specialises in grilled fish and bouillabaisse.

Resources

Tourist information

La Ciotat Office de Tourisme *bd Anatole France, La Ciotat (04.42.08.61.32/ www.tourisme-laciotat.com).* **Open** *June-Sept* 9am-8pm Mon-Sat; 10am-1pm Sun. *Oct-May* 9am-noon, 2-6pm Mon-Sat.

St-Cyr Les Lecques Office de Tourisme *pl de l'Appel du 18 Juin, Les Lecques (04.94.26.73.73/www.saintcyrsurmer.com).* **Open** *July, Aug, Dec* 9am-7pm Mon-Sat; 10am-1pm, 4-7pm Sun. *Sept, Oct, Mar-June* 9am-6pm Mon-Fri; 9am-noon, 2-6pm Sat. *Nov-Feb* 9am-5pm Mon-Fri; 9am-noon, 1-5pm Sat.

Wine Tour Cassis

Richard James recommends the pick of the local vineyards.

The small appellation of Cassis consists of a dozen estates spread around the eponymous seaside town. Most are a pleasant hike or cycle ride up the hill, away from the madding crowds that engulf Cassis in summer. Less than 200 hectares of vines are planted here, mainly with white varieties: ugni blanc (lacks character but gives freshness), clairette and marsanne (the two most interesting), doucillon or bourboulenc and sauvignon blanc. Over three-quarters of what's produced is white wine, making Cassis somewhat quirky in a southern context. Most of the rest is dry rosé, plus a tiny amount of red, both fashioned from grenache, cinsault, mourvèdre and syrah. With certain wines at €10 a bottle, great value doesn't spring to mind – but there are some interesting buys.

The Cassis tour includes four estates, two more or less in town and two out of town; you could visit all four in a day, or split them over two days. Start with **Clos Sainte Magdeleine**, owned by François Sack (av du Revestel, 04.42.01.70.28). It's located south-east of the harbour: take rue de l'Arène, then turn right. His whites are well worth trying if you haven't already discovered them in a local restaurant; the vines thrive on the sunny slopes of Cap Canaille. Afterwards, head back on yourself and this time go right on to Arène up to the roundabout, then right on to avenue de Provence where you'll find **Domaine du Bagnol** (12 av de Provence,

04.42.01.78.05). Jean-Louis Genovesi's whites and rosés are crisply refreshing, and partner seafood or tapas dishes very nicely.

A good hike north of Bagnol towards the station, **Domaine de la Ferme Blanche** (rte de Marseille, 04.42.01.00.74) is one of Cassis's best-known vineyards. Head west on avenue de Provence to the roundabout then north on avenue du 11 Novembre 1918, which feeds into avenue Joseph Liautaud. Follow this to the right and keep going onto avenue Auguste Favier, which in turn takes you on to Maréchal Foch and avenue Albizzi. The route de Marseille and entrance to Ferme Blanche are just past the roundabout; easy on foot or bike but tricky in a car, thanks to a confusing one-way system. Once you're there, enjoy François Paret's elegant white wines.

Next stop is **Château de Fontcreuse** (rte Pierre Imbert, 04.42.01.71.09, www.fontcreuse.com), where a rather exotic white wine is half-built from the seductive marsanne grape. The vineyard also makes some red (using an oddball cross-breed called caladoc) and rosé. To get there from the aforementioned roundabout, head north briefly towards the station then take a right on the twisty chemin de Bérard until it hits Emile Bodin. Go straight across on to chemin de la Douane, which forks right and comes out on the D559. Once you've turned left heading for La Ciotat, Jean-François Brando's understated chateau soon comes into view, set below the Couronne de Charlemagne rock face.

For further information on AOC Cassis, visit www.cassis.fr or www.vinscassis.com.

GETTING THERE & AROUND

By boat

The *Aquilade* (06.63.59.16.35, www.laciotat-ileverte.com) hops between La Ciotat's port and the Ile Verte from 10am to 5pm, April to September (hourly in July, Aug) for €9 return (€5 under-10s). The crossing take 15 minutes.

By bus

Cartreize (04.42.08.41.05) runs buses between Aix-en-Provence, Marseille, Cassis and La Ciotat stations. **Transport St-Cyr Tourisme** (04.94.26.23.71) runs from St-Cyr station to Les Lecques and La Madrague.

By car

Leave the A50 from Marseille at exits 8 for Cassis, 9 and 10 for La Ciotat and St-Cyr. The D559, from Marseille to Cassis, is wonderfully scenic, continuing along the coast past Les Lecques and Bandol to Toulon. The dramatic D141 route des Crêtes climbs from Cassis down to La Ciotat.

By train

Hourly trains between Marseille and Toulon stop at Cassis, La Ciotat and St-Cyr. Stations are each about 3km from the centre, and are connected to town by infrequent *navette* buses run by **TER** (08.91.70.30.00, www.ter-sncf.com).

Aix-en-Provence

For art-lovers, Aix marks the spot.

With its elegant golden stone mansions and elite opera festival, **Aix** epitomises the South of France at its most civilised. Yet despite its reputation as the haughty bastion of the bourgeoisie, this is a surprisingly young city, with some 40,000 students and a thriving café society. Summer also brings the prestigious Festival International d'Art Lyrique – though the recent opening of the Grand Théâtre de Provence and the daring Pavillon Noir dance centre (proof that the city can do contemporary as well as historic) mark its determination to be seen as an all-year cultural destination.

Just outside town, the **Montagne Ste-Victoire** is famed for its Cézanne connection, its triangular contours oddly familiar from his paintings. Hiking trails cross its wooded slopes, while the sheer cliffs are best left to climbers.

ABOUT THE CITY

An important Roman garrison town and thermal spa, thanks to its warm springs, Aquae Sextiae was founded in 122 BC by Roman consul Sextius, after he had defeated the Celto-Ligurians at Entremont (*see p168*). Sadly, little of Aix's Roman past survives, save the odd column recycled in later buildings; in 2004, archaeologists unearthed the ruins of an antique theatre, but the site remains closed to the public at present. Aix declined with the Roman Empire, but remained important enough to have a cathedral in the fifth century.

In the 12th and 13th centuries, the Counts of Provence held court in Aix, but it wasn't until the 15th century that the city saw a true resurgence. In 1409, the university was founded by Louis II of Anjou, and the city flourished under his artistically inclined son, Good King René, its court drawing artists such as Nicolas Froment and Barthélemy Van Eyck. After its absorption into France in 1486, Aix became the capital of the Parlement de Provence – the southern arm of a centralised administration.

The city boomed again in the 1600s as its newly prosperous merchant class built stylish townhouses, modelled on the Parisian fashions of the day. A new district, the Quartier Mazarin, sprang up to the south of the medieval town, virtually doubling the city's size.

In the 19th century, Aix was bypassed by the main railway line – unlike its rival Marseille, which embraced industrialisation. Even so, it remained an important university and legal city, with the creation of arts and law faculties and the new Palais de Justice.

The town has expanded rapidly in the past 20 years, as modern housing and business districts have swallowed up rural villages and the grandiose *bastides* built by the nobility outside the city. It's also home to a high-tech business park, numerous research institutes and France's second biggest appeals court.

SIGHTSEEING

Pedestrian-friendly central Aix divides neatly into Vieil Aix (the old town) and the later Quartier Mazarin. The two districts are set on either side of the stately cours Mirabeau, and encircled by a string of boulevards that trace the line of the old city ramparts; beyond lies the sprawl of the modern city.

Vieil Aix & cours Mirabeau

At the heart of the city, **cours Mirabeau** is a handsome, plane tree-lined avenue. Laid out in 1649, it soon became the favoured spot for local nobility to construct their mansions, and remains the epicentre of Aix's café society.

At No.53, the legendary **Deux Garçons** (*see p169*), a hangout of Cézanne and Zola's, remains an artistic and intellectual meeting place. Next door at No.55 was once the hat shop where Paul

Cézanne lived as a child. There are three fountains on the cours: the Fontaine des Neuf Canons, the Fontaine d'Eau Chaude (a mossy lump bubbling out water at 34°C) and the Fontaine du Roi René, with a statue by David d'Angers that portrays the wine-loving king holding a bunch of grapes.

At one end of the cours is place Charles de Gaulle, better known as **La Rotonde**. At its centre stands an elaborate 19th-century marble fountain with lions at the base and figures of Justice, Agriculture and Fine Art on the top.

North of cours Mirabeau lies the remarkably well-preserved maze of **Vieil Aix**, buzzing with small bistros, cafés and shops. Graceful squares and smart mansions alternate with more secretive, winding *ruelles*, while statues peer from niches and fountains dot the squares.

Parallel to cours Mirabeau runs rue Espariat, where the early 18th-century baroque church of **St-Esprit** nestles amid cafés and shops. From here, head to boutique-lined rue Fabrot via the cobbled place d'Albertas – a little enclave of splendid classical mansions, built in 1745. Almost opposite, behind an elaborately sculpted gateway, is the elegant Hôtel Boyer d'Eguilles (1672), now the town's **Muséum d'Histoire Naturelle**. Behind here on rue des Chapelliers, water spouts out of a carved head at the Fontaine des Bagniers; the fountain's bronze medallion of Cézanne was sculpted by Renoir.

Busy shopping streets rue Aude and rue Maréchal Foch lead to place Richelme, which comes alive every morning with fruit and vegetable stalls. On Maréchal Foch, note the doorway of the late 17th-century Hôtel Arbaud at No.7, framed by two muscular male slaves.

On beautiful place de l'Hôtel de Ville, the Gothic belfry with astrological clock and rotating figures of the seasons was once a town gateway, while the 17th-century **Hôtel de Ville** (04.42.91.90.00, closed Sat, Sun) was the historic provençal assembly. At the back, a double stairway leads up to the regional assembly room, adorned with portraits and mythological subjects; it was here that Cézanne

finally married his long-time companion Hortense Fiquet in 1886. The post office next door occupies a magnificent 18th-century former grain market, whose pediment, an allegory of the Durance and Rhône rivers by Chastel, is given a wonderful spark of life by a leg dangling lasciviously out of the frame.

Running north, rue Gaston de Saporta contains some of Aix's finest *hôtels particuliers*. Hôtel Etienne de St-Jean (No.17) houses the **Musée du Vieil Aix**; Hôtel de Châteaurenard (No.19), where Louis XIV stayed in 1660, has a staircase painted with trompe l'oeils by Daret (it now houses the city's social services, but you can visit the entrance hall); Hôtel Maynier d'Oppedé (No.23), with a fine 1757 façade, is now the Institute of French Studies – though concerts are sometimes held in its courtyard.

The street leads into the historic core of the university, and to the **Cathédrale St-Sauveur**, with its sculpted portals and fortified towers. Next door, the baroque archbishop's palace contains the **Musée des Tapisseries**; its courtyard hosts opera productions during the Festival International d'Art Lyrique.

West of the town hall, place des Cardeurs is lined with ethnic restaurants. Underground car park aside, it looks as ancient as any of the other squares: in fact, it was built in the 1960s, when an area of slums was demolished. From here, narrow streets lead to the **Thermes Sextius**, along with some fragments of medieval city wall on rue des Etuves and the last surviving tower on boulevard Jean Jaurès. West of the baths, the **Pavillon Vendôme** stands amid its formal gardens.

South-east of the town hall, the colonnaded Palais de Justice was built in the 1820s. In front of it, place de Verdun fills with bric-a-brac and book stalls on Tuesday, Thursday and Saturday mornings. It continues into place des Prêcheurs and place de la Madeleine, which resound to the city's main food market on the same days, in the shadow of the **Eglise de la Madeleine**. Further east lies the Villeneuve *quartier*, which replaced the royal gardens in the late 16th century. Several ornate *hôtels particuliers* remain on rue Emeric David and rue de l'Opéra: Cézanne was born at No.25. At No.17 is the Jeu du Paume, a real tennis court built in 1660 and transformed into the **Théâtre du Jeu de Paume** a century later.

⚫FREE Cathédrale St-Sauveur

rue Gaston de Saporta (04.42.23.45.65). **Open** 8am-noon, 2-6pm Mon-Sat; 9am-noon, 2-6pm Sun (closed during services). *Cloister* 9.30am-noon, 2-6pm Mon-Sat. **Admission** free.
With its semi-fortified exterior and Gothic central door, Aix cathedral is a hotchpotch of Romanesque, Gothic, Renaissance and baroque – reflecting its

---

INSIDE TRACK
LITERARY LICENCE

After meeting at school in Aix, Emile Zola and Paul Cézanne became inseparable. Some 30 years later, their friendship came to an abrupt end with the publication of Zola's *L'Oeuvre*, which centres on the struggles of a failed and frustrated artist. Recognising himself in Zola's protagonist, Cézanne was cut to the quick, and it's said he never spoke to Zola again.

on-off construction from the fifth to 18th centuries. At first sight the interior looks unremarkable, but it has two jewels. The first is off the right-hand nave: a polygonal, fifth-century Merovingian baptistery, with crisply carved capitals and traces of frescoes (the hole in the ground is a throwback to the days of total immersion baptism). The second gem is in the central nave: Nicolas Froment's 15th-century triptych *Mary in the Burning Bush*, with King René and Queen Jeanne praying in the wings. In the left nave, the 17th-century Corpus Domini chapel has a fine wrought-iron grille and a painting by Jean Daret.

FREE Eglise de la Madeleine

pl des Prêcheurs. **Open** 8-11.30am, 3-5.30pm daily. **Admission** free.

This former Dominican convent was rebuilt in the 1690s in the baroque style; its neoclassical façade, busy with swags and garlands, is a 19th-century addition. Inside are several altarpieces by Carlos Van Loo and a 15th-century *Annunciation* attributed to Flemish painter Barthélemy Van Eyck.

Musée des Tapisseries

pl des Martyrs de la Résistance (04.42.23.09.91). **Open** *15 Apr-15 Oct* 10am-6pm Mon, Wed-Sun. *16 Oct-14 Apr* 1.30-5pm Mon, Wed-Sun. Closed Jan. **Admission** €2.50; free students, under-25s. **No credit cards**.

On the first floor of the former bishop's palace, the tapestry museum displays 17th- and 18th-century tapestries discovered in situ in the 19th century.

Musée Granet. *See p167.*

MARSEILLE & AIX

Ballet Preljocaj – Pavillon Noir. *See p172*.

There's a particularly lively series of scenes from *Don Quixote*, woven in northern France between 1735 and 1744, along with costumes and model sets from opera productions at the Aix festival.

★ Musée du Vieil Aix

17 rue Gaston de Saporta (04.42.21.43.55). **Open** *Apr-Oct* 10am-1pm, 2-6pm Tue-Sun. *Nov-Mar* 10am-noon, 2-5pm Tue-Sun. **Admission** €4; €2.50 reductions; free under-14s. **No credit cards**. The collection focuses on folk art and popular traditions, with *santons* (Christmas crib figures) and crèche puppets, plus some fine lacquered furniture and faïence. The house, with its stately entrance hall, frescoes and tiny *cabinet* (antechamber), with an ornately carved and gilded domed ceiling, gives a glimpse of 17th-century aristocratic life.

Muséum d'Histoire Naturelle

6 rue Espariat (04.42.27.91.27/www.museum-aix-en-provence.org). **Open** 10am-noon, 1-5pm daily. **Admission** €2.50; free students, under-25s. **No credit cards**.
Mineralogy, ornithological and palaeontology collections, including dinosaur skeletons and hundreds of dinosaur eggs discovered on the Montagne Ste-Victoire, are displayed against painted backdrops, in this fine 17th-century *hôtel*.

Pavillon Vendôme

32 rue Celony or 13 rue de la Molle (04.42.91.88.75). **Open** *Mid Apr-mid Oct* 10am-6pm Mon, Wed-Sun. *Mid Oct-mid Apr* 1.30-5.30pm Mon, Wed-Sun. **Admission** €2.50; free students, under-25s. **No credit cards**.
Built in 1665 by Pierre Pavillon, this mini-pleasure palace, set in formal gardens, was where the Duc de Vendôme hid away with his mistress, Lucrèce de Forbin Solliès: the mascaron over the entrance is said to be her portrait. Giant atlantes hold up the balcony and the interior is adorned with 17th- and 18th-century furniture and portraits.

Thermes Sextius

55 cours Sextius (08.00.63.96.99/www.thermes-sextius.com). **Open** 8.30am-7.30pm Mon-Fri; 8.30am-1.30pm, 2.30-6.30pm Sat. **Credit** MC, V.
Behind wrought-iron railings and a classical façade, the Thermes now houses the glass and marble pyramids of an ultra-modern health spa. A small fountain still marks the warm spring of the original 18th-century bathing establishment, while to the right of the entrance is evidence of even earlier bathers – the remains of first-century BC Roman baths, fed by the Source Imperiatrice.

Quartier Mazarin

Laid out on a strict rectilinear grid plan in 1646, the Quartier Mazarin was conceived as a speculative venture and sold off in lots, masterminded by Mazarin, Archbishop of Aix and brother of Louis XIV's powerful minister Cardinal Mazarin. It gradually became the aristocratic quarter, and still feels very refined. There are few shops or restaurants, other than classy *antiquaires* and select designer fashion names, but plenty of fine doorways, balustrades and wrought-iron balconies.

The **Musée Arbaud** occupies a townhouse on rue du 4 Septembre, the main thoroughfare, which leads into place des Quatre Dauphins, with a baroque fountain depicting four playful dolphins. At the rear of an arcaded courtyard is the lovely Hôtel de Boisgelin (1650), while on nearby rue Cardinale, the Collège Mignet was where Zola and Cézanne went to school.

At the far end of rue Cardinale stands the **Eglise St-Jean-de-Malte**, built by the Knights of Malta at the end of the 13th century. Stark and almost unadorned, it was one of the earliest Gothic structures in Provence, with a broad nave and side chapels but no transept. Beside it, the Commanderie of the Knights of Malta now houses the **Musée Granet**, the city's fine art and archaeology collection.

Musée Arbaud

2A rue du 4 Septembre (04.42.38.38.95). **Open** 2-5pm Mon-Sat. **Admission** €3; free under-10s. **No credit cards**.
Old masters that belonged to the Mirabeau family hang amid provençal earthenware and manuscripts collected by scholar Paul Arbaud. Fine pieces of Marseille and Moustiers faïence are light years away from the rest of the tourist fodder made today.

★ Musée Granet

pl St-Jean-de-Malte (04.42.52.88.32/www.musee-granet-aixenprovence.fr). **Open** *June-Sept* 11am-7pm Tue-Sun. *Oct-May* noon-6pm Tue-Sun. **Admission** €4.
Housed in the 17th-century Palais de Malte, Aix's newly refurbished fine art museum has quadrupled in size. The impressive collection includes Italian and Flemish primitives, Dutch interiors and Flemish masters (among them a pair of portraits by Rubens), a motley crew of Italian baroque paintings and works by the weird Lubin Baugin. Don't miss some splendidly pompous 18th-century portraits by Hyacinthe Rigaud, or Ingres's magnificently malevolent *Jupiter and Thetis*. At the time of Cézanne's death, curator Henri Pontier haughtily refused to accept any of his works – an embarrassing omission now made up for by a room of seven small oil paintings, including a portrait of Cézanne's mother and a tiny study for *The Bathers*. Here, too, is the recent Philippe Meyer donation, which includes works by Bonnard, Mondrian, Picasso, Klee and Tal Coat, along with a room of Giacometti bronzes and oils.

The basement houses an interesting display of archaeological finds from the Oppidium d'Entremont

MARSEILLE & AIX

(*see p169*), with pottery, bronze tools and some extraordinary carved heads and fragments from a series of sculpted warriors. *Photo p165.*

Beyond the centre

South of La Rotonde fountain, a new business, residential and shopping district, **Quartier Sextius Mirabeau,** forms a bridge between old and new Aix. The allées de Provence, a pedestrian shopping street in provençal hues, leads to the stepped, pink stone-clad terraces of the new **Grand Théâtre de Provence** (*see p172*). Behind it are the striking black concrete **Ballet Preljocaj – Pavillon Noir** (*see p172*) and the **Cité du Livre** arts centre, which together form a dynamic new cultural hub.

Further out, the suburbs are dotted with former country villas and *bastides*, built in the 17th and 18th centuries by the nobles and parliamentarians of Aix. These include the Château de la Pioline, now a hotel, and the **Jas de Bouffon,** bought by Cézanne's father in 1859; here, too, is the **Fondation Vasarely**.

At Les Milles, the refectory of the prison camp where numerous intellectuals were interned during World War II is now the **Mémorial National des Milles**. Towards Marseille, beneath the perched village of Bouc-Bel-Air, are the romantic, Italian-influenced **Jardins d'Albertas,** dotted with statues.

North of Vieil Aix, past the pyramidal **Mausoleum of Joseph Sec** – a rare example of Revolutionary architecture dating from 1792, a time when there were more pressing things to do than build – a steep hill climbs to the Lauves. It's here that Cézanne built his last studio, the **Atelier Cézanne**. If you continue climbing, you'll come to a roundabout with the remains of an ancient city gate. Follow the signs along avenue Paul Cézanne to the spot where the artist painted many of his famous scenes of Montagne Ste-Victoire: a bit of a hike, but the view is worth it. The remains of the Celto-Ligurian **Oppidium d'Entremont**, site of Sextius's victory in the second century AD, lie just outside the city to the north-west.

Atelier Cézanne

9 av Paul Cézanne (04.42.21.06.53/www.atelier-cezanne.com). **Open** *Apr-June, Sept* 10am-noon, 2-6pm daily. *July-Aug* 10am-6pm daily. *Oct-Mar* 10am-noon, 2-5pm daily. **Admission** €5.50; €2 reductions; free under-12s. **Credit** AmEx, MC, V.
Cézanne built this studio in 1902, and worked here until his death in 1906. Then outside the town, with views of the triangular silhouette of the Montagne Ste-Victoire, it now overlooks post-war housing developments. Preserved just as it was in the artist's lifetime, the first-floor studio is an artistic clutter of easels and palettes, along with many of the props –

fruit, vases, a broken cherub statue – that are familiar from his still lifes. Visitors are advised to book in advance with the tourist office (*see p174*).

▶ *Don't miss the majestic Carrières de Bibémus (see p172) – a place of inspiration for Cézanne.*

FREE Cité du Livre

8-10 rue des Allumettes (04.42.91.98.88/ www.citedulivre-aix.com). **Open** noon-6pm Tue, Thur, Fri; 10am-6pm Wed, Sat. **Admission** free. Marked by a gigantic book at the entrance, this converted 19th-century match factory houses the historic Bibliothèque Méjanes (a public library and collection of rare manuscripts), the archives of Albert Camus and the Fondation St-John Perse, which includes a permanent display of manuscripts by the Nobel Prize-winning poet. A busy programme of events includes an annual literary festival in October and December's short film festival.

Fondation Vasarely

1 av Marcel Pagnol, Jas de Bouffan (04.42.20.01.09/www.fondationvasarely.fr). **Open** 10am-1pm, 2-6pm Tue-Sat. **Admission** €7; €4 reductions; free under-7s. **Credit** AmEx, MC, V.
At this 'centre architectonique', Hungarian-born abstract artist Victor Vasarely (1906-97) put his theories of geometrical abstraction and kinetic art into practice on a grand scale. The building itself is composed of hexagonal structures of black and white squares and circles that reflect off the water. Inside are large-scale paintings, tapestries and reliefs.

Jardins d'Albertas

N8, Bouc-Bel-Air (04.91.59.84.94/www.jardins albertas.com). **Open** *May, Sept, Oct* 2-6pm Sat, Sun, public holidays. *June-Aug* 3-7pm daily. Closed Nov-Apr. **Admission** €6; free under-16s. **No credit cards.**
The Marquis d'Albertas dreamed of constructing a lavish rural retreat – but then came the Revolution, and he was assassinated on 14 July 1790. The grand chateau was never built and only the formal gardens, laid out with magnificent terraces and pools, were ever completed. During the last weekend in May, an annual plant sale (along with talks and events) transforms the gardens into a burst of colour.

Jas de Bouffan

Reservation advised (04.42.16.10.08/information 04.42.16.11.61/www.aixenprovencetourism.com). **Open** 11.30am-5pm daily. **Admission** €5.50; €2 reductions; free under-12s.
This 18th-century country house, bought by the Cézanne family in 1859, marked the social ascension of Cézanne's father from hatmaker to banker. At last accepting his son's desire to be an artist, he had a studio constructed under the eaves. Here Cézanne produced many of his most celebrated works, painting the avenue of chestnut trees, the pond and

the two gardeners who posed for *The Card Players*. A multimedia presentation explores Cézanne's life and the history of the house. *Photo p170.*

FREE Oppidium d'Entremont

3km north-west of Vieux Aix via av Solari (D14), direction Puyricard (04.42.21.97.33/www. entremont.culture.gouv.fr). **Open** 9am-noon, 2-5.30pm Mon, Wed-Sun. **Admission** free.
This Celto-Ligurian hilltop settlement developed around the second century BC on the site of an earlier sanctuary, and was destroyed by Romans in the second century AD at the behest of the land-hungry Marseillais. Excavated sections reveal a grid plan, plus traces of shops, warehouses and workshops.
► *To get a better idea of the settlement, check out the archaeological finds at the Musée Granet (see p167).*

FREE Site Mémorial des Milles

Les Milles (04.42.24.34.68). **Open** 9am-12.15pm, 1-5pm Mon-Thur; 9am-12.15pm, 1-4pm Fri. **Admission** free.
Requisitioned as early as 1939 (before the German occupation), in a period of growing xenophobia and nationalism, this brick and tile factory became an internment camp for 'enemy subjects' in France. Prisoners were refugees from the Spanish Civil War and German and Austrian intellectuals, many of them Jewish, who had fled the Nazi regime. Among them were two Nobel Prize winners and the Surrealist painters Max Ernst and Hans Bellmer. After June 1940, Les Milles became a transit camp; nearly 2,000 Jews were deported from here to Auschwitz via Drancy. In the entrance, documents and archive photos tell the story of Les Milles, but it is the refectory that is the most telling witness, decorated with murals by prisoners that take a subtly satiric slant in the row of caricatured waiters painted in a parody of Leonardo's *Last Supper*. Across the road, at the former Gare des Milles, a railway wagon is a reminder of those sent to Auschwitz.

WHERE TO EAT

L'Amphitryon

2-4 rue Paul Doumer (04.42.26.54.10/www. restaurant-amphitryon.fr). **Open** noon-2.30pm, 7.30-10pm Tue-Sat. **Menus** *Lunch* €19-€22. *Dinner* €27-€36. **Credit** AmEx, MC, V.
Expect seasonal provençal cooking with cosmopolitan touches from chef Bruno Ungaro, founder of the Bistro Latin (*see right*). Eat in the sophisticated dining room or pleasant outdoor courtyard, or draw up a high chair at the counter and tuck into an entrecôte.

Antoine Côté Cour

19 cours Mirabeau (04.42.93.12.51). **Open** 7.30pm-midnight Mon; 12.30-2.30pm, 7.30pm-midnight Tue-Sat. **Menus** €15-€40. **Credit** DC, MC, V.

The fashionable folk of Aix flock to this Italianate restaurant, which serves great gnocchi and pasta. An ornate entrance off the cours Mirabeau leads to a beautiful courtyard, perfect for alfresco dining.

★ Bistro Latin

18 rue de la Couronne (04.42.38.22.88). **Open** noon-2.30pm, 7.30-10.30pm Tue-Sat. **Menus** €30-€60. **Credit** MC, V.
After 20 years, this charming, pared-down little bistro is still going strong. The prix fixe includes such delights as baby red peppers stuffed with *brousse* cheese, served with tapenade, or herby *daube d'agneau*.

★ Brasserie des Deux Garçons

53 cours Mirabeau (04.42.26.00.51). **Open** 7am-2am daily (meals noon-3pm, 7-11.30pm daily). **Menus** €20-€30. **Credit** AmEx, MC, V.
Alias 'les 2 G', the legendary Deux Garçons is named after the two waiters who bought it in 1840. Its interior is a delight, with tall mirrors, chandeliers, an old-fashioned cashier's desk and a salon to the side where you can read the papers or write your novel. There are two dining sections, one serving brasserie fare, the other a more ambitious restaurant.

Café Bastide du Cours

43-47 cours Mirabeau (04.42.26.10.06/www.cafe bastideducours.com). **Open** noon-1am daily. **Mains** €19.50-€28. **Credit** AmEx, MC, V.
One of the most charming restaurants in Aix, the Bastide has a sumptuous dining room and lovely heated terrace, with tables arranged around an enormous plane tree. The sophisticated cooking is rooted in provençal tradition: slow-roasted lamb shank with wild thyme is out of this world.

La Chimère Café

15 rue Brueys (04.42.38.30.00/www.lachimere cafe.com). **Open** 6.30pm-midnight Mon-Sat. **Menus** €21.50-€80.50. **Credit** V.
Local, fresh ingredients are inventively combined and stylishly presented at La Chimère, while the decor is a rococo mix of gilt and crimson, with a scattering of cherubs. The prices are fantastic and the cuisine excellent, making this a convivial place to spend an evening.

> **INSIDE TRACK**
> **SWEET THING**
>
> The town's culinary speciality is *calisson d'Aix*: diamond-shaped sweets made from almonds, sugar and preserved melon. Sample the best in town at **Confiserie Brisard** (16 rue d'Italie, 04.42.38.01.70) or **Leonard Parli** (35 av Victor Hugo, 04.42.26.05.71, www.leonard-parli.com).

MARSEILLE & AIX

★ Les Deux Frères
4 av Reine Astrid (04.42.27.90.32/www.les2 freres.com). **Open** noon-2pm, 8-9.30pm Mon-Fri; noon-2pm, 8-10.30pm Sat, Sun. **Menus** *Lunch* €17. *Dinner* €30. **Credit** V.

The Benchérif brothers – Stéphane in the kitchen, Olivier front of house – are behind this acclaimed eaterie, a ten-minute walk from the town centre. Modern Med cuisine is served in a chic minimalist setting, with video screens transmitting what's going on in the kitchen, and a spectacularly lit terrace.
▶ *The Benchérif brothers also run Le 37 (04.42.12.39.68) on place des Tanneurs, which serves more traditional cuisine.*

★ Le Formal
32 rue Espariat (04.42.27.08.31/www. restaurant-leformal.com). **Open** noon-1.30pm, 8-9.30pm Tue-Sat. **Menus** €15-€30. **Credit** MC, V.

Chef Jean-Luc Formal delivers beautifully presented, modern cuisine in his eponymous restaurant. Sample a summery starter of seasonal vegetables, edible flowers and red mullet fillets, or go for lamb in filo pastry with a shot of carrot juice. The barrel-vaulted cellars, with exposed stone, pale wood and modern paintings, are a welcome respite from the summer heat and tourist hordes. Book ahead.

Le Passage
10 rue Villars (04.42.37.09.00/www.le-passage. fr). **Open** 10am-midnight daily. **Mains** €12-€32. **Menus** *Lunch* €13. *Dinner* €23-€35. **Credit** AmEx, MC, V.

Reine Sammut of La Fénière in the Luberon is the *éminence grise* behind this stylishly converted sweet factory, which now contains a galleried restaurant, *salon de thé*, wine boutique and cooking school. A trio of young chefs keeps up her culinary vision in a pan-Mediterranean menu that takes in grilled fish with ratatouille, tartares and risotto.

Pierre Reboul
11 petite rue St-Jean (04.42.27.08.31). **Open** noon-1.30pm, 7.30-9.30pm Tue-Sat. **Mains** €60-€90. **Menus** €39-€110. **Credit** V.

Michelin-starred Pierre Reboul moved here recently from St-Rémy, and has been stirring up debate with his avant-garde cooking. This is as close as you'll get to molecular experimentation in largely traditional Aix, with modern decor to match.

★ Yamato (Koji & Yuriko)
21 av des Belges (04.42.38.00.20/www. restaurant-yamato.com). **Open** 7-10pm Tue; noon-2pm, 7-10pm Wed-Sun. **Menus** €48-€63. **Credit** MC, V.

Occupying an elegant 1930s house set in a Japanese garden, Yamato serves up what is probably the most authentic Japanese cuisine in southern France. As well as excellent sushi and sashimi and crisp, light

Jas de Bouffan. *See p168.*

tempura, you'll find good grilled fish and specialities like *uoroke* and *sukiyaki* (strips of beef simmered at the table over a flame, with vegetables and noodles).
▶ *Yôji (7 av Victor Hugo, 04.42.38.48.76) is another chic – but less pricey – Japanese eaterie.*

WHERE TO DRINK

★ Bar Brigand
17 pl Richelme (04.42.26.11.57). **Open** 9am-2am Mon-Sat; 2pm-2am Sun. **Credit** MC, V.

This is where Aix's hip young things come to have a few drinks, swap numbers and maybe slope off home with someone. For those who just want a beer, there are 40 varieties to choose from.

Le Bistrot Aixois
37 cours Sextius (04.42.27.50.10). **Open** 6.30pm-2am Tue-Sat. **Credit** AmEx, MC, V.

Renovated after a fire, the Bistrot has the BCBG (French Sloanes) students queuing to get in. Inside there are drinks, billiards and a small dancefloor.

Elfike
38 rue de la Verrerie (04.42.27.14.61/www.elfike. com). **Open** 3pm-2am Mon-Fri; 5pm-2am Sat; 8pm-2am Sun. **Credit** AmEx, MC, V.

Despite the dark medieval theming, the crowd is more varied than you might expect at this Goth haunt on a narrow street in Vieil Aix.

L'Orienthé

5 rue du Félibre Gaut (06.62.16.48.25). **Open** 3pm-1am Mon-Thur; 4pm-2am Fri, Sat; 3pm-2am Sun. Closed Sun in July, 1st 2wks Jan. **No credit cards**.

Leave your shoes at the door and relax over one of 50 varieties of tea and a delectable pastry at this exotic tea salon. Customers sit on pillows around low tables amid candles and incense.

Red Clover

30 rue la Verrerie (04.42.23.44.61). **Open** 8am-2am Mon-Sat. **Credit** MC, V.

The international student crowd hangs out at this boisterous pub, which serves a wide array of beers and whiskies. Don't expect to speak much French.

La Rotonde

2A place Jeanne d'Arc (04.42.91.61.70/www.la rotonde-aix.com). **Open** 8am-2am daily. **Menu** €18.50-€45. **Credit** MC, V.

Overlooking the fountain, this stylish address has a sleek terrace and boudoir-style interior. As the day goes on it morphs from breakfast and lunchtime gaff to clubby nightspot, with a DJ and a large array of champagnes, whiskies and cocktails (try the house Rotonde with vodka, rum, lime and raspberries).

Le Terminus

58 cours Mirabeau (04.42.27.69.25). **Open** 8pm-1am daily. **Mains** €18.50-€30. **Credit** MC, V.

The heated terrace at this friendly bar-restaurant is popular for an inexpensive meal (magret, steak, pizza), while inside is more of a drinking haunt.

NIGHTLIFE

Le Divino

4039 rte de Sisteron, 5km from town (04.42.99.37.08/www.divino.fr). **Open** *Club* 11pm-5am Thur-Sat. *Restaurant* 8pm-2am Thur-Sat. **Admission** *Club* €16. **Credit** MC, V.

More like a hip metropolitan club – think New York or Paris – Le Divino attracts Aix's fashionable set with its trendy decor and thumping house music.

Hot Brass Jazz Club

1857 rte d'Eguilles, Celony (04.42.21.05.57/ www.hotbrassaix.com). **Open** 10.30pm-dawn Fri, Sat. **Admission** €16-€19. **Credit** MC, V.

A short drive out of town, the Hot Brass offers live funk, soul, rock, blues and Latin bands (mainly local outfits). Reserve on the answerphone.

IPN

23 cours Sextius (04.42.26.25.17). **Open** 11.30pm-4am Thur-Sat. **Admission** €4 (members); €6 (non-members). **Credit** MC, V.

Always packed with students, this dance spot is set in an ancient cellar in the town centre. The ambience and music are great, while drinks are reasonable.

Le Mistral

3 rue Frédéric Mistral (04.42.38.16.49/www. mistralclub.net). **Open** 11.30pm-5am Tue-Sat. **Admission** €11-€15. **Credit** MC, V.

Behind a discreet entrance, Le Mistral is the long-established haunt of preppy students. The music is a mix of pop, house and techno, with visits from big-name DJs.

★ Le Sextius Mirabeau

2 cours Sextius (04.42.26.55.52). **Open** 5-11pm daily. **No credit cards**.

This casual bar has affordable drinks, a good wine selection and a small dancefloor. It's popular with students, who gather to hear live music and hang out with friends. Every Tuesday is reggae night.

SHOPPING

Aix offers some of the most sophisticated shopping in all of Provence; shops are open Monday to Saturday unless stated otherwise. Designer labels are centred around rue Fabrot, home to multi-label **Gago** (Nos.18 and 21, 04.42.93.28.32, www.gago-hommes.com) and adjoining rue Marius Reinaud, with **Zadig et Voltaire** at No.11 (04.42.38.65.08), **Robert Clergerie** shoes at No.2 (04.42.26.53.58) and **Intimoda** at No.8 (04.42.26.53.58). The more established **Agnès b** (No.2, 04.42.38.44.87) and **Paul Smith** (No.3, 04.42.26.53.88) are on rue Fernand Dol in the Quartier Mazarin.

A clutch of good childrenswear shops includes **Catimini** (9 pl des Chapeliers, 04.42.27.51.14, closed Mon morning), colourful **Marèse** (4 rue Aude, 09778 59856) and the excellent-value **Du Pareil au Même** (14 rue Maréchal Foch, 04.93.38.18.08, closed Mon morning). **Le Nain Rouge** (47 rue Espariat, 04.42.93.50.05, closed Mon morning) sells traditional wooden toys.

There are numerous antique and interior design shops on place des Trois Ormeaux and neighbouring rue Jaubert. **La Maison Montigny** (5 rue Lucas de Montigny, 04.42.96.51.52, closed Mon morning) has two floors of high-tech kitchen equipment, tasteful grey linen and burnished stainless steel. **Scènes de Vie** (3 rue Jaubert, 04.42.21.13.90, closed Mon morning) stocks sophisticated provençal pottery. Upmarket antique and fabric shops also congregate in the Quartier Mazarin, while **Décalé** at 14 rue d'Italie (04.42.53.32.65) has quirky household items and gifts. For details of regular *brocantes* and antiques fairs call 04.42.59.25.56 or 06.16.86.32.91.

Among Aix's bookshops, the **Librairie de Provence** (31 cours Mirabeau, 04.42.26.07.23) has a good fine art section; **Librairie Paradox** (15 rue du 4 Septembre, 04.42.26.47.99) stocks books in English and other languages. **Book**

in **Bar** (1 bis rue Joseph Cabassol, 04.42.26.
60.07) is a cosy anglophone bookshop and café
with a second-hand section upstairs.

ARTS & ENTERTAINMENT

Pick up *Le Mois à Aix*, a monthly listings
magazine published by the tourist office (also
online at www.aix-en-provence.com), or the
regional freebie weekly *César*, distributed in
hotels and bars, for up-to-date details of events.

3BisF
*Hôpital Montperrin, 109 av du Petit Barthélémy
(04.42.16.17.75/www.3bisf.com).* **Open** 9am-6pm
Mon-Fri. **Admission** €9; €4.50 reductions. **No
credit cards.**
Near the Cité du Livre, 3BisF is an exhibition space
and complex of artists' studios that hosts a vibrant
programme of contemporary dance and theatre productions and workshops.

★ Ballet Preljocaj – Pavillon Noir
*8-10 rue des Allumettes/530 av Mozart
(04.42.93.48.00/www.preljocaj.org).* **Tickets**
€6-€22. **Credit** MC, V.
This dramatic spider's web of black concrete and
glass, designed by architect Rudy Ricciotti, is home
to the Ballet Preljocaj and visiting dance companies.
Four rehearsal studios on the upper storeys are illu-
minated after dark so that passers-by can glimpse
works in progress, while the 378-seat auditorium is
buried underground. The programme includes public rehearsals and *apéro-danses*, where you can meet
the dancers over a drink after the performance.

Espace Musical Chapelle Ste-Catherine
20 rue Mignet (04.42.99.37.11). **Concerts** 7pm
Tue. **Tickets** vary. **No credit cards.**
This former church has been converted into a venue
for classical concerts – essentially chamber music
events, plus a festival in Holy Week.

FREE Galerie d'Art du Conseil Général
*21 bis cours Mirabeau (04.42.93.03.67/
www.cg13.fr).* **Open** *July-Sept* 10.30am-12.45pm,
2-6.30pm daily. *Oct-June* 9.30am-1pm, 2-6pm
daily. **Admission** free.
The exhibition space of the Conseil Général des
Bouches du Rhône showcases modern and contemporary art and photography.

Grand Théâtre de Provence
*380 av Max Juvénal (04.42.91.69.69/www.grand
theatre.fr).* **Box office** 11am-6.30pm Tue-Sat.
Tickets vary. **Credit** MC, V.
Part of the new arts hub in the Quartier Sextius
Mirabeau, this purpose-built modular auditorium
can seat up to 1,366. The busy line-up runs from
opera, classical concerts, stage musicals and international dance companies to big-name bands and
visiting jazz divas. The theatre also plays host to
free musical performances and other events.

Théâtre des Ateliers
29 pl Miollis (04.42.38.10.45). **Box office** 10am-
noon, 2-8pm Mon-Sat. Closed Aug. **Shows** 9pm.
Tickets €11.50; €5.50 reductions. **No credit
cards.**

Quarrying for Art

Let Cézanne be your guide to a newly-tamed wilderness.

A visit to the **Carrières de Bibémus**
quarries, with their blue-tinted pines and
burning colours shimmering in the summer
heat, is a bit like stepping inside one of
Cézanne's paintings. Works that seemed
proto-Cubist or even abstract suddenly
seem almost realist when you actually
see the disused stone quarries, with
their geometric planes and strange rock
formations, part natural, part man-made.
Set on the western flank of the Montagne
Ste-Victoire, this is a landscape of chaotic
rock falls and sculpted blocks, narrow
ravines and overhanging cliffs, in the
varying hues of red, cream and orange
that dominated Cézanne's palette.
Here, pine trees sprout at crazy angles,
interspersed with clumps of rosemary
and broom, backdropped by azure skies.

Between 1888 and 1904, Cézanne
was a frequent visitor to the site, where
he painted some 11 canvases and 16
watercolours. The quarries were opened
to the public in 2006, as part of the
celebrations marking the centenary of
Cézanne's death. Officials cut back the
undergrowth, laid out footpaths and
installed enamel plaques reproducing
certain canvases alongside the spot where
they were painted – but a wild, untamed
feel remains. As you wander amid the vast,
ochre-colour rocks, you can still glimpse
the wilderness and solitude that Cézanne
sought here.
The Carrières are open for guided visits;
reserve through the Office de Tourisme
(*see p174*). Admission costs €5.50, with
€2 reductions and free entry for under-12s.

A smallish theatre, Théâtre des Ateliers works on co-productions of new works with other subsidised theatre venues.

Théâtre du Jeu de Paume

17-21 rue de l'Opéra (04.42.99.12.00/box office 04.42.99.12.12/www.lestheatres.net). **Box office** 11am-6pm (in person noon-6pm) Tue-Sat. **Tickets** €20-€35. **Credit** MC, V.

Founded in 1756, this beautiful theatre reopened in 2000 after a major renovation. Director Dominique Bluzet brings in successful Paris plays, as well as touting companies from Marseille and elsewhere.

WHERE TO STAY

La Bastide du Cours

43-47 cours Mirabeau (04.42.26.10.06/www.cafe bastideducours.com). **Rates** €145-€320 double. **Rooms** 11. **Credit** AmEx, MC, V.

Located above a brasserie on the cours Mirabeau, 11 romantically themed rooms and suites are a feast of sumptuous fabrics and antique furniture. Some have canopied beds, others jacuzzis.

Hôtel Aquabella

2 rue des Etuves (04.42.99.15.00/www.aquabella. fr). **Rates** €165-€195 double. **Rooms** 110. **Credit** AmEx, DC, MC, V.

This modern hotel adjoining the Thermes Sextius may lack the character of Aix's older hotels, but compensates with its spacious, comfortable rooms and prime location. Facilities include a glass-walled restaurant and an outdoor pool.

Hôtel des Augustins

3 rue de la Masse (04.42.27.28.59/www.hotel-augustins.com). **Rates** €97-€240 double. **Rooms** 29. **Credit** DC, MC, V.

This appealing hotel occupies part of an Augustine monastery where Martin Luther stayed on his way back from Rome. It became a hotel in the 1890s; the reception is set in a spectacular vaulted space and the rooms are comfortable, though the provençal decor doesn't quite live up to the lobby's promise.

★ € Hôtel Cardinal

24 rue Cardinale (04.42.38.32.30/www.hotel-cardinal-aix.com). **Rates** €60-€110 double. **Rooms** 29. **Credit** MC, V.

Beloved by festival-going writers, artists and musicians, this little Quartier Mazarin hotel has bags of charm. Several rooms have stucco mouldings, a couple have original 18th-century painted overdoor panels, and all are decorated with high-quality fabrics, antiques, paintings and new bathrooms.

★ Hôtel Cézanne

40 av Victor Hugo (04.42.91.11.11/www.hotel aix.com). **Rates** €150-€290 double. **Rooms** 55. **Credit** AmEx, DC, MC, V.

Now under private management, the Cézanne has become the hippest hotel in town. The bar features scarlet banquettes and cool artwork, while the rooms are individually decorated, some with stainless-steel four posters, others in gold or candy pink; all have high-quality beds and great showers.

€ Hôtel de France

63 rue Espariat (04.42.27.90.15). **Rates** €57-€70 double. **Rooms** 27. **Credit** AmEx, MC, V.

This place is an inexpensive option in a town that has fewer central hotels than you might expect. Most rooms are of good size, and those at the front overlook the cafés of a busy shopping street in Vieil Aix.

Hôtel en Ville

2 pl Bellegarde (04.42.63.34.16/www.hotel enville.fr). **Rates** €95-€135 double. **Rooms** 10. **Credit** MC, V.

Behind an unassuming façade, this small boutique hotel is a calm hymn to warm earth tones and clean minimalist lines. Original artworks and modern bathrooms add to the appeal.

€ Hôtel Paul

10 av Pasteur (04.42.23.23.89/www.aix-en-provence.com/hotelpaul). **Rates** €40-€62 double. **Rooms** 24. **Credit** V.

In spite of the dated lobby and drab rooms, this is a fantastic bargain for travellers on a budget. It's set just north of the old town, down the hill from Cézanne's atelier. A shady garden offers respite on hot afternoons.

★ Hôtel Le Pigonnet

5 av du Pigonnet (04.42.59.02.90/www.hotel pigonnet.com). **Rates** €160-€340 double. **Rooms** 51. **Credit** AmEx, DC, MC, V.

Cézanne once painted the Montagne Ste-Victoire from the shady garden of this 18th-century mansion, about a kilometre outside town. Soaking up the sunshine by the pool is a joy, while rooms are comfortably floral; there's a very good restaurant too.

Hôtel des Quatre Dauphins

54 rue Roux Alphéran (04.42.38.16.39/www.les quatredauphins.fr). **Rates** €65-€120 double. **Rooms** 13. **Credit** MC, V.

The Four Dolphins has 13 simple but tastefully decorated – and air-conditioned – rooms. The hotel is a 17th-century building on one of the nicest streets in the Quartier Mazarin; book well ahead.

Hôtel St-Christophe

2 av Victor Hugo (04.42.26.01.24/www.hotel-saintchristophe.com). **Rates** €86-€125 double. **Rooms** 72. **Credit** AmEx, DC, MC, V.

Located just off La Rotonde, the St-Christophe has comfortable modern rooms behind a 19th-century façade, done up in art deco style or *à la provençale*; suites have views of the Montagne Ste-Victoire.

MARSEILLE & AIX

Villa Gallici
10 av de la Violette (04.42.23.29.23/www.villa gallici.com). **Rates** €350-€650 double. **Rooms** 22. **Credit** AmEx, DC, MC, V.
Slightly out of the centre in an elegantly renovated *bastide*, Villa Gallici offers plush comfort with Italianate trimmings. Some rooms have private gardens, and there's a swimming pool. Chef Christophe Gavot specialises in fish in the excellent restaurant.

RESOURCES
Hospital
Centre Hospitalier du Pays d'Aix Urgences, av Tamaris (04.42.33.50.00).

Internet
Virtualis *pl de l'Hôtel de Ville (04.42.26.02.30/ www.virtualis.fr).* **Open** 9am-midnight Mon-Fri; noon-midnight Sun. Closed Sat.

Police
av de l'Europe (04.42.93.97.00).

Post office
pl de l'Hôtel de Ville (04.42.17.10.40).

Tourist information
Office de Tourisme *2 pl du Général de Gaulle (04.42.16.11.61/www.aixenprovencetourism.com).* **Open** *June, Sept* 8.30am-7pm Mon-Sat; 10am-1pm, 2-6pm Sun. *July, Aug* 8.30am-9pm Mon-Sat; 10am-1pm, 2-6pm Sun. *Oct-Mar* 8.30am-7pm Mon-Sat; 10am-1pm, 2-6pm Sun.

GETTING THERE & AROUND
By bike
Aix's municipal bike hire system (www.vhello.fr) allows you to pick up a bike from one of 16 points around town and deposit it at another. Bikes can also be hired from **Cycles Zammit** (27 rue Mignet, 04.42.23.19.53, closed Mon).

By bus
The **Navette Aix-Marseille** (www.navette aixmarseille.com) is a high-speed (30 mins) shuttle service between Aix *gare routière* on av de l'Europe (04.42.91.26.80) and the Porte d'Aix in Marseille, with buses every five minutes at peak times. Aix is also served by six to ten buses daily to Avignon and an hourly shuttle to Marseille airport. Aix is also a stop on the Marseille to Nice airport service (three daily) run by **Phocéen Cars** (04.93.85.66.61). **La Diabline** is an electric minibus; there's an information and ticket desk (04.42.26.37.28) at the Office du Tourisme. Take the No.1 for Atelier Cézanne, No.20 for the Oppidium d'Entremont, No.16 for La Pioline and Les Milles, and No.4 from the old casino to the Fondation Vasarely.

By car
Leave the autoroute A8 at exits 29-31. Take the N7 from Avignon or St-Maximin-la-Ste-Baume. From Marseille, take the A51, which continues north towards Gap.

By train
Aix TGV station is 10km west of the city, served by regular shuttle buses from the *gare routière*. The old Aix station is on the slow Marseille–Sisteron line, with trains roughly every hour from Marseille-St-Charles, but is currently being modernised and replaced by a bus.

Around Aix

MONTAGNE STE-VICTOIRE
Looming over the plain if you arrive from the east, the triangular form of the Montagne Ste-Victoire is inextricably linked to Paul Cézanne. At once both familiar and far larger than in his paintings, the Montagne also offers rugged villages, wild landscapes and the changing colours that so obsessed Cézanne. He began going on long walks on the mountain when he was a schoolboy, and painted it in over 60 canvases and countless watercolours.

The best way to approach it is in a loop along the D17 to the south of the mountain and the D10 to the north. Cézanne rented a room to paint in at the Château Noir, just before Le Tholonet, from 1887, and later a hut at the Carrières de Bibémus quarry (*see p172* **Quarrying for Art**). Later he built his own atelier on the Lauves hill, with a view of the mountain. At Le Tholonet, the **Moulin Cézanne** (04.42.66.90.41, closed Sept-Apr) has an exhibition on local history and the friendship between Cézanne and Zola, with temporary painting and sculpture exhibitions upstairs.

Picasso is buried in the grounds of the privately owned Château de Vauvenarges under the mountain's northern flank, where he lived from 1959 to 1965. In summer 2009, the chateau will open to the public by appointment; call the Musée Granet (*see p167*) or the Aix tourist office (*see left*) for details.

If you're planning to do some hiking, it's much simpler to approach the mountain from its wooded, sheltered northern side than the more barren southern route, with its precipitous limestone cliffs. The GR9 climbs to the Croix de Provence at the western end of the ridge from Vauvenargues, and is also joined by a footpath from the attractive Col des Portes just further east, running along the top of the ridge to the highest point, the Pic des Mouches at 1,011 metres (3,317 feet), before descending near the town of Puyricard.

The Var

The **Grand Canyon du Verdon**.
See p222.

Introduction

From polished seaside chic to unspoilt scenery.

Glamorous St-Tropez hogs the spotlight, but there's more to this region than seaside glitz and crowded beaches. With large areas devoted to the vineyards of Bandol and the Côtes de Provence, or to military training grounds, the Var has suffered less at the hands of developers than much of the coast. Down steep caps accessible only by foot or boat, the odd hideaway remains – and away from the coast, it's easy to find seclusion amid the tiny hill villages.

Over the centuries, **St-Tropez** has been raided by Saracens, Signac and Brigitte Bardot – but you shouldn't let its showbiz reputation and appalling traffic jams scare you off. With charming markets and a much-frequented *pétanque* pitch, it still retains an undeniable fishing village charm. There are plenty of pleasant, quieter family resorts too, such as **Sanary-sur-Mer**, **Bormes-les-Mimosas** and **Le Lavandou**, while **Fréjus** boasts an impressive Roman heritage. Just inland, you soon find yourself in the wooded and remote-feeling Maures or the brick-red Estérel *massifs*.

To the west, **Hyères** was a belle époque hotspot, where aristocrats mixed with avant-garde artists; today, the Modernist Villa Noailles is a memento of its glory days. Just off the coast, the **Iles de Hyères** are car-free island idylls, covered with pine and eucalyptus trees and fringed with implausibly lovely beaches.

Back from the coast, the Green Var around **Brignoles** is renowned for its canoeing, hiking and organic produce. The wooded hills of the **Ste-Baume Massif**, meanwhile, shelter the mysterious cave where Mary Magdalene is said to have spent 30 solitary years, and the pilgrimage site of **St-Maximin-la-Ste-Baume**.

In the Var's mountainous northern reaches, perched villages such as **Tourtour**, **Aups**, **Salernes**, **Cotignac** and **Bargemon** cling perilously to the rock, and have barely changed in centuries. Here, too, are the dramatic **Gorges du Verdon**, with their twisting, narrow mountain roads, breathtaking vistas and challenging walking and rafting – heaven for outdoor types.

The Best of The Var

Standout sights, restaurants and hotels from across the region.

SIGHTSEEING

Wander the Roman ruins in **Fréjus** (*see p204*), then drive to Cocteau's **Chapelle Notre-Dame-de-Jérusalem** (*see p205*), hidden away in the forest. Another must-see is the angular, Modernist **Villa Noailles** (*see p187*) in Hyères – once home to wealthy art patrons Charles and Marie Noailles. Created in the same era, though ever-evolving, the **Domaine du Rayol** (*see p191*) is a stunning series of subtropical gardens near Le Lavandou.

Religion has also shaped the Var, with mighty abbeys and churches such as the imposing **Abbaye de Thoronet** (*see p218*) and the soaring **Basilique Ste-Marie-Madeleine** (*see p210*).

WHERE TO STAY

Bask on the private beach at the **Hôtel les Roches** (*see p191*) in Le Lavandou, or head inland to luxurious **La Villa Marie** (*see p201*), which has its own blissful spa.

Alternatively, snap up a bargain room at St-Tropez's **Le Colombier** (*see p197*), or book well ahead at the beachside **Le Refuge** (*see p201*)

PLACES TO EAT

Toulon is strong on seafood; try portside **Herrero** (*see p181*), or the beautifully-set **Restaurant Bernard** (*see p182*). To get even closer to the sea, eat on the beach at **plage de l'Estagnol** (*see p191*), near Brégançon. Gourmands flock to Alain Ducasse's **La Bastide de Moustiers** (*see p225*) – a Michelin-starred rural retreat with its own vegetable and herb gardens.

SPORTS & ACTIVITIES

Hike around the beautiful **Grand Canyon du Verdon** (*see p222*), or try a spot of canyoning or paragliding (*see p223*). If you need to unwind after all the excitement, **St-Tropez** is great for messing about in boats (*see p195*).

Toulon & the Western Côte

Step off the tourist trail and see a different side of Provence.

Best known as the French navy's most important Mediterranean base, **Toulon** isn't top of most tourists' itineraries. Intensive Allied bombing during World War II reduced much of the city to ruins, and some insensitive post-war reconstruction has done little to help it rise above its tough reputation. Nonetheless, pockets of the old town remain, while the busy daily market and harbour have a down-to-earth charm all of their own.

To the west of Toulon stretch a string of unpretentious family-friendly beach resorts, secluded hill villages and the justly famed **Bandol** vineyards, which produce some of the South's finest red and rosé wines.

THE VAR

TOULON

With its impressive harbour and surrounding crescent of hills, Toulon is a natural stronghold – and one that assumed increasing importance after 1481, when it became part of France. Louis XIV's military architect Vauban expanded the docks, fortified the town with star-shaped bastions and built the Fort St-Louis in Mourillon. Its stout defences saw off Anglo-Spanish battleships during the War of the Spanish Succession in 1707, but afforded little protection when the plague arrived from Marseille in 1720, wiping out half the citizens.

In 1789, as the Revolution spread across France, Toulon chose to join the royal camp. In the subsequent uprising, it fell to a then-unknown young officer called Napoleon Bonaparte in 1793, and narrowly escaped being razed to the ground. Facing defeat, the Royalists scuppered their own ships and blew up the shipyards to save them from the Revolutionaries' hands.

In a strange repeat of history, in November 1942 the French scuttled their fleet in the harbour to prevent Nazis troops from commandeering its battleships, torpedo boats and submarines. Two years later, a combination of Allied bombs and retreating Germans would lay the old town to waste.

Sightseeing

At the heart of what remains of Toulon's *vieille ville* is place Puget and the 18th-century Fontaine des Trois Dauphins, overgrown with tangled ivy and sprouting saplings. Home to a grain market in the 17th century, the café-lined square now hosts a small Friday morning book and antique market. South of here, contemporary and historic photography exhibitions are held in the **Maison de la Photographie**.

A stroll to the east of place Puget brings you to the **Cathédrale Ste-Marie-de-la-Seds** on place de la Cathédrale, with its Gothic interior and classical façade; construction began in the 11th century, but it wasn't finished until 1740. A few steps on is **cours Lafayette**, which becomes a vast market every morning except Monday. Its stalls overflow with local produce, from tiny radishes to plump peaches that stallholders squeeze tenderly to find you the perfect specimen. Towards the port, a snack stand sells *la cade* (chickpea crêpes) and *chichi freigi* (doughnuts). Here, too, is the diminutive **Musée du Vieux Toulon**, whose eccentric collection of historical relics ranges from lavishly embroidered religious robes to a carved coconut shell depicting Napoleon.

To the east of the old town, the remnants of Vauban's ramparts and the fortified Porte d'Italie are squeezed behind the Centre Mayol shopping centre and the Stade Mayol, home of Toulon's fast-rising rugby team. By the station, the sleek glass and steel **Zénith Oméga** (bd du Commandant Nicolas, 04.94.22.66.77, www.zenith-omega-toulon.com) puts on all kinds of rock concerts.

West of the old town lie the broad avenues and imposing squares of the 18th- and 19th-century new town. On place Victor Hugo, the **Opéra de Toulon** has an opulent red and gilt Third Empire auditorium, designed by Charles Garnier. At 6 rue Anatole France, a plaque marks where actor Raimu, star of Marcel Pagnol's 1930s film trilogy (*Marius*, *Fanny* and *César*), was born. He's also commemorated with various statues around town; on place Raimu, near the port, you can take a seat next to life-size bronzes of César and Panisse from the famous card game scene in *Marius*.

Towards the train station, the stately 19th-century former Var assembly building is now the **Hôtel des Arts**, hosting some excellent contemporary art and photography exhibitions. Across the street, the **Musée des Beaux-Arts** has a hotchpotch of work, running from Fragonard and marine paintings by Vernet up to post-war abstraction and the cartoon-influenced *figuration libre* of Combas and the Di Rosa brothers; currently under renovation, it's set to reopen in 2009.

Down by the harbour, the port and old town are divided by the avenue de la République housing project – an unlovely strip of boxy tower blocks. Beyond this, however, is a lively café-lined yachting marina. From here, you can take boat trips to the Iles de Hyères (*see p188*) or around the otherwise strictly off-limits military port. At the town hall annexe on quai Cronstadt, two 1657 atlantes by Pierre Puget shoulder the portal, embodying the agonising labour of early dock workers.

Over in the westerly Darse Neuve, the 'new dock' built in 1680, the **Musée de la Marine** houses figureheads, ship models and marine paintings. Its ornate doorway, with figures of Mars and Minerva, is the former dockyard entrance. To the right are the heavily guarded gates of the military port. Back from here, a couple of sex shops and bars with bored-looking, scantily clad girls lounging by the entrances are the last vestiges of Toulon's once-infamous red-light district. Known locally as 'Le Petit Chicago', the neighbourhood's narrow streets and shady squares are worth a stroll.

East of town, past the 17th-century Fort St-Louis, **Le Mourillon** is Toulon's upmarket beach suburb, with colourful old houses and bustling streets. Its chief draw is its long, sandy beaches, backed with shady lawns, play areas and laid-back restaurants, serving enormous bowls of moules-frites. The lovely *sentier des Douaniers*, once patrolled by Napoleon's customs agents, offers access to the most charming parts of the coast: small sandy coves and sheer cliffs topped with 19th-century villas. Two tiny coves, **Magaud** and **Méjean**, hide pristine fishing villages, wonderful views and waterside restaurants; Méjean is accessible by car. The 23 bus runs all along the coast, stopping at Le Mourillon, Méjean and Magaud.

Between Toulon and Le Mourillon, the **Musée des Arts Asiatiques** is a stylish showcase for treasures from China, Japan and South-east Asia: don't miss the Tibetan *thangka* cloths, painted with fierce, fiery-eyed deities. Close by on the littoral Fréderic Mistral, the tranquil **Jardins d'Acclimation** feature carefully labelled plants, lofty palm trees and a small playground.

Looming above town, **Mont Faron** provides a welcome escape from the summer heat. Its dense pine woods and limestone outcrops are criss-crossed with twisting footpaths and dotted with picnic tables; there are also two open-air restaurants. It's a nine-kilometre drive up the winding Corniche du Mont Faron, but the easiest way to get there is by taking the half-hourly 40 bus from rue d'Alger or place Louis Blanc to the **Téléferique** station, then ascending via cable car; the views are splendid. At the summit is a 19th-century fortress in

Opera de Toulon.

THE VAR

which the **Musée-Mémorial du Débarquement** commemorates the 1944 liberation of Provence, and the **Zoo du Mont Faron**. The latter specialises in wild cats and runs breeding programmes – though the magnificent snow leopards, panthers and lynxes, languidly sprawled in what seem very cramped enclosures, make for slightly uncomfortable viewing.

Another way to take in Toulon's exceptional geographic setting is to hop on a boat, for the price of a return bus ticket, to one of the four small towns around the bay. As the shuttles move outwards, they offer a wonderful view of the city and its backdrop of hills. Along the western shore in industrial **La Seyne-sur-Mer**, Fort Balaguier is where Napoleon completed the capture of Toulon in 1793, a feat honoured in the fort's **Musée Naval**. In **Les Tamaris**, there's contemporary art in the 1890s neo-Moorish **Villa Tamaris Pacha**. Another option is the sleepy, low-key fishing port of **St-Mandrier-sur-Mer**: walk across the peninsula to reach an unspoilt, rocky little cove, backed with pine trees and chirruping cicadas. Alternatively, **Les Sablettes**, a 1950s resort designed by architect François Pouillon, opens on to a broad sandy beach, perfect for a late afternoon swim; follow the coastal path south for the beach of Mar Vivo and the sweet Fabrégas cove.

FREE Hôtel des Arts
236 av Maréchal Leclerc (04.94.91.69.18/ www.var.fr). **Open** (during exhibitions) 10am-1pm Mon-Fri. **Admission** free.

FREE Maison de la Photographie
pl du Globe (04.94.93.07.59). **Open** noon-6pm Tue-Sun. **Admission** free.

FREE Musée des Arts Asiatiques
Villa Jules Verne, 106 bd Eugène Pelletan (04.94.36.83.10). **Open** noon-6pm Tue-Sat. **Admission** free.
▶ *For more Asian art gems, displayed in a 'floating' building designed by Kenzo Tange, visit Nice's Musée des Arts Asiatiques (see p258).*

FREE Musée des Beaux-Arts
113 bd du Maréchal Leclerc (04.94.36.81.00). **Open** noon-6pm daily (closed for renovations until Apr 2009). **Admission** free.

Musée de la Marine
pl Monsenergue (04.94.02.02.01/www.musee-marine.fr). **Open** *July, Aug* 10am-6pm daily. *Sept-June* 10am-6pm Mon, Wed-Sun. **Admission** €5; €3.50 reductions; free under-18s. **Credit** MC, V.

FREE Musée du Vieux Toulon
69 cours Lafayette (04.94.62.11.07). **Open** 2-5.45pm Tue-Sat. **Admission** free.

Musée-Mémorial du Débarquement
sommet du Mont Faron (04.94.88.08.09). **Open** *July-mid Sept* 10am-1pm, 2-6.30pm daily. *Mid Sept-end Sept* 10am-1pm, 2-6.30pm Tue-Sun. *Oct-Apr* 10am-1pm, 2-5.30pm Tue-Sun. *May, June* 10am-1pm, 2-6.30pm Tue-Sun. **Admission** €3.80; €1.55 reductions; free under-8s. **No credit cards**.

Musée Naval du Fort Balaguier
924 corniche Bonaparte, La Seyne-sur-Mer (04.94.94.84.72). **Open** *Mid June-mid Sept* 10am-noon, 3-7pm Wed-Sun. *Mid Sept-mid June* 10am-noon, 2-6pm Wed-Sun. **Admission** €3; €2 reductions; free under-5s. **No credit cards**.

Opéra de Toulon
pl Victor Hugo (04.94.92.70.78/www.operade toulon.fr). **Open** Box office 9.30am-12.30pm, 2-6pm Tue-Sat. Closed July, Aug. **Tickets** €15-€69. **Credit** V.

Téléphérique
bd Amiral Vence (04.94.92.68.25/www. telepherique-faron.com). **Open** *July-Aug* 9.30am-7.45pm daily. *June, Sept* 9.30am-7pm Tue-Sun. *Apr, May, Oct* 9.30am-12.15pm, 2-6pm Tue-Sun. *Feb, Mar, Nov* 9.30am-12.15pm, 2-5.30pm Tue-Sun. Closed Jan, Dec & windy days. **Admission** €6.30 return; €4.50 reductions; free under-4s. **No credit cards**.

FREE Villa Tamaris Pacha
av de la Grande Maison, La-Seyne-sur-Mer (04.94.06.84.00/www.villatamaris.fr). **Open** (during exhibitions) 2-6.30pm Tue-Sun. **Admission** free.

Zoo du Mont Faron
Mont Faron (04.94.88.07.89/www.telepherique-faron.com). **Open** *May-Sept* 10am-6.30pm daily. *Oct-Apr* 2-5.30pm Mon-Sat; 10am-5.30pm Sun. Closed on rainy days. **Admission** €8.50; €5 reductions; free under-4s. *Combined ticket* (Téléphérique & Zoo) €11.50; €7.50 reductions. **No credit cards**.

Cours Lafayette. See p179.

THE VAR

Where to eat

Au Sourd
10 rue Molière (04.94.92.28.52). **Open** noon-2pm, 7-10.30pm Tue-Sat; noon-2pm Sun. **Main courses** €9-€18. **Menu** €26. **Credit** MC, V.
Local dignitaries crowd to Au Sourd, set in the pedestrianised streets by the opera, for sautéed calamares and fresh fish from Hyères and La Ciotat, washed down with provençal wines.

★ € Bio et Terroir
3 rue Charles Poncy (04.94.22.59.32/www.lou frankou.fr). **Open** 10am-7pm Mon-Sat. **Main courses** €7.50-€12. **Credit** MC, V.
The star turn at this charming café are the generous platters of local specialities, starring such delights as duck confit with pine nuts, clementine-spiked green olive paste and juicy preserved figs. Even better, all of the ingredients are on sale in the enticing adjoining épicerie.

€ Bistrot de la Place
pl Gustave Lambert (06.03.12.36.39). **Open** noon-3pm Mon-Sat. **Main courses** €10-€15. **Credit** MC, V.
With its modish little terrace, set by a trickling fountain, and green-painted wrought-iron tables and chairs, this is a chic but inexpensive lunchtime stop-off. At €10, the plat du jour (an excellent chicken green curry, on our last visit) is a bargain.

Chez Daniel et Julia
plage de Fabrégas (04.94.94.85.13). **Open** 9am-4.30pm, 8-11pm Mon-Sat. Closed Nov. **Menus** €38-€90. **Credit** AmEx, MC, V.
This lovely restaurant is easier to reach than Restaurant Bernard, but just as peaceful. An appreciative crowd gathers here to devour home-smoked fish, lobster ravioli and Aups truffles on a tamaris-shaded terrace that overlooks the sea.

€ Les Enfants Gâtés
7 rue Corneille (04.94.09.14.67). **Open** *July, Aug* noon-3pm Mon-Fri. *Sept-June* noon-3pm Mon-Fri, 7.30-11pm Sat. **Main courses** €13.50-€21. **Credit** AmEx, MC, V.
The simple, seasonal menu at this friendly old town bistro ranges from seafood salads to steaks; the creamy risotto du jour is always worth a punt. Save room for the deeply tempting desserts though: panettone *pain perdu* with orange sorbet, a slab of chunky, own-made *tarte tatin*, or apricot crumble with honey ice-cream.

Herrero
45 quai de la Sinse (04.94.41.00.16). **Open** noon-3pm, 6-10pm Tue-Sun; noon-3pm Sun. **Main courses** €14-€34. **Menus** €19-€25. **Credit** AmEx, DC, MC, V.
Founded by ex-rugby international André Herrero, this waterfront eaterie has a devoted local following and modest prices. Seafood of every description is

THE VAR

Wine Tour Bandol

Richard James recommends the pick of the local vineyards.

You run into 'Le Rond-Point des Mourvèdres' off exit 11 of the A50, to the north of Bandol. A postage-stamp roundabout planted with mourvèdre vines, it's a sign of what's to come as you venture into Bandol territory (www.vinsdebandol.com). For the mythical mourvèdre grape lies at the very heart of the appellation, shaping not only its wines, but its growers' hearts and minds.

It's a meaty, late-ripening variety that needs plenty of sunshine and intimate handling. Elsewhere in the South, winemakers use less or no mourvèdre as they struggle to coax such a fine performance out of it. Yet to qualify as AOC Bandol, reds have to be at least half mourvèdre; some are 100 per cent. They're a good match for game, duck, pigeon or a good old-fashioned steak.

While Bandol's reputation stems from its reds (still the focus for the top estates), it produces two-thirds rosé – and a touch of often-overpriced white. The best rosés, which are full-bodied and dry, contain a fair amount of mourvèdre, along with cinsaut, grenache or syrah. They go particularly well with seafood, and Chinese or Thai cuisine.

The appellation encompasses the villages of Sanary, Le Castellet, La Cadière d'Azur and parts of St-Cyr-sur-Mer, Le Beausset, Evenos and Ollioules. Its vineyards stretch for ten kilometres around Bandol – where, ironically, you'd be hard-pressed to find a vine.

Heading east from the Rond-Point on the D66 towards Le Beausset, take the first right. **Domaine Tempier** (chemin des Fanges, Le Plan du Castellet, 04.94.98.70.21, www.domainetempier.com) is owned by the Peyrauds, who, in

the early days, were one of a handful who argued mourvèdre should be Bandol's central grape variety. Their rosé develops nicely and they make some fine reds. Two stand out: La Migoua (mourvèdre, cinsault, syrah, grenache) and La Tourtine (80 per cent mourvèdre), both sturdy and intense.

Next, follow the D559B through Le Plan, turn right underneath the motorway on to the chemin de l'Argile and follow it until you reach **Domaine Lafran-Veyrolles** (La Cadière d'Azur, 04.94.90.13.37, www.lafran-veyrolles.com), where you can sample some impressive reds and rosés.

Head back south on to the chemin de Fontanieu, then second right on to chemin de Pibarnon, which runs into chemin de la Paguette. Keep going until you hit chemin de la Croix des Signaux, home to the famed **Château de Pibarnon** (La Cadière, 04.94.90.12.73, www.pibarnon.com). Its vineyards lie on some of the highest slopes in Bandol, where the soil is very chalky and stony. Eric de Saint Victor and his father Comte Henri, who rebuilt the estate, believe this helps restrain the mourvèdre, making finer wines. Also recommended in La Cadière are **Gros'Noré** (675 chemin de l'Argile, 04.94.90.08.50, www.gros-nore.com) and **La Rouvière** (04.94.98.58.98).

Around Sainte-Anne-du-Castellet and Brûlat, try **Bastide Blanche** (367 route des Oratoires, 04.94.32.63.20) for muscular, concentrated reds and **Tour du Bon** (714 chemin de l'Olivette, 04.98.03.66.22, www.tourdubon.com) for elegant reds and one of the AOC's best white wines.

Head to Sainte-Anne-d'Evenos for the **Château Sainte Anne** (rte nationale 8, 04.66.82.77.41), which produces charming and sometimes unpredictable wines. Meanwhile, at **Domaine de la Laidiere** (426 chemin de Font Vive, 04.98.03.65.75), Freddie Estienne makes some of the finest wines in the appellation.

---

on the menu, from *amande de mer* clams and oysters to sea bass with fennel. Reserve in advance.

Restaurant Bernard

367 allée de la Mer, Anse de Magaud (04.94.27.20.62/http://restaurant-bernard.spaces.live.com). **Open** noon-2.30pm, 7.30-9.30pm Tue-Sat; noon-2.30pm Sun. Closed Oct-Mar. **Menus** €23-€40. **Credit** MC, V.

At the water's edge in the Magaud cove, Restaurant Bernard serves fresh grilled fish in a stylish beach shack. Book ahead, and be prepared for a steep scramble from the car park on avenue de la Résistance.

Restaurant Le Mayol

462 av de la République (04.94.41.39.36). **Open** noon-2pm, 7.30-10pm Mon-Sat; noon-2pm Sun. **Menus** €27.90-€39.50. **Credit** MC, V.

The best known of the seafood restaurants that line the port, Mayol, named after Toulon-born opera singer Félix Mayol, is a classic spot to scoff bouillabaisse and shellfish as you watch the sun setting over the sea.

★ € Le Resto des Artistes

10 rue de l'Humilité (04.94.29.91.03). **Open** noon-2pm, 7.30-10pm daily. **Main courses** €10-€15. **Menu** €18.50. **Credit** MC, V.

After an aperitif in place Puget, head for Le Resto's cluster of pretty, parasol-shaded tables. The three-course *formule* is a steal, with each dish lovingly described by the owner: tender squid salad, perhaps, or slices of magret (duck breast) with melon.

Le Richardi

25 bis rue de la Comédie (04.94.64.66.39). **Open** noon-1.45pm Mon; noon-1.45pm, 7.30-9.30pm Tue-Thur; noon-1.45pm, 7.30-10pm Fri, Sat. **Main courses** €14-€19.50. **Menus** *Lunch* €13.50. *Dinner* €21-€33. **Credit** MC, V.

Le Richardi serves artfully presented modern renditions of provençal classics in opulent surrounds (think crushed velvet seating, jewel-like lamps and baroque chandeliers). Dessert brings extravagant (and pricey) ensembles of artisan-made ice-creams.

Where to drink

113 Café

113 av Infanterie de Marine (04.94.03.42.41/ www.le113cafe.com). **Open** 8am-1pm Mon-Sat. **Main courses** €11-€19. **Menu** €25. **Credit** MC, V.

Set in a warehouse near the ferry port, this lively bar-restaurant hosts regular bands, Thursday-night salsa sessions and DJs on Fridays and Saturdays.

A Rhum Café

2 rue Beaussier (04.94.41.47.50). **Open** 6pm-1am daily. *Happy hour* Summer 6.30-8.30pm & 10.30-11.30pm. Winter 6.30-8.30pm. **Credit** MC, V.

Rum is de rigueur at this stylish little Le Mourillon lounge bar, with over 60 offerings served by the glass or bottle: flavours run from apricot to liquorice. A nightly happy hour gets the evening off to an inebriated start.

Bar à Thym

32 bd Dr Cuneo (04.94.41.90.10/www.barathym. com). **Open** 6pm-3am Mon-Sat. **Credit** MC, V.

Le Mourillon's studenty Bar au Thym is a great spot for post-beach beers or a late-night tipple; jam sessions and DJ sets draw an enthusiastic crowd.

Le Bizuth

69 quai de la Sinse (04.94.31.87.86/www.le bizuth.com). **Open** 8am-2am daily. **Main courses** €8-€15. **Menu** *Lunch* €10. **Credit** MC, V.

This slick portside restaurant and bar serves up mojitos and martinis until 2am; if you're feeling peckish, there's fish, pasta and inventive house salads – not to mention kangaroo fillets, and more traditional *entrecôtes*.

Where to stay

Best Western Le Corniche

17 littoral Frédéric Mistral (04.94.41.35.12/ www.bestwestern-hotelcorniche.com). **Rates** €110-€150 double. **Rooms** 30. **Credit** AmEx, MC, V.

Close to Le Mourillon's beaches, the Best Western is set on the coast road, behind a shady courtyard. Its airy rooms offer free Wi-Fi and some have balconies overlooking the bay; a rolling refurbishment is replacing the traditional decor with a modern cream and taupe colour palette and gleaming bathrooms.

★ € Celenya Hôtel

7bis rue de Chabannes (04.94.92.37.44/ www.hotel-celenya-toulon.com). **Rates** €55-€75 double. **Rooms** 29. **Credit** AmEx, MC, V.

Rooms at this chic, quirky hotel are themed around different cities and continents. London has a lovely little tiled bathroom and a silhouette of the city's skyline, while the North America suite has a glorious roof terrace and a stetson hanging on the wall. Not all rooms have air-conditioning.

€ Grand Hôtel Dauphiné

10 rue Berthelot (04.94.92.20.28/www.grand hoteldauphine.com). **Rates** €62-€66 double. **Rooms** 55. **Credit** AmEx, MC, V.

This friendly old-town hotel is a comfortable and conveniently-located option, seconds away from place Puget. Rooms are elegantly old-fashioned, with cream walls, red upholstery and freshly refurbished bathrooms; flat-screen TVs and free Wi-Fi access are nods to modernity, however.

€ Hôtel Lamalgue

124 rue Gubler (04.94.41.36.23/http://hotel. lamalgue.free.fr). **Rates** €41-€53 double. Closed mid Oct-June. **Rooms** 20. **Credit** MC, V.

Hidden away in the peaceful residential streets behind Le Mourillon's beaches, this is a no-fuss, no-frills option, with clean, simply furnished rooms and a friendly owner.

€ Hôtel Little Palace

6 rue Berthelot (04.94.92.26.62/www.hotel-littlepalace.com). **Rates** €54-€58 double. **Rooms** 23. **Credit** AmEx, MC, V.

Step out of the front door and you're in the very centre of the *vielle ville*. Inside, guestrooms are decorated in cheery red, orange and yellow tones, with rag-rolled walls and sparklingly clean bathrooms. Charming staff are happy to help out with restaurant recommendations and sightseeing advice.

THE VAR

Resources

Hospital
Hôpital Font Pré *1208 av Colonel Picot (04.94.61.61.61).*

Internet
Cybercafé Puget *pl Puget (04.94.93.05.54).* **Open** 8am-9pm daily.

Police
1 rue Commissaire Morandin (04.98.03.53.00).

Post office
rue Prosper Ferrero (04.94.18.51.00).

Tourist information
Office de Tourisme *334 av de la République (04.94.18.53.00/www.toulontourisme.com).* **Open** *Sept-June* 9am-6pm Mon, Wed-Sat; 10am-6pm Tue; 10am-noon Sun. *July, Aug* 9am-8pm Mon-Sat; 10am-noon Sun.

The Western Côte

BANDOL & AROUND

Long before the glitterati discovered St-Tropez, Bandol was a holiday hotspot for the intellectual set: Aldous Huxley, Thomas Mann and Marcel Pagnol all sojourned here. Today, the old town that fronts the quays is lined with palm trees and cafés, while the *ruelles* around 18th-century **Eglise St-François-de-Sales** buzz with shops and restaurants. The town's main market is held beside the port on Tuesday mornings, and there's a small nightly art market in summer. Westward towards the bay of Renecros sprawl elegant belle-époque homes and terraced vineyards (*see p182* **Wine Tour**): on the first Sunday in December, the Fête du Millésime sees proud vintners bear kegs of their three-month-old wines to the port for a public tasting, before putting them to bed in wooden casks for 18 months.

Offshore, tiny **Ile de Bendor**, bought by pastis magnate Paul Ricard in the 1950s, has been heavily cemented with apartments. Its main attraction is the **Exposition Universelle des Vins et Spiritueux,** comprising 8,000 bottles of alcoholic spirits but, sadly, no tastings. Ferries (04.94.05.54.88, €12, €8 reductions) sail hourly from Bandol port.

Inland from Bandol lie the pretty medieval hilltop villages of **La Cadière-d'Azur** and **Le Castellet**, a fortified village once owned by King René of Provence – ramparts and a stern 15th-century chateau remain, along with a sprinkling of arty shops. Outside the village, Formula One drivers test racing cars at the Circuit Paul Ricard.

The N8 continues east via the grey-stone village of **Ste-Anne-d'Evenos** and winds gently south along the River Reppe through the **Gorges d'Ollioules**, where steep cliffs are riddled with caves that once hid Gaspard de Besse, bandit-hero of local folklore. **Ollioules** is set amid terraced hills where locals tend olives, vines, citrus fruits and the blooms that end up in the town's wholesale flower market. Medieval streets climb from the massive 11th-century Romanesque church up to a ruined 13th-century chateau. In the eastern pine forests,

Sanary-sur-Mer.

CNCDC Châteauvallon presents a varied line-up of theatre, dance and music in a stunning open-air amphitheatre and indoor stage.

CNCDC Châteauvallon
795 chemin du Châteauvallon, Ollioules (04.94.22.74.00/www.chateauvallon.com). **Open** *Box office* 2-7pm Mon; 10am-7pm Tue-Sat. **Tickets** €22; €16 reductions. **Credit** MC, V.

FREE Exposition Universelle des Vins & Spiritueux
Ile de Bendor (04.94.05.15.61/www.euvs.org). **Open** *May-Oct* 10.30am-12.30pm, 3-7pm daily. **Admission** free.

Where to stay, eat & drink

In Bandol, escape the crowds on the private beach of the **Golf Hôtel** (plage Renécros, bd Lumière, 04.94.29.45.83, www.golfhotel.fr, closed mid Nov-mid Mar, double €54-€115), once the casino. Its beachside restaurant (04.94.29.99.89, mains €13-€19) is perfect for a laid-back lunch. Another seafront option is **Le Splendid** (83 av Maréchal Foch, 04.94.32.50.87, www.splendidhotel-provence.com, closed mid Nov-Mar, double €52-€134); the extra euros spent securing a sea view is money well spent.

A few streets back from the port, calm **Hôtel L'Oasis** (15 rue des Ecoles, 04.94.29.41.69, www.oasisbandol.com, closed Dec, double €58-€77) is a former parsonage. White linen tablecloths flap in the sea breeze at the chic **Auberge du Port** (9 allée Jean Moulin, 04.94.29.42.63, www.auberge-du-port.com, menus €38-€48), a lively seafood brasserie whose specialities include salt-baked fish.

In La Cadière, the lovely **Hostellerie Bérard et Spa** (av Gabriel Péri, 04.94.90.11.43, www.hotel-berard.com, closed Jan-mid Feb, double €91-€283) occupies several ancient houses and an 11th-century convent. The spa offers Carita and Décleor treatments, while the restaurant serves top-notch provençal fare (closed lunch Mon & Tue Oct-Apr, menus €49-€140). **Le Petit Jardin** (17 av Gabriel Péri, closed Wed & Thur, mains €14-€28), also part of the hotel, serves seasonal dishes on a veranda with a panoramic view.

In Ste-Anne-d'Evenos, Mme Dutheil de La Rochère offers *chambres d'hôte* at the **Château-Ste-Anne** vineyard (04.94.90.35.40, closed Oct, double €96). Surrounded by well-kept grounds, **Hôtel du Castellet** (3001 rte des Hauts du Camp, Le Beausset, 04.94.98.37.77, www.hotel ducastellet.com, double €320-€530) is an opulent affair, with its own golf course, Michelin-starred restaurant (closed lunch Mon, mains €40-€140) and luxuriously appointed rooms. In the rolling hills that surround Ollioules, **La Table du**

Vigneron (724 chemin de la Tourelle, 04.94.88.36.19, closed Mon, dinner Sun & Feb, menu €45) offers excellent seasonal cooking and tastings of its Domaine de Terrebrune wines.

Resources

Internet
Boss Cyber Café *9 rue des Ecoles, Bandol (04.94.29.03.03).* **Open** *July-mid Sept* 9am-1pm, 3-9.30pm Mon-Sat. *Mid Sept-June* 9am-1pm, 3-8pm Mon-Sat.

Tourist information
Bandol Maison du Tourisme *allée Vivien, Bandol (04.94.29.41.35/www.bandol.fr).* **Open** *July, Aug* 9am-7pm daily. *Sept-June* 9am-noon, 2-6pm Mon-Fri; 9am-noon Sat.
Ollioules Office du Tourisme *116 av Philippe de Hauteclogue, Ollioules (04.94.63. 11.74/www.ollioules.com).* **Open** *July, Aug* 9am-1pm, 4-7pm Mon-Sat. *Sept-June* 9am-noon, 2-6pm Mon-Sat.

SANARY-SUR-MER TO SIX-FOURS

Colourful boats bob beside the quay and fishermen still sew sardine nets along the palm-lined port of **Sanary-sur-Mer**, a bustling little seaside resort. In the 1930s, Sanary provided a refuge for German intellectuals escaping the Nazi regime; Aldous Huxley also lived here. At the western end of the port, in a 13th-century tower, the **Musée Frédéric Dumas** houses wine amphorae and ancient diving equipment – diving pioneer Frédéric was one of Jacques Cousteau's original 'trois mousque-mers'. There's a daily produce market and a flea market on the last Saturday of the month.

On the wind-battered Sicie peninsula, **Six-Fours-les-Plages** is a string of modern beach bars and restaurants, with a Saturday morning market. When the Mistral blows, angry waves make the so-called 'Brutal Beach' a surfers' paradise. On a hill to the north, the **Collégiale St-Pierre**, spanning the Romanesque and Gothic periods, is all that remains of the original village. A few miles north, the sixth-century **Chapelle Notre-Dame-de-Pepiole** is one of France's oldest Christian churches.

The modern beach resort of **Le Brusc** is on the site of the port of Tauroentium, founded by Phocaean Greeks from Marseille; today most visitors stay only long enough to get a ferry (04.94.05.54.88) to the **Iles des Embiez**, former salt-panning islands. The main island houses the **Institut Océanographique Paul Ricard**, a research centre into Mediterranean pollution, and offers miles of footpaths and cycle tracks; bikes can be hired on the quay.

THE VAR

FREE Collégiale St-Pierre

*montée du Fort Militaire, Six-Fours-les-Plages
(04.94.34.24.75).* **Open** *June-Sept* 10am-noon, 3-
7pm Mon, Wed-Sun. *Oct-May* 10am-noon, 2-6pm
Mon, Wed-Sun. **Admission** free.

FREE Musée Frédéric Dumas

*pl de la Tour, Sanary-sur-Mer (04.94.74.80.23/
www.scuba-museum.com).* **Open** *July-Aug* 10am-
12.30pm, 4-7.30pm daily. *Sept-June* 10am-
12.30pm, 3-6.30pm Sat, Sun. **Admission** free.

Where to eat, drink & stay

Ten minutes from Sanary's port, **Le Synaya**
(92 chemin Olive, 04.94.74.10.50, www.hotel
synaya.fr, double €65-€140, closed mid Nov-
late Mar) offers spacious rooms, stylishly kitted
out in dark wood and bold, modern fabrics,
and a delightful pool. In the same peaceful
residential neighbourhood, the flower-draped
Mas de la Frigoulette (130 av des Mimosas,
04.94.74.13.46, www.lafrigoulette.com, double
€50-€140, €15-€20 mains) is a convivial,
family-run hotel with a lovely restaurant
and bar on the terrace.

The **Hôtel-Restaurant de la Tour**
(24 quai Général de Gaulle, 04.94.74.10.10,
www.sanary-hoteldelatour.com, double €76-
€167) is right on the port; its rooms are slightly
old-fashioned, but the views are the real draw.
The restaurant (closed Tue, Wed & Dec, menus
€20-€30 lunch, €30-€44 dinner) serves gourmet
seafood. Sanary also has a healthy bar scene:
start at tiny **Café Mac'Sym's** (10 quai de
Gaulle, 04.94.74.45.34) before going clubbing
at **Mai-Tai** (1370 rte de Bandol, 04.94.74.23.92,
closed Mon-Thur, Sun).

In Six-Fours-les-Plages, Christian and Olivier
Blusset's **Bistro du Dauphin** (36 square des
Bains, plage de Bonnegrace, 04.94.07.61.58,
closed 2wks Feb, menus €30-€55) offers
inspired cooking at moderate prices. After
shopping at the market, the chef chalks up the
daily specials, with lots of fish and hearty meat
dishes (such as tripe or calf's head).

In Le Brusc, be sure to book ahead at **St-
Pierre** (47 rue de la Citadelle, 04.94.34.02.52,
www.lesaintpierre.fr, closed lunch Mon July &
Aug, dinner Sun & all Mon Sept-June, all Jan,
menus €18-€33.50), known for its grilled fish
and great bouillabaisse.

Resources

Internet

Cyber Espace @ Fenyx *8 rue Lauzet Ainé,
Sanary-sur-Mer (04.94.88.10.78).* **Open** *Jan-
June, Sept-Dec* 10.30am-1pm, 3-7pm Wed, Fri,
Sat; 3-7pm Sun. *July, Aug* 10am-1pm, 4-7.30pm,
9-11pm daily.

Tourist information

Sanary Maison du Tourisme *1 Quai
du Levant, Sanary-sur-Mer (04.94.74.01.04/
www.sanarysurmer.com).* **Open** *July, Aug* 9am-
7pm Mon-Sat; 9.30am-12.30pm Sun. *Apr-June,
Sept, Oct* 9am-noon, 2-6pm Mon-Fri; 9am-noon,
2-5pm Sun. *Nov-Mar* 9am-noon, 2-5.30pm Mon-
Fri; 9am-noon, 2-5pm Sat.
Six-Fours Office du Tourisme *promenade
Charles de Gaulle, plage de Bonnegrâce, Six-
Fours-les-Plages (04.94.07.02.21/www.six-fours-
les-plages.com).* **Open** *Apr-June, Sept* 9am-noon,
2-6.30pm Mon-Sat. *July, Aug* 9am-1pm, 2-7pm
Mon-Sat; 10am-1pm Sun. *Oct-Mar* 8.45am-noon,
2-5.30pm Mon-Fri; 9am-noon, 2-5.30pm Sat.

GETTING THERE & AROUND

By air

Toulon-Hyères airport is 35km (22 miles) from
the city centre.

By boat

Boat services (04.94.03.87.03, www.reseaumistral.
com) run from Toulon port to La Seyne, Les
Sablettes, Tamaris and St-Mandrier. Toulon is
also a ferry port to Corsica (04.95.32.95.95,
www.corsicaferries.com).

By bus

Société des Cars et Autobus de Cassis
(04.42.73.29.29) runs six buses a day between
Marseille and Bandol. **Littoral Cars**
(04.94.74.01.35) runs buses between Bandol and
Sanary, Le Brusc, Six-Fours, La Seyne and
Toulon. **RMTT** (04.94.03.87.03, www.reseau
mistral.com) runs buses from Toulon to Ollioules,
La Seyne and Sanary, and within Toulon (3, 13
and 23 go to the beaches at Le Mourillon; 40 to
the cable car). **Sodétrav** (08.25.00.06.50,
04.94.13.88.44) runs a service between Toulon
and Hyères.

By car

The A50 from Marseille in the west and the A57
from the east pour traffic directly into the centre
of Toulon. After decades of work, a cross-city
tunnel linking the two opened in 2003 – but only
in one direction. Leave the A50 at exit 12 for
Bandol, exit 13 to Six-Fours-les-Plages, Sanary-
sur-Mer and Ollioules and exit 14 for
Châteauvallon. The coastal D559 goes between
Marseille and Toulon via Bandol and Sanary.

By train

Toulon is on the main TGV line from Paris and is
also served by commuter trains from Marseille
and Nice. Local trains between Marseille and
Toulon stop at Bandol and Sanary-Ollioules,
although Sanary-Ollioules station is a dusty
2.5km walk from Sanary.

Hyères to Les Maures

From forested highlands to sub-tropical islands.

There are fewer English voices on this enticing seaside stretch than anywhere else on the southern coast. Yet the coastal road is one of the region's most handsome, winding through vineyards, sandy white coves and well-polished belle époque resorts. **Hyères** still evokes the glory days, with its stately palm trees, casino and 19th-century gardens. Offshore, **Porquerolles** and **Port-Cros** are breathtakingly beautiful, unspoilt island idylls.

Inland, the **Maures** mountains are packed with picturesque *villages perchés* and wild forests of chestnut and pine. Get off the beaten track and discover what the French have been keeping to themselves.

HYERES & GIENS

Palmy Hyères led the seaside brigade in the 19th century, when its mild climate was recommended for consumptives. It was particularly favoured by the British: even Queen Victoria paid a visit in 1892. But when the fashionable season changed from winter to summer, the town was marooned up on a hill five kilometres from the sea, while nearby Le Lavandou blossomed. Hyères is still in bloom, however, raking a living from cut flowers and date palms as well as tourism.

Hyères's medieval *vieille ville* is at the end of avenue Gambetta, the main drag from the coast, via the cafés on place Clemenceau or through the fortified Porte Massillon. The rue Massillon, lined with food shops, leads to the bustling square of place Massillon. Here the much-restored, barrel-vaulted **Tour St-Blaise**, used for exhibitions, is all that remains of a Templar monastery. Climb the steps from the square and take steep rue Ste-Catherine to **Collégiale St-Paul**, with its medieval bell tower and Renaissance doorway; the front room is crowded with naïve ex-voto paintings. On place de la République, the 13th-century **Eglise St-Louis** was once a Franciscan monastery where Louis IX prayed in 1254 on his return from the Crusades.

Climb up past the church to visit the **Villa Noailles**, a masterpiece of Modernist architecture that's now used for contemporary art and design exhibitions. All horizontal lines and Cubist stained glass, it was designed in 1924 by Robert Mallet-Stevens for avant-garde aristos Charles and Marie-Laure de Noailles. In its day, it was the scene of trysts and parties frequented by A-list bohemians, including Picasso, Stravinsky, Buñuel and Man Ray, who shot part of his film *Les Mystères du Château de Dé* here. Clips of his bizarre black and white flicks are shown in the screening room.

Continue up the montée de Noailles to the ruins of the 11th- to 13th-century castle of the Lords of Fos, stupendous fortifications that you're free to clamber around. It's surrounded by the **Parc St-Bernard** and the equally lush **Parc Ste-Claire**, home to the 19th-century castle where Edith Wharton once lived.

The charms of the modern town are distinctly faded, but near the town hall on avenue Joseph Clotis, fine belle époque houses have become arty restaurants and tearooms, and the **Casino des Palmiers** (1 av Ambroise Thomas, 04.94.12.80.80, www.casinodespalmiers.fr) still supplies a touch of glamour. The **Musée Municipal**, meanwhile, displays local paintings, archaeological finds and furniture.

Further along are the **Jardins Olbius Riquier**, where subtropical plants, a hothouse and a mini-zoo are set around a pseudo-Moorish villa. Sticking up on the Costebelle hill is the pierced concrete tower of **Eglise Notre-Dame-de-la-Consolation**, which replaced an ancient church bombed during World War II.

Beach territory below the town runs either side of a long, narrow isthmus. To the east, the **plage d'Hyères** is a long stretch of sand running from the busy marina along the Rade d'Hyères bay. In the Almanarre district to the west, the **Site Archéologique d'Olbia** (currently closed to the public) bears fragmentary traces of the Greek trading post of Olbia, along with Roman homes and baths, and part of a medieval abbey.

Jutting out between the two, the pretty **Giens** peninsula is the southernmost tip of the French Riviera, studded with tiny bays where local families hang out. On its west side, the four-kilometre **plage d'Almanarre** is popular with kite-surfers and kite-flyers, and hosts the heats of the world windsurfing championships. Between here and **La Capte** (a long, narrow stretch of sand, perfect for families) lie the disused Etang des Pesquiers salt pans, a salt-marsh moonscape and former source of Hyères's wealth. On summer afternoons after 5pm, the two narrow *départementale* roads accessing the beaches have some of the worst car jams around.

At the end of the isthmus is the hilltop village of **Giens** proper. Place Belvédère hosts a market on Tuesday morning and affords fantastic views. Escape the gaping throngs by hiking down the *sentier des Douaniers*, which winds through the backyards of Giens's hotels to rocky little **Port de Niel**. Locals come here to picnic or to dine on ultra-fresh fish at the excellent **Le Poisson Rouge** (*see 189*).

Boats leave for the islands from **La Tour Fondue**, a squat 17th-century fortress built by Cardinal Richelieu.

FREE Collégiale St-Paul

pl St-Paul, Hyères (04.94.65.83.30). **Open** *May-Sept* 10am-noon, 4-7pm Mon, Wed-Sun. *Oct-Apr* 10am-5.30pm Wed-Sun. **Admission** free.

FREE Musée Municipal

Rotonde du Parc Hôtel, entrance on av Foch, Hyères (04.94.00.78.42). **Open** *May-Sept* 10am-12.30pm, 4-7.30pm Mon, Wed-Sun. *Oct-Apr* 10am-noon, 2-5.30pm Wed-Sun. **Admission** free.

★ FREE Villa Noailles

montée de Noailles, Hyères (04.98.08.01.93). **Open** *June-Aug* 10am-noon, 4-7.30pm Mon, Wed-Sun. *Sept-May* 10am-12.30pm, 2-5.30pm Wed-Sun. **Admission** free.

Where to stay & eat

Hyères lacks the stylish accommodation of its elegant past, but the simple **Hôtel de Portalet**

(4 rue de Limans, www.hotel-portalet.com, 04.94.65.39.40, double €60-€90) in the old town has benefited from a recent makeover. On the beachfront by the hippodrome is **Lido Beach** (5 allée Emile Gérard, 04.94.01.43.80, www.lido-beach.com, double €60-€110), a little gem with its own stretch of sand.

Deep in the *vieille ville*, **Bistrot de Marius** (1 pl Massillon, 04.94.35.88.38, closed Mon, Tue, mid Nov-mid Dec & mid Jan-mid Feb, menus €18-€32) is a cut above the rest, with tables spilling out on to the square. Start with chilled oysters and finish with plums in red wine. **L'Eau à la Bouche** (3 pl Massillon, 04.94.35. 33.85) is as bohemian as Hyères gets, with exotic teas and huge salads dished up on the terrace. Carnivores can hit **Le Haut du Pavé** (04.94.35.20.98, www.le-haut-du-pave.com, closed Mon & Tue mid Oct-mid June, menus €26-€32) with its lipsmacking beef dishes and great lunchtime deals. Over in the modern area of town, **Les Jardins de Bacchus** (32 av Gambetta, 04.94.65.77.63, www.bacchushyeres. com, closed lunch Sat, dinner Sun, all Mon, 2wks Jan, June, menus €27-€55) is more formal, dishing up experimentally accented classics such as fois gras with rhubarb compôte.

La Capte is dotted with campsites and chain hotels – though halfway down the peninsula on the way to Giens, quirky **Les Ombrelles** (19 rte de Giens, 04.94.01.31.72, www.lesombrelles. com, double €42-€70) is a sweet option, set just by the beach. In Giens, the **Provençal** (pl St-Pierre, 04.98.04.54.54, www.provencalhotel.com, closed mid Oct-mid Apr, double €107-€168) has 1950s period charm, a pool and terraced gardens that descend to the sea. The **Tire Bouchon** (1 pl St-Pierre, 04.94.58.24.61, www.restaurantletirebouchon.com, closed Tue, Wed, mains €12-€26) stays true to its seafood roots and has breathtaking sea views.

For well-executed classic French fare with some inventive spicing, try **Lou Calabrun** (4 rue du Maquis Vallier, 04.94.48.50.35, closed Mon June-Aug, Mon, Tue and dinner Thur Sept-Nov & Feb-May, Dec-Jan, menus €25-€30).

INSIDE TRACK
HAUTE-COUTURE HYERES

Every spring, fashionistas, stylists and photographers flock to the Villa Noailles (*see left*) for the **Festival International de Mode et de Photographie**. There's free admission to its exhibitions, and a strong focus on emerging new talent as well as international names: in 1993, über-hip design duo Viktor & Rolf were one of its early discoveries.

Villa Noailles.

In the Port de Niel cove, highly recommended restaurant **Le Poisson Rouge** (04.94.58.92.33, www.restaurantlepoissonrouge.com, menus €27-€42) serves fish straight off the boat.

Resources

Tourist information

Office de Tourisme *3 av Ambroise Thomas, Hyères (04.94.01.84.50/www.hyeres-tourisme. com).* **Open** *July, Aug* 8.30am-7.30pm daily. *Sept-June* 9am-6pm Mon-Fri; 10am-4pm Sat.

THE ILES DE HYERES

Robert Louis Stevenson supposedly found inspiration for *Treasure Island* on the **Ile de Porquerolles**, the largest of the three islands strung across the entrance to Hyères bay. Colonised in the fifth century by the monks of Lérins (*see p241*), the islands were seized by the Saracens in 1160. The latter were turfed out by Francis I, who fortified Porquerolles with the Fort du Petit-Langoustier and the Fort Ste-Agathe, which looms over the yacht marina.

Up the hill from the port, Porquerolles village was built as a retirement colony for Napoleonic officers, and still resembles a colonial outpost. For 60 years from 1911, the village was the private property of Belgian engineer Joseph Fournier, who introduced the exotic flora; in 1971, much of the island was bought by the government, protecting it from developers. Smoking is banned in the park and on the beaches, and the island is car-free: instead, the well-dressed BCBG (*bon chic, bon genre*) French Sloanes who flock here cycle *en famille*. There are plenty of bike hire outlets in the port and village (€12 per day), which offer maps pointing out the quieter spots on the island.

No permit is required for the 6hp speedboats for hire (€90/day) on arrival in the port.

Village life centres on place d'Armes, planted with pungent eucalyptus trees and surrounded by cafés and food stalls. The white sand and lush backdrop of the plage d'Argent (west) or plage de la Courtade (east) are an easy ten- to 15-minute walk from the village through the pine woods. Forest tracks lead to the more mountainous southern half of the island and the Cap d'Arme lighthouse; note that these may be closed during high winds in summer due to the fire risk. Further inland, wine buffs can hunt down the Domaine de La Courtade (04.94.58.31.44, www.lacourtade.com, open 9am-noon, 1.30-4pm Mon-Fri), an all-organic vineyard in the centre of the island.

The second island is the lush and hilly **Ile de Port-Cros**, a nature reserve where cars and smoking are forbidden. It's criss-crossed with nature paths, including one that extends under the sea: close to Fort de l'Eminence, the *sentier sous-marin* (04.94.01.40.70, www.port crosparcnational.fr) enables swimmers and divers to discover the varied marine flora.

Eighty per cent of the **Ile du Levant** is still military property, though no longer a shooting range. The remaining area, Héliopolis, is a nudist colony where participating visitors, as opposed to voyeurs, are welcome.

Where to stay & eat

On Porquerolles, **Le Mas du Langoustier** (04.94.58.30.09, www.langoustier.com, closed Oct-Apr, double €179-€264/person half board) has luxurious rooms, beautiful gardens, fabulous fish, a helipad and a snooty reputation. Guests are met at the ferry by a minibus. Most charming of the hotels in the village is the **Auberge des**

THE VAR

Glycines (22 pl d'Armes, 04.94.58.30.36, www.auberge-glycines.com, double €99-€169), with provençal-style guestrooms.

Hotel-restaurant **L'Oustaou** (pl d'Armes, 04.94.58.30.13, www.oustaou.com, closed mid Nov-Apr, double €140-€195, mains €15-€22) serves pasta or *plats du jour* like squid cooked in ink. It also has six very pretty rooms, some with sea views. For serious seafood, try **L'Arche de Noé** (04.94.58.33.71, www.arche-de-noe.com, closed Oct-Mar, double €210-€335, menus €27-€45), which has mullet, bream and crustaceans from the local waters on the menu, plus two rooms, one with a delightful terrace. On Port-Cros, hotel **Le Manoir d'Hélène** (04.94.05.90.52, closed Oct-Apr, €150-€235 half board) has white turrets and calm, beautiful rooms. The restaurant serves Mediterranean classics (mains €30-€40, menus €43-€54), including sea bass with olives and grilled squid. Among the half-dozen hotels on Le Levant, **Le Ponant** (04.94.05.90.41, www.ponant.fr, closed Oct-May, double €90) has a whacking great terrace overlooking the sea.

Ferry services

There are frequent ferries in summer, and more limited services the rest of the year. **TLV** (04.94.58.21.81, www.tlv-tvm.com) runs ferries from La Tour Fondue in Giens to Porquerolles (20mins, €16 return, €14 reductions, free under-4s) and from Hyères to Port-Cros and Levant (60-90mins, €23.50 return, €20.50 reductions, free under-4s). **Vedettes Iles d'Or** (04.94.71.01.02, www.vedettes ilesdor.fr) runs boats from Le Lavandou to Port-Cros and Levant (35-60mins, €23.50 return, €19.60 reductions, free under-4s). There are also daily services to Porquerolles and Port-Cros from Cavalaire and Le Londe, and to Porquerolles from Toulon in summer.

BORMES-LES-MIMOSAS

Set above the coast in the hills, the village of **Bormes-Les-Mimosas** is a picturesque clutter of colour-washed houses. It's also the region's gastronomic capital, with a dining scene that's unrivalled on this stunning stretch of coast. The floral handle was added to its name in 1968, highlighting the fact that Bormes had the highest density of these scented, yellow, puffball-bearing trees on the Riviera. The mimosa blooms from January to March; the rest of the year, beautifully planted terraces drip with creepers and bougainvillea.

On the edge of the old village, next to the Wednesday marketplace, the **Chapelle St-François** was built in 1560 in thanks to St François de Paule, who delivered the village

from the plague in 1481. Place Gambetta, with its cafés and restaurants, leads into the main street, rue Carnot. From here, you can wander down streets full of local artisans like ruelle du Moulin and venelle des Amoureux, or climb the 83 steps of rue Rompi Cuou. Alternatively, head for the remains of the medieval castle of the Lords of Fos (closed to the public), which has panoramic views over the Med below.

The 18th-century **Eglise St-Trophime** contains some curious polychrome wood saints' reliquaries, as well as trompe l'oeil frescoes around the choir. Further down the hill, the **Musée d'Art et d'Histoire** displays some Rodin sketches, plus local paintings and historical artefacts. Bormes's beach suburb, **La Favière**, is a modern but inoffensive low-rise development with a marina, a diving club and plenty of shops for swimwear and picnic fare. There's a long, family-oriented sandy public beach, and a market on Saturday morning – and Monday evening in July and August.

The *sentier du littoral* coast path (marked in yellow) winds round the peninsula, which also offers some of the prettiest driving terrain in the South of France. The western part of the cape is home to the small hamlet of **Cabasson**, with its fine white sand bay and the heavily guarded 16th-century Fort de Brégançon, the French president's official summer retreat.

Cap Bénat, which juts out south-west of Bormes, is one of the least built-up stretches of coast in the Midi. There are no luxury villas to be seen – just the **Château de Brégançon**, source of a robust Côtes de Provence wine (*see p36*), woods, vineyards and a number of unspoiled beaches (you pay for the car park, but entrance is free). West of Brégançon, the **plage de l'Estagnol** is a lovely sandy strip. Shaded by pine woods, it has shallow waters, a café and a good fish restaurant (*see right*).

FREE Musée d'Art et d'Histoire de Bormes

103 rue Carnot, Bormes-Les-Mimosas (04.94.71.56.60). **Open** *June-Sept* 10am-noon , 2-6.30pm Tue, Thur-Sat; 2-6.30pm Wed; 10am-noon Sun. *Oct-May* 10am-noon, 2-5.30pm Tue, Thur-Sat; 2-5.30pm Wed; 10am-noon Sun. **Admission** free.

Where to stay & eat

On summer evenings Bormes becomes one large dining room. Stylish **Restaurant La Tonnelle** (23 pl Gambetta, 04.94.71.34.84, www.la-tonnelle-bormes.com, closed lunch, menus €27-€42) is a true discovery, thanks to chef Gil Renard's inventive, accomplished cooking. Rooms at the bustling **Hôtel-Restaurant La Bellevue** (5 pl Gambetta, 04.94.71.15.15, closed mid Nov-mid Jan, double

€42-€84) are among the least expensive in town and have splendid views over the valley below. The adjoining restaurant (menus €15-€36) has hearty servings of pigeon, rabbit and local seafood. Across the street, friendly **Café Le Progrès** (No.7, 04.94.46.00.19, menus €12-€17) is a good place for a pastis or a dish of moules-frites. Occupying an impossibly beautiful location under a medieval archway, **Lou Portaou** (rue Cubert des Poètes, 04.94.64.86.37, closed Mon, Tue Oct-May, closed 10 Nov-10 Dec, menus €30-€55) offers romantic dining at its best. For more daring fare book a table at **L'Escoundudo** (2 ruelle du Moulin, 04.94.46.42.56, closed lunch, Mon Sept-May, mid Nov-mid Jan, menus €33), where fois gras is blended with mango chutney and a red wine *jus*.

High above town, all the rooms at beautiful **Le Grand Hôtel** (167 rte du Baguier, 04.94.71.23.72, www.augrandhotel.com, closed Jan, double €50-€120) have views all the way to the Iles de Hyères. Down by the sea, **Hôtel de la Plage** (rond-point de la Bienvenue, La Favière, 04.94.71.02.74, closed Oct-Mar, double €55-€79) has simple rooms with balconies and terraces.

In Cabasson, **Les Palmiers** (240 chemin du Petit Fort, 04.94.64.81.94, www.hotel-palmiers.com, closed Nov-mid Feb, double €60-€200, menus €38-€76) has direct access to the beach and is resolutely provincial but reliable; half board is obligatory from July to September. At the lively **plage de l'Estagnol** (04.94.64.71.11, closed Oct-Mar, menus €20-€50), feast on superb fish and langoustines, grilled on a wood fire, and big vats of bouillabaisse. Reserve for dinner, when you'll have the beach to yourself.

Resources

Tourist information

Office de Tourisme *1 pl Gambetta, Bormes-Les-Mimosas (04.94.01.38.38/www.bormesles mimosas.com).* **Open** *Apr-Sept* 9am-12.30pm, 2.30-6.30pm daily. *Oct-Mar* 9am-12.30pm, 2-6pm Mon-Sat.

LE LAVANDOU TO CAVALAIRE

Although its pretty old town and wide sandy beach should not be discounted, **Le Lavandou** is one of the more unprepossessing towns in the region. Once a major fishing port, tourism is now its mainstay – with cheaper prices than you'll find in neighbouring resorts. The glitzy seafront is animated at night, and there's a huge market on Thursday mornings.

From Le Lavandou to Cavalaire-sur-Mer, though, the **Corniche des Maures** follows some of the coast's most unspoiled scenery. Finest of the blissfully undeveloped silver-

sand beaches are La Fossette, Aiguebelle, Cap Nègre and the plage de Pramousquier.

The village of **Le Rayol-Canadel** is home to the fabulous **Domaine du Rayol** gardens, created in 1910 by Parisian banker Alfred Courmes, who packed the grounds with exotic plants before losing all his money in the crash of 1929. Since 1989, gardening wizard Gilles Clément has added New Zealand and Asiatic subtropical gardens. Gullies, bowers and secret paths are dotted about this jungle of green, including a *sentier sous-marin* (undersea trail) around the baie du Figuier, which has to be booked in advance. On dry land, pick up the walks leaflet, which leads you on a treasure hunt for bottlebrushes, blackboys and other unusual species. Above Le Rayol-Canadel, admire the spectacular sea views from the Col du Canadel pass, which crosses over into the heart of the Maures. The idyll comes to a halt at **Cavalaire-sur-Mer**, a built-up sprawl with a long but unglamorous beach.

★ Domaine du Rayol

av des Belges, Le Rayol-Canadel (04.98.04.44.00/ www.domainedurayol.org). **Open** 9.30am-dusk year round. **Admission** €8; reductions €5. **Credit** MC, V.

Where to stay & eat

By Le Lavandou's *grande plage*, **Hôtel l'Ilot Fleuri** (bl du Front de Mer, 04.94.71.14.82, www.lilotfleuri.fr, double €55-€94) benefits from an unhurried charm and a leafy terrace to the rear. Next to the old port, simpler **Hôtel Le Rabelais** (2 rue Rabelais, 04.94.71.00.56, www.le-rabelais.fr, closed Nov-Dec, double €50-€105) has tranquil rooms a step back from the beachside bustle. For line-caught sea bass and other monsters of the deep, hit **Le Pecheur** (quai Gabriel Péri, 04.94.71.58.01, closed Mon, Wed & Fri lunch, Nov-Feb, menu €18.50-€45).

One-time meeting place of Churchill and Cocteau, luxurious **Hôtel Les Roches** (1 av des Trois Dauphins, plage d'Aiguebelle, 04.94.71.05.07, www.hotellesroches.com, closed Jan-Mar, double €240-€1,380) now plays host to presidents and A-listers. Its terrace, spa and infinity pool look out over the sea, where the hotel speedboat is moored. A step away from here is the Michelin-starred **Restaurant Mathias Dandine** (04.94.71.15.53, www.mathiasdandine.com, mains €48-€56, menus €55-€125), where the menu changes every week and the food is justly lauded.

In Le Rayol-Canadel, the unassuming-looking **Le Maurin des Maures** (29 bd de Touring Club, 04.94.05.60.11, mains €8.50-€48, menus €23.50-€29.50) is, in fact, a highly acclaimed restaurant, where bouillabaisse needs to be

THE VAR

ordered 24 hours in advance. Try the tartare of local fish and the tuna satay. Overlooking the lovely plage de Débarquement, **Hôtel de la Plage** (6, D559, 04.98.05.61.22, www.rayol hotelplage.com, closed Nov-Jan, double €42-€97) has a sun terrace, swimming pool and simple rooms, a stone's throw from the beach. On the equally lovely plage du Pramousquier, **Akwaba Beach** (04.94.71.23.93) and **Tamaris Plage** (06.26.16.60.25, both Easter-Sept) have free beachside parking, sun loungers and a scrummy barbecue menu. Nearby **Villa du Plageron** (chemin du Plageron, 04.94.05.61.15, www.plageron.com, double €90-€150) is the sort of beachside *chambre d'hôte* that travel journalists want to keep to themselves.

Resources

Tourist information
Le Lavandou Office de Tourisme *quai Gabriel Péri, Le Lavandou (04.94.00.40.50/www. lelavandou.com).* **Open** *May-Sept* 9am-7pm daily Mon-Sat; 10am-12.30pm, 4-6.30pm Sun. *Oct-Apr* 9am-noon, 3-6pm Mon-Sat.
Le Rayol-Canadel Office de Tourisme *pl Michel Goy, Le Rayol-Canadel (04.94.05.65.69/ www.tourismevar.com).* **Open** *May-Aug* 9.30am-12.30pm, 2-7pm Mon-Sat; 9.30am-12.30pm Sun. *Sept-Apr* 9.30am-12.30pm, 2.30-5.30pm Mon-Sat.

THE MASSIF DES MAURES

Take the D41 out of Bormes to Collobrières and you'll find yourself in a surprisingly feral mountain area, with a tortuous road that zigzags up to the Col du Babaou. The heart of the Massif, dotted with remote chapels and Neolithic menhirs, can only be reached on foot. It is crossed east–west by the GR9 and GR51 footpaths and north–south by the GR90. For the less ambitious, two short waymarked discovery footpaths leave from near the Office de Tourisme in Collobrières (*see right*), which also organises themed guided walks.

Surrounded by massive chestnut trees and the cork oak trees from which cork is hewn, **Collobrières** is Provence's chestnut capital. The **Confiserie Azuréenne** (bd Général Koenig, 04.94.48.07.20) sells marrons glacés and everything imaginable made with chestnuts, including soup, tea and ice-cream. Around 1850, Collobrières was an important logging centre, and 19th-century wood barons' houses contrast with higgledy-piggledy medieval streets. A ten-minute drive east, off the D14 to Cogolin, the isolated **Chartreuse de La Verne** looms like a fortress halfway up a remote hillside. Founded by Carthusian monks in 1170, it was burned down on several occasions in the Wars of Religion, and rebuilt each time in local stone.

Join tourists from a dozen different nations in the picture-perfect *village perché* of **Grimaud**. Window boxes and pavement cafés render this former Saracen and Templar stronghold more beautiful still, while arrows mark the route around its best sights. From the ruins of the 11th-century chateau that crowns it, there are panoramic views over a starkly contrasting landscape, as the sombre Maures mountains meet the brightly coloured villas and yacht-filled bay of St-Tropez.

Reached through the cork woods north of here, **La Garde-Freinet** is a lively stopping-off point where the main street, rue St-Jacques, and place Vieille abound with bistros, *brocantes* and designer gifts, and a superb old-fashioned *quincaillerie* (hardware store). Beyond the solid 15th- to 18th-century church, rue de la Planète is the start of an energetic climb to the ruins of the abandoned original village, inhabited until the 15th century and built on the foundations of a Saracen stronghold. At the same address as the tourist office (*see right*), the **Conservatoire du Patrimoine** (04.94.43.08.57, www. conservatoiredufreinet.org, closed Mon, Sun) has displays on the fortress and local heritage.

A busy crossroads between the Maures and St-Tropez, **Cogolin** wins no prizes for beauty, but it does qualify as a real town with an economy based around the manufacture of corks, briar pipes, bamboo furniture and carpet-making (the latter introduced by Armenian immigrants in the 1920s). Its claim to fame is the invention of the *tarte tropézienne*, a sweet brioche filled with cream that's now ubiquitous throughout the region. The Tarte Tropézienne (510 av des Narcisses, 04.94.43.41.20) still prepares it according to the original recipe, patented in the 1950s by Polish baker Alexandre Micka. Also worth a peek is the 11th-century church of St-Sauveur, with a lovely 16th-century altarpiece by Hurlupin. The market is on Wednesday and Saturday mornings, plus Monday and Friday in summer.

Chartreuse de La Verne
off D214 (04.94.43.45.41). **Open** *June-Aug* 11am-6pm Mon, Wed-Sun. *Sept-May* 11am-5pm Mon, Wed-Sun. Closed Jan. **Admission** €6; €3 reductions; free under-10s. **No credit cards**.

Where to stay & eat

In Collobrières, **Hôtel-Restaurant Notre-Dame** (15 av de la Libération, 04.94.48.07.13, closed Dec-mid Feb, double €37-€43, restaurant closed Tue, menus €18-€24) is a simple *pensione* located by a stream, dishing up hearty local classics. **Villa Naïs** (1568 rte de Martegasse, 04.94.71.28.57, www.villanais.com, double €69-€86), 20km (12 miles) west of La Môle airport on the D98, is a great pit stop, with a swimming pool, *pétanque* court and provençal country cooking (menu €27). In La Garde-Freinet, **Hotel Longo Mai** (14 rte Nationale, 04.94.55.59.60, www.hotel-longomai.com, double €43-€99) oozes rustic chic, with its parquet-floored, wooden-beamed guestrooms, some with large terraces. The fine *carte* includes wild boar stew, racks of lamb and local duck. Despite its name ('merry dove'), nearby **La Colombe Joyeuse** (12 pl Vieille, 04.94.43.65.24, closed Tue, 3wks Dec & 3wks Jan, menus €16-€26) has rabbit, fish and steak tartare on the menu.

Grimaud's **Café de France** (pl Neuve, 04.94.43.20.05, closed Mon, Nov-Feb, menus €17-€68) is classic French dining at its best, nestled under a vine-covered terrace. 'Simply done' sums up nearby **Le Clem** (3 bd des Micocouliers, 04.94.43.20.19, menus €9-€18.50), with moules-frites, steaks and huge salads.

In Cogolin, the elegant hideaway of **La Maison du Monde** (63 rue Carnot, 04.94.54. 77.54, closed mid Oct-mid Mar, double €75-€185) has 12 stylish rooms, a pool and garden; rooms near the road can be noisy. On place de la République, newly renovated **Bliss** (04.94.54.15.17, www.bliss-hotel.com, closed mid Oct-Dec, double €125-€175) is all contemporary chrome and subtle lighting.

Bormes-Les-Mimosas *See p190*.

La Petite Maison (34 bd Delattre de Tassigny, 04.94.54.58.49, closed Sun, 2wks late Oct, mains €16.50-€28) is a pretty restaurant with a garden, turning out home-made terrines and classic country dishes.

Resources

Tourist information

Cogolin Office de Tourisme *pl de la République, Cogolin (04.94.55.01.10/www. cogolin-provence.com).* **Open** *July, Aug* 9am-1pm, 2-6.30pm Mon-Sat. *Sept-June* 9am-12.30pm, 2-6.30pm Mon-Fri; 9am-1pm, 2-6.30pm Sat.
Collobrières Office de Tourisme *bd Caminat, Collobrières (04.94.48.08.00/ www.collobrieres-tourisme.com).* **Open** *July, Aug* 10am-12.30pm, 3-6.30pm daily. *Sept-June* 2-6pm Mon; 10am-noon, 2-6pm Tue-Sat.
La Garde-Freinet Office de Tourisme *Chapelle St-Jean, La Garde-Freinet (04.94.43.67.41/www.lagardefreinet-tourisme.com).* **Open** *July, Aug* 9.30am-1pm, 4-6.30pm Mon-Sat; 9.30am-noon Sun. *Apr-June, Sept* 9.30am-12.30pm, 3.30-5.30pm Mon-Sat. *Oct-Mar* 9.30am-12.30pm, 2-5pm Tue-Sat.
Grimaud Office de Tourisme *1 bd des Aliziers, Grimaud (04.94.55.43.83/ www.grimaud-provence.com).* **Open** *July, Aug* 9am-12.30pm, 3-7pm Mon-Sat; 10am-1pm Sun. *Apr-June, Sept* 9am-12.30pm, 2.30-6.15pm Mon-Sat. *Oct-Mar* 9am-12.30pm, 2.15-5.30pm Mon-Sat.

GETTING THERE & AROUND

By air

Toulon/Hyères airport (04.94.00.83.83) is near to Hyères port. High-rollers fly into La Môle (04.94.54.76.40), 15km (10 miles) from St-Tropez.

By bus

Sodétrav (08.25.00.06.50, www.sodetrav.fr) operates bus services between Toulon and Hyères and from Hyères to St-Tropez, stopping at Bormes, Le Lavandou, Le Rayol-Canadol and Cavalaire-sur-Mer; there are few buses on Sun. From June to Aug, a bus connects Bormes village and the beaches at La Favière and Le Lavandou.

By car

The A570 runs into Hyères before merging with the N98 coast road, which continues to Bormes and then cuts along the south of the Massif des Maures. The D559 at Bormes follows the coast to Le Lavandou and Cavalaire-sur-Mer.

By train

Nearest mainline stations are Toulon, Draguignan-Les Arcs and St-Raphaël. Hyères is on a branch line served by several trains a day from Toulon.

THE VAR

St-Tropez

A day in the life of le jetset.

Welcome to the land of high-octane glamour, where A-list celebs arrive on Vespas and doormen don't bat an eye as the evening's fifth Lamborghini cruises on up. But behind the glitz and the €15,000 per square metre real estate, a very real town awaits, with street markets, coastal walks and world-class dining.

On the St-Tropez peninsula, the idyllic villages of **Ramatuelle** and **Gassin** perch amid verdant vineyards and parasol pine-shaded hills, while white sandy beaches (and champagne-fuelled private beach clubs) stretch along the shoreline. This is God's own country – provided He could afford it, of course.

St-Tropez

Given St-Tropez's reputation for hedonism, it's fitting that arch-hedonist Nero should have put the place on the map. In the first century AD, the emperor had a Christian centurion, Torpes, beheaded in Pisa. His headless trunk was then set adrift in a boat with a rooster and a dog. When the boat washed up on the beach that was later named after the hapless centurion, the starving dog hadn't taken so much as a nibble of the corpse – a sure sign of sainthood.

In the Middle Ages, the small fishing community at St-Tropez was harried by Saracens until the 15th century, when 21 Genoese families were imported to show the pirates who was who. The place was still a tiny backwater in 1880, when Guy de Maupassant sailed his boat in to give the locals their first taste of bohemian eccentricity.

A decade later, post-Impressionist painter Paul Signac, driven into port by a storm, fell in love with St-Tropez and promptly moved in. He opened the famed Salon des Indépendants, and invited his friends (then unknowns, including Matisse, Derain, Vlaminck and Dufy) to exhibit. Wealthy holidaying Parisians stopped by to purchase works by the up-and-coming artists, and soon began buying homes of their own.

About the author

Kathryn Tomasetti *writes on the South of France for a worldwide array of publications, including* The Observer *and BA Highlife.*

Another wave of personalities washed up in 1956 after Roger Vadim and his young protégée Brigitte Bardot arrived to make *And God Created Woman*. In no time at all, St-Tropez became the world's most famous playboy haunt.

The millionaires and superstars are still there, but not all come out to play in the high season madness, remaining bolt-holed in their luxury sea-view abodes. When they do venture out, they are often whisked to an ultra-discreet HIP (Highly Important Person) room. Bardot herself, who alternates between her house in the hills and her seafront home-cum-animal-rights-HQ at La Madrague, is unlikely to be found mooching round the market these days. Instead, star-spotters must make do with a boat tour of the headland's A-list abodes (MMG leaves from Vieux Port, Apr-Sept daily, 04.94.96.51.00).

St-Tropez is at its most bacchanalian from June to August. Once the in-crowd has moved on to its next season fixture, the village becomes more family-oriented; in winter, it's pretty much deserted. Partying is not St-Tropez's only draw: Les Voiles de St-Tropez (www.ot-saint-tropez.com) is a September yacht fest that attracts large crowds, as does Les Bravades, a huge procession paying homage to the town's patron saint, Torpes, held each May.

Sightseeing

St-Tropez is built on a slope, with all the action sliding inexorably towards the Vieux Port. Here, the super-rich wine and dine on their enormous luxury yachts, in full view of the crowded café terraces, meaning that even the most sanguine holidaymaker is trapped as a gawping spectator.

East of the Vieux Port, the **Château de Suffren** (closed to the public) dates back to 972, and is the oldest building in town. Back from the quai Jean Jaurès a myriad of little galleries line the side streets, while the place aux Herbes is home to a small but lively daily market – get there around midday to lunch on fresh oysters, sea urchins and white wine. The steep rue de la Citadelle leads to a swarm of tourist-trap restaurants and the impressively walled 17th-century **Citadelle**, perched at the top of the village and with spectacular views from its ramparts. Below here, Roger Vadim is buried in the seaside **Cimetière Marin**.

Between the Vieux Port and the Nouveau Port, the **Musée de l'Annonciade** is a superb museum of early 20th-century art, housed in a 16th-century chapel; the collection includes works by Vuillard, Bonnard, Matisse, Braque and Vlaminck. Butterfly enthusiasts should also stop by the **Maison de Papillons**, comprising over 4,500 carefully catalogued species.

Behind the Vieux Port, St-Tropez's *pétanque*-playing fraternity hangs out on plane tree-lined place des Lices. Pick up a set at **Le Café** (*see right*) and you can join in. The square is also home to a market on Tuesday and Saturday, where fruit, vegetables, charcuterie, honey and wine fill the stalls and traders exchange gossip. On the hill, a kilometre south of town, the pretty **Chapelle Ste-Anne** (open to the public only on St Anne's day, 26 July) commands glorious views over the bay and southern Alps.

La Citadelle

Mont de la Citadelle (04.94.97.59.43). **Open** *Apr-Oct* 10am-6.30pm daily. *Nov-Mar* 10am-12.30pm, 1.30-5.30pm Mon, Wed-Sun. **Admission** €2.50; free under-8s. **No credit cards.**

Maison des Papillons

9 rue Etienne Berny (04.94.97.63.45). **Open** *Apr-Oct & Christmas holidays* 2-6pm Mon-Sat. Closed Nov-Mar. **Admission** €3; free under-8s. **No credit cards**.

Musée de l'Annonciade

pl Georges Gramont (04.94.17.84.10). **Open** *June-Sept* 10am-2pm, 3-7pm daily. *Oct-May* 10am-noon, 2-6pm Mon, Wed-Sun. Closed Nov. **Admission** *June-Sept* €6; €4 reductions. *Oct-May* €4; €3 reductions; free under-12s. **No credit cards**.

Activities

Boat hire

For smaller day boats, including a six-metre Stylmer (€400/day), try **Marine Services**

(06.20.80.01.22, www.marineservices.fr) at the eastern end of St-Tropez port. **Top Charter** (04.94.56.35.39, www.top-charter.com) in Port Grimaud is better for larger options like a skippered Leopard powerboat (€5,000/day). **Marine Air Sport** (rte de le Plage, 06.07.22.43.97, www.marine-air-sport.com) offers a similar range of boats for hire, as well as jet-ski rental and waterskiing lessons.

Scooter & bicycle hire

Two wheels can be better than four when exploring St-Tropez and the surrounding hill towns. **Holiday Bikes** (14 av du Général Leclerc, 06.13.31.14.89) rents bicycles from €12 a day and scooters from €26.

Where to eat & drink

★ Banh-Hoi

12 rue Petit St-Jean (04.94.97.36.29). **Open** *Late Mar-mid Oct* 7.30-11.30pm daily. Closed mid Oct-late Mar. **Main courses** €26-€30. **Credit** AmEx, MC, V.

One of a cluster of unassuming-looking eateries along rue Petit St-Jean, this place is prized by East Asian food fanatics. Critically acclaimed creations from chef Pham Van Ut include five-spice pork brochettes and Thai-style tuna tartare.

Bar du Port

7 quai Suffren (04.94.97.00.54). **Open** 7.30am-3am daily. **Credit** MC, V.

A vision of white and chrome, Bar du Port is a top spot to watch the A-list and the mega-rich pull up in their yachts to quaff a *café crème*.

Le Café

5 pl des Lices (04.94.97.44.69/www.lecafe.fr). **Open** 8am-midnight daily. **Main courses** €17-€32. **Menus** €30-€39. **Credit** AmEx, MC, V.

The terrace outside Le Café doubles as a stadium for watching the endless *boules* matches on place des Lices. There's hearty provençal dining in the evening, but most are happy to sink a *pression* of lager and tuck into a steak tartare or *hamburger et frites*.

INSIDE TRACK
MAKE MINE A MOKE

The coolest way to get around town is by renting a classic Mini Moke (think an open-sided Mini-meets-beach-buggy, and you'll get the picture). Originally designed for the British Army, but rejected as eminently unsuitable, the Moke has become a design icon. Pick yours up at **Garage Austin** (43 rte des Plages, 04.94.54.89.07) for €105 per day.

THE VAR

Café de Paris.

Café de Paris
15 quai Suffren (04.94.97.00.56). **Open** 7am-
3am daily. **Main courses** €30-€45. **Credit**
AmEx, DC, MC, V.
An unremarkable terrace gives little indication of
the plush, romantic interior. Designed by Philippe
Starck, the sushi bar and French diner exudes glamour with its backlit white drapes, chandeliers and
red velvet banquettes. It's the place to be seen.

★ Au Caprice des Deux
*40 rue Portail Neuf (04.94.97.76.78/www.au
capricedesdeux.com)*. **Open** Mid Feb-Nov 8pm-
midnight daily. Closed Dec-mid Feb. **Main
courses** €29-€36. **Menu** €59. **Credit** AmEx,
DC, MC, V.
Contemporary French cuisine at its best, infused
with a hint of new world flavour. The beef in the
salad is piquant, the cannelloni is stuffed with crab,
and you won't find cod with truffle emulsion on
many menus in St-Tropez.

L'Escale Joseph
*9 quai Jean Jaurès (04.94.97.00.63/www.joseph-
saint-tropez.com)*. **Open** noon-3pm, 7pm-midnight
daily. **Main courses** €39-€50. **Credit** MC, V.
A portside table at L'Escale means showmanship
with style. Incredibly flashy, it epitomises St-Tropez
chic. The menu is a delight, with only the finest cuts
to suit a demanding clientele: chateaubriand beef,
monkfish cheeks and tournedos Rossini.

€ Le Gorille
*1 quai Suffren (04.94.97.03.93/www.legorille.
com)*. **Open** July, Aug 24hrs daily. Sept-Dec, Feb-
June 8am-1am daily. Closed Jan. **Main courses**
€15-€25. **No credit cards**.
A portside favourite for the past 50 years. Simple,
inexpensive dishes predominate on the blackboard
menu: think steak-frites, salade niçoise and seafood
salads. The friendly staff keep the place open 24
hours a day in summer.

Grand Joseph
*1 place de l'Hôtel du Ville (04.94.97.01.66/
www.joseph-saint-tropez.com)*. **Open** noon-3pm,
7.30pm-midnight daily. **Main courses** €40-€60.
Credit MC, V.
The Franco-Japanese eaterie is a recent addition to
the fleet of restaurants owned by the eponymous
Joseph, a character as synonymous with St-Tropez
as Rick Stein is with Cornwall's Padstow. Simple
lunch options include tuna and beef carpaccios,
with more elaborate truffle and sashimi dishes on
the evening menu.

La Ponche
*pl du Revelin (04.94.97.09.29/www.laponche.
com)*. **Open** Mid Feb-Oct noon-2.30pm, 7-11pm
daily. Closed Nov-mid Feb. **Menus** €26.50-€40.
Credit AmEx, DC, MC, V.
Nestled by the plage de la Ponche, this place serves
high-end cuisine with an innovative twist. The filet
mignon is pork, not beef, while cod arrives with
'tagliatelled' vegetables. More classic provençal
dishes find their way on to the €40 *menu gas-
tronomique*. The adjoining Hôtel La Ponche has 18
stunning rooms (04.94.97.02.53, double €155-€570).

Spoon Byblos
*av Maréchal Foch (04.94.56.68.20/www.spoon
byblos.com)*. **Open** Mid Apr-June, Sept-mid Oct 8-
11pm daily. July-Aug 8pm-12.30am daily. **Menus**
€28-€42. **Credit** AmEx, DC, MC, V.
Pretentious and pricey though it may be, Alain
Ducasse's Spoon Byblos is beloved by the glitterati.
It's a wildly successful franchise of his Parisian
enterprise, with a menu that's split in two: signature
Spoon dishes can be found on the Origin menu, with
new culinary ideas on the Spoon New carte.

Nightlife

Les Caves du Roi
*Hôtel Byblos, av Paul Signac (04.94.65.68.00/
www.lescavesduroy.com)*. **Open** Easter-May, Sept
11pm-5am Fri, Sat. June-Aug 11pm-5am daily.
Closed mid Oct-Easter. **Admission** free.
Credit AmEx, DC, MC, V.
The paparazzi-free basement club at Hôtel Byblos
is one of the Côte d'Azur's most exclusive clubs.
Virtually impossible to get into unless you arrive
early or reserve a table in advance, Les Caves du

THE VAR

Roi has hosted private evenings for such luminaries as Elton John, and so always attracts a star-studded clientele.

Le Papagayo
résidences du Nouveau Port (04.94.97.07.56).
Open *Mar-May, Sept, Oct* 11.30pm-5am Fri, Sat. *June-Aug* 11.30pm-5am daily. Closed mid Nov-Feb. **Admission** free. **Credit** AmEx, MC, V.
With its port-side location and terrace, Le Papagayo is the perfect spot for people-watching (A-listers like P Diddy and Bono have been known to stop by for a drink). Younger and more energetic than St-Trop's other nightspots, the two-floor club also stages fashion shows and all manner of late-night dance beats.
► *In need of post-partying sustenance? Head to Le Gorille (see left) for a way-past-midnight feast.*

Le VIP Room
résidences du Nouveau Port (04.94.97.14.70/ www.viproom.fr). **Open** *July-Aug* midnight-5am daily. **Admission** free. **Credit** AmEx, MC, V.
This southern outpost of Jean Roch's Champs-Elysées club is where the gilded youths who slip between Paris and St-Tropez spend their pocket money. Music is boppy and feel-good.

Shopping

Designer boutiques pop up wherever there is space in St-Tropez, but rues Allard and Gambetta are the main fashion runways. The trademark at **Atelier Rondini** (16 rue Georges Clemenceau, 04.94.97.19.55, www.rondini.fr, closed Sun in summer, Sun & Mon in winter, mid Oct-mid Nov) is *sandales tropéziennes* – strappy handmade Spartacus sandals. Grab those goodies you've seen around town at **Galeries Tropéziennes** (56 rue Gambetta, 04.94.97.02.21), whose wares include olive oil soap, funky tablewear and multicoloured espadrilles. **La Tarte Tropézienne** (pl des Lices, 04.94.97.04.69, www.tarte-tropezienne-traiteur.com) is the place to try *la tropézienne*, a sponge cake filled with custard cream. Its picnics are fit for a millionaire: chilled Nile perch, smoked salmon blinis and other delicacies.

Where to stay

If you're planning to stay in St-Tropez during high season, book at least a month in advance.

B-Lodge
23 rue de l'Aïoli (04.94.97.06.57/www.hotel-b-lodge.com). **Rates** €80-€290 double. **Rooms** 10. **Credit** MC, V.
Located at the foot of the citadel, this freshly reno-vated hotel has style in spades. Minimalist rooms feature four-poster beds, sharp lines and black and white linen. The pricier guestrooms have balconies and terraces, and are good value in low season.

★ € Le Colombier
Impasse des Conquettes (04.94.97.05.31). **Rates** €70-€165 double. **Rooms** 11. **Credit** MC, V.

Vieux Port.

THE VAR

Nikki Beach. *See p200.*

This old *bastide* has 11 charming guestrooms and a delightful flower-filled garden. A little haven, it's set on a quiet cul-de-sac backing on to place des Lices.

Hôtel Byblos
av Paul Signac (04.94.56.68.00/www.byblos.com). Closed mid Oct-mid Apr. **Rates** €410-€850 double. **Rooms** 95. **Credit** AmEx, DC, MC, V.
Opened by Brigitte Bardot in 1967, and the site of Mick Jagger's proposal to Bianca, the perennially trendy Byblos has rooms and suites that emulate a Mediterranean village. With its swimming pool, fountain-filled gardens and restaurants – including Alain Ducasse's Spoon Byblos (*see p196*) – guests in search of St-Tropez luxury won't be disappointed.

€ Hôtel Lou Cagnard
18 av Paul Roussel (04.94.97.04.24/www.hotel-lou-cagnard.com). Closed Nov-late Dec. **Rates** €52-€122 double. **Rooms** 19. **Credit** MC, V.
A superb, inexpensive little option with a leafy garden for alfresco breakfasting. The provençal-themed rooms are clean and comfortable, although the first floor can get a little stuffy in summer. A one-week minimum stay policy operates in high season.

Pan Deï Palais
52 rue Gambetta (04.94.17.71.71/www.pandei. com). **Rates** €195-€970 double. **Rooms** 12. **Credit** AmEx, DC, MC, V.
Walk through the nondescript wooden entrance to find a foyer that resembles an avant-garde gentlemen's club, with club chairs, colourful vases and Persian rugs. Rooms are effortlessly stylish (cream walls, rich woods), while the mosaic-bottomed pool is an oasis of calm.

★ Pastis
61 av du Général Leclerc (04.98.12.56.50/ www.pastis-st-tropez.com). **Rates** €200-€600 double. **Rooms** 9. **Credit** AmEx, DC, MC, V.
Petite and perfectly formed, this harbourside hotel is owned by two former designers. Its rooms are wonderfully soothing, with pleasing attention to detail (including top-quality linen and bath products). With just nine rooms, often as not you'll have the funky lobby and heated outdoor pool all to yourself.

Le Sube
15 quai Suffren (04.94.97.30.04/www.hotel-sube.com). Closed 3wks Jan. **Rates** €115-€290 double. **Rooms** 28. **Credit** AmEx, DC, MC, V.
Smack in the centre of the old port, the woody Sube is a favourite with yachties. A fire burns in winter in the chesterfield-filled bar, and regulars vie for seats on its minuscule balcony overlooking the port.

Le Yaca
1 rue Aumale (04.94.55.81.00/www.hotel-le-yaca.fr). **Rates** €225-€1,270 double. **Rooms** 27. **Credit** AmEx, DC, MC, V.

This beautiful hotel makes an immediate impact, thanks to its contemporary art-filled foyer. A tranquil swimming pool forms the central oasis of the little complex, while the provençal-meets-Moorish guestrooms will break a few hearts on departure.

Resources

Tourist information
Office de Tourisme *quai Jean Jaurès, St-Tropez (08.92.68.48.28/www.ot-saint-tropez.com).* **Open** *Apr-June, Sept, Oct* 9am-12.30pm, 2-7pm daily. *July, Aug* 9.30am-8pm daily. *Nov* 9.30am-noon, 2-6pm Mon-Sat; 2-6pm Sun. *Dec-Mar* 9.30am-noon, 2-6pm daily.

ST-TROPEZ PENINSULA

Dotted with parasol pines and vineyards, with views down to pristine blue coves, the hills above town seem a world away from the chaos of the port. When the truly chic or truly rich airily talk about summering in St-Trop, often as not they actually mean hiding out in the hill villages in Garbo-esque seclusion, well away from the wannabees who frequent the old port.

Ramatuelle began life as a Saracen stronghold; razed in 1592 during the Wars of Religion, it was rebuilt in 1620. It still has a fortified feel, as tightly knit houses climb snail-like around the hill. A gateway by the church leads through to the partly pedestrianised old town, filled with leafy squares, olive oil shops and galleries. The street market on Thursdays and Sundays makes a popular day trip from St-Tropez, and it's packed out during its jazz and theatre festivals in July and August (*see p46*).

Ramatuelle is also just a short distance away from the **plage de Pampelonne** – five kilometres of sand, popular with the glitterati and naturist bathers alike. Among the chichi beach clubs, the famed **Club 55** (*see p200* **Join the Club**) was Brigitte Bardot's venue of choice to celebrate her retirement from films in 1974.

INSIDE TRACK
STORMING THE BEACHES

As you survey the sunworshippers basking in the heat and nubile lovelies cavorting in the shallows at St-Tropez's beaches, it's hard to imagine that soldiers once marched across these sands. In August 1944, though, this stretch of coast was one of the main Allied landing sites in **Operation Dragoon** (*see p22*) – a combined effort between Allied and French troops that led to the liberation of Cannes, Marseille and Toulon.

THE VAR

Join the Club

In a stretch awash with beach bar bacchanalia, here's where to head.

Each morning in summer, an armada of mega-yachts set off from their €50,000 per week berths in St-Tropez: arriving on a chartered Sunseeker is leagues cooler than parking up behind the plage de Pampellone's colourful cabanas. The shoreline here is lined with beach clubs, some purveying such rampant excess that even a Rolling Stone might blink with incredulity.

While some may find the sight of banking scions, Saudi princes and Ukrainian oligarchs running up €25,000 tabs in Krug champagne a tad excessive, for others it's a sure sign that it's party time. For a mere mortal to nuzzle into this world of fake boobs, booze and billionaires, it's best to act nonchalant but friendly. Arrive with a big smile, even bigger sunglasses and a very deep suntan.

A celeb-tastic experience necessitates your blacked-out AmEx card and a day at **Club 55** (04.94.55.55.55, www.leclub 55.com, sun lounger €17/day). It's the glammest club on the strip, so go for slinky, skin-hugging D&G rather than anything gypsy or boho. Paris Hilton and Bono have been known to soak up the elegant yet extravagant atmosphere.

A five-minute cut inland, **Nikki Beach** (04.94.79.82.04, www.nikkibeach.com, sun lounger €30/day) is a champagne-swigging hotspot for the young and beautiful. Board shorts are the thing here (lunchbox trunks are *so* passé). Disco music pounds all day long as the designer-clad euro crowd, who spend their winters at the original Nikki Beach in Miami, test out their best chat-up lines.

The birthplace of topless sunbathing, **La Voile Rouge** (04.94.79.84.34, sun lounger €25/day) is truly bacchanalian. If your idea of naughtiness is buying your partner a pair of sexy knickers, you'll be in for a wide-eyed wake-up call at this cocktail-fuelled, semi-naked orgy of a beach bar. Strip down and try not to gawp: expect your field of vision to include sights like string-clad beauties licking champagne off the odd (older) tummy.

Neptune Plage (04.94.79.81.52, www.plageneptune.com, sun lounger €25-€40/day) is one of Pampellone's top naturist beach clubs. It remains ever popular with an all-ages crowd, eating, sunbathing and playing beach tennis as naked as nature intended. The public stretch of sand to the south is like a Spencer Tunick art installation.

Further down is **Tikki Hutte** (*see p201*), with its rows of beachside cabanas. Although not a beach club as such, the complex has inexpensive bars and eateries that stay open in the evening, when the rest of plage de Pampelonne drifts back to St-Tropez central. This stretch is also a popular haunt for the metal-detecting fraternity, who appear at sundown in search of buried coins, lost engagement rings and a Swiss timepiece or two.

On the beach's southern shores, **Aqua Club** (04.94.79.84.35, www.aqua-club.fr, sun lounger from €16/day) is effortlessly chilled. Frequented by St-Trop locals and more discreet A-listers, kids aren't banned and boob jobs are restrained. Sport a pair of washed-out *Baywatch* boxers or a sun-bleached T-shirt to fit in with the regulars.

Nikki Beach.

Smaller **Gassin**, where Mick and Bianca Jagger honeymooned in the '70s, offers an incredible 360° view of the entire peninsula. Squeezing through ancient streets to its medieval fortress and church, it's easy to understand why Gassin has been named one of France's most beautiful villages. Surrounding vineyards all offer complimentary tastings – **Château Minuty** (04.94.56.12.09), with its chapel and Napoleon III-era mansion to nose around, is particularly recommended.

Slightly back from the coast, **La Croix-Valmer** is a residential town with fine views across cliffs dotted with the holiday villas of well-heeled French families. From here, there's easy access to the lovely plage de Gigaro and stunning coastal conservation area on the Cap Lardier. The golden sand beaches in the area are a world away from the hoi polloi of plage de Pampelonne, while coastal paths lead around the entire cape all the way back to St-Tropez.

Where to stay & eat

Heading out of Ramatuelle, 500 metres from Pampelonne beach, Christophe Leroy's **Les Moulins** (rte des Plages, 04.94.97.91.91, www.christophe-leroy.com, closed Oct-late April, double €140-€345, mains €28-€38) is a country inn with five cottage-type rooms. The provençal restaurant blends a few Thai and tempura dishes into the mix. **Les Girelles** (18 bd Patch, 04.94.79.86.69, closed mid Oct-Easter, double €69-€136) is a stone's throw from the shoreline, with a tranquil garden to the rear. Book ahead, as beach bums often reserve its 14 rooms months in advance.

To get even closer to the sea, book into one of the deluxe beachside cabanas at **Tikki Hutte** (plage de Pampelonne, 04.94.55.96.96, www.tiki-hutte.com, closed Nov-mid Mar, double €50-€355), where there's a one-week minimum stay.

La Villa Marie (chemin Val Rian, rte des Plages, 04.94.97.40.22, www.villamarie.fr, closed Oct-Apr, double €450-€790) is a glorious countryside retreat, with its own spa and lush, cypress-dotted gardens. The dining terrace looks out towards the distant plage de Pampelonne; after platters of lobster and Alaskan pincer crab claws, the Villa Marie's 4x4 can shuttle non-residents the four kilometres back to place des Lices.

In Ramatuelle, the vine-covered terrace of **Café de l'Ormeau** (pl de l'Ormeau, 04.94.79.20.20) is a superb spot to sit and soak up local life; next door, the **Cigalon** (04.94.79.21.08, closed Oct-Easter, menus €14-€31) is great for crêpes and cider. On rue Victor Léon, **La Forge** (04.94.79.25.56, closed Wed, Nov-mid Mar, menu €38) plies a gastronomic take on classic local cuisine. Far more low-key

is locals' joint **Chez Tony** (av Georges Clemenceau, 04.94.79.20.46), which also has the cheapest rooms in town (double €50-€65). Perched just below town, **Hostellerie Le Baou** (av Gustave Etienne, 04.98.12.94.20, closed mid Oct-Apr, double €195-€410) has spectacular views across the peninsula.

In Gassin, **Le Micocoulier** (pl des Barrys, 04.94.56.14.01, www.lemicocoulier.com, mid Oct-Apr, menu €29) and the **Bello Visto** (04.94.56.17.30, www.bellovisto.eu, closed Tue & Fri lunch, Nov-Feb, mains €26-€64) both serve up excellent traditional cuisine. The latter also has nine pretty rooms (double €60-€95).

The 19th-century **Château de Valmer** (rte de Gigaro, 04.94.55.15.15, www.chateau-valmer.com, closed mid Oct-mid Apr, double €190-€490), south-east of La Croix-Valmer, offers pure escapism. The pool is set amid vines and fruit trees, while a palm-lined path leads to the private beach, shared with sister hotel **La Pinède Plage** (04.94.55.16.16, www.pinede-plage.com, closed Oct-Apr, double €190-€470). The latter has a fine seafood restaurant looking out over the Med (mains €20-€60). At the end of the beach road, **Le Refuge** (04.94.54.28.97, closed mid Nov-Jan, double €60-€90) must rank among the world's best-placed *chambres d'hôtes*, but soon gets booked up. A higher-end B&B is the **3 Iles** (04.94.49.03.73, www.3iles.com, closed Nov-mid Mar, double €150-€230).

Resources

Tourist information

La Croix-Valmer Office de Tourisme
*esplanade de la Gare, La Croix-Valmer
(04.94.55.12.12/www.lacroixvalmer.fr).* **Open**
Mid June-Sept 9.30am-12.30pm, 2.30-7pm Mon-
Sat; 9.15am-1.30pm Sun. *Oct-mid June* 9am-noon,
2-6pm Mon-Fri; 9.15am-noon Sat, Sun.
Ramatuelle Office de Tourisme *pl de
l'Ormeau, Ramatuelle (04.98.12.64.00/www.
ramatuelle-tourisme.com).* **Open** *July-Aug* 9am-
1pm, 3-7.30pm daily. *May, June, Sept-mid Oct*
9am-1pm, 3-7pm Mon-Sat. *Mid Oct-Apr* 9am-
12.30pm, 2-6pm Mon-Fri.

PORT GRIMAUD & STE-MAXIME

In the bay west of St-Tropez, **Port Grimaud**
was designed in the late 1960s to look like a
miniature slice of the Venice lagoon. It's kitschly
pretty – and wonderfully surreal. Visitors must
park their cars and take in the watery lanes of
townhouses on foot or by boat. Kids will love
the electric boats that can be hired for a putter
around (cheekily, they are €25 per hour by the
car park, €20 per hour inside the city walls).

Ste-Maxime has lost the allure it exuded in
1930s posters, but is not without charm. Its
wide walkways and clean sandy beaches appeal
to families, and it's also an excellent base for
those who can't afford the rates in St-Tropez
or the Iles des Hyères: boats run by **Bateaux
Verts** (*see right*) serve both destinations for
€12 return and €20 return respectively. You
can also pick up one of 20 finely restored 2CVs
at **Escapa Deuche** (46 av Berthie Albrecht,
06.15.77.67.57, www.escapadeuche.com,
€200/day) and arrive in St-Tropez in style.

Where to stay, eat & drink

In Port Grimaud, the luxurious **Giraglia** (pl du
14 Juin, 04.94.56.31.33, www.hotelgiraglia.com,
closed Nov-Apr, double €275-€410) has a pool,
and a garden that's perfect for watching the
sunset over St-Tropez. **Hôtel Suffren** (16 pl du
Marché, 04.94.55.15.05, www.hotelleriedusoleil.
com, closed mid Nov-Mar, double €95-€250) has
balconies over the canals. For waterfront dining,
try **Le Bistroquet** (2 rue des Deux Ports,
04.94.56.42.77, closed Tue, menu €18).

The seafront at Ste-Maxime is lined with
brasseries and ice-cream parlours. The menu at
L'Hermitage (118 av de Gaulle, 04.94.96.04.05,
closed 2wks Jan, mains €20-€30) is a departure
from the norm, with swordfish carpaccio and
duck with peaches. Its owner also runs the new
Hôtel La Plage (36 av Général Touzet du
Vigier, 04.94.96.14.01, www.hotel-la-plage.fr,

double €65-€160) down the coast at Nartelle.
West of the centre, **Mas des Oliviers** (quartier
de la Croisette, 04.94.96.13.31, www.hotellemas
desoliviers.com, double €57-€160) has 20 rooms
plus studio apartments to let on a weekly basis,
as well as a pool, tennis courts and well-tended
grounds. By the golf club, **Hôtel le Beauvallon**
(bd des Collines, Ste-Maxime, 04.94.55.78.88,
www.lebeauvallon.com, closed Nov-mid Apr,
double €210-€560) is a plush establishment
where guests can lounge on the private beach,
gaze out from the infinity pool or whizz into
St-Tropez on the private speedboat. It has two
restaurants: **Les Colonnades** (menus €65-€85)
and a beachfront eaterie (mains €35-€65).

Resources

Tourist information

Port Grimaud Office de Tourisme *1 bd
Aliziers, Port Grimaud (04.94.55.43.83/www.
grimaud-provence.com).* **Open** *June-Sept* 9am-
12.30pm, 3-7pm Mon-Sat; 10am-1pm Sun. Closed
Oct-May.
Ste-Maxime Office de Tourisme
*promenade Simon Lorière, Ste-Maxime
(04.94.55.75.55/www.ste-maxime.com).* **Open**
9am-12.30pm, 2.30-7pm Mon-Sat; 10am-noon,
4-7pm Sun.

GETTING THERE & AROUND

By air
Private jets land on the Le Môle airstrip, 35km
(21 miles) from the Massif des Maures.

By boat
Les Bateaux Verts (04.94.49.29.39, www.
bateauxverts.com) runs hourly boat services
from Ste-Maxime to St-Tropez from Feb to Oct,
and every 20 minutes at peak times. **Trans
Côte d'Azur** (www.trans-cote-azur.com) has
daily summer departures from both Nice
(04.92.00.42.30) and Cannes (04.92.98.71.30).

By bus
Sodétrav (08.25.00.06.50, www.sodetrav.fr) runs
daily buses between St-Tropez and Toulon via
Hyères. There are four services a day between St-
Tropez, Ramatuelle and Gassin in July and Aug
and on Thur, Sat and Sun in Sept and June, and
daily services between St-Tropez and St-Raphaël,
via Grimaud, Cogolin and Ste-Maxime.

By car
Sweat it out on the N98 coast road. Ramatuelle is
on the D61 south of St-Tropez; for Gassin take
one of the signposted roads off the D61 or D559.
Ste-Maxime is on the D98 coast road or by A8
exit 36 and D25.

THE VAR

St-Raphaël & the Estérel

Affordable prices draw the seaside crowd to this sunny coastal stretch.

A sprawling resort town, anchored by a casino and a busy port, **St-Raphaël** is a major sailing centre. It was once the stomping ground of the fashionable set, as its grand hotels attest, but now it's just a friendly, affordable resort, geared more towards families than extravagant jet-setters.

The small town of **Fréjus** to the north is more interesting, boasting some of the most stunning Roman remains in France, while to the east the red volcanic rock of the **Massif de l'Estérel** looms over the deep blue sea.

ST-RAPHAEL

St-Raph, as the locals call it, is most famous for its five golf courses and Casino, where perma-tanned gents and leopardprint-clad ladies try their hand at blackjack or feed the slot machines. Back in 1799 it proved to be a lucky stop for a bedraggled Napoleon, who landed here after defeat in Egypt at the hands of the British; his arrival is commemorated by an Egyptian-style pyramid on avenue Commandant Guilbaud. But it fell to journalist Alphonse Karr (1808-90), exiled to Nice for his opposition to Napoleon III, to sort out the resort's PR: 'Leave Paris and plant your stick in my garden,' he wrote to a friend in 1864, 'next morning, when you wake, you will see it has grown roses.' Writers, artists and composers heeded the invitation, with Dumas, Maupassant and Berlioz among those who came here.

Following Karr's lead, the town's mayor, Félix Martin, transformed the village into a smart getaway. Illustrious guests found it an inspiring spot: Gounod composed *Romeo and Juliet* here in 1869, Scott Fitzgerald wrote *Tender is the Night*, and Félix Ziem painted. Following the 1920s craze for diving (Zelda, Fitzgerald's wife, used to dive drunk from the cliffs of their nearby hideaway), St-Raphaël gave birth to France's first dedicated sub-aqua club. A plethora of diving clubs remain; of the diving schools, try **Europlage** (port de Boulouris, rte de la Corniche, 04.94.19.03.26, www.europlage.fr, €50/half-day).

Despite its illustrious past, St-Raphaël can't compete with the other, more glamorous towns on the coast. The medieval and belle époque centre was largely destroyed by wartime bombing, bar a few old streets around the covered market on place de la République, and it simply lacks atmosphere; the jungle of neon around its outskirts certainly doesn't help.

Worth a visit, however, is the 12th-century church of St-Pierre-des-Templiers, which doubled up as a fortress against pirate attacks. It's home to a gilded wooden bust of St Peter, carried by fishermen in a torchlit procession to the Vieux Port on the first Sunday in August.

Next door, beside the remains of the Roman aqueduct, the **Musée Archéologique** has artefacts from the harbour, plus a display on underwater archaeology. If you dodge the in-line skaters, promenade René Coty offers a fine view of the sea and the twin rocks known as the Land Lion and the Sea Lion. The promenade, opened by Félix Martin in 1882, marked the beginning of St-Raphaël's tourist heyday; other remnants of the era include the Casino, the Hôtel Excelsior (built by the same architect, Pierre Aublé) and the 1914 Résidence Le Méditerranée. Modern-day St-Raphaëlites can be found at the daily food market; there's also an arts and crafts market on summer afternoons.

FREE Musée Archéologique

pl de la Vieille Eglise (04.94.19.25.75). **Open** *June-Sept* 10am-12.30pm, 2.30-7pm Tue, Wed, Fri-Sun; 10am-12.30pm, 2.30-9pm Thur. *Oct-May* 10am-12.30pm, 2.30-5.30pm Tue-Sat. **Admission** free. **No credit cards**.

Where to stay & eat

The **Excelsior** (193 bd Félix Martin, 04.94.95.02.42, www.excelsior-hotel.com, double €135-€170) is a seafront belle époque hotel with 34 smart but impersonal rooms and friendly staff. For longer stays, **Le Méditerranée** (1 av Paul Doumer, 04.94.82.10.99, www.le mediterranee.fr, double €315-€658/wk) is a large Victorian building divided up into airy apartments with their own kitchenettes. **Le Continental** (04.94.83.87.87, www.hotel-continental.com, double €150) is 150 metres from the port, and has comfortable, if rather floral, rooms. **La Thimothée** (375 bd Christian Lafon, 04.94.40.49.49, double €55-€75), in a residential area to the east of town, provides quiet, good-value accommodation. It has a pool and 12 rooms, two with sea views.

In the centre of town, **Le Jardin des Arènes** (31 av du Général Leclerc, 04.94.95.06.34, double €33-€51) is a charming place with stained-glass windows in the stairwell, a garden and very helpful staff. **Les Amandiers** (874 bd Alphonse Juin, 04.94.19.85.30, www.les-amandiers.com, double €35-€76) is an elegant building close to the marina with great views. Finally, the **Hotel San Pedro** (04.94.19.90.20, www.hotelsanpedro.fr, double €118-€160) is a charming country house with a large pool and a good restaurant.

Some of the best bouillabaisse on the coast can be found at **L'Arbousier** (6 av de Valescure, 04.94.95.25.00, www.arbousier.net, closed Mon, Tue, late Dec-mid Jan, menus €30-€59), where Philippe Troncy is one of St-Raphaël's most innovative chefs.

Resources

Tourist information

Office de Tourisme *210 rue Waldeck Rousseau, St-Raphaël (04.94.19.52.52/www.saint-raphael.com).* **Open** *July-Aug* 9am-7pm daily. *Sept-June* 9am-12.30pm, 2-6.30pm Mon-Sat.

FRÉJUS & ROQUEBRUNE-SUR-ARGENS

Having battled through the infernal traffic system to arrive at **Fréjus Plage**, you may end up wondering whether you ever actually left St-Raphaël. Don't despair: the Roman town up above is worth the effort. Founded as Forum Julii

by Julius Caesar in 49 BC, Fréjus became one of the most important naval bases in the Roman world – home to Augustus's swift-sailing galleys, which defeated Antony and Cleopatra at Actium in 31 BC. The harbour was guarded by two large towers; one, the Lanterne d'Auguste, still rises high on the site of the old port. But the town isn't just a living museum: with its ochre- and apricot-painted houses and squares draped with hanging baskets, it's also a pleasant place to while away an afternoon on a café terrace.

It takes the best part of a day to see the scattered Roman remains of Fréjus. Most impressive is the **Amphithéâtre Romain**, which still seats up to 10,000 for bullfights and plays. On the other side of the station, around the port, the Butte St-Antoine mound formed a western citadel; it has a tower that was probably a lighthouse. The Platforme, its counterpart on the east, served as military headquarters. Further north, the **Théâtre Romain** (rue du Théâtre Romain, 04.94.53.58.75) holds summer concerts.

Fréjus is also blessed with the unusual fortified **Cité Episcopale**, which contains a fascinating 15th-century bestiary painted on the ceiling of its two-tier, 13th-century cloisters. The carved doors at the entrance show Mary and Saints Peter and Paul amid scenes of Saracen butchery. Opposite is the fifth-century baptistery, where excavations have uncovered the original white marble pavement and pool. Upstairs, the **Musée Archéologique** has some outstanding Gallo-Roman antiquities recovered from digs at Fréjus. Emphasising that Fréjus is also a provençal town, the **Musée d'Histoire Locale et des Traditions** concentrates on artisan traditions and events such as the *bravade* bull run and grape harvest. Bringing things more up to date, the Port Fréjus yachting harbour opened in 1989 and is home to numerous restaurants and bars.

A kilometre north-east of Fréjus, the **Villa Aurélienne** (rte de Cannes, 04.94.53.11.30), a Palladian house in 22 hectares (54 acres) of gardens, hosts occasional photographic exhibitions. Further north, two surprising constructions evoke France's colonial past. On the N7 the **Pagode Bouddhique Hông Hiên** (13 rue Henri Giraud, 04.94.53.25.29, admission €2) is a Buddhist pagoda with an exotic garden and a collection of sacred animals and guardian spirits. Nearby, a war memorial rises above the graves of over 24,000 soldiers and civilians who died in Indochina. Jutting out amid pine woods stands the Mosquée de Missiri, a replica of the celebrated Missiri de Djenné mosque in Mali.

At **La Tour de Mare**, five kilometres north of Fréjus on the interior road to Cannes (RN7), is a curiosity of particular interest to art fans. Deep in a forest that enhances its mystical appeal, uniting nature and arcane symbolism, the **Chapelle Notre-Dame-de-Jérusalem** was designed by Jean Cocteau in 1961 as part of a proposed artist's colony that never took off. The octagonal chapel, built around an atrium (now glassed-in), incorporates the mythology of the First Crusade in its stained glass, floor tiles and frescoes. In the painting of the apostles above the main door, you might be able to pick out Coco Chanel, poet Max Jacob and Cocteau's lover, actor Jean Marais.

North-west of Fréjus, **Roquebrune-sur-Argens** is perched on a rocky peak at the foot of the Rocher de Roquebrune. Originally a stronghold, the *castrum*, located near the church, was once surrounded by a curtain wall (traces are still visible in boulevard de la Liberté) destroyed in the Wars of Religion in 1592. Tuesday and Friday are market days here.

The first left fork on the D7 north of town leads to the red sandstone **Rocher de Roquebrune**. At the summit stand three crosses that were made by the sculptor Bernar Veanet. Using the summit to symbolise Golgotha, Veanet's works recall crucifixions painted by Giotto, Grünewald and El Greco. Take the marked trail and (after a solid two-hour hike uphill) expect breathtaking views.

Amphithéâtre Romain

rue Henri Vadon (04.94.51.34.31). **Open** *Apr-Oct* 9.30am-12.30pm, 2-5.45pm Tue-Sun. *Nov-Mar* 9.30am-12.30pm, 2-4.45pm Tue-Sun. **Admission** €2. **No credit cards**.

Chapelle Notre-Dame-de-Jérusalem

av Nicolaï, La Tour de Mare (04.94.53.27.06). **Open** *May-Oct* 9.30am-12.30pm, 2-6pm Tue-Sun. *Nov-Apr* 9.30am-12.30pm, 2-5pm Tue-Sun. **Admission** €2. **No credit cards**.

▶ *Villefranche is home to another chapel by Cocteau, where his lively frescoes depict the life of St Peter; see p273.*

Cité Episcopale

58 rue de Fleury (04.94.51.26.30). **Open** *June-Sept* 9am-6.30pm daily. *Oct-May* 9am-noon, 2-5pm Tue-Sun. **Admission** €4.60; €3.10-€4.10 reductions; free under-18s. **No credit cards**.

Musée Archéologique

pl Calvini (04.94.52.15.78). **Open** *May-Oct* 9.30am-12.30pm, 2-6pm Tue-Sun. *Nov-Apr* 9.30am-12.30pm, 2-5pm Tue-Sun. **Admission** €2. **No credit cards**.

Musée d'Histoire Locale et des Traditions

153 rue Jean Jaurès (04.94.51.64.01). **Open** *Apr-Oct* 9.30am-12.30pm, 2-6pm Tue-Sun. *Nov-Mar* 9.30am-12.30pm, 2-5pm Tue-Sun. **Admission** €2. **No credit cards**.

Where to stay & eat

Inexpensive and superbly set in the heart of the old town, **Hôtel le Flore** (35 rue Grisolle, 04.94.51.38.35, www.hotelleflore.com, double

THE VAR

Amphithéâtre Romain.

€90) is a beautifully renovated private home. Another old town option is the **Aréna** (145 rue Général de Gaulle, 04.94.17.09.40, www.arena-hotel.com, double €80-€140), which offers a warm welcome, a garden and a pool; its restaurant (closed lunch Mon & Sat, menus €38-€58) serves the best provençal cuisine in Fréjus. **Hotel Cap Riviera** (3022 av de la Corniche, 04.94.81.21.42, www.frejus-hotel.com, closed Nov-Feb, double €52-€120) has charming sea- or garden-view rooms in a renovated family estate. The **Bellevue** (pl Paul Vernet, 04.94.17.12.20, double €55) is cheaper, with smallish rooms but good views over the square. Down on the beach is the modern, friendly **Sable et Soleil** (158 rue Paul Arène, 04.94.51.08.70, double €48-€60). Just outside Fréjus, **Hotel l'Estirado des Adrets** (Le Logis de Paris, Les Adrets, 04.94.40.90.64, www.estirado.com, closed Nov-Mar, double €72-€92) has airy, nicely decorated rooms and a cheery welcome.

Fresh pasta and crispy salads, steak-frites or home-made foie gras are just some of the choices at the centrally located restaurant **Les Micocouliers** (34 pl Albert Fevrier, 04.94.52.16.52, menus €17.80-€26.50). **La Cave Romaine** (114 rue Camelin, 04.94.51.52.03, closed lunch & Tue, menus €15-€30) serves pasta, pizza, grilled meat and fish. Hidden down a backstreet, tiny **Les Potiers** (135 rue des Potiers, 04.94.51.33.74, closed Tue Sept-June, 1wk Jan or Feb, menus €22.50-€33) benefits from the personal touch, courtesy of chef Richard François and his wife. Expect foie gras, the tenderest lamb and beef, and subtle desserts; the set menus are superb value. The **Bar du Marché** (5 pl de la Liberté, 04.94.51.29.09) offers a filling €9 *plat du jour*.

In Roquebrune-sur-Argens, **Les Templiers** (3 pl Alfred Perrin, 04.94.45.12.52, closed Mon, Sun, menus €15-€22) offers traditional French food; the *île flottante* (meringue on a sea of custard) is worth every guilty calorie.

Resources

For €8 you can buy a seven-day pass that grants you entry to five Fréjus attractions (excluding the Cité Episcopale).

Tourist information

Fréjus Office de Tourisme *325 rue Jean Jaurès, Fréjus (04.94.51.83.83/www.ville-frejus.fr).* **Open** *Apr-Aug* 9am-12.30pm, 2-7pm daily. *Sept-Mar* 9am-noon, 2-6pm Mon-Sat.
Roquebrune Office de Tourisme *rue Jean Aicard, Roquebrune-sur-Argens (04.94.45.72.70/www.ville-roquebrune-argens.fr).* **Open** *Apr-Sept* 9am-noon, 2-6pm Mon-Sat; 9am-noon Sun. *Oct-Mar* 9am-noon, 2-6pm Mon-Fri.

THE CORNICHE DE L'ESTEREL

The Corniche de l'Estérel (or, more prosaically, the RN98) will leave you breathless, thanks to its astonishing coastal views and terrifying hairpin bends. It's anybody's guess how the Touring Club de France got their jalopies along it when they opened the road a century ago.

Just out of St-Raphaël at **Boulouris** there are some pleasant beaches, but drive on to the **Pointe du Dramont**, ten kilometres east. In 1897 Auguste Lutaud bought the tiny Ile d'Or, just off the point. After building a four-storey mock-medieval tower he proclaimed himself King, Auguste I of the Ile d'Or and threw some of the wildest parties on the Côte. The plage du Dramont is famous as the strip of sand where the 36th Division of the US Army landed on 15 August 1944 (*see p23*). For a great view, take the signposted, one-hour walk up to the Sémaphore du Dramont. Another path descends to the port of **Agay**, a family resort with a sandy beach shadowed by the slopes of the Rastel d'Agay. The daredevil author of *Le Petit Prince*, Antoine de St-Exupéry, crashed his plane just around the bay in World War II.

The beach of **Anthéor** is dominated by the Plateau d'Anthéor, from which a path leads up to the Rocher de St-Barthélémy. Climbing to the Cap Roux peak is about a two-hour round trip. Further along the coast road, the Pointe de l'Observatoire offers views over the crags. Steep paths descend through the vegetation to secluded coves. It's blissful, but swimming can be dangerous when the tide is high.

Le Trayas has a pleasant, modest beach. The bay of La Figueirette, reached from the harbour of **Miramar**, was a tuna-fishing centre in the 17th century and has the ruins of a lookout tower. As you approach Miramar be prepared for a double-take when you see, perched high on the cliffs, Pierre Cardin's Le Palais Bulles, a James Bond villain's shag-pad that is open to the public for a jazz and theatre festival in July and early August. The views from the coast road at this point are among the most stunning of the Côte d'Azur, as you wind into **La Galère** and **Théoule-sur-Mer**, a friendly seaside town with some great fish restaurants and a Friday market. From here you can follow walking and mountain-biking trails up to the church of Notre-Dame-d'Afrique, a place of pilgrimage for the *pieds noirs*.

The chief curiosity at **Mandelieu-La Napoule** is the **Fondation Henry Clews** (Château de la Napoule, av Henry Clews, 04.93.49.95.05, www.chateau-lanapoule.com, tours Feb-Oct 11.30am, 2.30pm, 3.30pm, 5.30pm; Nov-Jan 2.30pm, 3.30pm, €6), a pseudo-medieval folly conjured out of the ruins of a Saracen

THE VAR

castle in 1917 by Henry Clews, a failed Wall Street banker-turned-sculptor. Today, it hosts artists' residencies and workshops. There's a market on Thursday and Saturday, and **L'Oasis** (*see below*) draws gastronomes, but the town is a bit of a downmarket Cannes, filled with yachting boors and retirement homes.

Where to stay & eat

Overlooking the Ile d'Or, near Agay, the isolated **Sol et Mar** (rte Corniche d'Or, 04.94.95.25.60, closed mid Oct-early Feb, double €95-€149, menus €30-€37) has large rooms, a saltwater pool and a provençal restaurant. At the straightforward **Hotel le Relais d'Agay** (bd de la Plage, 04.94.82.78.20, www.relaisd agay.com, double €47-€82), most of the rooms have beachfront views. Neighbouring **Hôtel Le Lido** (bd de la Plage, 04.94.82.01.59, www.lido agay.com, closed end Oct-Feb, double €70-€95) has a private beach and friendly service. With most rooms looking over the sea and a generous breakfast buffet, the **Beau Site Hotel** (1801 bd de la 36eme Division du Texas, 04.94.82.00.45, www.hotel-lebeausite.com, double €75-€150) is a lovely place to spend a few nights.

The enchanting **Relais des Calanques** (rte des Escales, 04.94.44.14.06, double €80-€120) near Le Trayas has clifftop gardens, a pool, a diving creek and a restaurant (closed Tue & Oct-Mar, *plat du jour* €15). **Le Trayas Youth Hostel** (9 av de la Véronèse, 04.93.75. 40.23, www.fuaj.org, closed Jan-mid Feb, rates €11.50/person) is two kilometres up the hill, with rooms for four to eight. Down in Port Miramar's marina, **La Marine** (04.93.75.49.30, closed Oct-Mar, menus €25-€50) is a fine fish restaurant with a lively bar. Pricier, but worth it for an Asian take on Mediterranean cuisine, is the **Etoile des Mers** at the **Miramar Beach Hôtel** (47 av de Miramar, 04.93.75. 05.05, www.mbhriviera.com, double €155-€265, menus €37-€82).

Further along the coast road, **La Tour de l'Esquillon** (Miramar, Théoule, 04.93.75.41.51, closed Nov-Mar, double €120-€140, menu €34), a 1920s hotel with marvellous views, recalls the era of Scott and Zelda. Théoule has plenty of tasty eating options, including fish restaurant **Le Marco Polo** (av de Lérins, 04.93.49.96.59, closed Mon Sept-June, menus €30) and **Nino's** (6 chemin Débarcadère, 04.92.97.61.11, closed Oct-Mar, mains €25-€50), where you can sit on the dock directly over the water and eat mouth-wateringly good wood-fired pizza.

In Mandelieu-La Napoule, **L'Ermitage du Riou** (av Henry Clews, 04.93.49.95.56, www.ermitage-du-riou.fr, closed Jan, double €126-€192, menus €39-€85) is a smart hotel with a private beach, pool and a good, highly atmospheric restaurant. At **L'Oasis** (rue Jean-Honoré Carle, 04.93.49.95.52, www.oasis-raimbault.com, closed 2wks Feb, Mon & dinner Sun mid Oct-Jan, menus €58-€115), splash out on Stéphane and François Raimbault's fine classical cooking and sumptuous desserts. A simpler option, **Boucanier** (port de Mandelieu, 04.93.49.80.51, www.boucanier.fr, menu €32), is down by the port; it's very French, very relaxed and serves great food.

Resources

Tourist information

Agay Office de Tourisme *pl Giannetti, Agay (04.94.82.01.85/www.esd-fr.com/agay).* **Open** *Apr-mid June* 9am-noon, 2-6pm Mon-Sat. *Mid June-Sept* 9am-8pm Mon-Sat. *Oct-Mar* 9am-noon, 2-5pm Mon-Fri.

Mandelieu Office de Tourisme *av Henry Clews, Mandelieu-La Napoule (04.93.49.95.31/ www.ot-mandelieu.fr).* **Open** *July, Aug* 10am-12.30pm, 2-7pm daily. *Sept-June* 10am-12.30pm, 2-6pm Mon-Fri.

Théoule Office de Tourisme *1 Corniche d'Or, Théoule-sur-Mer (04.93.49.28.28/www. theoule-sur-mer.org).* **Open** *May-Sept* 9am-7pm Mon-Sat; 10am-1pm Sun. *Oct-Mar* 9am-noon, 2-6.30pm Mon-Sat.

GETTING THERE & AROUND

By bus

Cars Phocéens (04.93.85.66.61) runs two services daily from Nice to St-Raphaël and from Marseille to Fréjus (12.45pm, Mon-Sat); from Hyères airport there are four buses a day to Hyères bus station, where you can catch a connection (eight daily) to St-Raphaël. **Estérel Bus** (04.94.52.00.50) runs between St-Raphaël and Draguignan, via Fréjus and Roquebrune (12 daily Mon-Sat; six Sun); there's also a service between St-Raphaël and Agay (15 daily Mon-Sat; ten Sun) and frequently from Le Trayas to Cannes, via Miramar and Théoule-sur-Mer. **Bus Azur** (04.92.99.20.05) runs nine buses daily between Mandelieu and Cannes.

By car

For St-Raphaël and Fréjus, come off the A8 at exit 37 or exit 38; St Raphaël is also accessible via the more scenic N98 coast road. The D2098 follows the coast. For Mandelieu-La Napoule, leave the A8 at exit 40.

By train

St-Raphaël is on the main coastal line, with TGV links from Paris, Nice and Marseille. Frequent trains from Nice and Marseille also stop at Fréjus and Mandelieu. Local trains on the St-Raphaël–Cannes line stop at Agay and Théoule-sur-Mer.

THE VAR

Brignoles & the Sainte-Baume

Celebrity-spotters and nature-lovers flock to the verdant Var.

In 2008, this area hit the headlines when Brad Pitt and Angelina Jolie decided to settle down at the sprawling Château Miraval. This hilly backwater now faces an interesting challenge: under siege from gawking fans and nosy reporters, can it preserve its age-old charm? Locals remain sanguine. While the latest arrivals may have stirred up a media storm and caused real estate rates to skyrocket, this area has always been quietly and discreetly upscale, as long-term part-time residents such as Johnny Depp and Bono can attest. When all the fuss dies down, life amid the rolling green hills should resume its former comfortable course.

BRIGNOLES & THE GREEN VAR

Despite its bucolic setting, Brignoles is the busy commercial centre of the western villages. A steady stream of traffic heads along the RN7 into town, though the new ring road keeps most of the noise and pollution away from the centre.

The town was once famed for its luscious preserved sugar plums, devoured by the royal courts of Europe; sadly, its fruit trees were destroyed in the 16th century. Bauxite mining proved a steadier source of income in the 19th century, while today the town is a centre of the Côtes de Provence wine industry.

A tree-lined river runs through the centre, while place Carami, given a facelift a few years ago, bustles with laid-back café life. The old town around it is quiet in winter, but lively enough in summer. The tourist office (*see p210*) can provide a walking tour map that takes you around the town's fine houses, towers and sturdy 13th-century ramparts. Market day is Wednesday, and there's a flower market on Saturdays – plus a flea market on the riverside promenade every second Sunday of the month.

Stroll up the covered rue du Grand Escalier, past **Eglise St-Sauveur**, to the Palace of the Counts of Provence. Built in 1264, it's now the **Musée du Pays Brignolais**, housing various provençal curiosities, an ancient sarcophagus, a reconstruction of a bauxite mine and a tiny plum tree (*la prune pistoline*), planted in the courtyard to commemorate the ancient delicacy.

Brignoles is also a springboard to the **Green Var** – a name inspired by the underground water sources that protect the region against drought. Take the D554 north from Brignoles, then the D45 at Châteauvert for the **Vallon Sourn**, a steep, rocky valley that's popular with rock-climbers, walkers and kayakers (*see right*). On the banks of the Argens river, **Correns** is the number-one organic village in France, with 95 per cent of its wines and produce grown organically. **Domaine des Aspras** (*see p36*), owned by the mayor, offers wine tasting in idyllic vineyards just south of town.

INSIDE TRACK
JOIN THE PARADE

To see Barjols at its liveliest, visit in mid January, when locals celebrate the **Fête de St-Marcel** – also known as the Fête des Tripettes. Drums beat as a high-spirited crowd jigs, sings and parades the saint's statue through town, after which a garlanded ox is roasted and eaten.

Barjols, 22 kilometres (13.5 miles) north of Brignoles, lies in a beautiful valley fed by fresh-water springs. An abundance of thick-hewn stone basins and mossy fountains have earned it the nickname 'the Tivoli of Provence'; pick up a map of the 28 fountains at the tourist office. North of the 11th-century Romanesque-Gothic **Eglise Notre-Dame-des-Epines**, 19th-century tanneries and watermills now house artists' workshops. Pretty terraces and café tables squeeze into the crooked streets, while on place de la Mairie, the largest plane tree in Provence has lifted up the cobblestones.

On the southern outskirts of Brignoles, by the D405, the tiny village of **La Celle** once attracted those seeking religious solace at the 12th-century **Abbaye Royale**. The refectory and ruined cloister remain, and are open to explore, while the simple Romanesque chapel still serves as the parish church. Another part of the abbey is now a luxury hotel-restaurant under the sway of super-chef Alain Ducasse, attracting pilgrims of a different sort (*see right*).

Tiny **La Roquebrussanne**, 15 kilometres south, is reached through woods beneath the odd-shaped rock formations of La Loube and sits on a plain of Coteaux Varois vineyards. The D64 leads east of here to the British-owned **Château des Chaberts** (04.94.04.92.05), a reliable rosé and reds producer that offers tastings. South of La Roquebrussanne, the D5 winds through more vineyards (try **Domaine du Loou**, 04.94.86.94.97, www.domaineduloou. com) to sleepy **Méounes-les-Montrieux**. With its meandering streets, trickling fountains and plane tree-shaded cafés, it's a pleasant spot to while away a morning; the market is on Sunday.

★ Abbaye Royale

La Celle (04.94.59.19.05). **Open** (Guided tours only) *Apr-Sept* 9am-12.30pm, 2-6pm daily. *Oct-Mar* 9am-noon, 2.5pm Mon-Fri; 9am-noon, 2-5.30pm Sat; 10am-noon, 2-5.30pm Sun. **Admission** €2.30. **No credit cards**.

Musée du Pays Brignolais

pl des Comtes de Provence (04.94.69.45.18/ www.museebrignolais.com). **Open** *Apr-Sept* 9am-noon, 2.30-6pm Wed-Sat. *Oct-Mar* 10am-noon, 2.30-5pm Wed-Sat; 10am-noon, 2.30-5pm Sat; 10am-noon, 3-5pm Sun. **Admission** €4; €2 reductions; free under-12s. **No credit cards**.

Activities

For kayaking or canoe trips, call **Provence Canoë** (D562 east of Carcès, 04.94.29.52.48, www.provence-canoe.com) – open daily during the summer and by appointment in April, May, and September to November. Hire costs from €15 to €44 per day.

Where to stay & eat

In Brignoles, **Hôtel de Provence** (pl du Palais de Justice, 04.94.69.01.18, closed 2wks Nov, Dec, Feb, double €50, menus €15-€30) is convenient and full of charm – if you ignore the roar of passing scooters. The hotel **Ibis Brignols** (ancien chemin du Val, 04.94.69.19.29, www. ibishotel.com, €70-€80 double) is clean and modern, with a nice garden setting. In the old town, arty *chambre d'hôte* **La Cordeline** (14 rue des Cordeliers, 04.94.59.18.66, www.la cordeline.com, double €70-€105) offers five beautifully decorated rooms in a 17th-century townhouse, plus deliciously sugary plum jam *à la brignolaise* for breakfast.

Just outside town, the five-guestroom **La Bastide de Messine** (chemin de Cante Perdrix, 04.94.72.09.06, www.bastide-messine. com, double €80-€100) is a 19th-century *bastide*, simply decorated and nestled in lovely grounds, with a huge swimming pool. The charming **Bastide de Valerian** (rte de vins, 04.94.59. 49.56, www.bastide-de-valerian.com, double €79-€85) is another out-of-town B&B. The exterior of **La Petite Nice** (9 rue Pierre Curie, rte de Brignoles, 04.94.77.26.75, www.lapetite nice.com, double €80) may be sweetly provençal, but the decor is more Italian, with rich colours and frescos. Outside is a little flower-filled garden.

Café le Central (pl Carami, 04.94.69.11.10, closed Mon, Sun, mains €7-€12) serves a good lunchtime *plat du jour* for €9. Also of note is **L'Hermine** (11 pl Carami, 04.94.78.33.07, closed Mon, Sun, mains €8-€15), serving up scrumptious crêpes and cider. Locals also favour **Lou Cigaloun** (14 rue de la République, 04.94.59.00.76, closed dinner Tue, Wed, meals €12) for unpretentious home cooking. **Au Vieux Pressoir** (RN7, rte de Marseille, 04.94.69.97.49, meals €10-€17 lunch, €27-€34 dinner) has eclectic decor, but some of the best *fois gras à l'armagnac* in the region. Brignoles also has one of the region's few worthwhile Asian restaurants: **Chez Lee** (18 av Dréo, 04.94.69.19.74, closed Tue, menus €21-€31).

Five kilometres east of Brignoles, the **Golf Club Barbaroux** (D79, rte de Cabasse, 04.94.69.63.63, www.barbaroux.com, double €82-€176, restaurant closed Sun, dinner Mon, mains €18-€25, menus €27-€49) is a hotel and restaurant set on an 18-hole golf course. Its modern rooms and two suites open on to private terraces and the woods.

Checking into one of the ten luxurious rooms at Alain Ducasse's **Hostellerie de l'Abbaye de La Celle** (10 pl du Général de Gaulle, La Celle, 04.98.05.14.14, www.abbaye-celle.com, double €205-€370) is the only way to go after a Michelin-starred candlelit dinner in the

THE VAR

THE VAR

adjoining Gothic convent (restaurant closed Tue, Wed, 2wks Jan-Feb, meals €42-€78).

In La Roquebrussanne, **Auberge de la Loube** (pl de l'Eglise, 04.94.86.81.36, closed 2wks Dec-Jan, double €70-€80, closed dinner Mon & Tue, meals €27-€57) is a classic inn with a lively bar and terrace restaurant. At Méounes, **La Source** (04.94.48.99.83, www. les-sourciers.net, double €50-€65, restaurant closed Tue, Wed, menus €12-€40) has four no-frills rooms and a terracotta-tiled restaurant, where the chef makes excellent use of seasonal local produce.

In outdoorsy Correns, you can live in the woods in elegant privacy at **La Terrasse** (04.94.59.57.15, www.terrasse-provence.com, double €90), which has four welcoming suites and a tranquil pool. Hardier types can pitch camp at the **Camping Municipal le Grand Jardin** (50 rte de la Barre, 04.94.37.21.95, wwwlegrandjardin.net, tent for two €18-€25, additional adults €3-€4.50). If camping's not your style, book into the 18th-century **Auberge du Parc** (pl Général de Gaulle, 04.94.59.53.52, www.aubergeduparc.fr, double €100-€130, restaurant closed Tue July, Aug, Sun night-Tue, June & Sept, Sun night-Thur Mar-Oct, menus €25-€35), which has six spacious rooms and a *fumoir*. Chef Onno Stijl creates a weekly-changing menu using market-fresh ingredients; the braised veal with pine nuts, truffles and cream is a typically good winter plate.

After hiking or climbing in Vallon Sourn, the shady courtyard of the picturesque **Auberge de Châteauvert** (rte de Barjols, 04.94.77.06.60, closed Tue, 3wks Oct, meals €9-€18) is a good place for a rest and a late-afternoon drink.

In Pontevès, the **Domaine-de-St-Ferréol** (west of Pontevès on D560, 04.94.77.10.42, closed Nov-Feb, double €62-€70) offers upmarket *chambres d'hôte* in an 18th-century farm that bottles its own wine and has a superb swimming pool.

Resources

Tourist information
Barjols Office de Tourisme *bd Grisolle, Barjols (04.94.77.20.01/www.ville-barjols.fr).* Open 9am-12.30pm, 2-5pm Tue-Sat.
Brignoles Syndicat d'Initiative *Hôtel de Clavier, 10 rue des Palais, Brignoles (04.94.69.27.51/www.ville-brignoles.fr).* Open 9.30am-12.30pm, 2-5.30pm Mon-Fri.
La Provence Verte Maison du Tourisme *carrefour de l'Europe, Brignoles (04.94.72.04.21/ www.la-provence-verte.org).* Open *Mid June-mid Sept* 9am-12.30pm, 2-7.30pm Mon-Sat; 10am-noon, 3-6.30pm Sun. *Mid Sept-mid June* 9am-12.30pm, 2-6.30pm Mon-Sat.

ST-MAXIMIN-LA-STE-BAUME & THE STE-BAUME MASSIF

Legend has it that after Mary Magdalene landed miraculously in Stes-Maries-de-la-Mer (*see p82*), she hid away in a cave in the Ste-Victoire mountains for the next 30 years. When she died, her remains were carried to a secret crypt in **St-Maximin** (by angels, some say), then promptly forgotten about until their rediscovery in 1279. In recognition of the increasing number of pilgrims coming to pay tribute to the holy remains, Charles II of Anjou, the flamboyant Duke of Provence, ordered a resplendent basilica to be built above the fourth-century sarcophagus where she lay. The good duke outdid himself: in the mostly flat farming country between Brignoles and Aix, the **Basilique Ste-Marie-Madeleine** rises like a divine beacon. It is the finest Gothic edifice in Provence and one of the few outposts of this style in the largely Romanesque South.

The interior is equally impressive, featuring some fascinating decoration by Dominican monks (including 94 wonderful carved walnut choir stalls). The altarpiece of the Passion by Antoine Ronzen, painted in 1520, is a highlight, while over the altar is a gilded plaster sunburst of cherubs and saints (1678-82) by Lieutaud. The 18th-century organ was saved from destruction during the Revolution by Lucien Bonaparte, Napoleon's youngest brother, who used it for spirited renditions of *La Marseillaise*.

Adjoining the basilica, the **Couvent Royal** is now a hotel (*see right*) – though you can visit the chapel, refectory and lovely Gothic cloister. Just south of here, rue Colbert runs through the 13th-century medieval quarter and along the sombre arcades of the Jewish district, founded in 1303 in this passionately Catholic town. Street life revolves around place Malherbe, where the Wednesday market brings an influx of shoppers, and **Café La Renaissance** (04.94.78.00.27) tries to keep up with the demand for *pastis* at its terrace tables.

Stretching south-west of St-Maximin are the forested limestone hills of the Massif-de-la-Ste-Baume. **Nans-les-Pins** is a hiking centre on both the *grande randonée* trail GR9 to Signes and the chemin des Rois royal pilgrimage route leading from St-Maximin to the Grotte Ste-Marie-Madeleine – the holy cave, or *santo baumo*, surrounded by ancient forests where legend has it that Mary Magdalene lived out the last 33 years of her life in solitary penitence.

On Good Friday, a procession led by Dominican monks climbs the mountain to hold a mass inside the cave; otherwise, contact the tourist office in Plan d'Aups (*see below*) for guided visits. The cave is hidden in the cliffs at 950 metres (3,100 feet), and can be reached by

Le Couvent Royal.

monastic cells (inhabited until 1957) have been converted into serene, stone-walled guestrooms. The restaurant occupies the arched vaults, with tables out in the cloister in summer.

Beween Nans-les-Pins and Plan d'Aups, the Benedictine convent of **Hôtellerie de la Ste-Baume** (D95, 04.42.04.54.84, dorm €7, double €25) offers rooms for pilgrims. At Nans-les-Pins, the **Domaine de Châteauneuf** hotel (rte N560, 04.94.78.90.06, www.domaine-de-chateauneuf.com, closed Nov-Mar, double €196-€390, restaurant closed lunch Mon-Fri, menus €38-€70), once a stopping point for Crusaders heading to the Holy Land, now sits amid the 18-hole Golf Club La Ste-Baume. Guests get free access to the green, and it also has a swimming pool and tennis courts. Across the N560, the elegant **Château de Nans** (04.94.78.92.06, www.chateau-de-nans.com, closed 1wk Nov, mid Feb-mid Mar, double €122-€183, restaurant closed Mon, Tue, menus €48-€59) serves gourmet delicacies, such as a seasonal risotto with summer truffles.

Resources

Internet
SMI St-Maximin Informatique *9 rue de la République, St-Maximin (04.98.05.92.70).* **Open** 9am-noon, 3-6.30pm Tue-Sat.

Tourist information
Nans-les-Pins Office de Tourisme *2 cours Général de Gaulle, Nans-les-Pins (04.94.78. 95.91/www.la-provence-verte.net).* **Open** *July, Aug* 9am-noon, 3-6pm Mon-Sat; 9am-noon Sun. *Sept-June* 9am-noon, 2-5pm Mon-Sat; 9am-noon Sun.
Plan d'Aups Office de Tourisme *pl de l'Hôtel de Ville, Plan d'Aups Ste-Baume (04.42. 62.57.57/www.la-provence-verte.net).* **Open** 9am-noon, 3-5pm Mon-Fri; 9am-noon Sat.
St-Maximin Office de Tourisme *Hôtel de Ville, St-Maximin-la-Ste-Baume (04.94.59.84.59/ www.la-provence-verte.net).* **Open** 9am-12.30pm, 2-6pm Mon-Sat; 10am-12.30pm, 2-6pm Sun.

GETTING THERE & AROUND
By bus
Autocars Blancs (04.94.69.08.28) runs six buses daily between Brignoles and St-Maximin and St-Maximin and Aix and daily services between Brignoles and Barjols; around two buses a day running towards Les Arcs stop at Correns. **Phocéen Voyages** (04.93.13.18.20) runs buses twice daily from Nice, and once a day from Marseille to both Brignoles and St-Maximin.

By car
Leave the A8 at exit 34 for St-Maximin, exit 35 for Brignoles; both are also on the N7.

climbing the short path from the **Hôtellerie de la Ste-Baume**. Flickering with candles and dotted with statues, it's eerily atmospheric. Across the road, the **Ecomusée de la Ste-Baume** (04.42.62.56.46) displays ancient crafts, such as wool dyeing and weaving. The forest was also long associated with fertility rites: the GR9 footpath follows an ancient mule track past the huge oval Cave of Eggs, where medieval mothers came to 'find' (conceive) their children.

On a barren mountain plateau, **Plan d'Aups** has a Friday market selling farmhouse goat's cheeses and jams, where robe-clad monks from the 11th-century church shop alongside the locals. At the eastern end of the massif, the village of **Mazaugues** for centuries sent ice (to preserve fresh fish) to Toulon and Marseille from its ice factories; the **Musée de la Glace** (Hameau du Château, 04.94.86.39.24, www. museeglace.free.st) explains its history.

🆓 **Basilique Ste-Marie-Madeleine**
pl de Prêcheurs, St-Maximin (04.42.38.01.78). **Open** 8am-11.30am, 3-5.30pm Mon-Sat. *Mass* 8am, 11am Sun. **Admission** free.

Where to stay & eat

At the 13th-century **Hôtellerie du Couvent Royal** (pl Jean Salusse, 04.94.86.55.66, www.hotelfp-saintmaximin.com, double €85-€153, menus €30-€39) in St-Maximin, former

Draguignan & the Central Var

Gorgeous gorges and hanging hilltop villages.

With the busy hub of **Draguignan** at its heart, the inland **Var** is a land of vineyards, truffle woods and charming *villages perchés*, set high on the hillsides. The **Gorges de Châteaudouble** offer spectacular scenery and free-roaming wild boar, while market town **Salernes** is the place to pick up terracotta *tomette* tiles.

Foodies head to truffle capital **Aups** and to **Cotignac**, famed for its centuries-old recipe for quince jelly. South of Draguignan, Côtes du Provence vineyards and olive groves line the gently sloping banks of the River Argens.

DRAGUIGNAN & AROUND

It has been a struggle for the self-proclaimed 'Artillery capital' of France, **Draguignan**, to shake its dull military image and transform itself into a tourist-drawing destination. The town centre is pleasant enough, though, with verdant flowers and trees lining the broad boulevards, laid out by Baron Haussmann as a dress rehearsal for his reworking of Paris.

To appreciate its charm from above, follow the pedestrianised montée de l'Horloge to the 17th-century bell tower (closed Sept-May), take a deep breath, and climb the 79 steps. Next, stroll up to place du Marché, where elegant but slightly dilapidated townhouses are adorned with blue shutters and hanging plants.

If you can face the crowds in the summer heat, come on a market day (all day Wed, Sat morning) when the square and surrounding alleys are perfumed with the scents of roasting chicken, thyme and goat's cheese. The **Musée Municipal** is housed in the summer palace of the bishop of Fréjus: besides a rather patchy collection of antiques and archaeology, it has some fine artwork, including *Rêve au Coin du Feu*, a marble sculpture by Camille Claudel, Renoir's *L'Enfant au Béguin* and 17th-century Italian master Panini's *St-Pierre de Rome*.

The **Musée d'Art et des Traditions Provençales** recreates traditional provençal life through displays of agricultural tools, glass, tiles and furnishings; there's also a collection of *santons*. The **Musée d'Artillerie** displays full-scale dioramas of battles, the personal effects of French war heroes and models of guns and ammunition from 1730 to 1945. US visitors might also be interested in the **American Memorial War Cemetery** on boulevard John Kennedy: 861 soldiers who participated in the 1944 landings are buried here.

The name Draguignan is derived from the dragon-slaying exploits of fifth-century St Hermentine. The beast's lair (according to legend) was north of town at the **Gorges de Châteaudouble**, now reached via the scenic D955. First stop, about a kilometre along, is the Pierre de la Fée (fairy stone), a giant dolmen dating from 2400 BC. Shortly thereafter, a dirt track on the right takes you to the beautiful **Domaine du Dragon** vineyard (*see right*), where the 12th-century fortified Castrum de Dragone of the Draguignan family once stood.

The D955 winds onwards along the gorge floor, passing **Rebouillon**, a hamlet built like a horseshoe around a central meadow on the banks of the Nartuby. From the gorge road, **Châteaudouble** (also reached directly by the D45) is like an eagle's nest, teetering on top of a 130-metre (427-foot) cliff overlooking the canyons. As its name suggests, there are two castles; one at the top of the village, the other by the riverbank. The village's wide staircases, vaulted passageways and sculpted façades, adorned with crosses and symbols of the knights of the Crusades, are a delight to explore. There are also some magnificent walks and prehistoric caves; the Grottes des Chèvres are the most interesting, with their strange stalactite figures.

West of Draguignan is a flatter landscape, ripe with vineyards and fruit trees. The D557 heads into the fortified village of **Flayosc**, encircled by a defensive wall of houses. Village life revolves around the little place de la République, with its timeworn mossy fountain. Fruit, vegetable and wine producers set up their stalls here on Monday mornings – also a good time to pick up some fresh pasta and fragrant, own-made pesto from nearby **Les Pâtes Flayoscaises** (23 bd Jean Moulin, 04.94.70. 41.52). The street also boasts a pretty, beamed *lavoir* (washing area); from here, you can take a pleasant stroll along the narrow canal and its walkway, skirting crumbling stone walls and shady gardens. There's also a 12th-century church, topped by a wrought-iron belfry.

![FREE] Musée de l'Artillerie
Ecole d'Artillerie, av de la Grande Armée, Draguignan (04.98.10.83.86). **Open** 9am-noon, 1.30-5.30pm Mon-Wed, Sun. Closed mid Dec-mid Jan. **Admission** free.

Musée des Arts & Traditions Provençales
15 rue Roumanille, Draguignan (04.94.47.05.72). **Open** 9am-noon, 2-6pm Tue-Sat; 2-6pm Sun. **Admission** €3.50; €1.50 reductions; free students under-25 (with ID), under-6s. **No credit cards.**

![FREE] Musée Municipal
9 rue de la République, Draguignan (04.98.10.26.85). **Open** 9am-noon, 2-6pm Mon-Sat. **Admission** free.

Where to stay & eat

The surrounding countryside is so seductive, it generally makes more sense to stay in a *chambre d'hôte* with a garden than in one of Draguignan's hotels, but old-fashioned **Hotel du Parc** (21 bd de la Liberté, 04.98.10.14.50, www.hotel-duparc. fr, double €58-€67) is a comfortable le address just outside the old town. The **Hotel le Victoria** (52 av Lazare-Carnot, 04.94.47.24.12, www.hotel-draguignan.com, double €59-€76), once a town-house, is now a modest hotel with a bar and billiards. A stone's throw outside town, **Les Oliviers** (rte de Flayosc, 04.94.68.25.74, closed 2wks Jan, double €56-€71) offers sparklingly clean rooms and a swimming pool in the garden. If you feel like splurging, the **Domaine du Dragon** (04.98.10.23.00, www.domainedu

dragon.com) has three handsome houses, nestled in its lovely vineyard, to rent out.

The **Restaurant du Parc** (bd de la Liberté, 04.94.50.66.44, closed Mon, Sun, mains €12-€23, menus €17.50-€32) has traditional cooking and a lively terrace, with tables sheltered under a huge plane tree. **Les Milles Colonnes** (2 pl aux Herbes, 04.94.68.52.58, closed Sun, 2wks Aug, dinner mid Aug-mid June, menu €20) is a classic brasserie, serving up *petits farcis niçois*, *rougets à la tapenade* and apple crumble.

In Châteaudouble, a good bet is the **Restaurant de la Tour** (pl Purgatoire, 04.94.70.93.08, closed Wed, menu €24). Try the excellent local game or the truffle omelette, if it's the season. **Le Restaurant du Château** (04.94.70.90.05, closed Mon, dinner Sun Oct-Mar, menus €26-€50) serves modern provençal cuisine, plus own-made foie gras, and has views over the Nartuby gorge.

Over in Flayosc, **L'Oustaou** (5 pl Brémond, 04.94.70.42.69, closed Mon, Wed, dinner Sun, menus €26-€42) is a well-regarded restaurant with a terrace, whose specialities include *daube provençale* and *pieds et paquets marseillais*. At **La Salle à Manger** (9 pl de la République, 04.94.84.66.04, closed Mon, lunch Sat, menus €25-€43), expect a more playful take on traditional dishes, served in elegant surrounds.

Resources

Hospital
Hôpital de Draguignan *rte de Montfarrat, Draguignan (04.94.60.50.00).*

Internet
NSP Internet *9 bd Jean Jaurès, Draguignan (04.99.68.42.94).* **Open** 2-7pm Mon; 10am-7pm Tue-Sat.

Police
Commissariat *1 allée Azémar, Draguignan (04.94.60.61.60).*

Post office
rue St-Jaume, Draguignan (04.94.50.57.35). **Open** 8am-noon, 2-7pm Mon-Fri; 8am-1pm Sat.

> **INSIDE TRACK**
> **HOT OFF THE PRESS**
>
> In a bucolic hamlet just north of Flayosc, the 13th-century **Moulin du Flayosquet** (Le Bastidon, rte d'Ampus, 04.94.70.41.45, closed Mon, Sun) is the oldest operating olive mill in the Var. Fifth-generation owner Max Doléatto offers tours and tastings of the delicious local olive oil.

THE VAR

La Muie.

Tourist information

Châteaudouble Office de Tourisme
Hôtel de Ville, pl de la Fontaine, Châteaudouble (04.98.10.51.35). **Open** 8-11.30am Mon-Fri.
Draguignan Office de Tourisme *2 av Lazare Carnot, Draguignan (04.98.10.51.05/www.tourisme-dracenie.com).* **Open** *July, Aug* 9am-7pm Mon-Sat; 9am-1pm Sun. Closed Sept-June.
Flayosc Office de Tourisme *pl Pied-Barri, Flayosc (04.94.70.41.31/www.ville-flayosc.fr).* **Open** *July, Aug* 9am-noon, 3-6pm Mon-Sat; 9am-noon Sun. *Sept-June* 9am-noon, 3-6pm Mon-Sat.

SALERNES, AUPS & TOURTOUR

A small town in the Bresque valley, **Salernes** is dominated by the ruins of its 13th-century chateau and famous for its iron-rich ceramics (little hexagonal red tiles called *tomettes*). It is set in a lush valley, surrounded by hills clad in pine, oak and olive trees.

A lovely 35-minute walking tour, marked by handmade tiles, takes you through the narrow streets of the old town and ends at the 13th-century ruins of the castle. Along the way you'll pass through the large central square, cours Théodore Bouge, home to centuries-old plane trees and a colourful market. On Wednesday and Sunday (market mornings), parking places and café seats are rare finds, especially at popular **Café de la Bresque** (04.94.70.67.22).

When not crammed with stalls selling fresh produce and pottery, the town is surprisingly quiet, even at the height of summer. As you explore its pretty backstreets and squares, don't miss the handsome place de la Révolution, which has a superb Roman fountain dribbling spring water. Down by the River Bresque, which flows along the southern side of the town, **La Muie** is a beautiful bathing site with crystal-clear water and sandy banks.

Renowned for its *tomette* floor tiles, the town still has 15 tile workshops and factories – most on the western outskirts of town. Check out **Jacques Brest Céramiques** (quartier des Arnauds, 04.94.70.60.65, closed Sun) and **Sismondini** (rte de Sillans, 04.94.04.63.06, closed Sun) for traditional tiles, **Carrelages Pierre Boutal** (rte de Draguignan, 04.94.70.62.12, closed Sun) for painted designs, and **Alain Vagh** (rte d'Entrecasteaux, 04.94.70.61.85) for colourful glazes and wacky creations.

A short drive north on the D31 brings you to **Aups**, walled by ramparts and spiralling outward in a sea of towers and tiled roofs. This is the truffle capital of the Var, so every Thursday at 10am late November to late February there is a high-stakes auction in the main square, where the precious commodity – all the more valuable as it is exempt from taxes – is sold out of car boots. The black fungi go for €700 to €800 per kilo; good examples should be fragrant and fairly clean (not coated with earth, which may hide gravel and other disappointing substances). If the thought of cooking so pricey a commodity makes you nervous, nearby Les Gourmets (*see right*) serves truffles year round.

Life in Aups revolves around pleasant, shady squares, tinkling fountains and cheerful little cafés on place Girard; sit at any of the terraces and try the *fougasse* – a local bread dressed with olive oil and lemon. From here, hit the boutiques hawking provençal goodies on adjoining rue Maréchal Foch. On avenue Albert 1er, don't miss the **Musée Simon Segal**. Housed in a former convent, it contains the work of the Russian-born painter, and other lesser-known artists of the Ecole de Paris. **Le Moulin à Huile** (montée des Moulins, 04.94.70. 04.66) displays ancient oil-extracting equipment and a video explaining the process, and offers tastings of its award-winning olive oil. For other local produce, the town's market is on Wednesday and Saturday mornings.

The seven-kilometre drive along the D557 from Aups to **Villecroze** offers breathtaking views of the Var's wooded landscape as far as the Maures mountain range. Just before the entrance to the town lies the 12th-century chapel of St-Victor, muffled by ancient cypresses and olive trees. The chapel is cared for by the **Académie Musicale de Villecroze** (9 rue Roger Maurice, 01.45.55.87. 26, www.academie-villecroze.com) whose pupils perform here in summer (8.30pm every other Fri, Apr-Oct). From the shop-lined main street, an attractive vaulted passage leads into the beautifully restored *vieille ville*, dotted with cafés.

Villecroze ('hollow town') is set against a cliff-face riddled with caves known as the **Grottes Troglodytes** (visits May-Sept; ask the tourist office, *see p216*) that a local lord turned into homes in the 16th century. A waterfall cascades down the cliff into a crystal-clear stream.

Just above Villecroze is the perched medieval village of **Tourtour**, reached by a twisting switchback road that gives credence to its title 'the village in the sky'. The boules pitch below the town hall has panoramic views over the countryside and is particularly picturesque on Wednesday and Saturday market days; higher still, the 11th-century church dominates the valley. The village also has a working 17th-century olive press, a *lavoir* and the medieval Tour Grimaldi watchtower.

Take the D51 out of Tourtour to reach the sleepy medieval hamlet of **Ampus**, where you'll find the 11th-century Romanesque chapel of Notre-Dame-de-Spéluque.

Musée Simon Segal

av Albert 1er, Aups (04.94.70.01.95). **Open** *Mid June-mid Sept* 10am-noon, 4-7pm Mon, Wed-Sun. **Admission** €2.50; €1.60 reductions; free under-10s. **No credit cards.**

Where to stay & eat

Just outside Salernes, the **Mas des Oliviers** (rte de Sillans la Cascade, 04.94.70.75.20, www. masdesoliviers-salernes.com, double €61)

Villecroze.

boasts a lovely pool and a friendly welcome. The **Framboisine** (pl de l'Eglise, 04.94.67.55. 32, closed dinner Sun, mains €12-€14, menus €15-€19) is a safe bet for delicious provençal cuisine and excellent espressos.

Aups comes alive in winter for the Fête des Truffes, on the fourth Sunday of January. Sample the fungi at **Les Gourmets** (5 rue Voltaire, 04.94.70.14.97, closed Mon, late June-mid July, 2wks Dec, menus €18-€32), a discreet gastronomic restaurant on the road to Tourtour. Truffles and foie gras are served year round; the rest of the menu changes seasonally to include game in winter, and morels in spring.

Further west, in tiny Moissac-Bellevue, is the comfortable **Bastide du Calalou** (rte d'Aups, 04.94.70.17.91, www.bastide-du-calalou.com, double €77-€259). Its large rooms boast plush furnishings, while the piano bar and library open on to acres of parkland and an inviting pool.

The best of the cafés and restaurants in Tourtour's main square is **L'Amandier** (pl des Ormeaux, 04.94.70.56.64, closed Mon, Nov-early Feb, menus €25-€37), serving up perfectly cooked fresh-caught perch, lightly flavoured with saffron; game is on the menu in winter. Just outside Tourtour, **Le Mas l'Acacia** (382 chemin des Peïroues, 04.94.70.53.84, double €50-€60) is a *chambre d'hôte* with spectacular views and a small pool. Laurent Guyon left the acclaimed Moulin de Mougins to open up **La Table de Tourtour** (traverse du Jas, Les Ribas, 04.94.70.55.95, closed Tue, menu €37): the sweet and sour scallop and prawn brochette, served with spiced vegetable *nems*, is a stunner.

On a hill below Tourtour, the **Mas des Collines** (camp Fournier, 04.94.70.59.30, double €80-€100, closed Nov-Mar, restaurant closed lunch, menus €22-€25) offers superb vistas from the balconies of its simple rooms, and has a pool.

A five-minute drive out towards Villecroze, **Les Chênes Verts** (04.94.70.55.06, closed June, double €100, restaurant closed Tue, Wed, menus €50-€125) is a gourmet restaurant where chef Paul Bagade does wonderful things with truffles; it also has three charming rooms. At **Au Bien Etre** (quartier Les Cadenières, 04.94.70.67.57, www.aubienetre.com, double €68-€75, closed lunch Mon-Wed, Sept-Mar, menus €24-€48) the welcome is as inviting as the food, the rooms cosy and comfortable. Owner-chef Michel Audier's creations include fois gras laced with artichokes and onion compôte, and spinach-stuffed roasted lamb glazed with rosemary *jus*.

Gourmets shouldn't miss the tiny, Michelin-starred **Fontaine d'Ampus** (04.94.70.98.08, closed Mon-Wed, menu €38) in Ampus. Owner and chef Marc Haye changes his set four-course menu weekly, depending on what's in season, and claims never to repeat himself; book ahead.

Resources

Tourist information

Ampus Office de Tourisme *Hôtel de Ville, Ampus (04.94.70.97.11/www.mairie-ampus.fr).* **Open** *June-Sept* 9.30am-12.30pm Mon-Fri.

Aups Office de Tourisme *pl Mistral, Aups (04.94.84.00.69/www.aups-tourisme.com).* **Open** *June, Sept* 8.30am-noon, 2-5.30pm Mon-Sat. *July, Aug* 9am-12.30pm, 3-6.30pm Mon-Sat. *Oct-May* 8.30am-noon, 1.30-5pm Mon-Fri; 9am-noon Sat.

Salernes Office de Tourisme *pl Gabriel Péri, Salernes (04.94.70.69.02/www.office tourisme-salernes.fr).* **Open** *July, Aug* 9.30am-7pm Mon-Sat; 9.30am-1.30pm Sun. *Sept-June* 9.30am-12.30pm, 2-6pm Tue-Sat; 10.30am-12.30pm Sun.

Tourtour Office de Tourisme *Château Communal, Tourtour (04.94.70.59.47/www.tourisme-tourtour.com).* **Open** *July, Aug* 9am-7pm Mon-Sat; 10am-1pm, 3-6pm Sun. *Sept-June* 9.30am-12.30pm, 2-6pm Wed-Sat; 11am-12.30pm Sun.

Villecroze Office de Tourisme *rue Ambroise Croizat, Villecroze (04.94.67.50.00).* **Open** *June-Sept* 9.30am-1pm, 4-6.30pm Mon-Sat. *Oct-May* 10am-1pm, 3-5pm Mon-Sat.

COTIGNAC & AROUND

Framed by a towering rock face, pierced with caves and topped with the ruins of a 15th-century castle, this lively town has long seduced the British, who buzz around its estate agents. It takes its name from *coing* (quince), traditionally made into jelly around these parts.

Locals and would-be locals lounge on shady café terraces along cours Gambetta; on flea market days (call 04.94.04.61.87 for dates), the town becomes one big bric-a-brac emporium. The general market, held on Tuesday mornings, is one of the best in the region.

To admire provençal Romanesque architecture in its purest form, visit the 12th-century **Eglise St-Pierre** in the town centre – though it is **Notre-Dame-des-Grâces** at the southern entrance that holds a special place in French history. A Parisian monk dreamed that the only way Louis XIII could have children was for Anne of Austria to carry out three novenas, including one at Cotignac. Lo and behold, Louis XIV was born after the queen left the town. To be on the safe side, Louis XIV paid his respects here in 1660 en route to marry the Infanta Marie-Thérèse in St-Jean-de-Luz.

Medieval rue Clastre has the oldest houses, while an exquisite 15th-century belfry stands on place de la Mairie. On and around the Grande Rue there are elegant 16th- and 17th-century townhouses, while place de la Liberté boasts the prettiest of Cotignac's fountains. The magnificent waterfall that cascades down the cliff from the River Cassole, La Trompine, provides hydroelectric power, and is a good picnic spot.

North on the D13 is lofty **Fox-Amphoux**, perched above superb forests of pines and oaks. First a Roman encampment, it later became a staging post of the Knights Templar. Locals still pronounce its name 'foks-amfooks' in true Provençal style – though there are precious few locals left in the village. In ruins a few decades ago, it's now full of over-restored second homes. Still, the 12th-century Romanesque church is intact on place de l'Eglise. Painter Bram van Velde spent a solitary year working here in 1958; thanks to the absence of cafés and shops, it's still an ideal refuge for those seeking peace and quiet.

Between Fox-Amphoux and Salernes, **Sillans-la-Cascade** is a refreshingly unrestored village with a sunny square, two restaurants facing the River Bresque and an all-day market on Fridays. Fragments of 11th-century fortifications surround the 19th-century chateau; the original Renaissance edifice was levelled in the Revolution after the owner refused to pay his taxes. In front of the old chapel, a wooden sign indicates the 30-minute hike to *la cascade*, a 42-metre (138-foot) waterfall that crashes down into a delightful pool.

One of the loveliest towns in the region, 11th-century **Entrecasteaux** (east of Cotignac on the D50) is dominated by the wonderful 17th-century **Château d'Entrecasteaux**. Having narrowly escaped destruction during the Revolution, it was in ruins when Scottish painter Ian McGarvie-Munn bought it and began repairs in the 1970s. Although very

THE VAR

is great for people-watching. Just off the square is popular seafood restaurant **La Gruppi** (8 rue St-Jean, 04.94.04.67.93, closed Mon, Sun, mains €12-€28), serving up fine grilled sea bass.

On a quiet street, **Maison Gonzagues** (9 rue Léon Gérard, 04.94.72.85.40, double €115) has five handsome, antique-furnished rooms in an 18th-century townhouse. On a hill on the outskirts of town, **L'Ensoleillado** (1298 chemin de la Colle de Pierre, 04.94.04.61.61, closed dinner Sun, Mon, 1wk Nov, 1wk Jan, mains €26-€36, menu €42) offers elegant food in a sophisticated setting, though the real luxury is the terrace overlooking the village and the cliffs.

A few minutes' drive from Cotignac, amid lush vineyards, the **Clos des Vignes** (rte de Monfort, 04.94.04.72.19, closed Mon, lunch Tue mid June-mid Oct, 2wks Jan, menus €28-€35) offers expertly prepared provençal dishes. Olives grow all around **La Radassière**, east of Cotignac (rte d'Entrecasteaux, 04.94.04.63.33, closed Jan, double €70), a friendly B&B where Maryse Artaud's huge breakfasts include preserved figs and quince jelly; ask for a room with a bay window. On the same road, Dany and Jean-Luc Delamarre offer a warm welcome at **La Bastide des Muriers** (04.94.04.70.92, double €78-€90, menu €18), with meals made with fruit and vegetables from their garden.

In Fox-Amphoux take a room with a view at the 11th-century **Auberge du Vieux Fox** (pl de l'Eglise, 04.94.80.71.69, closed Nov-Jan, double €65-€100, restaurant closed lunch Wed, Thur, menus €23-€32), whose meaty restaurant menu includes pork, duck and boar. At the foot of Fox-Amphoux, **Le Mas d'Aime** (04.94.80. 72.03, www.masdaime.com, double €79-€119) is a charming stone farmhouse with a lovely pool and four rooms. Another fine B&B is **Pierre de Lune** (quartier le Cléou, 04.94.80.77.53, www. de-lune.com, double €66-€79), where inviting rooms feature king-size beds, and breakfast brings home-made jam and local honey.

In Sillans-la-Cascade, **Hôtel-Restaurant Les Pins** (04.94.04.63.26, www.restaurant-les pins.com, double €45, menus €16-€34) offers pleasant rooms and meals in a rustic dining room. Try fish stew with *pistou* in summer, game in winter. Two kilometres from Entrecasteaux is **La Ferme du Grand Jas** (Château du Grand Jas, rte du Cotignac, 04.94.04.40.20, www. domainedugrandjas.com, double €80-€95), a beautifully restored farmhouse with charming rooms and hospitable owners.

Maison Gonzagues.

long, the structure is only one room deep; its small formal garden was designed by the renowned André Le Nôtre.

Château d'Entrecasteaux

Entrecasteaux (04.94.04.43.95/http://chateau. entrecasteaux.org/fr/). **Open** (guided tours) *Apr-July, Sept* 4pm Mon-Fri, Sun. *Aug* 11.30am, 4pm Mon-Fri, Sun. Closed Oct-Mar except for reserved bookings of over 20 people. **Admission** €7; €4 reductions; free under-12s. **No credit cards**.

Where to stay & eat

Lou Calen (1 cours Gambetta, 04.94.04.60.40, closed Mon, mains €8-€10) is one of Cotignac's oldest and best spots, with attractive, recently renovated rooms for €50 a night and a great Sunday brunch. Try the buffet of local appetisers (stuffed vegetables, grilled aubergine, sautéed mushrooms), followed by roasted lamb with ratatouille and puréed squash. A few doors down, **Trois Marches** (No.11, 04.94.04.65.99, closed Tue, Wed, mains €25-€35) serves delicious daily menus and piping hot, dripping-with-cheese pizza. **La Table de la Fontaine** (No.27, 04.94.04.79.13, closed Mon, dinner Sun, Nov-Apr, menus €20-€26) has a seasonally changing menu; order grilled fish with olive oil and lemon juice, or the huge side of grilled beef with home-cut fries. Across the square, the flower-filled terrace of the **Café de L'Union** (cours Gambetta, 04.94.04.60.19, mains €8-€14)

Resources

Tourist information

Cotignac Office de Tourisme *pont illuminé de la Cassole, Cotignac (04.94.04.61.87/www.la-provence-verte.net/ot_cotignac).* **Open** *Apr-Sept*

THE VAR

INSIDE TRACK
MONASTIC MUSIC

To hear Gregorian chants and mass in Latin is a rare and moving experience. Visit the impressive **Monastère St-Joseph-du-Bessillon** (D13, three kilometres outside Cotignac), whose cloister and dormitories have been lovingly restored by its 16 resident Benedictine nuns, where mass (11am) and vespers (5pm) are held daily.

9.30am-1pm, 3-6pm Tue-Fri; 9.30am-12.30pm, 2-5pm Sat. *Oct-Mar* 9am-1pm, 3-6pm Tue-Fri; 9am-1pm Sat.
Entrecasteaux Office de Tourisme *cours Gabriel Péri, Entrecasteaux (04.98.05.22.05/ www.si-entrecasteaux.com).* **Open** *June-mid Sept* 10am-noon, 3-7pm Tue-Sat. *Mid Sept-May* 9am-noon, 2-5pm Tue-Sat.
Sillans Office de Tourisme *Le Château, Sillans-la-Cascade (04.94.04.78.05).* **Open** *Mid Mar-June, Oct-Dec* 9am-noon, 2-6pm Wed-Sun. *July-Sept* 9am-noon, 3-7pm Wed-Sun. Closed Jan-mid Mar (except for last weekend of Feb).

THE ARGENS VALLEY & ABBAYE DU THORONET

South of Draguignan is Côtes de Provence territory, rich in vineyards. The most popular sport here is the vineyard crawl – best done by bicycle, with a solemn promise that you'll come back later with the car to pick up those 15 cases of rosé. Avoid, however, the dangerous and noisy N7, and stick to the small roads.

Most French think of **Le Muy** as the motorway exit for St-Tropez. But this small, flat, militantly working-class town has been caught in the crossfire of history a couple of times: once when locals failed to assassinate Holy Roman Emperor Charles V, and again when it was the parachute bridgehead for the August 1944 Allied liberation of Provence (*see p22*). The memorabilia-filled **Musée de la Libération** complements a visit to the American War Cemetery in Draguignan (*see p212*).

Between Le Muy and Les Arcs are the vineyards and chapel of the **Château Ste-Roseline** (D91 4km east of Les Arcs, 04.94.99. 50.30, www.sainte-roseline.com, chapel closed mornings). Saintly, aristocratic Roseline de Villeneuve (1263-1329) used to feed starving peasants during Saracen invasions; after her death, her corpse refused to decompose and has since reclined in a glass casket in the chapel. The mainly baroque chapel has some music stands by Diego Giacometti, brother of Alberto,

and a mosaic by Chagall. The chateau runs wine tastings and guided tours of its cellars (04.94.99.50.36, closed Sat, Sun, €4).

Les Arcs has a pretty medieval centre, twisting up towards the castle at Villeneuve. Don't miss the St Jean-Baptiste church, which has a wonderful baptism table dating from 1501 and a series of Louis Brea paintings. On the N7 south of town, the **Maison des Vins Côtes de Provence** (Les Arcs, 04.94.99.50.20, www. caveaucp.fr) is an excellent one-stop shop for those who don't have the time or patience to tour the vineyards; it also has maps and brochures for those who do. Just outside Taradeau, the **Château St-Martin** (rte des Arcs, 04.94.99. 76.76, www.chateaudesaintmartin.com, tastings €5-€15) has a sound and light show (in French or English, €5) in its 15th-century cellar, explaining the history of provençal wines.

The D10 north to Lorgues crosses the Argens river, passing the imposing **Château d'Astros** (04.94.99.73.00), which featured in Yves Robert's film of Pagnol's *Le Château de Ma Mère*.
Lorgues itself is a fortified town with a pleasant main street, lined with peeling plane trees, fountains and cafés; its market day is Tuesday. A 20-minute walking trail, marked by well-worn number plaques, wends its way along the medieval old town's ancient walls, defensive lines and vaulted passageways. Admire the multicoloured marble altar in the 18th-century **Collégiale St-Martin**, then wander up to the town's 12th-century clock and bell tower, topped with a 1623 wrought-iron campanile bell. The old town is also home to foodie destination **Chez Bruno** (*see p219*).

In the Darboussière forest, the Romanesque **Abbaye du Thoronet** is an imposing sight, its blocks of warm, pinkish stone held together by sheer gravity. Built in the 12th century, it was the first of the three great Cistercian foundations of Provence (with Silvacane and Sénanque). Its sparse, geometric lines reflect the austere lifestyle of the back-to-basics Cistercian order. The cloister, built on different levels to accommodate the sloping ground, has a charming fountain house, and one room houses a collection of 15th and 16th-century statues. This extraordinary haven is, however, under threat. Every day lorries loaded with bauxite from nearby mines shudder past, putting enormous pressure on the building. Sadly, experts are now advocating that concrete columns be used to reinforce the site – though as yet, nothing has been done about it.

Abbaye du Thoronet

04.94.60.43.90. **Open** *Apr-Sept* 10am-6.30pm daily. *Oct-Mar* 10am-1pm, 2-5pm daily. Closed Sun mass (noon-2pm). **Admission** €7; €5 reductions; free under-18s. **Credit** MC, V.

THE VAR

FREE Musée de la Libération

Tour Charles-Quint, Le Muy (04.94.45.12.79).
Open *Apr-June* 10am-noon Sun. *July, Aug* 10am-
noon daily. *Sept-Mar* by appointment.
Admission free.

Where to stay & eat

For views over the woods of Le Muy, stay in
Le Romarin (les hauts de la Combe, 04.94.45.
47.95, closed Nov, double €58-€68), which has
a few lovely rooms ahead at the pool.

In Les Arcs, book well ahead at **Le Logis
du Guetteur** (04.94.99.51.10, www.logisdu
guetteur.com, closed mid Jan-mid Mar, double
€130-€185), which occupies part of the
Villeneuve chateau; it has 13 charming rooms
and a restaurant in the vaults (menus €37-€60).
You can also just stroll in for a drink and look
round, as the (rather expensive) bar is open
to non-hotel patrons. The cheaper **Mas des
Amandiers** (882 chemin de Beon Seren, 04.94.
47.55.14, double €85-€100 is a cosy B&B with
welcoming hosts.

The jovial Boeuf brothers have the gourmet
scene in Vidauban sewn up: Alain runs hearty
La Concorde (pl de la Mairie, 04.94.73.01.19,
closed dinner Tue, all Wed, 2wks Nov, 2wks
Feb, menus €20-€55), while his brother Christian
owns the smart **Bastide des Magnans** (D48,
rte de La Garde-Freinet, 04.94.99.43.91, closed
Mon, dinner Wed, menus €29-€70); both offer
solid but elegant *cuisine de terroir*.

In Lorgues, the jet set flock to be ministered
to by truffle king Bruno Clément at **Chez
Bruno** (rue des Arcs, Campagne Mariette,
04.94.85.93.93, www.restaurantbruno.com,
closed Mon, dinner Sun, double €100-€306,
menus €65-€130) where the black fungus
appears in everything from lobster to ice-cream.

In a beautifully renovated 18th-century
olive mill, **La Table du Moulin** (5 rue des
Climènes, 04.94.73.98.87, closed Dec, Sat lunch,
Sun dinner, Mon, menu €18) specialises in fish.
The new hotspot on the market is **L'Okya** (24
rue Droite, 04.94.73.78.43, closed Mon, lunch
Sun, menus €13-€20), with a delightful terrace
and modern fusion cuisine.

Resources

Tourist information

Les Arcs Office de Tourisme *pl Général
de Gaulle, Les Arcs (04.94.73.37.30/www.lesarcs-
village.com).* **Open** *July-mid Aug* 9am-12.30pm,
1.30-7pm Mon-Fri; 10.30am-12.30pm, 4-7pm Sat.
Mid Aug-June 9am-noon, 1.30-5pm Mon-Fri.
Lorgues Office de Tourisme *pl
d'Entrechaux, Lorgues (04.94.73.92.37/www.ot-
lorgues.com).* **Open** 9am-noon, 3-6pm Mon-Sat;
10am-noon Sun.

Le Muy Office du Tourisme *6 rte de la
Bourgade, Le Muy (04.94.45.12.79/www.lemuy-
tourisme.com).* **Open** *July, Aug* 9am-noon, 4-7pm
Mon-Sat; 10am-noon Sun. *Sept-June* 9am-noon,
3-6pm Mon-Fri; 9am-noon Sat.

BARGEMON & BARGEME

Highway D25 slices through the countryside
towards Alpine Bargème, impressing motorists
with its display of olive groves, vineyards and
lavender before reaching the red-faced Gorge of
Pennafort. To the north, **Callas** is a tidy village
where hand-hewn stone houses cluster around a
Romanesque church and once-splendid castle,
and spectacular views radiate south to the
Maures and Estérel massifs.

Cross the Boussague Pass directly to
Bargemon or detour through woody ravines
past **Claviers**. On the main square, the clock
ticking in the church tower is one of the few
remaining from the Revolution. Enchantingly
leafy **Bargemon** was the last link in a chain
of six perched Roman fortified settlements
stretching east to Fayence and Montauroux,
built to ward off northern invaders. Today,
northern Europeans – much cherished for the
cash-flow tourism that long ago replaced local
shoe workshops – restore its stone houses and
stroll along the still-impressive ramparts, or
browse the Thursday morning market.

Cycling enthusiasts can visit the perched
villages by following a formidable 83-kilometre
(51-mile) tour from Bargemon to Seillan and
back; official tourist office prose suggests that
five hours and 23 minutes suffice to complete it.
The **Chapelle Notre-Dame-de-Montaigu**
(ask the priest next door for the key) in the
village centre has a giant golden altar and a
miraculous statue of the Virgin, brought out
once a year on Easter Monday. In the 14th-
century **Eglise St-Etienne**, built just outside
the town wall next to a so-called 'Roman' (in
fact, 12th-century) gate, is a fascinating
collection of votive letters.

North of Bargemon, there's a distinct change
of climate and vegetation as the D25 loops ever
upwards in hairpin bends to the Col de Bel
Homme. The road flattens out across the
military training grounds of Camp Canjuers,
where signs tell cars (perhaps unnecessarily) to
yield to tanks, and a couple of deserted villages
have been left behind for war-games.

Set at 1,097 metres (3,600 feet) on the
limestone cliffs, windswept **Bargème** is the
highest village in the Var. The Amis du Vieux
Bargème in the town hall run guided tours
(2.30-5.30pm daily July, Aug) of its fortified
gateways, 12th-century church and the ruins of
the Pontevès family chateau, destroyed during
the Wars of Religion. The village is remarkably

THE VAR

unspoiled (no tourist tat, no restaurants), with its natural beauty and the nearby GR49 footpath as its only draws.

Where to stay & eat

In Callas, shady place Clemenceau offers cool respite in the spray of the old fountain, at the café tables of **Les Sauveurs-le Moulin de Robert** (04.94.47.89.60, mains €15-€18). With 12 rooms and four suites, the **Hostellerie Les Gorges de Pennafort** (D25 S of Callas, 04.94.76.66.51, www.hostellerie-pennafort.com, closed mid Jan-mid Mar, double €185-€380, restaurant closed Mon, lunch Wed, menus €56-€72) cultivates manicured flowerbeds in a rocky gorge, far from the madding crowd. Phillippe da Silva cooks excellent regional dishes in classic cordon bleu mode, along with luscious desserts.

Hikers tramping through the gorges might try **Camping Les Blimouses** (D225, Callas, 04.94.47.83.41, closed mid Nov-mid Mar, €12-€17/two-man tent). In Claviers, **Auberge le Provençal** (2 pl du 8 Mai 1945, 04.94.47.80.62, closed Mon, Jan, menus €10-€20) is good for cheap sustenance, with simple French and Italian dishes (including wonderful pizzas).

In Bargemon, **Auberge L'Oustaloun** (2 av Pasteur, 04.94.76.60.36, www.oustaloun.fr, double €60-€70, closed Jan-Feb, restaurant closed Mon, Tue, menus €25-€28) is a family-run inn with plush, cosy rooms. Dine on trout and crayfish on the shady terrace in summer,

Callas. *See p219.*

or game by the fireplace in winter. Another good bet for tasty regional fare is **Restaurant La Taverne** (pl Chauvier, 04.94.84.09.17, closed dinner Wed, menus €16-€22), which has terrace tables by a fountain.

In tiny Bargème, Annie Noël offers *chambres d'hôte* and home-cooking at **Les Roses Trémières** (04.94.84.20.86, closed Dec-Mar, double €57, menu €19). In summer, she also runs a small lunchtime crêperie. Just off the GR49, **La Ferme Rebuffel** (La Roque Esclapon, 04.94.76.80.75, www.rebuffel.com, double €53-€68, menu €25, booking necessary) has spacious rooms on a working farm, complete with duck ponds and grazing sheep.

Resources

Tourist information
Bargème Office de Tourisme *Mairie, Bargème (04.94.50.23.00).* **Open** 2-5pm Mon, Tue, Thur, Fri.
Bargemon Office de Tourisme *av Pasteur, Bargemon (04.94.47.81.73/www.ot-bargemon.fr).* **Open** *May-Aug* 8.30am-12.30pm Mon; 2-5pm Mon, Tue, Thur, Fri; 9am-12.30pm Wed. *Sept-Apr* 9am-12.30pm Mon, Tue, Thur, Fri.
Callas Syndicat d'Initiative *pl du 18 Juin 1940, Callas (04.94.39.06.77).* **Open** 9am-noon, 2-6pm Mon-Fri; 10am-noon Sat.

FAYENCE TO MONTAUROUX

Antiques are the big draw at **Fayence**, another lofty fortified town. On Saturday mornings, locals both native and international shop at the market, then pour into the **Bistrot Fayençais** (04.94.85.02.72) on place de la République for a drink. The **Four du Mitan** (5 rue du Mitan, 04.94.76.19.85), an ancient bread oven, has a *tableau vivant* breadmaking display, while on place St-Jean-Baptiste, with its glorious mountain vista, the 18th-century **Eglise Notre-Dame** has a marble altarpiece by provençal mason Dominique Fossatti.

West of Fayence, the D19 passes the Romanesque **Chapelle Notre-Dame-de-l'Ormeau**, with its fine 16th-century altarpiece (visits 11am Thur; call Seillans tourist office, *see right*). Set against a dark forest, cream-coloured **Seillans** looks wonderfully romantic. Three Roman gates lead into the town, whose cobbled streets ascend to a chateau and tower. Its name derives from the Provençal *seilhanso* – the vats of boiling oil that villagers dumped on the heads of Saracen attackers. Today's less martial inhabitants concentrate their energies on honey and perfume. Max Ernst lived in the village at the end of his life, and 71 of his lithographs can be seen in a room on the first floor of the **Office de Tourisme** (04.94.76.

85.91, open 3-6pm, closed 2wks Nov, €2).

East of Fayence, **Tourrettes** is named after the two square towers of its chateau, another home of the powerful Villeneuve family. East of here, tiny **Callian** spirals up to an impressive feudal castle. In summer, cool your feet in the fountain on place Bourguignon, fed by the Roman aqueduct that supplied Fréjus.

Across the valley is **Montauroux**, famed for its sunny climate and Christian Dior connection; the Dior family once owned the 12th-century **Chapelle St-Barthélémy** (June-Sept 10am-noon Wed, 2-5pm Sat) above the village, bequeathing it to the community when the couturier died. Its market is held on Tuesday mornings, in the main square.

To cool off in the summer heat, make like the locals and head to the beautiful **Lac de St-Cassien**, a nature reserve six kilometres south-east of Montauroux that offers clean water, small beaches and kid-friendly cafés.

Where to eat & stay

The peaceful **Moulin de Camandoule** (chemin Notre-Dame-des-Cyprès, 04.94.76.00.84, www.camandoule.com, double €72-€190, restaurant closed dinner Wed Apr-Sept, Wed, Thur Oct-Mar, menus €30-€47) is a converted olive mill with 11 provençal-style rooms. Downstairs, you can dine on classic French cuisine amid ancient olive-pressing machinery.

In the heart of Fayence's pedestrianised old town, **La Sousto** (4 pl du Paty, 04.94.76.02.16, closed 1wk June, end Oct-early Nov, double €44-€53) offers a cheerful taste of village life. A short drive out, **Restaurant Le Castellaras** (rte de Seillans, 04.94.76.13.80, closed Mon, Tue, Jan, Feb, mains €24-€30, menus €46-€60) is the area's gourmet pull. Alain and Marie-Claude Carro offer upmarket classics (red mullet with ratatouille and fennel hearts, say) on a rose-planted terrace with magnificent views. As one of the only female chefs in Provence, their daughter, Hermance Carro, is under a lot of pressure to perform – and doesn't disappoint. Her restaurant, **Le Relais d'Olea** (1 pl Thouron, 04.94.60.18.85, www.lerelaisdolea.com, menus €28-€43) has big oak tables, placed to best advantage by the bay window looking out over the valley. Dishes might include shrimp-stuffed tomatoes, fish soup, pork baked with cep mushrooms or artichoke cassolette.

Just east of Montauroux, Eric Maio has won a Michelin star for his modern Mediterranean fare at the **Auberge des Fontaines d'Aragon** (D37, 04.94.47.71.65, www.fontaines-daragon. com, closed Mon, Tue, Jan, menus €37-€90); truffles often feature.

The **Four Seasons Resort Provence** (Domaine de Terre Blanche, Tourrettes, 04.94.

39.90.00, www.fourseasons.com, double €250-€1,600) is a luxury enclave with villas, a spa, a golf course, tennis courts and a swimming pool.

Resources

Tourist information

Fayence Office de Tourisme *pl Léon Roux, Fayence (04.94.76.20.08/www.paysdefayence. com).* **Open** *Mid June-mid Sept* 9am-12.30pm, 2-6.30pm Mon-Sat; 10am-noon Sun. *Mid Sept-mid June* 9am-noon, 2-5.30pm Mon-Sat.
Montauroux Office de Tourisme *pl du Clos, Montauroux (04.94.47.75.90/http:// tourisme.montauroux.com).* **Open** *Mid June-mid Sept* 9am-noon, 2-6pm Mon-Sat. *Mid Sept-mid June* 9-11.30am, 2-5.30pm Mon-Fri; 9am-noon Sat.
Seillans Office de Tourisme *pl du Thouron, Seillans (04.94.76.85.91/www. seillans-var.com).* **Open** *July, Aug* 10am-12.30pm, 3-6pm Mon-Sat; 10am-1pm, 3-6pm Sun. *May, June, Sept* 10am-12.30pm, 3-6pm Mon-Sat. *Oct-Apr* 10am-12.30pm, 3-6pm Tue-Fri; 3-6pm Sat.

GETTING THERE & AROUND

By car

The A8 runs along the Argens Valley. Take exit 36 (Le Muy) and then the N555 for Draguignan; the same exit and the N7 for Les Arcs and Lorgues. Salernes is west of Draguignan on the D557 and D560. Cotignac is south-west of Salernes on the D22. Bargemon is 25km (15.5 miles) north-east of Draguignan on the D562, D225 and D25. Fayence lies off the D562 between Draguignan and Grasse.

By train & bus

Les Arcs-Draguignan is on the main Paris–Nice line served by TGVs and slower trains between Nice and Marseille. **Les Rapides Varois** (04.94.47.05.05) runs hourly buses to Draguignan (fewer on Sun) from Les Arcs station timed to connect with trains; two to five buses a day (Mon-Sat) between Draguignan and Aups via Tourtour and Ampus; and buses from Les Arcs station to Lorgues and Le Thoronet (Mon-Sat, none Wed in school hols). **Autocars Blancs** (04.94.69.08.28) runs two buses a day between Draguignan and Marseille via Brignoles and Aix-en-Provence, and buses between Brignoles and Aups, Sillans, Villecroze, Salernes, Entrecasteaux, Cotignac and Lorgues. **Estérel Cars** (04.94.52.00.50) runs buses from Draguignan to St-Raphaël via Le Muy. **Transvar** (04.94.28.93.28) runs four buses a day (three on Sun) between Draguignan and Toulon via Les Arcs and Vidauban. **Gagnard** (04.94.76. 02.29) runs three buses a day Mon-Sat between Draguignan and Grasse, via Callas, Claviers, Bargemon and Seillans, Fayence, Callian and Montauroux. It also runs about four buses daily between Fayence and St-Raphaël.

THE VAR

Gorges du Verdon

Where the wild things are.

Local lore has it that when God finished with Creation, He took the best bits, made his own personal paradise – and called it the **Gorges du Verdon**.

There's no doubt that Europe's largest river canyon is one of France's greatest natural wonders. To brave the twisting, narrow roads is to reap rich rewards: astonishing views over sheer drops and dramatic scenery, with lofty villages and lonely chapels clinging to the rocks. To the west of the **Lac de Ste-Croix** the contours of the landscape soften, and lavender fields surround the tranquil town of **Riez**.

About the author
Sarah Fraser *has written for various publications at home and abroad, but keeps things local with the* Riviera Times.

THE VAR

THE GRAND CANYON

Until potholer Edouard Martel's explorations in 1905, few outside the local community knew about France's Grand Canyon – which is surprising, considering its scale: the chasm ranges in width from 215 to 1,650 metres (705 to 5,410 feet) in the eastern Upper Gorge, though it narrows dramatically in the lower section to between six and 108 metres (20 and 350 feet). The Grand Canyon proper runs for 21 kilometres (13 miles) from south of Rougon to the reservoir at the Lac de Ste-Croix.

Once the ravine was 'discovered', however, nature-lovers flocked to marvel at its beauty: jagged gorges carved into steep limestone cliffs by the emerald-green Verdon river, with sky-high bluffs in a forested wilderness. Even though one Parisian visitor suggested that the best thing to do with 'such a large, unproductive gash' would be to wall it up and make a dam, the sparsely populated but much-visited area was eventually made into a protected Parc Naturel Régional in 1977.

The *rive droite* and *rive gauche* (right and left banks) are the perilous roads perched on either side of the canyon, providing a dramatic 130-kilometre (80-mile) circuit fraught with hairpin bends. During high summer, traffic jams abound and tempers rise: the entire loop normally takes five to six hours, but can take a full day in July and August, partly owing to frequent stops along impossibly narrow roads for the superb photo opportunities. The best times to go are April, May, September or October, but even with the summer heat and congestion a visit is still worth the effort. The journey is best tackled from Castellane (take the Grasse exit from the A8 and follow the N85), where you can reach either *rive*: the D952 goes along the *rive droite*; turn left across the Pont de Soleil and follow the road past Trigance and you'll get to the *rive gauche*, the D71 (also called the Corniche Sublime).

Castellane is a small town on the route Napoléon that stands below a massive rocky outcrop. The ascent to the centre is an uphill 20-minute walk from the car park, but it's worth it to see the 18th-century shrine at the 11th-century Eglise St-Victor, built by monks from the Abbey de St-Victor in Marseille; note the large statue of the Virgin covered in ex-votos. The village itself is a tightly packed maze of streets, home to at least half a dozen companies running canyoning and rafting trips. It's also the departure point for excellent mountain bike trails into the Réserve Géologique de Haute-Provence. Napoleon paused for a bite in March 1815 at what is now the **Conservatoire des Arts et Traditions Populaires**, though the market (Wednesday and Saturday) better fulfils such needs nowadays. The **Musée Sirènes et Fossiles** has an impressive collection tracing the history of mythological mermaids via the fossils of sirenians, marine mammals that lived here when the sea still covered the region four million years ago. Ten minutes north of Castellane is the Vallée des Sirènes Fossiles, where the first of these fossils was discovered.

About 12 kilometres out of Castellane, the D952 Gorges road splits in two. Turn left along the D955 to the small town of **Trigance** – a tiny jumble of artists' studios and stone houses with an extraordinary chateau. Lovingly restored and rebuilt by Jean-Claude Thomas, who bought it in 1971, it's now a romantic hotel and restaurant (*see p224*).

Just after the chateau, take the narrow D90 for access to the **Corniche Sublime** (D71). Completed in 1947, it's a truly sublime feat of engineering, made up of heart-stopping twists and turns along the canyon's southern flank, with sheer drops to the bright ribbon of the river 800 metres (2,600 feet) below. There are plenty of scenic lookout points along the way, and – thankfully – most drivers are considerate. To reach the start of the Corniche Sublime, drive over the Pont d'Artuby (Europe's highest bridge until the opening of the Millau viaduct), suspended 650 metres (2,130 feet) above the Artuby torrent. (If a simple crossing isn't enough to set your pulse racing, local tourist offices will direct you to sports clubs that organise bungee jumping over the edge.)

The first glimpse of the canyon is from the Balcon de la Mescla lookout further along. Twisty and gut-clenchingly narrow, it winds above the gorge towards the splendidly perched town of **Aiguines**, which has the western entrance to the canyon on one side and the Lac de Ste-Croix, the largest of the four Verdon lakes, on the other. The fairytale castle – a faux-Renaissance pile with multicoloured towers – is not open to the public, but the tiny Chapelle de St-Pierre is. Dating from the tenth century, it's the oldest building in Aiguines, with a well-kept altarpiece, a tiny stained-glass window and breathtaking view over the valley.

The town was once famous for wood-carving, especially boules made from boxwood gathered by climbers at the base of the gorge. Climbing enthusiasts still flock here, and it's now an official climbing holiday centre; for courses, try La Corditelle (06.10.49.51.92, www.lacorditelle. com). For the less active visitor, there's a good local market on Fridays. Although the high fluorine content of the water makes it vibrant green (and undrinkable), the **Lac de Ste-Croix** is still a lovely spot to splash about in, unless the level is low, when it becomes muddy. Head down to the lakeshore beach at **Les Salles-sur-Verdon** for Verdon Loisirs (04.92.77. 70.26), which hires boats, pedalos and kayaks.

At the base of rocky cliffs in a narrow cleft lies **Moustiers-Ste-Marie**. Built around its 12th-century Romanesque church on the edge

of a precipice, it enjoys a Mediterranean climate despite its altitude. In the 17th and 18th centuries the town was renowned for its faïence, but after 200 years of production, it lost out to the fashion for porcelain and English bone china, and the last oven went cold in 1874. Recent attempts have been made to resuscitate the craft, and there are now 19 workshops, whose work is given the hard sell in the town's many craft and souvenir shops. The small but excellent **Musée de la Faïence** chronicles the industry's struggles, with delicate porcelains from the late 17th century. A small tourist train (04.92.77. 32.02, €5) runs past the town's sites while recounting its chequered history.

On a rock high above town is the **Chapelle Notre-Dame-de-Beauvoir**; dating back to the eighth century, it was beautifully restored in the 12th and 16th centuries. The steep path leading up to it is lined with 12 crosses, and has been used by pilgrims since 470. The 'crown of the village' is a star suspended from a chain between two rocks above the chapel. Locals say it was hung there by a knight, Sir Blacas, in thanks for his safe return from the Crusades.

Visitors looking for outdoor challenges should head for **Verdon Passion** (rue Frédéric Mistral, 04.92.74.69.77, www.verdon-passion. com) to try a spot of paragliding (€80-€200/day) or canyoning (€70/day).

Many of the towns here bill themselves as the gateway to the Gorges, but the tiny village of **La Palud-sur-Verdon** (further east along the D952) stands in its centre, just north of the

Lac de Ste-Croix.

THE VAR

Gorges' vertiginous drop. It's busy with hikers and climbers sporting baggy shorts and Birkenstocks, and has an international feel thanks to the many German and Dutch tourists. There are plenty of places in which to stay, and a friendly grocery store selling torches and gas for cooking; you'll see more hippie beads and long beards here than anywhere else in France. The market is on Sunday, and is a lively mix of produce and sporting gear. Just before La Palud, the D23 branches left to an airy circular route that climbs more than 500 metres (1,640 feet) before plunging halfway down the side of the canyon to the Chalet de la Maline, departure point for the Sentier Martel, a six- to nine-hour walk along the valley floor (*see p226* **The Right Altitude**). Just past La Palud, towards Castellane, you can enjoy the views from the aptly named Point Sublime.

Conservatoire des Arts et Traditions Populaires

34 rue Nationale, Castellane (04.92.83.71.80). **Open** *July-mid Aug* 10am-noon, 3-6pm daily. *Mid Aug-Sept* 10am-noon, 3-6pm Tue-Sun. *Oct-June* 10am-noon, 3-6pm Mon-Fri. **Admission** €2; €1.50 groups; free under-7s. **No credit cards**.

Musée de la Faïence

pl du Tricentenaire, Moustiers (04.92.74.61.64/ www.ville-moustiers-sainte-marie.fr). **Open** *Apr-Oct* 10am-12.30pm, 2-6pm Mon, Wed-Sun (until 7pm July, Aug). *Nov-Mar* 2-5pm Sat, Sun. **Admission** €3; €2 reductions; free under-16s & all Sat in July & Aug. **No credit cards**.

Musée Sirènes et Fossiles

pl Marcel Sauvaire, Castellane (04.92.83.19.23/ www.resgeol04.org). **Open** *May-Sept* 10am-1pm, 3-6.30pm Mon, Wed-Sat; 10am-noon Sun. *Oct-May* group bookings only. **Admission** €4; €2-€3 reductions; free under-8s. **No credit cards**.

Where to stay & eat

The Castellane commune abounds with mid-range hotels, *gîtes*, campsites and B&Bs. The **Hôtel du Commerce** (pl Marcel Sauvaire, 04.92.83.61.00, www.hotel-fradet.com, closed mid Oct-Feb, double €65-€95) has comfortable rooms and an excellent restaurant (closed lunch Mon-Wed, menus €23-€33), owned by a pupil of Alain Ducasse. **Canyons du Verdon** (bd St-Michel, rte de Digne, 04.92.83. 76.47, www.studi-hotel.com, closed Nov-mid Mar, double €39-€65) rents rooms and studio apartments for up to four people, and has a pool. In the old town, **La Main à la Pâte** (rue de la Fontaine, 04.92.83.61.16, closed Tue, Wed, mid Dec-mid Feb, mains €9-€15) is a friendly bistro serving pizzas and ace salads.

Moustiers-Ste-Marie. *See p223.*

Rooms at the **Auberge du Teillon** in the nearby hamlet of Garde (rte Napoléon, 04.92.83. 60.88, www.auberge-teillon.com, closed mid Nov-mid Mar, double €55) are fairly standard, but the restaurant (closed Mon Sept-June, dinner Sun Oct-Apr, menus €22-€48) is superb; book well ahead. **La Vieil Amandier** (montée de St-Roch, 04.94.76.92.92, http://levieil amandier.online.fr, double €55-€89) has nice rooms and a charming restaurant (mains €13-€23) with a huge fireplace. The grandest option is the medieval **Château de Trigance** (04.94. 76.91.18, www.chateau-de-trigance.fr, closed Nov-Mar, double €115-€175, menus €17-€38). Dominating the hilltop village of the same name, it has baronial halls, four-poster beds and a vaulted restaurant.

In Aiguines, the **Hôtel du Grand Canyon du Verdon** (04.94.76.91.31, www.hotel-canyon-verdon.com, double €110-€130) perches on the Corniche Sublime and has wonderful views from its restaurant. In the town centre, **Hôtel du Vieux-Château** (pl de Fontaine, 04.94.70. 22.95, www.hotelvieuxchateau.fr, closed Oct-Mar, menus €22-€29, double €55-€76) is a cosy alternative. The **Grand-Hôtel-Bain** in Comps-sur-Artuby (rue Praguillon, 04.94.76.90.06, www. grand-hotel-bain.fr, closed mid Nov-late Dec, menus €17-€38, double €55-€85) has been run by the same family for generations, and has plain, old-fashioned rooms and traditional fare.

Moustiers's **La Bouscatière** (chemin Marcel Provence, 04.92.74.67.67, www.la bouscatiere.com, double €160-€190, menu €30) is an exceptional B&B, with its different levels built into the rock. Terraces look out over the waterfall, and the cooking is rustic and filling. In the centre of town, **La Bonne Auberge** (04.92.74.66.18, www.bonne-auberge-moustiers. com, closed Nov-Mar, double €56-€80) has friendly owners and 19 cheerful rooms; **Le Relais** (pl du Couvert, 04.92.74.66.10, www. lerelais-moustiers.com, closed 1wk Oct, Dec-Feb, double €62-€81) is very comfortable; and solid 17th-century *bastide* **Le Baldaquin** (pl Clerissy, 04.92.74.63.92, www.baldaquin.fr, double €60-€73) is basic, quiet and clean.

Outside town, **La Ferme Rose** (04.92.75. 75.75, closed mid Nov-mid Mar except Christmas, double €78-€148, photos *p228*) favours a soft white palette and exposed beams, while **La Bastide des Oliviers** (04.92.74.61.10, www. la-bastide-des-oliviers.com, double €75-€125) is a tranquil B&B with a pool. Restaurant **Les Santons** (pl de l'Eglise, 04.92.74.66.48, closed dinner Mon, all Tue, mid Nov-Jan, menus €24-€33) is slightly pricey but well worth a visit (booking advised). For gourmet fare, head for superchef Alain Ducasse's country-house hotel/restaurant **La Bastide de Moustiers** (chemin de Quinson, 04.92.70.47.47, www. bastide-moustiers.com, closed Dec-Mar, double €160-€335, menu €48-€68).

At La Palud-sur-Verdon, **Le Panoramic** (rte de Moustiers, 04.92.77.35.07, double €59-€86, closed Nov-Mar, menus €13-€28) has 20 basic rooms and a good-sized pool.

Resources

Tourist information

Aiguines Office de Tourisme *av des Tilleuls, Aiguines (04.94.70.21.64/www.aiguines. com)*. **Open** *July-Aug* 9am-12.30pm, 2-5pm Mon-Sat. *Sept-June* 9am-noon, 2-5pm Mon-Fri.

Castellane Office de Tourisme *rue Nationale, Castellane (04.92.83.61.14/www. castellane.org)*. **Open** *July, Aug* 9am-12.30pm, 1.30-7pm Mon-Sat; 10am-1pm Sun. *Sept-June* 9am-noon, 2-6pm Mon-Fri.

Moustiers-Ste-Marie Office de Tourisme *Hôtel-Dieu, Moustiers-Ste-Marie (04.92.74.67.84/ www.ville-moustiers-sainte-marie.fr)*. **Open** *Mar-June* 10am-12.30pm, 2-6pm daily. *July, Aug* 9.30am-noon, 2-7pm daily. *Sept-Feb* 10am-noon, 2-5.30pm daily.

RIEZ & THE BASSES GORGES DU VERDON

West of the Lac de Ste-Croix, the cliffs are only half as sheer as in the Grand Canyon, and the land accommodates agriculture. Lavender is the main crop on the plateau de Valensole between the Basses Gorges and the town of Riez; it colours and perfumes the whole area in summer, and you're bound to stumble on a few lavender festivals in July and August.

Sleepy little **Riez**, dating from the first century AD, is pretty and unspoiled, even though it's the lavender capital of the area. An impressive main street suggests it has seen better days, while four seven-metre (23-foot) columns in a field on the western outskirts bear witness to the town's Roman past. Across the river stands a rare early Christian monument: a sixth-century Merovingian baptistery, with more plundered Roman columns. Inside, the **Musée Lapidaire** has an interesting collection of Gallo-Roman artefacts.

Ramparts surround the old town, which is dominated by a 16th-century clock tower. The western gate, the Porte St-Sols, opens on to the Grande Rue, where flamboyant Renaissance constructions include the Hôtel de Mazan at No.12, with its 16th-century staircase, and the **Musee de L'Abeille** (04.92.74.85.28, closed Mon, Sun, Oct-Apr, €2), with displays on bees, beekeeping and honey. The market (Wednesday and Saturday) is good for local truffles, honey, lavender and faïence. An easy hike up **Mont St-Maxime**, just behind the village, leads to a park with lovely views over the area.

Follow the D952 south-west along the River Colostre to the **Château d'Allemagne-en-Provence**, a part-13th-century, part-Renaissance splendour renowned for its fine, moulded-plaster chimneypieces; the guided visits are a delight. It also has five guestrooms (double €80-€140) or can be rented by the week.

The best approach to the Basses Gorges is from **Quinson** ('Pinson' in Provençal), 21 kilometres (13 miles) south-west of Riez. A walled city, now largely in ruins, it was built over the site of a prehistoric encampment. The discoveries unearthed were significant enough to inspire the ambitious **Musée de Préhistoire**. Opened in 2001, the elliptical building was designed by Norman Foster, and lies partially buried in the tiny village centre. A million years of prehistory are presented using clever reconstructions, including a mock-up cave complete with paintings, dioramas of Stone Age life and archaeological finds.

The twisty but scenic D82 winds south-west over the mountain to **Esparron de Verdon**, dominated by its fortified chateau, now a *chambre d'hôte* (*see p228*) and next to a lake used for watersports. The ancient spa town of **Gréoux-les-Bains** has a large choice of hotels, an old town crowded around a Templar castle, and the **Thermes de Gréoux-les-Bains**, a troglodyte spa (so as not to lose the therapeutic qualities of the calcium-, sodium-, sulphate- and magnesium-rich water through exposure to daylight). After a therapeutic

THE VAR

Walk The Right Altitude

Head for the hills for challenging hikes and breathtaking scenery.

The main points of contact for anyone who wants to explore the Gorges on foot are the regional tourist offices at Castellane or Moustiers-Ste-Marie *(for both see p225)*, where all manner of guides are available – from the written kind to the human-in-hiking-boots variety. Before you set out, get weather and safety information from the Parc Naturel Régional du Verdon (04.92.74.68.00, www.parcduverdon.fr).

WALK 1: THE COULOIR SAMSON
Length *2.5 kilometres (just over a mile).*
Time *Two hours (including pauses).*
Difficulty *Moderate: rain makes some sections slippery.*
Where to start: *The car park at the Point Sublime lookout.*
This is a family walk (sixes and over) through the Couloir Samson, just as lovely but much shorter than the Sentier Martel. The entrance to the trail, at the Point Sublime lookout, is well marked, and leads immediately to a cul-de-sac with picnic tables and public toilets. After having a quick look at the Gorges from the Cauvin viewpoint, follow the GR49 trail, indicated by a sign bearing a large green lizard.

The first stretch is a little steep and rocky; wear good shoes and be prepared to slide a bit. At the bottom, the trail follows the riverbed to the 17th-century Tusset bridge, which bears a resemblance to the Pont d'Avignon and is a good photo opportunity. After the bridge, follow the GR49 sign: the path twists and turns in a difficult climb to a clearing. Stop, breathe the pine-scented air, and take a break; after the clearing, the path is flatter. Don't miss the Rocher de la Renardière, a mysterious rock with a hole through it.

Shortly after, a splash of red paint on a tree means that the trail divides: one path continues up along the GR49, the other downwards to another viewpoint. Take the left (downwards) path, cross the stream and continue until you reach a large field. On the far side is the clifftop Rancoumas viewpoint. Black paint on the rocks shows the best places to stand for the most beautiful views – of the cliffs of L'Escales, over the Martel trail and to the village of Rougon. You'll need to backtrack to return to the parking lot, but the glorious scenery means you won't regret the effort.

WALK 2: THE SENTIER MARTEL
Length *14 kilometres (8.5 miles).*
Time *Six to nine hours (including breaks).*
Difficulty *Very strenuous. Do not do this one alone. Wear stout boots and bring lots of water, a map, sweater and torch. Arrange to have the use of two cars, parking one at the end to save a long walk back.*
Where to start *From the Chalet de la Maline. Strike out from the parking lot along the signposted GR4, first tackling the long descent and then working your way back up through the Samson Couloir to the Point Sublime car park.*
To get close to the Gorges instead of safely gawking at it from the car, tackle the Sentier Martel. But a word of advice: be in shape. This walk is best classified as a challenging adventure, sometimes passing over loose, shale-like ground and slick limestone at 45-degree angles.

Shortly after leaving the Chalet de Maline, the steep, narrow trail becomes difficult, with a sheer jagged rock wall on one side and, on the other, the void. To complicate matters, some sections of this initial part are covered in loose rubble and slippery, moss-covered stone. Take a deep breath, calm your racing heart and continue along the trail – and try not to worry: it widens up again about ten minutes later.

The path is very well marked, with two painted lines, white and red, splashed on the cliffside, on thick tree trunks or on rocks. After about three hours of

THE VAR

breathtaking views and some long downhill stretches (and the easy last half hour that has lulled you into smug security), you'll come suddenly to an impressive cliff with a series of iron ladder-stairs that you must clamber down. It's not a completely sheer drop to the chasm far below, although a difficult moment for vertigo sufferers. The ladder is divided up into five stages, with much-needed resting places along the way: there are around 240 rungs. (Dogs and children under ten will not be able to manage the ladders.) At the bottom, the trail gets a bit slippery again with loose rocks and shale, snaking down to the riverbed and the plage des Baumes Frères – which is not a beach at all, but a flat area with lots of pebbles.

Do not swim here. Because the Verdon river is controlled by two dams, the water levels can rise unexpectedly. Throughout this part of the trail you'll see disturbing signs of a stick figure running for its life before a tidal wave: this is to warn you to keep to the path or ensure you have a well-planned escape route. Check with the EDF electricity board, which controls the gates (recorded information 04.92.83.62.68).

The trail itself stays above the danger line at all times. It's a flat-ish, tree-covered path for about half an hour, then leads back upwards along another series of vertiginous cliffs – think 200-metre (660-foot) drops. Continue to follow the red and white trail markers until you reach an open plain filled with the wonderful scents of wild plants: raspberry bushes, ceps and mint. Moving ever upwards, you'll find a series of tunnels; put on that sweater and pull out your torch. The first tunnel is interesting for the iron rails left over from the era when the tunnels were being dug; the second is unremarkable; the last and longest has 'windows' that let you see out over the spectacular Verdon and towering cliffs. From here, keep on walking, controlling your fear as you tiptoe across a rather rickety footbridge over the Baou. Finish the hike by scrambling up to the Point Sublime car park, and sinking exhausted into your car.

The relatively quick drive back to the Chalet de la Maline to collect the other car should leave you plenty of time to have a well-earned victory drink at the bar.

massage, wander to the edge of town to see the **Crèche de Haute-Provence**, a doll-scale village constructed of natural materials that evokes the harsh beauty of windswept mountain life. Gréoux market is on Thursday.

Château d'Allemagne-en-Provence
(04.92.77.46.78/www.chateau-allemagne-en-provence.com). **Open** (Tours) *July-mid Sept* 4pm, 5pm Tue-Sun. *Apr-June, mid Sept-Oct* 4pm, 5pm Sat, Sun. **Admission** €6. **No credit cards**.

Crèche de Haute-Provence
36 av des Alpes (rte de Vinon), Gréoux-les-Bains (04.92.77.61.08). **Open** 9am-noon, 3-7pm Tue-Sun. Closed Jan, Feb. **Admission** €4; €2.50 reductions; free under-7s. **No credit cards**.

Musée Lapidaire
Baptistère, av Frédéric Mistral, Riez (04.92.77. 99.09). **Open** *Mid June-mid Sept* 6pm Tue, Fri, Sat. *Mid Sept-mid June* by appointment via tourist office (04.92.77.99.09). **Admission** €2. **No credit cards**.

★ Musée de Préhistoire des Gorges du Verdon
rte de Montmeyan, Quinson (04.92.74.09.59/ www.museeprehistoire.com). **Open** *Feb, Mar, Oct-Dec* 10am-6pm Mon, Wed-Sun. *July, Aug* 10am-8pm daily. *Sept* 10am-7pm Mon, Wed-Sun **Admission** €7; €5 reductions; free under-6s. **Credit** MC, V.

Thermes de Gréoux-les-Bains
av des Thermes, Gréoux-les-Bains (08.26.46. 81.85/www.chainethermale.fr). **Open** 6am-6pm daily (arrive before noon for 1-day visit). Closed mid Dec-Feb. **Admission** *1 day* €40. *6 days* €228. **Credit** AmEx, DC, MC, V.

Where to stay & eat

There isn't much choice of places in which to stay or eat in Riez itself: the **Carina** hotel (rue Hilarion Bouret, quartier St-Jean, 04.92.77.85.43, closed Nov-Mar, double €50-€58) has basic rooms and is prettier when looking out. Just outside town, on the D6 towards Valensole, the more impressive 16th-century **Château de Pontfrac** (04.92.77.78.77, www.chateaude pontfrac.com, double €70-€75) has a beautiful setting and serves simple, hearty meals (menus €28-€32). Quinson's bars are strong on hunting dogs and low on gourmet fare, but the museum, happily, has a café. The **Domaine de la Blaque** (04.94.77.86.91, www.lablaque.com, double €75), 13 kilometres from Quinson, is an elegant country estate with a generous slice of land and a fabulous pool.

THE VAR

La Ferme Rose. *See p225.*

At Esparron, sample the aristocratic lifestyle at the *chambre d'hôte* in the **Château d'Esparron** (Esparron de Verdon, 04.92.77. 12.05, www.esparron.com, closed mid Oct-mid Apr, double €130-€200), still in the hands of the Castellane family who built it in the 12th century.

Although it has something of a geriatric feel as curists come to take the waters, Gréoux-les-Bains has plenty of hotels and restaurants. Try **La Crémaillère** (rte de Riez, 04.92.70. 40.04, double €72-€78, menus €23-€32, closed mid Dec-mid Mar) or the **Villa Borghèse** (av des Thermes, 04.92.78.00.91, www.villa-borghese.com, closed mid Nov-mid Mar, double €80-€130), which has a lovely garden and a spa.

Resources

Tourist information

Gréoux Office de Tourisme *pl de l'Hôtel de Ville, Gréoux-les-Bains (04.92.78.01.08/ www.greoux-les-bains.com).* **Open** *Apr-June, Sept, Oct* 9am-noon, 2-6pm Mon-Sat; 9am-noon Sun. *July, Aug* 9am-12.30pm, 2-6.30pm Mon-Sat; 9am-noon, 2-6pm Sun. *Nov-Mar* 9am-noon, 2-6pm Mon-Fri; 9am-noon, 2-5pm Sat.

Riez Office de Tourisme *pl de la Mairie, Riez (04.92.77.99.09/www.ville-riez.fr).* **Open** *Mid-late June, early-mid Sept* 9.30am-12.30pm, 3-7pm Mon-Sat. *July, Aug* 9.30am-12.30pm, 3-7pm Mon-Sat; 9.30am-12.30pm Sun. *Mid Sept-mid June* 9.30am-12.30pm, 3-5pm Mon-Sat.

GETTING THERE & AROUND

By bus

Public transport is very limited. **Sumian Cars** (04.42.67.60.34) runs a daily bus from Marseille to Castellane via Aix, La Palud and Moustiers (Mon-Sat in July & Aug; Mon, Wed, Sat in Sept-June), and from Marseille to Gréoux-les-Bains via Aix (one daily, Mon-Sat). **VFD** (04.93.85.24.56) runs a service between Nice and Grenoble via Grasse and Castellane (Mon, Tue, Fri, Sat). **Guichard** (04.92.83.64.47) runs buses around the canyon (Sat, Sun in Sept-June; daily in July & Aug), linking Castellane with Point Sublime, La Palud and La Maline; it can also do customised tours or airport shuttles. Otherwise, the best option for the carless might be a day trip: try **Santa Azur** in Nice (04.97.03.60.00), which runs day trips to the Gorges on one Sunday a month (Apr-Oct).

By car

For the Grand Canyon, leave the A8 at exit 42 and take the N85 to Castellane via Grasse, or take exit 36 for Draguignan and then the D955. For Quinson, leave the A8 at exit 34 at St-Maximin and take the D560/D13. From Aix-en-Provence, take the A51 or D952 to Gréoux-les-Bains; the D952 continues to Moustiers.

The Riviera & Southern Alps

Introduction

Sunbathing, skiing – and a touch of celebrity-spotting

All that is best and worst about the South of France can be found in the Alpes-Maritimes *département*: a stunning coastline, swathed in some of the most banal concrete architecture of the postwar period; the glamour circuit of **Cannes**, **Monte-Carlo** and **St-Jean-Cap-Ferrat**; yachts, watersports and packed (and sometimes pebbly) beaches. The balmy, sub-tropical climate sustains citrus fruits, exotic gardens and **Menton**'s wintering pensioners, while the culinary scene embraces everything from niçois *socca* stands to the haute-cuisine extravaganzas of **Mougins**.

The cities dotted along the coast each have their own distinct character. If the champagne-fuelled swagger and ostentation of Cannes can be slightly *de trop*, **Nice** is more down-to-earth. Vibrant and cosmopolitan, it combines high culture with a lively bar and beach scene – despite its stony shoreline. The Lilliputian principality of **Monaco**, meanwhile, is an autocratic anomaly in the midst of fiercely Republican France. Famed for its Grand Prix circuit, glamorous casino and billionaire-friendly tax breaks, it's a fascinating place.

But to concentrate just on the Riviera coastal strip would be a mistake. Just back from the sea are ancient olive groves and picture-perfect villages such as **Haut de Cagnes**, **Peillon** and **Castellar**, where the pace of life is slow and the panoramas magnificent. Further inland, prosperous **Vence** and **St-Paul-de-Vence** are a mecca for art-lovers, while the scenery grows ever-wilder: highlights include the stalactite-hung **Grottes de St-Cézaire**, the dramatic **Gorges du Loup** and the **Parc National du Mercantour**, where wolves and wild boar roam.

The eastern half of the region is marked by its Italianate past, most evident in the Genoese palazzos of Vieux Nice and the Baroque churches of **Sospel** and the upper valleys. Echoes also linger in the region's sturdy peasant cuisine, with gnocchi and ravioli found on many on a menu in these parts.

The Best of The Riviera & Southern Alps

Standout sights, restaurants and hotels from across the region.

SIGHTSEEING
Check out the **Musée National Message Biblique Marc Chagall** and **Musée Matisse** (for both, *see p260*) in Nice, or head to St-Paul-de-Vence to immerse yourself in modern art at the **Fondation Maeght** (*see p301*). In Vence, pay homage to Matisse's genius at the **Chapelle du Rosaire** (*see p302*). On a somewhat larger scale is Nice's dazzling **Cathédrale St-Nicolas** (*see p258*) – a piece of Russian history embedded in the South.

PLACES TO EAT
Starry chefs include Alain Llorca at the **Moulin de Mougins** (*see p242*), Franck Cerutti at **Louis XV** (*see p284*) and Jacques Chibois at the **Bastide St-Antoine** (*see p294*). In a region famed for its hearty peasant food, though, you can eat well on a far more modest budget: try a humble slice of *socca* at **Chez René Socca** (*see p261*) or a dish of swiss chard gnocchi at **Acchiardo** (*see p260*).

WHERE TO STAY
The luxury hotels in these parts are the stuff of legend, from the inimitable **Hôtel Negresco** (*see p268*) to the classic swank of the **Hôtel Martinez** (*see p239*) or **Hôtel du Cap Eden-Roc** (*see p247*). A new wave of sleekly modern hotels, meanwhile, includes Nice's colourful **Hi Hôtel** (*see p267*) and Cannes's **Hôtel 3.14** (*see p239*).

NIGHTLIFE
Explore Cannes' nightlife hub, the Carré d'Or, at bars like **Le Chokko** and **Via Notté**, or hang out with *le jetset* at **Bâoli** (for all *see p238*). In Nice, quaff cocktails by the sea at **Hi Beach**, then party hard at **Le Klub** or **Ghost** (for both *see p265*).

SPORTS & ACTIVITIES
Juan-les-Pins is the place for **watersports** (*see p247*). Inland, there's climbing and hiking in the **Vallée des Merveilles** (*see p306*) and Alpine skiing around **Auron** and **Isola 2000** (*see p310*).

The Riviera & Southern Alps

© Copyright Time Out Group 2009

Cannes

Sprinkled with Hollywood stardust, Cannes basks in the spotlight.

At times, **Cannes** has a touch of unreality to it – and never more so than during the flashbulb frenzy of the two-week film festival each May. It brings a heady mix of pouting starlets, paparazzi, movie moguls and fame-hungry wannabes – not to mention the autograph hunters chasing in their wake. But even after the red carpet has been rolled up for another year, Cannes is far from shy and retiring. 'If you've got it, flaunt it', seems to be the motto in these parts, from the endless parade of sleek, low-slung sports cars along the Croisette to the surgically sculpted bodies, showcased to maximum effect in teeny designer bikinis.

For a welcome change of pace, take a boat trip out to the tranquil, pine-covered **Iles de Lérins**. Alternatively, head inland to explore the sophisticated yet sweetly rural hilltop village of **Mougins**.

CANNES

The smart set's love affair with Cannes started long before the festival began, or a bikini-clad Bardot frolicked on its sands. In 1834, the British lord chancellor Lord Brougham decamped here after an outbreak of cholera in Nice. He built a palatial villa in the then-modest fishing village, invited all his friends and came back every summer for the next 34 years. The aristocracy followed en masse, transforming this once-provincial backwater into a glitzy watering hole for Europe's rich and famous.

In 1939, Cannes was approached to host an International Festival of Cinema. World War II intervened, and it wasn't until 1946 that the festival was finally launched. These days, the city is a thriving European media festival hub, with events centring around the seafront's imposing 'new' Palais des Festivals, opened in 1982. It's busy year round hosting parties, festivals, conferences and conventions, keeping the glamour contingent high and the hotels full.

Yet beneath the superficial swank, the real Cannes remains: in the cafés around the market, say, or off the tourist trail in the town's oldest neighbourhood, Le Suquet.

Sightseeing

Curving around the coast, La Croisette is home to countless designer boutiques and the famed trinity of palace hotels: the **Majestic**, the **Martinez** and the **Carlton**. At No.47, **La Malmaison** is the only surviving wing of the 19th-century Grand Hôtel. Now home to art and photography exhibitions, it also hosts the film festival's Directors' Fortnight. Just off La Croisette, rue Commandant André and its surrounding streets are the city's nightlife hub, nicknamed the **Carré d'Or** ('golden piazza').

Stately palm trees line the promenade, while sun worshippers crowd the sandy beach below. Much of the stretch is sectioned off into private beaches, many owned by the big hotels, where you'll pay from around €18 to €38 a day for a sun lounger. Just before the Vieux Port is the famous **Palais des Festivals** (1 La Croisette, 04.93.39.01.01, www.palaisdesfestivals.com), its pavement indented with film stars' handprints and signatures; close by here, a little cluster of child-friendly attractions include a carousel

---

**INSIDE TRACK
BARE-ALL BATHING**

If you're after a top-to-toe tan, there is a straight and gay nudist beach, **La Batterie**, just off the N7 coast road between Cannes and Juan-les-Pins.

Cannes

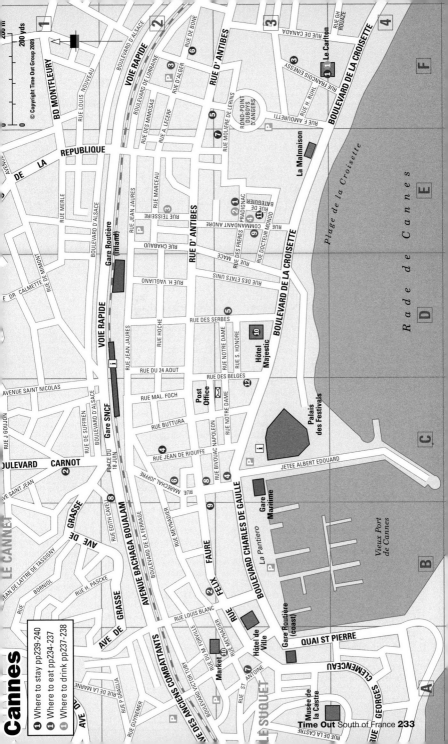

Where to stay pp239-240
Where to eat pp234-237
Where to drink pp237-238

LE CANNET

BD MONTFLEURY

VOIE RAPIDE

RUE D' ANTIBES

RUE D' ALGER

BOULEVARD D'ALSACE

RUE LOUIS NOUVEAU

RUE DE BONE

RUE DE CANADA

RUE G H ROUAZE

Le Carlton

RUE DE LORRAINE

RUE DES MIMOSAS

RUE A. LECERF

RUE DE LERINS

RUE H. RUHL

RUE FRANCOIS EINESSY

BOULEVARD DE LA CROISETTE

RUE E. MOUTTI

RUE F. MOUTTI

DE LA REPUBLIQUE

AVENUE

RUE MERLE

RUE DE MIMONT

E DR CALMETTE

RUE JEAN JAURES

RUE MARCEAU

RUE TEISSEIRE

RUE JEAN JAURES

RUE CHABAUD

RUE D' ANTIBES

RUE MACÉ

RUE DES FRERES

RUE DOCTEUR MONOD

RUE DE BATEGUIER

RUE COMMANDANT ANDRE

PRADIGNAC

ROND-POINT DUBOYS D'ANGERS

RUE MOLIERE

La Malmaison

Plage de la Croisette

Gare Routière (Miland)

Gare SNCF

RUE JEAN JAURES

RUE H. VAGLIANO

RUE DES ETATS UNIS

RUE DES SERBES

RUE HOCHE

RUE DU 24 AOUT

RUE MAL. FOCH

RUE BUTTURA

RUE NOTRE DAME

RUE S. HONORE

RUE NOTRE DAME

Hôtel Majestic

BOULEVARD DE LA CROISETTE

Rade de Cannes

AVENUE SAINT NICOLAS

RUE DE SUFFREN

RUE J GOUJON

BOULEVARD D'ALSACE

Post Office

RUE DES BELGES

RUE BIVOUAC NAPOLEON

Palais des Festivals

BOULEVARD CARNOT

RUE JEAN DE RIOUFFE

RUE MARECHAL JOFFRE

RUE MEYNADIER

PLACE DU 18 JUIN

BOULEVARD DE LA FERRAGE

AVENUE BACHAGA BOUALAM

JETEE ALBERT EDOUARD

Gare Maritime

La Pantiero

Vieux Port de Cannes

AVE DE GRASSE

RUE H. PASCKE

RUE BORNIOL

RUE DE LATTRE DE TASSIGNY

JEAN ST JEAN

RUE EDITH CAVEL

AVE SAINT JEAN

RUE FAURE

BOULEVARD CHARLES DE GAULLE

QUAI ST PIERRE

CLEMENCEAU

RUE GUYNEMER

RUE F GRAGLIA

RUE DE LA MARNE

RUE VICTOR TUBY

RUE DU M. FORVILLE

RUE MEYNADIER

BOULEVARD DES ANCIENS COMBATTANTS

Market

Hôtel de Ville

RUE ST ANTOINE

Musée de la Castre

RUE DE LA CASTRE

LE SUQUET

RUE GEORGES

200 yds
200 m

© Copyright Time Out Group 2009

and a small model-boating pond, where kids can race remote-controlled *petits bateaux* for €4 a pop.

Head past the port to reach Cannes's old town, **Le Suquet**. At its foot, the partly covered **Marché Forville** is one of the best food markets in the Midi. From here, the narrow streets climb upwards. **Rue St-Antoine** is packed with touristy restaurants, but the cobbled side streets, overlooked by shuttered, paint-peeling houses, are quietly atmospheric. At the top of the hill are the 16th-century **Notre-Dame-de-l'Espérance**, lit up like a beacon at night, and the **Musée de la Castre**, which occupies the ruins of the 12th-century castle. Inside is a hotchpotch of ethnic artefacts, weaponry and ceramics, amassed by an intrepid 19th-century aristocrat, Baron Lycklama.

On the flank of the hill is place du Suquet, dotted with restaurants and with a small boules pitch at its centre. Look out for **Sucrés des Lys** (8 rue St-Dizier, 04.93.99.73.45, closed Mon, Sun), a bijou florists' shop with two terrace tables. Here you can sample floral-infused syrups (lychee and rose petal, say), served with rose- and violet-scented biscuits. West of here, a long, sandy strip of public beach lines the **boulevard du Midi** – favoured by beach volleyball fanatics and a younger crowd.

On the other side of Cannes, the plush residential **Quartier de la Californie** is dotted with extravagant belle époque villas. Here, too, are the baroque **Chapelle Bellini** (in allée de la Villa-Florentina) and the blue-domed **Eglise Orthodoxe St-Michel Archange** (30 bd Alexandre III), famed for its choir's interpretations of Russian liturgy.

Inland, the hilltop village of **Le Cannet** has spectacular views and was once a magnet for painters: Renoir and Bonnard both bought villas here. Nowadays it is filled with less famous artists and their shops, along with expats in search of a slice of provençal life. From Le Cannet, the chemin des Collines is a lovely drive, winding through the hills above Cannes.

La Malmaison

47 La Croisette (04.97.06.44.90). **Open** *Apr-June* 10.30am-1pm, 2.30-6.30pm Tue-Sun. *July-mid Sept* 11am-8pm Tue-Thur, Sat, Sun; 11am-10pm Fri. *Mid Sept-Mar* 11am-8pm Tue-Sun. **Admission** €3; €2 reductions; free under-18s. **No credit cards.** **Map** p233 E3.

Musée de la Castre

Château de la Castre, pl de la Castre (04.93.38. 55.26). **Open** *Apr, May, Sept* 10am-1pm, 2-6pm Tue-Sun. *June-Aug* 10am-1pm, 3-7pm Tue-Sun. *Oct-Mar* 10am-1pm, 2-5pm Tue-Sun. **Admission** €3; €2 reductions; free under-18s. **No credit cards.** **Map** p233 A4.

Where to eat

Le 7ème Art Café

17 rue des Frères Pradignac (04.93.39.70.10). **Open** 7-11.30pm daily. Closed 5-22 Dec. **Main courses** €13-€37. **Menus** €23 (served until 9.30pm)-€35. **Credit** AmEx, MC, V. **Map** p233 E3 ❶

Set in the glitzy, bar-filled Carré d'Or area, Le 7ème is surprisingly good value for money. The cheaper early-evening *formule* is simple but inviting, while the €35 menu brings more elaborate fare: own-made foie gras in place of onion soup, for example, and a wider choice of desserts. A la carte, the focus is grilled meats – from juicy T-bones to meltingly tender lamb with garlic mash.

Al Charq Spécialités Libanaises

20 rue GH Rouaze (04.93.94.01.76/www.alcharq. com). **Open** 11am-11pm Tue-Sun. **Main courses** €15-€24. **Credit** AmEx, MC, V.

This busy and dependable Lebanese-run restaurant and deli serves some of the finest falafel in town. Drop in for lunch, or pick up some grilled aubergine, taboulleh and pitta-wrapped chicken for a picnic on the seafront.

★ Astoux et Brun

27 rue Félix Faure (04.93.39.21.87/www.astoux brun.com). **Open** noon-3pm, 7-11.30pm daily. **Main courses** €12-€79. **Credit** MC, V. **Map** p233 B2 ❷

Founded in 1953, this family-owned restaurant is famed for its sparklingly fresh seafood. Ignore the cramped tables and focus on what's on your plate: oysters shucked to order, followed by fish casserole or heaped platters of fruits de mer. Crisp white wines and good, brisk service complete the picture.

www.treesforcities.org

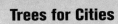

Trees for Cities
Charity registration number 1032154

Travelling creates so
many lasting memories.

Make your trip mean
something for years to
come - not just for you
but for the environment
and for people living in
deprived urban areas.

Anyone can offset their
flights, but when your
plant trees with Trees for
Cities, you'll help create
a green space for an
urban community that
really needs it.

Leave
Your
Mark
Create a green future for cities.

★ La Brouette de Grandmère

9bis rue d'Oran (04.93.39.12.10). **Open** 7.30-
10pm daily. **Menus** €33. **Credit** MC, V.
Map p233 F2 ❸
This convivial little bistro serves gloriously traditional French cuisine in a charming – and equally
old-fashioned – dining room. Pace yourself, as the
three-course set menu brings unstinting portions
of good, simple home-cooking (*pot au feu*, roasted
quail), along with wine, a shot of vodka and a glass
of champagne.

€ Café Los Farolles

1 rue Pré (04.93.39.20.32). **Open** 9am-9pm Mon-
Sat. **Main courses** €10-€13. **No credit cards.**
Call in for a drink before tackling the climb up to the
castle, or sample the selection of tasty, no-nonsense
plats du jour (omelette, steak, fish of the day) at this
unpretentious little bar. Amiable service and decent
wines make it an inviting spot to linger.

€ Caffè Roma

1 sq Mérimée (04.93.38.05.04). **Open** *Sept-June*
7.30am-2.30am daily. *July, Aug* 8am-12.30am
daily. **Menus** €15-€25. **Credit** AmEx, MC, V.
Map p233 C3 ❹
Day and night, the terrace at this perennially busy
café is prime people-watching territory. Service isn't
always sunny, but the espressos are nice and strong
and the pasta surprisingly good.

€ Cannelle

*Gray d'Albion, 32 rue des Serbes
(04.93.38.72.79).* **Open** 9am-7.30pm Mon-Sat.
Main courses €16-€20. **Menu** €20. **Credit**
AmEx, MC, V. **Map** p233 D3 ❺
Delectable quiches, salads and pasta dishes make
up the lunch menu at this smart café-cum-traiteur.
Its smattering of tables are soon snapped up, but
takeaways are also available.

★ € Dell'Arte

*6 rue du Maréchal Joffre (04.93.38.11.94/www.
ristorantedellarte.com).* **Open** noon-2.30pm, 7-
11pm Mon-Sat. **Main courses** €12-€14. **Credit**
MC, V. **Map** p233 C2 ❻
Presided over by the ebullient Dominique, this new
Italian eaterie is a delight. Its jumble of mismatched
chairs and vintage advertising has a quirky charm,
while the short, impeccably executed menu (gnocchi
with gorgonzola and nuts, spaghetti with clams) is
cooked by an Italian chef. The feast begins even
before you've ordered, with olive breadsticks,
crumbly chunks of parmesan, fresh-baked rolls and
fruity olive oil.

★ Le Jardin

*15 av Isola Bella (04.93.38.17.85/www.lejardin-
restaurant.com).* **Open** noon-2.30pm, 7.30-
11.30pm daily. **Main courses** €10-€26.
Menu *Lunch* (Mon-Sat) €17. **Credit** MC, V.

Though locals grumble about rising prices, they still
flock to the Jardin's tranquil courtyard, dotted with
fig trees and bougainvillea. Set to the north of town,
it feels a world away from the hectic Croisette; as
dusk falls, it's deliciously romantic. Food ranges from
well-executed fresh pasta and wood-oven pizzas to
grilled steaks and fish.

★ Le Mantel

22 rue St-Antoine, Le Suquet (04.93.39.13.10).
Open noon-2pm, 6.30-9pm Mon, Fri-Sun; noon-
2pm Tue, Thur. **Main courses** €25-€84. **Menus**
€27-€60. **Credit** AmEx, MC, V. **Map** p233 A3 ❼
Among the myriad touristy restaurants lining rue
St-Antoine, this quietly elegant restaurant remains
a mecca for foodies. Noël Mantel, whose CV includes
a stint with Alain Ducasse, delivers accomplished,
seasonal French fare; the risotto is legendary, as are
pâtissier Christian Gauthier's exquisite desserts.
▶ *At No.16, Le Mesclun (04.93.99.45.19) is
another fine choice along St-Antoine, with a
serious wine list and inventive cooking.*

O'tchan

4 rue Félix Faure (04.93.39.16.37). **Open** 9am-
7pm Mon-Sat. **Main courses** €14-€19. **Credit**
AmEx, MC, V. **Map** p233 C2 ❽
This airy, invitingly modern take on the *salon de thé*
has blends to suit every taste, from the cinnamon-
and cardamom-spiced Thé des Riads to an unusual
Sichuan yellow tea. Light lunch options range from
savoury waffles to salads (wasabi salmon with
beansprouts and lychees, say, or warm goat's cheese
with speck and apple).

Le Palme d'Or

*Le Martinez, 73 La Croisette (04.92.98.73.00/
www.hotel-martinez.com).* **Open** 12.30-2pm,
8-10pm Tue-Sat. **Main courses** €61-€95.
Menus €79-€180. **Credit** AmEx, DC, MC, V.
Having worked alongside Christian Willer for several years, Christian Sinicropi has taken over the
reins at Cannes's most prestigious address. He's
keen to make his mark (even the crockery is his own
design), and to hold on to his predecessor's Michelin
stars. His creative approach may have brought some
playful flavour combinations to the menu, but this
is serious gourmet dining with prices to match.

★ € Pastis

*28 rue Commandant André (04.92.98.95.40/
www.pastis-cannes.com).* **Open** 8am-2.30am
daily. **Main courses** €9-€30. **Menu** *Lunch* €13.
Credit AmEx, V. **Map** p233 E3 ❾
You'd be hard-pressed to find a more classic
brasserie than Pastis, with its leather banquettes,
dimly lit dark wood interior and inviting all-day
menu. Croque-monsieurs, omelettes, steaks and
seafood are all present and correct, along with the
splendid *formule midi* (€13): dish of the day or pizza
with either a glass of wine plus a coffee, or a dessert.

Le Restaurant Arménien

82 La Croisette (04.93.94.00.58/www.lerestaurant armenien.com). **Open** *July, Aug* 7-10pm daily. *Sept-June* 7-10pm Tue-Sun. Closed 10 Dec-2 Jan. **Menu** €45. **Credit** DC, MC, V.

This Armenian eatery has won a loyal following with its warm service, strong wine list and quality cooking. Meze include kebabs, ravioli with mint and stuffed vine leaves, with plenty of vegetarian options and some idiosyncratic menu translations, such as the mysterious 'laminated ones with cheeses' and 'aubergines vapours'.

€ La Taverne Lucullus

4 pl Marché Forville (04.93.39.32.74). **Open** 5am-3pm Mon-Sat. **Main courses** €11. **No credit cards. Map** p233 A3 ⑩

Overlooking the market, this low-key bistro opens in time to fortify the stallholders before the day's work begins, then closes after lunch. A splendid dish of the day is rustled up from the market's spoils, while locals quaff beers and talk football.

★ € La Terrasse

Hôtel Oxford, 148 bd de la République (04.93. 68.40.83/www.oxfordhotel.fr). **Open** noon-2pm Tue-Fri; 7-10pm Fri, Sat. **Main courses** €12-€17. **Menus** €17-€23. **Credit** AmEx, MC, V.

Set on a shady veranda, this unpretentious little hotel restaurant is worth the walk from the seafront. Home-cooked provençal classics are its forte, matched by a concise and pleasingly local wine list. You won't find better value than the €17 *assiette de terrace*, which includes a glass of wine and dessert.

Where to drink

★ Le 72 Croisette

72 La Croisette (04.93.94.18.30). **Open** *Apr-Oct* 7am-2.30am daily. *Nov-Apr* 7am-8pm daily. **Credit** AmEx, MC, V.

Of all the bars along the Croisette, this remains the most unpretentious and feistily French. Nab a ringside seat to watch the rich and famous arriving at the iconic Martinez (*see p238*) next door.

Amiral Bar

Le Martinez, 73 La Croisette (04.92.98.73.00/ www.hotel-martinez.com). **Open** 9am-2am daily. **Credit** AmEx, DC, MC, V.

With its grand piano and expert mixologists, the bar at Le Martinez is a seductively swanky place to sip a cocktail or two. Drinks don't come cheap, but it's worth the expenditure. Metal plaques around the bar are engraved with the names of those lucky (and loaded) enough to be counted among its regulars.

Amiral Bar.

★ Bar des Célébrités

Le Carlton, 58 La Croisette (04.93.06.40.06/
www.ichotelsgroup.com). **Open** *June-Aug* 10am-
2am daily. *Sept-May* 10am-1am daily. **Credit**
AmEx, DC, MC, V. **Map** p233 F3/4 ❶
The sea-facing terrace, live jazz sessions and killer
cocktails at the Carlton's bar are the epitome of old-
time Riviera glamour. You may not spot a celebrity,
but you're guaranteed to feel like one for the duration of your drink.

Le Chokko

15 rue des Frères Pradignac (06.18.09.70.28/
www.chokko-cannes.com). **Open** 6pm-2.30am
daily. **Credit** AmEx, DC, MC, V. **Map** p233
E3 ❷
Run by the owners of Tantra and Loft and set in the
heart of the 'golden piazza', this plush lounge bar is
a hit with Cannes's bright young things. Evenings
kick off with sushi-nibbling and drinks, hotting up
as the DJs start spinning electro, rock and disco.

Morrison Lounge

10 rue Teisseire (04.92.98.16.17/www.morrisons
pub.com). **Open** 5pm-2am Mon-Fri; 1pm-2am Sat,
Sun. **Credit** DC, MC, V. **Map** p233 E2 ❸
Part Irish pub, part lounge-style club, Morrison's is
a heady cocktail of carousing and dancing. The madness peaks on St Patrick's Day, but it's never what
you might call sedate.

★ Via Notté

13 rue Commandant André (06.22.92.23.58/
www.vianotte.fr). **Open** 6pm-2am daily.
Admission free. **Credit** AmEx, DC, MC, V.
Map p233 E3 ❹
Via Notté is one of the hottest spots du jour: while
less fashionable establishments struggle to fill their
tables, this place is heaving. A young, lively crowd
sips cocktails on the street-side terrace, then dances
to pounding house once midnight strikes.

Nightlife

Bâoli

Port Pierre Canto (04.93.43.03.43/www.lebaoli.
com). **Open** *Mid Apr-mid Nov* 8pm-5am daily.
Mid Nov-mid Apr 8pm-5am Fri, Sat. **Admission**
varies. **Credit** AmEx, MC, V.
Many an A-lister has passed through these hallowed
portals, from Kylie to Jay-Z. Stately palm trees, low-
level lighting and canopy-tented tables create a suitably seductive backdrop for champagne-fuelled
flirting and dancing.

FREE Le Loft

13 rue du Dr Monod (06.20.79.46.81/www.
dalton-group.com). **Open** 11pm-2.30am Wed-Sat.
Admission free. **Credit** AmEx, MC, V.
A major player on Cannes's clubbing scene, the Loft
lures its clientele on to the dance floor with a crowd-

pleasing playlist of house, hip hop and electro.
Downstairs is Tantra, a concept restaurant serving
sushi, sashimi and Asian-influenced cuisine.

★ Le Palais

1 La Croisette (04.92.99.33.33/www.palais-club.
com). **Open** *July, Aug* 11pm-5am. **Admission**
€30-€60. **Credit** MC, V.
This summer-only club attracts a stellar line-up of
DJs (Erick Morillo, Roger Sanchez, David Vendetta)
and has panoramic views across the bay.

Shopping

Lined with glossy designer boutiques, La
Croisette, rue d'Antibes and the streets that link
the two are a label-lovers' paradise. Along La
Croisette, there's **Céline** (No.24, 04.92.99.20.12),
Dior (No.38, 04.92.98.98.00) and **Chanel** (No.5,
04.93.38.55.05) for starters; if you need some
sparkle to complete the look, staff at **Chopard**
(No.9, 04.92.98.07.07) will be more than happy
to assist. Along with more designer brands, rue
d'Antibes adds some high street names to the
mix, including **Mango** (No.84, 04.97.06.63.63)
and CD and book chain **Fnac** (No.83, 08.25.02.
00.20); **Princesse Tam Tam** (No.67, 04.92.18.
81.86) sells deliciously pretty, flirty lingerie.
   Marché Forville, behind the old port, is a
magnificent covered market, selling produce
every morning except Monday, when it turns
into a *brocante* (flea market). After a browse,
head for a coffee at the **Cannoise des Cafés**
(17 pl du Marché Forville, 04.92.98.82.25, closed
Sun afternoon, Mon), with its magnificent array
of coffee beans: there are over 25 blends to
purchase or sample on site, from Arabica doux
to the heady Jamaican Blue Mountain bean.
   Rue Meynadier is another foodie mecca. The
queues outside long-established deli **Ernest**
(No.52, 04.93.06.23.00, closed Sun afternoon,
Mon) speak for themselves, while a blackboard
describes the daily specials: rabbit with olives,
salmon and spinach quiche and other own-made
delicacies. At No.36, **L'Atelier Jean Luc
Pelé** (04.93.38.06.10) is even more enticing, its
gleaming glass counter full of jewel-like mini-
macaroons, chocolates and lavish fruit-topped
gateaux, each bearing their maker's name on
an edible chocolate tag. **Ceneri Fromager**
(No.22, 04.93.39.63.68, closed Mon, Sun),
meanwhile, has some heavenly cheeses.
   Cannolive (16 & 20 rue Venizelos,
04.93.39.08.19, closed Mon, Sun) is the place
for regional goodies – olive oil, lemon and
raspberry honey and rosewater. If you're
more interested in intellectual fodder, head
for **Cannes English Bookshop** at 11 rue
Bivouac Napoléon (04.93.99.40.08). All shops
are open from Monday to Saturday, unless
stated otherwise.

Where to stay

Special (that's to say, vastly inflated) rates apply during the Film Festival; book as far ahead as possible to secure a room.

Le Carlton

58 La Croisette (04.93.06.40.06/www.ichotels group.com). **Rates** €250-€950 double. **Rooms** 343. **Credit** AmEx, DC, MC, V. **Map** p233 F3/4 ❶

Built in 1910, the Carlton looms over the Croisette with sublime self-assurance. Its iconic façade oozes old-fashioned glamour: check out the twin *coupoles*, modelled on the breasts of the famous courtesan la Belle Otéro. Renovations are scheduled for winter 2008, though the hotel is set to reopen by early 2009.

Le Cavendish

11 bd Carnot (04.97.06.26.00/www.cavendish-cannes.com). Closed mid Dec-mid Jan. **Rooms** 34. **Rates** €190-€310 double. **Credit** AmEx, DC, MC, V. **Map** p233 C1 ❷

Once the Riviera residence of Lord Henry Cavendish, this chic boutique hotel remains an opulent bolthole. Its belle époque façade, art deco lift and Carrera marble staircase remain, while rooms are exquisitely furnished and finished. Personal touches include a nightly turndown service, where sheets are sprinkled with lavender water.

Château de la Tour

10 av Font-de-Veyre (04.93.90.52.52/www.hotel chateaudelatour.com). Closed Jan. **Rates** €125-€200 double. **Rooms** 35. **Credit** AmEx, MC, V.

On the outskirts of Cannes, this converted chateau is a peaceful alternative to the more showy palace hotels along the Croisette. The formal gardens and pool are stunning, while its rooms boast ornate bedsteads and artfully subdued colour schemes.

Hôtel 3.14

5 rue François Einessy (04.92.99.72.00/www.3-14hotel.com). **Rates** €200-€545 double. **Rooms** 96. **Credit** AmEx, DC, MC, V. **Map** p233 F3 ❸

The most self-consciously hip of the city's hotels is a visual feast, with five floors loosely themed around different continents: Asia features dark wood and geometric lines, while Africa is a riotous mix of rich, jewel-like colours. A cool private beach and rooftop pool add to the playful but pampering vibe.

★ € Hôtel Alnea

20 rue Jean de Riouffe (04.93.68.77.77/www. hotel-alnea.com). **Rates** €60-€90 double. **Rooms** 11. **Credit** MC, V. **Map** p233 C2 ❹

Bright and breezy decor and a central location make the Alnea an appealing budget choice: there's free Wi-Fi and air-conditioning in the rooms too. Owners Noémie and Cédric are charming hosts, and you can hire bikes to explore the city for €14 a day.

Hôtel Canberra

120 rue d'Antibes (04.97.06.95.00/www.hotel-canberra-cannes.cote.azur.fr). **Rates** €170-€420 double. **Rooms** 35. **Credit** AmEx, DC, MC, V. **Map** p233 F2 ❺

Set behind a discreet door amid the bustle of rue d'Antibes, this neoclassical hotel oozes low-key luxury. Renovated in 2008, its rooms are decorated in calm neutrals and greys, with the odd splash of hot pink and all mod cons (enormous beds, crisp linen, flat-screen TVs). Out back, the heated pool and teak-decked terrace are unexpectedly tranquil.

Hôtel Embassy

6 rue de Bône (04.97.06.99.00/www.embassy-cannes.com). **Rates** €130-€210 double. **Rooms** 56. **Credit** AmEx, DC, MC, V. **Map** p233 F2 ❻

Set just back from rue d'Antibes, this is a peaceful but central base. Rooms are a decent size and well equipped, with Wi-Fi and flat-screen TVs. Best of all, there's a little rooftop pool and sunny patio.

★ Hôtel Martinez

73 La Croisette (04.92.98.73.00/www.hotel-martinez.com). **Rates** €285-€1,000 double. **Rooms** 412. **Credit** AmEx, DC, MC, V.

Behind its gleaming white art deco façade, the Martinez is a no-expense-spared affair. Its sleekly renovated rooms ooze old-school opulence, with 1930s-style prints and grand marble bathrooms. Other luxuries include the Givenchy spa, octagonal outdoor pool (heated year round), superb Palme d'Or restaurant (*see p236*) and a lovely private beach.

€ Hôtel Oxford

148 bd de la République (04.93.68.40.83/ www.oxfordhotel.fr). **Rates** €60-€80 double. **Rooms** 11. **Credit** AmEx, DC, MC, V.

If you don't mind the 20-minute walk to the seafront, the Oxford is outstanding value for money. Rooms are comfortable and stylish, with elegant grey and claret decor, free Wi-Fi and flat-screen TVs. (Bathrooms can be on the small side, though.) Outside is a verdant garden, free parking and a terrace restaurant (*see p237*).

€ ★ Hôtel de Provence

9 rue Molière (04.93.38.44.35/www.hotel-de-provence.com). **Rates** €79-€119 double. **Rooms** 30. **Credit** AmEx, DC, MC, V. **Map** p233 E3 ❼

Set in a beautifully maintained garden, with soaring palm trees and lush flowers, this place feels wonderfully peaceful. Tasteful colour schemes and white-painted antiques lend its rooms a fresh, airy feel: ask for a garden view.

Hôtel Renoir

7 rue Edith Cavell (04.92.99.62.62/www.hotel-renoir-cannes.com). **Rates** €125-€320 double. **Rooms** 26. **Credit** AmEx, DC, MC, V. **Map** p233 C2 ❽

THE RIVIERA & SOUTHERN ALPS

Looking smart and thoroughly modern after a recent makeover, the Renoir has large, well equipped rooms (flat-screen satellite TV, Wi-Fi) and helpful staff. Secure parking and 24-hour room service are typical of the hotel's willingness to go the extra mile.

Hôtel Splendid
4-6 rue Félix Faure (04.97.06.22.22/www. splendid-hotel-cannes.fr). **Rates** €133-€264 double. **Rooms** 62. **Credit** AmEx, MC, V. **Map** p233 B2 **9**
With its wedding-cake façade and flags fluttering in the breeze, this stately establishment harks back to the golden days of the belle époque. Inside, grand brass bedsteads, cast-iron radiators and intricately tiled bathrooms evoke days gone by – although satellite TV and broadband internet access are a nod to the 21st century.

Majestic Barrière
10 La Croisette (04.92.98.77.00/www.majestic-barriere.com). Closed mid Nov-Dec. **Rates** €260-€1,090 double. **Rooms** 305. **Credit** AmEx, DC, MC, V. **Map** p233 D3 **10**
The Majestic r-opened its doors in 2008, with stage one of its ongoing renovations complete. The vast guestrooms are classic without being fussy, with crisp, masculine stripes, immense TVs and echoing marble-clad bathrooms – perfect for the industry folk who flock here in festival-time. At the time of writing, the pool and spa remained closed.

★ € Le Romanesque
10 rue du Batéguier (04.93.68.04.20/www.hotel leromanesque.com). **Rates** €70-€190 double. **Rooms** 8. **Credit** AmEx, DC, MC, V. **Map** p233 E3 **11**
This once-down-at-heel address reopened in 2008 as a gorgeous little boutique hotel. Set off an elegant antique stairwell, each of the eight individually named rooms has its own unique features: a private terrace, perhaps, or an ornately carved four-poster. (Charlotte, with its white-painted antique bed and freestanding bath, is wonderfully romantic.)

€ Villa d'Estelle
14 rue des Belges (04.92.98.44.48/www.villa destelle.com). **Rates** €95-€260 double studio. **Rooms** 23. **Credit** AmEx, DC, MC, V. **Map** p233 C3 **12**
The elegant Villa d'Estelle offers 23 self-catering studios, apartments and suites. Kitchenettes, marble bathrooms and flat-screen TVs are among the home comforts, along with an attractive pool; for larger groups, there's the four-bedroom penthouse duplex.

Resources

Hospital
Centre Hospitalier de Cannes
04.93.69.70.00/www.hopital-cannes.fr.

Internet
Dre@m Cyber-Café *6 rue Commandant Vidal (04.93.38.26.79).* **Open** 10am-8.30pm Mon-Sat.

Police
Commissariat *1 av de Grasse (04.93.06.22.22).*

Post office
22 rue Bivouac Napoléon (04.93.06.26.50). **Open** 8am-7pm Mon-Fri; 8am-noon Sat.

Tourist information
Office de Tourisme *esplanade Georges Pompidou, Cannes (04.92.99.84.22/www.cannes-on-line.com).* **Open** *Sept-June* 9am-7pm daily. *July, Aug* 9am-8pm daily.
Other locations *Gare SNCF, rue Jean Jaurès, Cannes (04.93.99.19.77).* **Open** *Sept-June* 9am-1pm, 2-7pm Mon-Sat. *July, Aug* 9am-7pm Mon-Sat.

St-Honorat. *See p241.*

Around Cannes

ILES DE LERINS

The Iles de Lérins are only a 15-minute boat ride from the old port of Cannes. Known to the ancients as Lero and Lerina, the islands were renamed St-Honorat and Ste-Marguerite after the siblings who founded monastic communities here in the fourth century.

Today, **St-Honorat** is a beautiful backwater, home to a tiny community of Cistercian monks who live, work and pray in a 19th-century monastery. A short walk around the coastal path, the **Monastère Fortifié** was built by the monks in 1073 to protect themselves from Saracen attack. Visitors can wander through forests of pine and eucalyptus and swim discreetly off the rocky outcrops. There's also a simple café, **La Tonelle** (04.92.99.18.07).

The island of **Ste-Marguerite** is larger and more touristy. A maze of little *sentiers* (forest paths) lead through copses of fragrant pine and eucalyptus, emerging at tiny beaches and coves. True, there are yachts anchored further out in the azure waters – but there's always a hidden nook to be found, if you're prepared to clamber along a rocky ledge or two. Kiosks sell snacks and drinks, and there are two restaurants: **L'Escale** (04.93.43.49.25, closed mid Oct-mid Mar, mains €18-€31) and **La Guérite** (04.93.43.49.30, closed end Oct-mid Apr, mains €30-€50).

The former stronghold and prison of the Fort is now home to the **Royal Musée de la Mer**. Its collection includes Roman remains and cargo retrieved from shipwrecks, but most visitors are here to see the prison cell of the Man in the Iron Mask, held captive during Louis IV's reign and made famous by novelist Alexandre Dumas. Close by are two little graveyards. One, overgrown with trees, has rocks marking the plots; the other is more orderly, with wrought-iron gates bearing the word 'Tombés' ('fallen'), in memory of the Crimean soldiers buried there. It's beautifully tranquil, as lizards bask on the sun-warmed walls and the sea glints behind.

Monastère Fortifié

St-Honorat (04.92.99.54.00). **Open** *July-mid Sept* 10.30am-12.30pm, 2.30-5pm daily. *Mid Sept-June* 8.30am-6pm daily. Mass 9.50am Sun. **Admission** *Oct-June* free. *July-Sept* €2. **No credit cards**.

Musée de la Mer

Fort Royal, Ile-Ste-Marguerite (04.93.43.18.17). **Open** *June-Sept* 10am-5.45pm daily. *Oct-Mar* 10.30am-1.15pm, 2.15-4.45pm Tue-Sun. *Apr, May* 10.30am-1.15pm, 2.15-5.45pm Tue-Sun. **Admission** €3; €2 reductions; free students, under-18s. **Credit** AmEx, MC, V.

Getting to the islands

Planaria (04.92.98.71.38, €11 rtn to St-Honorat) and **Trans Côte d'Azur** (04.92.98.71.30, €11 rtn to Ste-Marguerite) run boats from quai Laubeuf in Cannes old port between 7.30am and 6.30pm daily. **Compagnie Estérel Chantelclair** (04.93.39.11.82) runs crossings to Ste-Marguerite from promenade La Pantiero (€10 rtn, 7.30am-5pm, until 7pm July & Aug). Vintage boats, complete with a skipper, can be hired at Port Canto's **Olympique Nautique** (06.14.89.24.57).

MOUGINS

The hilltop village of Mougins is an extraordinary sight, carpeted in flowers and bushes, with narrow lanes and restored houses built along the outlines of medieval ramparts. In the interwar period, it was discovered by the Surrealists, among them Cocteau, Picabia and Picasso, who came here in the company of Dora Maar and Man Ray. Local lore has it that cash-strapped Picasso covered his room with murals to pay for his board and lodging; the enraged owner made the still-obscure artist whitewash over them the next day. Undaunted, Picasso settled here in 1961 with his wife Jaqueline, and spent much of his time in the area until his death in 1973. Their house, **L'Antre du Minotaur** (the Minotaur's Lair), can be seen just opposite the strikingly beautiful chapel of **Notre-Dame-de-Vie** (closed except for mass, 9am Sun), a mile south-east of Mougins.

Today, Mougins bristles with galleries, painters, and wealthy second-homers, as the closed-circuit cameras peeping out from behind the bougainvillea attest. (One notorious former resident was Haitian dictator Baby Doc Duvalier, who had a pied-à-terre here.) Upstairs in the town hall, the **Musée Maurice Gottlob** explores the history of Mougins, while **Le Lavoir** (av Charles Mallet, 04.92.92.50.42, closed Nov-Feb), once the village laundry, showcases local artists. Next to the 12th-century **Porte Sarrazine**, the **Musée de la Photographie** displays antique cameras, along with some photos of Picasso by André Villers, and works by Doisneau and Lartigue.

South-east of Mougins on the A8 is the **Musée de l'Automobiliste**, a glass and concrete temple to racing cars and motorbikes.

Musée de l'Automobiliste

772 chemin de Font-de-Currault, access Aire de Bréguières on A8 (04.93.69.27.80/www.musauto. fr.st). **Open** *Apr-Sept* 10am-6pm daily. *Oct-mid Nov, mid Dec-Mar* 10am-1pm, 2-6pm daily. Closed mid Nov-mid Dec. **Admission** €7; €5 reductions; free under-12s. **Credit** AmEx, MC, V.

THE RIVIERA & SOUTHERN ALPS

FREE Musée de la Photographie

Porte Sarrazine (04.93.75.85.67). **Open** *July-Aug* 10am-8pm daily. *Sept, Oct, Dec-June* 10am-6pm Mon-Fri; 11am-6pm Sat, Sun. Closed Nov. **Admission** free.

FREE Musée Maurice Gottlob

1 pl Commandant Lamy (04.92.92.50.42). **Open** 9am-5pm Mon-Fri; 11am-6pm Sat, Sun. Closed Nov. **Admission** free.

Where to stay & eat

Mougins may be small, but it packs a gastronomic punch. Most famous of all is Alain Llorca's **Moulin de Mougins** (av Notre-Dame-de-Vie, 04.93.75.78.24, www.moulin-mougins. com, double €160-€290, menus €59-84). Foodies flock to the old mill's chandelier-lit dining room to sample Llorca's sun-drenched Mediterranean cuisine: scampi with thyme flowers, say, or red mullet with saffron and fennel compôte.

Set in an 18th-century *mas*, Serge Gouloumes's **Restaurant Candille** (Hôtel le Mas Candille, bd Clement-Rebuffel, 04.92.28.43.43, closed lunch Mon, Tue, double €395-€635, menus €54-€130) is another culinary heavyweight. His Italian-provençal creations are inventive without being too outré; tatin of foie gras and armagnac is one of his signature dishes. The rooms are

Le Feu Follet.

suitably luxurious, as are the manicured grounds and Shiseido spa. **Les Muscadins** (18 bd Courteline, 04.92.28.43.43, www.hotel-mougins-muscadins.com, double €130-€260), where Picasso fell in love with Mougins back in 1936, has also now become part of the Le Mas Candille empire.

A stately 19th-century manor house, **Manoir de l'Etang** (66 allée du Manoir, 04.92.28.36.00, www.manoir-de-letang.com, double €150-€275) is a secluded idyll in the hills, with lovely views over a pond covered in lotus flowers. If you're after something more intimate, **Les Rosées** (238 chemin de Font Neuve, 04.92.92.29.64, www.lesrosees.com, double €260-€310) is a chic B&B with four über-stylish suites.

Le Feu Follet (pl Commandant Lamy, 04.93.90.15.78, www.feu-follet.fr, closed Mon, lunch July & Aug, mid Dec-mid Jan, menus €26-€55) offers sophisticated cooking, with a beautiful (and busy) terrace. On the same square, the **Brasserie de la Mediterranée** (04.93.90.03.47, menus €39-€50) is strong on seafood. **Le Bistrot de Mougins** (pl du Village, 04.93.75.78.34, closed Wed, lunch Thur & Sat, menus €21 lunch, €34-€47 dinner) serves good, rustic cooking in a vaulted cellar.

Resources

Tourist information

Office de Tourisme *Parking du Moulin de la Croix, Mougins (04.93.75.87.67/www. mougins-coteazur.org).* **Open** *Mid June-mid Sept* 9am-8pm daily. *Mid Sept-mid June* 9am-5.30pm Mon-Fri; 9am-5pm Sat.

GETTING THERE

By bus

Cannes's main bus station, which is by the port, serves coastal destinations: **RCA** (08.20.48.11. 11, www.rca.tm.fr) goes to Nice via the villages along the coast and to Nice airport (every 30mins, Mon-Sat). From the SNCF station RCA goes to Grasse (every 30mins Mon-Sat, hourly Sun) via Mougins. **Phocéen Cars** (04.93.39.79.40) runs three services a day (Mon-Sat) to Marseille and Aix-en-Provence.

By car

Leave the A8 at exit 41 or 42, or take the N7 direction Cannes. Mougins is 3.5km north of Cannes on the N85. For Vallauris, leave the A8 at exit Antibes and follow the signs from the D435. The N7/N98 coast road runs through Golfe-Juan.

By train

Cannes is served by the TGV from Paris (5hrs 10mins). There are regular trains along the coast to Juan-les-Pins, Antibes and Nice.

Antibes to Cagnes

The glamour of days gone by endures along this sandy stretch.

Twinned they might be, but **Antibes** and **Juan-les-Pins** are by no means identical. Juan-les-Pins struts around like a rebellious, spiky-haired teenager while Antibes, the impeccably groomed sibling, sighs and shakes her head. What they have in common is a love of hedonism, from the all-night beach parties at Juan-les-Pins to the relentless spending at the Hôtel du Cap Eden Roc. If you've come to the Riviera for natural beauty, Juan-les-Pins might fill you with horror, but a walk around the amazing Cap d'Antibes at sunset will make amends.

Thick with traffic and factory outlets, the road between Cagnes and Antibes might seem best avoided. Look beyond the eyesores, though, and you'll find some gems: the medieval citadels of **Villeneuve-Loubet** and **Haut-de-Cagnes**, say, or the village of **Cros de Cagnes**, where fishermen still return each day with buckets of fish in shades of silver, pink and gold.

ANTIBES & JUAN-LES-PINS

The Greeks set up the trading post of Antipolis in the fifth century BC. Ligurian tribes fought hard to get their hands on the town over the following centuries, forcing Antibes's residents to turn to Rome for protection in 154 BC. But the fall of Rome left Antibes prey to attacks from every passing marauder, from Barbarians to Vandals, Visigoths to Franks. In the tenth century, Antibes fell into the hands of the Counts of Grasse before passing to the bishops of Antibes and, at the end of the 14th century, to the Grimaldis of Monaco. It remained theirs until 1608, when Henri IV of France purchased Antibes, turning it into his front-line defence against the Savoy kingdom across the bay in Nice. This opposition partly explains the striking architectural differences between the old towns of Nice and Antibes: the latter has a certain austerity, with its stone houses and grey-blue shutters, while Vieux Nice, painted in pink and ochre with jade-green shutters, has a more flamboyant Italian feel.

To host the trickle of wealthy Europeans seeking winter sunshine, a local entrepreneur opened the **Grand Hôtel du Cap** in 1870. But Antibes and Juan-les-Pins became a year-round playground only in 1923, when consummate hosts Gerald and Sara Murphy – friendly with the likes of Picasso, Hemingway and Rudolf Valentino – persuaded the hotel to stay open all year, not just in winter. That same summer, US tycoon Frank Jay Gould spotted the area's potential and began buying property to create hotels and a casino, while Coco Chanel launched a flowing, casual look for women that earned Juan-les-Pins the name 'Pyjamopolis'. Picasso painted masterpieces here, waterskiing was invented and women bared skin on the beach; Antibes-Juan-les-Pins became the Riviera's first chic summer resort.

These days, yachties and zillionaires mix with artists and easyJetsetters to create a genuinely cosmopolitan atmosphere. Juan-les-Pins is unashamedly touristy and near-dead in the winter, but Antibes buzzes with markets, culture and café society all year; both throng with crowds in the summer heat.

The conurbation of Antibes-Juan-les-Pins is a mainly unappealing mass wedged between the sea and the A8 motorway. The old districts are best approached from **Fort Carré**, which stands on the point separating the St-Roch inlet from Baie des Anges – or, even better, by sea. The fort was constructed in the 16th century to counter the Savoy threat; in the 17th century, Louis XIV's military architect, Vauban, gave it its eight-pointed star shape. South of here, Port Vauban is Europe's largest yacht marina,

THE RIVIERA & SOUTHERN ALPS

harbouring grand pleasure crafts and glitzy boutiques, where you can hire – sorry, charter – your own craft and join the yachterati. In June, the **Voiles d'Antibes** (*see p46*) fills the bay with splendid sailing vessels and motor yachts.

Hidden behind the ancient walls of the quay is **plage de la Gravette**, a free sandy beach with gently shelving waters. At the other end of the ramparts is the **Musée d'Histoire et d'Archéologie**, containing reminders of the town's multi-faceted past, including Greek and Etruscan amphorae. Also squeezed within the ramparts is the **Eglise Notre-Dame-de-l'Immaculée-Conception** (04.93.34.06.29), a rich mix of marble virgins, baroque stylings and deep ochres, lapis blues and blood-red walls.

The **Château Grimaldi** next door follows the plan of the earlier Roman fort, despite rebuilding in the 16th century. In 1946, when Picasso rented a cold, damp room on the second floor, it belonged to a certain Romuald Dor and already housed a small archaeological collection. Dor had ulterior motives in his offer of such prime Riviera studio space; the works Picasso left behind in lieu of rent enabled him to upgrade his lacklustre collection and re-baptise it the **Musée Picasso**. It now houses over 300 works by Picasso, alongside pieces by Miró, Calder and Léger; the first floor displays temporary exhibitions and 147 paintings by Russian-born artist Nicolas de Staël.

Inland from the castle, cours Masséna plays host to one of the region's liveliest (and priciest) produce markets, the **Marché Provençal** (every morning, except Mon in winter); market gardeners sell local produce down the centre aisle. Another foodie stop-off is **Balade en Provence** (25bis cours Masséna, 04.93.34.93.00), stocking olive oils, *pistou*, honey, hams and absinthe. This area of the old town, a hive of Anglo-Frenchness, is also home to **Heidi's English Bookshop** (24 rue Aubernon, 04.93.34.74.11). In place Nationale, comic artist Raymond Peynet's **Musée Peynet** is dedicated to cartoon art.

The old town can become frenzied in high season, but wander into its more residential streets and you'll be amazed at how peaceful it feels. Don't miss the area known as the **Commune Libre du Safranier**, which has its own 'mayor', Zézé Marconi, and mission: to preserve local traditions while raising money for the poor with events such as giant street feasts. It's beautifully kept, with flowers cascading from the bright blue shuttered windows of the stone houses along rues du Safranier, du Bas Castelet and du Haut Castelet.

Heading south out of Antibes, the scenery changes dramatically from built-up citadel to leafy lap of luxury. The **Cap d'Antibes** peninsula is a playground for the super-rich, although most of the houses are of the classic, understated variety rather than the glitzy *Footballers' Wives* type. Rent a bike from one of the many outlets along boulevard Wilson and take in the views as you wend your way up to the **Jardin Botanique de la Villa Thuret**, established in 1856. If cycling sounds like too much exertion, take advantage of the Cap's long stretches of public beach at **plage de la Salis** and **plage de la Garoupe**. Both are within walking distance of Antibes and Juan-les-Pins.

Between the two, and a fair hike uphill, the **Sanctuaire de la Garoupe** displays a great collection of unlikely ex-votos. At the southern tip of the peninsula, the **Musée Naval et Napoléonien** has model ships and charts and mementos of the great man. Next to it stands another historical landmark: the magnificent **Hôtel du Cap**.

To the west of the peninsula, **Juan-les-Pins** has no pretensions to history: a sandy, deserted bay until the 1920s, it was conceived for – and still attracts – a hedonist crowd. The centre is a seething mass of boutiques and restaurants; if it seems frantic during the day, you should see it on a summer's night. The beautiful beach has both public and private sections.

East of Antibes (a ten-minute drive by the N7, or a five-minute walk from Biot train station), **Marineland** is a major tourist draw. Visitors can get close to sharks (in a 30-metre tunnel), penguins, giant turtles, sea lions and falcons, but the main attractions are the playful dolphins and rather more daunting-looking orcas, which perform synchronised feats in a 4,000-seater stadium. The complex also houses three other amusement parks; in summer, it's worth paying extra for Aquasplash, whose 13 giant slides, wavepool and newly added Pirate Island provide welcome relief from the heat.

Fort Carré
av du 11 Novembre (06.14.89.17.45). **Open**
Mid June-mid Sept 10am-5.30pm Tue-Sun. *Mid
Sept-mid June* 10am-4pm Tue-Sun. **Admission**
€3; €1.50 reductions. **No credit cards.**

FREE Jardin Botanique
90 chemin Raymond (04.97.21.25.00). **Open**
Apr-Oct 8am-6pm Mon-Fri. *Nov-Mar* 8.30am-
5.30pm Mon-Fri. **Admission** free.

Marineland
*306 av Mozart (04.93.33.49.49/www.marine
land.fr).* **Open** *July-Aug* 10am-11.30pm (last entry
at 10.30pm) daily. *Feb-June, Sept-Nov, mid Dec-
early Jan* 10am-5.30pm daily. *Nov-mid Dec* 10am-
5.30pm Wed, Sat, Sun. Closed early Jan-early Feb.
Admission *Marineland* €35; €26 reductions;
free under-3s. **Credit** MC, V.

Musée d'Histoire et d'Archéologie
Bastion St-André, 3 av Mezière (04.92.90.54.37).
Open *Jan-June, Sept-Dec* 10am-noon, 2-6pm Tue-
Sun. *July-Aug* 10am-noon, 2-6pm Tue, Thur, Sat,
Sun; 10am-noon, 2-8pm Wed, Fri. **Admission**
€3; free under-18s. **Credit** MC, V.

Musée Napoléonien
bd Kennedy (04.93.61.45.32). **Open** *June-Sept*
10am-6pm Tue-Sat. *Oct-May* 10am-4pm Tue-Sat.
Admission €3; free under-18s. **No credit cards.**

Musée Peynet
chemin Raymond, pl Nationale (04.92.90.54.30).
Open *Sept-June* 10am-noon, 2-6pm Tue-Sun. *July,
Aug* 10am-noon, 2-6pm Tue, Thur, Sat, Sun; 10am-
noon, 2-8pm Wed, Fri. **Admission** €3; €1.50
reductions; free under-18s. **No credit cards.**

★ Musée Picasso
Château Grimaldi, pl Mariejol (04.92.90.54.20).
Open *15-30 June, 1-15 Sept* 10am-6pm Tue-Sun.
July & Aug 10am-6pm Tue, Thur, Sat, Sun; 10am-
8pm Wed, Fri. *Mid Sept-mid June* 10am-noon,
2-6pm Tue-Sun. **Admission** €6; free under-18s.
Credit MC, V.

Where to eat & drink

Antibes's cosmopolitan old town is lined with
cafés and bistros – the trick is finding the good
ones, many of which close for lunch or, rather
oddly, during August.

The most talked-about new restaurant in
town is **Le Figuier de Saint-Esprit** (14 rue
St-Esprit, 04.93.34.50.12, closed Tue, lunch
Wed, mains €30-€40), where renowned chef
Christian Morrisset cooks up innovative dishes
such as squid and clam cannelloni with squid
ink and shellfish *jus*. Dinner is pricey, but
there are affordable lunch menus and a €49
set evening menu. Another chic choice is
Les Vieux Murs (25 prom Amiral de Grasse,
04.93.34.06.73, closed lunch Mon-Sat mid June-
mid Sept, all Mon & lunch Tue mid Sept-mid
June, mains €32-€39), whose young chef
Philippe Tribet previously worked with
Morrisset. His pared-down cooking highlights
seasonal ingredients; sample the *menu des
gourmets* for €42.

For a coffee in atmospheric surrounds, drop
by the age-old **Pimm's** (3 rue de la République,
04.93.34.04.88, http://pimmscafe.ifrance.com),
which still has a few writers and lovers hiding
in the woodwork, or head to the place Nationale,
cours Masséna or boulevard d'Aguillon
café strips. **L'Oursin** (16 rue République,

Commune Libre du Safranier.

THE RIVIERA & SOUTHERN ALPS

Plage de la Garoupe. *See p244.*

04.93.34.13.46, www.restaurant-loursin.fr, closed Mon Nov-Apr, mains €12-€55) is a seafood institution founded in 1962; try the classic fish soup or salade niçoise with fresh tuna, followed by an oyster or mixed seafood platter.

Le Brûlot (3 rue Frédéric Isnard, 04.93.34.17.76, www.brulot.com, closed Sun, lunch Mon-Wed, mains €12) is famous for its *socca* (chickpea pancake), grilled meats and fish, all cooked in a wood-fired oven.

La Taverne du Safranier (1 pl du Safranier, 04.93.34.80.50, closed mid Nov-mid Feb, all Mon & dinner Sun Sept-June, all Mon & lunch Tue July-Aug, mains €20-€25) is a bastion of local cuisine, serving sardine fritters, *petits farcis* (stuffed vegetables) and seafood pasta.

Classy **Oscar's** (8 rue du Dr Rostan, 04.93.34.90.14, www.oscars-antibes.com, closed Mon, Sun, 1st 2wks in June, end Dec-mid Jan, mains €20-€28) has a sleek, all-white interior. Its most expensive set menu is a five-course affair featuring lobster, caviar and truffles.

L'Ancre de Chine (26 bd d'Aguillon, 04.93.34.27.70, closed lunch Sat, menus €14-€21), the best Chinese in town, is justifiably busy, while next door **L'Eléphant Bleu** (28 bd d'Aguillon, 04.93.34.28.80, mains €15-€40) serves excellent Thai food.

Stylish foodies flock to sample knockout bouillabaisse or platters of langoustines at the venerable **Bacon** (bd de Bacon, 04.93.61.50.02, www.restaurantdebacon.com, closed Mon, lunch Tue, Nov-Feb, menus €49-€79); looking out over the Baie des Anges, the almost all-white dining room has a tented ceiling that is rolled back in summer. **Les Pêcheurs** (10 bd Maréchal Juin, Cap d'Antibes, 04.92.93.13.30, www.lespecheurs-lecap.com, closed Tue, lunch July-Aug, Tue-Wed Sept-June, mains €40-€60), a beach resort with a new luxury hotel that's due to open in May 2009, serves stunning local ingredients sniffed out by chefs Francis Chauveau and Hervé Busson, with a view of the Esterel and the Iles de Lérins.

At Juan-les-Pins there are plenty of beach establishments. The family-friendly **Plage Epi Beach** (bd Guillaumont, 04.93.67.27.84, closed Wed Sept-June, mains €12-€22) specialises in fish (including bouillabaisse), lobster and provençal food. Lively **La Bodega** (16 av du Dr Dautheville, Antibes, 04.93.67.59.02, mains €8-€26) stays open until the early hours in summer to feed revellers from local nightlife haunts. **Bijou Plage** (bd du Littoral, Juan-les-Pins, 04.93.61.39.07, www.bijouplage.com, mains €22-€30), offers reliable seafood, such as prawns flambéed with cognac, on the seafront.

For a touch of crustacean class, visit **Festival de la Mer** (146 bd Wilson, Antibes, 04.93.61.04.62, closed lunch mid June-mid Sept, mains €20-€30) which serves buckets of oysters, scallops and snails. The highly regarded **Perroquet** (3 av Georges Gallice, 04.93.61.02.20, closed Nov-26 Dec, mains €17-€45) is possibly Juan-les-Pins's finest, with an emphasis on traditional French cuisine.

Nightlife

With a club scene that's more affordable than in St-Tropez or Monaco, Juan-les-Pins has some of the liveliest nightlife on the Côte. The best club is **Le Village** (pl de la Nouvelle Orléans, 1 bd de la Pinède, 04.92.93.90.00, closed Mon-Thu, Sun, admission €16). DJs play a mix of pop and house, and the vast monastic interior is *très* cool – though hefty drinks prices quickly blow a hole in the pocket. Nearby, Juan icon **Whisky à Go Go** (5 av Jacques Léonetti, La Pinède, 04.93.61.26.40, closed Nov-Mar, admission €16) is showing its age with a kitsch 1970s disco feel. Young upstart **Minimal** (142 bd Président Wilson, 04.93.67.78.87, closed Sun-Thur, admission varies) is dedicated to house music.

The suavest hangout for drinks is the **Hôtel St-Charles Lounge** (4 rue St-Charles, 04.93.61.18.82, www.hotelsaintcharles.fr, closed Jan, Feb), where DJs try to tempt cocktail drinkers on to the dancefloor from 10pm onwards. A superb club and casino on the seafront east of Antibes is **La Siesta-Le Pearl** (rte du Bord de Mer, 04.93.33.31.31, www.pearl-lasiesta.com, admission €10), where you can dance to pop and house in the open air and people-watch on the terrace. **Xtrême Café** (6 rue Aubernon, 04.93.34.03.80) is a fashionable bar for cocktails, aperitifs and nibbles, while **Café Cosy** (3 rue Migranier, 04.93.34.81.55, closed Mon) is a mellow place to listen to jazz and blues. For a wilder soirée, visit the **Absinthe Bar** (25 cours Masséna, 04.93.34.93.00), where you can steep yourself in the history of this much-maligned spirit.

Activities

Water sports & yacht hire

It was in Juan-les-Pins, they say, that waterskiing was invented in the 1930s at the beach of the glamorous Hôtel Belles-Rives, which still has its own waterskiing club. The **Ecole de Ski Nautique** (Plage Bretagne, 06.13.61.51.17) is another waterskiing specialist. For diving, **Golfe Plongée Club** (port de Golfe-Juan, 06.09.55.73.36) offers beginners' courses, while **Côté Plongée** (bd Maréchal Juin, 06.72.74.34.94, www.cote plongee.com) on Cap d'Antibes runs children's courses, and exploratory and night dives. On the Antibes side of the Cap, the **Club Nautique** (quai du Fort Carré, Port Vauban, 04.93.65.80.00, http://cna.antibes.free.fr) is a professional set-up with dinghies and catamarans to hire or learn on.

If a cruise is your idea of nirvana, stop by **Yachtbrokers International** (21 rue Aubernon, 04.93.34.04.75, www.ybi1.com, closed Sat, Sun), which can provide an eight-berth, 23-knot motorboat with a captain and two crew (from €3,500 a day, plus fuel, port fees, food and drink). **Arthaud Yachting** (61 chemin de l'Ermitage, Cap d'Antibes, 04.93.61.51.00, www.arthaudyachting.com) organises excursions to hidden corners of the Côte d'Azur that are accessible only by boat.

Where to stay

Of all the hotels on the French Riviera, the **Hôtel du Cap Eden-Roc** (bd Kennedy, Cap d'Antibes, 04.93.61.39.01, www.edenroc-hotel.fr, closed mid Oct-mid Apr, double €460-€620) is probably the most exclusive, and certainly the most expensive. Set back from the coast in 25 acres of woodland, the hotel can be irritatingly overrun by celebrities and their bodyguards. Smartly dressed non-residents can use the restaurant, bar and pool, but expect a hefty fee if you so much as glance at a sunlounger.

A wallet-friendly alternative is the **Hôtel Beau Site** (141 bd Kennedy, 04.93.61.53.43, www.hotelbeausite.net, double €90-€155), offering clean, simple accommodation and a pool. More affordable still is **Hôtel La Jabotte** (13 av Max Maurey, Cap d'Antibes, 04.93.61.45.89, www.jabotte.com, double €66-€96), minutes from a sandy beach but so welcoming that you might not want to leave its leafy garden, particularly between 6pm and 8pm, when the owners serve the house aperitif. Each of the ten rooms has nautical wood panelling and its own soothing colour.

In a central but peaceful location by Antibes's main square, former coaching inn **Le Relais du Postillon** (8 rue Championnet, 04.93.34.20.77, www.relaisdupostillon.com, closed 2wks Nov-Dec, double €63-€89) has cheery, recently renovated rooms. Nearby, the **Modern Hôtel** (1 rue Fourmilière, 04.92.90.59.05, www.modernhotel06.com, closed mid Dec-mid Jan, double €66-€85) has comfortable rooms with a slightly 1980s feel. Somewhat cosier is the **Hôtel Le Ponteil** (11 impasse Jean Mensier, 04.93.34.67.92, www.leponteil.com, closed mid Nov-Feb, double €79-€94), with a leafy exterior.

For thalassotherapy spa treatments, stop by the modern **Thalazur Hôtel Baie des Anges** (770 chemin des Moyennes Bréguières, Antibes, 04.92.91.82.00, double €93-€139), which uses water pumped up from the sea. **Hôtel Juan Beach** (5 rue de l'Oratoire, Juan-les-Pins, 04.93.61.02.89, www.hoteljuanbeach. com, closed Oct-Mar, double €93-€127), a five-minute walk from the nightlife action, has acquired a lovely pool, outdoor lounge area and new bathrooms under its current owners.

The **Hôtel Castel Mistral** (43 rue Bricka, Juan-les-Pins, 04.93.61.21.04, closed Oct-Mar, double €76-€94) is a charmingly dilapidated place, handy for the beach, with a pretty terrace out front. To do Juan in style, though, stay at the **Hôtel Juana** (La Pinède, av Gallice, 04.93.61.08.70, www.hotel-juana.com, double €220-€335), a refined art deco jewel, two minutes from the sea. Run by the same owners, the classic **Hôtel Belles-Rives** (33 bd Edouard Baudoin, 04.93.61.02.79, www.belles rives.com, double €145-€740) has retained its 1920s style and furnishings. Unwind in the luxurious bars and lounges, or try your hand at water sports on the private beach. Inexpensive charm, antiques and a sunny terrace make **La Marjolaine** (15 av du Dr Fabre, 04.93.61.06.60, closed Nov-mid Dec, double €50-€70), steps from Juan-les-Pins station, a delightful find.

Resources

Internet

Cybercafé Bang Lounge Bar *av de Cannes, (04.93.67.60.60).* **Open** 9am-midnight daily.

Tourist Information

Accueil Touristique du Vieil Antibes *32 bd d'Aguillon (04.93.34.65.65).* **Open** *July, Aug* 10am-9pm daily. *Sept, June* 10am-noon, 1.30-6pm Mon-Fri; 10am-noon Sat.

Antibes Office de Tourisme *11 pl de Gaulle, Antibes (04.97.23.11.11/www.antibes-juanlespins.com).* **Open** *July, Aug* 9am-7pm daily. *Sept-June* 9am-12.30pm, 1.30-6pm Mon-Fri; 9am-noon, 2-6pm Sat; 10am-noon Sun.

Juan-les-Pins Office de Tourisme *51 bd Guillaumont, Juan-les-Pins (04.97.23.11.10/ www.antibes-juanlespins.com).* **Open** *July, Aug* 9am-7pm daily. *Sept-June* 9am-12.30pm, 1.30-6pm Mon-Fri; 9am-noon, 2-6pm Sat; 10am-noon Sun.

BIOT

Picturesque **Biot** (pronounced Bee-ot) is best known for its glassware – a trade that has flourished here since the 1950s, when the **Verrerie de Biot** fired up its furnaces. Half working factory and half gallery, the Verrerie is just off the main D4 road, below the town walls. Visitors can watch the unique Biot 'bubble glassware' (*verre bullé*) being blown, and there are plenty of chances to buy both here and in the village, where rue St-Sébastien is lined with glassware shops. One of the best is **Raphaël Farinelli** (465 rte de la Mer, 04.93.65.17.29 (workshop), 24 rue St-Sébastien, 04.93.65.01.89 (shop)). The **Galerie Internationale du Verre** (chemin des Combes, 04.93.65.03.00)

is also worth a visit, with its collection of highly sculptural glass by US and European artists.

Biot is also home to the wonderful **Musée National Fernand Léger**. Reopened in 2008 after years of renovations, the low-slung building is set in undulating sculpture gardens. It traces the work of the restless, politically committed artist from his first Impressionist stirrings in 1905, through his boldly coloured 'machine art' of the 1920s and '30s to the later murals, stained glass, ceramics and tapestries.

The village is a vivid mix of galleries, cafés and a tangle of little lanes; on Tuesday mornings a market is held on rue St-Sébastien and the pretty place des Arcades; the square is surrounded by Italianate loggias – a home-from-home touch brought by Genoese settlers who moved in to repopulate Biot after the Black Death. The pretty church has good altarpieces by Louis Bréa and Giovanni Canavesio.

The **Musée d'Histoire et de la Céramique Biotoises** has a patchy but charming collection of local costumes and artefacts. On the way out of Biot, pick up tips and buy plants at the **Bonsai Arboretum**, a collection of over 1,000 bonsai in a 2,000 square-metre (21,500-square-foot) Japanese garden, tended by two generations of the Okonek family.

Bonsai Arboretum

299 chemin du Val de Pôme (04.93.65.63.99/ http://museedubonsai.free.fr). **Open** 10am-noon, 2-6pm Mon, Wed-Sun. **Admission** €4; €2 reductions; free under-6s. **No credit cards.**

Verrerie de Biot.

Musée d'Histoire et de la Céramique Biotoises

9 rue St-Sébastien (04.93.65.54.54). Open July-Sept 11am-7pm Wed-Sun. *Oct-June* 2-6pm Wed-Sun. **Admission** €2; €1 reductions; free under-16s. **No credit cards.**

★ Musée National Fernand Léger

chemin du Val de Pôme (04.92.91.50.30/ www.musee-fernandleger.fr). Open June-Oct 10am-6pm Mon, Wed-Sun. *Nov-Apr* 10am-5pm Mon, Wed-Sun. **Admission** €6.50; €5 reductions; free under-18s.

La Verrerie de Biot

chemin des Combes (04.93.65.03.00/www. verreriebiot.com). Open July, Aug 9.30am-8pm Mon-Sat; 10am-1pm, 10.30am-1.30pm, 2.30-7.30pm Sun. *Sept-June* 9.30am-6.30pm Mon-Sat; 10am-1.30pm, 2.30-6.30pm Sun. **Admission** €3.

Where to stay & eat

The charming **Hôtel des Arcades** (16 pl des Arcades, 04.93.65.01.04, www.hotel-restaurant-les-arcades.com, closed mid Nov-mid Dec, 10 days Jan, double €55-€100, restaurant closed Mon, dinner Sun, mains €16-€23) is a 15th-century mansion that mixes ancient (huge fireplaces, four-posters) and modern. The owner is a collector, and the gallery-cum-restaurant displays works by artists including Vasarely, Léger and Folon. Provençal classics (hearty *daube de boeuf*; aïoli on Fridays) are made with local produce, and staff are delightfully friendly.

Laid-back **Le Jarrier** (30 passage Bourgade, 04.93.65.11.68, www.lejarrier.com, closed Mon, Sun, mains €27-€37), set in a converted jar factory, serves Mediterranean dishes laced with truffles, spices and fruit. On central rue St-Sébastien, **Le Piccolo** (No.30, 04.93.65.16.91, closed Wed, menus €19-€25) dishes up pizza, pasta and provençal dishes on its shady terrace.

A lively locals' hangout is **Le Bar du Coin** (29 rue St-Sébastien, 04.93.65.10.72, mains €12-€15), where enormous salads and grilled meats can be washed down with local wine and a healthy selection of beers. On the same street, the long-established **Crêperie du Vieux Village** (2 rue St-Sébastien, 04.93.65.72.73, closed Thur, menu €13.50) serves a wide selection of crêpes, including the 'deadly sin' (involving Calvados, apple, hazelnuts, caramel and crème Chantilly).

Tucked away in what was a 16th-century potter's workshop, stylish **Les Terraillers** (11 rte du Chemin Neuf, 04.93.65.01.59, www.les terraillers.com, closed Wed, Thur, Nov, mains €39-€48) has a delightful atmosphere and a host of provençal dishes, with a €39 menu at lunch. **La Pierre à Four** (15 rte de Valbonne, 04.93.65.60.00, closed lunch Mon, Wed & Fri

July & Aug, Mon, Tue & dinner Sun Sept-June, menus €19-€35) has no terrace, but makes up for it with an unbeatable-value set menu, which sometimes features foie gras. Near Sophia-Antipolis, **L'O Vive** (329 rte d'Antibes, 04.93.65.07.83, closed Sun, Sat lunch, mains €13-€18 lunch, €22-€24 dinner) serves creative Mediterranean cuisine in a stylish setting. Out-of-town elegance can be found at the **Domaine du Jas** (625 rte de la Mer, 04.93.65.50.50, www.domainedujas.com, closed Nov-Feb, double €100-€235), a ten-minute drive towards the sea. It has a mosaic-bottomed pool, palm trees and several homely reception rooms.

Resources

Tourist information

Office du Tourisme *46 rue St-Sébastien, 06410 Biot (04.93.65.78.00/www.biot.fr). Open July, Aug* 10am-7pm Mon-Fri; 2.30-7pm Sat, Sun. *Sept-June* 9am-noon, 2-6pm Mon-Fri; 2-6pm Sat, Sun.

VILLENEUVE-LOUBET & CAGNES

Zip through the beachside resorts between Antibes and Nice and you'll be missing out. Just a few kilometres inland lie the medieval centres of Villeneuve-Loubet and Haut-de-Cagnes, where vine-covered houses and traditional restaurants meet fine views and few tourists.

The graceful lanes of **Villeneuve-Loubet** hide more than their fair share of galleries, cafés and attractive squares. In fact, it's so peaceful that holidaying rock and film stars have taken to hiding here from the silly-season paparazzi on the coast. The **Musée de l'Art Culinaire** celebrates one of Villeneuve's most famous sons, Auguste Escoffier, who turned cooking from a trade to an art and became head chef of the Savoy in London. If you're inspired to attempt some culinary feats of your own, the town's market is on Tuesday and Friday mornings. At the foot of the old town is the **Musée d'Histoire et d'Art**, where military relics rub shoulders with a handful of portraits and an exhibition space devoted to regional artists.

Three kilometres away, the purpose-built resort of **Villeneuve-Loubet Plage** stretches

---

INSIDE TRACK
HOOKED ON CLASSICS

The village church of **Biot** makes a wonderfully atmospheric venue for the summer **Festival des Heures Musicales de Biot**. For details of the programming, see www.heuresmusicalesdebiot.com.

THE RIVIERA & SOUTHERN ALPS

around the **Marina Baie des Anges**, an enormous (and some might say hideous) 1960s apartment complex. Shaped like a giant wave, it can be seen for miles around; weekly visits are organised by the tourist office (10am Wed July & Aug, €3). The seafront teems with seafood and pizza joints, water sports activities and a long pebbly beach, packed out with families.

Cagnes, a few kilometres down the coast towards Nice, is, in fact, three separate entities: seafront Cros-de-Cagnes; the Cagnes-sur-Mer, which is actually inland; and medieval Haut-de-Cagnes. Perched on high, the latter is home to the UNESCO-sponsored **Festival International de la Peinture** each summer (contact the tourist office for details, *see right*).

Cros-de-Cagnes started life as a fishing village but today is better known for its crowded pebbly beach, water sports hire and beachfront string of restaurants and hotels. On the other side of the busy A8 lies **Cagnes-sur-Mer**, home to Auguste Renoir's estate, **Les Collettes**. The artist had the house built in 1908 after his doctor prescribed a drier, warmer climate for his rheumatoid arthritis. Although Renoir painted his *Grandes Baigneuses* here, he complained that the sun was too dazzling and turned to sculpture, working up until his death in 1919 and battling against the growing paralysis in his hands. The house is preserved pretty much as he left it, and there's also a collection of paintings of the artist by his friends, as well as a few of his own works.

The town also has a wonderful food and clothes market on rue du Marché that leads to the **Cité Marchande**, a covered mornings-only market (closed Mon). On the slip road between the A8 and Cagnes-sur-Mer is the **Atelier des Parfums** (43 chemin des Presses, Cagnes-sur-Mer, 04.93.22.69.01, www.atelier-des-parfums. com) perfume factory. Guides give you a free tour of the factory and let you sample one of scores of different scents; there are also perfume-making workshops. More exhilarating is the **Hippodrome Côte d'Azur** (04.93.22.51.00, www.hippodrome-cotedazur.fr, closed mid Mar-June, Sept-mid Dec). In summer racing is a chariot style known as 'le Trot'; the Cannes to Nice train stops here during racing season.

High on the hill within walking distance of Cagnes-sur-Mer, or reached by a shuttle bus from Cagnes bus station, is the wonderfully unspoilt **Haut-de-Cagnes**. It's a favourite spot for contemporary artists of all persuasions, drawn by an annual arts festival but also by the **Musée Mediterranéen d'Art Moderne** and the **Donation Suzy Solidor** (a collection of 40 portraits by Cocteau, Dufy and Lempicka), both of which are housed in the dramatic **Château-Musée Grimaldi**, part Renaissance residence, part 14th-century fortress. In the town centre,

the **Eglise St-Pierre** has fine stained glass and a marble font. To the east is the stunning **Chapelle Notre-Dame-de-Protection**, where statues and a host of wonderful arches are backdropped by warm-hued frescoes.

★ **Château-Musée Grimaldi**

pl Grimaldi, Haut-de-Cagnes (04.92.02.47.30). **Open** *May-Sept* 10am-noon, 2-6pm Mon, Wed-Sun. *Oct-Apr* 10am-noon, 2-5pm Mon, Wed-Sun. Closed 3wks Nov. **Admission** €3 (€4.50 with Musée Renoir); €1.50 reductions; free under-18s. **No credit cards**.

Musée Escoffier de l'Art Culinaire

3 rue Auguste Escoffier, Villeneuve-Loubet Village (04.93.20.80.51/www.fondation-escoffier.org). **Open** *July, Aug* 2-7pm Mon, Tue, Thur, Sat, Sun; 10am-noon, 2-7pm Wed, Fri. *Sept-June* 2-6pm Mon-Fri, Sun. Closed Nov. **Admission** €5; €2.50 reductions; free under-11s. **No credit cards**.

Musée d'Histoire et d'Art

pl de l'Hôtel de Ville, Villeneuve-Loubet Village (04.92.02.47.30). **Open** *May-Apr* 10am-noon, 2-6pm Mon, Wed-Sun. *Oct-Apr* 10am-noon, 2-5pm Mon, Wed-Sun; 9am-12.30pm Sat. Closed 2wks Nov. **Admission** €3; €1.50 reductions; free under-18s. **No credit cards**.

Musée Renoir, Les Collettes

chemin des Collettes, Cagnes-sur-Mer (04.93.20.61.07). **Open** *May-Sept* 10am-noon, 2-6pm Mon, Wed-Sun. *Oct-Apr* 10am-noon, 2-5pm Mon, Wed-Sun. Closed 2wks Nov. **Admission** €3 (€4.50 with Château-Musée Grimaldi); €1.50 reductions; free under-18s. **No credit cards**.

Where to stay, eat & drink

The area's most luxurious accommodation can be found at **Le Cagnard** (54 rue Sous-Barri, 04.93.20.73.22, www.le-cagnard.com, double €135-€310) in Haut-de-Cagnes, set in a gorgeous 12th-century building, with spectacular views. Try roast pigeon, duck or lamb under the coat-of-arms-studded ceiling of the restaurant (closed lunch Mon, Tue, Thur, mid Nov-mid Dec, menus €56-€96), which opens dramatically to reveal the sky.

The **Villa Estelle** (5 montée de la Bourgade, Haut-de-Cagnes, 04.92.02.89.83, www.villa-estelle.com, double €100-€145) is a medieval coaching inn with a handful of rooms; the newly added suite Estelle has a private terrace. The modern, almost cool **Grimaldi** (6 pl du Château, Haut-de-Cagnes, 04.93.20.60.24, www.hotelgrimaldi.com, double €125-€185) overlooks the main square and has a reliable restaurant (closed Tue, mains €20-€29).

THE RIVIERA & SOUTHERN ALPS

Haut-de-Cagnes's dining scene is centred on the steep montée de la Bourgade and the place du Château at the top. **Fleur de Sel** (85 montée de la Bourgade, 04.93.20.33.33, www.restaurant-fleurdesel.com, closed Wed, lunch Thur, 2wks Jan, 2wks Oct/Nov, mains €20-€25) serves updated provençal cooking, such as slow-cooked John Dory fillet with aubergine caviar and chorizo *jus*. **Entre Cour et Jardin** (102 montée de la Bourgade, 04.93.20.72.27, closed Mon, lunch Tue & Sat, 2wks Jan, 1wk June, 1wk Oct, mains €18-€28) is also innovative, serving variations on oysters, foie gras and quail, and classic steak.

On nearby rue Hippolyte Guis, Italian **Il Melograno** (04.93.73.92.80, www.restaurantil melograno.fr, closed lunch, Thur, 1wk Nov, 1wk Feb, mains €16-€18) serves dishes from Piedmont, such as roasted veal in fig sauce or rabbit in white wine sauce. Near the busy main square, friendly **Les Baux** (2 pl du Château, 04.93.73.14.00, closed Mon June-Oct, dinner Nov-May, 2wks Dec, mains €12-€16) offers home-style French cooking. The owners also run a B&B (www.loustalounet.com, double €70).

At Cros-de-Cagnes port, **La Réserve aka Lou Lou** (91 bd de la Plage, 04.93.31.00.17, closed Sun, lunch Sat, mains €29-€38) is a justly acclaimed restaurant. Crustaceans stud the menu, from prawns in ginger to lobster *à l'armoricaine*. At the pleasantly bourgeois **La Bourride** (Port de Cros de Cagnes, 04.93.31.07.

75, closed Wed, mains €30-€40), chef Hervé Khobzi serves classic *bourride* (monkfish stew flavoured with aïoli) and more creative dishes on the glassed-in terrace or shady patio. For more down-to-earth moules-frites, head to **La Caravelle** (42 bd de la Plage, 04.93.20.10.09, closed lunch Mon, Jan, mains €15-€20).

In Villeneuve-Loubet, **L'Auberge Fleurie** (13 rue des Mesures, 04.93.73.90.92, closed July & Aug Wed, Sept-June Wed, Thur, mid Nov-mid Dec, mains €18-€25) cooks up hearty dishes in traditional surroundings.

Resources

Tourist information
Cagnes-sur-Mer Office de Tourisme
6 bd Maréchal Juin, Cagnes-sur-Mer, Villeneuve-Loubet (04.93.20.61.64/www.cagnes-tourisme.com). **Open** *July, Aug* 9am-12.30pm, 2-6pm Mon-Fri; 9am-12.30pm Sat. *Sept-June* 9am-noon, 2-6pm Mon-Fri; 9am-noon Sat.
Villeneuve-Loubet Plage Office de Tourisme *16 av de la Mer (04.92.02.70.16/ www.ot-villeneuveloubet.org).* **Open** *July, Aug* 9am-7pm Mon-Sat; 10am-1pm Sun. *Sept-June* 9am-noon, 2-6pm Mon-Fri; 9.30am-12.30pm Sat.
Villeneuve-Loubet Village Office de Tourisme *Annexe rue de l'Hôtel de Ville, Villeneuve-Loubet (04.92.02.66.16/www.ot-villeneuveloubet.org).* **Open** *July, Aug* 9.30am-12.30pm Mon-Sat. *Sept-June* 9am-noon, 3-5pm Mon-Fri; 9.30am-12.30pm Sat.

GETTING THERE & AROUND
By bus
RCA (04.93.85.64.44) bus No.200 between Cannes and Nice runs every 15mins Mon-Sat, every 30mins Sun, stopping at Antibes, Juan-les-Pins, Villeneuve-Loubet, Biot and Cagnes. Shuttle bus 10A runs hourly between Antibes station and Biot. Call Antibes bus station (08.00.06.01.06). **TAM** (04.93.85.61.81) buses run from Cannes to Nice, serving Biot, Antibes, Cannes, Vence and St-Paul.
By car
For Antibes-Juan-les-Pins, leave the A8 at exit 44, or drive along the prettier N98 coast road. Juan-les-Pins is west of Cap d'Antibes; Villeneuve-Loubet and Cagnes are east of Antibes. In summer, avoid the N7 Antibes to Nice at the Biot junction, which becomes one long car park when Marineland is emptying out. For Biot, take the N7 and then D4 Biot–Valbonne road, 3km after Antibes.
By train
Antibes is served by high-speed TGVs from Paris and more frequent local trains, which also stop at Juan-les-Pins, Biot, Cagnes-sur-Mer, Cros-de-Cagnes and Villeneuve-Loubet Plage. Shuttle buses connect Cagnes-sur-Mer and Haut-de-Cagnes and Villeneuve-Loubet Plage and old town.

Chapelle Notre-Dame-de-Protection.

Nice

Exuberant, Italianate Nice has an inimitable charm.

Its beach may be painfully pebbly, but **Nice** has never let such minor details stand in its way. A winter retreat for pampered aristocrats in the 18th and 19th centuries, thanks to its mild climate and gift for self-promotion, it has thrived on the tourist trade ever since. Yet while visitors flock here from every corner of the globe, the city remains remarkably unfazed by all the attention. Less glossy than its counterparts along the coast, Nice has never bartered its soul to the tourist dollar.

Inland from Nice, the **Arrière Pays**, are a quietly delightful mini-wilderness of olive groves, pine woods, wild flowers and precariously perched villages, offering cooling summer breezes, spectacular panoramas and rustic cuisine.

ABOUT THE CITY

The promenade des Anglais, crowned by the flamboyant Hôtel Negresco, is the city's most famous sight, dotted with sun-drenched palm trees and flanked by the turquoise bay. Following its curve takes you to the Old Town, with its shuttered, ochre-hued buildings, pretty churches, gallery-filled alleys and busy bars.

Yet the city has always had a darker side, and a reputation for organised crime. 'Avoid the region of Nice,' Graham Greene advised his readers in 1982, describing it as 'the preserve of some of the most criminal organisations in the South of France.' This shady image stems in part from the financial shenanigans of its late, long-time mayor, Jacques Médecin (who ended up fleeing to Uruguay).

Yet although Nice is said to have a high crime rate, figures show it is only slightly more dangerous than Paris and less crime-ridden than Cannes or Antibes. In recent years, the Old Town has cleaned up its act considerably – although night-time festivities often lead to slurred 3am shouting matches (most of them in English), which echo along the narrow streets.

Culturally, there is plenty happening here, from the summer jazz festival to the packed programme at the Opéra de Nice. The number of art galleries and museums is also dazzling – with free entry to municipal museums as of summer 2008. There's also a year-round line-up of festivals, including the Carnaval in the run-up to Lent and the Fête des Mais in May.

History

Prehistoric man set up camp some 400,000 years ago at the site known as Terra Amata at the foot of Mont Boron, not far from where Sir Elton John's hilltop villa now perches. In the fourth century BC, Phocaean Greeks from Marseille sailed into the harbour and founded a no-expense-spared trading post around another prominent hill (now the Colline du Château), naming it Nikaïa.

The Romans arrived in 100 BC and built an imposing city on a third hill that they called Cemenelum (today's Cimiez). The town's prime location made it an obvious target in the Dark Ages for invading Saracens and Barbarians, who left it in ruins, but by the 14th century it was thriving once again.

In 1382, Jeanne, Queen of Sicily and Countess of Provence, was smothered to death on the order of her cousin Charles of Durazzo, Prince of Naples. He and another cousin, Louis of Anjou, then staked their claims on the rich area – but after sizing up the balance of power, the wily Niçois decided to shun both, and allied themselves with the Counts of Savoy.

Apart from a brief period of control by Revolutionary forces between 1792 and 1814, Nice belonged to Savoy until 1860. Italian art, food and culture became intrinsic to the region. France tried to reclaim Nice several times, finally succeeding when Napoleon III signed the Treaty of Turin in 1860 with the King of Sardinia; the treaty was later ratified in a plebiscite, though the result (some 25,700 pro-French to 260 anti-French votes) had a strong smell of election-rigging about it.

Over a century before that, Nice was discovered by wealthy British travellers seeking winter warmth. In 1822, they raised a subscription for the building of the seafront esplanade still called the promenade des Anglais, and smart hotels sprang up to cater to the demand. When Queen Victoria and her entourage descended in the 1890s, the town's fashionable status was assured.

In the early 1960s, Nice became a cutting-edge artistic hub, thanks to the impetus of New Realists Yves Klein and Arman. Other artists flourished under the aegis of this movement; works by Venet, César and Ben can be seen at MAMAC (the Musée d'Art Moderne et d'Art Contemporain) and dotted around the city.

Former mayor Jean Médecin (father of the more controversial Jacques) has left his mark, too: the city's main shopping street is named after him, and you'll still see his book on niçois cuisine in local bookshops. The city's current mayor is the centre-right Christian Estrosi, elected in 2008: so far, his biggest headline-grabbing moment has been signing the birth certificates for new Riviera residents Angelina Jolie and Brad Pitt's twins.

SIGHTSEEING

Vieux Nice, Colline du Château & Vieux Port

Bordered by the Baie des Anges and Colline du Château, **Vieux Nice** is the most colourful quarter of the city. Faded, pastel-painted buildings line its labyrinthine alleys, opening up into café-filled squares. Once shunned as crime-ridden and poverty-stricken, it's now much sought-after among young property-hunters and second-homers, who live alongside lifelong residents. The latter quietly go about their business, negotiating the tourist-filled streets with remarkable tolerance and maintaining the old ways of life: religious festivals, such as the procession on Palm Sunday, are still taken very seriously indeed.

The heart of the *vielle ville* lies just back from the seafront, along lively **cours Saleya**. Here, cut flowers perfume the air and fruit and vegetable stalls operate from dawn to lunchtime, Tuesday to Sunday; on Mondays, *brocanteurs* take over, selling a jumble of antiques, junk and second-hand clothes.

Presiding over the square is the **Chapelle de la Miséricorde**, with its superb baroque interior, decorated with soaring blue and gold

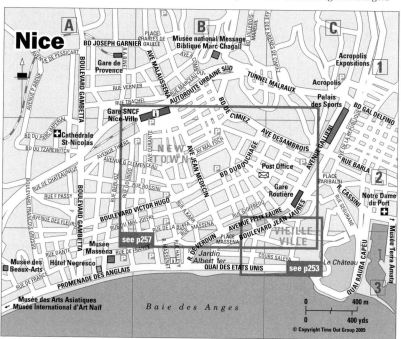

© Copyright Time Out Group 2009

THE RIVIERA & SOUTHERN ALPS

columns, lavish frescoes and a 15th-century Louis Bréa altarpiece. Also of note (though not open to the public) is the faded yellow building at 1 place Charles Félix, at the end of cours Saleya, home to Henri Matisse from 1921 to 1938. Towards the seafront, the 19th-century **Opéra de Nice** is grandly belle époque. Nearby, on the quai des Etats-Unis, the **Galerie de la Marine** and **Galerie des Ponchettes** exhibit changing exhibitions of contemporary art in airy, tranquil surrounds.

The **Centre du Patrimoine** (75 quai des Etats-Unis, 04.92.00.41.90, closed Sat, Sun) celebrates Nice's heritage, and runs a superb weekly programme of guided walks. For €3 you can learn about the city's art deco legacy, follow the course of its hidden river, or explore Cimiez's Queen Victoria connection; pre-book for the ever-popular tour of Nice's Russian monuments (€6).

Café-filled place Rossetti is home to two places of pilgrimage: the **Cathédrale de Ste-Réparate**, a loving tribute to Nice's patron saint that is remarkable for its glazed-tile roof, and the legendary **Fenocchio** (2 pl Rossetti, 04.93.80.72.52, www.fenocchio.fr, closed Dec & Jan) ice-cream parlour. No fewer than 90 different flavours are on display, making for much last-minute indecision as you near the front of the queue; avocado, black olive and chewing gum are among the more outré scoops.

On rue de la Poissonnerie, the baroque **Chapelle de l'Annonciation** is known locally as the Chapelle Ste-Rita, out of respect for an Italian saint still venerated in Nice as a miracle healer of terminal diseases. A few streets north-east of here, gallery-lined rue Droite shelters the tiny, Jesuit-built **Eglise du Jésus** (pl du Gesù, open 2.30-5.30pm Tue, Thur), a masterpiece of baroque artistry. A short stroll on, **Palais Lascaris** is a treasure trove of Flemish tapestries and 17th-century furniture.

On the corner with rue Collet, a queue often stretches outside **Lou Pilha Leva** (10 rue Collet, 04.93.13.99.08, mains €8-€12), waiting to order a paper plate of *socca* or a slice of *tourte de blettes*. Past here, rue Droite feeds into rue

St-François, thronged with clothes shops and tourist trinket-sellers; place St-François is the site of a small fish market (daily, except Tue).

Marking the Old Town's northern boundary is the elegantly arcaded place Garibaldi, laid out in the 18th century and later named after the hero of Italian unification, born in the Vieux Port in 1807. Restaurants huddle beneath its arches; stop by **Pâtisserie Cappa** (Nos.7-9, 04.93.62.30.83, closed Mon, Sept) for heavenly pastries, mousse cakes and *tourtes de blettes*.

East of the Old Town looms the **Colline du Château**, a craggy, pine-shaded hill and park. Two ancient cemeteries occupy its northern reaches; one Christian, one Jewish. The park itself is a tranquil spot to escape the tourist crush in the Old Town, with terrific views across the bay. Steps ascend from rue du Château or rue Ste-Claire, but if you don't fancy the 90-metre (295-foot) slog, there's a lift (8am-6pm daily, €1.10) by the 19th-century Tour Bellanda.

Following the curve of quai Rauba Capeu from the Old Town takes you past the imposing **War Memorial** on place Guynemar, hewn out of the rock face and inscribed with the names of *les fils morts* of the two World Wars. Keep walking around the headland to reach the Vieux Port. Lined with tall, multicoloured houses, it has plenty of simple cafés where you can snack on a *pan bagnat* and watch ferries leaving for Corsica. Here, too, is the neo-classical church of **Notre-Dame-du-Port** (8 pl Ile de Beauté, 04.93.89.53.05). A few streets back from the church is another buzzing *socca* hotspot, **Chez Pipo** (13 rue Bavastro, 04.93.55.88.82, closed Mon in Sept, Oct, Dec-June, Sat in July, Aug). After lunch, browse through the bric-a-brac at the **Marché des Puces** (pl Robilante, closed Mon, Sun), where you can pick up everything from long-stopped grandfather clocks to 1960s handbags and Chinese fans.

East of the Colline du Château, the Parc Forestier le Mont Boron is an idyllic spot for a picnic, with winding paths through acres of pines and breathtaking views down to the coast. Between the two hills, in an area dotted with 19th-century villas, the **Musée Terra Amata** documents the area's earliest settlement. Next to it, the Castel des Deux Rois is a perfect park for children, with a petting zoo, water jets, mini-golf and playgrounds galore.

**INSIDE TRACK
SECRET SUNBATHING**

Across the road from the war memorial on quai Rauba Capeu, between the Old Town and the port, steps lead down to a sun-baked bathing area, with blocks of rock to bask on and a ladder descending into the deep, crystal-clear water. Even at the summer peak, it's far less hectic than the public beaches.

★ FREE **Cathédrale de Ste-Réparate**
pl Rossetti (04.93.62.34.40). **Open** 8.30am-noon, 2-6pm daily. **Admission** free. **Map** p255 C2.
With its stucco façade and ceramic-tiled dome, the ochre-hued 17th-century cathedral dominates the Old Town. It's named after the city's patron saint: a 15-year-old girl, martyred in the Holy Land in 250 AD, whose decapitated body washed up in the Baie des Anges in a flower-laden boat.

FREE Chapelle de l'Annonciation (Chapelle Ste-Rita)

1 rue de la Poissonnerie (04.93.62.13.62). **Open** 7.30am-noon, 2.30-6.30pm daily. **Admission** free. **Map** p255 C2.

Follow a steady trickle of locals into this gilded baroque gem and light a candle for St Rita – the patron saint of hopeless causes – with whom the chapel is popularly associated.

FREE Galerie de la Marine & Galerie des Ponchettes

59 & 77 quai des Etats-Unis (Galerie de la Marine 04.93.91.92.90/Galerie des Ponchettes 04.93.62.31.24). **Open** 10am-6pm Tue-Sat. **Admission** free. **Map** p255 B3 & C3.

Transformed into two municipal art galleries in the 1950s, Nice's ancient fish and flower markets now showcase up-and-coming local and international talents; exhibitions change every three months.

FREE Musée d'Histoire Naturelle de Nice

60 bd Risso (04.97.13.46.80/www.mhnnice.org). **Open** 10am-6pm Tue-Sun. **Admission** free.

If you like London's Horniman Museum, you'll love this place. Lurking in its display cases are the dried remains of all kinds of slippery, slithery monsters (cephalopods feature prominently, including squids of all shapes and sizes), guaranteed to induce shivers of delighted horror in junior visitors. There's talk of a move to new premises in the Parc Phoenix, but for the moment the museum is staying put.

FREE Musée Terra Amata

25 bd Carnot (04.93.55.59.93/www.musee-terra-amata.org). **Open** 10am-6pm Tue-Sun. **Admission** free.

Find out what Riviera life was like 400,000 years ago. The highlights of this modest museum, built on an excavation site, include a reconstituted prehistoric cave, a human footprint in limestone and records of ancient elephant hunters.

FREE Palais Lascaris

15 rue Droite (04.93.62.72.40). **Open** 10am-6pm Mon, Wed-Sun. **Admission** free. **Map** p255 B2.

Exhibits at this magnificent Genoese-style villa include an 18th-century pharmacy, preserved in its entirety, and a collection of antique musical instruments. Simply wandering through the still, dimly lit second-floor rooms is a delight, though, as ornate baroque furniture, heavy Flemish tapestries and frescoed mythological scenes evoke the gilded opulence of the villa's heyday.

Promenade des Anglais & the beaches

Along the seafront, west of the Old Town, the quai des Etats-Unis segues into the **promenade des Anglais**, 19th-century Nice's most famous landmark. A chaotic parade of in-line skaters, joggers, street performers and strolling sun-worshippers, it's busy from dawn until dusk, when families dawdle over last ice-creams and couples watch the sun setting over the bay. The promenade is lined with grandiose belle époque

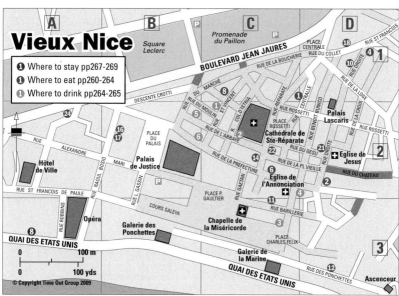

Vieux Nice

❶ Where to stay pp267-269
❶ Where to eat pp260-264
❶ Where to drink pp264-265

© Copyright Time Out Group 2009

and art deco palaces, including the domed **Hôtel Negresco** and the newly opened **Musée Masséna**. The imposing **Palais de la Méditerranée** is another of the strip's architectural icons. Built by American millionaire Frank Jay Gould in 1929, it was shamefully gutted in the 1990s, preserving only the art deco façade, and has now been reborn as a luxury hotel and casino.

The beach below is a broad expanse of sun-bleached pebbles, curving around the azure bay. While stretches are open to anyone, the rest is carved up into private beaches, where you'll pay €10-€15 for a sun-lounger for the day. One of the nicest is **Castel Plage** (8 quai des Etats-Unis, 04.93.85.22.66, closed mid Sept-mid Mar, sun lounger €15/day), sheltered by the headland. With its art deco signage, the venerable **Beau Rivage** (107 quai des Etats-Unis, 04.93.80.75.06, www.nicebeaurivage.com, closed Nov-Mar, sunlounger €17/day, mains €40-€45) is a chic spot to bask on blue and white loungers, or lunch at linen-clad tables.

The hottest spot to sun yourself, though, is newcomer **Hi Beach** (*see p265*). Equipped with Wi-Fi, hammocks, a massage area and shady, fabric-walled *cabanes* for families, it oozes laid-back chic. At €20 per day for a lounger it's a few euros more than its rivals, but the beautiful crowd are undeterred. As night falls, it morphs into a buzzing bar and restaurant.

FREE Musée Masséna

65 rue de France/35 promenade des Anglais (04.93.91.19.10). **Open** 10am-6pm Mon, Wed-Sun. **Admission** free. **Map** p253 A3.
Reopened in 2008 after a massive renovation, the museum occupies a sumptuous late 19th-century Italianite villa, built as a winter residence for the aristocratic Victor Masséna. Elaborate mosaics and freizes, ornate carvings and marble pillars evoke its owner's life of moneyed ease in a series of carefully restored rooms. Upstairs, exhibits and paintings recount Nice's history; all signs are in French.

The New Town

Laid out in the 18th and 19th centuries, the New Town's orderly grid of streets and stuccoed apartments seem a world away from the crowded alleys of the *vielle ville*. In reality, it's just a hop, skip and a jump across the Jardins Albert 1er and place Masséna – crossing the sleek new tramline as you go.

It may have entailed years of building work and disruption, but the first line of the tramway finally opened in November 2007, carving a gleaming path through the heart of the New Town. Once a traffic-choked roundabout, **place Masséna** has become a vast pedestrianised piazza – a little spartan for some tastes, but

Cathédrale St-Nicolas. *See p258.*

imposing nonetheless. It's currently home to one of the artworks commissioned to line the tramway, Jaume Plensa's *Conversation in Nice*. Sitting cross-legged atop ten-metre poles, seven fibreglass male figures gaze over the square; at dusk, they glow with slowly shifting colours.

Glossy boutiques cluster on nearby rues de Paradis, de Suède and Alphonse Karr, while the pedestrianised eastern end of rue de France is lively with boutiques, restaurants and pizzerias. Slicing north-west from place Masséna, avenue Jean Médecin – now traversed by trams, and traffic-free – is Nice's prime shopping street.

North-east of place Masséna, the mighty **MAMAC (Musée d'Art Moderne et d'Art Contemporain)** squares up to another cultural heavyweight: the **Théâtre de Nice**, which is breathing new life into the niçois performing arts scene.

A few blocks back from the promenade des Anglais, broad boulevard Victor Hugo is lined with belle époque villas. Further west, the **Musée des Beaux-Arts** has a small but notable collection, including a plaster study for Rodin's *Le Baiser*. A kilometre further on is the **Musée International d'Art Naïf Anatole Jakovsky**, while just before the airport, the **Musée des Arts Asiatiques** nestles among the lush botanical species and giant hothouses of the marvellous **Parc Floral Phoenix** (405 promenade des Anglais, 04.92.29.77.00).

At the far end of Jean Médecin is the main train station. North of here, along avenue Malaussena and boulevard Joseph Garnier, is the **Marché de la Libération** (mornings, closed Mon), its stalls piled high with courgette flowers, yellow-fleshed peaches and Cavaillon melons. It's more down-to-earth than cours Saleya, and locals with tartan wheelie shoppers far outnumber snap-happy tourists. On rue Flaminius Raibereti, stallholders at the indoor **Cité Marchand** sell meat, cheese and deli goods, including slabs of *tourte de blettes*.

West of the train station, across boulevard Gambetta, the **Cathédrale St-Nicolas** is Nice's most-visited attraction. Further north, **Villa Arson** displays adventurous contemporary art in a lovely garden setting.

★ Cathédrale St-Nicolas (Eglise Russe)

av Nicolas II (04.93.96.88.02/www.acor-nice. com). **Open** *May-Sept* 9am-noon, 2.30-6pm daily. *Oct-May* 9.30am-noon, 2.30-5pm daily. **Admission** €3; free under-12s. **No credit cards. Map** p258 A2.

Built between 1903 and 1912, this beautiful pink and grey marble, brick and tile Russian Orthodox cathedral is a wonderfully incongruous addition to Nice's skyline. Five brilliantly hued onion-domed cupolas announce its presence from afar; inside, the visual feast continues with intricate carvings and frescoes, and a marvellous iconostasis. A strict dress code bans shorts, short skirts and T-shirts. *Photo p257.*

★ FREE MAMAC (Musée d'Art Moderne et d'Art Contemporain)

promenade des Arts (04.97.13.42.01/www. mamac-nice.org). **Open** 10am-6pm Tue-Sun. **Admission** free. **Map** p258 D2.

This colossus of a museum is devoted to European and American art from the 1960s onwards. New Realism and Pop Art are well represented, with plenty of pieces from the Nice School (Arman, César, Klein), plus a room of Niki de Saint Phalle's flamboyant works. The roof terrace, dotted with Klein's minimalist sculptures, affords panoramic city views.
▶ *Another of Niki de Saint Phalle's resplendent statues stands in front of the Hôtel Negresco (see p268) – a glittering, mosaic-clad Miles Davis.*

★ FREE Musée des Arts Asiatiques

405 promenade des Anglais (04.92.29.37.00/ www.arts-asiatiques.com). **Open** *May-mid Oct* 10am-6pm Mon, Wed-Sun. *Mid Oct-Apr* 10am-5pm Mon, Wed-Sun. **Admission** free. **Credit** V.

Influential Japanese architect Kenzo Tange designed this coolly minimalist white marble and glass structure, whose select collection of rare pieces ranges from a 12th-century Japanese Buddha to the latest in Asian high-tech design. Don't miss the tea ceremonies under the gingko trees (3pm Sun, €10; for reservations call 04.92.29.37.02).

★ FREE Musée des Beaux-Arts

33 av des Baumettes (04.92.15.28.28/ www.musee-beaux-arts-nice.org). **Open** 10am-6pm Tue-Sun. **Admission** free. **Map** p258 A3.

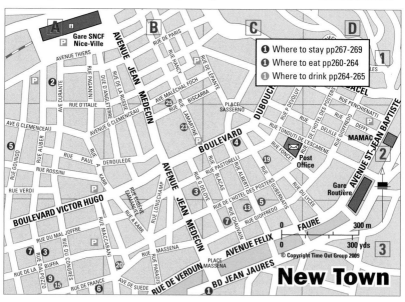

© Copyright Time Out Group 2009

New Town

A steep climb up the Baumettes, this picturesque museum is housed in a grand, Genoese-style villa, built for a Ukrainian princess in 1878. Its impressive collection of 15th- to early 20th-century art made it a target for thieves in summer 2007, who escaped with works by Monet, Brueghel and Sisley. Look out for pieces by the likes of Raoul Dufy, Pierre Bonnard and Jules Cheret. Lesser-known niçois symbolist Gustav-Adolf Mossa's watercolours are not to be missed; scenes of death and corruption, presided over by languid, darkly erotic sirens.

Musée International d'Art Naïf Anatole Jakovsky

Château Ste-Hélène, av du Fabron (04.93.71.78.33). **Open** 10am-6pm Mon, Wed-Sun. **Admission** €4; €2.50 reductions; free under-18s. **No credit cards**.
Once the home of perfume creator René Coty, this stately pink villa now houses a fine collection of naïve art. Some 600 works trace the history of the artistic movement, from the 18th century to the present; artists include Rousseau, Séraphine, Rimbert and Grandma Moses.

FREE Villa Arson

20 av Stephen Liégeard (04.92.07.73.73/ www.villa-arson.org). **Open** *July-Sept* 2-7pm Mon, Wed-Sun. *Oct-June* 2-6pm Mon, Wed-Sun. **Admission** free.
Set in sprawling parkland, with an 18th-century villa at its heart, Villa Arson is at the cutting edge of avant-garde art. There's an art school on site, as well as an exhibition space: after looking round, you can listen to heated discussions in the café (closed Aug & Sept).

Cimiez

Perched on a hillside to the north of the city centre, lofty Cimiez is Nice's most affluent neighbourhood, swathed in large villas, Roman ruins and sweeping belle époque apartments. The walk from Vieux Nice or place Masséna takes half an hour; alternatively, take bus No.15 from place Masséna, towards Cimiez.

Just off the lower reaches of the boulevard de Cimiez is the splendid **Musée National Message Biblique Marc Chagall**, showing the Belarusian painter's large-scale biblical works. Further up, sweeping round the corner of boulevard de Cimiez and avenue Régina, you can't miss the Excelsior Régina Palace. Designed by Biasini, the hotel where Queen Victoria once stayed and Matisse lived between 1938 and 1943 is now a smart apartment block.

At the top of the hill, the **Musée Matisse** stands behind the ruins of the Roman amphitheatre and the **Musée d'Archéologie**. Here, too, is **L'Eglise Notre-Dame-de-Cimiez** and its 16th-century Franciscan monastery,

Musée des Arts Asiatiques

flanked by a glorious, rose-perfumed garden and the cemetery in which Matisse and Dufy are buried. Further down rue Grammont is Nice's most unusual church: designed by Jacques Droz, **Ste-Jeanne d'Arc** is a radical 1930s reinforced-concrete structure, nicknamed 'the egg'.

FREE L'Eglise et le Monastère Notre-Dame-de-Cimiez

pl du Monastère (04.93.81.00.04). **Open** *Church* 9am-12.30pm, 2-6pm daily. *Museum* 10am-noon, 3-6pm Mon-Sat. **Admission** free.
A heavy-handed 19th-century reworking of a 16th-century building, this church's main draw is its triptych of Louis Bréa altarpieces. Next door are some intriguing muralled cloisters and the Musée Franciscain; after learning about the uncomfortable ends of Franciscan martyrs, stroll under the monastery's cypress-shaded walkways and take in the spirit-lifting views.

FREE Musée Archéologique de Nice-Cimiez

160 av des Arènes (04.93.81.59.57/www.musee-archeologique-nice.org). **Open** 10am-6pm Mon, Wed-Sun. **Admission** free. **No credit cards**.
This smart archaeological museum charts Nice's history from 1100 BC up to the Middle Ages through an impressive array of ceramics, sculpture, jewellery and tools. Outside are the first- to fourth-century

remains of Cemenelum, with vestiges of the public baths, paved streets and a 4,000-seat amphitheatre – now used as a venue during the Nice Jazz Festival.

★ FREE Musée Matisse
164 av des Arènes (04.93.81.08.08/www.musee-matisse-nice.org). **Open** 10am-6pm Mon, Wed-Sun. **Admission** free. **Credit** MC, V.
Matisse's 17th-century villa (and its modern extension) houses a fascinating collection of paintings, drawings, engravings and sculptures, tracing the artist's development from dark, brooding early works through to the colourful paper cut-outs.
▶ *Check out the preparatory sketches for the Chapelle du Rosaire, then visit the real thing in Vence; see p302.*

★ Musée National Message Biblique Marc Chagall
av du Dr Menard (04.93.53.87.20/www. musee-chagall.fr). **Open** *May-Oct* 10am-6pm Mon, Wed-Sun. *Nov-Apr* 10am-5pm Mon, Wed-Sun. **Admission** €6.50-€8.50; €4.50-€6.50 reductions; free under-18s. Free to all 1st Sun of mth. **Credit** MC, V. **Map** p253 B1.
Dedicated to long-time Riviera resident Chagall, the museum displays a complete set of canvases interpreting episodes from three Old Testament books, notably the *Song of Songs*. Chagall provided mosaics, sketches and stained glass for the gallery, which also hosts temporary exhibitions and small-scale acoustic concerts in its lovely amphitheatre.

Bellet

On the western side of town, Nice's industrial outskirts give way to wooded countryside as you drive up the steep route de Bellet. A small sign, 'Vignobles de Bellet', indicates you're entering France's smallest AOC (*appellation d'origine contrôlée*). The pretty little vineyard enclave of Bellet (www.vinsdebellet.com) lies on the steep slopes in the Alpine foothills, and is easily explored in a morning trip.
Made from little-known grape varieties such as la folle noire and braquet, Bellet's rosés and reds are hard to find outside the local area. A

trio of producers to hunt out are **Château de Crémat** (442 chemin de Crémat, 04.92.15.12.15, www.chateau-cremat.com), **Château de Bellet** (chemin de Saquier, Les Séoules, 04.93.37.81.57) and **Clos Saint Vincent** (collet des Fourniers, 04.92.15.12.69, www.clos-st-vincent.fr). Almost all of Nice's wine shops stock wines from Bellet producers: try the long-established **Caves Bianchi** (*see p266*).

WHERE TO EAT

Le 22 Septembre
3 rue Centrale (04.93.80.87.90/www.le22 septembre.com). **Open** 7-11pm Tue-Sat. **Main courses** €9-€15. **Menus** €14-€17. **Credit** MC, V. **Map** p255 C/D1 ❶
Savvy students and budget city-breakers flock to this cheap-as-chips Old Town eatery, where you can feast on beef stroganoff or sea bass with basil butter for under a tenner.

★ Acchiardo
38 rue Droite (04.93.85.51.16). **Open** noon-1.30pm, 7-10pm Mon-Fri. Closed Aug. **Main courses** €13-€14. **No credit cards**. **Map** p255 D2 ❷
Wood panelling, gingham curtains and a bargain-priced wine list make for a convivial buzz at this family-run eatery. The menu sticks to well-executed niçois classics, from *petits farcis* (stuffed veg) to the offputtingly named *merda di can* (dog poo): swiss chard gnocchi with tomato, *pistou* or gorgonzola.

★ L'Allegro
6 pl Guynemar (04.93.56.62.06). **Open** noon-1.45pm, 8-10pm Mon-Fri; 8-10pm Sat. Closed Aug. **Main courses** €29-€56. **Menus** €19-€54. **Credit** MC, V.
Close to the harbour, this long-established Italian is an ever-popular spot. Under the watchful eyes of characters from the frescoed commedia dell'arte, customers savour exquisite own-made ravioli, risotto and fresh pasta. It's best to book in advance.

L'Auberge de Théo
52 av Cap de Croix (04.93.81.26.19/ www.auberge-de-theo.com). **Open** noon-2pm, 7-10.15pm Tue-Sat; noon-2pm Sun. Closed mid June-mid July. **Main courses** €7-€19. **Menus** €16.50-€30.50. **Credit** MC, V.
In an area where restaurants are far from plentiful, this trattoria is an ideal pitstop between the Chagall and Matisse museums. Italian specialities include beef *tagliata* and creamy escalope Valdostana.

Au Petit Gari
2 pl Garibaldi (04.93.26.89.09/www.aupetitgari. com). **Open** noon-2pm, 7-10pm Mon-Fri. **Main courses** €15-€30. **Menus** *Lunch* €13. **Credit** MC, V.

INSIDE TRACK
FAST FOOD NIÇOIS

You can't leave Nice without sampling its street food specialities. *Socca* is a strangely addictive chickpea pancake, served hot from the oven, while *tourte de blettes* is a hearty, no-nonsense pie filled with swiss chard and pine nuts, which comes in both sweet (*sucrée*) and savoury (*salé*) incarnations.

You can't go wrong with the lunchtime *plat du jour* at this sweetly old-fashioned bistro: a mere €13, with a glass of wine and a coffee thrown in. It might be anything from a piled-high plate of mussels to fresh fish; regulars still remember the glorious day when truffle-stuffed chicken breast was served.

La Baie d'Amalfi

9 rue Gustave Deloye (04.93.80.01.21/www.baie-amalfi.com). **Open** noon-2pm, 7-10.15pm daily. Closed July. **Main courses** €15-€30. **Menus** *Lunch* €17-€20. *Dinner* €31. **Credit** MC, V. **Map** p258 B2 ❸

Pizza, pasta and fish enthusiasts are in heaven in this bustling old-style mansion. Try the risotto San Remo with courgette flowers and scampi, or gnocchetti with mozzarella.

Bar du Coin

2 rue Droite (04.93.62.32.59). **Open** noon-2pm, 7-10pm Tue-Sat. **Main courses** €10-€16. **Credit** MC, V. **Map** p255 D1 ❹

Enormous thin-crust pizzas, authentically blackened at the edges, keep this Old Town pizzeria thronged. All the classics are present and correct, along with more innovative offerings such as the reblochon, potato and ham-topped Madame Plouck. Huge salads and heaped plates of pasta complete the menu, with a very quaffable house rosé to wash it all down.

Bio et Cie

12 rue Alberti (04.93.01.94.70/www.bio-et-cie.com). **Open** noon-2.30pm Mon-Fri; noon-2.30pm, 7.30-10pm Sat. **Main courses** €9.50-€15. **Menus** €14-€18. **Credit** MC, V. **Map** p258 C2/3 ❺

Organic produce and carefully sourced meat are mainstays of the ever-changing menu at this thriving New Town restaurant, along with a selection of lactose-, gluten- or wheat-free dishes.

Le Bistrot d'Antoine

27 rue de la Préfecture (04.93.85.29.57). **Open** noon-2pm, 8-10pm daily. **Main courses** €12-€16. **Credit** MC, V. **Map** p255 C2 ❻

See p264 **A Corking Night Out.**

★ Caffè Bianco

9 rue Chauvain (04.93.13.45.12). **Open** noon-2pm, 7-10pm Tue-Fri; 7-10pm Sat, Sun. **Main courses** €14-€25. **Menus** €26. **Credit** MC, V. **Map** p258 C3 ❼

With its flickering candles and red velvet banquettes, Caffè Bianco is perfect date terrain. Chalked up on the blackboards, a concise menu runs from vegetarian-friendly pastas and risottos to *poisson du jour* or classic meaty fare: braised lamb shank, say, or duck with pan-fried foie gras.

Casa Mia

4 rue Pontin (04.93.85.51.72/www.casamia nice.com). **Open** 7-10pm Mon, Tue, Thur-Sat;

noon-2pm Sun. **Main courses** €13-€16. **Menus** *Lunch* €13-€15. *Dinner* €24-€27. **Credit** MC, V. **Map** p255 C1 ❽

Service is genial, if occasionally forgetful, at this colourful little trattoria. The simple, seasonal menu is a delight, with good-value set menus and superb fresh pasta: spinach and ricotta-stuffed parcels in creamy sage sauce, perhaps, or tagliatelle with squid. Generous portions mean you may struggle to manage dessert – though the silky caramel panna-cotta is hard to resist.

La Cave de l'Origine

3 rue Dalpozzo (04.83.50.09.60). **Open** noon-2pm, 7-10pm Tue-Sat. **Main courses** €8-€28. **Credit** MC, V. **Map** p258 A3 ❾

See p264 **A Corking Night Out.**

Cave de la Tour

3 rue de la Tour (04.93.80.03.31/www.cave delatour.com). **Open** 7am-7pm Tue-Sat; 7am-noon Sun. **Main courses** *Lunch only* €10-€12. **Credit** MC, V.

See p264 **A Corking Night Out.**

Le Chantecler

Hôtel Negresco, 37 promenade des Anglais (04.93.16.64.00). **Open** 12.30-2pm, 7-10.30pm Wed-Sat. Closed Jan. **Menus** *Lunch* €45. *Dinner* €90-€130. **Credit** AmEx, DC, MC, V.

Having taken the helm in Le Chantecler's Michelin-starred kitchen, young wonderchef Jean-Denis Rieubland has introduced some modern touches to its menu. Foie gras might be served with raspberries, cardamom-infused rhubarb and balsamic syrup, for example, with almond-crusted bass and artichoke mousse to follow.

★ Chez Palmyre

5 rue Droite (04.93.85.72.32). **Open** noon-2pm, 7-10pm Mon-Sat. **Menu** €13. **Credit** MC, V. **Map** p255 D1 ❿

This tiny eatery offers an inimitable taste of niçois home cooking – if you can squeeze in on one of its handful of tables. The lucky few feast on a bargain four-course *formule*: dishes change daily, but on our last visit included deep-fried courgette flowers, followed by grilled, herby pork with *ratatouille niçoise*. Regulars recommend the tart for afters.

★ Chez René Socca

2 rue Miralheti (04.93.92.05.73). **Open** 9am-10pm Tue-Sun. Closed Jan. **Main courses** *(socca)* €2-€8. **No credit cards.**

Wooden tables spill out into the street from Vieux Nice's oldest and most popular address for *socca*. Stern waiters slam down your drinks and you have to fetch the piping-hot niçois specialities yourself – but you're here for the food, not for airs and graces. If a slice of chickpea *socca* doesn't appeal, try the *petits farcis* or onion-topped *pissaladière*.

Delhi Belhi

22 rue de la Barillerie (04.93.92.51.87/www.
delhibelhi.com). **Open** 7pm-midnight daily. **Main**
courses €9-€21. **Menus** €19-€29. **Credit** MC,
V. **Map** p255 C2/3 ⓫

Ignore the unfortunate name; Delhi Belhi dishes up
confident renditions of classic curries in a softly lit
dining room just behind the cours Saleya. To sample several dishes, order a thali – a vegetarian version is available.

Don Camillo Créations

5 rue des Ponchettes (04.93.85.67.95/www.don
camillo-creations.fr). **Open** noon-2pm, 7-11pm
Tue-Sat. **Main courses** €26. **Menus** €26-€80.
Credit AmEx, MC, V. **Map** p255 D3 ⓬

In a smart dining room with crisp white linen tablecloths, chef Marc Laville delivers a playful take on
niçois classics – a *pissaladière* roulade with pan-fried
foie gras, perhaps, or lobster and beef carpaccio with
tempura-battered courgette flowers. At €26, the
weekdays-only lunchtime *menu du marché* is a steal.

Emilie's Cookies

9 rue Alberti (04.93.13.89.58/www.emilies
cookies.com). **Open** 8am-6.30pm Mon-Fri; 9am-
6.30pm Sat. Closed 2wks Aug. **Main courses**
€4-€10. **No credit cards. Map** p258 C3 ⓭

Savouries include home-baked bagels with a stellar
array of fillings, but it's hard to resist going straight
for the sweets. Towering, golden-topped muffins
and the namesake cookies are impossible to ignore.

L'Escalinada

22 rue Pairolière (04.93.62.11.71/www.
escalinada.fr). **Open** noon-2.30pm, 7.30-10.30pm
daily. **Main courses** €12-€23. **Menu** €24. **No**
credit cards.

With its cosy, beamed interior and tables perched
along sloping rue Pairolière, this pretty little restaurant is a bastion of niçoise cuisine. Specialities range
from own-made *gnocchi au pistou* (garlic, basil and
olive oil) and stuffed sardines to more carnivorous
delights such as *tripes à la niçoise*.

L'Estrilha

11-13 rue de l'Abbaye (04.93.62.62.00). **Open**
noon-3pm, 7-11pm Mon-Sat. **Main courses** €11-
€22. **Menus** €19.50, €23.50. **Credit** AmEx, MC,
V. **Map** p255 C2 ⓮

Set menus are good value at this Vieux Nice restaurant, kicking off with an amuse-bouche of pungent
tapenade with tiny, crunchy croutons. Dishes feature plenty of local produce (stuffed rabbit, perhaps,
or brebis cheese with fig marmalade), while the à
la carte speciality is the *amphore*: a fish, tomato,
white wine and basil stew, baked in a clay pot.

Le Grand Café de Turin

5 pl Garibaldi (04.93.62.29.52/www.cafede
turin.com). **Open** 8am-10pm Mon, Tue, Thur-

Lou Pistou.

Sun. **Main courses** €8-€30. **Menus** *2-person*
platters €70-€95. **Credit** AmEx, DC, MC, V.

Serving sparklingly fresh seafood, this classic
brasserie is tucked away under the colonnades of
place Garibaldi. Since it opened in 1910 it has been
jammed with locals slurping oysters; service can be
testy, but the atmosphere is the real thing.

★ Keisuke Matsushima

22ter rue de France (04.93.82.26.06/www.kei
sukematsushima.com). **Open** 7.30-10pm Mon,
Sat; noon-2pm, 7.30-10pm Tue-Fri. **Main courses**
€30-€35. **Menus** *Lunch* €35. *Dinner* €65-€130.
Credit AmEx, MC, V. **Map** p258 A3 ⓯

One of the most respected chefs in town, Michelin-
starred Kei Matsushima is going from strength to
strength. His minimalist dining room is a mecca for
gastronomes and expense-accounters, while the
Mediterranean cuisine combines innovative flavours
with artful presentation.

Lou Pistou

4A rue Raoul Bosio (04.93.62.21.82). **Open**
noon-2pm, 7-10pm Mon-Fri. **Main courses**
€13-€19. **Credit** MC, V. **Map** p255 B2 ⓰

With its sweet lace curtains, diminutive premises
and strictly regional menu, Lou Pistou is a splendid
place to sample local recipes: *farcis niçois*, perhaps,
or *tripes à la niçoise* with chunky strips of deep-fried
chickpea *panisse*. Next door is the equally good –
and equally small – Le Merenda (*see right*).

★ La Merenda
4B rue Raoul Bosio (no phone). **Open** noon-2pm,
7-10pm Mon-Fri. Closed 3wks Aug. **Menus** €25-
€30. **No credit cards. Map** p255 B2 ⑰
Shoebox-sized and invariably packed, the legendary
La Merenda serves the ultimate version of every
niçois classic. To reserve, stop by in person.

Oliviera
*8bis rue du Collet (04.93.13.06.45/www.oliviera.
com).* **Open** 12.30-2.30pm, 7.30-9.30pm Tue-Sat;
12.30-2.30pm Sun. **Main courses** €12-€22. **No
credit cards. Map** p255 D1 ⑱
Much-loved by local foodies, Nadim Beyrouti's shop
and restaurant is lined with gleaming vats of local
olive oil. Freshly made dishes, based around
regional produce, might range from lentil and swiss
chard soup to rabbit; each stars a different olive oil.

La Part des Anges
17 rue Gubernatis (04.93.62.69.80). **Open** noon-
8pm Mon-Thur; noon-2pm, 7-10pm Fri, Sat. **Main
courses** €10-€15. **Credit** AmEx, MC, V. **Map**
p258 C2 ⑲
See p264 **A Corking Night Out.**

★ Les Pêcheurs
*18 quai des Docks (04.93.89.59.61/www.les
pecheurs.com).* **Open** *Apr-Sept* 12.15-2.15pm,
7.15-10.15pm Mon, Tue, Fri-Sun; 7.15-10.15pm
Thur. *Oct-Mar* 12.15-2.15pm, 7.15-10.15pm Wed-
Sun. **Main courses** €24-€52. **Menus** €26-€36.
Credit AmEx, MC, V.
You'll find all the usual Mediterranean seafood (sardines, octopus, sea bream) at this accomplished portside brasserie, but often with an Asian or Creole
touch – so prawns are fried with ginger and lemon-
grass and served with curry-spiked courgette purée.
Fish soup, a niçoise classic, is prepared with just the
right mix of rockfish and plenty of saffron.

La Petite Maison
*11 rue St-François-de-Paule (04.93.85.71.53/
www.lapetitemaison-nice.com).* **Open** noon-2pm,
7.30-11.30pm Mon-Sat. **Main courses** €10-€35.
Credit AmEx, MC, V.
This venerable restaurant draws colourful locals at
noon, models and movie stars by night. An indul-
gent menu features lashings of truffles and foie gras,
while simpler fare includes garlicky oven-baked
king prawns and the famed salt-baked sea bass.

La Pizza Cresci
*34 rue Masséna (04.93.87.70.29/www.crescere.
fr).* **Open** 11am-1am daily. **Main courses** €8-
€19. **Credit** MC, V. **Map** p258 B3 ⑳
Top-notch pizzas, cooked in a wood-fired oven, and
democratic pricing ensure this pizzeria is perennially busy. At No.43, sister operation Le Québec
(04.93.87.84.21) is an equally easygoing brasserie,
delivering steaks, pizzas, pasta and omelettes.

Restaurant du Gésu
1 pl du Gésu (04.93.62.26.46). **Open** noon-2pm,
7.30-10.30pm Mon-Sat. **Main courses** €6-€13.
No credit cards. Map p255 D2 ㉑
Set in a pretty Old Town square, the terrace here is
jammed year round with locals and tourists. The
secret of its success is simple delicious niçois cooking, with everything prepared on the premises –
including the fresh gnocchi.
▶ *If you're struggling to score a table, pop up the
road and try the excellent Acchiardo (see p260).*

Resto Wine Notes
*6 rue Ste-Réparate (04.93.53.09.79/www.resto
winenotes.com).* **Open** 5pm-1am Tue-Sun. **Main
courses** €13-€28. **Menu** €30. **Credit** MC, V.
Map p255 C2 ㉒
See p264 **A Corking Night Out.**

Le Speakeasy
7 rue Lamartine (04.93.85.59.50). **Open** noon-
2pm Mon-Sat. **Main courses** €9-€10. **Menus**
€13.50-€15.50. **Credit** MC, V. **Map** p258 B2 ㉓
Its narrow entrance bedecked with the stars and
stripes, this American-owned vegan eatery is one of
a kind. Cooking is surprisingly inventive, and portions generous; on our last visit, a rich, crispy-topped
sweet potato pie was sublime. Organic spelt or malt
beer is a perfect accompaniment.

★ L'Univers de Christian Plumail
*54 bd Jean Jaurès (04.93.62.32.22/www.christian
plumail.com).* **Open** noon-2pm, 7.30-10pm Mon-
Fri; 7.30-10pm Sat. **Main courses** €30-€32.
Menus €22-€70. **Credit** AmEx, MC, V. **Map**
p255 A2 ㉔
This smart Old Town address remains a destination
dining spot, thanks to renowned niçois chef
Christian Plumail. His simple but beautifully executed Mediterranean cuisine has won him a Michelin
star, and there's a cracking wine list. Sample the
affordable lunchtime menu if you're on a budget.

Vinivore
32 av de la République (04.93.26.90.17). **Open**
9am-11pm Mon-Sat (dinner Fri, Sat only). **Main
courses** €12-€16. **Credit** MC, V.
See p264 **A Corking Night Out.**

★ Vin/Vin
*18bis rue Biscarra (04.93.92.93.20/www.
restaurant-20survin.com).* **Open** noon-2.30pm,
7-10.30pm Mon-Sat. **Main courses** €11-€21.
Credit MC, V. **Map** p258 B1/2 ㉕
See p264 **A Corking Night Out.**

La Zucca Magica
*4bis quai Papacino (04.93.56.25.27/www.lazucca
magica.com).* **Open** noon-2.45pm, 7pm-midnight
Tue-Sat. **Menus** *Lunch* €17. *Dinner* €27. **No
credit cards.**

Pumpkin plays a starring role on the menu – and in the eccentric decor – at this portside vegetarian restaurant. The Piedmontese chef serves up a no-choice five-course menu: Italian cheeses generally feature heavily, so make sure you're hungry.

WHERE TO DRINK

Le Bar des Oiseaux

5 rue St-Vincent (04.93.80.27.33/www.bar desoiseaux.com). **Open** noon-2pm Mon-Wed; noon-2pm, 7.30-11pm Thur-Sat. **Main courses** €13-€14. **Credit** MC, V. **Map** p255 C2 ❶
Expect plenty of local atmosphere at this popular restaurant, bar and theatre. There are live bands, snippets of theatre, and uproarious comic sketches.

★ Bliss Bar

12 rue de l'Abbaye (04.93.16.82.38/www.my space.com/blissbar06). **Open** 8pm-2am Mon-Sat. **Credit** MC, V. **Map** p255 D2 ❷
A large but amiable doorman presides over who steps through the sliding glass doors at this sleekly appointed bar; don't make the painful mistake of trying to saunter in before he's pressed the button. Inside, Nice's beautiful crowd quaff mohitos, flirt and party in air-conditioned comfort, while DJs spin funk and soul from Wednesday to Saturday.

Café Borghèse

9 rue Fodéré (04.92.04.83.83). **Open** 8am-midnight Mon-Sat. **Menus** €12-€25. **Credit** MC, V.

THE RIVIERA & SOUTHERN ALPS

A Corking Night Out.

Raise a toast to the rise of the wine bar.

Chilled rosé is a must in Nice, particularly in summer (when it's perfectly acceptable to throw a few ice cubes into the glass). Yet rosé is not the star at the new wine bars that are popping up all over the city. As in Paris, the emphasis is increasingly on *vins naturels*: wines produced with a minimum of chemicals and sulphites, many of them organic or biodynamic. Because there are few local producers of *vin naturel*, you're more likely to sip a crisp white from the Loire or a blackberry-scented red from the Rhône Valley than the ubiquitous rosé.

Responsible for launching the trend in Nice is Olivier Labarde, whose shop and wine bar **La Part des Anges** (*see p263*), just outside the Old Town, puts many of the country's best natural wine producers on display: look for names such as Gramenon, Breton, Richaud and Lapierre. Take advantage of the lack of corkage fee to indulge in an exceptional bottle of Burgundy, or try something more unusual such as vin de pays from the Ardèche; at lunchtimes and on Friday and Saturday nights you can nibble on cheese or charcuterie or choose from a handful of delicious hot dishes.

La Part des Anges recently opened a second wine bar, **Vinivore** (*see p263*), run by the genial Bonaventure Blankstein. Bonaventure, or Bono as he is known, previously worked at **Vin sur Vin** (*see p263*), a knowledgeably staffed *bistro à vins* with a terrace on a pedestrian street in the New Town. Here, wines are stored in a temperature-controlled 'cellar' in the back of the dining room, which you can visit with the sommelier to select your bottle. Organic wines are available, while the meaty menu changes with the seasons – if you can, try the courgette blossom fritters or steak tartare.

Perhaps the most stylish new wine bar in town, though, is **La Cave de l'Origine** (*see p261*), run by Carlo Ferreira and Isabelle Ponsolle. It's a peaceful space with a red and grey colour scheme and a small *épicerie* at the front, where you'll find everything from smoked tuna belly to handmade nougat. At mealtimes, the two dining rooms fill up with a cheerful French and foreign crowd that appreciates the fresh, often-organic ingredients from the market and the uncommon wines selected by Isabelle.

Wine-lovers should also check out two new Old Town bistros. At **Le Bistrot d'Antoine** (*see p261*), succulent grilled meats such as duck magret or steak and the occasional fish dish provide the foil for wines selected from small producers and sold at reasonable prices, starting at €13 a bottle. **Resto Wine Notes** (*see p263*), where you might sample wine from the tiny Bellet region in the western hills of Nice, has a more contemporary bistro menu: think kangaroo fillet with mole negro sauce. If this sounds too modern, visit the long-established **Cave de la Tour** (*see p261*) on the other side of the Old Town, where the mostly male regulars linger around the bar sipping surprisingly good wines and snacking on *pissaladière*, the local onion tart.

In the shadow of Notre-Dame-du-Port, this easy-going bar is open all day, seamlessly sliding from afternoon cappuccinos to evening aperitifs. The food is good, too, with enormous salads and copious portions of gnocchi and ravioli.

La Civette du Cours
1 cours Saleya (04.93.80.80.59). **Open** 7.30am-2.30am daily. **Main courses** €5-€13. **Credit** DC, MC, V. **Map** p255 C3 ❸
Set in prime people-watching territory on the corner of cours Saleya, La Civette is the perfect spot to bask in the last rays of early-evening sun. It's one of the cheaper places on the square for an aperitif, served with olives and squares of salty *pissaladière*. Service is rushed but amenable.

★ Les Distilleries Idéales
24 rue de la Préfecture (04.93.62.10.66). **Open** 9am-midnight daily. **No credit cards**. **Map** p255 C/D2 ❹
Known to its regulars as L'Idéal, this quirky corner bar strikes the perfect balance between cool and casual. The decor is louche and slightly Gothic, while seats at the tables lining the street are like gold dust on summer evenings.

★ Hi Beach
47 promenade des Anglais (04.97.14.00.83/ www.hi-beach.net). **Main courses** €21-€35. **Open** 9am-midnight daily. **Credit** AmEx, MC, V.
Opened in summer 2008, Hi Hotel's beach bar and restaurant immediately became the place to be seen. The menu, masterminded by none other than Kei Matsushima (*see p262*), is on the pricey side, but drinks aren't too steep – and it's a lovely spot to sip a caipirinha as the sun sets over the bay.

Tapas la Movida
2 rue de l'Abbaye (04.93.62.27.46). **Open** 9pm-3am Mon-Fri; 5am-midnight Sat, Sun. **Credit** MC, V. **Map** p255 B2 ❺
Vodka and tequila shots by the metre (12 shots) or half-metre (six) are the speciality at this backstreet bar and gig venue – though if drinks by the dozen seems excessive, single shots are a mere €1.60 each. A much-pierced and dreadlocked crowd loiters in the alleyway out front; head inside for ear-splitting punk and alternative bands.

Wayne's
15 rue de la Préfecture (04.93.13.46.99/www. waynes.fr). **Open** noon-1am daily. **Admission** free. **Credit** AmEx, MC, V. **Map** p255 B2 ❻
A mecca for anglophones in Vieux Nice, Wayne's attracts young partygoers with copious boozing, raucous live bands and theme nights (ranging from toga evenings to 1980s parties). The website's gallery of girls with their boobs out pretty much sums up the spirit of the place.

Ghost.

NIGHTLIFE
For concert venues, notably the **Palais Nikaïa**, *see p267.*

Le Blue Whales
1 rue Mascoïnat (04.93.62.90.94). **Open** 5.30pm-4.30am daily. **Admission** free. **Credit** DC, MC, V.
A laid-back, friendly crowd frequents this better-than-average pub, where there's generally a DJ or band in situ. Sound levels make meaningful conversation tricky, so you're best off turning your attentions to playing pool, dancing and drinking.

Ghost
3 rue Barillerie (04.93.92.93.37). **Open** 8pm-2.30am daily. **Admission** free. **Credit** DC, MC, V.
This tiny, dimly lit club has a speakeasy vibe (you need to ring the bell to get in) and a broad playlist: anything goes, from trip hop and drum 'n' bass to no-nonsense house.

★ Le Klub
6 rue Halevy (06.60.55.26.61/www.leklub.net). **Open** midnight-5am Wed-Sun. **Admission** free-€14. **Credit** MC, V.
The hottest gay nightspot in Nice, Le Klub throws open its doors to clubbers of all orientations. Its line-up of DJs is one of the best on the Riviera, mixing local talent with global big-hitters; look out, too, for quirky regular nights, like the cabaret evening.

INSIDE TRACK NIGHTLIFE
DOLLY MIXES

The hottest party in town is the itinerant **Dolly Party**, a riotous gay electro night that travels around the French Riviera. To find out when it's next dropping by Nice, check online at www.dollyparty.com.

Odace

29 rue Alphonse Karr (04.93.82.37.66/ www.odaceclub.com). **Open** 11pm-5am Tue-Sat. **Admission** free. **Credit** AmEx, MC, V.
The sleek, oriental-inspired decor at Odace oozes opulence, and attracts a champagne-sipping clientele. There's a decent restaurant, but most people come here for the decadent party atmosphere that cooks up later on as DJs take to the decks.

Le Smarties

10 rue Défly (04.93.62.30.75/http://nice smarties.free.fr). **Open** 7am-2am Mon, Thur-Sun. **Admission** free. **No credit cards.**
Billing itself as a 'bar electro-lounge', Smarties is an appealingly lo-fi affair, decorated with low-slung divans and 1970s television sets. Look out for themed nights and the odd extended happy hour.

SHOPPING

If you're planning a serious designer splurge, you're probably better off heading to Cannes than shopping in Nice. That said, Nice has all the basics covered, with the major chains (department store Galeries Lafayette, book and record shop Fnac et al) all present and correct on avenue Jean Médicin, along with the split-level Etoile shopping mall. Luxury labels congregate on rue Paradis, avenue de Suède and avenue de Verdun. For a cherry-picked selection of labels, try the **Espace Harroch** (7 rue Paradis, 04.93.82.50.23, closed Mon, Sun), a sleek showcase for the likes of Paul Smith, Helmut Lang and Yohji Yamamoto.

The Old Town is home to some delightfully quirky specialists. **Glove Me** (5 rue du Marché, 04.93.79.75.63, closed Mon, Sun) is devoted to elegant, Italian-made leather gloves, in every hue and style. Behind a deliciously old-fashioned shopfront, **Maison Bestagno** (17 rue de la Préfecture, 04.93.80.33.13, closed Mon, Sun & Aug) sells classic umbrellas, walking sticks and pretty ruffle-edged parasols. For mid-range fashion, head for **Une Cabane sur la Plage** (37 rue Droite, 04.93.76.82.46, closed Mon), where stylish womenswear labels include Danish Noa Noa and the Italian Lino Factory. If you prefer a simpler summer look, nearby **Blanc du Nil** (11 pl du Marché, no phone,

closed winter) has rails of undyed white cotton garments, from men's trousers to plain frocks.

Vieux Nice also offers rich pickings for foodies. **Alziari** (14 rue St-François-de-Paule, 04.93.13.44.97, www.alziari.com.fr, closed Mon, Sun) specialises in olive oil, with large capacity cans for the serious addicts. A few doors down at No.11, Clément Bruno's **Terres de Truffes** (04.93.62.07.68, www.terrsdetruffes.com, closed Mon) is a deli and bistro devoted to all things truffle-related: stock up on puréed truffles and truffle oil, then scoff a tuber-topped salad or baked potato. On the same street, **Auer** (No.7, 04.93.85.77.98, www.maison-auer.com, closed Mon), founded in 1920, sells gorgeous candied fruits and chocolates. Next door, its tearoom serves loose-leaf teas, cakes and light lunches.

If you're self-catering, head to pasta shop **Barale** (7 rue Ste-Réparate, 04.93.85.63.08, closed Mon), where goodies range from thick strands of spinach tagliatelle or ricotta-stuffed ravioli to plump *panisses*, made with chickpea flour. To wash the feast down, pop into **Caves Bianchi** (7 rue Raoul Bosio, 04.93.85.65.79). A wealth of wines awaits at this historic wine shop, and staff are happy to advise.

Although the Old Town's **cours Saleya** market (mornings, except Mon) is a foodie must, the Niçois tend to favour the **Marché de la Libération** (*see p258*): it's set past the train station, on the new tram route.

Finally, if you're running short of reading material, drop in at the New Town's **Librairie de la Presse** (103 rue de France, 04.93.44. 41.96, closed Sun). It has stacks of second-hand bargains, in English and French, ranging from classics by Camus and Pagnol to contemporary Brit-lit – along with a sprinkling of pulp fiction paperbacks from the 1960s, sporting wonderfully lurid covers.

ARTS & ENTERTAINMENT

For music and theatre listings, buy the weekly French-language *Semaine des Spectacles* or pick up *Le Pitchoun*, a free French-language guide to what's on.

Acropolis

1 esplanade Kennedy (04.93.92.83.00). **Open** varies. **Tickets** vary. **Credit** MC, V.
This modern mega-structure hosts special events, conventions, concerts, ballet and opera.

Casino Ruhl

1 promenade des Anglais (04.97.03.12.33). **Open** *Slot machines* 10am-5am daily. *Gaming rooms* from 8pm Mon-Fri; from 5pm Sat, Sun. **Admission** (over-18s only, bring ID) *Slot machines* free. *Gaming rooms* €12. **Credit** AmEx, MC, V.

A modern, spawling expanse of gaming rooms, offering French and English roulette, blackjack, punto banco, craps and clanging slot machines.

Cinémathèque de Nice
3 esplanade Kennedy (04.92.04.06.66/ www.cinematheque-nice.com). **Open** varies. **Tickets** €2; €18 10-film pass. **No credit cards.** Nice's cinémathèque puts on an international selection of classic films and recent releases, screened in *version originale* with French subtitles. A membership card (€1) is necessary to attend screenings.
▶ *Cinéma Rialto (4 rue de Rivoli, 04.93.88.08.41, €7) also shows English-language new releases.*

Opéra de Nice
4-6 rue St-François-de-Paule (04.92.17.40.00/ www.opera-nice.org). **Open** *Box office* 9am-6pm Mon-Thur; 9am-8pm Fri; 9am-5pm Sat. **Tickets** €8-€85. **Credit** MC, V.
This 19th-century gem of an opera house, on the edge of Vieux Nice, is decked out in sumptuous red velvet, with crystal chandeliers and lashings of gilt. First-rate visiting artists perform symphonies and ballet as well as opera.

Palais Nikaïa
163 rte de Grenoble (04.92.29.31.29/bookings 08.92.39.08.00/www.nikaia.fr). **Open** *Box office* 1-6pm Mon-Fri. **Tickets** vary. **Credit** MC, V.
This massive, state-of-the-art, modular concert hall and stadium hosts crowd-pleasing rock and classical stars, plus sporting events.

Palais des Sports Jean Bouin
2 rue Jean Allègre (04.97.20.20.30). **Open** varies. Closed Aug. **Admission** *Pool* €4.40; €3.60 reductions. *Ice rink* €4.30; €3.50 reductions (skate hire €2.70). **No credit cards.**
The star attractions at this vast municipal complex are its well-kept, Olympic-sized indoor pool and impressive, good-value ice rink.

FREE Théâtre de la Photographie et de l'Image
27 bd de Dubouchage (04.97.13.42.20/ www.tpinice.org). **Open** 10am-6pm Tue-Sun. **Admission** free.
Formerly a theatre, this is now a slickly appointed photography gallery. Temporary exhibitions are usually well chosen, showcasing emerging talents as well as big-name artists.

Théâtre National de Nice
promenade des Arts (04.93.13.90.90/www. tnn.fr). **Open** *Box office* 2-7pm Tue-Sat. **Tickets** *Grande Salle* €7.50-€30. *Petite Salle* €16-€20. **Credit** AmEx, DC, MC, V.
The Théâtre National de Nice stages high-profile productions of French and foreign classics, along with a robust programme of contemporary drama.

WHERE TO STAY

A luxurious alternative to staying in a hotel is to hire an apartment through the super-helpful **Nice Pebbles** (09.52.78.27.65, www.nice pebbles.com, €50-€200/night). Properties range from elegant, antique-dotted hideaways to slick, super-modern renovations with home cinema systems and immense walk-in showers. The pick of the bunch include the quirky Katja (a hip mix of modern design and flea market finds) and Vincent, an opulent Old Town pad (best feature: a magnificent Philippe Starck bath at the foot of the bed).

★ Hi Hôtel
3 av des Fleurs (04.97.07.26.26/www.hi-hotel. net). **Rates** €215-€435 double. **Rooms** 38. **Credit** AmEx, DC, MC, V.
With its experimental living spaces in jellybean colours, this place remains the funkiest place to stay in Nice. The tiny rooftop pool has a lovely view, interiors are by up-and-coming designer Matali Crasset and there are DJ soirées on weekends.

Hôtel Albert 1er
4 av des Phocéens (04.93.85.74.01/www.hotel-albert-1er.fr). **Rates** €90-€145 double. **Rooms** 72. **Credit** AmEx, MC, V. **Map** p255 C3 ❶
Overlooking the gardens of the same name, this belle époque hotel exudes old-world charm. Its rooms feature oak bedsteads and antique armoires, while floor-to-ceiling windows look out on the sea or over the gardens.

Hi Hôtel.

Hôtel Negresco.

Hôtel Beau Rivage

*24 rue St-François-de-Paule (04.92.47.82.82/
www.nicebeaurivage.com).* **Rates** €210-€400
double. **Rooms** 118. **Credit** AmEx, DC, MC, V.
Matisse once lived in the Beau Rivage, but he probably wouldn't recognise it in its sleek, modern rein-
carnation. Rooms are kitted out with neutral colour
schemes, plasma TVs and crisp linen, along with
light switches that can lead to confusion after one
too many drinks from the minibar. The hotel has its
own beach, but no sea views.

€ Hôtel Belle Meunière

*21 av Durante (04.93.88.66.15/www.belle
meuniere.com).* Closed Dec-Jan. **Rates** €45-€57
double; €15-€22 dorms. **Rooms** 17. **Credit** MC,
V. **Map** p258 A1 ❷
Minutes from the train station, this elegant, stucco-
fronted house offers clean, simply furnished rooms
for budget travellers. The shady garden is a popular spot for youthful guests to kick back, flirt and
swap backpacking tales.

Hôtel les Cigales

*16 rue Dalpozzo (04.97.03.10.70/www.hotel-
lescigales.com).* **Rates** €110-€220 double. **Rooms**
19. **Credit** AmEx, MC, V. **Map** p257 A3 ❸
Rooms are cheerfully decorated at this friendly, old-
fashioned former *hôtel particulier;* some have small
balconies looking over the garden. The New Town
location is conveniently central, and there's a pleasant little roof terrace where guests can relax after a
hard day's sightseeing.

Hôtel Ellington

*25 bd Dubouchage (04.92.47.79.79/www.
ellington-nice.com).* **Rates** €195-€260 double.
Rooms 119. **Credit** AmEx, MC, V. **Map** p258
C2 ❹
An elegant newcomer on the city's hotel scene, the
Hôtel Ellington opened at the end of 2006. Its lofty,
chandelier-lit lobby and lounge evoke the glamour
of a bygone age, while the bar is a stylish spot for a
snifter. The well-equipped guestrooms are more
modern in style (and less chic), and can be on the
small side.

Hôtel de la Fontaine

*49 rue de France (04.93.88.30.38/www.hotel-
fontaine.com).* **Rates** €90-€125 double. **Rooms**
29. **Credit** AmEx, MC, V.
Spruce, friendly and great value, the Fontaine's best
feature is its flower-decked inner courtyard. Rooms,
while nothing fancy, are comfortable and welcoming, and rates include an ample buffet breakfast.

Hôtel Negresco

*37 promenade des Anglais (04.93.16.64.00/
www.hotel-negresco-nice.com).* **Rates** €285-€570
double. **Rooms** 145. **Credit** AmEx, DC, MC, V.
Nothing succeeds like excess, as this domed, pink
and white icon proves. The sumptuous bedrooms
and suites are a visual feast, with themes ranging
from art deco to Louis XIV pomp, while public
spaces are dotted with artworks from the owner's
impressive private collection. Dinner at the famed
Chantecler (*see p261*) is a must.

€ Hôtel Oasis
23 rue Gounod (04.93.88.12.29/www.hoteloasis-nice.com). Rates €67-€105 double. **Rooms** 34. **Credit** AmEx, MC, V. **Map** p258 A2 ❺
Set in a quiet but central location, this tranquil hotel prides itself on its 'home from home' atmosphere, and is a dependable budget option. Larger rooms overlook a shady courtyard, planted with palm and fig trees, where breakfast is served in summer.

★ Hôtel la Pérouse
11 quai Rauba Capeu (04.93.62.34.63/www.hotel-la-perouse.com). Rates €170-€525 double. **Rooms** 62. **Credit** AmEx, MC, V.
Clinging to the colline du Château, La Pérouse offers fabulous views across the Baie des Anges. Rooms are immaculate, with marble-clad bathrooms and fresh orchids, while suites are wonderfully plush; the one above the restaurant has the biggest terrace, with superb sea views. The sun terrace and pool are set against the sheer, rocky hillside, adding to the sense of a romantic hillside eyrie.

Hôtel du Petit Palais
17 av Emile Bieckiert (04.93.62.19.11/www.petit palaisnice.com). Rates €80-€170 double. **Rooms** 25. **Credit** AmEx, MC, V.
Set amid the mansions of Cimiez, the belle époque Petit Palais has spacious rooms, panoramic views and plenty of character. It's a steep walk from the centre of town, but the reward is glorious tranquility: you're more likely to be woken by birdsong than urban bustle.

★ € Hôtel Solara
7 rue de France (04.93.88.09.96/www.hotel solara.com). Rates €50-€90 double. **Rooms** 14. **Credit** MC, V. **Map** p258 A3 ❻
Once you've ascended in the impossibly narrow and decidedly shaky lift, the Solara proves to be a little gem, with bright, air-conditioned rooms and free Wi-Fi access; rooms on the fifth floor also have charming private terraces with views across the New Town. For such a central location, it's great value.

Hôtel Splendid
50 bd Victor Hugo (04.93.16.41.00/www.splendid-nice.com). Rates €175-€255 double. **Rooms** 128. **Credit** AmEx, MC, V.
Set in a modern high-rise building, this smart, long-established four-star hotel has plenty to recommend it, not least its heated rooftop pool and terrace. On the ground floor, its newly opened spa incorporates a small hammam and jacuzzi, with two treatment rooms. Rooms are spacious and comfortable; the pricier ones have balconies.

Hôtel Suisse
15 quai Rauba Capeu (04.92.17.39.00/www.hotels-ocre-azur.com). Rates €79-€195 double. **Rooms** 42. **Credit** AmEx, DC, MC, V.

Standing on the headland of the Baie des Anges, where it basks in the late afternoon sun, the Hôtel Suisse is perfectly located for the beach and Old Town. Its rooms are kitted out in a subtle, modern style; some are small-ish, but magnificent panoramas across the bay more than compensate. For those with a terrace, breakfasting outside is de rigueur.
▶ *Neighbouring Hôtel la Pérouse (see left) has similarly spectacular views over the bay.*

€ Hôtel Villa La Tour
4 rue de la Tour (04.93.80.08.15/www.villa-la-tour.com). Rates €49-€139 double. **Rooms** 14. **Credit** AmEx, MC, V.
This bijou Old Town hotel occupies a converted 18th-century convent. The buffet breakfast is a lively affair, rooms are individually decorated, and there's an enchanting little roof terrace.

Hôtel Windsor
11 rue Dalpozzo (04.93.88.59.35/www.hotel windsornice.com). Rates €90-€175 double. **Rooms** 54. **Credit** AmEx, MC, V. **Map** p258 A3 ❼
This cult address is a mecca for bohemian types. Avoid the cheaper 'standard' rooms and check into one of the 25 artist-decorated rooms: each is unique, from the stripped-down simplicity of Oliver Mosset's design to the primary-coloured scribbles of niçois artist Ben. There's also an exotic garden and a chic fitness suite with a hammam and sauna.

Mercure Marché aux Fleurs
91 quai des Etats-Unis (04.93.85.74.19/www.mercure.com). Rates €95-€145 double. **Rooms** 49. **Credit** AmEx, MC, V. **Map** p255 A3 ❽
The seafront location is the main attraction at this link in the Mercure hotel chain – you're seconds from the beach. Rooms are clean and comfortable enough, though sometimes on the small side.

Le Palais de la Méditerranée
13-15 promenade des Anglais (04.92.14.77.00/www.concorde-hotels.com). Rates €280-€550 double. **Rooms** 188. **Credit** AmEx, DC, MC, V.
Behind a listed art deco façade, the Palais is a thoroughly modern, no-expense-spared establishment. The sea views are extraordinary, as is the heated open-air pool on the third floor. Locally inspired haute cuisine comes courtesy of chef Philippe Thomas in the hotel's restaurant, Le Padouk.

Resources

Hospital
Hôpital St-Roch *5 rue Pierre Dévoluy (04.92.03.77.77/www.chu-nice.fr).*

Internet
E-mail Café *8 rue St-Vincent (04.93.62.68.86).* **Open** 7.30am-7pm Tue-Sat; 10am-7pm Mon, Sun.

THE RIVIERA & SOUTHERN ALPS

Hotspot Internet Café *1 rue de l'Ancien Sénat (04.93.81.96.79).* **Open** noon-10pm Mon, Wed-Sun.

Police
1 av Maréchal Foch (04.92.17.22.22). **Open** 24hrs daily.

Post office
21-23 av Thiers (04.93.82.65.00). **Open** 8am-7pm Mon-Fri; 8am-noon Sat.

Tourist information
Office du Tourisme et des Congrès
5 promenade des Anglais (08.92.70.74.07/www.nicetourisme.com). **Open** 8am-8pm Mon-Sat; 9am-7pm Sun.
Office de Tourisme *Gare SNCF, av Thiers (04.93.87.07.07).* **Open** *June-Sept* 8am-8pm Mon-Sat; 9am-7pm Sun. *Oct-May* 8am-7pm Mon-Sat; 10am-5pm Sun.

Getting there

From the airport
Nice airport is 8km west of the city centre. Bus No.98 runs between the airport and the *gare routière* (bus station), while No.99 runs between the airport and the main SNCF station (every 20mins Mon-Sat, every 30mins Sun). No.23 from terminal 1 goes only to St-Maurice via the station. A taxi to the city centre will cost about €35.

By bus
The *gare routière* (5 bd Jean Jaurès, 04.93.85.61.81) is the hub for most Côte d'Azur coach services, among them the international buses that run via Nice from Rome to Barcelona and from Venice to Nice via Milan. **Phocéen Cars** (08.10.00.40.08) on place Masséna runs buses between Marseille and Nice via Aix and Cannes (five daily, Mon-Sat; three on Sun), and to Toulon, via Cannes and Hyères (two daily, Mon-Sat). **RCA** (04.93.85.64.44, www.rca.tm.fr) runs regular buses along the coast to and from Cannes and Menton.

By car
You can leave the A8 at exit 54 or 55, but it's more scenic to take the N7 or N98 along the coast (though expect traffic jams in summer and during rush hour).

By train
The main **SNCF** railway station (3 av Thiers, www.sncf.com) is served by frequent trains from Paris and Marseille. Local services to Menton also stop at Gare Riquier, near the port and in the Old Town. The Gare St-Augustin is near the airport. The private **Gare de Provence** (4bis rue Alfred Binet, 04.97.03.80.80), just north of the main station, is the departure point for the narrow-gauge **Train des Pignes**, which heads into the Alps – for details, *see p312.*

Getting around

By bus
An extensive bus network, including four Noctambus night buses, is run by **Ligne d'Azur** (10 av Félix Faure, 08.10.06.10.06, open 7.15am-7pm Mon-Fri; 8am-6pm Sat; 29 av Masséna, open 7.45am-6.30pm Mon-Fri; 8.30am-6pm Sat). Tickets cost €1. Bus-hop passes (€4, daily; €15, weekly), are available from Ligne d'Azur, tabacs and newsagents.

By taxi
Nice's taxis are notoriously expensive. To order a taxi, call **Central Taxi Riviera** (04.93.13.78.78).

By tram
Tickets for the tram (www.tramway-nice.org) cost €1, and can be bought from machines at each stop. Ligne 1 traces an 8.7km U-shape through the city, from Comte de Falicon to the pont Michel.

THE ARRIERE-PAYS

Mere minutes from Nice, the hinterlands known as the Arrière-Pays seem a world away from the fast-paced energy of the Côte d'Azur's urban centres and seaside throngs.

Just 18 kilometres (11 miles) north of Nice on the D2204/D15, **Contes** juts out from a steep slope overlooking the Paillon de Contes river. Once a Roman settlement, this quiet village found itself in the limelight in 1508 when the Bishop of Nice was called in to rid it of a nasty plague of caterpillars. The good bishop triumphed, giving the townsfolk reason to build the Chapelle Ste-Hélène in 1525; don't miss the tiny Renaissance fountain in its courtyard. This area is also famous for its olives – olives are still pressed (Dec-Mar) in a 17th-century watermill at the Site des Moulins (04.93.79.19.17, open 9.30am-12.30pm, 2-5pm Sat). Olive oil, salted olives and tapenade are on sale at the Gamm Vert agricultural co-operative (rte de Châteauneuf, 04.93.79.01.51, open 8.30am-noon, 2.30-6pm Tue-Sat).

In tiny **Châteauneuf-de-Contes**, 4.5 kilometres to the west, the 11th-century Madone de la Vielle Ville church is worth a look. A well-marked half-hour walk leads to the atmospheric ruins of vieille Châteauneuf.

On the main square of **Coaraze**, self-styled *village du soleil* ('village of the sun'), the town hall bears a dazzling yellow sundial by Jean Cocteau. Its name supposedly derives from *caude rase* ('cut tail'): wily medieval inhabitants caught Old Nick napping and grabbed hold of him, obliging him to shed his tail to escape. A modern pavement mosaic illustrates the tale, while the village itself is a maze of vaulted passageways, cypress-lined gardens and fountains. Also of interest is the unusual Chapelle Notre-Dame-de-la-Pitié, otherwise known as the 'Blue Chapel' for its monochrome scenes depicting the life of Christ. In the old cemetery at the top of the village, cement boxes are provided for burials, as the rocks are too hard even for pickaxes.

Travel 16 kilometres north-east of Nice on the D2204/D21 and you'll find **Peillon**, isolated on a rocky spur above olive groves. It's an unspoilt, photogenic huddle of grey stone houses and narrow, cobblestoned streets, with an unbeatable panorama over the valley. Not to be missed is the minuscule **Chapelle des Pénitents Blancs** at the entrance to the village. It's kept closed to protect the 15th-century frescoes of the Passion, attributed to Giovanni Canavesio, although the works can be viewed through a grating by means of coin-operated lights.

Further upstream – or a lovely 90-minute ridge walk from Peillon – **Peille** is a quiet village with handsome Romanesque and Gothic doorways and a ruined feudal castle. Its feisty inhabitants, who accepted numerous excommunications in the Middle Ages rather than pay taxes to the bishop, speak their own dialect, known as Pelhasc.

At the bottom of the Peillon Valley, the agricultural township of **L'Escarène** was once an important staging post on the route du sel ('salt road') from Nice to Turin; for once, a piece of modern engineering – the viaduct of the Nice–Sospel railway – complements the view of the Old Town. Further up the route du sel, the fortified medieval crossroads of **Lucéram** is worth a detour for its 15th-century Eglise Stes-Marguerite-et-Rosalie (closed Mon, Tue), which has a striking Italianate, onion-domed, yellow and pink belfry. Outstanding altarpieces by the Bréa School recount the story of St Marguerite, a shepherdess-martyr who was burned at the stake. She was also one of Joan of Arc's favourite voices-in-the-head.

Where to stay & eat

In Coaraze, book in at the **Auberge du Soleil** (5 chemin Camin de la Beguda, 04.93.79.08.11, closed Nov-mid Feb, double €68-€92, menus €23-€28), where the bucolic vista is matched by splendidly rustic cuisine; try the *giboulette de lapin* (rabbit stew). Rooms are simple but comfortable, and overlook the valley. At the edge of the village, the **Relais de Feuilleraie** (rte du Soleil, 04.93.79.39.90, www.relais-

feuilleraie.com, double €49-€60) offers five cosy rooms, a panoramic terrace and a pool.

In Peillon, the **Auberge de la Madone** (2 pl Auguste Arnulf, 04.93.79.91.17, www.chateauxhotels.com/madone) double €95-€200, closed early Nov-Jan) is a romantic hideaway with 14 rooms and a Michelin-starred restaurant (closed Wed, lunch Thur & Nov-Jan, menus €32-€62). Chef Christian Millo and his son Thomas, who trained under super-chef Alain Ducasse, deliver refined Nissart specialities; the view from the flower-lined terrace is one of the best in the Arrière-Pays.

In Peille, stop for a pastis and *pissaladière* at the café **Cauvin Chez Nana** (5 pl Carnot, 04.93.79.90.41, closed dinner Mon, Thur & Sun, all Tue, Wed, dinner reservations required, menus €18-€25).

Resources

Tourist information

Coaraze Office du Tourisme *7 pl Ste-Catherine, Coaraze (04.93.79.37.47).* **Open** *Apr-Sept* 10am-12.30pm, 3-6pm Tue-Fri. *Oct-Mar* 10am-12.30pm, 3-6pm Tue-Fri; 10am-12.30pm Sat.
Contes Syndicat d'Initiative *pl Dr Albert Olivier, Contes (04.93.79.13.99/www.ville-contes.fr).* **Open** 2-5pm Mon-Fri.
Lucéram Maison du Pays *pl Adrien Barralis, Lucéram (04.93.79.46.50).* **Open** 10am-noon, 2-6pm Tue-Sat.
Peille Syndicat d'Initiative *Mairie, pl Carnot, Peille (04.93.91.71.71).* **Open** 9am-noon Mon-Fri.
Peillon Syndicat d'Initiative *Mairie, 620 av de l'Hôtel de Ville, Peillon (04.93.79.91.04).* **Open** 8.30am-noon Mon, Tue, Thur; 8.30am-noon, 2-5.30pm Wed, Fri.

Getting there

By bus

There are buses from Nice to Peille (three daily, Mon-Sat), to L'Escarène and Lucéram (four daily, Mon-Sat) and to Contes and Coaraze (two daily, Mon-Sat); for details call Nice's *gare routière* (04.93.85.61.81).

By car

The starting point for getting to the Arrière-Pays by car is the D2204 Paillon valley road, which begins at the Acropolis roundabout in Nice as bd J-B Verany.

By train

The Nice–Sospel line (between four and six trains daily) stops at Peillon, Peille and L'Escarène, but only L'Escarène has a station within easy reach of the town; Peillon and Peille are a 5km walk from their respective stations.

The Corniches

Beaches and boats on Europe's wealthiest stretch of coast.

The vast yachts moored up on either side of **Cap-Ferrat** say it all: this is where Europe's elite come to play, unaffected by economic malaise or the price of oil.

Yet this divine stretch of coast is also the South of France at its most democratic, ringed with coastal paths and equipped with something special to suit any budget. You can enjoy a hotel with a sun terrace in **Cap-d'Ail** for the price of a starter at a ritzy restaurant in **Beaulieu**, and both are equally wonderful.

THE CORNICHE ROADS

The three Corniche roads that wind between Nice and Menton – low (Basse), middle (Moyenne) and high (Grande) – offer enticing glimpses of azure sea, manicured gardens and gorgeous villages.

The **Basse Corniche** (D6098, also known as the Corniche Inférieure) hugs the coast, passing through all the towns and resorts. To take some of the strain, the wider **Moyenne Corniche** (D6007) was hacked through the mountains in the 1920s. The highest route, the **Grande Corniche** (D2564), follows the ancient Roman Aurelian Way, and is the most spectacular of the three. It's a favourite with would-be racing drivers, masochistic cyclists and scenery-lovers.

The glamour of the Corniches has its tragic side too. On 13 September 1982, a car carrying Princess Grace of Monaco and her youngest daughter, Stéphanie, swerved off the N53, a treacherous descent full of hairpin bends that runs from the Grande Corniche to the Moyenne Corniche. Stéphanie survived; her mother did not. After Grace's mysterious death, Rainier retreated from the public eye. Fresh flowers can generally be seen by the roadside at the scene of the accident, and a second memorial stands halfway along the Nice to Villefranche Basse Corniche road.

About the author

Riviera resident **Tristan Rutherford** *writes about the Côte d'Azur for the British press, including* The Independent *and* The Sunday Times Travel Magazine.

Basse Corniche

VILLEFRANCHE-SUR-MER

Used as a natural shelter by the Greeks and Romans, Villefranche proper was founded in the 14th century by Charles II of Anjou as a duty-free port. The town's pink, ochre and apricot houses and trompe l'oeil frescoes are wonderfully photogenic, and you might still see elderly men mending fishing nets beside the tiny, cobbled port. In the old town, the eerie, vaulted rue Obscure has hardly changed since the Middle Ages.

The deep harbour between the headlands of Mont Boron to the west and Cap-Ferrat to the east was used as a US naval base until 1966; the quayside, lined with brasseries and overlooking a long, sandy beach, is now a haven of high-class entertainment. At the western end of the port is the minuscule **Chapelle de St-Pierre-des-Pêcheurs**; in 1957, Jean Cocteau covered it in lively frescoes depicting the life of St Peter.

At the top of the old town, the 18th-century **Eglise St-Michel** (04.93.76.69.94) is a handsome, Italianate church. Its impressive organ, built in 1790, is still played for Sunday mass. West of the church is the 16th-century Citadelle, built by the Dukes of Savoy; it houses the voluptuous female figures of local sculptor Antoniucci Volti (in the **Musée Volti**) and 100 minor works by artists such as Picasso, Hartung, Picabia and Miró (in the **Musée Goetz-Boumeester**). A coastal path leads around the Citadelle's walls from the harbour to the port of Darse, home to scores of colourful yachts and a sheltered beach. On the quayside,

Eco-Loc (06.63.91.16.77, €30 per day, closed Oct-May) rents electric bikes, and **Dark Pelican** (04.93.01.76.54, €120-€500/day) can rent you a speedboat with or without a prior licence.

Villefranche buzzes all year round, especially during the provençal market, held on place du Marché on Saturday mornings, and the Sunday antiques market on avenue Albert 1er.

★ Chapelle de St-Pierre-des-Pêcheurs
quai Courbet (04.93.76.90.70). **Open** *Apr-Sept* 10am-noon, 3-7pm Tue-Sun. *Oct-mid Nov, mid Dec-Mar* 10am-noon, 2-6pm Tue-Sun. Closed mid Nov-mid Dec. **Admission** €2; free under-12s. **No credit cards**.

FREE Musées Volti, Musée Roux & Musée Goetz-Boumeester
Citadelle, av Sadi Carnot (04.93.76.33.27). **Open** *July, Aug* 10am-noon, 2.30-7pm Mon, Wed-Sun. *June, Sept* 9am-noon, 2.30-6pm Mon, Wed-Sun. *Oct, Dec-May* 9am-noon, 2-5.30pm Mon, Wed-Sun. **Admission** free.

Where to stay & eat

The refined **Hôtel Welcome** (3 quai Amiral Courbet, 04.93.76.27.62, www.welcomehotel. com, double €96-€218) is a splendid yellow and blue portside establishment; it has little in common with the hotel of the same name where Cocteau fraternised with sailors amid opium fumes in the 1920s. Two minutes up the hill is the simple **Hotel Provençal** (4 av Maréchal Joffre, 04.93.76.53.53, www.hotelprovencal.com, double €56-€118), half of whose rooms have tiny balconies overlooking the bay. The nine rooms of the **Hotel Villa Vauban** (11 av Général de Gaulle, 04.93.55.94.51, www.hotelvillavauban. com, double €65-€185), four with sea-view balconies, are charming. For the best value rooms on the Riviera, try **Hotel Patricia** (av de l'Ange Gardien, 04.93.01.06.70, www.hotel-patricia.riviera.fr, closed Dec, double €32-€57). Staff are as friendly as can be, and there's a gorgeous shared garden and private parking.

The row of restaurants on the quayside all have deals with the boats moored up alongside, thus ensuring the freshest catch. The **Fille du Pêcheur** (3 quai Courbet, 04.93.01.90.09, mains €16-€45) and **L'Oursin Bleu** (11 quai Courbet, 04.93.01.90.12, closed Jan, Tue Nov, Dec, mains €30-€55) sit side by side; raw tuna steaks and seared scallops are a winner at the former, with more experimental cuisine at the latter. On place Amélie Pollonais, trendy **Le Cosmo** (04.93.01. 84.05, mains €12-€27) is packed with locals, and serves some of the best *salade niçoise* on the Riviera. It's also great for a shared starter and beers at sundown. The latest place to be seen at,

is **La Mayssa** (pl Wilson, 04.93.01.75.08, closed Mon, mains €23-€35) on the port building's large roof terrace. It does cosmopolitan dishes such as fillet of John Dory with a jasmine tea infusion.

Resources

Tourist information
Office de Tourisme *Jardin François Binon, Villefranche-sur-Mer (04.93.01.73.68/www. villefranche-sur-mer.com).* **Open** *July, Aug* 9am-7pm daily. *June, Sept* 9am-noon, 2-6.30pm Mon-Sat. *Oct-May* 9am-noon, 2-6pm Mon-Sat.

CAP-FERRAT

The lush peninsula jutting out between Villefranche and Beaulieu is a millionaires's paradise of high-hedged mansions, once a haunt of Somerset Maugham, Keith Richards and the Agnelli family; today's new neighbours are more likely to be Russian oligarchs. The promontory is a walker's dream, with a stunning path (*see p276* **A Walk on the Wealthy Side**).

The approach to the Cap is dominated by the **Villa Ephrussi-de-Rothschild**, an Italianate extravaganza built for Beatrice de Rothschild in the early 1900s. Here, Beatrice had appropriate settings recreated for her vast, largely 18th-century art collection. The villa is surrounded by fountain-filled Spanish, Japanese and Italian gardens, with arresting views.

On the eastern side of the peninsula, luxury yachts have replaced many of the fishing boats at St-Jean-Cap-Ferrat. Still, it's a delightful spot for an evening drink, followed by a stroll along the marina and Port St-Jean. Further west, the **Zoo du Cap-Ferrat** is home to some 300 species, from flamingos to otters and zebras.

★ Villa Ephrussi-de-Rothschild
1 av Ephrussi-de-Rothschild (04.93.01.33.09/ guided group visits 04.93.01.45.90/www.villa-ephrussi.com). **Open** *July, Aug* 10am-7pm daily. *Mid Feb-Oct* 10am-6pm daily. *Nov-mid Feb* 2-6pm Mon-Fri; 10am-6pm Sat, Sun. **Admission** €10; €7 reductions; free under-7s. **Credit** AmEx, MC, V.

Zoo du Cap-Ferrat
117 bd du Général de Gaulle (04.93.76.07.60/ www.zoocapferrat.com). **Open** *Apr-Sept* 9.30am-7pm daily. *Oct-Mar* 9.30am-5.30pm daily. **Admission** €15; €11 reductions; free under-3s. **Credit** MC, V.

Where to stay & eat

The stately **Grand-Hôtel du Cap-Ferrat** (71 bd du Général de Gaulle, 04.93.76.50.31, www.grand-hotel-cap-ferrat.com, double €550-€1,550) occupies acres of manicured grounds at the tip of the peninsula. Its rooms are exquisite, while head chef Didier Anies's daring creations have won him a Michelin star at the **Le Cap** restaurant (04.93.76.50.26, mains €72-€82) in 2008. Friendly and affordable **Hôtel Clair Logis** (12 av Prince Rainier III de Monaco, 04.93.76.51.81, www.hotel-clair-logis.fr, double €80-€170) has clean, comfortable rooms and lovely gardens; former guests include Gregory Peck and Charles de Gaulle. The **Hôtel Brise Marine** (58 av Jean Mermoz, 04.93.76.04.36, www.hotel-brisemarine.com, closed Nov-Jan, double €150-€172) is a delightful ochre- and turquoise-trimmed villa with a tangled garden, between St-Jean and Paloma beach. On a quiet backstreet between St-Jean and Beaulieu, **Résidence Bagatelle** (11 av Honoré Sauvan, 04.93.01.32.86, hotelbagatelle.free.fr, double €80-€150, closed Oct-Mar) has simple rooms with sea views and an overgrown citrus garden.

Overlooking St-Jean port from place Georges Clemenceau, Laurent Poulet's **Table du Cap** (04.93.76.03.97, closed lunch Mon-Thur, mains €37-€56) has seafood-oriented modern French cuisine and splendid views along the coast. Two restaurants stand out on the quayside: the sublime (and self-explanatory) **Gourmet Italian** (04.93.76.08.57, closed Mon & lunch Tue, mains €12-€38) and seafood specialist **Le Sloop** (04.93.01.48.63, closed Wed, menu €37). Join St-Jean locals in the **Restaurant du Port** (7 av Jean Mermoz, 04.93.76.04.46, closed Tue) for three-course feasts (€21) of flambéed prawns, grilled sea bream and sardines.

Resources

Tourist information
Office de Tourisme *59 av Denis Séméria, St-Jean-Cap-Ferrat (04.93.76.08.90).* **Open** *July, Aug* 9am-6pm daily. *Sept-June* 9am-6pm Mon-Sat.

BEAULIEU-SUR-MER

A charming belle époque resort that has long been a hit with European aristocrats, **Beaulieu** still has an old-world feel. Well-heeled strollers and their yapping dogs loiter on the scenic promenade Maurice Rouvier, which links the port to St-Jean-Cap-Ferrat via the public beach. Gustave Eiffel and Gordon Bennett, director of the *New York Herald Tribune*, lived here, as did archaeologist Theodore Reinach, so fond of ancient Greece that he built an extraordinary replica of a fifth-century BC Athenian house. Set in front of the Baie des Fourmis (named after the ant-like black rocks dotted about), the **Villa Kérylos** is now a museum, with a sunken marble bath and antique-looking frescoes galore.

On the beachfront, the **Casino**, a turn-of-the-19th-century jewel offering roulette, blackjack and baccarat, is deliciously retro. The Basse Corniche continues eastwards through the quiet seaside resort of **Eze-sur-Mer** and on to **Cap-d'Ail**. The latter has an easy coastal path that runs past the former homes of press magnate Lord Beaverbrook and actress Greta Garbo to the splendid pebbly plage Mala. This stretch

Villefranche-Sur-Mer. *See p272.*

is prized by the Monaco jetset and Italian daytrippers alike; the wearying trek down the steps (and up again) ensures that it's almost entirely child-free.

Casino de Beaulieu-sur-Mer
4 rue Fernand Dunan (04.93.76.48.00/www. partouche.com). **Open** 11am-4pm Mon-Thur, Sun; 11am-5pm Fri, Sat. **Admission** *Over-18s only; ID required* free. **Credit** AmEx, DC, MC, V.

★ Villa Kérylos
impasse Gustave Eiffel (04.93.01.01.44/www. villa-kerylos.com). **Open** *July, Aug* 10am-7pm daily. *Mid Feb-June, Sept, Oct* 10am-6pm daily. *Nov-mid Feb* 2-6pm Mon-Fri; 10am-6pm Sat, Sun. **Admission** €8.50; €6.20 reductions; free under-7s. **Credit** AmEx, MC, V.

Where to stay & eat

Celebrities and royalty still flock to the fin-de-siècle **Florentine Hôtel La Réserve** (5 bd Leclerc, 04.93.01.00.01, www.reservebeaulieu. com, closed mid Oct-mid Dec, double €580-€3,395); Olivier Brulard's highly acclaimed restaurant here (closed Mon, dinner mid Dec-May, menus €175-€270) serves excellent modern French cuisine. Two great cheapies by the train station and bus stop make Beaulieu a good base from which to explore the Corniches. **Hôtel Le Havre Bleu** (29 bd du Maréchal Joffre, 04.93.01.01.40, www.lehavrebleu.com, closed 1wk Dec, 1wk Jan, double €60-€82) is a blue and white villa with simple rooms; **Hôtel Marcellin** (18 av Albert 1er, 04.93.01.01.69, www.hotel-marcellin.com, double €60-€99) has a stone-paved garden and antique-laden foyer.

Restaurant Les Agaves (4 av Maréchal Foch, 04.93.01.13.12, closed lunch, mid Nov-mid Dec, menu €38) is upmarket and fun, with daily market specials and spring rolls on its menu. In the harbour, the retro-colonial **African Queen** (port de Plaisance, 04.93.01.10.85, average €50) is an institution, serving huge fish platters and pizzas from its wood-fired oven.

On Eze-sur-Mer's seafront, **La Villa sur la Plage** has hip apartments to rent by the week (06.27.40.08.48, €750-€1,280). With great views and large terraces, Cap-d'Ail's **Hôtel Miramar** (126 av du 3 Septembre, 04.93.78.06.60, double €43-€63), a ten-minute hike above plage Mala, is one of the Riviera's best deals. Further down the hill, the **Hôtel de Monaco** (1 av Pierre Weck, 04.92.41.31.00, www.hoteldemonaco.com, double €160-€180) is another gem, with wood-panelled mini-suites, a roof terrace and a sauna. Plage Mala has two chic seafront eateries: **La Reserve** (04.93.78.21.56, closed Oct-Easter, mains €18-€43) and **L'Eden** (04.93.78.17.06, closed Oct-Easter, mains €11-€52).

Finally, you don't have to be young to stay at Cap-d'Ail's **Relais de la Jeunesse** (2 av Gramaglia, 04.93.78.18.58, closed mid Oct-mid Mar, single bed €17), set in a belle époque villa in a prime waterfront location.

Resources

Tourist information
Office de Tourisme *pl Georges Clemenceau, 06310 Beaulieu-sur-Mer (04.93.01.02.21/www. ot-beaulieu-sur-mer.fr).* **Open** *June-Sept* 9am-12.30pm, 2-7pm Mon-Sat; 9am-12.30pm Sun. *Oct-May* 9am-12.30pm, 2-6pm Mon-Sat.

Moyenne Corniche

EZE

A picturesque eagle's nest of a place, with views to match and a profusion of tour buses, **Eze** is perched 430 metres (1,410 feet) above the shimmering Med. The village started life as a Celto-Ligurian settlement, passing from Phoenicians to Romans and Lombards to Saracens. Its glorious vistas inspired Nietzsche, who would stride up here in the 1880s from his Eze-sur-Mer home, planning the third part of *Thus Spake Zarathustra.* The steep mule path he took (now called sentier Frédéric Nietzsche) snakes through olive and pine groves; allow 75 minutes and take a bottle of water for the uphill slog from the Basse Corniche.

Other than metal workshops, souvenir shops, galleries and perfectly rejuvenated lanes, there is little of substance to see in Eze. In what remains of the castle, at the top of the village, the **Jardin Exotique** is a prickly blaze of flowering cacti and succulents, enjoying a sweeping view over red-tiled roofs to the coast.

Jardin Exotique
rue du Château, Eze (04.93.41.10.30/www.eze-riviera.com/village/jardin_exotique.htm). **Open** *July, Aug* 9am-8pm daily. *Sept-June* 9am-5.30pm daily. Closing times vary, depending on daylight. **Admission** €5; €2.50 reductions; free under-12s. **No credit cards.**

Where to stay & eat

The sumptuous rooms at the **Château de la Chèvre d'Or** (rue du Barri, 04.92.10.66.66, www. chevredor.com, closed Dec-mid Mar, double €270-€725) have sweeping views. Enjoy dining on the terrace (menus €95-€210) on Michelin-starred chef Phillipe Labbé's gastronomic fare. **Château Eza** (rue de la Pise, 04.93.41.12.24, www.chateaueza.com, closed Nov-mid Dec, double €150-€890), had a royal makeover, and has a Michelin-starred restaurant of its own (menus €45-€105). Beyond the city walls, the

Hôtel Arc en Ciel (av du Jardin Exotique, 04.93.41.02.66, www.arcencieleze.fr, double €62-€89) offers simple, modern rooms. Enjoy classic French cuisine with a provençal twist in the vintage interior of **La Troubadour** (4 rue du Brec, 04.93.41.19.03, closed Mon, Sun, mid Nov-mid Dec, menus €35-€48).

Resources

Tourist information
Office de Tourisme *pl du Général de Gaulle, 06360 Eze (04.93.41.26.00/www.eze-*

A Walk on the Wealthy Side

Take the Cap-Ferrat trail to stunning views and fabulous houses.

The belle époque casino by Beaulieu's Joffre bus stop stands at the foot of the Cap-Ferrat trail, its rococo splendour a taste of things to come. The ten-kilometre loop around Europe's richest spit of land starts at the promenade Maurice Rouvrier, to the west of plage des Fourmis – a family-friendly stretch of sand, but not a patch on five other magnificent beaches dotted around the Cap.

The first – and easiest – section of the walk curves past the **Royal Riviera** hotel, a popular summer retreat for wealthy Russians. Walk on for 500 metres, with the Med on your left, to the fairytale pink mansion **Le Fleur du Cap**, former home of David Niven (and Charlie Chaplin before him). The path continues for another 500 metres, past several private jetties, to St-Jean's sandy town beach.

You pass a Spar and a bakery as you walk through the village along avenue Jean Mermoz, handy for stocking up on hiking food. There's also a handful of estate agents, proferring 'price on application' mansions. The castle-like structure after Le Voile d'Or hotel at No.21 is the former retreat of Hungarian Princess Wilma Lwoff-Parlaghy, and boasted one of the first swimming pools in France.

Another 100 metres on, at the end of avenue Jean Mermoz, head down chemin de St-Hospice if you want to to take the additional two-kilometre coastal route to **Paloma beach**, one of the Cap's finest. The trail meanders past the gardens of some of the world's most expensive residences. The manicured grounds of **La Fiorentina**, former home of South African mining magnate Sir Edmund Davis and generally regarded as one of the Riviera's most elegant homes,

can be glimpsed from this verdant coastal path. The two beautiful beaches of **Les Fosses** and **Les Fossettes** mark the final leg of the loop, which delivers you back at the end of avenue Jean Mermoz at its intersection with avenue Claude Vignon.

Avenue Claude Vignon leads to the chemin de la Carrière, the narrow, five-kilometre path around the Cap's southernmost peninsula. The further you go, the more savage the scenery. Ocean rollers crash at the land's tip, as Monte Carlo comes into view on your left. The rocks are rawer, too: a sea-battered, sun-bleached moonscape dropping into the Med. Midway round the point, the Grand-Hôtel du Cap-Ferrat's **Club Dauphin** is a striking sight. If you're tiring, you can leave the path at the lighthouse 500 metres further on. A towering 1862 landmark construction, it was built by orders of Napoleon III, when trade, not tourism, was the Riviera's big earner. (If you do head inland here, look out for Somerset Maugham's house, **La Mauresque**, at 52 boulevard Général de Gaulle. Peek over the gate at the mansion, which once played host to Winston Churchill, Lord Beaverbrook and the Aga Khan.) There are no buses back into Beaulieu or Villefranche from here, so you'll need to have arranged a lift.

If you feel like carrying on, you'll see the coast's towering topography mirrored by underwater rocks and ridges from the precipitous path's final three kilometres. Dive boats are testament to the rapidly deepening sea, which makes for the best scuba diving on the Riviera. Strong swimmers can have a dip here, but others should carry on until Villefranche's medieval

riviera.com). **Open** *Apr-Oct* 9am-7pm daily.
Nov-Mar 9am-6.30pm Mon-Sat.

Grande Corniche

LA TURBIE

Dominating the Grande Corniche is **La Turbie**,
a spectacularly located village that is often
shrouded in mountain mist. Sleepily charming,
it consists of little more than a row of ancient,
ochre houses, two town gates and the 18th-

castle is in view, then wander past fig trees,
Aleppo pines, samphire and cacti to a series
of little coves, blessed with azure seas.

After rejoining the Cap's crowds at the
sheltered plage de Passable, wander up the
chemin du Roy and the chemin de Passable
to **Les Cèdres**. The mansion was home
to King Leopold II of Belgium. The largest
landowner the world has ever known, he
owned much of the Cap in the 1890s.
Avenue Grasseuil takes you 500 metres to
the Basses Corniche, where you can catch
the No.100 bus to earthier surroundings.

century church of **St-Michel-Archange**,
with its host of 'attributed to' and 'school of'
works. What puts the village on the map is the
Roman **Trophée des Alpes**, a partly restored
curve of white Doric columns set in a hilltop
park. The Trophée was erected in 6 BC to
celebrate Augustus's victory over local tribes;
it bears a copy of an inscription praising him,
though the huge statue that once adorned the
monument has long since gone. Inside the
adjoining museum is a scale model of the
original, and artefacts unearthed on the site.
Star-gazers should head north of La Turbie
to **Eze Astrorama** (rte de la Revère,
04.93.85.85.58, www.astrorama.net), a popular
astronomy show with a planetarium, telescopes
and videos; check the website for regular
'Spectacle aux Etoiles' star-gazing nights (€9).

Trophée des Alpes
18 av Albert 1er, La Turbie (04.93.41.20.84).
Open *Mid May-mid Sept* 9.30am-1pm, 2.30-6pm
Tue-Sun. *Mid Sept-mid May* 10am-1.30pm, 2.30-
5pm Tue-Sun. **Admission** €5; €3.50 reductions;
free under-18s. **No credit cards**.

Where to stay & eat

As well as luxurious bedrooms and a vine-clad
exterior, La Turbie's **Hôtellerie Jérôme**
(20 rue de Compte de Cessole, 04.92.41.51.51,
closed Nov-mid Feb, double €95-€150) has a
swish restaurant (closed Mon & Tue, menus
€65-€120) serving regional fare with a Ligurian
twist. The very good **Café de la Fontaine** (4
av Général de Gaulle, 04.93.28.52.79, closed Mon
Sept-May, mains €13, menu €25) does gourmet
niçoise food just off the main square. A short
drive back along the Grande Corniche towards
Nice, the **Hôtel Hermitage** (1951 av Diables
Bleus, 04.93.41.00.68, www.ezehermitage.com,
double €75-€125) is a vine-covered inn with a
poolside restaurant that serves decent regional
cuisine (menus €25-€48).

GETTING THERE & AROUND
By bus
RCA (04.93.85.64.44, www.rca.tm.fr) runs useful
buses: No.100 plies the Basse Corniche between
Nice and Menton; No.112 (Nice–Beausoleil) stops
in Eze (Mon-Sat); and No.116 runs five times a
day (Mon-Sat) between Nice and Peille via La
Turbie. **Ligne d'Azur** (08.10.06.10.06,
www.lignedazur.com) runs the No.81 bus from
Nice to Cap-Ferrat, and its No.83 shuttles
between Eze-Bord-de-Mer and Eze village.

By train
Villefranche, Beaulieu, Eze-Bord-de-Mer and Cap-
d'Ail are served by regular trains from Nice.

THE RIVIERA & SOUTHERN ALPS

Monaco & Monte-Carlo

Heaven for racing demons, and a haven for the super-rich.

Red Ferraris and Bentleys gleam in the sunlight in front of the Hôtel de Paris or tear round the hairpin bends in this playground for the rich and famous, where tower blocks loom over 19th-century villas and roads disappear into tunnels in an effort to maximise every last inch of possible space.

This densely packed two square kilometres of rock is one of the last three remaining autocratic states in Europe (the others being Lichtenstein and the Vatican). Portraits and photos of the sovereign prince hang in every shop and hotel, and although nominally a constitutional monarchy since 1911, with its own minister of state (the equivalent of a prime minister), Monaco's prince still holds executive power and signs all ordinances.

MONACO

The Grimaldi family has ruled this tiny state since 1297, when François Grimaldi sneaked in disguised as a monk and took over what was then a Genoese colony. The Grimaldis' historic territory included neighbouring Roquebrune and Menton, until they voted to join France in 1861, thus losing the state's main source of revenue: a tax on lemons. Two years later, Charles III gave the Société des Bains de Mer (SBM), headed by businessman François Blanc, permission to open a casino in the new part of town named after him, Monte-Carlo. Monaco's destiny was made. The SBM, today 69 per cent owned by Monaco state (the royal family), still runs Monte-Carlo's grandest hotels, restaurants, casinos, nightclubs and spas.

Under Prince Rainier III, sovereign prince from 1949 to 2005, the tiny principality was transformed from a sedate gambling resort into a glamorous, billion-dollar tax haven, increasing its GDP 180-fold. With no income tax levied, it became home to racing drivers, tennis stars and millionaires of every stripe. The prince's marriage to Hollywood star Grace Kelly, which brought Monaco into the post-war glamour circuit, and the subsequent antics of their offspring Caroline, Albert and Stéphanie,

have kept the francophone gossip press busy since 1956. Princess Grace's fatal car crash in 1982 is still shrouded in myth (although you can now follow a Grace trail around town).

Monaco is best enjoyed with a fortune, or at least the semblance of one – many of those Bentleys and Ferraris have just been hired for a few days. For those here on the cheap, though, there are a smattering of two- and three-star hotels near the train station and just across the border in France (you can tell by the postboxes). Dining and going out needn't break the bank either: most (glitzy if bland) nightspots only charge entrance at weekends, and few have strict dress codes. The free public beach at Larvotto has a reasonably clean stretch of sea, with fish swimming almost up to the water's edge. These attractions and a handful of sights are accessible by a cheap, frequent bus service and a network of public lifts. Hard to spot on the free maps distributed at key spots around the principality, the latter make light work of the punishing inclines from seafront to clifftop.

Sightseeing

Monaco is divided into five districts: Monaco-Ville, La Condamine, Monte-Carlo, Fontvieille and Monaghetti. The principality is only four kilometres long, but its steep hills and complicated system of tunnels mean it's worth checking out which district you're heading for before setting out.

The first thing you will want to see is the twin-turreted **Casino de Monte-Carlo** (*see p286*). Along with the adjoining opera house, it presides over the fountains, parked-up super-cars and manicured greenery of place du Casino. The square is home to Monaco's finest lodgings (**Hôtel de Paris**) and restaurant (**Louis XV**), along with the people-watching terrace of the **Café de Paris**. Braided flunkies

abound. This is the Monaco you came for: the Monte-Carlo of legend, and the *Persuaders* locations you used to watch on Sunday afternoons. It won't disappoint.

On avenue Princesse Grace, a pretty Japanese garden provides a calm oasis of water gardens, gravel, stepping stones and red bridges before the glass and metal **Grimaldi Forum** cultural centre. Across the street is the **Musée National Automates et Poupées** (Villa Sauber, 19 av Princesse Grace, +377-93.30.91.26, www. nmnm.mc, €6) – a museum devoted to dolls and frequented almost entirely by small girls

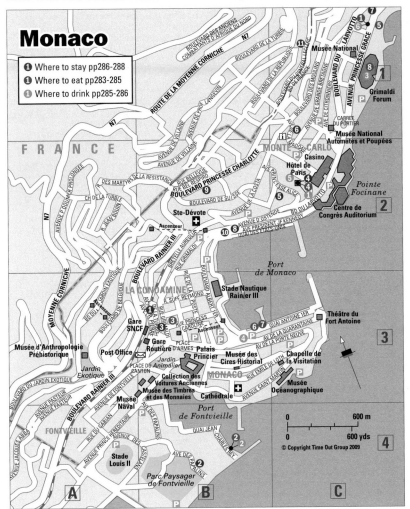

THE RIVIERA & SOUTHERN ALPS

THE RIVIERA & SOUTHERN ALPS

A Walk in the Fast Lane

Following Monaco's famous Grand Prix route on foot.

No sport can compete with the prestige and glamour of Formula 1. And no other racing circuit boasts the thrill of speeding €20,000,000 cars around the world's most exclusive piece of real estate. The tightness and complexity of Monaco's Grand Prix circuit was described by three-times F1 champion Nelson Piquet as 'like trying to cycle around your living room'. But it's also the one to win: 'the greatest race in the world and the greatest track,' according to 2008 Monaco GP champion Lewis Hamilton.

A 45-minute hike around the 3.3-kilometre circuit isn't quite in the same league as Michael Schumacher's 74-second lap record, but walking it does allow you to savour the finest moments of Monaco GP history. You can spot the starting grid markings under the traffic heading east on boulevard Albert 1er. On race day the din is intolerable: with such a tight track, burning rubber at the lights is a necessity, and the procession of 20 cars scream as they push out 18,000rpm apiece.

The tight right 100m (330ft) ahead takes you past the bronze cast of William Grover-Williams in his Bugatti. The winner of the inaugural GP in 1929, Grover-Williams went on to work for the British secret service during World War II. The track is essentially the same then as it is now, although the early races were an invitation-only affair, with a liberal sprinkling of daredevil aristocrats.

Avenue d'Ostende is the first chance to run up through the gears before a harsh left at Massenet pushes you around the seaward side of the Hôtel de Paris and spits you out at Casino square. It's habitually lined with Ferraris, Lamborghinis and Aston Martins (although parking here is technically free, police will politely ask you to move on if your vehicle is crap). Back on the race route, the descent down avenue des Spelugues to Mirabeau corner is headlong, the altitude testing drivers' spatial skills harder than any of the other, flatter, courses on the F1 circuit.

The speed is cruelly curtailed down to 48kmh (30mph) by a tortuous double-hairpin by the Fairmont Hotel, then ramped up again as the road bends around and tunnels back underneath the hotel. These chicanes may quash the circuit's average speed down to a lowly 125km/h (80mph), but they keep the excitement at boiling point.

Dozens of drivers have been befuddled by the sun as they emerge from the tunnel at 290km/h (180mph) on the fastest part of the track. In 1955, Alberto Ascari's Lancia drove wide and ended up in the harbour. The superstitious driver spun off and died at Monza a few days later while wearing teammate Eugenio Castellotti's white helmet: his own lucky blue one was having a new chinstrap fitted following his spectacular Monaco crash.

Burning down to Tabac corner, the circuit shoots past the boats in the quay. Over the long weekend of testing, qualifying and racing, a chartered super-yacht here will set you back around €250,000. As the circuit runs south of the open-air swimming pool, there's a bust of Louis Chiron, the only local-born Monaco GP winner, back in 1931. Plenty of other drivers have lived in the principality for tax reasons, though, not least record six-time winner Ayrton Senna, who retired to his apartment immediately after crashing out of first place in the 1988 race.

The penultimate turn bends around the Rascasse restaurant to a brass sculpture of five-time F1 champion Juan Manuel Fangio, standing astride his Mercedes-Benz. The obvious photo op requires a hop inside the Argentine ace's vehicle for a celebratory post-circuit snap.

and their mothers. Beyond lie the public beach at Larvotto, a couple of vast luxury hotels and **Le Sporting Club** (*see p285*).

The other main draw is the **Port Hercule** at La Condamine, with its gin palace yachts bobbing in the water. The quaysides form half of the Grand Prix circuit (*see p280* **A Walk in the Fast Lane**) each May. Lined with downmarket terrace bars at sea level on quai Albert Ier, and landmark destinations – **Quai des Artistes, Stars 'n' Bars** – on quai Antoine 1er, it's busy noon and night. On quai Albert 1er, the open-air public swimming pool becomes an outdoor ice rink in winter, while the terrace is used for everything from funfairs and fireworks to international showjumping. Behind here lies the homeliest part of the principality, with a few streets of 19th-century shops and houses and the pink and yellow arcaded place des Armes, home to a mornings-only market.

Looming over the harbour is Monaco-Ville or Le Rocher itself, the original fortified medieval town – an easy walk or bus ride up from the place des Armes. Its chief attractions are the **Palais Princier**, where changing of the guard takes place at 11.55am daily in the cannon-lined square, the **Cathédrale** and the popular **Musée Océanographique**. This is the oldest part of the principality – and tourist central, with souvenir shops touting Ferrari tat and stamp collections. On the edge of the promontory overlooking the sea, the remains of the **Fort St-Antoine** are now an outdoor amphitheatre, used for theatre performances in summer.

The tunnel on bus routes Nos.5 and 6 brings you to the harbour at Fontvieille on the western side of the rock. This is the heart of the Fontvieille district, built on reclaimed land in the 1980s. It's home to sprawling apartment complexes, along with a shopping centre that has a handful of toytown museums on its roof, the best of which is the **Collection des Voitures Anciennes**. There's also a mini-zoo, the **Jardin Animalier** (terrasses de Fontvieille, +377-93.50.40.30, closed noon-2pm daily, €4, €2 reductions), set up by Prince Rainier after a visit to Africa in 1954. Here, too, are the **Stade Louis II** (3 av des Castelans, +377-92.05.74.73, www.asm-fc.mc, €4, €2 reductions), home to premier division football club AS Monaco, the heliport and the 4,000 rose bushes of the Princesse Grace rose garden.

The other, if not only, major sight is the prickly **Jardin Exotique** on the way out of town. The nearby 1920s Villa Paloma (56 bd du Jardin Exotique, Monaghetti, +377-98.98.19.62, www.nmnm.mc) will open from the end of 2009 as the **Nouveau Musée National Monaco**, providing a temporary home for part of the art collection destined for a new national museum, set to open by 2015 near Larvotto beach.

FREE Cathédrale de Monaco

av St-Martin, Monaco-Ville (+377-93.30.87.70/ www.cathedrale.mc). **Open** *July-Sept* 8.30am-7pm daily. *Oct-June* 8.30am-6pm daily. **Admission** free (no entry during mass). **Map** p279 B3
Monaco's cathedral was built in 1875 in a sort of Romanesque, kind of Byzantine style. It contains a 15th-century altarpiece by Louis Bréa, a grandiose marble altar, some relics of St Dévote and the simple slab tombstone of Princess Grace, joined in 2005 by that of Prince Rainier III.

Collection des Voitures Anciennes

terrasses de Fontvieille, Fontvieille (+377-92.05. 28.56). **Open** 10am-6pm daily. **Admission** €6; €3 reductions; free under-8s. **No credit cards.** **Map** p279 B3
It is revealing that Monaco's most substantial museum should be devoted to the royal car collection, which ranges from a 1903 de Dion-Bouton to a 1986 Lamborghini Countach. A recent addition is the ALA 50, a prototype sports car made in Monaco and presented to Prince Albert II for his 50th birthday in 2008.

FREE Eglise Ste-Dévote

pl Ste-Dévote, La Condamine (+377-93.50.52. 60). **Open** 8.30am-6.30pm daily. **Admission** free. **Map** p279 B2
Now curiously marooned under a series of bridges and flyovers, this little church was built in 1870 on the site where, according to legend, Monaco's patron saint was guided ashore in the fourth century by a dove after surviving a shipwreck off Africa. Dastardly medieval pirates stole the saint's relics, only to be caught and their ship set on fire; in commemoration, a replica ship goes up in flames in front of the church each year on January 26.

★ Jardin Exotique et Grotte de l'Observatoire/Musée d'Anthropologie Préhistorique

62 bd du Jardin Exotique, Monaghetti (+377-93.15.29.80/www.jardin-exotique.mc). **Open** *Mid May-mid Sept* 9am-7pm daily. *Mid Sept-mid May* 9am-6pm or sunset daily. **Admission** €6.90; €3.60 reductions; free under-6s. **Credit** MC, V. **Map** p279 A3
Spectacularly planted over the cliff-face, this wonderland of nearly 7,000 bizarrely shaped cacti and succulents has everything from giant Aztec agaves to ball-shaped 'mother-in-law's cushion' cacti. At the bottom of the cliff is a stalactite- and stalagmite-lined cave (open on guided visits) and the anthropology museum, which traces the story of Stone Age life on the Riviera. Its displays feature bones galore from long-extinct animal species and impressive Cro-Magnon skeletons, all found in the Grimaldi caves (which can be visited in Balzi Rossi, just over the border in Italy).

THE RIVIERA & SOUTHERN ALPS

Musée de la Chapelle de la Visitation

pl de la Visitation, Monaco-Ville (+377-93.50. 07.00). **Open** 10am-4pm Tue-Sun. **Admission** €3; €1.50 reductions; free under-12s. **No credit cards**. **Map** p279 C3

This 17th-century baroque chapel is an appropriate setting for religious paintings by Rubens, Zurbaran, Ribera and Italian baroque masters.

Musée des Souvenirs Napoléoniens et Collection des Archives Historiques du Palais

pl du Palais, Monaco-Ville (+377-93.25.18.31). **Open** *June-Sept* 9.30am-6.30pm daily. *Oct, Nov* 10am-5pm daily. *Dec-May* 10.30am-noon, 2-4.30pm Tue-Sun. Closed mid Nov-mid Dec. **Admission** €4; €2 reductions; free under-8s. **No credit cards**. **Map** p279 B3

Bonaparte buffs should head for the southern wing of the Palais Princier, where they can peruse a vast array of artefacts from the First Empire, including the little man's hat and a bust by Canova.

Musée Océanographique

av St-Martin, Monaco-Ville (+377-93.15.36.00/ www.oceano.mc). **Open** *Apr-June, Sept* 9.30am-7pm daily. *July, Aug* 9.30am-7.30pm daily. *Oct-Mar* 10am-6pm daily. **Admission** €12.50; €6 reductions; free under-6s. **Credit** MC, V. **Map** p279 C3

Set in an imposing fin-de-siècle building, on 85m (279ft) of sheer cliff rising from the sea, the aquarium was founded by Prince Albert I, a keen oceanographer, in 1910. The old-style museum on the first floor is dedicated to his activities, with whale skeletons, original equipment and meticulously surveyed maps of Arctic islands. The aquarium includes reconstructed coral reefs, bright with tropical fish.

★ Palais Princier

pl du Palais, Monaco-Ville (+377-93.25.18.31/ www.palais.mc). **Open** *Apr-May* 10.30am-6pm daily. *June-Sept* 9.30am-6.30pm daily. *Oct* 10am-5pm daily. Closed Nov-Mar. **Admission** €7 (€9 with Napoleonic museum); €3.50 (€4.50 with Napoleonic museum) reductions; free under-8s. **No credit cards**. **Map** p279 B3

The sugary palace, built over a 13th-century Genoese fortress, is closed when the prince is in residence (signalled by a red and white banner). The well-presented free 30-minute audio guide takes in the frescoed Galerie d'Hercule, bedrooms, state apartments with Venetian furnishings and the throne room. The courtyard is used for classical concerts in summer.

Trips & tours

The **Ferrari Monaco Tour** (06.28.34.62.15, www.f1monaco-racing.com) allows you to fulfil your dream of taking a red Ferrari around the hairpin bends of Monaco (20mins as driver €85; as passenger €45). Meanwhile, **Héli Air Monaco** (Héliport, av des Ligures, Fontvieille, +377-92.05.00.30, www.heliairmonaco.com) runs ten-minute helicopter tours of the principality; four passengers are required for everyone to pay the minimum fare of €55 each. A slightly less glamorous way to see the sights is to hop on board one of the kitsch little tourist trains run by **Monaco-Tours** (38 quai Jean-Charles Rey, +377-92.05.64.38, €7, free under-5s), running from the Musée Océanographique to 18 key spots around the principality.

Where to eat

★ Bar Boeuf & Co

Le Sporting, av Princesse Grace, Monte-Carlo (+377-98.06.71.71/www.alain-ducasse.com). **Open** 8pm-1am daily. **Main courses** €38-€58. **Credit** AmEx, DC, MC, V. **Map** p279 C1 ❶

In 2008, Alain Ducasse's meat and fish concept Bar et Boeuf gained a new name, new decor and new chef Nicolas Lamstaes, fresh from the Louis XV kitchens (where he returns in winter). Although *bar* (sea bass) and *boeuf* (beef) remain the focus, the '& Co' means that other dishes, such as spicy chicken tagine, now get a look-in too. There are lovely sea views from the terrace, while service offers just the right degree of laid-back formality.

Beef Bar

42 quai Jean-Charles Rey, Fontvieille (+377-97.77.09.29/www.beefbar.com). **Open** noon-3pm,

8pm-midnight daily. **Menu** *Lunch* €18-€25.
Main courses €14-€28. **Credit** AmEx, DC,
MC, V. **Map** p279 B4 ❷
Although the name must owe more than a little
inspiration to Bar Boeuf (*see p283*), this sleek contemporary brasserie is all about meat eating, with
different cuts of beef from different breeds and origins (Argentina, Netherlands, USA).

€ Huit et Demi

4 rue Princesse Caroline, La Condamine (+377-
93.50.97.02/www.huit-et-demi.com). **Open** noon-
2.30pm, 7-11pm Mon-Fri; 7-11pm Sat. **Main**
courses €14-€20. **Credit** AmEx, DC, MC, V.
Map p279 B3 ❸
Red velvet Fellini-esque surroundings and a huge
terrace harbour gaggles of gossiping Italians,
English and Monégasques. Superbly fresh Franco-
Italian fare includes *beignets de courgettes* and sea
bream *en papillotte*; the soup of fresh fruits with
own-made lemon sorbet is divine.

★ Louis XV

Hôtel de Paris, pl du Casino, Monte-Carlo
(+377-92.06.88.64/www.alain-ducasse.com).
Open 12.15-1.45pm, 8-9.45pm Mon, Thur-Sun; 8-
9.45pm Wed (late June-late Aug). Closed mid Feb-
early Mar, late Nov-late Dec. **Menus** €105-€190.
Credit AmEx, DC, MC, V. **Map** p279 C2 ❹
This jewel box of a dining room offers one of the
most glamorous outdoor terraces in the world. Alain
Ducasse's first restaurant is still his best, although
now he flies in to supervise, and the kitchen is in the
hands of his protégé Franck Cerruti. The food is a
luxurious contemporary update of the sturdy, peasant food native to the coast and hinterlands from
Nice to Genoa, complemented by a remarkable cellar. Dress code: jacket and tie recommended for men.

★ La Note Bleue

plage Larvotto, av Princesse Grace, Monte-Carlo
(+377-93.50.05.02/www.lanotebleue.mc). **Open**
Mid May-mid Sept 9am-11pm daily. *Mar-mid*
May, late Sept-mid Dec varies. **Live music** *June-*
mid Sept Thur-Sun. Closed Jan-Feb, Thur in Nov.
Main courses €14-€28. **Credit** DC, MC, V.
Map p279 C1 ❺
Beachside Note Bleue is a great place to enjoy a
leisurely lunch or to squander a balmy summer
night. The kitchen serves up modern Mediterranean
cuisine, such as chicken with ceps and risotto, grilled
squid and pasta with Italian ham. By day, you can
rent a lounger on its private section of beach; by
dusk, tea lights transform the terrace into a romantic bar, with free jazz every weekend in summer.

Quai des Artistes

4 quai Antoine 1er, La Condamine (+377-
97.97.97.77/www.quaidesartistes.com). **Open**
noon-2.30pm, 7.30-11pm daily. **Main courses**
€14-€35. **Menus** *Lunch* €22 Mon-Fri. *Dinner*
€48-€56. **Credit** AmEx, DC, MC, V. **Map** p279
B2/3 ❻
Beside the Marlborough Gallery, this spacious terrace brasserie overlooking the harbour is a little too
formal to transform the quai Antoine 1er into an arty
hangout. Still, the seafood is superb, the €22 lunch
deal a bargain and the service first-class.

Karé(ment).

★ € Stars 'n' Bars

6 quai Antoine 1er, La Condamine (+377-97.97.95.95/www.starsnbars.com). **Open** *July, Aug* 10am-5am daily. *Sept-June* 11am-midnight Mon-Thur; 11am-2am Fri-Sun. **Main courses** €14-€19. **Credit** AmEx, DC, MC, V. **Map** p279 B2/3 **❼**

Everyone comes to this American restaurant-sports bar, with its four-square island bar surrounded by crash barriers and racing cars suspended from the ceiling. Drivers' overalls are inlaid into the tables, heaving with humongous hamburgers and Tex-Mex specialities, although in summer it's the large harbourfront terrace that draws the crowds.

Zébra Square

Grimaldi Forum, 10 av Princesse Grace, Monte-Carlo (+377-99.99.25.50/www.zebrasquare. com). **Open** noon-3pm, 8pm-midnight daily. Closed Feb. **Main courses** €20-€35. **Credit** AmEx, DC, MC, V. **Map** p279 C1 **❽**

Cool sister operation of its namesake counterpart in Paris, Zébra Square is a trendy bar-restaurant atop the Grimaldi Forum (take the lift by the main entrance). The small after-hours lounge bar is a destination in itself, but most are here for modern provençal cuisine, served in the low-lit dining room and on the seaview terrace.

Where to drink

Monaco's most famous nightclub remains the long-standing **Jimmy'z** at Le Sporting (*see right*), but there are plenty of late-night clubs and bars for the less glitzy punter. The harbour has two levels of unpretentious quayside venues, plus the catch-all **Stars 'n' Bars** (*see above*).

Bar Américain

Hôtel de Paris, pl du Casino, Monte-Carlo (+377-92.16.28.64). **Open** 10.30am-2am daily. **Credit** AmEx, DC, MC, V. **Map** p279 C2 **❶**

This old-school cocktail bar and café overlooks the Casino, with tables spilling out into the exquisite lobby of the Hôtel de Paris (*see p287*). Inside, a jazz trio plays in the corner while immaculately attired bar staff serve pricey (€22) cocktails, rare armagnacs and bottles of local Monaco beer in frosted glasses (€11). Smart dress please, at any time, with jacket and tie required as the evening wears on.
▶ *Other swish hotel bars include the Lobby Bar at Le Métropole and the 24-hour L'Intempo at the Méridien Beach (for both, see p287).*

Gerhard's Café

42 quai Jean-Charles Rey, Fontvieille (+377-92.05.25.79). **Open** 7.30am-3am daily. **Credit** MC, V. **Map** p279 B4 **❷**

At aperitif time, Gerhard's is the place of choice on Fontvieille harbour for an eclectic range of international expats and leathery-skinned seadogs, who

---

> **INSIDE TRACK**
> **BOARDING THE BUS-BOAT**
>
> **Riviera Navigation** (quai des Etats-Unis, +337-92.16.15.15, www.riviera-cruise. com) is an eco-friendly 'bus-boat' service that links Monaco-Ville to Monte-Carlo via an electric-powered boat. It's a great way to discover Monaco from the sea – and peep at the luxurious yachts docked in the harbour. Departures leave every 20 minutes, and tickets cost a mere €1.

down wine, German beers and nibbles perched along the bar, or around small tables amid the unselfconsciously dated decor.

★ Karé(ment)

Grimaldi Forum, 10 av Princesse Grace, Monte-Carlo (+377-99.99.20.20/www.karement.com). **Open** 9am-5am daily. **Credit** AmEx, DC, MC, V. **Map** p279 C1 **❸**

This hip cocktail and tapas bar, with a terrace from which to view passing cruise ships, has been packed since it opened in 2004. Cocktails (€15) are only served until 11pm, after which a DJ keeps the crowd busy on the dancefloor and the lip-shaped furniture.

La Rascasse

1 quai Antoine 1er, La Condamine (+377-93.25.56.90/www.larascasse.mc). **Open** 11am-4.45am Mon-Fri; 8pm-4.45am Sat, Sun. **Map** p279 B2/3 **❹**

A restaurant by day, La Rascasse morphs into a music venue and bar by night, with rock bands (mostly covers) from 11.30pm downstairs and DJs upstairs. It's on the tricky Rascasse bend of the F1 circuit (expect to pay around €2,500 for lunch with a grandstand view on race day).

Moods

Under the Café de Paris, pl du Casino, Monte-Carlo (+377-98.06.20.08/www.montecarlo resort.com). **Open** 7pm-2am Tue-Sat. **Credit** AmEx, DC, MC, V. **Map** p279 C2 **❺**

The latest addition to the live music scene is a two-level 'studio and music bar', which sees itself as Monaco's answer to London's Marquee and Ronnie Scott's. Classic rock, jazz and blues dominate.

Le Sporting Club

av Princesse Grace, Monte-Carlo (+377-92.16.22.77). **Open** *July-Aug* 8.30pm-late daily. *Sept-June* 8.30pm-late Wed-Sun. **Admission** *Concerts/shows* €60-€145 (incl 1st drink). **Credit** AmEx, DC, MC, V. **Map** p279 C1 **❻**

This vast seaside complex is frequented by models, pop stars, Middle Eastern princes, businessmen on expense accounts and miniskirted demoiselles,

THE RIVIERA & SOUTHERN ALPS

adorned with Cartier. Jimmy'z (+377-92.16.36.36, closed Mon & Tue Sept-June), the disco for beautiful people, requires chic attire and an ample wallet. Le Sporting d'Eté summer festival guarantees a star-studded setlist for a jet-set audience (Diana Ross and Alanis Morissette graced the stage in 2008).

Shopping

Luxury knows no bounds in Monte-Carlo (though not on a par with Cannes), from Chanel, Dior and a rash of glittery jewellery shops on avenue des Beaux-Arts and place du Casino to the designer boutiques along boulevard des Moulins and avenue Princesse Grace, where the choice ranges from Karen Millen and Chloé to the Bentley and Lamborghini concessions.

In place du Casino, the **Galerie du Métropole** is an upscale three-storey mall, home to the realistically priced Fnac CD, book and hi-fi store and various fashion stores. True Monégasques shop at La Condamiue market and in the **Centre Commerciale** in Fontvieille, a large shopping mall with a mega-supermarket.

Arts & entertainment

Le Cabaret du Casino

pl du Casino, Monte-Carlo (+377-98.06.36.36). **Show** 10.30pm Wed-Sat. Closed mid June-mid Sept. **Admission** *Show & drink* €25. *Show & dinner* €74. **Credit** AmEx, DC, MC, V. **Map** p279 C2.
Slick cabaret shows offer an alternative to gambling in a red-velvety nightclub atmosphere, with different dance-based spectaculars each season.

★ Casino de Monte-Carlo

pl du Casino, Monte-Carlo (+377-98.06.21.21/ www.casino-monte-carlo.com). **Open** (over-18s only, ID essential) *Slot machines* 2pm-late Mon-Fri; noon-late Sat, Sun. *Salons privés* 4pm-late daily. *Club Anglais* 10pm-late daily. **Admission** €10. *Salons privés & Club Anglais* €20. **No credit cards**. **Map** p279 C2.
The ornate gambling house was dreamed up in 1863 by Monaco's prince to generate revenue. Old-fashioned rules still apply: no clergymen or Monégasque citizens are allowed into the gaming rooms. For men, a sports jacket and tie are de rigueur. Roulette has a €5 minimum bet, while stakes are higher in the salons privés and Club Anglais, which offer chemin de fer, trente-et-quarante, blackjack and craps.

Grimaldi Forum

10 av Princesse Grace, Monte-Carlo (+377-99. 99.30.00/www.grimaldiforum.com). **Open** *July, Aug* 10am-8pm Mon-Sat. *Sept-June* noon-7pm Mon-Sat. **Admission** varies. **Credit** AmEx, DC, MC, V. **Map** p279 C1.

This glass and steel exhibition and cultural centre is used for everything from concerts and art exhibitions to trade shows, as well as performances by the acclaimed Ballets de Monte-Carlo, directed by choreographer Jean-Christophe Maillot. The Forum also features destination restaurant Zébra Square and nightspot Karé(ment), each with their own lift by the main entrance; for both, *see p285.*

Monte-Carlo Country Club

155 av Princesse Grace, Roquebrune-Cap Martin (04.93.41.30.15/www.mccc.mc). **Open** *July, Aug* 8am-9pm daily. *Sept-June* 8am-8pm daily. **Admission** (1-day pass) €40; €29 reductions. **Credit** AmEx, MC, V. **Map** p279 B2/3.
The swankiest sports club on the Riviera has clay tennis courts, squash, a gym and a heated open-air pool (open May-Oct) with airjets, waterfalls and a counter-current basin for aquatic workouts.

Open Air Cinema

26 av Princesse Grace, Monaco-Ville (08.92.68.00.72/www.cinemasporting.com). **Open** *Mid Aug-mid Sept* 9.30pm daily. **Admission** €10; €7 reductions. **No credit cards**.
On a warm summer evening, sit under the stars with a glass of rosé and catch the latest big release at the largest open-air screen in Europe. Seating is on cushioned chairs, or slightly more expensive reclining sun-loungers with tables for your drinks. Films are screened in their original language.

Opéra de Monte Carlo

Salle Garnier, Casino de Monte-Carlo, pl du Casino, Monte-Carlo (+377-98.06.28.28/www. opera.mc). **Open** *Nov-Apr* €20-€110. **Credit** AmEx, DC, MC, V. **Map** p279 C2.
Constructed in the 1870s, Charles Garnier's opera house has played host to everyone from Adelina Patti and Shaliapine to Placido Domingo, as well as Diaghilev's Ballets Russes. After a painstaking restoration it reopened in 2006, replete with stucco, gold leaf and grand chandeliers, and remains the place for a glamorous evening out.

Where to stay

Note that hotels for miles around shoot up their rates for the Monaco Grand Prix in May, and book well ahead to secure a room.

Hôtel Ambassador-Monaco

10 av Prince Pierre, La Condamine (+377-97.97.96.96/www.ambassadormonaco.com). **Rates** €165-€195 double. **Rooms** 35. **Credit** AmEx, DC, MC, V. **Map** p279 B3 **❶**
The white stucco-fronted Ambassador is an old-fashioned hotel near the train station, with light, good-sized rooms, a 1930s lobby and an Italian restaurant, Malizia.

THE RIVIERA & SOUTHERN ALPS

Hôtel Columbus

23 av des Papalins, Fontvieille (+377-92.05.90.
00/www.columbushotels.com). **Rates** €280-€335
double. **Rooms** 181. **Credit** AmEx, DC, MC, V.
Map p279 B4
This hip hotel, set on the harbour, has given a con-
temporary spin to Monaco's old-world image. Its
rooms are decked out in soft, cool colours and feature
luxurious leather upholstered beds. The cocktail bar
is a haunt of Formula 1 drivers, presided over by
part-owner David Coulthard.

€ Hôtel de France

6 rue de la Turbie, La Condamine (+377-
93.30.24.64/www.monte-carlo.mc/france).
Rates €90 double. **Rooms** 26. **Credit** MC, V.
Map p279 B3 ❸
Located on a narrow street in La Condamine, this
welcoming budget option is a long way from Monte-
Carlo glitz. There's no lift and the air conditioning
comes courtesy of ceiling fans, but the bedrooms are
clean and cheerfully decorated. Book well ahead, as
there aren't many budget options in these parts.

★ Hôtel de Paris

pl du Casino, Monte-Carlo (+377-92.16.30.00/
www.montecarloresort.com). **Rates** €410-€1,480
double. **Rooms** 182. **Credit** AmEx, DC, MC, V.
Map p279 C2 ❹
The grande dame of Monaco's luxury hotels was
opened in 1864, right next to the Casino. Famous
guests – Verdi, Alexandre Dumas, General Grant –
flooded in. Extended seven times, it now boasts
three restaurants, including the exquisite Louis XV
(*see p284*) and the equally elegant Bar Américain
(*see p285*). There's also direct access to Les Thermes
Marins spa, if you fancy a spot of pampering.

Hôtel Hermitage

sq Beaumarchais, Monte-Carlo (+377-92.06.40.
00/www.montecarloresort.com). **Rates** €370-
€940 double. **Rooms** 280. **Credit** AmEx, DC,
MC, V. **Map** p279 C2 ❺
A flouncy wedding cake of a hotel, the belle époque
Hermitage had two new floors added in 2004, but
the centrepiece is still the winter garden with its
stained-glass dome by Gustave Eiffel. Guests can
enjoy exquisite seafood at the rooftop restaurant, Le
Vistamar, and access to Les Thermes Marins.

Hôtel Métropole Monte-Carlo

4 av de la Madone, Monte-Carlo (+377-93.15.
15.15/www.metropole.com). **Rates** €400-€600
double. **Rooms** 141. **Credit** AmEx, DC, MC, V.
Map p279 C1 ❻
The 1880s Métropole has been refurbished in sumptuous fashion by decorator Jacques Garcia (of Hôtel
Costes and L'Hôtel in Paris fame) and now features
opulent fabrics, mahogany and marble bathrooms,
an ESPA spa, a seawater swimming pool, and a gastronomic restaurant, conceived by Joël Robuchon.

★ Le Méridien Beach Plaza

22 av Princesse Grace, Monte-Carlo (+377-93.
30.98.80/www.lemeridien.com). **Rates** €240-€375
double. **Rooms** 403. **Credit** AmEx, DC, MC, V.
Map p279 C1 ❼
The Méridien has a prime location by the city beach
at Larvotto, as well as indoor and outdoor pools, a
private beach and a beauty and fitness centre. High-
tech curved rooms in the mirror towers have
panoramic views, while top-floor suites offer person-
alised service. Lounge on curved red sofas over tea,
or watch the chefs at work in the circular open
kitchen of the 24-hour L'Intempo restaurant and bar.

Casino de Monte-Carlo.

★ € Hôtel Miramar

*1 av Président J-F Kennedy, La Condamine
(+377-93.30.86.48/www.hotel-miramar.mc).*
Rates €115 double. **Rooms** 11. **Credit** MC, V.
Map p279 B3 ❽

Miramar's 11 nautically styled rooms (lots of wood
and seagrass) offer perhaps the one true bargain in
Monaco – you're almost next to the Port Palace, for
a fraction of the price. Some of its rooms have balconies, and all offer great views across the Port
Hercule to the Palais Princier. Staff are friendly, and
there's a bar-brasserie downstairs.

Novotel Monte-Carlo

*16 bd Princesse Charlotte, Monte-Carlo (+377-
99.99.83.00/www.novotel.com).* **Rates** €160-€400
double. **Rooms** 218. **Credit** AmEx, DC, MC, V.
Map p279 B2 ❾

This recent arrival, designed by architect Jean-
Michel Wilmotte in cream stone, wood and glass, is
a decidedly upmarket outpost of the Novotel hotel
chain. Bedrooms are kitted out in businesslike, minimalist beiges, and there's a swimming pool, sea-
view terrace and restaurant.

Port Palace

*7 av Président J-F Kennedy, La Condamine
(+377-97.97.90.00/www.portpalace.com).* **Rates**
€265-€390 double. **Rooms** 50. **Credit** AmEx,
DC, MC, V. **Map** p279 B3 ❿

Hermès design director Leila Menchari is responsible for the sleek interior of this super-stylish contemporary hotel (check out the sharkskin walls in the
lift). The sixth-floor terrace restaurant serves
Mediterranean cuisine, while the spa uses the Clé de
Peau Beauté range, rarely seen outside Japan. All
superior to executive rooms have harbour views.

€ Villa Boeri

*29 bd du Général Leclerc, Beausoleil (04.93.78.
38.10/www.hotelboeri.com).* **Rates** €63-€78
double. **Rooms** 29. **Credit** AmEx, DC, MC, V.
Map p279 C1 ⓫

Within a short walk of the Casino, you won't find
cheaper than the small, friendly Boeri. It's the last
of a line of budget lodgings a few doors across the
border in Beausoleil, and provides clean, comfortable rooms, some with sea-facing balconies.

▶ *The recently renovated Olympia at No.17bis
(04.93.78.12.70) has rooms in the €100 range.*

Resources

Monaco has its own **phone cards**, **stamps**
and **dialling code**, 377. To reach Monaco, dial
your international access code (00 from the UK
or France, 011 from the US) or a '+' symbol,
followed by 377 and the number; you don't need
this prefix when calling internally. To call
France from Monaco, dial 00.33 or +33 before
the number. The currency is the euro.

Hospital

Centre Hospitalier Princesse Grace
av Pasteur (+377-97.98.99.00).

Internet

Stars 'n' Bars *see p285.*

Police

Police Municipale *pl Marie (+377-
93.15.28.26).*

Post office

Postes et Télégraphes *1 av Henri Dunant
(+377-99.99.80.80).* **Open** 8am-7pm Mon-Fri;
8am-noon Sat.

Tourist information

**Direction des Tourismes et des
Congrès de la Principauté de Monaco**
*2A bd des Moulins, Monte-Carlo, Monaco
(+377-92.16.61.16/www.visitmonaco.com).*
Open 9am-7pm Mon-Sat; 10am-noon Sun.

GETTING AROUND

The six-line colour-coded bus network is easy
and cheap. Lines 1 and 2 go to Monaco-Ville from
the Casino area. Single tickets (€1) and one-day
tourist passes (€3) are available on board.
  There are taxi ranks on place des Moulins,
square Beaumarchais and avenue PrésidentJF
Kennedy; otherwise, call 08.20.20.98.98. Note
that only cars registered in Monaco or the Alpes-
Maritimes (06) can enter Monaco-Ville.

GETTING THERE

By air

The nearest airport is at Nice (*see p270*), 16km
away. Take the bus from here to bd des Moulins
(€12.50, 50mins). Héli Air Monaco (*see p283*) runs
a helicopter service (€85, €50 reductions, free
under-2s), which takes seven minutes. A bus
(€4, 15mins) runs from Nice airport to the station;
from here, take the train to Monaco Monte-Carlo.

By bus

A regular bus service runs between the Nice and
Menton *gares routières*, stopping at bd Albert Ier
by La Condamine harbour.

By car

Leave the A8 autoroute at exit 57 or 58 or take
the coastal N98 (Basse Corniche) from Nice to the
west and Cap Martin and Menton in the east.

By train

Monaco Monte-Carlo station is served by the
Cannes–Nice–Menton–Ventimiglia line. From Nice,
the journey costs €3.10 and takes under 15mins. A
few TGV trains connect directly with Paris (6hrs).

Roquebrune to Menton

The cap of luxury.

The pine, fir, olive and mimosa trees that swathe **Cap-Martin** seem to have been planted by God with the express purpose of concealing the luxury hideaways that abound in these parts. The illustrious (Churchill, WB Yeats) and notorious (African dictator Emperor Bokassa) have all been drawn to the beautiful Cap-Martin promontory, while **Menton**, the last stop on the French coast before Italy, exudes faded elegance. The town is also famed for its lush gardens, which flourish in the subtropical microclimate.

ROQUEBRUNE-CAP-MARTIN

About an hour's walk straight up from the sea, the tiny village of **Roquebrune** was built into the hill's soft-looking pudding stone in the tenth century; its stone buildings still cling valiantly to the rock, offering matchless views. It started life as a fortified Carolingian fiefdom, then for five centuries from 1355 belonged to the Grimaldis, before being incorporated into France in 1860. It is crowned by the **Château de Roquebrune**, which would have been Disneyfied by its English owner in the 1920s had the locals not kicked up a fuss. It has four floors of historical displays, including armour and a dungeon.

The well-maintained **Le Corbusier walk** (formerly the Sentier Douanier) winds around the edge of the peninsula, passing by Le Corbusier's tiny modular beach shack, **Le Cabanon** (call the tourist office for visits, 10am Tue & Fri), set just before the Pointe de Cabbé. To the west, the curved **plage du Golfe Bleu** is a favourite landing spot for hang-gliders. It was here that Le Corbusier drowned while out for a swim in 1965; luckily, he had the foresight to design himself an impressive memorial, which stands in the village cemetery.

For the energetic, the **Sentier Massolin** is little more than a giant staircase leading from Roquebrune down to the coast via **Carnolès**, a popular seaside suburb that sprawls between

the Cap and Menton, with a bustling shingle beach. There are two more secluded beaches just below Cap-Martin Roquebrune railway station, and plenty of tiny paths to the water.

Château de Roquebrune
pl William Ingram (04.93.35.07.22). **Open** 10am-12.30pm, 2-6pm daily. **Admission** €3.70; €1.60 reductions; free under-7s. **No credit cards**.

Where to stay & eat

Opened in 1929, the **Monte Carlo Beach Hotel** (av Princesse Grace, 04.93.28.66.66, www.montecarlobeachhotel.com, double €265-€655) looks on to a sheltered cove just outside Monaco. Its private beach plays host to a varied line-up of DJs from mid May to August (4pm-midnight). Meanwhile, the luxurious **Vista Palace** (1551 rte de la Grande Corniche, 04.92.10.40.00, www.vistapalace.com, double €250-€700) is getting a bold new look care of Norman Foster, and is set to reopen in early 2010.

In the thick of the seafront action, the freshly renovated **Hôtel Reine d'Azur** (29 promenade du Cap-Martin, 04.93.35.76.84, www.reinedazur.com, closed Nov, double €58-€87) has modest rooms and a gravelly garden – ask for a sea-facing balcony. On the eastern tip of Cap-Martin, the **Hôtel Alexandra** (93 av Winston Churchill, 04.93.35.65.45, www.hotel-alexandra.net, double €60-€184) is a friendly, modern option; most rooms have jacuzzis and balconies with views towards the bay of Menton.

In Roquebrune, **Au Grand Inquisiteur** (18 rue du Château, 04.93.35.05.37, closed Jan, dinner Mon-Fri July-Sept, mains €18-€20) serves up top-notch cuisine in an old sheepfold carved out of the rock. For breathtaking sea views, book a table on the terrace of the **Hôtel-Restaurant des Deux-Frères** (1 pl des Deux Frères, 04.93.28.99.00, www.lesdeuxfreres.com, double €100-€110). The elegant restaurant (closed Mon, lunch Tue & dinner Sun, menus €28-€48) serves provençal cuisine with an international twist (turbot with avocado oil and broad beans sautéed with chorizo, say) and the small rooms are exquisitely romantic. The neighbouring tearoom **Fraise et Chocolat** (06.67.08.32.20, closed Fri & mid Nov-mid Dec), adorned with children's drawings, is a fine choice; children love the giant strawberry marshmallows. Across the square, atmospheric troglodyte café **La Grotte** (3 pl des Deux Frères, 04.93.35.00.04, closed Wed, dinner Tue, mains €10-€12) offers salads, *plats du jour* and pretty good pizza.

Resources

Tourist information
Office de Tourisme *218 av Aristide Briand, Carnolès, Roquebrune (04.93.35.62.87/www. roquebrune-cap-martin.com).* **Open** *July, Aug* 9am-7pm Mon-Sat; 10am-5pm Sun. *June, Sept* 9am-12.30pm, 2-6.30pm Mon-Sat. *Oct-May* 9am-12.30pm, 2-6pm Mon-Sat.

MENTON

Each year the town springs to life for the two-week **Fête du Citron** (*see p48*), which celebrates the small but prized harvest with kitsch parades. The town's festive calendar otherwise extends to a street theatre and young musicians' fair in May, classical music evenings in July, the prestigious Festival de Musique in August and a Mediterranean garden event in mid September. The streets feel sedate even in high season, bar the lively pedestrian rue St-Michel, which attracts the hordes with sunny café terraces, ice-cream shops and lurid soaps.

After more than six centuries of Monégasque domination, Menton voted to become French in 1861. In the same year, British physician Henry Bennet recommended the town for its healthy air. An influx of wealthy Britons and Russians arrived, bringing tearooms, botanical gardens and grand belle époque hotels (now demolished or turned into flats, sadly). Writers, artists and musicians – among them Monet, Maupassant, Flaubert and Liszt – also sojourned here.

The tone of present-day Menton is still set by its dilapidated belle époque villas, but there's modernity too: artist-aesthete-poet Jean Cocteau certainly left his mark. With the mildest climate on the Côte d'Azur – and therefore in France – the town is also a plant-lover's paradise. The garden of the **Villa Maria Serena** is said to be the warmest in France, with the temperature never lower than 5°C (41°F); among its rarities are a Canary Islands dragon tree. Meanwhile, Europe's biggest citrus tree collection mingles with contemporary sculptures in the garden of the **Palais Carnolès**, the 18th-century summer retreat for the Princes of Monaco.

The **Musée des Beaux-Arts** in the Palais Carnolès has European paintings ranging from Italian primitives and a beautiful Virgin and Child by Louis Bréa to modern artists including Graham Sutherland. In a 17th-century bastion on the edge of the old port, the **Musée Jean Cocteau** was the artist's last work before his death. Cocteau also decorated the **Salle des**

Menton.

Mariages in the Hôtel de Ville (pl Ardoïno, 04.92.10.50.00, closed Sat, Sun) with images of eternal love. North towards Gorbio, the **Eglise Russe** (12 rue Paul Morillot, 04.93.35.70.57, services 5pm Sat, 10am Sun) is worth a look.

★ Jardin de la Villa Maria Serena
21 promenade Reine-Astrid (04.92.10.33.66). **Open** Guided tours only; call the Service du Patrimoine (*see right*). **Admission** *Tour* €5. **No credit cards.**

FREE Musée des Beaux-Arts
3 av de la Madone (04.93.35.49.71). **Open** 10am-noon, 2-6pm Mon, Wed-Sun. **Admission** free. *Garden tour* €5. **No credit cards.**

Musée Jean Cocteau
Vieux Port (04.93.57.72.30). **Open** 10am-noon, 2-6pm Mon, Wed-Sun. **Admission** €3; free under-18s. **No credit cards.**

Where to stay & eat

The belle époque **Hôtel Aiglon** (7 av de la Madone, 04.93.57.55.55, www.hotelaiglon.net, double €88-€212, menu €29.90), set back from the beach towards Carnolès, is the epitome of faded Riviera charm. It has a garden with towering banana palms, rooms with frescoes and a pool. Owned by the same family since 1908, **Hôtel Paris-Rome** (79 av de la Porte de France, 04.93.35.73.45, www.paris-rome.com, closed Nov & Dec, double €60-€95) faces Garavan Bay, a 15-minute walk from the old town. It houses a restaurant serving inventive Mediterranean food and a very chic piano bar, decorated with contemporary sculptures; the rooms (except the two junior suites) have a more traditional look. On the same strip, the **Hôtel Napoléon** (No.29, 04.93.35.89.50, www.napoleon-menton.com, double €94-€149) targets a younger clientele with modern furniture, bright colour schemes, an outdoor pool and an ice-cream parlour on the beach. The vintage '50s lobby of **Hôtel Moderne** (1 cours Georges V, 04.93.57.20.02, www.hotel-moderne-menton.com, double €63-€90) would look at home in a gallery, but the rooms are plainly furnished – though they do have balconies.

On the edge of Menton is **Le Mirazur** (30 av Aristide Briand, 04.92.41.86.86, www.mirazur.fr, closed Mon, lunch Tue-Fri mid July-Aug; Mon & Tue Sept-mid Oct, Mar-June; mid Oct-Feb, menus €35-€90), run by young Argentinian-Italian chef Mauro Colagreco. Here, the finest local ingredients meet haute cuisine technique in dishes that look almost too beautiful to eat.

In the old town, stone-vaulted **A Braijade Meridiounale** (66 rue Longue, 04.93.35.65.65, www.abraijade.com, closed lunch July & Aug,

Wed Sept-June, mains €17-€25) is famous for its flambéed vertical brochettes. Just off rue St-Michel, **Le Bouquet Garni** (1 rue Palmaro, 04.93.35.85.91, closed Mon, Sun, mains €15) is a good-value bistro serving local specialities such as *barbajuan* (fried ravioli). The most coveted terrace on the place aux Herbes is that of **Le Balico** (04.93.41.66.99, closed Mon & Sun July & Aug, Tue & Wed Sept-June, mains €15-€20), where the salads, grilled meats and fish are reliably good. **La Coquille d'Or** (1 quai Bonaparte, 04.93.35.80.67, closed Tue, mains €12-€30) serves excellent provençal-style seafood in glitzy surroundings.

Resources

Internet
Café des Arts, 16 rue de la République (04.93. 35.78.67). **Open** *July, Aug* 7.30-10pm Mon-Sat. *Sept-June* 7.30am-noon, 2-10pm Mon-Sat.

Tourist information
Office de Tourisme Palais de l'Europe
8 av Boyer, 06500 Menton (04.92.41.76.76/ www.villedementon.com). **Open** *Mid June-mid Sept* 9am-7pm daily. *Mid Sept-mid June* 8.30am-12.30pm, 2-6pm Mon-Sat; 9am-12.30pm Sun.
Service du Patrimoine *Hôtel d'Adhémar de Lantagnac, 24 rue St-Michel (04.92.10.97.10).* **Open** 10am-12.30pm, 1.30-6pm Tue-Sat.

Getting there

By bus
The Ligne d'Azur No.100 bus runs along the coast between Nice and Menton every 15mins, taking just over 1hr (€1). **RCA Menton** (08.20. 42.33.33) runs an hourly service from Menton's *gare routière* (by the train station) along the Basse Corniche to Nice airport, stopping at Carnolès, Roquebrune and Monaco, and hourly shuttle buses from Carnolès to Roquebrune.

By car
Leave the A8 at exit 58 and follow the Grande Corniche to Roquebrune, exit 59 for Menton (last exit before Italy), or one of the three Corniches from Nice. Gorbio is 9km north-west of Roquebrune-Cap-Martin on the narrow D23. For Ste-Agnès, take rte des Castagnins from Menton, which becomes the D22 (13km). Castillon is 10km up the D2566 Sospel road from Menton. Castellar is 6km up the D24.

By train
Local trains on the Nice–Ventimiglia line stop at Roquebrune-Cap-Martin (just before the headland), Carnolès (just beyond), Menton and Menton-Garavan stations. There are also daily TGV connections between Paris and Menton.

Grasse & the Gorges du Loup

Head to the hills for stunning views – and perfumes galore.

Set between the sea and the mountains, the ancient town of **Grasse** is best known as the perfume capital of France. Tourists still flock here for the perfume museum, factory discounts and ornate bottles of scent, but there's more to the area than eau de toilette. The Romanesque cathedral and crooked streets of the *vielle ville* are a delight to explore, while the surrounding limestone hills harbour unspoilt medieval villages and hidden grottos.

To the north-east of Grasse, the breathtaking **Gorges du Loup** canyon slices through the hills. Here, outdoor types can try their hand at canyoning, or hike across the dramatic terrain.

GRASSE

Since 2004, when a 25-minute rail connection to Cannes was put back on track, Grasse has been determined to polish up its rather tattered image of dilapidated houses, graffiti and suburban gangs. A sweeping clean-up operation has transformed much of the town – the *vielle ville*, in particular. Yet unlike picture-perfect Valbonne or Mougins, Grasse's town centre offers up a genuine glimpse into the lives of real people: there are children playing in the streets, washing hanging from the windows and men of all ages loitering in tiny squares, sipping pastis and playing *pétanque*.

Grasse's fortunes took off in the 16th century, when fragrance-loving Catherine de Medici sparked a vogue for perfumed leather gloves. The town's balmy microclimate and established tanning industry made it ideal for combining perfume production with glove-making. When gloves went out of style, the Grassois continued making perfume, perfecting the art until the cosmetic world sat up and took notice. Today, the town's factories extract precious floral essences for the likes of Dior, Chanel and Saint Laurent.

A few decades ago, the fields of the Plan de Grasse were filled with flowers ready for harvest, but these days the view of the valley is less romantic, with more factories than freesias.

Nonetheless, around 120 rose and 20 jasmine farms remain: savvy Grasse has also moved with the times, branching out into the manufacture of synthetic scents.

Factories aside, Grasse has plenty of old-world charm. Steep staircases with hidden doorways jostle for space with the tacky glitz of the boulevard du Jeu de Ballon, which climbs up past the municipal casino, and the grand plazas filled with plane trees are magnificent. The main square, place du cours Honoré Cresp, has a cluster of museums around it (park underneath and continue on foot to avoid traffic jams). First up is the **Musée International de la Parfumerie**, reopened in 2008 after three years of renovations. The exhibition space has doubled in size – all the better to show off the 4,000-piece collection, which includes some fabulous 19th-century advertising and extravagant antique perfume bottles. In the rooftop greenhouse, you can touch and smell different plants, flowers and herbs.

For an insight into the lives of the 19th-century provençal bourgeoisie, visit the **Musée d'Art et d'Histoire de Provence** – set, very appropriately, in a beautifully renovated old *hôtel particulier*. Almost directly opposite, in the 18th-century Hôtel Pontevès-Morel, is the **Musée de la Marine**, dedicated to Admiral François Joseph Paul (1722-88), Count of Grasse, whose defence of Chesapeake Bay during the siege of Yorktown helped bring the American War of Independence to an end. Inside are miniatures of naval ships and maps.

From here, wander through the touristy shops of rue Jean Ossola to the **Musée Provençal du Costume et du Bijou**, housed in the beautiful 18th-century home of the Marquise de Clapiers-Cabris. The house itself is worth the visit, although a cursory jaunt through the collection of delicate lacework, Indiana cloth and simple dresses worn by peasants, craft workers and farmers' wives is also of interest. Next, turn right down rue Gazan into place du Petit Puy, dominated by the **Cathédrale Notre-Dame-du-Puy**. It's a prime piece of Lombard-influenced Romanesque architecture, mauled in the 17th and 18th centuries but now meticulously restored to its former glory. In its right aisle are several paintings by a young Rubens; it also houses *The Washing of the Disciples' Feet*, a rare religious work by local painter Fragonard.

Head down the steps to the side of the Hôtel de Ville towards the place des Herbes, once Grasse's herb and vegetable market, and now a good place to pause for a coffee. From here, take rue Droite (crooked, despite its name), looking out for the remarkable Renaissance stairwell at No.24. At the top of the street, the portal and Gothic window of the old Oratory Chapel are incorporated into the façade of Monoprix. Turn left for the cobbled place aux Aires, with its lovely three-tiered fountain and cafés. Every morning except Monday it hosts a not-to-be-missed flower and produce market.

At the far end of the public garden stands the **Villa-Musée Fragonard**, an elegant 17th-century mansion where artist Jean-Honoré Fragonard (1732-1806) sought refuge from the Revolutionary powers. Born in Grasse, the son of a not-very-successful glove-maker, Fragonard took himself to Paris. There, his voluptuous paintings found favour with Louis XV's aristocratic, pleasure-loving circle; alas, they were little liked by the children of the Revolution who, after all, decapitated most of his clients. The villa has sketches and etchings, plus trompe l'oeil murals by Fragonard's 13-year-old son, Alexandre, and a verdant garden.

Grasse's three big perfume houses (**Fragonard**, **Galimard** and **Molinard**) all offer factory tours, demonstrating the distilling and blending process. Fragonard also displays a collection of stills and perfume bottles at its 18th-century Historic Factory, though perfume production has shifted to the modern Fabrique des Fleurs. At Galimard's **Studio des Fragrances** you can concoct your own fabulous creation (€45), which is then funnelled into a charming glass bottle.

The flowers at the heart of Grasse's perfume success are celebrated in the Expo-Rose in May and the Jasmine Festival on the first weekend of August; call the tourist office (*see p295*) for details. At other times of year head to the **Jardin de la Princesse Pauline** on avenue Thiers, which has spectacular views amid its jasmine and rose bushes. Alternatively, drive to nearby Plascassier to visit the **Domaine de Manon** (36 chemin du Sevran, 04.93.60.12.76, www.domaine-manon.com, €6), which offers seasonal tours (May-Sept) of its fragrant fields of jasmine and roses.

Musée d'Art et d'Histoire de Provence
2 rue Mirabeau (04.93.36.80.20/www.musees degrasse.com). **Open** *June-Sept* 10am-12.30pm, 1.30-6.30pm daily. *Oct, Dec-May* 10am-12.30pm, 2-5.30pm Mon, Wed-Sun. Closed Nov. **Admission** €4; €2 reductions; free under-10s. **Credit** MC, V.

★ Musée International de la Parfumerie
8 pl du cours Honoré Cresp (04.93.36.80.20/ www.museesdegrasse.com). **Open** *June-Sept* 10am-7pm daily. *Oct-May* 10am-12.30pm, 2-5pm Mon, Wed-Sun. **Admission** €4; €2 reductions; free under-10s. **No credit cards**.

Musée de la Marine
2 bd du Jeu de Ballon (04.93.40.11.11). **Open** 10am-noon, 2-5pm Mon-Fri. **Admission** €3; €1.50-€2.50 reductions; free under-12s. **No credit cards**.

FREE Musée Provençal du Costume et du Bijou
2 rue Jean Ossola (04.93.36.44.65). **Open** *Feb-Oct* 9am-6pm daily. *Nov-Jan* 9am-12.30pm, 2-6pm daily. **Admission** free.

FREE Parfumerie Fragonard
Historic Factory *20 bd Fragonard (04.93.36.44.65/www.fragonard.com)*. **Open** 10am-4pm daily. **Admission** free. **Fabrique des Fleurs** *Les Quatre Chemins, 17 rte de Cannes (04.93.77.94.30)*. **Open** *Feb-Oct* 9am-6.30pm daily. *Nov-Jan* 9am-12.30pm, 2-6pm daily. **Admission** free.

FREE Parfumerie Galimard
Factory *73 rte de Cannes (04.93.09.20.00/ www.galimard.com)*. **Open** *May-Oct* 9am-6.30pm daily. *Nov-Apr* 9am-noon, 2-6pm Mon-Sat. **Admission** free. **Studio des Fragrances** *rte de Pégonas (04.93.09.20.00)*. **Open** by appointment. **Admission** €35. **Credit** AmEx, MC, V.

THE RIVIERA & SOUTHERN ALPS

FREE Parfumerie Molinard

*60 bd Victor Hugo (04.93.36.01.62/www.
molinard.com).* **Open** *Apr-Sept* 9am-6.30pm
daily. *Oct-Mar* 9am-12.30pm, 2-6pm Mon-Sat.
Visits finish 1hr before closing. **Admission** free.

Villa-Musée Fragonard

*23 bd Fragonard (04.97.05.58.00/www.musees
degrasse.com).* **Open** *June-Sept* 10am-6.30pm
daily. *Oct, Dec-May* 10am-12.30pm, 2-5.30pm
Mon, Wed-Sun. Closed Nov. **Admission** €4;
€2 reductions; free under-10s. **Credit** MC, V.

Where to stay & eat

There are great views at the quiet, out-of-the-
way **Auberge La Tourmaline** (381 rte de
Plascassier, 04.93.60.10.08, double €84-€104)
and friendly, central **Hôtel des Parfums** (bd
Eugène Charabot, 04.92.42.35.35, www.hoteldes
parfums.com, double €96-€126), which has a
pool and gym. **Hôtel Le Victoria** (7 av Riou
Blanquet, 04.93.40.30.30, closed Jan, double
€52-€79) is a child-friendly hotel with a pool,
a decent gym and a reasonable restaurant.

The Michelin-starred **Bastide St-Antoine**
(48 av Henri Dunant, 04.93.70.94.94,
www.jacques-chibois.com, double €235-€650,
menus €53 lunch, €130-€170 dinner) is set
in a century-old olive grove just below Grasse.
Jacques Chibois is renowned for his wonderful
flavour combinations – including an exceptional
fois gras and truffle cream soup. Its 16 elegant
rooms and suites look over the grounds, which
feature a pool and *pétanque* pitch.

Its unhappy location by the *gare routière*
aside, **Café Arnaud** (10 pl de la Foux,
04.93.36.44.88, closed Sun, mains €25-€33,
menus €20-€40) is one of the oldest restaurants
in Grasse, serving unpretentious food with a
provençal slant; try the home-made fois gras.

A creative approach and consistently good
food have made cosy **Le Gazan** (3 rue Gazan,
04.93.36.22.88, mains €19-€32, menus €19.50-
€32, closed Sun, Dec-Jan, dinner Mon-Thur in
Sept-Nov, Feb-July) a must-eat destination: lean
steak with a violet-infused *jus* and scalloped
potatoes is one of the highlights. Locals and
tourists alike lunch at **La Voûte** (3 rue du
Thouron, 04.93.36.11.43, mains €12.50-€24,
menus €22-€25), tucking into local specialities
and French classics (the steak tartare is great).

Set in a converted, candle-lit olive mill,
Le Moulin des Paroirs (7 av Jean XXIII,
04.93.40.10.40, www.lemoulindesparoirs.com,
reservations necessary Sat & Sun, closed Mon,
end Sept-mid Oct, menus €20-€60) is a romantic
choice, with enticing set menus and seasonal
specialities. Good curry is rare on the Côte
d'Azur: those with a craving should try **Le New
Punjab** (3 rue Fabreries, 04.93.36.16.03, mains

€9-€15). In the Casino, **Le Perchoir** (bd Jeu
de Ballon, 04.93.36.91.00, closed lunch, all day
Mon & Tue, menus €28-€79) has a certain Vegas
charm; have a drink in the kitsch lounge bar and
eat steak-frites before gambling the night away.

Just outside town, the **Clos des Cyprès** (87
chemin de Canebiers, 04.93.40.44.23, www.clos
descypres.fr, double €99-€125) offers five
guestrooms in a lovely 19th-century villa,
set amid pine, olive and cypress trees. South-
west Grasse, meanwhile, has the delightful
(if pricey) **Bastide St-Mathieu** (35 chemin
Blumenthal, 04.97.01.10.00, www.bastidest
mathieu.com, double €290-€380). The building
dates back to the 18th century and its decor is
elegantly traditional; outside there's a vast pool,
set amid lovely gardens.

Near Auribeau-sur-Siagne, a short drive out
of town, the **Moulin du Sault** (rte de Cannes,
Moulin Vieux, 04.93.42.25.42, closed Mon, mains
€26-€40, menus €28-€46) is perfect for special
occasions, with its stunning terrace and superb
food; try the grilled sea bass with lemon and
olive oil. Five minutes on foot up the route

Villa-Musée Fragonard.

Napoléon towards Digne, the **Mandarina** (39 av Yves Emmanuel Baudoin, 04.93.36.10.29, www.mandarinahotel.com, double €60-€68) is a former Carmelite hospice. The terrace has sea views and the welcome is friendly.

Resources

Internet
Le Petit Caboulot 8 pl de la Foux (04.93.40.16.01). **Open** 8am-7.15pm Mon-Sat.

Tourist information
Office de Tourisme 22 cours Honoré Cresp, Grasse (04.93.36.66.66/www.grasse-riviera.com). **Open** July-Sept 9am-7pm Mon-Sat; 9am-1pm, 2-6pm Sun. Oct-June 9am-12.30pm, 2-6pm Mon-Sat.

WEST OF GRASSE

Northwest from Grasse along the route Napoléon (N85, rte de Digne) is a surprising hinterland; you soon find yourself climbing through impressive, arid mountain scenery. After about 12 kilometres you'll reach the medieval village of **St-Vallier-de-Thiey**, which sits on the plateau de Caussols – a good vantage point for spotting *bories*, the dry-stone igloos once occupied by shepherds. The 12th-century Romanesque church on the place du Tour is one of the oldest in the *département*, with a beautifully carved entrance portal. The village also has a large playground, sporting complex and equestrian centre (for details, call the Maison des Jeunes et de la Culture on 04.93.60.76.29). Nearby is the **Souterroscope de Baume Obscure**, where underground waterfalls crash past stalactites and stalagmites. (Bring a sweater, as it's a constant 12°C.) Further north towards Castellane and the Gorges du Verdon (*see p222*) the scenery becomes more Alpine, dotted with pine forests.

South of St-Vallier towards Cabris are the **Grottes des Audides**, where 279 steps carved out of the rock lead down to the spring, nestled amid soaring stalactites and stalagmites. Inhabited in prehistoric times, the cave system was discovered by a shepherd in 1988. In the adjoining Parc Préhistorique, dioramas illustrate the lives of these original inhabitants.

Cabris itself is a prosperous village, with cafés and restaurants squeezed around its central square, and splendid mansions nestled against the mountain face. The English Cabris Cricket Club (www.cabriscricket.com) plays matches on the village green, drawing all the expats in the area.

Perched above the River Siagne is the unspoilt medieval village of **St-Cézaire-sur-Siagne**, famed for its perfectly preserved architecture and magnificent views. Check out the Gallo-Roman sarcophagus in the entrance to its 12th-century chapel before heading to the **Grottes de St-Cézaire**. The rust-red stalagmites and stalactites are famous for their curious shapes, ranging from toadstools to animals and flowers; some emit an eerie musical sound when struck.

Grottes des Audides
1606 rte de Cabris (04.93.42.64.15/http://grottes desaudides.free.fr). **Open** July, Aug 11am-6pm Tue-Sun. Sept-June 2-6pm Wed-Sun. Closed late Aug-early Sept. **Admission** Caves €5; €3 reductions; free under-4s. Parc Préhistorique €3; €2.50 reductions; free under-4s. **Credit** AmEx, DC, MC, V.

★ Grottes de St-Cézaire
9 bd du Puit d'Amon (04.93.60.22.35/www.les grottesdesaintcezaire.com). **Open** June, Sept 10.30am-noon, 2-6pm daily. July, Aug 10.30am-6.30pm daily. Oct 2.30-5pm daily. Nov, Jan 2.30-5pm Sun. Feb, Mar 2.30-5pm daily. Apr, May 2.30-5.30pm daily. Closed Dec. **Admission** €6; €3-€4.50 reductions; free under-6s. **Credit** AmEx, MC, V.

Souterroscope de Baume Obscure
chemin Ste-Anne, St-Vallier-de-Thiey (04.93.42.61.63). **Open** May-June, Sept 10am-5pm Mon-Sat; 10am-6pm Sun. July, Aug 10am-6pm daily. Oct-Apr 10am-5pm Tue-Sun. Closed mid Dec-mid Feb. **Admission** €7.65; €3.80 reductions; free under-4s. **Credit** MC, V.

Where to stay & eat

In St-Vallier-de-Thiey, **Le Relais Impérial** (85 rte Napoléon, 04.92.60.36.36, www.relais imperial.com, double €41-€73) is cosy and clean, with a restaurant that serves up filling, basic fare (mains €19-€26). The friendly **Le Préjoly** (pl

---

**INSIDE TRACK
ON THE OLIVE TRAIL**

Perfume aside, Grasse's other fragrant speciality is olive oil. It's a serious business, with the same sort of tastings, auctions and ratings found in the wine world; the local *olive de Nice* has been awarded an *Appellation d'Origine Contrôlée*, so only olive oil from this region can be labelled 'from Nice'. Of the local farms, one of the best is the **Moulin à Huile Conti** (138 rte de Draguignan, 04.93.70.21.42, closed Sun). The shop is open year round, while the mill itself springs into action during pressing season (Nov-Jan).

THE RIVIERA & SOUTHERN ALPS

Cavalier Fabre, 04.93.60.03.20, www.prejoly.com, closed Jan, double €38-€77) is a country inn of some 50 years' standing. Its restaurant (04.93.42.60.86, closed Tue evening & Wed in winter, menus €16.50-€24.50) serves good-quality classic cuisine; try the salmon, grilled over an open fire. Towards St-Cézaire, **L'Hostellerie des Chênes Blancs** (2020 rte de St-Vallier, 04.93.60.20.09, www.chenes-blancs.com, closed Sept-Apr, double €67-€129) has a pool, tennis courts and a good restaurant (menus €21.50-€29.50), where hearty mains include *ravioli à la daube*.

In Cabris, the charming **Mas du Naoc** (chemin du Migranié, 04.93.60.63.13, www.le masdunaoc.com, double €110-€145) oozes style, with its airy, gorgeously appointed rooms, tranquil gardens and pool. In the centre of the village, **L'Horizon** (100 promenade St-Jean, 04.93.60.51.69, closed mid Oct-Mar, double €80-€130) has a pool, terrace and good-sized rooms. **Le Vieux Château** (pl du Panorama, 04.93.60.50.12, www.aubergeduvieuxchateau.com, double €85-€135, restaurant closed Mon, Tue & Jan, menus €24 lunch, €37 dinner) is a beautiful hotel-restaurant carved out of the old castle, with provençal food and four double rooms; book well ahead. The cuisine at **Le Petit Prince** (15 rue Frédéric Mistral, 04.93.60.63.14, www.lepetitprince-cabris.com, closed Dec-mid Jan, menus €20-€29) is traditional with a twist; try the braised duck with pepper and rose petal sauce. **Le Mini Grill** (5 pl du Puits, 04.93.60.55.58, closed Wed, dinner Tue, menu €18-€21), with its off-road terrace and no-fuss menu, is handy for children.

Resources

Tourist information

Cabris Office de Tourisme *4 rue Porte Haute, Cabris (04.93.60.55.63)*. **Open** *May-Sept* 9am-12.30pm, 2-5.30pm Mon-Sat. *Oct-Apr* 9am-12.30pm, 1.30-5pm Mon-Sat. Closed Christmas.
St-Cézaire Office de Tourisme *3 rue de la République, St-Cézaire-sur-Siagne (04.93.60.84.30/ www.saintcezairesursiagne.com)*. **Open** 10am-noon, 3-6.30pm Tue-Fri; 10am-noon Sat, Sun.
St-Vallier Office de Tourisme *10 pl du Tour, St-Vallier-de-Thiey (04.93.42.78.00/www. saintvallier.com)*. **Open** *Mar-June, Sept, Oct* 9am-noon, 3-6pm Mon-Sat. *July, Aug* 9am-noon, 3-6pm Mon-Sat; 10am-noon Sun. *Nov-Feb* 9am-noon, 3-5pm Mon-Sat.

THE GORGES DU LOUP

Known as the 'violet village', **Tourrettes-sur-Loup** is built on a rocky peak surrounded by precipices. Producing so many violets that it has a festival devoted to them in early March (the Fête des Violettes), the fortified medieval town is also a mecca for sculptors, potters and painters, with over 30 workshops and galleries. The main drag, the Grand'Rue, is lined with overly earnest – and expensive – shops. The 15th-century church has some beautiful altarpieces, including scenes from the life of the Virgin, and a Louis Bréa triptych. Afterwards, call in at **Confiserie Florian** (pont du Loup, 04.93.59.32.91, www.confiserieflorian.com) for traditional sweets and chocolates flavoured with violets, lemon verbena and citrus.

Set on a hillside surrounded by beds of jasmine, orange trees and violets, **Le Bar-sur-Loup** is a charming medieval village. Its narrow streets wind around a massive 16th-century castle with four corner towers and a ruined keep. The Gothic church of St-Jacques contains a 15th-century altarpiece, as well as a famous *danse macabre*, portraying tiny courtly dancers being shot by Death, judged unworthy by St Michael, then promptly hurled into hell. When he's in the area, a less saintly Michael (Schumacher) has been known to take a spin at **Fun Kart** (plateau de la Sarée, rte de Gourdon, 04.93.42.48.08, www.fun-karting.com, €20/20 mins, closed Sun).

Tortuous bends and overhanging cliffs, accompanied by the sound of crashing water, lead you into the **Gorges du Loup**, where the sport du jour is canyoning. Consisting of climbing down slippery cliffs (or jumping off them), it's a dangerous pursuit, so hire a guide. **Destination Nature** (69 rue Georges Clemenceau, La Colle-sur-Loup, 04.93.32.06.93, www.loisirs-explorer.com/destination-nature) is affordable (€45) and reliable, and can also organise mountain hiking. If you're experienced enough to do it on your own, consult *Les Guides Randoxygène* at tourist offices.

Along the D6, amid lush vegetation, a huge monolith marks the entrance to the spectacular Saut du Loup. The waters of the Loup swirl furiously through this enormous, eroded cauldron, gushing down through vegetation petrified by the lime carbonate of the spray.

Perched between Grasse and the Loup Valley is **Gourdon**, a medieval citadel that kept watch against marauding Saracens. The 13th-century **Château de Gourdon** blends French and Italian Romanesque influences and has gardens laid out by André Le Nôtre in the 17th century. It houses the Musée Historique (the usual weaponry and torture implements, plus a Rembrandt and a Rubens) and the Musée de la Peinture Naïve (Douanier Rousseau-type daubs, and one example of the real thing).

Château de Gourdon

Gourdon (04.93.09.68.02/www.chateau-gourdon. com). **Open** *June-Sept* 11am-1pm, 2-7pm daily. *Oct-May* 2-6pm Mon, Wed-Sun. **Admission** €4; €3 reductions; free under-12s. **No credit cards.**

THE RIVIERA & SOUTHERN ALPS

Where to stay & eat

In Tourrettes-sur-Loup, **Chez Grande Mère** (pl Maximin Escalier, 04.93.59.33.34, closed Wed, lunch Sat, Nov-mid Dec, menus €18-€24) has a cosy fire and serves wonderful home-made dishes, with bread still warm from the oven. **Bacchanales** (21 Grand'Rue, 04.93.24. 19.19, closed Mon evening, all Tue, Wed, early Dec, mid Jan-Feb, menus €35-€48) is a local favourite for traditional provençal dishes like stuffed tomatoes, and is good for vegetarians.

Les Belles Terrasses (1315 rte de Vence, 04.93.59.30.03, http://bellesterrasses.free.fr, double €73-€110) lives up to its name and has nice, if basic, rooms. **Le Mas des Cigales** (1673 rte des Quenières, 04.93.59.25.73, double €72-€105) is a charming B&B with a pool and tennis courts. **Relais des Coches** (28 rte de Vence, 04.93.24.30.24, closed Mon & Tue, Jan, lunch July & Aug, menu €38) offers trad French fare, along with a Sunday roast cooked by a Yorkshire chef (noon-6pm, €25).

A panoramic terrace, large pool and floral rooms make the **Residence des Chevaliers** (521 rte du Caire, 04.93.59.31.97, closed Oct-Mar, double €120-€190) a comfortable place to stay. **Auberge de Tourrettes** (11 rte de Grasse, 04.93.59.30.05, www.aubergedetourrettes.fr, closed Jan, Feb, double €112-€130) has a lovely terrace and an excellent restaurant (menus €45-€80), serving local dishes such as rabbit baked with olive paste. Nearby **Le Foulon** (4220 rte de Grasse, 04.93.24.41.38, www.le-foulon.com, double €100-€166, menu €28) is a delightful hideaway, with friendly owners and a wonderful setting; the restaurant serves appealing Italian-provençal fare.

Restaurants are few and far between in Le Bar. Try **La Jarrerie** (av Amiral de Grasse, 04.93.42.92.92, www.restaurant-la-jarrerie.com, closed Tue, lunch Wed, Jan, menus €27-€49) for smart provençal fare (duck breast with honey and morel mushrooms, say). In Gourdon, the **Auberge de Gourdon** (04.93.09.69.69, menus €18-€24, closed evenings & all Mon) is a bar, tabac and eaterie with local charm, heavy provençal accents and simple, honest cuisine.

Le Mas au Loup (1389 ancienne rte Vence Grasse, 04.93.59.32.68, www.lemasauloup.com, double €60-€75) has two snug rooms and lovely views. Campers should try the **Camping Rives du Loup** (2666B rte de la Colle, pont du Loup, 04.93.24.15.65, €15-€25/pitch).

Resources

Tourist information

Le Bar Office de Tourisme *pl Francis Paulet, Le Bar-sur-Loup (04.93.42.72.21/www.lebarsur loup.fr).* Open *Apr-June, Sept* 3-6pm Mon; 10am-1pm, 3-6pm Tue-Fri; 10am-1pm Sat. *July, Aug* 10am-1pm, 3-7pm Tue-Sun. *Oct-Mar* 9.30am-noon, 3-5pm Tue-Fri; 3-6pm Mon; 10am-1pm Sat.

Gourdon Syndicat d'Initiative *pl Victoria, Gourdon (04.93.09.68.25/www.gourdon-france.com).* Open *July, Aug* 9.30am-1pm, 3-7pm. *Sept-June* 10.30am-1pm, 2-6pm daily.

Tourrettes-sur-Loup Office de Tourisme *2 pl de la Libération, Tourrettes-sur-Loup (04.93.24. 18.93/www.tourrettessurloup.com).* Open *Oct-June* 9.30am-6pm Mon-Sat. *July-Sept* 9.30am-6pm daily.

Confiserie Florian.

VALBONNE

Designed by the monks of Lérins, as part of a 17th-century bid to repopulate an area devastated by plague, **Valbonne** was planned on a neat chequerboard design. Its symmetrical rectangles are a far cry from the twisting, narrow streets of nearby medieval villages. Clearly inspired by Roman town planning, the village is bordered by 'rampart houses', with an entrance gate on each of its four sides and lookout points to spot approaching enemies.

At the heart of the village is place des Arcades, where the Fête du Raisin celebrates the late-ripening servan grape at the end of January. For the rest of the year, locals and tourists gossip and people-watch on the café terraces. The parish church is to the right of the plaza; once part of Chalaisian Abbey, it is in the form of a Latin cross and has a square chevet. The abbey, now beautifully restored after six years of work, contains the small **Musée des Arts et Traditions Populaires**. The village is also home to several glass workshops, notable for their handmade perfume flasks.

In the shadow of Valbonne lies **Sophia-Antipolis**, a perfectly landscaped, perfectly soulless science park where 20,000 people from more than 60 countries work in R&D-intensive companies, keeping the already high property prices in the area bubbling over.

Musée des Arts et Traditions Populaires

rue Paroisse, Valbonne (04.93.12.96.54). Open *May-Sept* 3-7pm Thur-Sun. Closed Oct-Apr. **Admission** €2; €1 reductions. **Credit** AmEx, MC, V.

Where to stay & eat

In Valbonne, the 17th-century **Hôtel Les Armoiries** (pl des Arcades, 04.93.12.90.90, www.hotellesarmoiries.com, double €89-€159)

offers comfortable, traditionally decorated rooms (though some are on the small side). Just outside town, **Château la Bégude** (rte de Roquefort-Les-Pins, 04.93.12.37.00, closed mid Nov-mid Dec, double €80-€328) is a carefully restored manor with 34 beautiful guestrooms and a terrace restaurant (closed dinner Sun Nov-Mar, menus €31 lunch, €43 dinner) overlooking the golf course. The **Bastide de Valbonne** (107 rte de Cannes, 04.93.12.33.40, www.bastide-valbonne.com, double €95-€250), with four charming rooms and a large pool, is also surrounded by golf courses.

The **Bistro de Valbonne** (11 rue de la Fontaine, 04.93.12.05.59, closed Mon lunch, Sun, Thur lunch mid June-mid Sept, Sat lunch mid Sept-mid June, mains €18-€33) serves French classics and is renowned for its superb smoked wild Baltic salmon. At **Lou Cigalon** (4-6 bd Carnot, 04.93.12.27.07, closed Mon & Sun, mains €34-€46, menus €31 lunch, €56-€115 dinner) owner-chef Alain Parodi gets stellar reviews for his modern spin on provençal cuisine; roasted veal with pistachio and wild rice, perhaps, or spiced octopus with chorizo.

Resources

Tourist information

Valbonne Office de Tourisme *1 pl de l'Hôtel de Ville, Valbonne (04.93.12.34.50).* Open *Mid June-mid Sept* 9am-12.30pm, 1.30-5.30pm Mon-Sat. *Mid Sept-mid June* 9am-12.30pm, 1.30-5.30pm Mon-Fri; 9am-12.30pm Sat.

GETTING THERE & AROUND

By bus

Rapides Côte d'Azur (04.93.36.08.43) runs buses daily between Grasse and Cannes, Nice airport, Vence, Grasse and St-Cézaire, some of which stop at Cabris, and between Grasse and St-Vallier-de-Thiey (Mon-Sat). For the Gorges du Loup, take No.511 from Grasse to Pont du Loup. **TACAVL** (04.93.42.40.79) operates several services (Mon-Sat) between Grasse and Le Bar-sur-Loup. **STCAR** (04.93.12.00.12) No.3VB runs from Cannes direct to Valbonne about every hour (less on Sun) and the No.5VB (four buses Mon-Fri) goes via Sophia-Antipolis. **Sillages** (04.92.28.58.68, www.sillages-stga.tm.fr) also runs buses in the area.

By car

The N85 (rte Napoléon) between Cannes and Grasse heads towards Digne via St-Vallier-de-Thiey. From Nice take the D2085 at Cagnes towards Le Bar-sur-Loup and Grasse. For Cabris, take the D4 out of Grasse, then the D13 to St-Cézaire. The D2210 winds from Vence towards Grasse via Tourrettes-sur-Loup and Le Bar, with side roads turning off up the Gorges du Loup.

INSIDE TRACK
ANCIENT AND MODERN

South-west of Valbonne in Mouans-Sartoux, the grounds of a 16th-century chateau are the unlikely home of the sleek **Espace de l'Art Concret** (Château de Mouans-Sartoux, 04.93.75.71.50, www.espacedelartconcret.fr, closed Mon Sept-June €5), founded in 1990. A mecca for fans of geometric, abstract and minimalist art, its permanent collection includes works by Honegger, Albers, André, LeWitt and Morellet.

Vence & St-Paul

A rich artistic heritage has paid dividends for Vence and St-Paul.

Even when its streets are clogged with tourists clutching ice-cream cones and cameras, it's easy to understand why the beautiful village of **St-Paul-de-Vence** has attracted so many artists over the years: the intent *pétanque* players in front of the Café de la Place are a painting in themselves. These days it's home to numerous art galleries – and one of France's finest contemporary art museums.

The more understated town of **Vence**, with its laid-back medieval *vieille ville*, is better suited to lingering on a café terrace and savouring the slow pace of provençal life.

VENCE

A Ligurian tribe was already calling this part of France home long before Emperor Augustus and his sandalled hordes marched in and named it Vintium. Set in a strategic position ten kilometres from the sea, Vence was a bishopric from the fourth to the 19th centuries, and has two patron saints. The first was fifth-century Bishop Véran, who organised the town's defences against Visigoth invaders (though Saracens would later succeed where the Barbarians had failed, razing the cathedral and much of Vence to the ground). The second, 12th-century Bishop Lambert, defended the town's rights against its rapacious new baron, Romée de Villeneuve, setting a trend of rivalry between nobility and clergy that was to last until the bishopric was dissolved after the Revolution.

In the 1920s, Vence became popular with artists and writers, including Paul Valéry, André Gide and DH Lawrence, who died here in 1930. A simple plaque in the cemetery marks the place where Lawrence lay for five years; he was then cremated at the behest of his widow, and his ashes shipped to New Mexico. (Though some say that Frieda Lawrence's lover, Ravagli, who was given the task, dumped the ashes somewhere between Marseille and Villefranche to save himself the trouble.)

Walls still encircle some of the medieval *vieille ville*, which has retained its old-world feel despite the modern sprawl outside; boulevard Paul André follows the old ramparts and offers sweeping views to the Alps. Outside the western Porte Peyra, one of five original town gates, place du Frêne is named after its giant ash tree, planted to commemorate a visit from Pope Paul III in 1538. The gate leads into place Peyra, site of the Roman forum. Between the two squares, the 17th-century **Château de Villeneuve** was the long-time residence of the Lords of Villeneuve, Provence and Vence. It's now occupied by the **Fondation Emile Hugues**, which organises exhibitions of major modern artists who visited or resided in Vence, such as Matisse and Chagall.

At the centre of the *vieille ville*, the **Ancienne Cathédrale Notre-Dame-de-la-Nativité**, undergoing restoration at the time of writing, was built on the site of a Roman temple to Mars in the fourth century. Little of the original structure remains, although there are Roman fragments worked into the baroque façade on place Clemenceau; St Véran is said to have been buried in the pre-Christian sarcophagus in the third chapel on the right. The baptistery is decorated with Chagall's vibrant mosaic of Moses (1979); look out also for Jacques Bellot's charmingly irreverent 15th-century carvings on the choir stalls. Outside, place Clemenceau is home to the town's morning market, with stalls selling everything from second-hand clothes to piping hot *socca* (chickpea pancake).

Just outside the medieval town, **place du Grand Jardin** is edged with cafés. Residents pause to gossip over coffee or cast a practised eye over the *pétanque* players in the square, and it's here that you really get a feel for local life. To see Vence at its liveliest, though, come in July, when the **Nuits du Sud** (*see p47*) bring a month of salsa, jazz and French-Arabic music.

The town's prime attraction is the **Chapelle du Rosaire** (*see p302* **Matisse's Final Masterpiece**). It's a 15-minute walk from town, well marked from Porte Peyra and with breathtakingly lovely views on the way.

To the north-east of Vence, **St-Jeannet** is a wine-producing village dominated by the dramatic rock outcrop known as Le Baou, which can be ascended by a waymarked path. Fifteen kilometres east of Vence is sleepy **La Gaude**, a friendly little hillside village that dates from 189 BC. It's the starting point for six marked walks, including one to Vence (which takes just over an hour) and a 90-minute hike to Le Baou; the tourist office (*see p303*) has maps.

★ Chapelle du Rosaire

466 av Henri Matisse (04.93.58.21.10). **Open** 10am-11.30am, 2-5.30pm Tue, Thur; 2-5.30pm Fri, Sat; mass 10am Sun. Closed mid Nov-mid Dec. **Admission** €3; €1.50 reductions; free under-6s. **No credit cards**.

Château de Villeneuve Fondation Emile Hugues

2 pl du Frêne (04.93.58.15.78). **Open** 10am-12.30pm, 2-6pm Tue-Sat. **Admission** €5; €2.50 reductions; free under-12s. **No credit cards**.

Where to stay & eat

On the eastern edge of Vence, the delightful **Hôtel Miramar** (167 av Bougearel, plateau St-Michel, 04.93.58.01.32, www.hotel-miramar-vence.com, double €68-€148) is set in an ancient manor house with a pool, terrace and panoramic views of St-Jeannet, the sea and the hills. Art-lovers might prefer **La Maison du Frêne** (1 pl du Frêne, 06.88.90.49.69, www.lamaisondufrene. com, double €150-€180), a vividly coloured B&B in the centre of Vence, filled with works by local artists. Another central option is the sweet **Hôtel Le Provence** (9 av Marcellin Maurel, 04.93.58.04.21, closed mid Jan-mid Feb, double €42-€68), set in a flower-filled garden.

Slightly out of the centre, the charming **Hôtel Villa Roseraie** (51 av Henri Giraud, 04.93.58.02.20, www.villaroseraie.com, double €87-€147) has a magnificent garden with a swimming pool. An upmarket hotel since 1970, the luxurious **Château du Domaine St-Martin** (av des Templiers, 04.93.58.02.02, www.chateau-st-martin.com, €320-€500 suite) provides elegant accommodation, ranging from junior suites with balconies and sea views to private villas. The hotel also has stunning views and a fine Italian-influenced restaurant.

Located on a quiet, wooded hill, the **Hôtel Cantemerle** (258 chemin Cantemerle, 04.93.58.08.18, www.relais-cantemerle.com, double €190-€210) offers various spa therapies,

including shiatsu, reflexology and Thai massage. Other facilities include indoor and outdoor pools and a Turkish bath – plus a bar and restaurant for the evening retox.

L'Auberge des Templiers (39 av Joffre, 04.93.58.06.05, www.restaurant-vence.com, closed Mon, Tue & Wed in summer, mains €27-€33) has great mod Med cuisine, cooked by internationally trained, Vence-born chef Stéphane Demichelis and served in the sun-dappled garden in summer. A la carte is pricey, but there's a €39 set menu. The 15th-century **Auberge des Seigneurs** (pl du Frêne, 04.93.58.04.24, closed 2wks Jan, double €85-€95) has been an inn since 1895 and is wonderfully cosy in winter. Its restaurant specialises in roast meats, cooked over a grill in the dining room's huge fireplace (closed Mon, lunch Tue-Thur, mains €15-€20).

The culinary event of 2008 was the opening of **Les Bacchanales** (247 av de Provence, 04.93.24.19.19, closed Tue, Wed & 3 wks Nov-Dec, menus €32-€45). Chef Christophe Dufau's succinct, daily changing menu puts an inventive spin on local ingredients, and the setting is heavenly: a sun-filled villa with sculptures in the garden, ten minutes' walk from Vence.

At **La Litote** (4 rue de l'Evêché, 04.93.24. 27.82, www.lalitote.com, closed Mon & Sun in July & Aug, Wed, Thur & lunch Sun Sept-June,

La Colombe d'Or. *See p303.*

mains €13), chef Stéphane Furlan takes great pride in his reasonably priced contemporary French food – foie gras with mango, perhaps, or lobster raviole.

Outside La Gaude, **L'Orangeraie de la Baronne** (66 chemin du Maoupas, 04.92.12. 13.69, www.orangeraie.fr, double €75-€95) is a B&B with four rooms and an apartment, set on a farm that produces clementines, kumquats, avocados and olives. Breakfast and dinner make the most of the organic fruit and vegetables grown on the farm.

Resources

Tourist information
La Gaude Office du Tourisme
8 rue Louis Michel Féraud, La Gaude (04.93.24.47.26/www.mairie-lagaude.fr). **Open** 9am-12.30pm Mon, Sun; 9am-12.30pm, 2.30-5pm Tue-Fri; 9am-4pm Sat.
St-Jeannet Syndicat d'Initiative *rue Charles François Euzière, St-Jeannet (04.93.24. 73.83/www.saintjeannet.com).* **Open** *June-Sept* 9am-6pm daily. *Oct-May* 9.30am-noon, 2.30-5pm Tue-Sat.
Vence Office de Tourisme *8 pl du Grand Jardin,Vence (04.93.58.06.38/www.vence.fr).* **Open** *July, Aug* 9am-7pm Mon-Sat; 10am-5pm Sun. *Sept-Oct, Mar-June* 9am-6pm Mon-Sat. *Nov-Feb* 9am-5pm Mon-Sat.

ST-PAUL-DE-VENCE & LA COLLE-SUR-LOUP

St-Paul might have been just another picture-perfect village, dotted with olive and orange trees and circled by crumbling ramparts, were it not for its extraordinary artistic heritage. Its fortunes changed forever in the early 20th century, when a flood of artists, including Picasso, Matisse, Braque and Dufy, pitched up after World War I, paying for their board and lodging at **La Colombe d'Or** (*see p303*) with paintings that still adorn its walls. Then, in the '60s, art collectors Aimé and Marguerite Maeght created the Fondation Maeght (*see below*) to house their remarkable collection; it's now one of France's most important modern art museums.

St-Paul's narrow medieval lanes are jammed with daytrippers in high season and lined with bougainvillea, jasmine and geraniums – along with hard-sell artists' studios and shops plying antiques, crafts and souvenirs. Between the tourist tat on **rue Grande**, look out for some fabulously smart foodie shops selling perfectly packaged olive oil and designer chocolates.

In the **Eglise Collégiale** on place de la Mairie, only the choir remains from the original 12th-century building; later adornments include St Clément's chapel, a masterpiece of baroque stucco, and a painting of St Catherine of Alexandria attributed to Tintoretto.

Sip wine and snack on low-cost local cuisine under the plane trees at **Café de la Place** (pl Général de Gaulle, 04.93.32.80.03), which affords a prime view of France's most famous *terrain de boules*. Celebrities line up to challenge local champions, and players travel from as far afield as Japan for tournaments, but rookies are also welcome; a set of boules can be rented from the tourist office for €5 an hour. Walk round the ancient ramparts for panoramic views of the sea and surrounding hills, sprinkled with luxury villas. The Port de Nice leads to a cemetery overlooking the sea, where Chagall is buried.

The **Chapelle des Pénitents Blancs** was one of Belgian artist Jean-Michel Folon's last projects before his death in 2005. Bright, airy and peaceful, it celebrates the charitable works of the White Penitents brotherhood, which once occupied the 17th-century chapel. On one wall is a spectacular mosaic, made of over a million pieces that were hand cut in a Milan studio.

In a pine forest just north-west of St-Paul, the **Fondation Maeght** is one of the Côte's star attractions. This extraordinary low-slung construction, set in grounds bristling with artworks, was designed by Catalan architect José Luis Sert in 1964 to house Aimé and Marguerite Maeght's art collection – some 9,000 items. The Fondation is a maze, with no fixed route or hanging plan – although some works

Matisse's Final Masterpiece

Simple lines speak volumes at the Chapelle du Rosaire.

On the outskirts of Vence, the unassuming little Chapelle de le Rosaire (*see p300*) is a place of pilgrimage for art-lovers. This is Matisse's final work – a labour of love that he started in 1947, at the age of 77, and worked on for the next four years.

Not conventionally religious, as he himself admitted ('I don't know whether I believe in God or not – I think, really, I'm some sort of Buddhist'), Matisse designed the chapel by way of thanks to a Dominican nun, Sister Jacques-Marie, who cared for him when he had cancer. He supervised every element of its design, from the stained-glass windows to the priest's brightly coloured vestments.

Although the chapel is white, it is saturated with colour. As light streams through the glowing stained-glass windows, its smooth Carrara marble and white tiles are dappled with colour – an effect best seen in the morning sunlight. On one wall, a vast, black line drawing of St Dominic, painted on ceramic tiles, is striking in its simplicity; alongside it, Mary holds out the infant Jesus, surrounded by flowers. On the east wall is a scrawled, powerful Stations of the Cross.

Three years after its completion Matisse died, having described the chapel as his masterpiece: 'The culmination of a whole life dedicated to the search for the truth.'

have places of their own by virtue of being part of the fabric of the place: a Miró labyrinth peopled with sculptures and ceramics, say, or the Giacometti figures in the courtyard. The more portable Braques and Légers, Kandinskys and Mirós, Bonnards and Chagalls go into storage to make way for temporary exhibitions.

Near the Fondation, the more commercial **Galerie Guy Pieters** (chemin des Trious, 04.93.32.06.46, www.guypietersgallery.com) was opened by Belgian gallery owner Pieters in 2000. It exhibits and sells American pop art and French nouveau réalisme, with pieces by Christo, Niki de Saint Phalle and Robert Indiana. For truly modern art, head to to the **Galerie Catherine Issert** (2 rte des Serres, 04.93.32. 96.92, www.galerie-issert.com, closed Sun), which shows all manner of cutting-edge works. The **Bogéna Galerie** (24 rue Grande, 04.93.32. 53.60, www.bogena-galerie.com) specialises in the work of contemporary artists such as Jeff Bertoncino, Carl Dahl and Mary Mackey.

South-west of St-Paul-de-Vence, unspoilt **La Colle-sur-Loup** has an attractive 17th-century church, but is best known for antiques. The main run of shops on rue Yves Klein open

Tuesday to Sunday (3.30-6.30pm), and there's an antiques market every second Sunday of the month. The **Maison des Arts** (10 rue Maréchal Foch, 04.93.32.32.50, www.maisondesarts.com) offers residential art and 'creative thinking' courses in a beautiful 18th-century house, and showcases local artists. What really puts La Colle on the map, though, is L'Abbaye, a 12th-century monastery that's now a stunning hotel.

Chapelle des Pénitents Blancs

pl de l'Eglise (04.93.32.86.95). **Open** 3-6pm daily. **Admission** €5; free under-12s. **No credit cards**.

★ Fondation Maeght

Monté des Trious (04.93.32.81.63/www. fondation-maeght.com). **Open** *June-Sept* 10am-7pm daily. *Oct-May* 10am-6pm daily. **Admission** €11; €9 reductions; free under-10s. **Credit** AmEx, MC, V.

Where to stay & eat

Accommodation is expensive in St-Paul, but the **Hostellerie les Remparts** (72 rue Grande, 04.93.32.09.88, closed Nov & Jan, double €45-

€95) combines style and value, with rooms facing the stunning countryside to the west or the old town's winding streets. The Hostellerie manages two restaurants, the best of which, **Les Remparts de Saint Paul** (closed dinner Sun, all Mon, Nov & Jan, menu €30), features tasty traditional delights such as *beignets de fleurs de courgettes*, as well as local wines.

In summer, expect to have to book two months ahead for a room, and at least ten days ahead for a table, at **La Colombe d'Or** (pl du Général de Gaulle, 04.93.32.80.02, www.la-colombe-dor.com, closed late Oct-mid Dec, 2wks Jan, mains €50-€60, double €300-€380). The hotel is famed for the artistic treasures left here in lieu of payment by former clients, including Picasso, Modigliani, Miró, Matisse and Chagall. A meal on the fig-shaded terrace is still a treat, with its mix of earthy food and jet-set clientele.

A deluxe hotel in the centre of the town, **Le Saint Paul** (86 rue Grande, 04.93.32.65.25, www.lesaintpaul.com, double €220-€320, closed Jan-mid Feb) is a 16th-century mansion with a superior restaurant (mains €40-€50) run by chef Ludovic Puzenat. On place du Tilleul, **Le Tilleul** (04.93.32.80.36, mains €9-€16) has a stunning terrace under a century-old lime tree. Drop in for a light lunch, afternoon tea (with great ice-creams), or the creative dinner menu.

Hostellerie de la Fontaine (10 montée de la Castre, 04.93.32.80.29, closed Tue in Oct-May, Jan, mains €12-€16) is a down-to-earth wine bar specialising in *tartines* (open sandwiches). Eat in the art-decked dining room, or on the sunny terrace. For the best ice-cream in town (and superior coffee), try the friendly **Dolce Italia** (13 pl de l'Eglise, 04.93.24.09.95). In a former oil mill, family-run **Le Vieux Moulin** (rond-point Ste-Claire, rte de Vence, 04.93.32.10.45, mains €16-€20) dishes up provençal specialities, made with market-fresh ingredients.

Chagall once stayed at the **Hôtel le Hameau** (528 rte de La Colle, 04.93.32.80.24, www.le-hameau.com, closed Nov-mid Feb, double €150-€170), which has 17 provençal-themed rooms. The flower-covered terrace is perfect for leisurely breakfasts, or lounging by the pool.

The *Jungle Book*-worthy B&B **Orion** (impasse des Peupliers, chemin du Malvan, 04.93.24.87.51, www.orionbb.com, closed Jan-Mar, double €150-€180) has four dizzying tree houses, one ground-level cabin and a pool; book several months ahead for a minimum of a week in summer, or two nights in low season. It feels miles away from the tourist crush in town.

Set in a 19-acre park with views of the sea, **Le Mas d'Artigny & Spa** (chemin des Salettes, 04.93.32.84.54, www.mas-artigny.com, double €159-€450) has rooms, self-catering apartments and villas with private pools and gardens, plus an outdoor pool, heated year

round. Award-winning chef Francis Scordel heads up its restaurant, **Le Bougainvillier** (mains €28-€36). Another outstanding hotel, ideal for celeb-spotting, is **Le Mas de Pierre** (rte des Serres, 04.93.59.00.10, www.lemasde pierre.com, double €230-€440), an oasis of tranquillity in the valley to the west of St-Paul. If you like faded grandeur it might all seem a trifle new, but there's no arguing with the superb service: jars of own-made marshmallows in the lobby and a super-helpful concierge. The restaurant (mains €40-€55) is run by the Alain Ducasse-trained Frédéric Garnier, and does a good-value lunch menu for €50.

In La Colle-sur-Loup, **L'Abbaye** (541 bd Honoré Teisseire, 04.93.32.68.34, www.hotel abbaye.com, double €135-€185) is a romantic medieval monastery. The cloisters, vaulted cellars and chapel are wonderfully atmospheric, and there's a lovely pool. A great B&B in the village is **Un Ange Passe** (419 av Leonardi, 04.93.32.60.39, www.unangepasse.com, double €80-€130), surrounded by a riot of tropical vegetation on the edge of the Gorges du Loup. The swimming pool draws water from a nearby spring, so chemicals are kept to a minimum.

On the road leading up to La Colle from Cagnes, **La Clé des Champs** (822 rte de Cagnes, 04.92.02.86.09, closed Tue, lunch Wed, mains €18-€22) serves hearty fare such as *bagna cauda* (crudités with anchovy dip) and chicken with pastis and fennel; the chef-owner closes when he feels like it, so call ahead.

Resources

Tourist information
La Colle-sur-Loup Office du Tourisme
28 rue Maréchal Foch, La Colle-sur-Loup (04.93.32.68.36/www.ot-lacollesurloup.com). **Open** *Mid June-mid Sept* 9am-7pm Mon-Fri, 9am-noon, 3-7pm Sat, Sun. *Mid Sept-mid June* 9am-noon, 2-6pm Mon-Sat.
St-Paul-de-Vence Office de Tourisme
2 rue Grande, St-Paul-de-Vence (04.93.32.86.95/ www.saint-pauldevence.com). **Open** *June-Sept* 10am-7pm daily. *Oct-May* 10am-6pm daily.

GETTING THERE

By bus
From Nice, **Transport Alpes-Maritimes** (www.cg06.fr/tam-html) runs a regular bus service (No.400) to Vence via St-Paul.

By car
Exit the A8 at junction 48 and follow the D7 to St-Paul. Continue north until the D7 becomes the D2, when you arrive in Vence. Coming from the north, exit the N202 at Carros and continue on the D2210 to Vence, turning south on to the D7 to St-Paul.

THE RIVIERA & SOUTHERN ALPS

Into the Alps

The height of natural beauty.

For many visitors to the Côte d'Azur, the mountains
serve only as a picturesque backdrop to the glamour
of the coast. Yet those who take the time to wend
their way into the deeply scored valleys of the
Roya, **Tinée**, **Vésubie** and **Haut Var**, whether
by car, train or bus, reap rich rewards.

Hiking boots are de rigueur, and provençal
mas give way to no-frills chalets; hearty pasta and
meat dishes provide fuel for hours of exertion. For
sporty types there are walking trails, canyoning,
climbing, mountain biking and skiing, but even the
less active can appreciate the benefits of the cool
mountain air and the beauty of the villages, some clinging perilously to craggy
rocks. Here you'll find colourful markets selling delicate-tasting olive oil and
Alpine honey, and tiny baroque chapels with frescoes worthy of the best museums.

THE ROYA & BEVERA VALLEYS & THE VALLEE DES MERVEILLES

In 1860, Savoy and the rest of the County of
Nice officially became a part of France under
the reign of Napoleon III, but the upper valleys
of the Roya and its tributary the Bévéra were
granted to Vittorio Emanuele II, sovereign of
the new kingdom of Italy – a nice little gesture
between the rulers, since they were Vittorio's
favourite hunting grounds. The inhabitants of
the valleys stubbornly remained essentially
French, at least in spirit, but it was not until
1947 that they were allowed to decide which
side of the border they wanted to be on.

The **Train des Merveilles**, a dramatic
railway line linking Nice with Piedmont,
completed in 1928, crawls up (and down) the
Roya and Bévéra valleys from Nice Ville train
station between May and October. Some of the
main stops are Peille, Sospel, Breil-sur-Roya,
Fontan-Saorge, St-Dalmas-de-Tende, La Brigue
and Tende; in ski season the **Train des
Neiges** follows the same track, with bus links
to Casterino. For more information, *see p312*.

Charming **Sospel**, a sleepy, sprawling town
beside the River Bévéra, is the gateway to the
Roya Valley, and a great place to stock up on
the outstanding local olive oil and honey; there's
a food market on Thursday mornings on place
du Platane, and one on Sunday mornings on
place du Marché. Sospel was the second largest

city in the County of Nice in the 13th century,
thanks to its key location on the Mediterranean
salt route. The 11th-century Vieux Pont still
spans the river in two graceful arcs; its tower
(now the tourist office) was once the toll gate
that gave passage, for a price, to a steady stream
of mules on the salt trail from Nice to Turin.

The town is split in two by the river. On the
south bank the oldest house is the Palais Ricci,
which bears a plaque commemorating Pope
Pius VII's stay here. The streets abound with
charming squares and sculpted fountains; the
most imposing one, on place de la Cabraïa, has
two levels, and was used as a drinking trough
for the goats once auctioned here. The highlight,
though, is the floridly baroque **Eglise St-
Michel** on place St-Michel, with its stucco
façade, trompe l'oeil murals and François Bréa's
splendid early 16th-century *Immaculate Virgin*.

From the church, cross to the north bank to
visit place St-Nicholas, which has old houses
with beautifully carved stone lintels and an
elegant fountain. From here, you can hike ten
minutes or so south of the village on the D2204
to the **Musée du Fort St-Roch**, a fascinating
relic of the Maginot Line. Built in 1932 as part
of a defensive line along France's borders, this
underground complex was a high-tech marvel.
Through what appears to be the entrance to a
garage in the cliffside, visitors embark on a trip
through seemingly endless galleries, containing
officers' quarters, munitions, a hospital, kitchens
and (of course) a wine cellar.

North-west of Sospel, the narrow D2566 climbs alongside the Bévéra river through the Turini forest, rich in maple, beech, chestnut and spruce trees. Several roads meet at the 1,604-metre (5,262-foot) **Col de Turini**, a popular spot from which to start hiking or cross-country skiing at the edge of the Parc National du Mercantour. For a wonderfully scenic drive, take the D68, which runs through the Authion Massif. The **Monument aux Morts**, a few kilometres along, pays tribute to those who died in the Austro-Sardinian war of 1793 and against the Germans in 1945. Further along are the Cabanes Vieilles, stark ruins of a Napoleonic military camp that was damaged in the fighting in 1945. At the **Pointe des Trois-Communes** at the far edge of the camp, there's a marvellous panorama of the peaks of the Mercantour and the Pré-Alpes. The Col de Turini is a popular spot for car rallies, so don't be surprised if you meet noisy race cars speeding along the roads.

North of Sospel is the D2204, which ascends the 879-metre (2,884-foot) Col de Brouis before dropping into the Roya Valley proper at **Breil-sur-Roya**. A tranquil village of red-tiled pastel houses and picturesque streets, it has survived practically intact since the Middle Ages. Breil has several small industries (leather, olives and dairy farming), each well represented at the market on Tuesdays and Saturdays. It has also become an internationally renowned centre for canyoning, rafting and kayaking.

The main square, place Bracion, is flanked by two churches. The façade of the **Chapelle Ste-Catherine** is Italian Renaissance in style, with two Corinthian columns flanking the portal. The more flamboyant 18th-century church of **Sancta-Maria-in-Albis** (closed noon-2pm daily) is home to one of seven historic, finely decorated organs in the area, put into service every summer during the Les Baroquiales baroque music festival. Also of note is the colourful A Stacada, a festival that takes place in July every four years (the next is 2009), when villagers in medieval costume parade through town, periodically stopping to perform scenes portraying the abolition of the *droit de seigneur*. For details, contact the tourist office (*see p307*).

Originally a Ligurian settlement and then a Roman colony, **Saorge** lies in a fiercely rugged setting. The most spectacular of the Roya villages, its cluster of Italianate houses and bell towers, with shimmering fish-scale-tile roofs, cling to the mountainside at the entrance to the breathtaking Roya Gorge. A narrow cobbled street winds up to the 15th-century **Eglise St-Sauveur**, which was built by hauling stones up on the back of mules. Inside is a magnificent organ, built in 1847 by the Lingiardi of Pavia, shipped from Genoa then carried to Saorge by mule. The village remains resolutely low-key: there are no boutiques, and only two restaurants.

South of Saorge is the not-to-be-missed **Couvent des Franciscains**, whose lovely cloister is filled with painted sundials and 18th-century frescoes depicting the life of St Francis. Beyond the monastery's cypress-lined terrace, a mule track leads to the Madone del Poggio, a ruined Romanesque abbey (closed to the public).

The last stop before the climb over into Italy, **Tende**, 20 kilometres (65 miles) from Saorge, is surrounded by peaks that become seriously Alpine. Tende is a market town (there's a municipal market on Wednesday and a farmers' market on Tuesday, Saturday and Sunday) where hikers and nature-lovers gather to gear up before heading off into the Mercantour or Vallée des Merveilles. Anyone intending to visit

THE RIVIERA & SOUTHERN ALPS

Saorge.

the Vallée des Merveilles should visit the **Musée des Merveilles**, which has a diorama and interactive exhibits as well as Bronze Age artefacts. It's dry stuff, but informative.

The **Vallée des Merveilles** itself is an isolated valley, enclosed on all sides by mountains and dominated by the 2,872-metre (9,423-foot) Mont Bégo. It takes two and a half hours on foot from Casterino to reach its famed Bronze and Iron Age engravings, so it may be worth staying overnight in the area and hiring a licensed guide for a 4x4 tour (you should still expect about three hours of walking). For a list of qualified guides, see www.tendemerveilles.com; a day costs €65 per person, a half-day €45. Casterino's Chalet d'Accueil (04.93.04.89.79) can help you plan your visit. Western access is from Madone de Fenestre in the Vésubie Valley (*see right*), via the high-altitude Refuge de Nice.

The Vallée des Merveilles contains at least 50,000 engravings, most dating from 2500 BC to 500 BC, although there are some more recent examples. Bronze and Iron Age shepherds chipped away at the red rocks to depict familiar objects – cattle, ploughs, field systems. One of the most famous is the so-called Sorcerer, a bearded giant who appears to be shooting lightning bolts from his hands.

Downstream from Tende, a side road leads east to picturesque **La Brigue**. Once a mighty medieval stronghold, the village nestles under the ruin of its chateau in a pretty valley on the River Levense. It has three wonderful baroque churches, though only the 15th-century **La Collégiale St-Martin**, with its fine primitive paintings of the Nice School, is open to the public. The real treat lies further east, where the mountain chapel of **Notre-Dame-des-Fontaines**, a site of pilgrimage since antiquity, houses a series of frescoes that has earned it the nickname the 'Sistine of the Alps'. The nave frescoes by Giovanni Canavesio push beyond Gothic into a touching, though still primitive, foretaste of the Renaissance. To arrange a visit, contact La Brigue tourist office (*see right*).

★ Couvent des Franciscains

Saorge (04.93.04.55.55). **Open** *Apr-Oct* 10am-noon, 2-6pm Mon, Wed-Sun. *Nov-Mar* 10am-noon, 2-5pm Mon, Wed, Sun. **Admission** €4.60; free under-18s. **No credit cards.**

Musée du Fort St-Roch

16 pl Guillaume Tell, Sospel (04.93.04.00.70). **Open** *Apr-June, Sept, Oct* 2-6pm Sat, Sun. *July, Aug* 2-6pm Tue-Sun. **Admission** €5; €3 reductions; free under-5s. **No credit cards.**

FREE Musée des Merveilles

av du 16 Septembre 1947, Tende (04.93.04.32.50/ www.museedesmerveilles.com). **Open** *May-mid* *Oct* 10am-6.30pm Mon, Wed-Sun. *Mid Oct-Apr* 10am-5pm Mon, Wed-Sun. **Admission** free. **Credit** AmEx, MC, V.

Where to stay & eat

Along the route to Sospel from Nice is the highly recommended **Pierrot-Pierrette** (pl de l'Eglise de Monti, Menton, 04.93.35.79.76, www.pierrotpierrette.com, closed Mon, Dec-mid Jan, double €67-€77) with scrumptious regional cuisine (closed Mon, menus €28-€39.50) and a well-tended garden with a pool. Just outside Sospel, the homely wood-and-whitewashed interior of **L'Auberge Provençale** (rte du Col de Castillon, 04.93.04.00.31, www.auberge provencale.fr, double €65-€110, menus €21-€34) offers a cosy welcome.

In town, the leisurely **Bel Aqua** restaurant (closed lunch Tue & Wed, Dec-Feb, menus €21-€31) of the **Hôtel des Etrangers** (7 bd de Verdun, 04.93.04.00.09, www.sospel.net, closed Dec-Feb, double €72-€85) is a local institution; the food, including a tank of justifiably worried-looking trout, is first class. The 27-room hotel has a swimming pool, wading pool and indoor jacuzzi. Alternatively, **Le St-Pierre** (14 rue St-Pierre, 08.75.71.43.73, www.sospello.com, double €78-€90) is a charming *chambre d'hôte* with two wonderfully old-fashioned rooms; meals (€25) are available on request.

At the Col de Turini, the modern, log cabin-like **Les Trois Vallées** (04.93.04.23.23, www.les3vallees-turini.fr, double €59-€67) also has a restaurant (menus €15.50-€41). Rustic **Le Ranch** (04.93.91.57.23, www.ranch-turini.com, closed mid Nov-mid Dec, Mar, double €40-€45), with no TV or telephones, is ideal for getting away from it all: the chef is proudly Lyonnais, and the bread home-baked (mains €10-€15).

Out of Breil-sur-Roya, the **Hôtel Restaurant Castel du Roy** (146 rte de l'Aigora, 04.93.04.43.66, www.castelduroy.com, closed Nov-Mar, double €80-€105), surrounded by a two-hectare park along the Roya river, has comfortable rooms, a swimming pool and fine regional cuisine; try sea perch with a provençal tian or local trout (menus €25-€35, closed Mon). A youthful, sporty option is the Gîtes de France B&B **Lisa**, with seven rooms accommodating one to six people (392 chemin du Foussa, 04.93.04.47.64, half board €38/person). A week-long canyoning holiday, including a monitor and meals, costs around €470 per person in a quadruple room.

Near Saorge, restaurant **Le Bellevue** (5 rue Louis Perrissol, 04.93.04.51.37, closed Mon dinner, Tue lunch, mid Nov-mid Dec, mid Jan-mid Feb, dinner Nov-Apr, mains €10.50-€23) has a panoramic view. There are no hotels in Saorge, but trekkers flock to the freshly renovated **Gîte de Bergiron** (04.93.04.55.49, bergiron.free.fr, closed Oct-Apr, €25-€30/person) by the monastery; it has a six-person dorm with bunkbeds and a pleasant double room. Half board costs an extra €15 per day, and the entire house can be rented by the week.

In Tende, **L'Auberge Tendasque** (65 av du 16 Septembre 1947, 04.93.04.62.26, closed dinner, mains €15) serves the famous *truite au bleu*, where the fish hardly pauses between tank and plate. **Tentes Autour du Monde** (04.93. 04.88.90, www.lestentesautourdumonde.com, four-person tent €35/person) offers something completely different: six tents in five different styles (Mongolian, Berber, medieval, Inuit and teepee) and a jacuzzi, with Italian/French food and a world-themed meal once a week (menus €15-€20). The owners will pick up guests from Nice airport or Tende train station.

St-Dalmas-de-Tende's **Hôtel Restaurant Le Prieuré** (av Jean Médecin, 04.93.04.75.70, www.leprieure.org, double €49-€64, mains €7-€15) is part of a centre that provides work for the disabled, and offers pristine rooms and immaculate grounds – a comfortable stop for those allergic to mountain refuges. **Le Mouton Dort** (28 av des Martyrs de la Résistance, 04.93. 79.18.08, www.lemoutondort.com, closed mid Nov-mid Dec, double €55-€70) has seven tasteful rooms with private entrances and terraces, spectacular views of the mountains and a covered pool. The classiest hotel in Casterino is **Le Chamois d'Or** (04.93.91.58.31, www.hotelchamoisdor.net, closed Nov-mid Dec, double €88-€122), with toned-down mountain decor and an attractive beamed restaurant. If you want to try one of the Vallée des Merveilles refuges, contact **Club Alpin Nice** (04.93.62. 59.99, www.cafnice.org, dorm €15.50).

At La Brigue, **La Cassolette** (20 av Général de Gaulle, 04.93.04.63.82, closed Mon, dinner Sun, Mar, mains €12-€25) is a tiny, convivial bistro, chock-a-block with statuettes of barnyard birds. It serves gnocchi and ravioli, divine foie gras, duck confit and desserts; book ahead. **Hôtel Restaurant Le Mirval** (3 rue Vincent Ferrier, 04.93.04.63.71, www.lemirval. com, closed Nov-Mar, double €50-€70, restaurant closed dinner, menus €20-€35) has utilitarian but spacious modern accommodation.

Resources

Tourist information
Breil-sur-Roya Office de Tourisme *17 pl Bianchéri, Breil-sur-Roya (04.93.04.99.76/ www.breil-sur-roya.fr).* **Open** 9am-noon, 1.30-5pm Mon-Fri; 9am-noon Sun.
La Brigue Bureau de Tourisme *pl St-Martin, La Brigue (04.93.79.09.34/www. labrigue.fr).* **Open** 9am-noon, 2-5pm daily.

Sospel Office de Tourisme *19 av Jean Médecin, Sospel (04.93.04.15.80/www.sospel-tourisme.com).* **Open** 9.30am-12.30pm, 2-6.30pm Mon-Sat; 9.30am-12.30pm Sun.
Tende Office de Tourisme *103 av du 16 septembre 1947, Tende (04.93.04.73.71/www. tendemerveilles.com).* **Open** *June-Sept* 9am-noon, 2-6pm Mon-Sat; 9am-noon Sun. *Oct-May* 9am-noon, 2-5.30pm Mon-Sat; 9am-noon Sun.

THE VESUBIE VALLEY

Fed by the snows of the Alpine ranges, the Vésubie river flows through one of the most beautiful valleys above Nice. The best way into the upper valley is the D19 out of Nice, which rises almost imperceptibly past villas and pastures to the village of **Levens**, a cluster of stone houses with an excess of burbling fountains. The town hall contains some amusing 1950s frescoes, in the style of strip cartoons, on the life of Marshal Masséna, and there's a stunning view from near the War Memorial that extends out over the junction of the Var and the Vésubie. Beyond Levens the mountains begin with a vengeance, as the road clings to the side of the Gorges de la Vésubie – which can also be negotiated on the lower D2565 route. Soon after the two roads meet is the turn-off for **Utelle**, a village that projects like a balcony over the Vésubie Valley below. This isolated village has kept its character: old houses with sundials and a church with a Gothic porch and doors carved with scenes from the life of local boy St Véran.

The nearby **Chapelle des Pénitents-Blancs** has a carved wooden version of Rubens's *Descent from the Cross*, while the shrine of **Madone d'Utelle** stands on a barren peak six kilometres further on; try to visit in the morning, before the clouds roll in. A plain

INSIDE TRACK
PARK LIFE

The stunningly beautiful **Parc National du Mercantour** (www.mercantour.eu) stretches across the northern part of all four valleys, criss-crossed with some 600 kilometres (373 miles) of marked footpaths. As well as free-roaming, bell-clanking sheep and goats, you'll find chamoix and marmots, rare imperial eagles, eagle owls, snow grouse and the recently reintroduced lammergeyer (a bearded vulture that lives mainly on bones), along with the Alpine ibex or *bouquetin* that roam between the Mercantour and the adjacent Parco Naturale delle Alpi Marittime in Italy.

terracotta church, it owes its existence to a ninth-century shipwreck on the patch of sea that, on a clear day, can be seen far below. Believing they had been saved from drowning by the Virgin, who appeared on the mountainside bathed in light, grateful Spanish mariners climbed up here to build a shrine.

The road up to St-Martin-Vésubie continues past Lantosque to **Roquebillière**, a crumbling old village with a modern offshoot opposite, built after a landslide in 1926 that claimed 17 lives. By the river on the same side as the modern village is the unusual church of **St-Michel-de-Gast-des-Templiers**. Built by the Knights Templar and later taken over by the Knights of Malta, it is full of abstruse Templar symbolism. The altarpiece from the Nice School is dedicated to St Anthony, and there is a fine collection of priestly vestments in the sacristy. The key is kept by Madame Périchon, who lives in the house opposite.

At **Berthemont-les-Bains** you'll find a modern spa. The sulphurous 30°C (86°F) waters were used by the Romans to treat respiratory diseases and rheumatism; today, they're funnelled into various indoor pools where clients relax after a therapeutic massage at the **Station Thermale de Berthemont-les-Bains** (04.93.03.47.00, closed Oct-Apr, half-day €42-€79, week €235-€290).

St-Martin-Vésubie is a good place to refuel and pick up supplies and information. The pocket-sized place Félix Faure links the main valley road with rue Cagnoli, St-Martin's pedestrian backbone. A little paved channel of water, known as a *gargouille*, runs the length of the steeply inclined street.

The road west to the church of **Madone de Fenestre** criss-crosses a mountain stream. Push on to the end, where a mountain refuge and tin-roofed church are surrounded by a cirque of high peaks. The church is only two centuries old, but its miraculous icon of the Madone de Fenestre (kept in St-Martin in winter) dates from the 12th century. Allow at least an hour and a half for the rewarding walk up past a lake to the Col de Fenestre on the Italian border.

Perched on a rocky spur that overlooks St-Martin, **Venanson** is home to the tiny **Chapelle Ste-Claire** on place St-Jean, which has lively 15th-century frescoes of the life of St Sebastian. If it's closed, collect the key from the Hôtel Bellavista (04.93.03.25.11) opposite.

West of St-Martin, the D2565 continues up to the **Col St-Martin** (1,500 metres/4,921 feet), which links the Vésubie and Tinée valleys. Just right from the Col is a *via ferrata*, a protected climbing route with a handrail that will get your pulse racing. There are three routes, blue, black and red, depending on difficulty; even the easiest takes an hour and a half. Ask at the

tourist office (*see right*) for equipment and details. Just below the pass is **La Colmiane**, where, in June and July, you can career down the mountain on a *trottinerbe*, a sort of scooter with huge soft tyres, from the top of the Pic de Colmiane lift. In winter, it's a small ski resort.

The charms of **St-Dalmas-de-Valdeblore**, the first village over the pass, are more sedate. The **Eglise de l'Invention de la Ste-Croix**, a fine Romanesque church with its very own piece of the Holy Cross, once belonged to a powerful Benedictine priory.

Where to stay & eat

Above Utelle on the Madone d'Utelle road, **Le Bellevue** (5 rte de la Madone, 04.93.03.17.19, closed Wed, Jan, dinner, mains €9-€18) has views that live up to the name and serves traditional home-cooking. The owners also rent out six holiday apartments with a shared pool in **Les Résidences de Bellevue**. In nearby Lantosque, **L'Ancienne Gendarmerie** (Le Rivet, 04.93.03.00.65, closed Nov-Feb, double €65-€110, restaurant closed Mon & dinner Sun, menus €17.90) was once a police station (hence the sentry box outside), and offers eight rooms and a small swimming pool perched above the river. The **Bar des Tilleuls** (04.93.03.05.74, menus €17-€22) is a good place for a pastis or a pizza under the lime trees.

In Roquebillière, the friendly *chambre d'hôte* **Ferme les Cartons** (Quartier Gordon, 04.93. 03.47.93, double €50) has lovely views and lovely old-fashioned rooms. The **Hôtel des Thermes** in Berthemont-les-Bains (04.93.03. 43.38, closed Apr-Oct, double €50-€60), site of the only hot springs in the Alpes-Maritimes, has 12 rooms with a charming garden and terrace.

Towards the top of the main street in St-Martin-Vésubie, **La Treille** (68 rue Cagnoli, 04.93.03.30.85, closed Jan-Mar, Mon in July & Aug, Wed & Thur in Sept-June, mains €10-€15) is a friendly restaurant with good wood-fired pizzas (dinner only), classic meat and fish dishes and a panoramic, vine-shaded terrace. Rustic **La Bonne Auberge** (98 allée de Verdun, 04.93.03.20.49, www.labonneauberge06.fr, closed mid Nov-mid Feb, double €52-€57) lives up to its name, offering solid mountain hospitality (mains €8-€22) in a cheerful building overlooking the valley. The slightly more luxurious **Edward's Parc Hôtel La Chataigneraie** (allée de Verdun, 04.93.03.21.22, www.raiberti.com/hotel-la-chataigneraie, closed Oct-May, double €60-€70) is a little frayed, but still a good place in which to relax, with the aid of a heated outdoor pool and a restaurant (menus €16-€18.50).

Near Colmiane, at an altitude of 1,800 metres (5,900 feet), **Le Pic Assiette** (Valdeblore,

Parc National du Mercantour. *See p307.*

THE RIVIERA & SOUTHERN ALPS

06.21.01.63.68, closed weekdays in spring & autumn, menus €14-€24) is renowned for its spectacular mountain views and generous buffet of local specialities. The owners also organise hikes with a local botanist to pick edible wild plants, followed by a cookery class.

Resources

Tourist information
Bureau des Guides du Mercantour *pl du Marché, St-Martin-Vésubie (04.93.03.31.32/ www.guidescapade.com).* **Open** 10.30am-12.30pm, 4-5.30pm daily. Closed Sept-June.
St-Martin-Vésubie Office de Tourisme *pl Félix Faure, 06450 St-Martin-Vésubie (04.93. 03.21.28/www.saintmartinvesubie.fr).* **Open** *July, Aug* 9am-1pm, 2.30-7pm daily. *Sept-June* 9am-noon, 2-6pm Mon-Sat; 9am-noon Sun.

THE TINEE VALLEY

Most Niçois see this road as a bit of scenery on the way to the ski resorts of Isola 2000 or Auron (*see p310* **Frozen Assets**), but the upper reaches of the Tinée Valley are worth a visit in their own right. The Tinée flows into the Var just where the latter changes direction to head south to Nice. A few side roads wind their way up to the *villages perchés* of **La Tour** and **Clans**. The former has some vivacious 15th-century scenes of vices and virtues in the Chapelle des Pénitents-Blancs and an ancient but working oil mill. In well-preserved medieval Clans, the Chapelle de St-Antoine features frescoes of the life of the saint. On the east side of the valley, **Marie** is a pretty medieval hamlet of only 60 inhabitants.

Approaching **St-Sauveur-sur-Tinée**, the iron-rich cliffs turn a garish shade of puce – quite a sight at sunset. St-Sauveur is a one-horse town with little to retain the visitor, but it is also the jumping-off point for a stunning route west via the ski resort of **Valberg** into the Haut Var Valley, whose source lies just below the Col de Cayolle, one of the finest of all the gateways into the Mercantour.

Above St-Sauveur, the Tinée Valley heads north through the Gorges de Valabre before broadening out below **Isola**, a siesta of a village amid chestnut groves, with a solitary 15th-century bell tower and, rather unexpectedly given the pace of life around these parts, **Aquavallée** (04.93.02.16.49, admission €4.50-€10), a covered fun pool with a 30-metre (98-foot) slide, children's pools, sauna, gym, steam room and squash courts. Further incongruities lie in wait up the side road that ascends the Chastillon torrent to the ski resort of **Isola 2000**. The 1970s British design of this blight on the landscape has not aged well, but from here you can walk into the surrounding high peaks or continue by car over the Col de la Lombarde pass into Italy.

St-Etienne-de-Tinée, near the head of the valley, is a surprisingly lively market town of tall, pastel houses and Gothic portals, which celebrates its shepherding traditions in the Fête de la Transhumance on the last Sunday in June. It has a cluster of interesting frescoed churches, though you need to go on a tour organised by the tourist office to see them. For information on tours and the Fête de la Transhumance, contact the tourist office direct (*see p311*).

The prize for the most unexpected sight in the Alpes-Maritimes must go to the **Chapelle**

Frozen Assets

There's more to the South of France than sun, sand and sea.

THE RIVIERA & SOUTHERN ALPS

Californians who think they have a monopoly on the 'ski in the morning, surf at sunset' aesthetic have obviously never heard of **Isola 2000** (www.isola2000.com) – and they're not alone. The purpose-built resort is less famous than more northerly Alpine destinations such as Chamonix or Val d'Isère; not surprising, given that its handful of hotels and restaurants lie in the shadow of just 120 kilometres (75 miles) of skiable pistes, stretched across less than 1,000 metres (3,280 feet) of elevation – but that doesn't stop the hordes making the journey from Nice for sun-drenched tumbles in the soft stuff.

Experts will soon exhaust the area's potential, although the Mesclun black, accessed by the Mene chair, is long and decidedly hair-raising, and there's off-piste potential at the back of the 2,603-metre (8,540-foot) Cîme de Sistron. It's best suited to beginners and early intermediates, though, thanks to a wealth of excellent blue and red runs. Many of those accessed via the Pelevos and Coq gondolas wind atmospherically through the trees before depositing skiers back in the valley, with the highest points offering clear-day views all the way to the sparkling Mediterranean.

The one problem is space; Isola's defiant popularity makes for huge peak-season crowds, which is why those in the know often head for neighbouring **Auron** (www.auron.com). Founded in the 1930s, the resort retains a wholesome rusticity largely absent in Isola – and offers a slightly larger ski area, well served by three cable cars and a raft of chairlifts, including some new high-speed six-seaters. Of the four separate areas, Las Donnas and Sauma Longue offer the most challenging runs – including some unpisted

black itineraries and the nippy Colombier red; beginners and early intermediates will find a network of leisurely blues and non-threatening reds fanning out between the Demandols and Lieuson areas.

Isola 2000 and Auron are both family-friendly, with crèches, kids' clubs and off-slope activities aplenty; there's also a good range of summer activities, from mountain biking to parapenting and a thrilling *via ferrata* mountain trail. There's also a third associate resort, **St-Dalmas-le-Selvage** (www.saintdalmasleselvage.com), which lacks downhill pistes but has a huge number of cross-country ski tracks.

Visitors seeking true hidden gems should head to one of the tiny resorts lying further south. **Gréolières-les-Neiges** (www.greolieres.fr) and **L'Audibergue** have just 26 kilometres (16 miles) of runs apiece, each offering a handful of barely connected green, blue and red pistes for beginners and early intermediates. Where they excel is character, their small town centres teeming with rustic wooden buildings and mercifully short on tourists of any nationality: it's not unusual to be among the only people on the slopes at the tail end of the season. They're also extremely cheap (ski passes from €21 and €15 per day respectively), a short drive from any number of cultural attractions, and offer stunning views of the Med: on a clear day it's possible to see all the way to Corsica from Gréolières. The only concern is snow quantity: with so southerly an orientation, the seasons are short (Jan-Mar) – but the potential rewards far outweigh the risks. For the latest on weather conditions at any of these resorts, call **Météo Neige** (08.92.68.10.20) or **Météo France** (3250, from France only).

de St-Erige (open by appointment; collect the key from the tourist office, *see right*) in the ski resort of **Auron**. The little wooden chapel – commissioned by wealthy parishioners in the 15th century, when this upland plain was covered in summer cornfields – is almost overwhelmed by the faux-Swiss-chalet hotels that surround it. Inside, it's another story – a series of stories, in fact, told in vivid frescoes dating back to 1451. Scenes of the life of Mary Magdalene alternate religious mysticism with the secular spirit of the troubadour poets.

North of St-Etienne, the D2205 becomes the D64 to Barcelonnette, the highest paved road in Europe. When the pass is open (June-Sept) bikers, motorists and even cyclists slog up to the Col de la Bonette, where the road loops to encircle the bare peak of Cime de la Bonette. From the highest snack bar in Europe (2,802 metres/9,193 feet), a short path takes you up to the viewing platform at 2,860 metres (9,383 feet) for a spectacular panorama.

Alternatively, leave the D2205 north of St-Etienne and head left to the ravishingly pretty village of **St-Dalmas-le-Selvage**, the highest in the Alpes-Maritimes. Most of the houses still have their original larchwood roofs, open under the eaves where corn was traditionally laid out to dry. The church has two early 16th-century altarpieces, and inside the tiny **Chapelle de Ste-Marguerite** are frescoes by Jean Baleison, discovered behind the altar in 1996.

Where to stay & eat

In Isola 2000, **Hôtel La Diva** (04.93.23.17.71, www.hotelladiva.fr, closed mid Apr-mid Dec, double €140-€180) has spacious rooms with balconies and is so close to the slopes that you can leave the hotel on skis. At the foot of the Immeuble St-Pierre, **La Marmotte** (04.93.23. 98.65, www.lamarmotteisola2000.com, mains €12-€18) is a cheerful restaurant that brings a touch of originality to mountain cuisine, with specialities such as a whole camembert baked with garlic and parsley, and Australian fondue (with kangaroo meat). The comfortable **Hôtel Le Régalivou** in St-Etienne-de-Tinée (13 bd d'Auron, 04.93.02.49.00, double €45-€68) has a summer restaurant (closed Sept-June) serving solid regional dishes (menus €13-€25). The town also has a well-run municipal campsite, with a swimming pool on a small watersports lake (Plan d'Eau des Trinitaires, 04.93.02.41.57, closed Oct-May, €8.50/two people).

In Auron, the centrally located **Hôtel Chastellarès** (pl Centrale, 04.93.23.02.58, www.chastellares.com, double €90-€215 with half board) has lovely balconies and a good restaurant. More luxurious is the **Chalet d'Auron** (La Voie du Berger, 04.93.23.00.21,

www.chaletdauron.com, closed weekdays May-June, Sept-Nov, double €126-€315), a stylish chalet with a cosy piano bar, hammam, indoor pool, sauna and restaurant serving regional specialities (mains €21-€28). There's also a homely 40-bed **Gîte d'Etape** (04.93.02.44.61, dorm €15) in the village, designed for walkers tackling the GR5 long-distance path but open to anyone. In St-Dalmas-le-Selvage, the **Hôtel Restaurant des Amis** (1 rue du Val-Gelé, 04.93.02.40.30, closed mid Nov-mid Dec, double €43-€58) has eight comfortable rooms and a restaurant that serves good pasta (mains €12).

Resources

Tourist information

Auron Office de Tourisme *Grange Cossa, Auron (04.93.23.02.66/www.auron.com)*. **Open** *July, Aug* 9am-12.30pm, 2.30-6.30pm daily. *School hols* 9am-6pm daily. *Sept-June* (except hols) 9am-noon, 2-6pm Mon-Fri.

Isola 2000 *Immeuble Le Pélevos, Isola (04.93. 23.15.15/www.isola2000.com)*. **Open** *July, Aug, mid Dec-Apr* 9am-noon, 2-7pm daily. *School hols* 9am-7pm daily. *Sept-June* (except hols) 9am-noon, 2-6pm daily.

St-Etienne-de-Tinée Office de Tourisme *Maison du Mercantour, St-Etienne-de-Tinée (04.93.02.41.96)*. **Open** *July, Aug* 9.30am-12.30pm, 2-6.30pm daily. *Sept-June* 9am-noon, 2-6pm daily.

THE UPPER VAR VALLEY

The River Var flows into the Mediterranean next to Nice airport at St-Laurent-du-Var, but in the upper reaches it offers Alpine scenery and perilously perched villages. Although you can follow the route by the N202 from Nice airport, the trip on the **Train des Pignes** (*see p312*) is worth the journey in itself. Built in 1891-1900 between Nice and Digne-les-Bains in the sparsely populated Alpes de Haute-Provence, it was part of an ambitious plan to provide a direct rail link between the Alps and the Côte d'Azur. The one-metre narrow-gauge track runs over 31 bridges and viaducts and through 25 tunnels, climbing to an altitude of 1,000 metres (3,280 feet).

Beyond Plan du Var, the mountains close in on either side at the forbidding **Défilé de Chaudan**, beyond which the Var abruptly changes direction, heading west. **Villars-sur-Var** is a *village perché* with some good Renaissance art in the church of **St-Jean-Baptiste**; it also produces good Côtes de Provence wine. At **Touët-sur-Var**, space is so tight that the village church straddles a mountain stream. The valley opens out a little at **Puget-Théniers**, an old Templar stronghold and birthplace of Auguste Blanqui, one of the leaders of the Paris Commune of 1871; he's commemorated by a stirring Aristide Maillol monument on the main road. Take the road towards Beuil from Touët-sur-Var to reach the small but unspoilt ski resort of Valberg (turn left at Beuil for Valberg, right for Auron and Isola 2000, which are in the Tinée Valley).

Cradled in a curve of the river, **Entrevaux** is a handsome fortified village. Perched way above on a ridge is a fortress built by Louis XIV's military architect Vauban in the 1690s; until 1860, this was a border town between France and Italy. The twin towers that guard the entrance to the village across a single-arched bridge are almost Disney-picturesque, but inside it's a sturdily practical place, with tall houses, narrow lanes and a 17th-century cathedral built into the defensive walls. The castle is a steep, appetite-building climb from the town; it's an atmospheric old pile, with dungeons to explore.

Beyond Entrevaux, the Train des Pignes continues towards **Digne-les-Bains** via the old town of **Annot**, where the houses are built right up against huge sandstone boulders, and **St-André-les-Alpes** on the Lac de Castellane. The Var Valley backtracks again in a route that can be traced by the D2202 along the dramatic red-schist Gorges de Dalious to its source way north in the Parc de Mercantour.

Where to stay & eat

Near Puget-Théniers, organic market gardener and chef Benoît Poulet and his English wife Maria have put the tiny town of La Penne on the map with the **Auberge de La Penne** (1 rue de Pontis, 04.93.05.09.81, by reservation, closed dinner Mon-Fri in Sept-June, menus €25-€31), a country inn where the food is prepared with unusual care. In Valberg, **Le Chalet Suisse** (av de Valberg, 04.93.03.62.62, www.chalet-suisse.com, closed Apr-May, Oct-Nov, double €86-€100) has comfortable rooms decorated in provençal style, plus a restaurant (menu €25), sauna and hammam. Across the street, **Le Valbergan** (04.93.02.50.28, closed Sun & Mon off-season, mains €10-€15) satisfies hearty appetites with its *pierrades* – meats cooked at the table on a stone, served with a variety of sauces – and raclettes. **Le Chant du Melé** (970 rte des Huerris, 04.93.02.57.88, www.chambres-hotes-valberg.com, double €69-€78) has five homely rooms, with teddy bears and free Wi-Fi; half board is available on request.

Resources

Tourist information
Puget-Théniers Office de Tourisme-Maison de Pays *2 rue Alexandre Barety, Puget-Théniers (04.93.05.05.05).* **Open** *Mar-*

Oct 9am-noon, 2-6pm Mon-Fri; 9am-7pm Sat, Sun. *Nov-Feb* 9am-noon, 2-5pm daily.

GETTING THERE & AROUND
By bus
It's easiest to reach the Roya Valley by train or car, but **TAM** runs a bus service by request between Breil-sur-Roya and St-Dalmas-de-Tende (Tue-Sat; call 08.00.06.01.06 with your requested date and time, leaving your name and phone number). **TRAM** (04.93.89.47.14) buses run between Nice and St-Martin-Vésubie (twice daily Mon-Sat, once Sun); some buses continue to Colmiane. Infrequent buses also serve Le Boréon and Madone de Fenestre in summer. **Santa-Azur** (04.93.85.92.60) runs daily services between Nice, St-Etienne-de-Tinée and Auron, and between Nice, Isola and Isola 2000. TAM also runs a Nice–Auron and Nice–Isola service.

By car
For the Roya and Bévéra valleys take the D2566 from Menton to Sospel, then the D2204 north for Breil-sur-Roya. Alternatively, the Roya Valley can be ascended from Ventimiglia in Italy on the S20, which crosses into France at Olivetta San Michele, 10km before Breil. The N202 follows the Var Valley from Nice airport; the D2565 branches off here along the Vésubie Valley (also reached by D2566/D70 from Sospel via the Col de Turini); the D2205 follows the Tinée Valley.

By train
The **Train des Merveilles** (04.93.04.92.05) runs from Nice to Tende daily June-September and on weekends and holidays in May and October; if you're planning a hike in the Vallée des Merveilles, a bus runs from St-Dalmas-de-Tende and Tende to Casterino (where the trails begin) in July and August. The 9am train from Nice has live commentary in French and English. The **Train des Neiges** runs every weekend on the same line, 5 Jan-23 Mar, with bus links to Casterino. From July to September the most economical ticket is the €12 Carte Isabelle, which is valid for a day on all the region's trains. An alternative to the Train des Merveilles is the regular Nice–Cuneo line, with about five trains a day and connections in Italy to Turin. There's also a service from Ventimiglia to Cuneo that passes through Breil-sur-Roya and Tende.

The **Train des Pignes** (04.97.03.80.80) departs from the Gare de Provence in Nice (4bis rue Alfred Binet) and arrives at the Gare Digne-les-Bains. There are four daily departures in each direction; at the time of writing part of the line was closed for repairs and had been replaced by a bus service. Trains are modern, if small, but steam trains still ply the route between Puget and Théniers on Sunday from May to October.

Directory

Cours Mirabeau.
See p163.

Getting There & Around

ARRIVING BY AIR

Airlines

Airlines providing direct flights are detailed below. From the USA, most flights involve a Paris connection.

Air France *UK 0871 663 7777/ USA 1-800 237 2747/France 08.20.82.08.20/www.airfrance.com.* Paris to Avignon, Marseille, Montpellier, Nice and Nîmes.
British Airways *UK 0844 493 0787/US 1-800 247 9297/ France 08.25.82.54.00/ www.britishairways.com.* Gatwick to Marseille and Montpellier; Heathrow, Gatwick and Birmingham to Nice.
British Midland *UK 0870 607 0555/France 01.41.91,87.04/ www.flybmi.com.* Heathrow and Nottingham to Nice.
Delta *UK 0845 600 0950/ US 1-800 221 1212/France 08.11.64.00.05/www.delta.com.* Daily from New York JFK to Nice.
Easyjet *UK 0871 244 2366/ France 08.25.08.25.08/ www.easyjet.com.* Gatwick, Stansted, Aberdeen, Bristol, Liverpool and Luton to Nice; Gatwick to Marseille.
Ryanair *UK 0871 246 0000/ France 08.92.23.23.75/ www.ryanair.com.* Luton and Stansted to Nîmes.

Airports

See *pp2-3* for airport locations.

Aéroport Avignon-Caumont *04.90.81.51.51/www.avignon. aeroport.fr.* Air France flies in from Paris Orly.
Aéroport de Nîmes-Arles-Camargue *04.66.70.49.49/ www.nimes.aeroport.fr.* 10km (6 miles) south-east of Nîmes; 20km (12 miles) from Arles.
Aéroport Marseille-Provence *04.42.14.14.14/www.marseille. aeroport.fr.* Situated 28km (17 miles) north-west of town in Marignane; buses run

every 20mins to Marseille station, every 30mins to Aix-en-Provence.
Aéroport Montpellier Méditerranée *04.67.20.85.00/ recorded times 04.67.20.85.85/ www.montpellier.aeroport.fr.*
Aéroport Nice-Côte d'Azur *08.20.42.33.33/04.89.88.98.28/ www.nice.aeroport.fr.* France's second airport, located 7km west of central Nice. Most airlines use Terminal 1; Air France flights use Terminal 2.
Aéroport de Toulon-Hyères *04.94.00.83.83/www.toulon-hyeres. aeroport.fr.* Near Hyères port.

Helicopter services

Helisecurite *04.89.98.50.10/ www.helicopter-saint-tropez.com.* Scheduled flights Cannes–Nice €115 one way or €230 return. Private charters are also available.
Héli-Air Monaco *+377-92.05. 00.50/www.heliairmonaco.com.* Nice–Monaco €115 one-way or €195 return.
Nice Hélicoptères *04.93.21.34.32.* A Cannes–Nice return costs around €160 plus tax.

BY TRAIN

French trains are run by the **SNCF** state railway (www.sncf.com).

Train lines

Mainline services The **TGV** (high-speed train) runs to the South from Paris Gare de Lyon and Lille, via Lyon, to Avignon. There it splits down to Nîmes and east to Aix-en-Provence, Marseille, Toulon, Draguignan-Les Arcs, St-Raphaël, Cannes, Antibes, Nice, Monte-Carlo and Menton (not all trains stop at all stations). Note that the highest-speed track currently only reaches Marseille and Nîmes.

It takes around 2hrs 40mins to Avignon, 3hrs to Aix, Marseille and Nîmes, 5hrs 30mins to Nice. On slower, long-distance trains from

Menton and Nice, you can travel overnight by *couchette* (a bunk-bed sleeping car, shared with up to five) or *voiture-lit* (a comfier sleeping compartment for up to three). Both are available in first- and second-class, and must be reserved ahead.

Eurostar *UK 01233 617575 or 0870 518 6186/France 08.92.35. 35.39/www.eurostar.com.* For the Eurostar to the South of France, change on to the TGV at Lille or Paris. July to September, a weekly Eurostar goes direct from London St Pancras International to Avignon Central in just 6hrs.

Local trains The local SNCF network is most extensive in the Rhône Valley and along the coast. Out-of-town stations usually have a connecting *navette* (shuttle bus) to the town centre. Sometimes SNCF runs buses (marked 'Autocar' in timetables) to stations where the train no longer stops; rail tickets and passes are valid on these. **Métrazur** runs along the coast, stopping at all stations between Marseille and Ventimiglia in Italy. There's also a Marseille–Aix–Gap line and two mountain lines from Nice: the Roya Valley line via Sospel, and the privately run Train des Pignes (from Gare de Provence).

Fares & tickets

You can buy tickets in all **SNCF** stations from counters or by French-issued credit cards at automatic ticket machines, also from some travel agents. Phone bookings can be made on 3635 or 08.92.35.35.35 (7am-10pm daily). Bookings can be made online at www.sncf.com or www.tgv.com, and paid online or at ticket machines; certain tickets can be printed out at home. The **TGV** can be booked up to two months ahead; seats must be reserved in advance. For all journeys, you must *composter votre billet* – date-stamp your ticket in the orange *composteur* machine on the platform before you depart.

In the UK, tickets for through travel can be booked from any mainline station or travel centre. Otherwise try the **International Rail Centre** (08700 841 410, www. international-rail.com) or the **Rail Europe Shop** (179 Piccadilly, London W1V OBA, 08448 484064, www.raileurope.co.uk).

Fares & discounts Fares vary according to whether you travel in normal (*période normale*) or peak (*période de pointe*) hours; discounts are sometimes still available within these times, but first-class travellers pay the same rate at all times. *Découverte à deux* gives a 25% reduction for two people travelling together on a return journey, and there are discounts for up to four adults travelling with a child under 12. Every Tuesday www.sncf.com advertises special *dernière minute* offers, while a *prem* (available every day) gives low prices for selected cities if bought in advance. You can also save 25%-50% by buying special discount cards for under-12s, 12-25-year-olds and over-60s. Children under four travel free.

International passes A Eurodomino pass allows unlimited travel on France's rail network for a 3-8 day duration within a month, but must be bought before arriving in France. There are discounted rates for children aged between four and 11, young people between 12 and 25 and for the over-60s. Passes for North Americans include Flexipass, Eurailpass and Saver Pass, which can be bought in the USA.

Bicycles on trains For long-distance train travel, bicycles need to be transported separately, and must be registered and insured. They can be delivered to your destination, though this may take several days. On Eurostar bikes can be transported as hand luggage in a bike bag, or checked in up to 24hrs ahead of your journey. Bikes can be transported on many local trains (indicated by a bicycle symbol in timetables). You can also consult *SNCF Guide Train + Vélo*.

BY BUS & COACH

Travelling round France by bus takes some determination.

Eurolines

UK 0870 514 3219/France 08.92. 89.90.91/www.eurolines.com. Coaches from London Victoria to Avignon, Marseille, Toulon and Nice.

Local buses The coastal area is reasonably well served by buses, and city centres have regular services. Services are more limited in the country and are run by myriad local companies. Rural buses often cater for schools and workers, meaning there may be just one bus in the morning, one in the evening and none on Sundays and school holidays. Towns of any size should have a bus station (*gare routière*) – often near the rail station.

BY CAR & MOTORBIKE

Much of Europe heads south during July and August. Coast roads and motorways crawl at a snail's pace, especially around St-Tropez or between Cannes and Menton. Roads are at their worst on Saturdays and around the 14 July and 15 August public holidays. Look for BIS (Bison Futé) signs, which attempt to ease summer traffic by suggesting diversions on backroads.

Car ferries & the Eurotunnel

Brittany Ferries *UK 0871 244 0744/France 08.25.82.88.28/ www.brittanyferries.com.* Poole to Cherbourg, Plymouth to Roscoff, Portsmouth to St-Malo or to Caen.
Eurotunnel *UK 0870 535 3535/France 08.10.63.03.04/ www.eurotunnel.com.* The Eurotunnel takes cars from Folkestone to Calais, through the Channel Tunnel.
Hoverspeed Norfolkline *UK 0870 164 2114/www.hoverspeed. com.* High-speed Seacats run Dover to Calais and Newhaven to Dieppe.
P&O Stena Line *UK 0870 598 0333 or 0871 664 5645/France 08.25.12.01.56/www.poferries.com.* Dover to Calais and Portsmouth to Cherbourg or Le Havre.
SeaFrance *UK 0871 423 7119 or from outside the UK +44 870 571 1711/www.seafrance.com.* Dover to Calais.

Driving in France

Autoroutes & tolls The distance from Calais to Nice is 1,167km (725 miles); from Caen to Nice 1,161km (721 miles). Dieppe to Avignon is 854km (531 miles), Calais to Avignon 965km (600 miles). For Provence, the quickest route from Calais is via Paris (but avoid the Périphérique ring road at rush hour) and the A6 Autoroute du

Soleil to Lyon and the Rhône Valley. A less-trafficked route to western Provence is the A10–A71–A75 via Bourges and Clermont-Ferrand. www.viamichelin.com, www. mappy.fr and www.autoroutes.fr can help you plan your route. Call 08.92.68.10.77 or tune into Radio 107.7 FM for traffic information.

French autoroutes are toll (*péage*) roads, although some sections – especially around major cities – are free. At *péage* toll-booths, payment can be made by cash or credit card. From Calais to Menton, expect to spend around €80 on tolls. Nice airport to Monaco costs €3.20, Aix-en-Provence to Nice €14.

There are *aires* (rest stops) every 20-30km (10-20 miles) or so; simple ones offer picnic tables and toilets, while larger ones may have 24hr petrol stations, cafés, shops and sometimes tourist information.

Motorail A comfortable though pricey option is the Motorail: put your car on the train in Calais or Paris and travel overnight down to the coast. Services do not run every day, except in high summer; you may have to travel on a different day to your car. Couchettes are mandatory. For UK bookings, contact **Rail Europe** (0844 848 4064, www.frenchmotorail.com).

Paperwork If you bring your car to France, you'll need to bring the relevant registration and insurance documents and your driving licence. New drivers need to have held a licence for at least a year.

Roads French roads are divided into autoroutes (motorways, marked A8, A51 etc), *routes nationales* (national 'N' roads, marked N222 etc), *routes départementales* ('D' roads) and tiny rural *routes communales* ('C' roads).

Speed limits In normal conditions, speed limits are 130kph (80mph) on autoroutes, 110kph (69mph) on dual carriageways and 90kph (56mph) on other roads. In heavy rain and fog, these limits are reduced by 20kph (12mph) on autoroutes, 10kph (6mph) on other roads; limits are also reduced on days of heavy air pollution. The limit in built-up areas is 50kph (28mph), sometimes 30kph (17mph). Speed limits are rigorously enforced; automatic radars have been installed all over France since 2003, which can automatically send off a speeding fine for breaking the speed limit by as little as 6kph.

Breakdown service The AA and RAC do not have reciprocal arrangements with French organisations, so take out additional breakdown insurance, for example with **Europ Assistance** (UK 0870 737 5720). Local 24hr breakdown services include **Dépannage Côte d'Azur** (04.93.29.87.87). Autoroutes and routes nationales have emergency telephones every 2km (1.2 miles). *See also p320* **Emergencies**.

Driving essentials

● It is now obligatory to carry a luminous (Hi-Glow or DayGlo) vest in your car; you have to put it on before even stepping out on the hard shoulder, so don't keep it in the boot or anywhere inaccessible. Fines for failure to comply can be severe.
● At intersections where no signposts indicate the right of way, the car coming from the right has priority. Roundabouts follow the same rule, though many now give priority to those on the roundabout: this will be indicated either by stop markings on the road or by the message '*Vous n'avez pas la priorité*'.
● Drivers and all passengers must wear seat belts.
● Children under ten are not allowed to travel in the front, except in baby seats facing backwards.
● You should not stop on an open road; pull off to the side.
● When drivers flash their lights at you, they are warning that they will not slow down and you should keep out of the way. Oncoming drivers may also flash lights to warn when there are *gendarmes* lurking on the other side of the hill.
● Carry change, as it's quicker to head for the exact-money queue on *péages*; but cashiers do give change and *péages* accept credit cards.
● Motorbikes must have headlights on while in motion; cars must have their headlights switched on in poor visibility.
● All vehicles have to carry a full spare set of light bulbs, and drivers who wear spectacles or contact lenses must carry a spare pair.
● The French drink-driving limit is 0.5g alcohol per litre of blood (about a small glass of wine). Above 0.8g/l, you can have your licence confiscated on the spot.
● Key phrases include:
Cédez le passage Give way.
Vous n'avez pas la priorité Give way, you do not have right of way.
Passage protégé No right of way.
Rappel Reminder.

Fuel Only unleaded (*sans plomb*) and diesel (*gasoil*) are available, but a special unleaded petrol is available for cars that run on leaded fuel. Petrol tends to be most expensive on autoroutes, so many drivers fill up at the supermarkets. Petrol stations can be scarce in rural areas (it's especially hard finding one that opens on a Sunday), though some supermarket stations have 24hr pumps that accept Carte Bleue.

Parking In high season, you have to get up very early to get a parking space at the beach. Inland, some highly touristed villages now have compulsory car parks, and car parks are often the best option in the main cities. Parking meters have now largely been replaced by *horodateurs* (pay-and-display machines), which take either cards, available from tabacs, or coins. Parking may be free over lunch, on Sundays and on public holidays. Check exact details on the machine or display panels.

Vehicle hire

To hire a car, you must normally be 25 or over and have held a licence for at least a year. Some hire firms will accept drivers aged 21-24, but a supplement of €8-€15 per day is usual. Remember to bring your licence and passport with you.

Hiring a car in France is expensive. Consider fly-drive packages; it can be cheaper if you arrange car hire before leaving home. SNCF offers a train/car rental scheme, in assocation with Avis. There are often good weekend offers (Friday evening to Monday morning). Week-long deals are better at the bigger hire companies – with Avis or Budget it costs around €250/wk to hire a small car, with insurance and 1,700km (1,000 miles) included. Most international companies will allow the return of a car in other cities or even countries. Low-cost operators, such as ADA, may have a high excess charge for dents or damage. Rates with EasyCar vary according to demand.

ADA France *01.48.06.58.13 or 08.25.16.91.69/www.ada.fr.*
Avis UK *0870 010 0287/France 08.20.05.05.05/www.avis.co.uk.*
Budget UK *0870 153 9170/from outside the UK +44 1344 484 100/ www.budget.fr.*
Europcar France *08.25.35.23.52/www.europcar.com.*

EasyCar *No phone reservations/www.easycar.com.*
Hertz UK *0870 850 2654/ France 01.41.91.95.25/ www.hertz.fr.*
Interrent France *08.99.70.02.92/www.interrent.fr.*

BY BICYCLE

Cycling is an excellent way to see Provence, but if you bring a foreign-made bike, pack some spare tyres – French sizes are different.

Bike hire

Holiday Bikes *www.holiday-bikes.com*
Franchise network with 20 branches along the Côte d'Azur, between Bandol and Menton, plus Avignon and Forcalquier. Bicycles, scooters and mopeds can be hired at individual agencies or on the web. Prices start at €12/day.

SNCF Bikes can be rented from some SNCF stations (around €15/day plus €150 deposit), and returned to any station in the scheme. *See also p315.*

ON FOOT

Provence is crossed by several well-signposted, long-distance *sentiers de grande randonnée* (GR), as well as local footpaths, all described in Topo guides, available from bookshops and newsagents. On the coast, some of the most beautiful *caps* (headlands) have waymarked paths, while walking in the Calanques gives access to spectacular unspoilt beaches. The best periods for walking are spring and autumn; access may be limited during the height of summer in areas where there is a high risk of fire. Be sure you have plenty of water and sun protection. *See also p321* **Maps** and *p323* **Sport & activity holidays**.

HITCH-HIKING

Allô-Stop *30 rue Pierre Sémard, 75009 Paris (01.53.20.42.42/ www.allostop.net).*
A safer method of hitchhiking than taking your chances on the kerb with a waved thumb and a smiley cardboard sign, this agency puts hitchhikers in touch with drivers. You should call several days in advance. There's a fee of €4.50-€10.50, depending on distance; you then pay €0.36/10km to the driver (Paris to Nice costs around €36).

Accommodation

Book ahead in summer, especially on the coast. Outside the peak period of mid July to mid August, you shouldn't have too much trouble.

Many hotels and campsites close from November to March; some reopen for Christmas. Some tourist offices offer a free booking service and, if you arrive with nowhere to stay, most will know which hotels have last-minute vacancies.

CAMPING

French campsites (*les campings*) can be surprisingly luxurious. Prices range from around €8-€26 per night for a family of four, with car, caravan or tent. Camping rough (*camping sauvage*) is discouraged, but you may be given permission if you ask. Be careful when camping in areas that may be a fire risk.

Campsites are graded from minimal-comfort one-stars to four-star luxury. To get back to nature look out for campsites designated '*Aire naturelle de camping*', where facilities will be minimal, with prices to match. Some farms also offer camping pitches, designated '*Camping à la ferme*' – once again, facilities are usually limited.

The French Federation of Camping and Caravanning *Guide Officiel* (www.campingfrance.com) lists 11,000 sites nationwide. The *Michelin Green Guide – Camping/Caravanning France* is also good.

CHAMBRES D'HOTES

Chambres d'hôtes, in private homes with a maximum of five bedrooms, are the French equivalent of British bed and breakfasts. Sometimes dinner *en famille* is also available. Staying in a *chambre d'hôte* can be an inexpensive alternative to a hotel, but it can also be an upmarket (and pricey) option; many are set in beautiful rural farmhouses (*mas*) or impressive chateaux.

The following guides, available from tourist offices, provide listings. Most tourist offices will also have a local list, but it's worth just keeping an eye out for roadside signs, especially in rural areas. We also list selected *chambres d'hôtes* in the **Where to stay** sections.
● *Chambres et tables d'hôtes*: listings for 14,000 French B&Bs.

● *Chambres d'hôtes prestige*: 400 luxury B&Bs, plus 100 luxury gîtes.
● *Châteaux accueil*: a selection of B&Bs in private chateaux.

GITES & HOLIDAY RENTALS

Self-catering accommodation ranges from simple farm cottages to grand manor houses: even the odd chateau. Tourist offices will usually have lists of rental properties.

On the coast, rentals range from luxury villas to purpose-built (and often cramped) flats or *résidences de Tourisme* in the newer coastal resorts. Rentals are usually by the week or month and normally run Saturday to Saturday; book ahead for July and August. Weekend rentals may be possible in winter.

Fédération des Gîtes Ruraux de France Maison des Gîtes de France, *59 rue St-Lazare, 75009 Paris (01.49.70.75.75/ www.gites-de-france.com)*. Note that some gîtes will be off the beaten track and the use of a car, or at the very least a bicycle, is usually essential. You'll often be expected to supply your own bed linen.

Properties are given an *épi* (ear of corn) classification from one to five according to level of comfort; prices average around €250-€460/wk in August for a two- to four-person gîte. Some are far cheaper – but may be correspondingly basic.

Brittany Ferries (0870 536 0360) is the UK agent for Gîtes de France, although its brochure only lists a small selection.

Clévacances *05.61.13.55.66/ www.clevacances.com*. This association of holiday flats, houses and *chambres d'hôtes* doesn't exist in all *départements*, but is well reputed.

GITES D'ETAPE & REFUGES

Gîte d'étape accommodation – often found in mountainous areas, or along long-distance footpaths – is intended for overnight stays by hikers, cyclists, skiers or horse-riders. The gîtes tend to be spartan, with bunks and basic facilities; it is always wise to book. *Gîtes de neige*,

gîtes de pêche and *gîtes équestre* are all variations on the *gîte d'étape*, for skiers, anglers and horse riders.

Mountain *refuges* (shelters) range from large and solid stone houses to basic huts. All have bunk beds and many offer food. Often only open from June to September, they should always be booked in advance. Prices vary from €6 to €14 per person. Lists are available from local tourist offices or from **Club Alpin Français** (www.ffcam.fr).

HOTELS

Along with Paris, the South of France is one of the most expensive places to stay in France. Hotels are graded from no stars to four-star, according to factors such as room size, lifts and services, but the star system does not necessarily reflect quality or welcome, nor facilities such as air-conditioning or Wi-Fi: an old building may lack a lift but be otherwise charming. For this reason we do not list star ratings.

Prices & reservations

You can usually get a decent room from around €60 for two, though prices are much higher on the coast. Prices are usually given per room rather than per person, and will be posted on the back of the door.

We quote the price for double rooms, but many hotels will also have triples, quadruples or suites suitable for families, or can provide an extra bed or cot (there may be a supplement). Breakfast generally isn't included: expect to pay from €6 in a budget hotel to €25 in a luxury hotel. All hotels charge an additional room tax (*taxe de séjour*) of 15¢-€1/person per night. During peak season hotels may insist on *demi-pension* (with lunch or, more usually, dinner included).

When booking, you may be asked for a deposit; most places accept a credit card number.

YOUTH HOSTELS

To stay in most *auberges de jeunesse* you need to be a member of the International YHA or the **Fédération Unie des Auberges de Jeunesse** (27 rue Pajol, 75018 Paris, 01.44.89.87.27, www.fuaj.org).

Resources A-Z

DIRECTORY

ADDRESSES

Addresses in France have a five-figure postcode before the town's name, starting with two numbers that indicate the *département*. This may be the only address in small rural communes; bigger places have street names; major cities are divided into *arrondissements*.

AGE RESTRICTIONS

You must be 18 or over to drive and 16 to consume alcohol in a public place. The age of consent is 15.

BEAUTY SPAS

Thalassotherapy

The French will often devote an entire holiday to thalassotherapy – therapeutic seawater massage and seaweed treatment. Children are generally not welcome, although some spas offer babysitting services and postnatal packages.

Biovimer Spa Marina *Baie des Anges, Cros-de-Cagnes (04.93.22.71.71/www.biovimer.fr).* **Thalassa Hyères** *allée de la Mer, La Capte, Hyères (04.94.58.00.94).* **Thalazur Antibes** *770 chemin des Moyennes Bréguières, Antibes (04.92.91.82.00).* **Thermes Marins de Monte-Carlo** *2 av de Monte-Carlo (+377-98.06.69.00).*

Inland spas

Aix's thermal spa (*see p167*) concentrates on beauty and fitness, while Gréoux (5 av des Marronniers, Gréoux-les-Bains, 08.26.46.81.85) is more focused on medical treatments.

Grape cures are available in the Vaucluse (contact Avignon's Office de Tourisme, 04.32.74.32.74, www.avignon-tourisme.com).

BUSINESS

Business people in France prefer to meet in person, even to discuss something that could easily have been dealt with over the phone. Shake hands and remember that French is a more formal language than English: use the *vous* form, unless it's someone you know well.

Most major banks can refer you to lawyers, accountants and tax consultants; several US and British banks provide expatriate services. The standard English-language reference is *The French Company Handbook*, published by the International Herald Tribune.

Dailies *La Tribune* and *Les Echos*, and the weekly *Investir*, are trusted media sources. *Capital*, its sister magazine *Management* and the weightier *L'Expansion* are worthwhile monthlies.

Conventions & conferences

Acropolis *1 esplanade Kennedy, Nice (04.93.92.83.00).* **Centre des Congrès Auditorium** *bd Louis II, Monte-Carlo, Monaco (+377-93.10.84.00).* **Centre de Rencontre Internationale** *13 bd Princesse Charlotte, Monte-Carlo (+377-93.25.53.07).* **Palais des Congrès** *Parc Chanot, 2 bd Rabatau, Marseille (04.91.76.16.00/www.parc-chanot.com).* **Palais des Festivals** *La Croisette, Cannes (04.93.39.01.01/ www.palaisdesfestivals.com).*

Couriers & shippers

DHL *08.20.20.25.25/www.dhl.com.* **FedEx** *08.20.12.38.00/ www.fedex.com.*

Office services

Accents *Pauline Beaumont, 120 chemin des Serres, Gattières (04.93.08.38.38/pauline.beaumont @worldonline.fr).* Translations. **Gale Force** *13 av St-Michel, Monte-Carlo (+377-93.50.20.92/ www.galeforce.com).* Computer assistance in English. **Loca Centre** *1330 av Guilibert de la Lauzière, Europarc de Pichaury, Bâtiment B5, Aix-en-Provence (04. 88.71.88.35/www.locacentre.com).* Rentals of laptops, PCs and printers.

Useful addresses

British Chamber of Commerce *17 Le Vert Clos, 594 Chemin des Combes, Antibes (08. 74.76.03.53/www.bccriviera.com).*

CHILDREN

Plenty of kids' activities are laid on in France, and many hotels have family rooms or can add a cot (*lit bébé*). Disposable nappies (*couches jetables*) are easy to find.

Activities & sightseeing

The beach and the sea are the easiest places to amuse children, and private beach concessions with sunloungers and parasols are the easiest of all: just book your parasol close to the shore and watch the kids make sandcastles. Main resorts and beaches are monitored by trained lifeguards in summer.

Be careful with the intense midday sun: most French families leave the beach between noon and 3pm.

In cities, many theatres and museums run activities for children, especially on Wednesdays and Saturdays. Museums and sights usually have reduced rates for kids: under-18s get free entry at state museums. Family-friendly attractions include Marineland at Antibes (*see p245*) and the Aquarium in Monaco (*p283*). Even small villages often have playgrounds, which can be a good place to meet other families.

Eating out

Eating out with kids is a normal part of French life. It's especially easy during the day at cafés or restaurants with a terrace. Many places offer a children's menu, will split a *prix fixe* between two kids or will give you an extra plate so that you can share with your children.

Transport

When hiring a car, be sure to book baby and child seats in advance. For train fares, *see p314.*

CUSTOMS

Custom declarations are not usually necessary if you arrive from another EU country and are carrying legal goods for personal use. The amounts given below are guidelines only: if you come close to the maximums in several categories, you may still have to explain your personal habits to an interested but sceptical customs officer.
● 800 cigarettes, 400 small cigars, 200 cigars or 1kg loose tobacco.
● 10 litres of spirits (more than 22% alcohol), 90 litres of wine (less than 22% alcohol) or 110 litres of beer.

Coming from a non-EU country or the Canary Islands, you can bring:
● 200 cigarettes, 100 small cigars, 50 regular cigars or 250g (8.82oz) of tobacco.
● 1 litre of spirits (more than 22% alcohol) or 2 litres of wine or beer (more than 22% alcohol).
● 50g (1.76oz) of perfume.
● 500g coffee; 100g tea.

Beware of bringing in any fake designer goods from the markets across the border in Italy at Ventimiglia and San Remo. The goods may be confiscated and you may have to pay a fine.

Tax refunds (détaxe)

Non-EU residents can claim a refund on VAT (TVA) on some items if they spend over €175 in one day. Ask for a *bordereau de vente à l'exportation* form in the shop and, when you leave France, have it stamped by Customs. Then, post the form back to the shop.

DISABLED

Holidays & accommodation

Tourist offices should be able to provide information on accessible sights and hotels. Disabled parking is indicated with a blue wheelchair sign; the international orange disabled parking disc is also recognised. To hire a wheelchair or other equipment, enquire at the local pharmacy. In Nice, part of the public beach has been adapted for wheelchairs with ramp access and a concrete platform.

Gîtes Accessibles à Tous (Gîtes de France, 59 rue St-Lazare, 75009 Paris, 01.49.70.75.75, www. gites-de-france.fr) lists holiday rentals equipped for the disabled. The *French Federation of Camping and Caravanning Guide* and the *Michelin Green Guide: Camping/ Caravanning France* both list campsites with disabled facilities.

Travel & transport

SNCF runs train carriages designed to hold wheelchairs. For information, call 08.00.15.47.53. People accompanying handicapped passengers get free travel or reductions, as do guide dogs.

Taxi drivers cannot legally refuse to take disabled people or guide dogs, and must help them into the taxi.

Location de Véhicules Equipés et Automatiques *51 rue Celony, 13100 Aix-en-Provence (04.42.93.54.59/www.lvea.fr).* Rents cars specially adapted for disabled drivers; around €100/day.
Eurotunnel *03.21.00.61.00/ UK 0870 535 3535/www.euro tunnel.com.* The Channel Tunnel car-on-a-train allows disabled passengers to stay in their vehicles and get a 10% discount.
Groupement pour Insertion des Handicapés Physiques (GIHP) *01.43.95.66.36/ www.gihpnational.com.* The GIHP provides information on disabled transport.

Useful addresses

Association des Paralysés de France *01.40.78.69.00/ www.apf.asso.fr.*
RADAR (Royal Association for Disability & Rehabilitation) *Unit 12, City Forum, 250 City Road, London EC1V 8AF, UK (7250 3222/ www.radar.org.uk).*

DRUGS

Possession of drugs is illegal in France – and being caught in possession of even a small amount of cannabis could land you in jail and incur a large fine.

ELECTRICITY & GAS

Electricity in France runs on 220V. Visitors with UK 240V appliances can use a converter (*adaptateur*), available at hardware shops.

For US 110V appliances, you will need to use transformer (*transformateur*), available at Fnac and Darty chains.

EMBASSIES & CONSULATES

For general enquiries, passports or visas, you usually need the consulate rather than the embassy. A full list of embassies and consulates appears in *Pages Jaunes* under 'Ambassades et Consulats' (or see www.pagesjaunes.fr).

Consulates in the South

Canada *10 rue Lamartine, Nice (04.93.92.93.22).*
Great Britain *24 av du Prado, Marseille (04.91.15.72.10).*
Ireland *24 av Roi Albert, La Californie, Cannes (06.77.69.14.36).*
USA *pl Varian Fry, Marseille (04.91.54.92.00); 7 av Gustave V, Nice (04.93.88.89.55).*

Embassies in Paris

Australia *01.40.59.33.00/ www.france.embassy.gov.au.*
Canada *01.44.43.29.00/ www.amb-canada.fr.*
Great Britain *01.44.51.31.00/ www.amb-grandebretagne.fr.*
Ireland *01.44.17.67.00/ www.embassyofirelandparis.com*
New Zealand *01.45.01.43.43/ www.nzembassy.com/france.*
South Africa *01.53.59.23.23/ www.afriquesud.net.*
USA *01.43.12.22.22/ france.usembassy.gov.*

DIRECTORY

DIRECTORY

EMERGENCIES

Police *17.*
Fire (Sapeurs-Pompiers) *18.*
Ambulance (SAMU) *15.*
EDF/GDF *08.10.12.61.26.*
Emergencies from a mobile phone *112.*
See also below **Health**.

GAY & LESBIAN

France is a generally gay-tolerant country and the Riviera has long been a stamping ground for pink people. Gay bars, saunas and discos abound in Nice, Toulon, Marseille, Nîmes, Aix and Avignon, there are Gay Pride marches in Marseille and Cannes, and an infrastructure of groups is slowly developing. Nice's Coco Beach is a 24hr cruising point. Other gay beaches include the ritzy plage de St-Laurent-d'Eze and lage St-Aygulf at Fréjus. La Batterie, just outside Cannes, is a straight and gay nude beach (*see p232*).

Associations & information

Centre Gai et Lesbien
*24 rue Porte De France,
Nîmes (04.66.67.10.59).*
Open *7-9pm Thur.*
Support and advice.
www.gay-provence.org
Lists gay-friendly hotels and B&Bs, activities and associations.
www.france.qrd.org
France-wide directory of gay and lesbian associations and events.

HEALTH

All EU nationals staying in France are entitled to use the French Social Security system, which refunds up to 70% of medical expenses (but sometimes much less, for example for dental treatment).

In January 2006 the E111 was replaced by the European Health Insurance Card (EHIC). It is easiest to apply for one online at www.dh. gov.uk (provide your name, date of birth and NHS or NI number). The E112 form is still valid for those already receiving medical care, such as routine maternity care. Fees and prescriptions are paid in full, then reimbursed in part on receipt of a completed *fiche*. Non-EU nationals should take out insurance before leaving home.

Accident & emergency

For emergency numbers, *see above* **Emergencies**. Note that the Sapeurs-Pompiers (fire brigade),

who are also trained paramedics, will usually be called to accidents rather than the SAMU.

Complementary medicine

Most pharmacies sell homeopathic medicines. For alternative medicine practitioners, ask in the pharmacy or check www.pagesjaunes.fr.

Contraception & abortion

To obtain the pill (*la pilule*) or a coil (*stérilet*) you will need a prescription. Visit a GP (*médecin généraliste*) or gynaecologist (*gynécologue*); look in the Pages Jaunes (www.pagesjaunes.fr) or ask at a local pharmacy for a recommendation. You can buy condoms (*préservatifs*) and spermicides from pharmacies.

French pharmacies also dispense the morning-after pill (*pilule du lendemain*) without a prescription. Abortion (*avortement* or *interruption volontaire de la grossesse*) is legal up to 12 weeks and can be reimbursed by French Social Security; consult a gynaecologist or look for the local 'Planning Familial' centre in the telephone directory.

Doctors & dentists

A complete list of practitioners can be found in the Pages Jaunes under 'Médecins Qualifiés'. To get a Social Security refund, choose a doctor or dentist with 'Médecin Conventionné' after the name. Consultations cost at least €20, of which a proportion can be reimbursed if you are entitled to use the French Social Security system (*see left*). A *médecin généraliste* is a general practitioner, though you are also free to go to the specialist of your choice – whose fees may be two or three times higher.

Helplines & house calls

In cases of medical emergency, dial 15 for an ambulance or, in most large towns, ring the Service d'Aide Médicale d'Urgence (SAMU) – the numbers will be given at the front of telephone directories. The Sapeurs-Pompiers (fire brigade) also have trained paramedics.

Alcoholics Anonymous South of France *08.20.20.02.57.*
Centre Anti-Poisons *04.91.75.25.25.*
Nice Médecins *04.93.52.42.42.*
Local doctor service for home visits.

SOS Help *01.46.21.46.46.*
Open 3-11pm daily.
Paris-based helpline in English.
SOS Médecins
*Marseille 04.91.52.91.52;
Nice 08.10.85.01.01.*
Can send a doctor on a house call. A home visit before 7pm starts at €38 if you don't have French Social Security, €23 if you do; the fee goes up after 7pm.

Hospitals

For a complete list, consult the Pages Blanches (www.pages blanches.fr) under 'Hôpital Assistance Publique'.

Opticians

Any optician can make small repairs and, if you bring your prescription, supply new glasses. Drivers are required by law to carry a spare pair.

Pharmacies

Pharmacies, which sport a green neon cross, have a monopoly on issuing medication. Most open from 9am or 10am to 7pm or 8pm. Staff can provide basic medical services such as disinfecting and bandaging wounds, attending to snake or insect bites (for a small fee) and will indicate the nearest doctor on duty. French pharmacists are highly trained; you can often avoid visiting a doctor by describing your symptoms and seeing what they suggest. They are also qualified to identify mushrooms, so you can take in anything you aren't sure about.

Towns have a rota system of *pharmacies de garde* at night and on Sundays. Any closed pharmacy will have a sign indicating the nearest open pharmacy.

STDs, HIV & AIDS

SIDA Info Service
08.00.84.08.00. **Open** *24hrs daily.*
Confidential AIDS information in French; some bilingual counsellors.

ID

You are required to keep your passport or *carte de séjour* with you at all times.

INSURANCE

Insurance is often required for sporting activities. *See also left* **Health**.

INTERNET

Big youth- and student-oriented cities such as Aix and Marseille have plenty of cybercafés, but availability in rural areas and villages is much more variable. Wi-Fi is now available in many hotels and airports; in general, free wireless access isn't common, but there are several places in the South of France that do offer the service – listed at http://wififreespot.com.

ISPs

Club-Internet
www.club-internet.fr.
Free *www.free.fr.*
Orange *www.orange.fr.*

LANGUAGE

See p326 **Essential Vocabulary**; for food terms, *see p327* **Decoding the Menu**. For courses, *see p323*.

LEGAL ADVICE

Mairies (town halls) may be able to answer legal enquiries; phone for details of free *consultations juridiques*. They will also be able to recommend an *avocat* (lawyer) or *notaire* (solicitor), both are addressed as 'Maître'. English Language Yellow Pages can give names of English-speaking lawyers in the Côte d'Azur over the phone (08.92.68.83.97).

LOST & STOLEN PROPERTY

To report a crime or lost belongings, visit the local *gendarmerie* or *commisariat de police* (*see p322* **Police & crime**). If you want to make an insurance claim, you'll need a police report. Phone numbers are given at the front of local directories; in an emergency dial 17. If you lose a passport, report it first to the police, then to the nearest consulate (*see p319* **Embassies & consulates**).

MAPS

Tourist offices can usually provide free town maps (*plans*). The large-format Michelin Atlas or 1:1,000,000 (1cm:10km) No.989 sheet map (*carte routière et touristique*) for the whole of France are good for driving. Michelin Carte Régionale No.528 Provence, Côte d'Azur is a good 1:200,000 (1cm:2km) all-purpose map of the region. For walking or cycling, the

Institut Géographique National (IGN) maps are invaluable. Top 100 (1:100,000, 1cm:1km) and Top 50 (1:50,000, 2cm:1km) maps mark all roads and most footpaths; the IGN blue series 1:25,000 (4cm:1km) has even greater detail.

MEDIA

English-language press

Most of the major British and US papers, including the Paris-based *International Herald Tribune*, can be picked up from newsagents (*maisons de la presse*) in major towns, at train stations and at airports.

Local English press

The *Riviera Reporter* (04.93.45.77.19, www.rivierareporter.com) is a glossy magazine aimed at foreign residents, carrying news, local information and small ads; it can be picked up at English bookshops. The monthly *Riviera Times* (04.93.27.60.60/www.rivieratimes.com) has local news, events and classifieds. *The Connexion* is an A4-sized news and ads freebie.

French press

As well as the French national dailies *Le Monde* (centre-left), *Libération* (left), *Le Figaro* (right) and sports daily *L'Equipe*, the French are attached to their local papers: *Nice-Matin* (www.nicematin.com), *La Provence* (www.laprovence.com), *Var-Matin* (www.varmatin.com), *Le Dauphiné Vaucluse* and *La Marseillaise* cover most of Provence and the Côte d'Azur. Free news dailies are booming in Marseille, with *20 Minutes* and *Metro*, plus free *La Marseillaise* offshoot *Marseille Plus*.

A vast range of magazines includes news weeklies *L'Express*, *Nouvel Observateur*, *Le Point* and *Marianne*, women's mags *Elle*, *Marie-Claire*, *Jalouse*, *Vogue*, and gossip essentials *Paris Match*, *Gala* and *Voici*.

Radio

FM radio

Note that stations' wavelengths often vary from area to area.

87.8 France Inter State-run, MOR music and international news.
91.7/92.1 France Musique State classical music channel with concerts and jazz, and lots of talk.

93.5/93.9 France Culture Highbrow state culture station.
105.5 France Info 24hr news, economic updates and sports. Broadcasts repeat every 15mins, so it's good for learning French.
RTL The most popular French station, mixing music and talk.
Europe 1 News, press reviews, sports, business and interviews.
NRJ Very popular pop channel.
Nostalgie Golden oldies.
Rire et chansons French comedy acts, mixed with pop.

88.8 FM Radio Grenouille Marseille station, with hip coverage of culture, events and new music.
98.8 FM Radio Monte-Carlo
106.3/106.5 FM Riviera Radio Parochial English-language radio, with small ads and local news and gossip.
BBC World Service 6.195 to 12.095 MHz shortwave.

Television

Terrestrial channels France has six terrestrial channels. The biggest, **TF1**, features movies, reality shows, soaps and news with star anchors Patrick Poivre d'Arvor and Claire Chazal. **France 2** is a similar state-run version, minus the reality shows. **France 3** has regional news, sports, documentaries and Sunday's **Cinéma de Minuit**, with classic films screened in their original language (VO). **Canal+** is a subscription channel, with recent movies, exclusive sport and late-night porn. **Arte** is a Franco-German hybrid specialising in intelligent arts coverage, films and themed evenings. Its wavelength is shared with educational channel **La Cinquième** (6.45am-7pm). **M6** rotates music videos, imported series and some excellent magazine programmes.

Cable & satellite channels Cable and satellite channels include **LCI** for 24hr news and business bulletins; documentaries on **Planète**, **Histoire and Voyages**; **Téva** for women's programmes and good sitcoms in VO; **Mezzo** for classical music and dance; **Eurosport** for sport; **Canal Jimmy**, **13e Rue**, **Série Club**, **RTL9** for sitcoms and police series; and **TMC** for sitcoms and classic movies. Foreign-language channels include **BBC World**, **BBC Prime** and **CNN**.

MONEY

The euro (€)

The euro (€) is the official currency in France and 14 other participating European Union nations. Coins exist in 1, 2, 5, 10 and 50 centime denominations; notes are in 5, 10, 20, 50, 100, 200 and 500 denominations. Try to avoid €200 and €500 notes as few shops are willing to accept them.

ATMs

If your cash-withdrawal card has the European Cirrus symbol, withdrawals can be made from bank and post office cash machines by using your PIN. Credit card companies charge a fee for cash advances, but rates are often better than bank rates.

Cash machines are widespread in major cities and towns, but can be few and far between in rural areas.

Banks

French banks usually open from 9am to 5pm Monday to Friday (some close for lunch between 12.30pm and 2.30pm); some also open on Saturday. All close on public holidays (usually from noon on the previous day).

Bank accounts

To open an account (*ouvrir un compte*) you need proof of identity, regular income and an address in France. You'll probably have to show your passport or *carte de séjour*, a utility bill in your name and a payslip or a letter from your employer. Students need a student card and may need a letter from their parents. French banks are tough on overdrafts, so try to anticipate any cash crisis in advance and work out a deal for an authorised overdraft (*découvert autorisé*). Depositing foreign-currency cheques is slow, and incurs high charges, so use wire transfer or a bank draft in euros.

Credit cards

Major international credit cards are widely used in France, especially Visa (linked to the French Carte Bleue); American Express and Diners Club coverage is more patchy. French-issued cards have a security microchip (*puce*) that enables them to be slotted into a card reader and transactions

authorised by keying in a PIN; non-French cards generate a credit slip to sign.

In case of credit card loss or theft, call the following 24hr services, which have English-speaking staff.

American Express
01.47.77.72.00.
Diners Club *08.20.00.07.34.*
MasterCard *08.00.90.13.87.*
Visa *08.92.70.57.05.*

NATURAL HAZARDS

For details on heat and floods, *see also p326* **Climate**.

Insects

For every tourist there is at least one mosquito in the South, particularly in the Camargue. Plug-in vaporisers are a good defence and are available in most supermarkets. Campers should beware of a spider that bites exposed skin at night, producing an itchy rash. Black scorpions are sometimes found from late spring to autumn.

Fire

Fire is a major risk during the dry summer period, and each year there are usually several serious fires, some of them caused deliberately. Always be careful when walking or cycling on open mountain or in woodland; campfires are strictly banned and certain paths are closed in high summer or on windy days.

OPENING TIMES

Shops are generally open 9.30am-7pm, earlier for food shops. The sacred lunch hour is still largely observed, which means that many shops and offices close at noon or 1pm and reopen at 2pm or later.

Many shops also close for the morning or all day on Monday. Hypermarkets (*grandes surfaces*) usually stay open through lunch. Most shops close on Sundays, though *bureaux de tabac* (stamps, (cigarettes) and newsagents are often open Sunday mornings, and *boulangeries* (bakers) may be open every day. Public offices and *mairies* (town halls) usually open 8.30am-noon, then 2-6pm; for banks, *see left* **Banks**. Except in peak season, many museums close for lunch. They also close on certain public holidays, notably 1 Jan, 1 May and 25 Dec. National museums usually close on Tuesday.

POLICE & CRIME

Police in urban and rural areas come under two different governmental organisations. The **Gendarmerie nationale** is a military force serving under the Ministère de la Défense and its network covers minor towns and rural areas. The **Police nationale** serve under the Ministère de l'Intérieur in main cities. Some cities also have **Police municipale**.

Beware of car crime. Police advise leaving nothing visible in parked cars. In Nice there has also been a spate of car jackings (car theft as people are parking); petrol theft is not unknown in rural areas. If you are robbed, make a statement at the police station or *gendarmerie* for your insurance claim.

POSTAL SERVICES

Postes (post offices) are usually open 9am-noon and 2-7pm Monday to Friday, and 9am-noon on Saturday. In main post offices, individual counters are marked according to the services they provide; if you just need stamps, go to the window marked 'Timbres'.

If you need to send an urgent letter or parcel overseas, ask for it to be sent through 'Chronopost', which is faster but more expensive. Chronopost is also fastest for parcels within France; packages up to 25kg are guaranteed to be delivered within 24hrs.

For a small fee, you can arrange for mail to be kept poste restante, addressed to Poste Restante, Poste Centrale (for main post office), then the town postcode and name. You will need to present your passport when collecting mail.

Stamps are also available at tobacconists (*bureaux de tabac*) and other shops selling postcards and greetings cards. For standard-weight letters or postcards (up to 20g within France and 10g within the EU) a 50¢ stamp is needed.

Telegrams can be sent during *poste* hours or by phone (24hr); to send a telegram abroad, dial 08.00.33.44.11.

Fax and photocopying facilities are often available at post offices and at newsagents. Many supermarkets also have coin-operated photocopiers.

RELIGION

The presence of the British in the South of France over the past two centuries means that there are

several Anglican churches.
For more information contact:

**Intercontinental Church
Society** *1 Athena Drive, Tachbrook
Park, Warwick CV34 6NL (0192
643 0347/www.ics-uk.org).*
Holy Trinity Church *2-4 av
General Ferrie, Cannes (04.93.94.
54.61/www.holytrinitycannes.org).*
Service 10.30am Sun.
**Monaco Christian
Fellowship** *9 rue Louis Notari,
Monaco (+377.93.30.60.72/www.
mcfellowship.com).* **Service** 11am
Sun.
**St Michael's Anglican
Church** *11 chemin des Myrtes,
Beaulieu (04.93.01.45.61/www.
stmichaelsbeaulieusurmer.org).*
Service 10am Sun.

REMOVALS

For international removals use
a company with experience in
France that is a member of the
International Federation of
Furniture Removers (FIDI) or
the Overseas Moving Network
(www.omnimoving.com).

Overs International *Unit 8,
Abro Development, Government
Road, Aldershot GU11 2DA
(01252 343646/www.overs.co.uk).*

SMOKING

The French remain enthusiastic
smokers, but only behind closed
doors and in the streets: smoking is
now banned in most public spaces
around the country. Cigarettes are
officially only on sale in *tabacs*,
which tend to close at 8pm (or 2pm
on Sundays).

SPORT & ACTIVITY HOLIDAYS

Enquire at local tourist offices
about swimming and tennis; there
is also useful information online at
www.crt-paca.fr.

Climbing

Les Guides randoxygène (available
from main tourist offices) are
excellent guides for climbers and
walkers, with detailed trails in the
region. Dozens of climbing clubs
provide courses, plus guides and
monitors for day outings.

Club Alpin Français *14 av
Mirabeau, Nice (04.93.62.59.99/
www.cafnice.org); 3 rue St-Michel,
Avignon (04.90.82.66.17).*

Cycling

Taking your own bike (*vélo*) to
France is relatively easy (*see
p315*). Some youth hostels also
rent out cycles and arrange tours;
for details, contact the **YHA**.

Package cycling holidays are
offered by various organisations;
luggage is normally transported
each day to your next destination.
The IGN 906 Cycling France map
gives details of routes, cycling clubs
and places to stay. The **Cyclists
Touring Club** (0844 736 8450,
www.ctc.org.uk) can provide
members with cycle and travel
insurance, detailed touring
itineraries and information sheets
about France; its tours brochure
lists trips to the region. The club's
French counterpart is the
**Fédération Française de
Cyclotourisme** (01.56.20.88.88,
www.ffct.org).

Golf

For Provence's golf courses, contact
the **Fédération Française de
Golfe** (01.41.49.77.00, www.ffg.org).
French Golf Holidays (01277
824100, www.yourgolfholiday.com)
offer golf holiday packages out of
the UK.

Horse riding

Horse riding and pony trekking are
popular, with *centres équestres* all
over the region (for the Camargue,
see p82 **Wild Horses**).

Foxcroft Travel (01834 831841,
www.foxcrofttravel.co.uk) offers
French equestrian holidays out of
the UK. For further information,
contact the **Association Drôme
à Cheval** (04.75.45.78.79, www.
drome-a-cheval.com) or the **Ligue
Régionale de Provence des
Sports Equestres** (298 av du
club Hippique, Aix-en-Provence,
04.42.20.88.02, www.provence-
equitation.com).

Skiing

There are several ski resorts in the
Alpes-Maritimes; the three with the
best facilities are Auron, Valberg
and Isola 2000 (*see p310*).

Fédération Française de Ski
04.50.51.40.34/www.ffs.fr.

Watersports

Antibes and Cannes are major
watersports centres, and there's
great diving at the Iles de Lérins,

the Iles de Hyères and the
Calanques. Canoes and rafts are
popular in the Gorges de Verdon
and on the River Argens.

For detailed listings of local
operators, pick up the *Watersports
Côte d'Azur* brochure or go to
www.france-nautisme.com.

**Comité Régional de Voile
Alpes-Provence** *46 bd
Kraemer, Marseille
(04.91.11.61.78).*
**Comité Régional de Voile
Côte d'Azur** *Espace Antibes,
2208 rte de Grasse, Antibes
(04.93.74.77.05).*
**Fédération Française de
Canoë-Kayak et des Sports
Associés en Eau-Vive**
01.45.11.08.50/www.ffck.org.
**Fédération Française
d'Etudes et de Sports
Sous-Marins** *24 quai Rive-
Neuve, Marseille (04.91.33.99.31/
www.ffessm.fr).*
**Ligue Régionale Canoë
Alpes-Provence** *14 av Vincent
Auriol, Bagnols-sur-Cèze (04.66.89.
47.71/www.canoe-paca.fr).*

Walking

Each *département* has its own
ramblers' organisation that
arranges guided walks. The Club
Alpin Français in Nice (*see left*
Climbing) organises day-long
hikes with coach/minibus transport.
See also p321 **Maps**.

**Fédération Française
de Randonnée Pédestre**
01.44.89.93.93/www.ffrandonnee.fr

STUDY & STUDENTS

Language courses

Actilangue *2 rue Alexis Mossa,
Nice (04.93.96.33.84/
www.actilangue.com).*
Alliance Française *310 rue de
Paradis, Marseille (04.96.10.24.60);
2 rue de Paris, Nice (04.93.62.
67.66/www.alliance-francaise-
nice.com).*
Azurlingua *47 rue Herold,
Nice (04.97.03.07.00/www.azur
lingua.com).*
**Centre International
d'Antibes** *38 bd d'Aguillon,
Antibes (04.92.90.71.70/www.
cia-France.com).*
**ELFCA (Institut
d'Enseignement de la
Langue Française sur la
Côte d'Azur)** *66 av de Toulon,
Hyères (04.94.65.03.31/www.
elfca.com).*

DIRECTORY

DIRECTORY

International School of Nice
15 av Claude Debussy, Nice (04.93.21.04.00/04.93.21.84.90/ www.isn-nice.org).

Student discounts

To claim discounts in museums, cinemas and theatres you need an **International Student Identity Card**. ISICs are only valid in France if you are under 26.

Under-26s can also get discounts of up to 50% on train fares with the **Carte 12/25**.

Universities

The **Université d'Aix-Marseille** has arts, humanities and law faculties located in Aix, and science and mathematics faculties in Marseille; Aix-Marseille III (04.42.21.59.87) is the most international part.

Contact the **Institut d'Etudes Françaises pour Etudiants Etrangers** (23 rue Gaston de Saporta, Aix-en-Provence, 04.42.21.70.90, www.iefee.com) about courses for foreign students.

Other major universities in the South of France include **Avignon** (04.90.16.25.00, www.univ-avignon.fr), **Toulon** (04.94.14.20.00, www.univ-tln.fr) and **Nice-Sophia Antipolis** (04.92.07.60.60, www.unice.fr).

Useful organisations

British Council's Central Bureau for Educational Visits & Exchanges *10 Spring Gardens, London SW1A 1BN (7389 4004).*
Centre des Échanges *Internationaux Club des 4 Vent, 1 rue Golzen, 75006 Paris (01.40.51.11.71/www.cei4vents.com).* A non-profit organisation, running sporting and cultural holidays, and educational tours for 15- to 30-year-olds.
Erasmus Programme *British Council, 28 Park Place, Cardiff, CF10 3QE (029 2039 7405/ www.britishcouncil.org/erasmus).* Launched in 1987, the Erasmus scheme enables EU students with a reasonable standard of written and spoken French to spend a year of their degree taking appropriate courses in the French university system.

The central UK office publishes a brochure, but applications must be made through the appointed Erasmus co-ordinator at your home university.

TELEPHONES

Telephone numbers are always ten figures, written in sets of two, e.g. 01.23.45.67.89. If you want numbers to be given singly rather than in pairs as is customary, ask for *chiffre par chiffre*.

Regional telephone numbers are prefixed as follows: Paris & Ile de France 01; North-west 02; North-east 03; South-east and Corsica 04; and South-west 05. Mobile phones start with 06.

When calling from abroad, omit the zero. The code for dialling France is 33; for Monaco it is 377.

Public phones

Public phone boxes use phone cards (*télécartes*), which are available from post offices, stationers, stations, *tabacs* and some cafés. To make a call from a public phone box, lift the receiver, insert the card, then dial the number. To make a follow-on call, do not replace the receiver but press the green 'appel suivant' button and dial.

International calls

Dial 00 or the plus symbol, then the country's international code.

Australia *61.*
Canada *1.*
Ireland *353.*
Monaco *377.*
New Zealand *64.*
South Africa *27.*
UK *44.*
USA *1.*

Special rates

In France numbers that start with the following prefixes are charged at special rates:

0800 Numéro vert Freephone.
0801 Numéro azur 9¢ first min, 34¢/min.
0802 Numéro indigo I 12¢/min, then 11¢/min.
0803 Numéro indigo II 15¢/min, then 11¢/min.
Cheap rates Within France cheap rates apply between 7pm and 8am both on weekdays and at weekends.

Mobile phones

France has just three mobile phone operators, offering various subscriptions and prepaid cards. The operators are SFR, Bouygues, and France Telecom/Orange.

Phone directories

Phone directories can be found in all post offices and in most cafés. The Pages Blanches provides a listing of people and businesses in alphabetical order. Pages Jaunes lists businesses and services by category. Both are available on www.pagesjaunes.fr.

24-hour services

French directory enquiries (*renseignements*) *12.*
International directory enquiries *32 12 then country code (eg. 44 for UK, 1 for USA).*
Telephone engineer *13.*
International news (French recorded message, France Inter) *08.36.68.10.33 (34¢/min).*
To send a telegram: *international 08.00.33.44.11; within France 36.55.*
Speaking clock *36.99.*

TIME

France is one hour ahead of Greenwich Mean Time (GMT) and six hours ahead of New York. The clocks change between summer and winter time on the same date as the UK. The 24hr clock is frequently used in France when giving times: 8am is *huit heures*, noon (*midi*) is *douze heures*, 8pm is *vingt heures* and midnight (*minuit*) is *zéro heure*.

TIPPING

By law a service charge of 10-15% is included in the bill in all restaurants; leave a small extra tip of 50¢-€2 on the table if you are particularly pleased. In taxis, round up to the nearest 50¢ or €1; give €1-€2 to porters, doormen, hairdressers and guides. In a bar or café, just leave small change.

TOILETS

Anyone may use the toilet in a bar or café, although it's polite to at least have a *café* at *le zinc*. Ask for *les toilettes* or *le WC* – pronounced 'vay say'. You may have to get a token (*jeton*) from the bar. Public toilets vary; some are still squats.

TOURIST INFORMATION

France has an efficient network of tourist information offices (Office de Tourisme or Syndicat d'Initiative), often present in even tiny villages, with information on accommodation, sporting facilities, cultural attractions and guided visits; some also have hotel booking and ticket reservation services.

For information before you travel, there are French government Tourist Offices in the UK (Lincoln House, 300 High Holborn, London, WC1V 7JH, 0906 824 4123) and USA (825 Third Avenue, New York, NY, 1-514 288 1904).

Otherwise, you can consult the French Government Tourist Office's official internet site at www.franceguide.com.

VISAS

To visit France, you need a valid passport. Non-EU citizens require a visa, although USA, Canada, Australia and New Zealand citizens do not need a visa for stays of up to three months. If you are in any doubt, check with the French consulate in your country.

If you intend to stay in France for more than 90 days, then you are supposed to apply for a *carte de séjour*.

WEIGHTS & MEASURES

France uses the metric system. Remember that all speed limits are in kilometres per hour. One kilometre is equivalent to 0.62 mile (1 mile = 1.6km). Petrol, like other liquids, is measured in litres (1 UK gallon = 4.54 litres; 1 US gallon = 3.79 litres).

WHEN TO GO

Climate

The climate is generally hot and dry, except for spring, when there may be heavy rainfall, and November, which can be blustery, cold and wet. The coast has a gentle Mediterranean climate with mild winters (minimum daytime temperatures of 10°C/50°F) and hot summers (30°C/86°F or more). Temperatures can rise into the 40s°C (100s°F) in the middle of the day. Stay in the shade, wear a sunhat and drink plenty of water.

In Provence, the Mistral, a harsh, cold wind, blows down the Rhône Valley and howls through the streets of Arles, Avignon and Marseille, bringing winter (and at times spring) temperatures down dramatically. It usually lasts three or four days, but can go on as long as ten days. The area has also seen dramatic storms in recent years,

causing flash floods in autumn. The high mountains usually have snow from November to March. Although summer is generally dry, there are often dramatic thunderstorms along the Riviera in late August. Average sunshine on the French Riviera is six hours in January, 12 hours in July.

Information For local forecasts dial 08.92.68.12.34 followed by the *département* number. Otherwise, look at www.meteo.fr, www.la chainemeteo.com and www.meteo consult.com, or dial 3201.

Public holidays

On public holidays, banks, post offices and public offices will be closed. Food shops – in particular *boulangeries* (bakeries) – will still open, even on Christmas Day. It is common practice, if a public holiday falls on a Thursday or Tuesday, for French businesses to *faire le pont* ('bridge the gap') and take Friday or Monday as a holiday too. The most fully observed holidays are 1 Jan, 1 May, 14 July, 15 Aug and 25 Dec.

1 Jan New Year's Day (Nouvel an). **Easter Monday** (Lundi de Pâques). **1 May** Labour Day (Fête du Travail). **Ascension Day** a Thur, 40 days after Easter (Ascension). **8 May** Victory Day (Fête de la Libération), marking the end of World War II. **14 July** Bastille Day (Quatorze Juillet). **15 Aug** Assumption Day (Fête de l'Assomption). **1 Nov** All Saints' Day (Toussaint). **11 Nov** Armistice Day (Fête de l'Armistice). **25 Dec** Christmas Day (Noël).

WOMEN

Women need feel no more threatened in the South of France than in any other European country; indeed, women who are here alone will be more comfortable than in many places. The usual safety precautions should be taken in big cities at night. Be careful on trains, especially sleepers. You may receive compliments – more a cultural difference than sexual harrassment. A polite '*N'insistez pas!*' ('Don't push it!') should turn off any unwanted attention. For contraception and abortion, *see p320*.

International Women's Club of the Riviera
06.21.46.54.93/www.iwcr.org.
Coffee mornings for newcomers.

SOS Viol Informations
08.00.05.95.95.
Freephone service in French, dealing with rape.

WORKING IN THE SOUTH OF FRANCE

Anyone coming to work in France should be prepared for bureaucracy. Documents regularly required include a passport and a legally approved translation of your birth certificate (embassies have lists of translators).

Carte de séjour

Officially, EU citizens and non-Europeans alike who are in France for more than three months must apply at the *local mairie* (town hall) for a *carte de séjour*, valid for five years. Those who have had a *carte de séjour* for at least three years, have been paying French income tax, can show proof of income and/or are married to a French national can apply for a ten-year *carte de résident*.

Job-hunting

All EU nationals can work legally in France, but must apply for a *carte de séjour (see above)* and a French social security number from the Caisse Primaire d'Assurance Maladie. Some ads can be found at branches of the **Agence National Pour l'Emploi** (ANPE, www.anpe. fr), the French national employment bureau. This is also the place to sign up as a *demandeur d'emploi* and thereby qualify for French unemployment benefit. Offices are listed under Administration du Travail et de l'Emploi in the Pages Jaunes. Alternatively, the European Commission lists employment opportunities across Europe on their website (www.europa.eu.int/eures).

Seasonal employment

Foreign students can get an *autorisation provisoire de travail* (a temporary work permit) for part-time work during the holidays.

Some seasonal work is available – mainly in the tourist industry, for which you'll need to be able to speak decent French.

Other work possibilities include gardening, house-sitting and teaching English. Grape- and fruit-picking in the harvest (*vendange à main*) is very difficult to set up in advance. A good search engine for jobs is www.pacajob.com.

Vocabulary

In French, the second-person singular ('you') has two forms. Phrases here are given in the more polite *vous* form. The *tu* form is used with family, friends, young children and pets; you should be careful not to use it with people you don't know sufficiently well. You'll also find that courtesies such as monsieur, madame and mademoiselle are used much more than their English equivalents. *See right* Decoding the Menu for food terms.

GENERAL EXPRESSIONS

● yes *oui*; no *non*; OK *d'accord/ça va*
● good morning/good afternoon/hello *bonjour*; good evening *bonsoir*; goodbye *au revoir*
● how are you? *comment allez vous?/vous allez bien?*; how's it going? *comment ça va?/*(familiar) *ça va?*
● Sir/Mr *monsieur (M, Mr)*; Madam/Mrs *madame (Mme)*; Miss *mademoiselle (Mlle)*
● please *s'il vous plaît*; thank you *merci*; thank you very much *merci beaucoup*
● sorry *pardon*; excuse me *excusez-moi*
● do you speak English? *parlez-vous anglais?*; I don't speak French *je ne parle pas français*; I don't understand *je ne comprends pas*; please speak more slowly *parlez plus lentement, s'il vous plaît*; leave me alone *laissez-moi tranquille*
● how much?/how many? *combien?*; have you got change? *avez-vous de la monnaie?*; I would like... *je voudrais...*
● I am going *je vais*; I am going to pay *je vais payer*
● it is *c'est*; it isn't *ce n'est pas*
● good *bon(ne)*; bad *mauvais(e)*; small *petit(e)*; big *grand(e)*; beautiful *beau/belle*; well *bien*; badly *mal*; expensive *cher*; cheap *pas cher*
● a bit *un peu*; a lot *beaucoup*; very *très*; with *avec*; without *sans*
● and *et*; or *ou*; because *parce-que*
● who? *qui?*; when? *quand?*; which? *quel?*; where? *où?*; why? *pourquoi?*; how? *comment?* at what time? *à quelle heure?*

● forbidden *interdit/défendu* out of order *hors service/en panne* daily *tous les jours (tlj)*; except Sunday *sauf le dimanche*

ON THE PHONE

● hello (telephone) *allô*; who's calling? *c'est de la part de qui?/qui est à l'appareil?*; hold the line *ne quittez pas/patientez s'il vous plaît*

GETTING AROUND

● when is the next train for...? *c'est quand le prochain train pour...?*
● ticket *un billet*; station *la gare*; train station *gare SNCF*; platform *le quai*; bus/coach station *gare routière*; bus/coach *autobus/car*
● entrance *entrée*; exit *sortie*; left *gauche*; right *droite*; interchange *correspondence*
● straight on *tout droit*; far *loin*; near *pas loin/près d'ici*
● street *la rue*; street map *le plan*; road map *la carte*
● bank *la banque*; is there a bank near here? *est-ce qu'il y a une banque près d'ici?*
● post office *la Poste*; a stamp *un timbre*

SIGHTSEEING

● beach *une plage*; bridge *un pont*; cave *une grotte*; wine cellar *une cave*; church *une église*; market *marché, les halles*; museum *un musée*; mill *un moulin*; town hall *l'hôtel de ville/la mairie*; exhibition *une exposition*; ticket (for museum) *un billet*; (for theatre, concert) *une place*; free *gratuit*; reduced price *un tarif réduit*; open *ouvert*; closed *fermé*

AT THE HOTEL

● do you have a room (for this evening/for two people)? *avez-vous une chambre (pour ce soir/pour deux personnes)?* full *complet*; room *une chambre*; bed *un lit*; double bed *un grand lit*; (a room with) twin beds *(une chambre) à deux lits*; with bath(room)/shower *avec (salle de) bain/douche*; breakfast *le petit déjeuner*; included *compris*; lift *un ascenseur*; air-conditioned *climatisé*; swimming pool *piscine*

AT THE CAFE OR RESTAURANT

● I'd like to book a table (for three/at 8pm) *je voudrais réserver une table (pour trois personnes/à vingt heures)*; the bill, please *l'addition, s'il vous plaît*
● lunch *le déjeuner*; dinner *le dîner*
● coffee (espresso) *un café*; white coffee *un café au lait/café crème*; tea *le thé*; wine *le vin*; beer *la bière*; a draught beer *une pression*; mineral water *eau minérale*; fizzy *gazeuse*; still *plate*; tap water *eau du robinet*

BEHIND THE WHEEL

● give way *céder le passage*; it's not your right of way *vous n'avez pas la priorité*; residents only *sauf riverains*; no parking *stationnement interdit/stationnement gênant*
● pedestrian *piéton*; toll *péage*; speed limit 40 *rappel 40kph*
● petrol *essence*; unleaded *sans plomb*; diesel *gasoil*
● traffic jam *embouteillage/bouchon*; speed *vitesse*

NUMBERS

● 0 *zéro*; 1 *un, une*; 2 *deux*; 3 *trois*; 4 *quatre*; 5 *cinq*; 6 *six*; 7 *sept*; 8 *huit*; 9 *neuf*; 10 *dix*; 11 *onze*; 12 *douze*; 13 *treize*; 14 *quatorze*; 15 *quinze*; 16 *seize*; 17 *dix-sept*; 18 *dix-huit*; 19 *dix-neuf*; 20 *vingt*; 21 *vingt-et-un*; 22 *vingt-deux*; 30 *trente*; 40 *quarante*; 50 *cinquante*; 60 *soixante*; 70 *soixante-dix*; 80 *quatre-vingts*; 90 *quatre-vingt-dix*; 100 *cent*; 1,000 *mille*; 1,000,000 *un million*

DAYS, MONTHS & SEASONS

● Monday *lundi*; Tuesday *mardi*; Wednesday *mercredi*; Thursday *jeudi*; Friday *vendredi*; Saturday *samedi*; Sunday *dimanche*
● January *janvier*; February *février*; March *mars*; April *avril*; May *mai*; June *juin*; July *juillet*; August *août*; September *septembre*; October *octobre*; November *novembre*; December *décembre*
● spring *printemps*; summer *été*; autumn *automne*; winter *hiver*

DIRECTORY

INDEX

INDEX

INDEX

Advertisers' Index

Please refer to the relevant pages for contact details

INDEX